STEPPING STONES

STEPPING STONES

Interviews with

SEAMUS HEANEY

Dennis O'Driscoll

FARRAR, STRAUS AND GIROUX

New York

Farrar, Straus and Giroux
18 West 18th Street, New York 10011

Distributed in Canada by Douglas & McIntyre Ltd.
Printed in the United States of America
Originally published in 2008 by Faber and Faber Limited, Great Britain
Published in the United States by Farrar, Straus and Giroux
First American edition, 2008

Library of Congress Cataloging-in-Publication Data
O'Driscoll, Dennis.
    Stepping stones : interviews with Seamus Heaney / Dennis O'Driscoll.
      p.   cm.
    First published in 2008 by Faber and Faber, London.
    Includes bibliographical references and index.
    ISBN-13: 978-0-374-26983-8 (hardcover : alk. paper)
    ISBN-10: 0-374-26983-1 (hardcover : alk. paper)
      1. Heaney, Seamus, 1939– —Interviews. 2. Poets, Irish—20th century—
Interviews. I. Heaney, Seamus, 1939– II. Title.

PR6058.E2Z82 2008
821'.914—dc22
[B]
                                                          2008041252

www.fsgbooks.com

            1   3   5   7   9   10   8   6   4   2

Contents

CONTENTS

Introduction

'A wise man's wisdom needs to be extracted', Bertolt Brecht remarks in his poem about the cross-examining Customs man who seizes on the knowledge which the sage Lao Tsu is smuggling into exile. On 9 September 2001, Seamus Heaney called to my office in the International Branch of Irish Customs, around the corner from Dublin Castle, once the centre of English power in Ireland and now the powerhouse of Ireland's Revenue and Customs service. In my cramped room, at the end of the long, low, crepuscular corridor – resembling a smugglers' tunnel more than the fifth-floor passage-way of a modern office block – Heaney, having already agreed in principle to an interview book I had proposed by letter (citing auspicious precedents: *Conversations with Czesław Miłosz*, Vaclav Havel's *Disturbing the Peace*, Eugène Guillevic's *Living in Poetry*), elaborated on his ideas for the project. It cannot have been easy for him to face an extensive series of interviews, knowing that this would add further pressures to a life in which literary acclaim has been accompanied by massive claims on his time.

Had he inclined towards refusal, I would not have pursued the matter. Having witnessed for myself the daily arrival by green An Post van of a sackful of requests, invitations, proofs, academic enquiries, personal letters, manuscripts-in-progress and glossy new books, to a house where neither phone nor fax enjoys a moment's respite, I knew he had strong grounds for hesitation. His presence at a book launch, his speech at an art-gallery opening, his place at a Friday-night dinner table; his reading, his lecture, his review, his blurb, his oration, his nomination, his reaction to some public event – everyone has plans that involve snatching him away from his poems.

Now here I was, embarking on a project which would encroach on his dream time even further. What I told myself in mitigation, and what I hope this book bears out, is that a volume of linked interviews with Seamus Heaney would be a substantial addition to his oeuvre rather than merely a subtraction and distraction. Moreover, I decided from the start not to propose, let alone impose, any deadline for completion of the book. The priority for the poet must be his poetry; and the poetry must determine the agenda and dictate the deadline. Happily, it was during the years in which this book was under way that Heaney wrote virtually all of the poems in *District and Circle* (2006). Some poems ('Anahorish 1944', 'Tate's Avenue' and 'Home Help', for instance) drew their initial inspiration from the ongoing interviews; others were excerpted directly from Chapter 8 as the opening sections of 'Found Prose' and 'Out of This World'. As more recent poems also began to emanate from these interviews, Heaney referred to the book as 'a potent stirrer-up of memories'. Poems apart, *The Burial at Thebes*, his version of Sophocles' *Antigone*, opened in the Abbey Theatre, Dublin in 2004; *Finders Keepers*, a generous selection from his lifetime's output of autobiographical and critical prose, was published in 2002; and translations, essays and lectures continued to appear. Not surprisingly, there were lengthy periods when no progress with this book was feasible.

At Seamus Heaney's own request, the interviews were conducted principally in writing and by post. But – at the risk of some small overlap with previous chapters (which are themselves not without unavoidable overlaps) – Chapter 15 combines the transcripts of two interviews we recorded (one publicly, the other privately) in Santa Fe, under the auspices of the Lannan Foundation, in October 2003; and several of the remarks relating to *District and Circle* in Chapter 13 originated on the spacious stage of the Queen Elizabeth Hall, London, in April 2006, where I interviewed Heaney before an audience. My original plan had been to visit the poet on a specific day each week to record material which I would then transcribe. However, given the relentless demands he already faced – and, until an illness in 2006, his frequent absences on foreign literary and academic travel – this was not a practical proposition.

I therefore began to prepare the written questions and observations which form the basis of these interviews. The questions provided 'multiple choice' options in that Heaney could decide which ones to answer and which to ignore, and could rearrange the order in which he responded to them. It would have been unrealistic to expect responses to all of these countless questions: my first set, confined to the themes of childhood and the early writing years, consisted of sixty-two packed pages; many hundreds of additional pages – interlaced with question marks – would eventually reach the poet who, for all his unfailing patience with this project, must sometimes have questioned his wisdom in laying himself open to such a grand inquisition.

In the process of working together towards a final text – reviewing responses, filling gaps, remedying omissions, adding narrative links, augmenting connective tissue – the conversational dimension of the material, though already evident (especially after the opening, orienting chapters), was further heightened. Each suite of questions was either bound by a thematic thread or – more usually – based around a specific collection of Heaney poems. I wanted to avoid a slavishly chronological approach; collection-centred questions fostered variety and flexibility, allowing for a blend of contemporaneous commentary and retrospective recollection. If this resulted in some anomalies – for instance much of Heaney's reminiscence about his secondary schooling precedes the detailed focus on his primary schooling (for which the *Station Island* chapter presented an appropriate context) – it seemed a quirky price worth paying, especially since the pay-off is more true to the manner in which normal conversation loops and meanders, advances and retreats, than any strictly chronological account could hope to be.

While this book does not therefore conform to biographical convention, the fact that Seamus Heaney has not been the subject of a biography was itself a stimulus to this work. But chronological biographies of famous writers almost inevitably become as predictable as the check-in routines at international airports once the author's gifts have been recognized and he or she is subsumed into the world of honours and awards and intercontinental literary travel. The adoption of a collection-based approach left me free at any stage to ask Heaney (whose books have all included eidetic evocations of childhood) about aspects of his growing up and his development as a writer. To avoid losing contact with the essential inner poet, especially when we touched on the periods in which the 'smiling public man' began striding the literary world, was a constant objective. I tend to think of Seamus Heaney as a poet whose childhood – notwithstanding its 'sorrowing' aspects, discussed in this book – had its Edenic dimensions: certainty and security, calendar customs and feast days, agrarian cycles and ecclesiastical rites. The wound of expulsion from that tried, tested and trusted world hurt him into a poetry of evocation, yearning and elegy.

Ian Hamilton, the English critic and poet, regarded Heaney as 'the most over-interviewed of living poets'. Yet what initially prompted me to undertake this book was precisely the opposite view: a conviction that he was under-interviewed in more senses than one. It seemed to me that a major poet who has been a consistently engaging literary interviewee should be encouraged to expound his ideas and expand his recollections beyond the meagre word-counts of a newspaper or literary journal; also, that a broader range of themes should be explored than was usual in the past (when the contents of the latest Heaney publication, or the implications of the Ulster Troubles for his work, were the staple interrogative fare). Aside from a handful of exceptions – including the interview by his friend Karl Miller (Between the Lines, 2000) and the *Paris Review* interview (Fall 1997) by his fellow poet Henri Cole – Heaney interviews, though fascinating in themselves, have been too narrow in scope to present a comprehensive portrait of the man and his times.

Writers are not necessarily articulate simply because language is their stock in trade. If poets spoke poetry, they would not need to write it; if the poems they wrote in the heat of creation attained instant perfection, they would not need to be repeatedly revised, rethought and rewritten. But Seamus Heaney – as anyone who has heard him interviewed on radio, or who has been the fortunate addressee of one of his handwritten letters or postcards will know – has the rare capacity to improvise sentences which are at once spontaneous and shapely, playful and profound, beautiful and true. The same extemporaneous eloquence is a feature of these interviews.

While it took some years for the book as a whole to accumulate, the individual tranches tended to be completed very quickly, whenever an opportunity for tranquil recollection unexpectedly presented itself and Heaney could concentrate on a chapter over a few days in Glanmore Cottage. His remarks combine the swiftness and immediacy of an oral interview with the coherent and considered qualities of good autobiographical writing. Patrick Kavanagh – among Seamus Heaney's early exemplars as a poet – was always tempted as oral interviewee (and indeed when cross-examined in the law courts during the libel action he inadvisedly pressed) towards the impetuous overstatement and the reckless generality; yet even the volatile Kavanagh appreciated the importance of more measured responses: 'When we – or at any rate when I – speak impromptuously, we tend to speak on the surface, expressing the surface irritations of the moment. Out of repose the truth springs.' A similar point about interviews was made by the more guarded J. M. Coetzee: 'Truth is related to silence, to reflection, to the practice of *writing*. Speech is not a fount of truth but a pale and provisional version of writing.'

My own role here is that of prompter rather than interrogator – the book was in no sense envisaged to be a 'tell all' account of Seamus Heaney's life. I can think of no compelling reason why writers should feel obliged to discuss publicly the more private and intimate details of their lives or to air material which they plan to explore artistically. Yet never during my interviewing did I sense that he had withheld or suppressed anything that would be of significance to readers; and this is very much a book for readers of his oeuvre, on whose behalf I hope to have asked the kinds of questions which they might themselves have wished to pose.

The only stipulation made at the outset by the poet was that he would not engage in detailed analytical discussion of individual poems. In this respect, one is reminded again of J. M. Coetzee and also of another Nobel laureate, George Seferis. Alluding to the latter, his translator Edmund Keeley wrote: 'However accommodating a poet may feel toward a student or critic or interviewer, if he is as wise as George Seferis, he will be reluctant to allow the richness of his work to be restricted by the kind of detailed commentary on specific poems that seems to carry the imprint of the poet's approval, especially if this comment is meant for public consumption . . .' J. M. Coetzee, having observed in an interview that the author of his novels 'either isn't me or is me in a deeper sense than the words I am now speaking are me', warned that any comment he might make on his own work would be 'said from a position peripheral, posterior to the forever unreclaimable position from which the book was written'.

This book does not pretend to be an authorized 'reader's guide' to Seamus Heaney's poems but rather a survey of his life, often using the poems as reference points. It offers a biographical context for the poems and a poetry-based account of the life. It reviews the life by re-viewing it from the perspective of Heaney's late sixties: a life which has itself been monitored – sometimes almost as closely as his books have been reviewed – by critics and journalists. Seamus Deane, a friend since their schooldays, recalled – in his *New Yorker* memoir of Heaney – that he once sent a letter to the poet 'with his name in quotation marks on the envelope – "Seamus Heaney" ': 'He liked that', Deane went on. 'But Heaney was aware, too, of the chemistry that alters a writer who has gained fame and transforms him from what he is to what his reputation is.' My hope is that this dialogue will go some distance towards unshackling the poet from the quotation marks and releasing him back into an unhampered life of his own:

> And there I was, incredible to myself,
> among people far too eager to believe me
> and my story, even if it happened to be true.

Little wonder that Seamus Heaney identifies with 'Borges and I', a 'parable' by Jorge Luis Borges which begins: 'It's the other one, it's Borges, that things happen to . . . News of Borges reaches me through the mail and I see his name on an academic ballot or in a biographical dictionary.' In this book, the 'other' Heaney, the mythologized public figure, is reunited with the Heaney of the first person singular; the 'intended, complete' poet sits down to break-fast with the husband and householder; the artist of *Field Work* demonstrates the art of saving hay. We see how haphazard the writing process can be for a poet who does not immure himself in an ivory tower, how much the writing has had to compete with the living and breadwinning.

Seamus Heaney is himself given to the interrogative path to wisdom, in both prose and poetry, never shying from the big existential questions. One of the deepest sources of his profundity as a writer, and one of the characteristics which (along with a gift for recreating childhood epiphanies) he shares with Czesław Miłosz – the poet he identified as the 'giant at my shoulder' – is the need to respond to an insistent inner voice which asks 'What did you do with your life, what did you do?' In *The Spirit Level*, he wonders aloud of an antecedent, the 'journeyman tailor' of 'At Banagher': 'Does he ever question what it all amounts to / Or ever will?' Similarly, he imagines his brother asking 'is this all? As it was / In the beginning, is now and shall be?' Questions hovering over other collections include 'What do we say any more / to conjure the salt of our earth?'; 'Where does spirit live?'; 'who's to know / How to read sorrow rightly, or at all?' And central to Heaney's endeavours have been the 'preoccupying questions' he raises on the first page of his first volume of prose, *Preoccupations*: 'How should a poet properly live and write? What is his relationship to be to his own voice, his own place, his literary heritage and his contemporary world?'

These are among the questions which recur here, explicitly and implicitly, as we follow in Seamus Heaney's footsteps on what he called, in his Nobel Prize speech, 'a journey into the wideness of language, a journey where each point of arrival – whether in one's poetry or one's life – turned out to be a stepping stone rather than a destination'. This book aims at a stocktaking, not a summing up: it retraces the stepping stones; but the stream itself is in full spate.

Dennis O'Driscoll

Acknowledgements

Together with Seamus Heaney, I warmly acknowledge a deep debt of gratitude to J. Patrick Lannan and the Lannan Foundation, whose very generous support and encouragement of this book proved crucial to its preparation and progress. Patrick's ongoing personal interest – as unfailing as it was unobtrusive – acted as an inspiration and a stimulus. Warm thanks are also due to Frank C. Lawler, Vice President of the Lannan Foundation, and to Jo Chapman, Program Officer for Literature. Chapter 15 was recorded, partly before a public audience, under the auspices of the Lannan Foundation in Santa Fe, on 1 and 2 October 2003.

Chapter 13 incorporates part of a public interview at the Queen Elizabeth Hall, London, on 22 April 2006. Thanks are due to the organizer, Ruth Borthwick, former Head of Literature at the South Bank Centre.

Glossary

Seamus Heaney's distinctive vocabulary often draws on vernacular words (Hiberno-English, Ulster Scots and Gaelic) and on dialect usages from south County Derry in Northern Ireland. While it would be impracticable to gloss all of the words in this book with which non-Irish readers will be unfamiliar (and, it should be added, many of those words will be readily found in dictionaries), the following brief guide is offered to some of the words and terms used, and some of the organizations and institutions referred to:

aisling: vision or dream poem in the Gaelic tradition, often presenting Ireland in the guise of a beautiful woman.

Aosdána: Irish academy of artists, elected members of which are entitled, under certain conditions, to receive an annual stipend.

B-Specials: part-time police reserve force of the Royal Ulster Constabulary [RUC].

Bloody Friday: Friday 21 July 1972 in Belfast, when twenty-six IRA bombs were set off, causing eleven deaths and one hundred and thirty serious injuries.

Bloody Sunday: Sunday 30 January 1972 in Derry, during which thirteen unarmed men were shot dead and seventeen wounded by the Parachute Regiment.

cailleach: witch-like old woman or crone.

cairn: heap or mound of stones forming a monument.

céilí: (i) casual visit to friends/neighbours, or a gathering of such people; (ii) an Irish dancing event accompanied by Irish music.

Croppy: originally derived from the cropped hair characteristic of the United Irishmen in the 1798 Rebellion, the term became more generally applied to nationalists, Republicans and Catholics in Northern Ireland.

dinnseanchas: genre of Irish writing which draws on the lore of place names.

dúchas: heritage, birthright, patrimony, traits.

fíor-Ghael: true, or archetypal, Irish person.

GAA: Gaelic Athletic Association, which promotes 'Gaelic games' (hurling, camogie and Gaelic football mainly).

Gaeltacht: Irish-speaking districts of Ireland.

The Group: writing workshop in Belfast, founded and directed (October 1963 to March 1966) by Philip Hobsbaum and later directed by Seamus Heaney.

Inst.: The Royal Belfast Academical Institution, a grammar school for boys.

loaning: small country lane, road or pathway.

march (in relation to land): a boundary between holdings; or, as verb, to border, to be bordered by, to be situated alongside.

moss: peat bog.

The Movement: term applied in the 1950s to a group of English poets (including Philip Larkin, Kingsley Amis, Elizabeth Jennings and Donald Davie) whose work was considered to be characterized by scepticism, irony, adherence to traditional forms, a 'common sense' presentation of everyday subject matter and resistance to modernism.

rann: stanza, verse, song.

RTE: Radio Telefís Éireann, the public-service broadcaster of radio and television in Ireland.

RUC: Royal Ulster Constabulary; the police force of Northern Ireland from 1922 to 2001.

sally (in relation to trees): willow (from Latin *salix*).

seanchas: storytelling, conversation.

shuler: wanderer, tramp.

street: yard in front of, or behind, a dwelling house.

Taoiseach: Prime Minister of the Republic of Ireland.

trig: neat, tidy.

turf: peat.

Twelfth of July/The Twelfth: Date on which the defeat of the
 deposed Catholic King James II by the Protestant King William
 III at the Battle of the Boyne (1690) is commemorated in
 Northern Ireland with marches and parades by Protestants.

UDR: Ulster Defence Regiment; a reserve military unit in
 Northern Ireland from 1970 to 1992. Envisaged as a
 replacement for the B-Specials, its membership was drawn
 almost exclusively from the Northern Irish Protestant
 community.

Chronology

1939 On 13 April, Seamus Heaney [SH] born at Mossbawn farm, near village of Castledawson, Co. Derry, to Margaret Kathleen (née McCann) and Patrick Heaney. He is the first of their nine children, two daughters and seven sons. Patrick Heaney's sister, Mary, is also part of the household.

1944 American forces from the 82nd Airborne Division stationed at an aerodrome at Creagh, near the Heaney household.

1944–51 Attends Anahorish Primary School. He is taught in junior classes by Miss Catherine Walls; in senior classes by school principal, Bernard ('Master') Murphy.

1951–7 Passes eleven-plus examination and wins scholarship to St Columb's College, Derry, where he boards for six years. Enjoys, in particular, classes in A-level Latin and English. John Hume and Seamus Deane are fellow pupils. Awarded State Exhibition scholarship to university.

1953 Death of younger brother Christopher in road accident.

1954 Heaney family move from Mossbawn to The Wood, outside the village of Bellaghy, Co. Derry – a farm bequeathed to Patrick Heaney by his uncle, Hugh Scullion.

1957–61 Undergraduate at Queen's University Belfast [QUB]. Honours degree course in English Language and Literature. Graduates with first-class honours. At Queen's he publishes his first poems in student magazines Q and Gorgon in 1959.

1958 First journey abroad: sponsored by aunt as member of Derry Diocesan Pilgrimage to Lourdes.

1961–2 Completes diploma course in teaching at St Joseph's College of Education, Andersonstown, Belfast. Teaching practice at St Thomas's Secondary Intermediate School in the Ballymurphy area of Belfast. Short-story writer Michael McLaverty, headmaster of the school, lends him Patrick Kavanagh's *A Soul for Sale*, in which he first reads 'The Great Hunger'.

1961 Publishes first article, 'Shall We Jive This Jig?', in the *Irish Digest*.

1962 Takes summer holiday job in Passport Office in London. Appointed to staff of St Thomas's. Increased reading of contemporary Irish and British poetry leads to renewed commitment to writing. Poems published in the *Belfast Telegraph*.

1963 Poems published in the *Irish Times* and the *Kilkenny Magazine*. Appointed Lecturer in English at St Joseph's College of Education. Philip Hobsbaum, lecturer at QUB and poet, initiates The Group poetry workshop. SH a member, along with Michael Longley, Edna Longley, James Simmons, Stewart Parker, Joan Newmann, Bernard MacLaverty. Other important artistic friendships, from this time onwards, with poets John Hewitt and Derek Mahon, painters T. P. Flanagan and Colin Middleton, and singer/film-maker David Hammond.

1964 In pre-Christmas issue of *New Statesman*, literary editor Karl Miller publishes three of SH's poems, leading to an invitation from Faber and Faber to submit a manuscript.

1965 Marries Marie Devlin. *Eleven Poems*, a pamphlet, published in Festival Publications series from Queen's University Festival.

1966 *Death of a Naturalist* published by Faber and Faber; wins Eric Gregory Award. Birth of first child, Michael. On departure of Philip Hobsbaum, SH appointed to faculty of QUB as lecturer in English. Takes over chairmanship of The Group, which meets irregularly until he leaves for California in 1970. In this capacity, and in his role as lecturer, SH will eventually meet – as students and young poets – Frank Ormsby, Paul Muldoon, Medbh McGuckian, Ciaran Carson.

1967 In Dublin briefly as lecturer at Summer School in Trinity College; meets Patrick Kavanagh. SH now a regular speaker in Ireland and Britain at summer conferences for teachers. First meets Ted Hughes at such a conference in Hereford. Also beginning to contribute to arts and education broadcasts on BBC Radio, and will continue to do so on a regular basis until the early 1980s. Cholmondeley Award for *Death of a Naturalist*.

1968 Second son, Christopher, born. While taking part in Room to Rhyme, a poetry and song tour with Michael Longley and David Hammond, SH is introduced to Paul Muldoon. Visited by George Mackay Brown in Belfast. Attends Thomas Hardy Festival in Dorchester, seeing Hardy's birthplace and his grave at Stinsford church; also T. S. Eliot's burial place at East Coker, Somerset. Claddagh Records issue *The Northern Muse*, a recording of John Montague and SH reading their poems. Takes part in some of the first protest marches and meetings following the RUC baton-charging of the Civil Rights march in Derry on 5 October. Reports on the new political mood in 'Old Derry's Walls' in *The Listener*. Somerset Maugham Award and Geoffrey Faber Memorial Award for *Death of a Naturalist*.

1969 *Door into the Dark* published. First visit to United States, to read to literary group in Richmond, Virginia. En route meets poet Padraic Colum, anthologist William Rossa Cole and his wife Galen Williams in New York. SH, accompanied by his family, is abroad during summer in fulfilment of terms of Somerset Maugham Award: first in Bas Pyrénées region of France, subsequently in Madrid with Marie Heaney's sister. Regular visits to Prado, trips to Ávila, Toledo; attends a bullfight. Guest-edits issue of *Threshold* in which Paul Muldoon is first published.

1970–1 SH and family in California, where he is visiting lecturer at University of California, Berkeley. Befriended by Thomas Flanagan and meets Conor Cruise O'Brien, who is briefly on campus as Regents' Lecturer. Attends poetry readings by Gary Snyder, Robert Bly, Robert Duncan, Robert Creeley. Returns home during the week in which internment without trial introduced in Northern Ireland.

1972 *Wintering Out* published. Bloody Sunday shootings in Derry and Bloody Friday bombings in Belfast. SH resigns lectureship in QUB and moves with family to Glanmore Cottage in Co. Wicklow, which he rents from Synge scholar Ann Saddlemyer. Meets Robert Lowell in London. Meets Joseph Brodsky at Poetry International festival in London. Begins work on translation of *Buile Shuibhne*. Edits *Soundings*, an anthology of new Irish poetry. Presents a weekly book review programme (*Imprint*) on RTE Radio and will do so for the next five years.

1973 Birth of daughter, Catherine Ann. Goes to Scotland for first time, attending poetry event at St Andrews. Meets Norman MacCaig and Iain Crichton Smith. Visits Copenhagen, meets P. V. Glob, author of *The Bog People*. Travels in Jutland, views Tollund Man in Silkeborg Museum and Grauballe Man in Aarhus. Participates in performance of John Montague's *The Rough Field* at the Roundhouse, London, with music by the Chieftains. Appointed member of Irish Arts Council, a position he will hold until 1978. American Irish Foundation Literary Award. Denis Devlin Memorial Award.

1974 First visit to Grasmere, presenting TV programme about Dove Cottage in the BBC's 'Writers' Houses' series. Delivers 'The Fire i' the Flint' as the British Academy's Chatterton Lecture. Edits *Soundings 2* anthology.

1975 *North* and the pamphlet *Stations* published. Returns to teaching, as Lecturer in English at Carysfort College of Education in Dublin. E. M. Forster Award from American Academy of Arts and Letters. Organizes and introduces poetry reading series at Kilkenny Arts Week, hosting Robert Lowell, Norman MacCaig, Richard Murphy, Derek Mahon. Second cousin Colum McCartney is victim of random sectarian assassination by Loyalist paramilitaries at the time of this event.

1976 Granted leave of absence from Carysfort to return to University of California, Berkeley, as Beckman Professor. Delivers 'Englands of the Mind' as Beckman Lecture. At Kilkenny Arts Week, hosts Eugène Guillevic, Judith Herzberg, Sorley Maclean, Máirtín Ó Direáin. W. H. Smith Award. Duff Cooper Memorial Award for 1975 presented to SH by Robert Lowell.

1977 Reads at Rotterdam Poetry Festival; is visited in Ireland by fellow participant Les Murray and his wife Valerie. Tours Newgrange and Knowth megalithic passage tombs with the Murrays and other friends. Delivers address at Robert Lowell's memorial service in London. Visits Hugh MacDiarmid at his home in Biggar, Scotland.

1978 First visit to Struga Festival in Macedonia, later recalled in his poem 'Known World'.

1979 *Field Work* published. Spends spring semester as visiting lecturer in Harvard University, where he is accompanied by his family. Friendship with Helen Vendler, first established a few years earlier at the Yeats International Summer School in Sligo, strengthens. Meets Elizabeth Bishop frequently and forms lasting friendships with other poets, artists and writers in the Boston area. Also meets Bernard McCabe, a Professor of English at Tufts University: McCabe and his wife Jane will become important friends. Summer spent with family in Thomas Flanagan's house on Long Island and begins revision of *Sweeney Astray*. In December, takes part in panel on 'Current Unstated Assumptions about Poetry' at MLA Convention in San Francisco.

1980 *Preoccupations: Selected Prose 1968–1978* published. Meets Derek Walcott in New York. Judge, along with Ted Hughes, Philip Larkin and Charles Causley, of first Arvon Foundation Poetry Competition, for which 35,000 poems were entered. Guest-edits issue of *Ploughshares*.

1981 Becomes a director of Field Day Theatre Company, founded in 1980 by Brian Friel and Stephen Rea. Resigns from staff of Carysfort College. On holiday with family in France and Spain during culmination of IRA hunger strikes in Long Kesh prison. Later in summer, attends an international poetry festival in Morelia, state capital of Michoacán province in Mexico. Jorge Luis Borges, Octavio Paz, Vasko Popa, Marin Sorescu, Tadeusz Różewicz, Michael Hamburger, Tomas Tranströmer, Allen Ginsberg also on the programme.

1982 Begins temporary arrangement with Harvard University whereby he will teach there during spring semester for the next three years. Honorary degrees from QUB and Fordham University, New York, where SH delivers the commencement address in verse. Visits Orkney for first time; meets George Mackay Brown again. *The Rattle Bag*, anthology co-edited with Ted Hughes, published.

1983 *An Open Letter* published in Field Day pamphlet series, as SH's response to his inclusion as a 'British' poet in *The Penguin Book of Contemporary British Poetry*. *Sweeney Astray* published by Field Day. In summer, teaches a creative writing course at College of Notre Dame in Belmont, near San Francisco; while there, meets Czesław Miłosz for first time, in company of Robert Pinsky and Robert Hass.

1984 *Station Island* published. Death of SH's mother, Margaret
Kathleen. Harvard appointment alters from temporary contract
to tenured position as Boylston Professor of Rhetoric and
Oratory. Writes 'Alphabets' as Phi Beta Kappa poem for
Harvard. *Hailstones*, a limited edition of new poems, published
at The Gallery Press by SH's friend, the poet/editor Peter
Fallon. Guest-edits another issue of *Ploughshares*.

1985 Attends Festival of Youth and Students in Moscow on
invitation of Yevgeny Yevtushenko. Reads poems in Moscow,
then proceeds as guest poet for short trip to Soviet Republic of
Azerbaijan. PEN Translation Prize for *Sweeney Astray*.

1986 Takes part in celebration of 350th anniversary of founding
of Harvard College. Writes 'Villanelle for an Anniversary', in
response to a commission, and recites it to a convocation of
over 20,000 Harvard graduates and guests on 5 September.
Delivers the T. S. Eliot Memorial lectures at University of Kent,
Canterbury. Death of SH's father Patrick in October.

1987 *The Haw Lantern* published. Remembrance Day bombing in
Enniskillen. First visit to Japan, taking part in poetry festival at
Kanto Gakuin University. While in Tokyo, SH, accompanied by
the Irish ambassador, is granted audience with Crown Princess
(later Empress) Michiko, the first of several such meetings.

1987–8 Spends the full academic year in Harvard with wife
Marie, son Christopher and daughter Catherine Ann.

1988 *The Government of the Tongue* published. Delivers the first
Richard Ellmann Memorial Lectures at Emory University,
Atlanta, under the general title 'The Place of Writing'.
International Writers' Conference in Dun Laoghaire, during
which SH and fellow participants Joseph Brodsky, Les Murray
and Derek Walcott are recorded in discussion by the BBC.

1988–9 On sabbatical leave for year. Ann Saddlemyer sells
Glanmore Cottage to the Heaneys. To celebrate his fiftieth
birthday, SH and Marie visit Rome for the first time; during
summer he is elected as Professor of Poetry in Oxford
University. Joint celebratory poetry reading at Gate Theatre,
Dublin, for John Montague at sixty and SH at fifty.

1990 Prepares a version of Sophocles' *Philoctetes*, premiered by
Field Day Theatre Company as *The Cure at Troy*. Lannan
Literary Award.

1991 *Seeing Things* published. First performance, at Cibéal Festival in Kenmare, Co. Kerry, of 'The Poet and The Piper' – SH's collaborative event with *uilleann* piper Liam O'Flynn.

1993 Publishes *The Midnight Verdict*, translations from Ovid and Brian Merriman, at The Gallery Press. Elected as Foreign Honorary Member of American Academy of Arts and Letters.

1994 IRA ceasefire in late August. SH responds with article in *Sunday Tribune*, which is published while he is in Denmark, coincidentally, on a visit to Tollund Bog. Visits Krakow for launch of a Polish edition of his poems, translated by Stanisław Barańczak.

1994–5 Year's leave of absence from Harvard.

1995 *The Redress of Poetry: Oxford Lectures* published, as is *Laments* by Jan Kochanowski, co-translated by Stanisław Barańczak and SH. Undertakes translation of *Beowulf*. Visits Greece with Marie and friends Dimitri and Cynthia Hadzi. Award of Nobel Prize to SH announced while they are in Pylos in the Peloponnese. Ceremony in Stockholm in December, at which Nobel medal presented by King Carl XVI Gustaf of Sweden.

1996 *The Spirit Level* published. Attends Joseph Brodsky's memorial service in New York. Resigns as Boylston Professor and is appointed Emerson Poet in Residence at Harvard, a non-teaching role requiring a six-week visit on alternate years. Opens Bellaghy Bawn visitors' centre, which includes exhibits of SH books, recordings and memorabilia. QUB names its new library in honour of SH and he lays the foundation stone. Many other celebrations of Nobel Prize at local and international level: Harvard University, Bellaghy GAA Club, Magherafelt Rural District Council. SH delivers opening address at Frankfurt Book Fair, participates in L'Imaginaire Irlandais festival in France and gives Poetry Day reading at the Art Institute of Chicago. Elected to membership of Royal Irish Academy. Meets with Vaclav Havel on his presidential visit to Ireland.

1997 *The School Bag*, anthology co-edited with Ted Hughes, published. *The Spirit Level* wins Whitbread Book of the Year Award.

1998 *Opened Ground: Poems 1966–1996* published. Omagh bombing. Death of Ted Hughes. SH attends Hughes's funeral in

North Tawton, Devon, on his return from first session at
Harvard as Emerson Poet in Residence. Elected as *saoi*, the
highest honour of Aosdána, the Irish academy of artists.

1999 Translation of *Beowulf* published. SH's second visit to
Mexico; readings in Mexico City and Oaxaca. Delivers address
at Ted Hughes's memorial service in Westminster Abbey. *Diary
of One Who Vanished* premiered at Dublin Theatre Festival.
Wins Irish Times Literature Prize for *Opened Ground*.

2000 *Beowulf* wins Whitbread Book of the Year Award. SH
attends St Patrick's Day party in White House as guest of
President Bill Clinton. Lectures and reads at several millennial
celebrations, including Harvard Commencement. Visits
Denmark and reads from *Beowulf* at Lejre, reputed site of
Hrothgar's Hall. The Seamus Heaney Lectures (on education)
are inaugurated at St Patrick's College Dublin. On
31 December, SH and Marie travel to Stinsford church to read
Thomas Hardy's 'The Darkling Thrush' (dated 31 December
1900) at his grave.

2001 *Electric Light* published. Delivers tribute at R. S. Thomas's
memorial service in Westminster Abbey. Delivers first Darcy
O'Brien Memorial Lecture at University of Tulsa. Takes part in
three-day programme devoted to his work at Lincoln Center,
New York: a reading of *Beowulf*; a performance of 'The Poet
and The Piper' with Liam O'Flynn; and a presentation of *Diary
of One Who Vanished*. Golden Wreath awarded at International
Poetry Festival, Struga, Macedonia. Visits South Africa; reads
and lectures at Rhodes University, Grahamstown; in Cape Town
meets Kader Asmal – formerly of Trinity College Dublin – who
is Minister for Education in the South African government.
Attends centenary celebrations of Nobel Prize in Stockholm.

2002 Publishes *Finders Keepers: Selected Prose 1971–2001*.
Delivers Tanner Lectures on Human Values at Clare Hall,
Cambridge. Opens exhibition centre at Sutton Hoo
archaeological site in Suffolk for National Trust. Visits Prague,
reads at Charles University and travels on to Vilnius as guest of
Lithuanian Writers' Union. Gives first Hugh MacDiarmid
Lecture in Langholm, Scotland, MacDiarmid's birthplace.

2003 Trip to Russia: readings/lectures in St Petersburg and
Moscow; presents Joseph Brodsky tribute in the House on the

Fontanka, former home of Anna Akhmatova, and visits Brodsky's home apartment and other literary landmarks. *Finders Keepers* receives Truman Capote Award for Literary Criticism. Attends centenary celebrations for Rafael Alberti and Pablo Neruda in Residencia des Estudiantes, Madrid. Presents Amnesty International's Ambassador of Conscience Award to Vaclav Havel in Abbey Theatre, Dublin. 'The Poet and the Piper' recording by SH and Liam O'Flynn issued by Claddagh Records.

2004 Opening of SH Centre for Poetry, Queen's University. *Burial at Thebes*, SH's version of Sophocles' *Antigone*, premiered by Abbey Theatre. In Delphi on two occasions: at conference of writers speaking about the Greek influence on their work; then at celebrations of 2,500th anniversary of the birth of Sophocles. 'The Poet and the Piper' in Iceland. Attends funeral of Czesław Miłosz in Krakow. Holidays in Sicily and visits Greek Temples in Agrigento. Delivers centenary lecture in memory of Patrick Kavanagh at Inniskeen, Co. Monaghan. Features on stamps issued jointly by the postal services of Ireland and Sweden to celebrate 'Irish Nobel Literary Laureates'.

2005 Takes part in celebrations to mark Derek Walcott's seventy-fifth birthday. Visits and lectures in Asturias. Opens exhibition of material associated with Ragnarök in Silkeborg Museum. Also opens the Wordsworth Trust's Jerwood Centre in Grasmere. Receives Irish PEN Award. SH and Marie visited in Glanmore Cottage by Emperor and Empress of Japan. Lectures and reads at Bread Loaf Writers' Conference, Middlebury, Vermont. Premio Lerici Pea Award, Lerici, Italy.

2006 *District and Circle* published. Attends Hong Kong Literary Festival. Other readings in Ireland, USA, Rotterdam, Stratford-upon-Avon, Grasmere, Edinburgh. Suffers mild stroke in late August and is admitted to Royal Hospital, Donnybrook, Dublin. Complete recovery inside six weeks but engagements for next twelve months cancelled.

2007 *District and Circle* wins T. S. Eliot Prize and Irish Times Poetry Now Award. Delivers Ted Hughes Memorial Lecture at Ways with Words Festival, Dartington, the only engagement of the year he did not cancel. Resigns as Emerson Poet in Residence at Harvard. Elected to the Polish Academy of Arts and Sciences.

Visits classes in Anahorish School. The Gallery Press publishes *The Riverbank Field*, a limited edition of new poems.

2008 Attends *Poesia* poetry festival in Milan. Presented with Cunningham Medal, the 'premier award' of the Royal Irish Academy. Attends the unveiling by Queen Elizabeth II of a stone carved with his stanza commissioned to mark the centenary of the foundation of QUB.

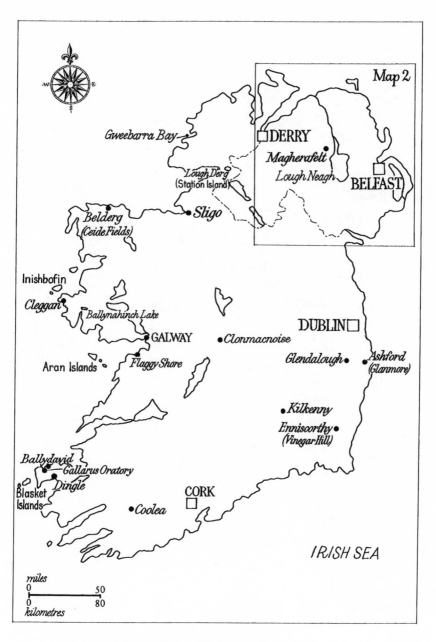

Map 1 Ireland (places referred to)

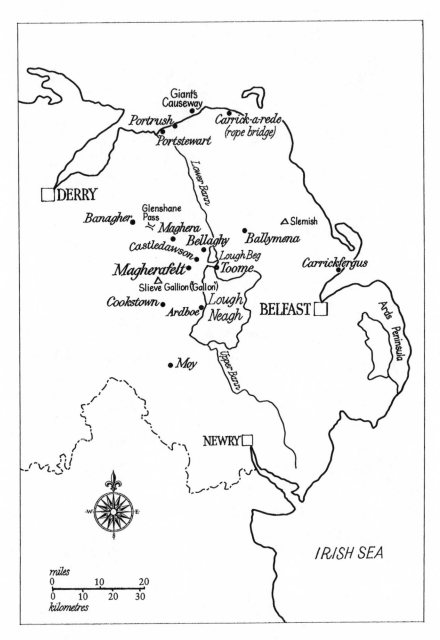

Map 2 Northern Ireland (places referred to)

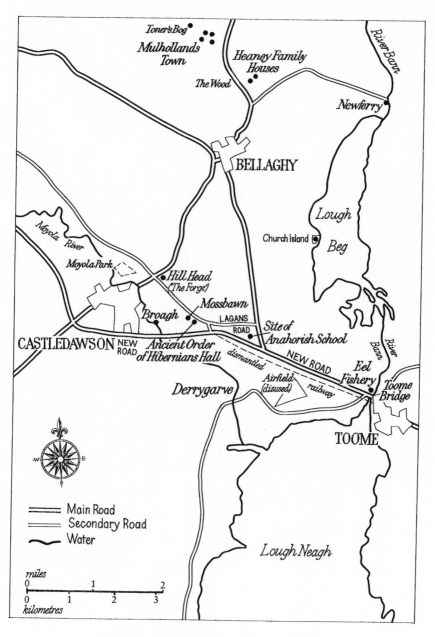

Map 3 South County Derry (detail)

I

BEARINGS

I

From Home to School

~

*You've said that, having so often read that you were born on a
farm in County Derry in 1939, you scarcely believe it any more.
Can public life as a prominent writer rob you of your private life?
If so, does poetry restore that missing life or at least provide some
recompense?*

Many of the poems are doing something like that. You end up drop-
ping back through your own trapdoors, with a kind of 'they-can't-
take-this-away-from-me' feeling. There's a paradox, of course, since
the poems that provide the recompense are the very ones that turn
your private possessions into images that are – as Yeats once said –
'all on show'. Yet a poem saves as well as shows. The remark about
not believing I was born on a farm comes less from the poems than
from reading too many 'Notes on Contributors' . . .

*Before we talk about your books and how you came to write
them, could I take a guided tour around your first place,
Mossbawn?*

We're talking about a one-storey, longish, lowish, thatched and
whitewashed house, about thirty yards in from the main road.
Parallel to the road. Somebody riding past on a bike would have
seen it through a thorn hedge and a screen of young alder trees
growing on a bank just behind the hedge. Beyond the alders was
what we called 'the front garden' – a mini-field of sorts – and
between the front garden and the house was a boxwood hedge.
The lane, or loaning, went straight in from the road and formed
one end of that front garden. So you walked down the lane, with

3

beech trees on either side of you, and turned left on to 'the front street'. Then, if you stood facing the front door, you had on your right the front window of the 'kitchen' or living room; farther along on your right was the front window of the 'upper bedroom'. On your left, you had the front window of the 'lower bedroom' and, beyond that, the stable door – since the stable was 'under the roof' with the dwelling house.

What kind of traffic is on the road in the forties?

Cars, now and again. Buses, backwards and forwards, morning, noon, afternoon, evening, night. We were on the main route between Belfast and Magherafelt, Belfast and Cookstown, Belfast and Derry, and were very conscious of the buses since there was a bus stop at the end of the Broagh Road, not far from the end of the lane. There were bicycles too, a few regular pedallers and the occasional traveller from farther up or down the country. Kathleen Garvin going to her job in Castledawson. Paddy McNicholl going to do yardwork in Gribbin's of Anahorish. RUC men now and again. But the most spectacular was definitely Master Pollock, a schoolmaster, a recreational cyclist in shorts, pelting along on his 'racer' – he always created a bit of a stir. Then there were the lorries – coal lorries, cattle lorries, quarry lorries, sand lorries, door-to-door grocery vans and butchers' vans. Horses and carts, donkeys and carts even, though they were rare enough.

Was there a family car?

We never had a car when we lived at Mossbawn. All that had to wait until we moved to The Wood farm in the 1950s. At that stage my father learned to drive and we had a succession of big heavy saloons – big because the family was big, but also because he needed a big boot for ferrying bales of hay and bags of meal and newborn calves. At different times there was an Austin 16 and a Vauxhall Victor and a Humber Hawk, all second-hand. And of course all of them ended up hard to start and needing to be pushed, so that was one way the Heaney family used to come together, shoulder to shoulder, gathering momentum, waiting for the engine to fire.

How did your father manage to conduct his cattle-dealing business – travelling to farms and cattle fairs – before becoming a driver?

He got a lot of lifts. When I was very young, his partner in the trade was another farmer-dealer called Patsy McWilliams, who lived three miles down the road at Toomebridge. Patsy had a car and was always pulling up on the front street or tooting his horn at the end of the lane. A bit later on, my father teamed up with another dealer from Maghera called Jim McKenna, who had a car I remember very well: a Triumph Mayflower – a rather smooth, well-polished grey saloon; classy for a cow-man. Jim drove me and my parents in the Mayflower when I went for the first time to St Columb's College, forty miles away in Derry. He also drove me home from college on the day I got the news that my brother Christopher had been killed in a road accident – at that bus stop, incidentally, at the end of the Broagh Road . . .

. . . which must have tainted the stop dreadfully for the family.

It did. But what was to be done? My mother still had to get to Castledawson.

That's where she did the shopping?

Yes. She was a bus-taker – whether for the mile and a half to 'the town', as we called the village, for the main weekly shopping, or to the larger shopping centres of Magherafelt or Cookstown. In each of those towns she had houses to call in: my grandfather and grandmother's place in New Row in Castledawson; my uncle Peter's – her brother's – in Magherafelt; and her sister Sarah's in Cookstown. So there was a social edge to the shopping outings, and a place to wait for 'the service bus', as it was called. It also meant that, as children, we could travel with her and then be left off in those family houses while she made her purchases.

Did your mother cycle sometimes?

Aunt Mary, my father's sister, who lived with us, was the bicycle woman. She would ride to Mass in Bellaghy on a Sunday. My mother might have used the bike very early on, but she was physically a heavier woman, more encumbered, less lightsome than Mary. When it came to shopping, there was a fair amount of walking involved. I suppose there were three ratings in the shopping experience: first of all, 'wee shops' out on their own in the country, like Biddy Gribbin's in Anahorish, or Kealey's at Hillhead, where the ad hoc shopping was done. Sweets and cigarettes. Tide-me-over purchases of cooking stuff. Then in Castledawson there were the fuller scale provisioners, places where – as I've said – the rations were bought week by week. Farther afield, in Magherafelt and Cookstown in one direction, and Ballymena in the other, there were the exotic drapery emporia and larger shoe shops. Suits of clothes for the children, new 'rig-outs' for the women, materials for curtains, purchases like wedding presents or finer household goods – those things usually involved special trips by bus.

But sugar, tea, bacon, lard, self-raising flour, dried fruit and other desultory things – wool or thread or pot-menders or shoelaces or the local papers – were shopped for closer to home. I often walked to Gribbin's and Kealey's and for that matter to Castledawson. My aunt Mary occasionally went on her bike, but never for the full rations. Her domain was more yard and dairy, milking and baking.

What about the travelling shop? Was there barter of any sort – trading of eggs, for example?

I'd forgotten about the eggs. Our travelling grocery van came from County Antrim and was run first by a man called McCartney, but 'the egg man' was our name for him. It wasn't a case of barter: he bought and paid for the eggs every week and my mother bought and paid for whatever she needed. I remember dry goods and tinned goods on little narrow shelves that ran round the inside of the van, fitted with laths to retain the cans and jars and bottles.

In latter days, incidentally, when people had their own cars and the mobile shop was being knocked out of business, some shopmen diversified by turning themselves into poteen distributors – their most faithful clientele would anyhow have included old bachelors living at the end of long lanes, ideal customers for a drop of the clear stuff. There was a big illicit trade going on in those days.

Any brand names – of groceries I mean, not poteen! – that continue to resonate?

Colman's mustard, in powder form, say; Camp Coffee – liquid 'essence of coffee', with a wonderful illustration on the label of a British officer in full regalia, kilt and all that, being served his coffee by an Indian batman. HP sauce. Tate and Lyle's Golden Syrup in broad round tins. Biscuits: Arrowroot and Rich Tea, a great luxury when buttered. Saxa Salt and indeed Carrick Salt, from Carrickfergus. The Carrick Salt packet used to have this great illustration of a woman running after a hen, trying to throw salt on its tail – the belief being that salt on the tail would halt a hen in flight.

Maybe we should store away the groceries and resume the tour . . . When I reach the farmyard, what outbuildings do I see? What's inside them? What's in the yard?

Well, as you come down the lane, you're looking into the first farm building, the one we called simply 'the shed'. It stood at the gable end of the house, a wooden-framed, zinc-roofed job, open at one end, the other walls made from flattened-out tar barrels. Old tar barrels, for some reason, were in plentiful supply. They'd had the bottoms knocked out of them and were unriveted and unrolled so as to make a tin panel that could then be nailed up on a wooden frame. Inside the shed there might be some bags of grain or potatoes or fertilizer or a farrowing crate. It had a clay floor. A smell of old meal. Implements in the corners. Swallows' nests up on the rafters.

And besides the shed?

Walk on with the gable of the house on your left and the shed on your right and you're into the back yard. One side of that is defined by the dwelling house and opposite, on the other side, say fifteen yards away, you have the byre and – later on – a pig house. The byre was an old structure, a cow house, no windows; cow stalls on your left when you went in, with room for four cows; stalls again on your right, although these weren't used for cattle in my time, more for storage of fodder. Beast smells and manure smells. A 'groop', as it was called, a sunk trench in the concrete floor running to a back outlet, to drain the piss and catch the cow dung. Cleaning the byre involved barrowing out the contents of the groop, sluicing it down and rebedding it with clean straw. Then wheeling that barrowful of stuff out to the dunghill, or the *duchull*, as we pronounced it – to rhyme more or less with Ahoghill, except that that won't be much of a help to anybody who doesn't know the pronunciation of Ahoghill . . .

Where do I find the omphalos, as you've called the pump?

It stood immediately outside the back door and, when you were pumping, you faced a windbreak of sorts, a couple of old hawthorn trees. They made a little division between the yard proper and the hen run and hen house. There was an outside toilet, set back in its own quiet corner. Also a kitchen garden where my aunt Mary used to work at growing vegetables – and sweet peas on a netting-wire fence. Then too there was the haggard – the stackyard, with cocks of hay for fodder, straw for bedding and, at a certain time of the year, stacks of the unthreshed corn. It sounds very idyllic, but it was a small, ordinary, nose-to-the-grindstoney place. A subsistence-level life.

If I stand still for a minute in the yard, what sounds might I hear?

Hens. Cackles and clucks. Coming up to Christmas, turkeys or geese. All year round the occasional roar of a calf or a cow. Maybe a train shunting at the station in Castledawson – because we had the railway, running parallel to the road, about a hundred yards away at the end of the field behind the byre. Later on, in the early fifties, when we began to keep pork pigs, you'd hear them grunting too, although the earliest pig calls I recollect were screams coming from the Gribbin slaughterhouse in Anahorish, a quarter of a mile away. The Gribbins were in the pig trade, and on a Tuesday morning they killed. Then too, there would have been the factory horn of Clarke's Mill in Castledawson, every morning and evening – and an occasional thud of explosion from a quarry somewhere or other on the horizon, maybe at Lavey, maybe farther away at Glenshane Pass. One sound that struck me as special, even at the time, was the rat-a-tat of a pony and cart driven by a man called Bob Cushley: Bob always kept the jennet going at a really fast lick and brought a kind of storybook glamour to the place. Every other horse and cart lumbered and lock-stepped along but Bob seemed to have some kind of Phaethon complex and to be always trying for lift-off.

Were horses important to you as a child? Which breeds did the family favour?

In Mossbawn we always had one horse, but we had the use of Mackle's mare any time a second horse was needed – to yoke in a mowing machine, say, or a potato digger. When I was very young, the horse was called Neddy, a big black carthorse with a white spot on his forehead. One of my very first memories is of going out to the field with a handful of corn stalks and holding them up to Neddy's nose. They must have tickled him or irritated him in the eye, for he lifted one of his front hoofs and pushed me – pushed, I still think, rather than kicked me to the ground.

I have no sense of what breed the horses were – the breed names I heard then had to do with cattle – nor can I remember what happened to Neddy. He must have been sold, probably to an old horse dealer or drover who used to call with us now and again on his journeys between fairs. He'd be taking a couple of horses long distances and would occasionally lie out overnight in the shed – a great mystery to us youngsters. At any rate, we then had a second horse, but only briefly, a mare that had to be put down. She had bolted suddenly in the field, torn off with a saddle-harrow still harnessed to her, and eventually ended up with a broken leg in a roadside drain. A beautiful young chestnut creature. I'll never forget her standing at the gable of the house that evening, although I cannot remember how they managed to get her from the roadside to the yard. She was on the spot where the horses always used to be clipped, standing high and quiet while the man with the portable electric shears buzzed under and round and bared the veins on the belly. But this time she was shivering and shivered more vehemently still when the man put the humane killer to her brow and dropped her with one hard smart crack.

After that, we had a big, broad-backed, good-natured white pony called Ben, and I used to ride Ben now and again, going from the field to the stable, say, or the stable to the field. I also used to ride Mackle's mare, Kate, usually with one of the Mackles leading her and one walking at her side. There was always an element of the treat, and just the slightest element of anxiety, when you were near horses. They were approached with circumspection. But then, it's hard for any operation with horses not to have a certain ceremonial aspect to it. Even catching one in the field, putting the winkers on, putting the collar on – it was an investiture every time.

Having collared your horse, what was it used for? Was it a case of the cart being put after the horse – and then the tractor arriving as a replacement to the horse?

The horses were used for carting stuff from field to barn, or from shop to farm – grain, potatoes, provisions; or for work in the fields – ploughing, harrowing, drilling, grubbing, rolling, mowing, potato digging, drawing in hay or corn or turf. And yes, of course, the tractor gradually replaced them. In our case, there was an interim period when we had no horse and no tractor of our own; instead we used the services of local farmers who 'worked to the country'. The pace of farm work speeded up greatly with the tractor: on those small-holdings, a man who owned a tractor could do his ploughing in less than half the time it had taken previously; as a result, he was free to hire himself and the machinery to neighbours. It was really just an updating of the old system of helping out with horses and hands at busy times of the year.

Did you ever use a pony and trap?

There was an old broken-down trap in the shed when I was very young. By the early forties, the pony and trap were well on their way out, although I do remember being in a trap somewhere and enjoy-ing the clip and lightness and elegance of the ride. The nearest thing to the sensation that I've experienced since was in Hagi, in Japan, when Marie and I were given a run in a rickshaw. A visitor's treat; but, even so, it still felt a bit wrong. On a rickshaw you have a god's-eye view of labouring humanity, the bowed head and the bent back. But there's also this borne-aloft, speedy, airy propulsion – the same thing that made a pony and trap such an attractive get-up.

How dependent was the house on rainwater? How was it collected? Where did your drinking water come from?

Rainwater! Amazing to be answering these questions, ending up as your own anthropological specimen. Rainwater we collected off the byre roof, since the byre was covered with corrugated iron and had a spouting. There was no way of collecting it off the dwelling-house thatch; and, besides, with all the smoke it absorbed from the chimney, the thatch would have polluted anything that seeped through. The rainwater was prized because it was soft and made excellent suds. It was carried in from the barrel as needed, and heated in big pots and saucepans on the stove.

Drinking water came from the pump at the back door, but it was hard water, and if you washed with it the soap ended up in a grimy line around the basin. It also built up a hard lining inside the kettle, so we would keep a marble in the kettle to prevent it from silting up too quickly. Drinking water sat in a bucket on a stool in the scullery. And the scullery was located in a tiny extension, a little brick box built at the back door, one part scullery and one even smaller part pantry. No running water, no inside toilets. None of that until the mid-fifties, when we built a new two-storey house down at The Wood.

The pantry and the scullery – what roles did they play?

The dishes were washed in the scullery, the vegetables prepared, the wellington boots worn in the yard kept behind the door there, the Primus stove, the oilcans, the water bucket. Then too there was a separate basin for washing hands and faces and general toiletries. Plus a small bath where the washing of clothes was done. In the pantry, the milk and butter, the flour I think, although that too may have been in the scullery. We're talking about very small spaces.

What's it like inside the Mossbawn kitchen?

Well, you come in through the front door, and immediately on your right there's a jamb wall, a wooden partition that reaches into the kitchen for about four or five feet, making a little hallway of sorts. Hooks for coats on the wall there, and on top of the partition, a shallow storage space where, for example, the first hank of tow would be kept – every year that first flax to be scutched would be brought home from the mill, as a matter of course, for general inspection and admiration, to be combed out and tested for strength. As you proceed into the kitchen, the door to the lower bedroom is on your left, then and, opposite you, the back door to the scullery. A stove and chimney breast on the inside to your right. An armchair. A sofa under the front window. A cot for the baby on the inside of the jamb wall. Ordinary bow-backed kitchen chairs.

On the walls, a holy calendar and two embroidered pictures, done years before by my aunt Sarah. One of Dunluce Castle in County Antrim, the other of Carrickfergus Castle. And a kind of little shrine picture, to commemorate the Eucharistic Congress in Dublin in 1932 – the three patron saints of Ireland on it, Patrick, Brigid and Colmcille, and little ornamental medallions with motifs of round towers and Celtic crosses. A tiny red glass lamp on the mantelpiece kept lit for the Sacred Heart. Saint Brigid's crosses behind the pictures.

It's small, I suppose, but I didn't particularly feel that at the time. The floor is cement – concrete would be too hard-and-fast a word for the generally gravelly composition – it's smoothy-crumbly, and at one place there's a little corroded hollow where we pour out the milk for the cats. For light, the front door's open in the summer, the usual mote-slants in the bedrooms from the windows. At night, candles in the bedrooms, an oil lamp on the wall in the kitchen, maybe a hurricane lamp in the scullery. The Tilley lamp and the Aladdin came later.

What's cooking? Is it a house where you have your 'dinner' in the middle of the day?

On the stove, there'd be feeds for the fowl and the animals: potatoes to be mashed up for hen food, gruels for calves, that kind of thing; sometimes big pots of washing, white fabrics being boiled for extra whiteness. The kettle kept on the boil. Stewing. Baking. Scones on the griddle at a certain time of the day. Scones or cakes in the oven. Women's work was never done . . . Getting us out to school, getting a breakfast: porridge, bread and butter mostly, maybe a boiled egg – but that was more for my father. Then we had a man who worked about the farm and he would get his own special midday meal. Also there was the children's 'dinner', when we came home from school, at half-three, four o'clock. Then a supper around seven. And with my father out at the fairs, and his irregular hours, there was no telling when a place would have to be set for him. Saturdays and Sundays were a bit more regular. A late lunch or, you're right, 'dinner', usually a stew. On Sunday, a pot roast. And often a salad on Sunday evening. Our own lettuce. Our own hard-boiled eggs. Home-made egg mayonnaise. Home-grown scallions. Tinned salmon, maybe.

Your mother must have had a hectic life. Did she manage to sit down with you at the meals?

My mother rarely sat down with us, she tended to hover, or would come to the table late. But maybe I'm remembering how it was when we were all a bit bigger, in the new house in The Wood. My father did have his place at the top of the table all right. But we were rarely all assembled round the table at the one time. We made an event of it, mind you, on Christmas Day. The upper bedroom would be turned into a kind of dining room, since there was a leaf table there that could be opened up to accommodate us, and it was always a great occasion: tablecloth, special dinner service, the canteen of cutlery opened, a fire in the grate, the goose, the apple sauce . . .

A dinner service sounds posh.

Well, maybe I should say a dinner *set*: it had been a wedding present and some of it was kept on the top shelf of the dresser and some in the cupboard part at the bottom. My sister still has several plates from it, sixty years on, a gravy jug and a sauce boat also. It had a pattern of autumn leaves, deep tans on a creamy-golden ground, with a gold edging on every piece. China, so it was treated carefully and rarely used: for visitors maybe; or at holidays, Easter or Christmas. Custom and ceremony, as the poet would have said. Otherwise we made do with more durable stuff: blue-ringed mugs and bowls; white crockery plates and soup plates. Although there were always a few big white china cups and saucers. I suppose that's why that poem of Padraic Colum's stays in the memory: 'A dresser filled with shining delph, / Speckled and white and blue and brown!'

'I could be quiet there at night, / Beside the fire and by myself, / Sure of a bed and loth to leave / The ticking clock and the shining delph'. Is that how it was in the evenings?

The clean-swept floor, the closed doors that let the heat gather, the shut-in safety of the kitchen, it was all there. But what I remember is more huddled and snug, less highlighted and gleaming than in Colum's poem. It was an atmosphere created by grown-ups winding down. My father tended to stretch out on the sofa, my mother to be in the armchair, my aunt at the table maybe. A big luxury for my mother was to bathe her feet at night – there was real appeasement in the sound of hot water from the kettle stroop going into the basin of cold stuff. No private bathroom then. No cricket on the hearth either, by the way, since we had a terrific little iron stove called – imagine – 'The Modern Mistress', a coal-burner that gave off a fierce heat when it was stoked up. One of the big thrills was to see the round iron lids redden up as it overheated. The open hearth and the turf fire were part of the attraction of the house in The Wood where my aunt Grace and uncle Hughie lived.

Can I take a peek into the different rooms, see what's in them: iron beds, maybe, big old wardrobes, chests of drawers . . . And what about the floors and floor coverings, the wallpaper and the cubbyholes?

One thing I remember early on is the pleasure of tearing wallpaper off the wall beside the bed. There was pink distempered plaster underneath that made the perfect surface for writing on with a pencil . . . 'The lower room' had a 'cement' floor with linoleum and a couple of rugs. The upper bedroom had a wooden floor, and there was a sheepskin rug in front of the fireplace, and a wardrobe, not very big or gaunt; probably an acquisition by the newlyweds, although it did have its mysteries – that soft, lavish feel of hanging clothes, womany fragrances, everything always on silent hold. 'Down the room' there were indeed three of those big iron-frame beds that would eventually end up as makeshift gates, brass-turreted jobs, real old jinglers, as broad as ruck-shifters. They more or less filled the room. There was also a screened-off corner with shelves and hangers that had to do as a wardrobe for my aunt's clothes and the youngsters'.

When I think of it, I can hardly believe that we all fitted in. The infant was in a pram in the upper bedroom where my parents slept. And the next baby was up there too, in a cot. In the lower room, my sisters slept with my aunt Mary, and the rest of us divided ourselves out in the other two beds.

Which of the rooms is the one in which, as a baby in your cot, your feet touch the floor?

It wasn't a bedroom, it was in the kitchen, on the other side of the jamb wall from the little hallway. And that was a different cot from the one in the room where the baby slept. A much sturdier job. Joe Ward, the carpenter, who lived across the road from us, made it and it was used by every one of the family as they came along – in fact, Marie and I had it in Glanmore Cottage thirty years later, when Catherine was born. Plywood ends, rails and dowel rods for sides, set on little rockers, so it was just that bit up off the floor. The bottom was made of boards, removable, not nailed down, just laid

14

across as slats, so when you got to a certain age you could lift one or two of them out and step down on to the ground. Antaeus Óg, just touching base.

Did you really hear rats on the ceiling boards above your head in the bedroom, as described in 'An Advancement of Learning'? What other sounds could you catch in your bedroom?

There was thatch on the roof, don't forget, then a tongue-and-groove ceiling, so yes, there'd often be this scratching and scuttling. Mice, presumably. But every now and again there would be a more substantial traveller on the boards, most unwelcome, and we'd presume it to be Mr Rat. But the comfort sound in the bedroom was the horse beyond the wall. You'd hear these occasional big body rolls and foot stamps in the stable. Big flubby snorts of contentment. There was contentment and security also from the voice of the newsreader on the wireless and talk going on in the kitchen. Sometimes a train passed at night, or the dog would bark, maybe at a drunk man out on the road.

When you look out through the different windows of the house, what do you see?

Not very much, really. For a start, the windows are small, and set comparatively low. From the back window, you'd see the yard and the byre; from the front, the boxwood hedge with a young chestnut tree in it, the front garden, the alder trees along the road. If you were outside you could look south-west to Slieve Gallon on the horizon: our hill of longing.

Are there any animals slaughtered on the farm? How much of the comestibles are home produced?

One of my abiding memories is of my father reaching down into a tea chest full of salt and pulling out a lump of home-cured bacon. That must have been just after the end of the war, and I have a feeling there was an element of contraband about it. I think it was a pig of our own that had been killed and cured and kept. He was taking out a bit to sell to a neighbour . . . But that was a rare moment. Hens and chickens would have had their necks pulled now and again and been boiled. Geese killed and plucked at Christmas, turkeys later on. Much of the beef was bought from travelling butchers' carts. On the other hand, most of the vegetables were home grown – not necessarily in the garden; along one side of the potato field, there'd be a few drills of turnips, cabbage, carrots, parsnips maybe, cauliflower, Brussels sprouts. In the garden, you'd have early potatoes, coming ahead of the main field crops. Arran Peaks and Arran Banners were crop potatoes with us, Golden Wonders often in the garden, Kerr's Pinks too.

Speaking of vegetable plots, in both Stations *and* Preoccupations *you recall being lost among pea drills. Were the peas grown for use by the household or were they grown commercially? And why did your getting lost prove such a* cause célèbre *in your family?*

I don't actually have a clear memory of the moment; but I do have clear memories of them talking about it, so that's how the story originates. On the other hand, I know exactly where it happened and often saw peas growing there. It wasn't in the garden, for some reason, but at the side of the field between our back yard and the railway. There was an old well under a hawthorn bush, just beside the cart track, and in front of the well there was an earthen slipway of sorts, about fifteen or twenty feet of softish clay ramp, and for some reason my aunt Mary grew peas there. A little place of her own. It was by no means a commercial venture, in fact I believe the place was more like a flower bed to her than a vegetable patch. Anyhow, I loved the rods and the whole profusion of stalks and leaves and pods, and must have felt the attraction very early on. So that was where I got to and, since it was out of the yard and a wee bit beyond the known world, so to speak, it took them a while to find me. A *cause célèbre*, I suppose, because of unforgettable panic: the child was lost!

Did the butter-making of 'Churning Day' actually take place in Mossbawn? Why did you need to get that activity into such exact, evocative words so early in your life? Was it because you – or even Ireland as a whole – had begun to lose contact with that way of life?

Nothing as general or sociological was at work. It was more a case of personal securing, the kind of thing you mentioned at the start, an entirely intuitive move to restore something to yourself. You're also dealing with the unpredictable, the way one memory can unexpectedly open the writing channels and get you going. The churning experience was already inscribed in me, if you'll excuse the expression, from the time I used to take my turn with the churn-staff. No dairy, by the way, but a churn in the middle of the kitchen floor – it was usually kept out in the scullery but there was no room in the scullery to get at the action. A plunge churn, hooped and lidded, the timber lid with a hole in the middle of it to let it down over the staff. It was hard work but social work, whoever was in the house giving a hand, needing to keep the slush and slap of it going. You could never be sure how long the job would take: the moment the butter appeared was always special, but the wait for it was always tinged with anxiety. No wonder there used to be all those old superstitions about neighbours blinking the cow or the milk.

In terms of barns, outhouses, acreage, are we talking about an average holding for the locality?

My father's land consisted of two small farms he had inherited. One in Mossbawn, and one in Broagh, which I haven't mentioned because it had no dwelling house and we had no sense of domestic connection with it. Broagh was where my Heaney grandparents had lived – and died relatively early – and in Broagh we had three good stone outhouses. One was called 'the barn' – a very dry place where grain could lie and often did – although never for long, given the rat problem. I remember wheat being 'lashed' over a roller barrel in the corner of it: handful by handful, they threshed the grain off the heads of the crop in such a way as to keep the actual stalks unbroken for thatching. Then too there were a couple of cattle sheds in the Broagh, where hay and straw would often be stored. Those sheds, incidentally, were also erotic shrines of a sort, very snug and silent and warm and much favoured by courting couples after dark. The next day you'd come on these nice big haynests with sweet wrappers and orange peelings scattered all over the place. Amazing how early you 'begin to take notice' – as they used to observe in their decorous way.

How far was Broagh from Mossbawn?

Half a mile, maybe more. I'm not sure. There were different ways to go. Down the field, up the railway, through the fields again. Or round by the side road, twisting and turning. If we went by the road, we passed quite a few of our own fields. Broagh, as you know, is the Irish for riverbank, *bruach*, and a bit of our ground came up to the bank of the Moyola – 'the long rigs', 'the riverbank field' and 'the half acre'. Then there was 'Brian's field' and 'the field at Mackle's' and 'the field in front of Mary McErlean's'. These last three were scattered among other people's land, but at Mossbawn we had seven fields all contiguous – small, mind you, but all of a piece, a region to ramble in . . . All in all, I think the land amounted to something like forty acres. By no means 'a big farm' but bigger by ten or fifteen acres, I'd say, than others around us.

Was there any hint of class distinction between the people with larger and smaller holdings? Between Catholics and Protestants, for that matter?

We were at eye level, socially, with most neighbours. And in fact, in that part of the country – I'm speaking very particularly – the Protestant neighbours weren't really all that well off. Willie Evans over the road from us was a labouring man, and had no land. Sandy and Rachel Evans had a bungalow-type house with roses and a certain style, but owned no more than a couple of fields. The Gilmores and Dawsons farther up the main road had no land to mention either.

But we were on very good terms with all of these people. Respectable neighbours, you know, all part of something settled. The Garvins, for example, would have been more or less the same kind of family as we were, in terms of the size of the farm, the nonsectarian disposition of the household, and a general un-anxiousness about where they stood. And then there were those two other Evans men I mention here and there in the poems, George and Alan, very easy in their way of going on, very friendly. They had been in the army during the war and brought my father a big set of rosary beads from Rome after they were demobbed. Their remark about having stolen the beads off the Pope's dresser was much quoted.

Where was the flax dam positioned in relation to the family house? Where was Anahorish School? Maybe you'd situate me again?

Suppose the Mossbawn house is a short horizontal line on the face of a clock, on the level between nine and three: you look out the front door and you're looking over the main road straight up at twelve o'clock. Behind you at six, but only a field away, is the railway, another horizontal line parallel to the house. At nine o'clock, to your left along the main road, is Hillhead. At three o'clock, straight down it, is Toomebridge. Somewhere between one and two – along a side road called Lagans Road – is Anahorish School. Don't forget now, you're still standing facing twelve: the River Moyola is off the clock behind you, down below six o'clock, half a mile beyond the railway at the end of the Lower Broagh Road. And the flax dam is along that lower road. Aren't you sorry now that you asked?

Now that I know – to the last second! – the whereabouts of Anahorish School, I must ask what memories you retain of the place, of learning to read there, for instance.

Yes, my memory of learning to read goes back to my first days in Anahorish School, the charts for the letters, the big-lettered reading books. But I don't think I showed any particular promise or volubility as a child – certainly nobody ever recorded my first words. I cried on the first morning I went to school, of course. My father was shaving, getting ready to go to a fair. Phil McNicholl, a girl a year or two older than me who lived just beyond the carpenter's house, had the job of bringing me but I let up the bawl the minute she came to the door and my father had to pretend to be angry – although it didn't seem like pretence then. I went off very sorrowfully. When we got near the school, I was surprised to see so many children running about the place at that time of the morning, then the old breadcrumby smell of the porch, the bareness and extent of the rows of coat hangers. I remember also being embarrassed about my schoolbag – it wasn't new and it wasn't strictly speaking a schoolbag. Something better, maybe, but it wasn't what others had, so it bothered me. It was a hand-made leather shoulder pouch, the kind of thing bus conductors used to collect fares in; it had belonged to my uncle Peter, I think, who drove a bread cart and had to have a shoulder bag for his money. What I liked best about those first days, I have to say, was being taken care of by Phil, having a special closeness to her. First love, I suppose.

What did you see and hear on the road to school?

It was a bit of a nature trail, in its way: a side road with mostly high hedges, going through boggy ground, bog holes, shrubs and briars and rushes in the meadows alongside. One of those old lonely byways with grass growing on the crown of it, daisies and dandelions, foxgloves and primroses at different times of the year at the roadside. Birds' nests in the springtime. Often, too, gypsies camped in the shelter of the hedge – or rather tinkers, which was not then a demeaning term, by the way, but one that still carried a whiff of its tinsmith, repairman associations. Brightly painted caravans, tents made of old tarpaulins draped over bent sapling branches, fires burning, the ponies hobbled here and there in gaps. All very storybooky, no doubt, but just the usual thing at that time. Then in the summer, in the afternoons, there would be this parked car with the windows steamed up and, for all the stillness surrounding it, you knew there was action going on in the back seat. That clandestine thing always gave us a charge.

The road was called Lagans Road and there was a little hill on it, called Mulholland's Brae. From the top of Mulholland's Brae, depending on the weather, you could see Slemish mountain in County Antrim – a volcanic lump, but fabulous because St Patrick was said to have herded sheep there for a farmer called Miliucc, after he was first brought to Ireland as a slave. You could always see the shine of Lough Beg, just a mile away, and the spire above trees on Church Island – a definite landmark.

Can you remember missing school because of illness? Did you have all the usual childhood complaints?

All of them. I remember being in bed all day and the curtains pulled on the window when I had the measles. And having the extraordinary experience of 'raving', as they called it. Fever and rambling and a sort of hallucination. It was scaresome but it was a high. The elders were there at the bedside trying to calm you and, even though you couldn't be calmed, their presence made you feel safe. Then too there were the mumps. Big scarves wrapped round the big swellings. And 'swollen glands', whatever they were. I don't hear of youngsters with that complaint nowadays. There was the fear of diphtheria too, very strongly, and the inoculation against it that was done at the school. And there were boils. By God, there were boils. At times the classroom looked like a field hospital, there were so many bandaged necks.

Did you have any awareness of illness among the grown-ups?

Not a great deal. You heard about old people being 'a-waiting on' – on their deathbed. You heard the word 'stroke'. And the word 'decline'; but that particular 'decline' didn't refer to people losing ground in the course of an illness. It was a hush-hush word for tuberculosis. And it usually came up in conversations about the past that you'd overhear but not quite follow. It belonged to the vocabulary of dread. Several of my father's siblings had died of TB, or consumption, in the 1920s and I suppose fear of the disease was constantly haunting that whole generation.

Were there locals who were reputed to have cures and traditional remedies?

There were people who had the cure of ringworm, certainly. I remember my brother Hugh being taken to some man or woman in County Antrim for whatever rites or words and applications were called for. And I think his recovery was attributed to that visit. Ringworm was a constant scourge on farms at that time, very easy to pick up from posts or walls or gates or whatever the cattle had been in contact with. And very distressful, itchy and raw by turns. Then there was a big woman called Trea McWilliams who could cure a stye in the eye. I often heard them talk about what she did, but again have only the vaguest recollection. I think it involved the sign of the cross and the thorn from a gooseberry bush, and Trea's disappearance to the bedroom in the course of the visit, presumably to pray. She was a bit of an exotic in the district anyhow, a wife who had come from the shores of Lough Neagh, more of a fisher woman than a farm woman.

We have, so far, been concentrating mainly on the Mossbawn part of your upbringing. But one of the most dramatic moments in your childhood must have been your family's move from Mossbawn to the farm at The Wood. How far away from Mossbawn was The Wood?

Oh, four or five miles. Less as the crow flies.

A relocation of that nature is extremely unusual for a farmer's family.

There were two main reasons for the move. The first was that my father inherited the farm at The Wood when his uncle Hughie died, round about 1952 or 53. The second was the fact that there was a bad feeling about staying on so close to the road where Christopher was killed in February 1953.

Would you mind saying something more about that accident? The poem 'Mid-Term Break' is so well known.

I wasn't there on the evening it happened, but I do have a clear picture of it in my mind. It was at the bus stop a little up the road from our lane. Christopher and my brother Hugh were on one side of the road, posting a letter on the bus for Belfast – it used to be you could hand a letter to the conductor and it would be mailed later that evening in the city; it saved a trip to the post office. Anyhow, at that same moment, my brothers Pat and Dan were walking up the road on the other side, on an errand to fetch a gallon of paraffin oil from a house farther along. As the bus moves off, Christopher – who is three and a half years old – sees the two boys on the other side and immediately starts across the road towards them. But while the bus is pulling away, a car is coming in the opposite direction, and Christopher runs out from behind the bus straight into the side of the car and is knocked down. The driver hadn't a chance. What happens next I can hardly bear to think about: Hugh lifts him and holds him, bleeding and probably unconscious; then the man who is a passenger in the car comes and takes Christopher and carries him the thirty or forty yards to our lane, Hugh behind him, weeping all the time. My mother, who is out at the clothes line, hears it and comes round to the street and sees what has happened. All in a few minutes. He was taken to the Mid-Ulster Hospital in Magherafelt and died a couple of hours later.

I can well imagine the dread your parents must have had of that bus stop and road afterwards.

I remember a lot of talk about the danger of the traffic, but that wasn't the only reason why we moved to The Wood. I think my father's heart had always been in The Wood – for this reason: he went there after his parents' deaths and was taken care of by the Scullion uncles, who were my grandmother Heaney's brothers. Basically there were three points on my father's family compass:

Broagh, where he was a child, where his Scullion mother had gone after she married his father, James Heaney. The Wood, where his mother came from, and where he went after she died. And Mossbawn, which he inherited as a young man, where Mary lived and where he went to live after he got married.

But what about the rest of the family – who would not have had your father's connectedness to the place?

I was actually away at college when we moved during the spring of 1954. I was aware all right that it was going to happen, since we often overheard it discussed. My younger brothers have a more vivid recollection of the actual flitting, how it took two different lorries, one load carried in George McGinley's cattle truck and the other, smaller stuff in the furniture removal van. The Wood house was familiar, all the same, certainly to me, since I was often down there, and would even stay over for a night or maybe two with my aunt Grace and my uncle – strictly my great-uncle – Hughie. After Hughie's death, Grace moved to another old place of theirs 'across the fields'. My aunt Sarah also lived at The Wood when I was smaller, but sometime in the late forties or early fifties she bought a house of her own in the village of Bellaghy.

So while there was a definite strangeness after the move, I personally didn't experience any significant wrench. I already knew the neighbours and the lie of the land very well. My brothers had more problems, since they were changing school. My sister Sheena, however, was already at secondary school in Magherafelt and continued to go there, just as I continued in St Columb's. Ann, my second sister, who was always a bit delicate as a youngster, was taken special care of and went in my aunt Sarah's car to Ballynease School where Sarah taught. Probably the one who bore most of the brunt was my mother – a wife coming into the husband's home ground, surrounded by even more of his family.

Was there much difference in the size of the farm or the religious mix? Was there any sense of what would now be termed 'upward mobility' about the move?

No sense of that. And even though that whole area – the townland of Tamlaghtduff, that is, adjacent to Ballyscullion and Ballymacombs – even though it would probably have been thought of as mostly

Catholic, I suddenly realize that The Wood farm was actually marched by land belonging to three Protestant farmers. Junkin's (old Johnny Junkin appears in 'The Other Side') and McIntyre's and – in a much lesser way – Sands's. We probably had ten or twelve acres more in The Wood than in Mossbawn, but we were very much on a par with the McIntyres and Junkins and Mulhollands, fifty-, sixty-acre farms with cattle and a good yard and outbuildings. My father, of course, had lived in the area in earlier years and my aunts and great-uncle had been there all along, so that meant there was no sense of outsiderishness.

How did the house at The Wood compare with the old Mossbawn homestead?

The old Wood house was also a single-storey thatched job, with three bedrooms and several other sheds and dairy rooms and calf houses all under the one long run of roof. When we went there, we got a stove put in; until then, there had been a turf fire on an open hearth. The old house was very much a transitional arrangement: from the moment we left Mossbawn, the plan was to build a new, two-storey dwelling house, and that was started fairly soon after we landed. Everybody was growing up.

Was the Mossbawn house then put up for sale?

Mossbawn was sold, yes, and the Broagh farm also. That's how we could afford to build the new house. Mossbawn was renovated soon after that by the new owners, although the basic shape of the old dwelling house was retained and is still there. The beech trees were cut down, the outbuildings greatly extended – if you see the place now, it's completely different, looks like a small industrial estate. Hedges between the fields have been taken out, the railway has gone, and in general – not just round Mossbawn but all over the country – that old sense of tillage and season and foliage has disappeared. Once trees and hedges and ditches and thatch get stripped, you're in a very different world. You're deserting the ground for the grid.

Would you regard the loss of Mossbawn as having been a corner-stone of your poetic imagination?

Definitely. Not that I had any sense of that at the time. Loss wouldn't have been in the vocabulary then. Adolescence is an awkward time anyway, and when we moved to the other end of the parish, into the environs of the village of Bellaghy, I didn't know many people in my own age group, boys or girls. Then too, except for six weeks in the summer and a couple of weeks at Christmas and Easter, I was away all year at college in Derry. I never got properly moulded into the Bellaghy ground. There was always an ingredient of at-homeness missing – I don't mean inside the family house, but in the social milieu. For example, I had no affection for the Bellaghy GAA team: I was a natural supporter of Castledawson and continued to play for the Castledawson minor team even after we moved. In Mossbawn I'd had companions like Henry Gribbin and Jim Shivers; if we'd stayed, I might have shared some kind of teenage herd life with them, but nothing like that materialized around The Wood. It could be, of course, that the out-of-placeness of those in-between years mattered as much for the poetry life as the in-placeness of childhood. And I should beware of exaggerating: I had a gang life of sorts around Queen's University, I had good friends at St Columb's, but around The Wood the memory that remains is of being out of it.

When you write about childhood, is it to Mossbawn that memory leads you? Can you give me examples of poems which are set in The Wood, or poems that fuse the two settings?

'The Other Side', as I say, is set on the ground of The Wood farm, and Toner's Bog in 'Digging' belongs in that terrain also. When we moved we had turbary rights, and those summer days in the moss were among the most idyllic of my life. A lot of the peat reverie in a poem like 'Kinship' derives from those sessions on Toner's Moss. And a confession here, something I'd almost forgotten: when I wrote 'Digging', I made my great-uncle Hughie into a grandfather – in the years before we moved, on a couple of occasions when I was staying in The Wood, I went with Hughie to the bog. Rode with him up in the cart – he's present as 'the god of the waggon' in the fifth section of 'Kinship' – and when we came home helped to build the turf up in a stack. To me he was always the ur-ancestor on the Heaney side of the family. Even so, the setting is almost always Mossbawn, Broagh, that other end of the parish.

Then too there are poems very specifically set in 'the new house'. In *Seeing Things* 'The Ash Plant' imagines what my father saw from his upstairs bedroom window. And one of the twelve-liners recollects my father's vision of what the new house would be like: 'big, straight, ordinary . . .' – a vision he certainly managed to realize. It was one of those 1950s take-me-or-leave-me dwelling houses, facing the road, bare faced, built on a bare field. The age of Formica triumphing in farmland. Tarmac and kerbstones.

Who were your godparents? Did you have regular contact with them?

My aunt Sarah, or Sally as the family called her, was my godmother. And very constant and responsible about it. Sally was my father's schoolteacher sister, single, very thorough, very kind, very defined. She had a kind of Artemis quality about her. Handsome, always very well turned out, tweed suits, silk blouses, a cameo brooch. Capable at needlework and gardening, the driver of her own car – a Standard Eight – from the moment I remember her. There was, for example, a piano in the old Wood house that belonged to her. When she moved into her own house in the village of Bellaghy, I used to go down from Mossbawn on a Saturday to help her with her garden. I weeded and did a bit of digging. Aged ten or eleven, I suppose.

I was close to her, and when I showed some academic promise she kept me in view. It was in her house I got a feel for books – she had a bookcase with sets of Hardy and Kipling that she'd bought as a young teacher, and it was always strange to see my own initials on the inside flyleaf of all of them: 'S. Heaney, 1925'. Sally it was, too, who bought me a lovely big glass-doored bookcase for my twenty-first birthday, and who gave Marie and me five hundred pounds, after we got married, for a deposit on our first house. I could go on about her. She was a great woman, an emotional as well as a material provider.

And your godfather?

Eddie Heaney, no relation, was one of a namesake family who either hailed from Scotland or had returned from there, since they all had Scottish accents. Eddie was a farmer, and famous for being easy-going. A very affable man, always late with his sowing and harvesting, always welcome wherever he went, somebody my father and mother were both very fond of. A remark he made in the last days of his life has come to mean more and more to me. My brother Hugh visited him in hospital and said something like, 'Oh,

Eddie, you can have no regrets, you were always good to people.'
'Far too bloody good to them, Hugh,' said Eddie. 'Far too bloody
good.'

Your grandparents?

I never knew my Heaney grandparents. They had died when my
father was young. And, oddly enough, I never missed them. As far
as we were concerned, Granny and Granda were in Castledawson
and that was that. My grandfather McCann was like any central-
casting grandfather of that era: shining bald head, shining wire-
rimmed glasses, shining-backed dark waistcoat, collarless shirt
sporting its front stud, reading the paper at the end of the table,
gazing at you over the glasses.

Did you have a grandchild's special relationship with him?

I have a distinct memory of only one thing he said and I remember
it only because he made a mistake. I was up in Castledawson – I
must have been nine or ten – to see the film of *Treasure Island*
which was being shown in St Malachy's Hall, just across the street
from the grandparents' house. There's a great scene near the end
of the book, you remember, when Jim Hawkins is up on the rigging
and this sinister crewman called Israel Hands is coming after
him with a knife. Well, my grandfather says to me when I come
back in from the picture, 'Well, son, did you see Isaac Hands?'
Somehow in that little slip I was vouchsafed a glimpse of the
mysterious gulf between childhood and old age – I mean I had
an intuition that I can only now put into words. What that
shift from Israel to Isaac told me was that he had read *Treasure
Island* decades before, and that it had stayed with him and was
a part of everything that had happened to him in between and
the fleetness of all that was somehow processed into his slip of
memory.

Your grandmother McCann is the old woman in 'Electric Light'?

That's her, with her mangled thumb and grey overall and whispery
voice and unzipped slippers. She was lucky in the intelligence and
kindness of her family, in particular my aunt Annie who lived in
those days in the New Row house and attended to her. As did my
uncle Sonny and my uncle Paddy.

Was Seamus a family name?

My grandfather Heaney was called James, so that must have been one reason for my being Seamus. Why the name was given in its Irish form, I'm not sure. Everything in Northern Ireland sends a signal, of course; but I don't think my name was meant to signify any special defiance, since neither my father nor my mother was actively Republican. My mother would certainly have had a more energetic attitude, more alert to the sectarian strains, readier to be provoked by the hidden operations of the system. She had a critical, disaffected attitude, but my father tended to sail through many of those aggravations as if he didn't notice. When it came to community, he belonged as much with the cattle dealers as with the Catholics. It may be that the self-possession came from something in his background – the Scullion uncles he was reared with in The Wood were prosperous old boys, and so he'd always lived on land and owned land, was always on a social par with the smallholders and the not so small. He would have considered himself a cut above 'the men of no property', whereas there was something in my mother that identified with the working class and the labouring class. She felt the inequalities more acutely.

You don't think she would have pressed for the Irish form of the name?

I don't think so. She had no particular orientation towards the Gaelic side of things. I said elsewhere that my father's background was suggestive of that old native Irish cattle-herding culture, whereas hers was closer to modernity, to the flower bed and the terrace-house. The Heaney sisters – Mary, Grace and even the schoolteacher Sarah – belonged more naturally in a farm kitchen than she ever did. Their mother's name had been Scullion – from the Irish, Ó Scoileáin: nothing to do with the English scullery word 'scullion', but coincidentally right for women who were familiar with big pots full of cattle feed. My mother, on the other hand, would have been more at home near a polished stove with a cake baking in the oven.

All the same, when I remember that my name was misspelled in the registry of births and that my birth certificate gave it as 'Shamus', the mother part in me sees it as another official refusal to concede the Irish dimension, whereas the father part puts it down to the ignorance of some wee clerk who just happened to be the daughter of an Orangeman and therefore knew no better.

Was it a burden to be called Seamus in Unionist Ulster?

More like a badge of honour. Seriously, the name signified confidence and if it entailed provocation for the Unionists, well, too bad. The 'call me Seán' factor was something you learned to live with – to a certain class of Loyalist, one Irish name was much the same as another. It was the Ulster form of 'they all look alike', but it would still be wrong to see 'Seamus' as some kind of flag-waving or Gaelic flaunt. Neither I nor anyone in the family would have regarded it like that. My sister Sheena, for example, who comes after me in the family, was christened Jane Pauline. And my own second name is Justin, taken from the liturgical calendar. The feast of Justin Martyr falls on the day after my birthday.

What were the names of your brothers and sisters?

Sheena, Hugh, Patrick, Charles, Colm and Daniel. Ann, who came after Sheena, died in 2002. And Christopher was between Colm and Daniel.

Which of them are you closest to?

Equiclose, so to speak, to all of them. Which also means, I suppose, equidistant. Being the eldest and then being off from the age of twelve to boarding school and university, I shifted into a kind of separateness, but also a kind of privilege. A slight element of *in loco parentis* crept in early on. To take a very simple example: in my early teens, when I no longer believed in Santa Claus, I used to do some undercover work for my mother. I took a hand in getting some of the Santa stuff for the younger ones. There was always a free day in St Columb's College on 8 December, the Feast of the Immaculate Conception; the boarders would be allowed out for the afternoon into the city of Derry. I'd roam the counters of Woolworth's and Littlewood's to pick up small stocking-filler things to bring home a fortnight later. That's just one instance of my 'special relationship'.

Another?

Well, there was the case of milking the cows, which I never did after I went to Derry. When we moved to The Wood, we started to send milk to the creamery. Not in any very big way, but even so, cows had to be milked every morning and evening and the milk be out at the road in cans by a certain time. Over the years Hugh and Pat and Charlie and Colm got the milking job, since they were at home – although Pat eventually followed me to St Columb's. But even when I came home on holidays, I was allowed my lie-in and they got up – partly because St Columb's itself was regarded as a kind of hard-labour regime.

Would you say therefore that you grew away from your siblings during those Derry years?

That would be putting it too strongly. At the beginning, I was closest to my sister Sheena, because she was the first sibling I had. When she started school, for example, I was in charge of her. In later life, I've been able to keep up separate relations and good relations with all of them. A different mixture of irony and affection pertains in each case. But even so, I'm still a bit out beyond. When Ann was alive, I'd stay with her any time I went back to County Derry, since she lived on her own in her own house and tended to be at the centre of the extended family.

Were you the only one to go to university? Was it the 1947 Education Act which enabled you to do so; or, if necessary, would some other means have been found?

Without the scholarship system inaugurated at that time, I don't think I'd ever have got to university. The teachers at primary school told my parents I was a clever boy, so I was entered for the new qualifying exam, and got it – in 1950. But because I was still only eleven, it was decided it would be better to have the scholarship deferred, with the result that I had an extra year of preparation for secondary school. I came in early to Master Murphy and was given my first lessons in Latin – something I go back to in one of the sections of 'Station Island'. He also made a stab at teaching me algebra and Irish, but I was so nervous and he was so abrupt and unclear, and the one-to-one sessions such an ordeal, it was all to little avail.

My sympathy in this whole area goes to my younger brothers, who suffered a wobble in their education at that crucial moment, just before they should have been entered for the eleven-plus, as the new exam was known. The move from Mossbawn to The Wood entailed a change of primary school for them – Hugh would have been round about eleven years old, Pat ten and so on. There was some mishandling and mistiming about it all. Pat did get entered for the exam and eventually studied for a history degree at Queen's. My sister Sheena qualified as a teacher at a college of education in Rugby. Dan, my youngest brother, qualified with a BEd in Belfast. All thanks to the system put in place by that Labour government in Britain.

In a previous interview, you said you'd had a happy and secure childhood. Yet you added, 'I think everybody recollects their earliest life as somehow in the middle of a space that is separate and a little sorrowing.' I'd like to hear you elaborate a bit on that.

What's to be said? I was trying to express what it felt like when I thought back to my earliest self. Something like that is necessarily vague, and it's bound to be affected by ways of knowing and feeling that literature and culture offer you. I must have had this image of the little me as the *animula*, the little soul alone. Or the image from Plato's parable, as Yeats calls it, of the soul at birth separated from its other half, and seeking and yearning for it ever after. When I recollect myself as a young child, I have a sense of being close to that unsatisfied, desiring, lonely, inner core. It – or he – hasn't disappeared but nowadays he dwells farther in, behind all kinds of socialized defences, barriers he learned to put up in order to keep the inwardness intact but which ultimately had the effect of immuring it.

'Standing in the middle of a space that is separate and a little sorrowing': a literal explanation of that would be to say it's about seeing myself in a field when I was small, looking up and listening to a lark. Larks were plentiful, ordinary, everywhere until I was well into my teens, and without being quite conscious of it, your romantic soul responded to all that ardency. One of the first modern poems I took to, for example, was a poem to a skylark by Cecil Day Lewis. I came on the old Penguin Poets selection of Day Lewis the other day, and was surprised to see I had bought it in August 1957, the summer before I went to Queen's University. The poem to the skylark is the last one in that book and it reminded me of how wide open I had always been to what the poem calls 'heaven's noon-wide reaches'.

'Intimations of immortality': can you recall visionary moments of that kind at any later stage of your life?

Out in the country, on starlit nights in Glanmore, pissing at the gable of the house, I had the usual reveries of immensity. But on a couple of other occasions that I specifically recollect, it was more a case of being overwhelmed by the work of mortal men. One morning in Berkeley, on the top floor of Wheeler Hall where the English Department is located, I was standing out on a balcony. The bricks were already warm in the sun, it was clear and summery and light-drenched; you could see the white terraces and tower blocks of San Francisco across the bay and the green trace of trees and gardens in between, and I had this visitation of – well, I don't know what to call it . . . Humanist joy? Awe? A tremendous sense of what human beings had achieved on earth. Something akin to Wordsworth's revelation on Westminster Bridge.

Across the bay, poets like Ginsberg and Snyder were having their apocalyptic vision of the cost of this urban civilization; but, in answer to your question, I'm only attesting here to my own epiphany. And something similar, some sense of the beauty and magnitude of what has been wrought by the sons of men, as the Bible might say, came to me one morning years after that in Manhattan. We were staying in an apartment in midtown; I was up at dawn and looking out at skyscrapers so close you felt you could have reached out and touched them through the smoky glass. Everything was magnificent and still and outlined with a kind of oxyacetylene definition against the dawn light. Something in me swam out to it all and at the same time something from it swam into me. It was like being an inhabitant of the empyrean.

Was there ever a moment of self-consciousness, of awareness, in the course of your childhood, a moment when you realized that this would always be a touchstone period of your life?

The sword of sorrow swung widely on the day I went as a boarder to St Columb's College. That was a definitive moment. Nothing altogether prepared any one of us for what was happening. My father and mother were out of it too, I know: going to Derry, going into the college, into the president's corridor, the president's room, the strangeness and diffidence they would have felt there in the clerical presence, the relative grandeur of the milieu, leather desk, carpeted hush, book-lined walls and so on. At this stage of my life I feel I know the uncanny sense of their own individuality and responsibility that must have been with them that day. They were consigning me to an unknown and we were all growing up. The fog was lifting. Imagine this: the pathetic phrase I used to hear in those days before I left was, 'They get a good dinner.' That was the extent of the understanding country people had about St Columb's College as a boarding school. And the extent of the expectation! The real meaning of what was happening came for all concerned when my father and mother simply had to say goodbye and walk away from the front door of Junior House, down the central walk to the main gate of the college, and I stood watching them, brimming with grief. Unblaming, unavailing grief. A space that was separate and, for sure, not a little sorrowing.

2

Growing into Poetry

~

Were you unusually responsive to poetry as a child?

I don't think so. I can't remember much about the poems we were taught early on. William Allingham's 'The Fairies', certainly: 'Wee folk, good folk, / Trooping all together; / Green jacket, red cap, / And white owl's feather!' And those images of 'crispy pancakes / Of yellow tide-foam'. Then there was another we used to recite about ducks dabbling – not the one by Allingham about four ducks on a pond, but something much more ebullient about ducks with their tails in the air, their heads in the water. The whole class would chant it out together. But by the time we were in 'the master's room', poems were incidental to reading lessons. You made do with whatever appeared in the reading book – 'Young Lochinvar' and 'Oh, to be in England' and 'The Inchcape Rock'. The poem that I remember best from that time is Wordsworth's 'Fidelity': 'A barking sound the Shepherd hears, / A cry as of a dog or fox . . .' It's about a dog that stays for weeks in this lonely dale in the mountains, keeping watch by the body of its master after he has fallen to his death off a cliff. What got to me was the description of the fells and the tarn and the sinister atmosphere.

Were there poems or nursery rhymes at home? You've written about your mother rhyming off the Latin prefixes and suffixes which she'd learned at school.

Oh yes. She also used to belt out a verse of Longfellow's – I think it was Longfellow – that her own father had relayed to her: ''Tis the idle that grow weary, / Gaily sounds each busy note. / 'Tis a pleasure

34

to be working . . .', or words to that effect. Good muscular-Christian stuff. And it was she who first taught us 'There was a naughty boy / And a naughty boy was he . . .' One of the great delights of reading Keats, when I was an undergraduate, was to discover that he had written those lines impromptu during his tour of Scotland, in a letter to his young sister Fanny. Until then, it was just another anonymous rhyme – which is a big compliment to it.

What effect did those rhymes and poems have on you?

I'm not sure. The main thing is that they stay with you for a lifetime. Poems learned early on, poems with a truly imaginative quality, end up being sounding lines out to the world and into yourself. I was thinking recently, for example, about a two-line poem that has been in my head since I was a youngster: 'Two sticks standing and one across / Spells Willie Brennan in the Hillhead Moss'. It's what you'd call an 'unlettered' performance but I've come to realize it links up with Stephen Dedalus's meditation on Sandymount Strand, the bit where he thinks 'Signatures of all things I am here to read . . .'

Whoever made up the Hillhead Moss poem was reading the signatures of the world as artfully as any Martian poet. There are the two sticks standing and the one across; underneath them, of course, there would be the remains of a turf fire, telling us that Willie Brennan had been in the moss all day and this little contraption he'd set up to boil a can of water for his tea was his signature. I'm not sure what I felt when I first heard the thing, over sixty years ago, but it animated and instigated something in the poetry part of me.

Were you the kind of pupil whose essays were held up by the teacher as a shining example to the rest of the class?

Far from it. I had the name for being good at sums. And as I went up the ranks, I enjoyed the parsing and general analysis side of 'English' better, the spelling tests and so on. I had no particular gift for writing what were called 'compositions', and no particular enjoyment of it. But I do remember a moment, early on at St Columb's, when the topic was 'A Day at the Seaside' and I made a connection between the performative student in me and a more inward creature, the writer-in-waiting, if you like. In the middle of the list of usual, expected activities such as diving and swimming, neither of which I could do, I wrote about going into an amusement arcade to escape from a shower and being depressed by the wet footprints on the floor and the cold, wet atmosphere created by people in their rained-on summer clothes. This had actually happened to me, so the image and the recording of it had a different feel. Something in me knew that I was on the right, intimate track – but it took me years to follow up.

Robert Lowell's '. . . why not say what happened?' was still somewhere in your future.

Sometimes when I'm talking to students about writing, about the necessity to open that inner path, I go back to that 'Day at the Seaside' essay. In it, I wrote about buying a bucket and spade, and provided all the expected detail – except in this case it was all made up, probably because there was a slight element of shame or humiliation involved. Again, I ought to have said what happened, because what happened was far more interesting. My mother, like many another country woman in those days, regarded buckets and spades as 'catchpennies', flashy things not worth spending the money on. So what she did was to buy a couple of wooden spoons that we could use in the sand if we wanted to; they could then be brought home and used all year round in the kitchen. It was meant to be good for us, but I still remember the disappointment of it, the embarrassment, the sheer refusal to break with the usual. And eventually I came to recognize something of my mother's down-to-earthness in myself, or rather an old suspicion of too much up-in-the-airness . . .

. . . which relates to your remark that, when you first read Robert Frost, you recognized 'a certain blunt, plonked-down thing' in his poetry that appealed to you. Did you read Frost early on?

I believe the first Frost poem I read was 'Out, Out –', the one about the boy losing his hand in an accident in a farmyard, having it cut off suddenly while he's working with a buzz-saw and there and then, just like that, dying. The thing in itself is sudden and powerful but it had an extra force for me because my brother Christopher had also died suddenly in an accident. Anyhow, Frost's head-on treatment of the way it just happens was unforgettable. I must have read 'Out, Out –' when I was twenty or so, probably in my second year or maybe my third year in Queen's University. So it was late enough. By that time I was already a slave to Hopkins.

Can you remember your first encounter with Hopkins's poetry?

It was in St Columb's College, when we were studying the prescribed poems in an anthology called *A Pageant of English Verse*. It was a matter of sensation, little ricochets and chain reactions within the nervous system. Lines like 'As tumbled over rim in roundy wells / Stones ring' or 'rose-moles all in stipple upon trout that swim; / Fresh-firecoal chestnut-falls; finches' wings'. I once said it was like getting verbal gooseflesh. And, naturally enough, when I wrote my first poems as an undergraduate a few years later, I wrote in Hopkins-speak.

Had Hopkins any hand, as it were, in your early 'Lines to Myself' (quoted in your essay, 'Feeling into Words')? Do you still feel responsive to your own advice in that poem to 'attempt concrete compression, / Half guessing, half expression'?

That first appeared in a student magazine called *Gorgon* in later 1960 – with a misprint, of course. 'Compression' appeared as 'expression' . . . I was twenty-one at the time; and, yes, I suppose that devotion to the concrete and the condensed was reinforced by Hopkins. And I've never turned my back on that kind of effort. There was another misprint, by the way – or better say misspelling – in that *Gorgon*: Seamus was printed as Sheamus. And the same mistake appeared in 'Sheamus' Deane's name. Seamus had two terrific flag-flying contributions in that issue, a poem and an essay on Wallace Stevens. The misspellings are a nice example of the reminders of their not-quiteness that people from a nationalist background were issued with in those days, entirely unconsciously and entirely effectively.

Was that why you chose to write under the name Incertus?

Not at all. The pseudonym had nothing to do with disguising my origins. It had all to do with a lack of writerly self-confidence.

Were those early Incertus poems written in conscious homage to Hopkins, or were they simply your best attempts at the time to write your own poetry?

Both, I suppose – although there was one called 'October Thought' which was very much a self-aware Hopkins imitation. So many things were at work beneath the surface, and it's so long ago, it's hard to know. But the farther away I get, the more I remember about different bits of reading that prompted different attempts. We'd read Housman in First Arts at Queen's, for example, and it's possible that some of those hayfield scenes in *A Shropshire Lad* led me to an Incertus poem called 'Harvest Heat'. And there was something about the clean quick diction in Hemingway that spoke to me and maybe spoke through Incertus also, although Hopkins was the main man.

How did the fact that Hopkins was a Catholic priest influence your attitude to the man or the work, or indeed to the Catholic Church and the priestly vocation?

The fact that Hopkins had been a priest was incidental – we used to laugh at one of the older lay teachers who'd always refer to him as Father Hopkins. There were too many priests all round us for holy orders to be impressive as such. More to the point was the general Catholic thing, the fact that the theology and doctrines that Hopkins embraced were the ones that embraced me and my generation. First, at primary school, we were introduced to the catechism. Then, at St Columb's, the formation became more systematic; we had a textbook called *Hart's Christian Doctrine*, and went on afterwards to a book on apologetics, Aquinas's proofs for the existence of God and so on.

For five years we had an annual religious knowledge exam, and at the same time we were living the liturgical year in a very intense way: a Latin Mass every morning; aware, from the missal, of the feast day and the order of the feast; going to confession and communion; alert to the economy of indulgences; offering up little penitential operations for the release of the suffering souls in purgatory; adjudicating the moment when sexual fantasy passed from being a 'temptation' to being the deliberate 'entertainment of impure thoughts' – not to mention the full surrender to the mortal sin of the job itself. What you encounter in Hopkins's journals – the claustrophobia and scrupulosity and religious ordering of the mind, the cold-water shaves and the single iron beds, the soutanes and the self-denial – that was the world I was living in when I first read his poems.

So yes, you're right that it wasn't simply a matter of the phonetics taking over, it wasn't just the fireworks in phrases like 'shining from shook foil'. It was the fact that the height and depth of Hopkins's understanding matched my own. The end of 'As kingfishers catch fire . . .', for example, those lines about Christ playing 'in ten thousand places' to 'the Father through the features of men's faces' – to us that was just a kind of illuminated text celebrating the doctrine of the mystical body of Christ, a teaching that was part and parcel of our Religious Knowledge classes.

Did the fact that Hopkins was a troubled man increase your sense of the interplay between suffering and art?

When I was at Queen's, I used to carry around the old Penguin edition of Hopkins's poems edited by W. H. Gardner; it had selections from the letters and notebooks and I got to know that material fairly well also. By then I suppose 'life' and 'literature' were beginning to connect. I'd come out of the cocoon of a Catholic boarding school but my whole way of thinking and feeling was still structured by that discipline, and the discipline, when all's said and done, was essentially a preparation for religious vocation. The ideal conclusion to such a schooling would have been entry into a seminary. Going to Queen's was a matter of going out into the world, and for us 'the world' carried negative associations that it wouldn't have had for others. For us it belonged in a triad of danger that involved 'the world, the flesh and the devil'. It wasn't so much a secular challenge, an entry into opportunity, but a testing ground for the soul, an arena that called for the exercise of heroic virtue.

Does this link up somehow with the phrase in 'Singing School' about 'lineaments of patience'?

Passive suffering and the meaning of it: that didn't preoccupy me in any abstract way. But the idea that your own travails could earn grace for others, for the souls in purgatory, for instance, was appealing; my mind worked on those lines all right, my sense that there was value in selfless endurance. It also probably sprang from sympathy for my mother's situation. I could see that religion was a powerful compensation for her. There she was, doomed to biology, a regime without birth control, nothing but parturition and potato-peeling *in saecula saeculorum*, and the way she faced it and, in the end, outfaced it was by prayer and sublimation, toiling on in the faith that a reward was being laid up in heaven. She didn't have any simple-minded trust in this but went with the fiction of it, as it were, lived it as a wager rather than an insurance. It was defiance as much as devotion . . . Anyhow, the whole theology of suffering, the centrality of sacrifice, of the cross, of losing your life to save it, all that fitted in with what I saw in her. And it's at the very core of Hopkins's thought. The sestet of 'The Windhover', as far as I'm concerned, is a versified enunciation of that attitude.

Talk of versifying and enunciating reminds me of those remarks in 'Feeling into Words' about the connection you perceived between the 'heavily accented consonantal noise' of Hopkins's poetic voice and the Northern Irish accent. You must be glad not to have grown up in a place given to 'standard English'.

I'd taken my degree in English Literature and couldn't miss learning that the iambic pentameter had been put on the defensive by Ezra Pound and co. from early on. Talk of free verse and sprung rhythm was simply a given of the seminar-speak when we were undergraduates. Then too, in those days, I read a good bit of Lawrence's poetry; and not just the poetry – the essay on 'Poetry of the Living Present', for example. I'd got my hands on a big second-hand hardback of Lawrence's literary criticism and for a while was reading nothing else. At the same time, there was Eliot's *Selected Prose*. I just went with the orthodox idea that the age demanded a roughening up of the utterance, an avoidance of smooth numbers – you were meant to hit the stride of living speech.

When I eventually encountered Kavanagh's 'Great Hunger' and Ted Hughes's 'View of a Pig' and so on, part of the excitement was in their spoken force. So that's what I was after in those early poems: 'Docker', for example: 'That fist would drop a hammer on a Catholic – / Oh yes, that kind of thing could start again'. Iambic maybe – but, you know, hearable on the street. And all this was going on before I got linked up with The Group and received more explicit encouragement from Philip Hobsbaum to roughen up. When I was an undergraduate, there was a general, Leavisitey prejudice in favour of 'felt life', in favour of an Anglo-Saxon diction, and there was also the fact that I did have a genuine response to the Old English poetry we had to study. I think 'The Wanderer' and 'The Seafarer' and 'The Battle of Maldon' might have established some sort of a register for me.

As a young poet from a nationalist background you might have been expected to resist the Anglo-Saxon stresses, in Hopkins and elsewhere, in favour of the assonances of Gaelic poetry. Were you tempted in that direction? I don't get the impression that Austin Clarke was ever your exemplar.

The cultural politics of all that came home to me gradually. I'd been introduced to Daniel Corkery's notion of *The Hidden Ireland* in my fifth year at St Columb's. Our Irish teacher read out extracts from the book and I was taken by the pathos of the scenario and could consider myself an heir to the Irish speakers in the cabins, one of Eoghan Ruadh Ó Suilleabháin's and Aodhagán Ó Rathaille's 'audience in posterity'. In fact, I remember giving a lecture on Daniel Corkery at one of the first Queen's University Festivals in the early sixties and Stewart Parker being in the audience. Most of what I knew then about poetry in Irish came from the school books. And, as someone from the nationalist side, I certainly had a strong sense of the importance of the Irish heritage and went looking for books about Irish poetry. But you have to remember that this was the late 1950s, early 1960s, in Northern Ireland, and in the County Londonderry library system there were damned few texts relating to matters Gaelic.

I did a lot of my reading in the summer and the only book I could get on the subject of Irish poetry in the Magherafelt branch of the County Library was one by Robert Farren called *The Course of Irish Verse*. It took the Thomas MacDonagh line, saw the course of Irish verse in English flowing from native sources, commended Austin Clarke's assonances for being continuous with Gaelic practice and generally prescribed this course of development. So all that was in my head early on as theoretical baggage of a sort, but it didn't have any regulatory force when I came to write. The writing current has to flow in your limbs and joints and the linguistic experiences that threw my switches were in English. What happened subsequently was a process of squaring this experiential fact with the cultural and political pieties I grew up with. There were always those old nationalist tests hovering over you: could you be an Irish writer if you wrote in English? Of course you could, but you were still faced with that screening process.

Again in light of your nationalist background, I'm surprised that you gravitated – even graduated – towards Queen's University in Belfast, rather than University College or Trinity College in

Dublin. Did the Catholic Church's ruling against attendance by Catholics at Trinity College influence your decision?

Dublin just wasn't on the horizon. Even Belfast was far away to me. In those days, I was outside the loop, my family had no familiarity with universities, no sense of the choices that were there, no will to go beyond the known procedures, no confidence, for example, about phoning up the local education authority and seeking clarification about what was possible – no phone, for God's sake. As far as we were concerned, Dublin didn't mean University College and Trinity College; it meant Croke Park where the All Ireland football final and the All Ireland hurling final were played. What happened to me in the first three decades of my life wasn't quite a matter of personal decision, it was more or less typical and generational. People of my age from that background were all just carried along on the conveyor belt of the times: the 'qualifying exam' and eleven-plus scholarship, the boarding school – chosen, by the way, because there was no specifically Catholic secondary school in the mid-Ulster area where I could attend as a day pupil. Then the university scholarship. Then graduation, the job, the wedding, the mortgage, the car, the family. Then – well, then the question asked by Plato's ghost: *What then?*

No vocational guidance was given at St Columb's?

No. 'Vocation' in that time and place meant a call to the priesthood, and that you had to discover for yourself. When I was leaving St Columb's, the students who were going on for the priesthood went straight to Maynooth and students going out into the world went off in other directions. Those from the Donegal side of the border followed the Donegal County Council's procedures and aimed for University College or Galway, and the successful ones within the Northern system generally followed the scholarship trail to Queen's – unless there was some family capacity or concern to do otherwise. In my own case, the ban on Catholics going to Trinity didn't enter. Trinity just didn't come up on the screen. But for Michael Longley and Derek Mahon, the situation was very different. Their school, the Royal Belfast Academical Institution, had a long history of sending its pupils to Trinity. The Inst.–Trinity axis was as natural as the St Columb's–Maynooth one, and for the same reasons – cultural and religious bonds, teachers in the school who were graduates of the university, a general sense that this was the tradition.

Did you ever regret not having headed south? Were there sectarian divides, for example, operating against you in Queen's?

I've never regretted going to Queen's, and I should say that the quality of life the students had invented for themselves was on the whole more civil than life outside the university. The divide was there, yes, no denying it. There was the Bible Union and the Catholic Students' Society, the Irish Society/Cumann Gaelach and the Officers' Training Corps, but there were also more open arenas such as the 'Literific' – the debating society – and the billiard rooms of the Student Union, and the Drill Hall for the Saturday-night hops.

The discrimination operated more blatantly elsewhere, in the staffing at ground level – the porters and kitchen staff and groundsmen – and at administrative levels. But in our group of honours English students we had terrific come-and-go, a certain breeziness and style in handling all of the noxious stuff. I think we were an education to ourselves in that regard. I have a strong trust in the connections and friendships made at the time across the religious divide – enduring still, I'm sure, on all sides, even though we've not met for forty years. We may have been a lucky year, but I can't believe we were all that exceptional. Probably the characters who end up doing English are just that bit more sympathetic and maybe even that bit more transgressive. On the other hand, there were plenty of people who went through Queen's and came out as thick-witted and bigoted as when they went in.

Had you given serious thought to taking up Law or Medicine or Engineering at Queen's and reserving your aptitude for English, your taste for literature, as a more private pursuit? Or indeed had you considered studying another language?

In my First Arts year I actually took French and Latin, as well as English, but when I was admitted to the honours English course, these were dropped. But no, I never did conceive of myself as a lawyer or a doctor. And I wonder if I had sufficient self-awareness or detachment at the time even to think of myself as having a 'taste for literature'. At that stage, I would have thought of myself as acquiring qualifications rather than developing a taste.

Did you engage in any political activity, formally or informally, at Queen's?

No, nothing like that. I don't know how you'd have gone about it then.

Would the Irish Society and the Catholic Students' Society not have had a political dimension, however subtle? Did you sometimes speak Irish with other students, for example?

At the meetings of An Cumann Gaelach, yes, Irish was often spoken, but not always. And I took part in Irish-language plays, one-acters that were put on by the Irish Society and were entered in inter-university drama competitions. I remember us travelling to Dungannon and once, I think, to Dublin. But I don't remember much about the actual plays. You're right, all the same, to see a political colouring in that kind of affiliation, although the immediate motive was cultural, or perhaps better say counter-cultural . . . I also went with a group of Celtic Department students to the Gaeltacht at Easter in, I think, my third year at Queen's.

And the Catholic Students' Society?

Well, again, that was more strictly religious than political, but admittedly it was hard to separate the two categories completely in that place at that time. Undoubtedly the Catholic chaplaincy existed first and foremost in order to keep the students in touch with their religious practice. There were retreats, pilgrimages to Lough Derg and so on – my first couple of trips to Lough Derg were CSS outings, bus trips at the end of the year. The chaplain held these weekly 'sodality meetings', as they were called – homily, prayers and benediction. Not every Catholic student attended – far from it – but quite a number, nevertheless, did turn up. The chaplaincy, it's fair to say, functioned as a second – almost an alternative – student union. It was a social centre: cups of tea and reading rooms; photographs of the students in each year on the walls. It was frequented mostly by country boys and convent girls finding their feet in the new surroundings.

We were all in digs in those days, with landladies on the premises, and no great facilities for relaxation when you went home in the evenings. So in your first and second year, especially, after a stint in the library in the evening, you tended to go round to the chaplaincy and flirt with the girls.

Your early poem 'Twice Shy' refers to 'mushroom loves' that had 'puffed and burst in hate'.

That overstates it drastically – 'hate' is there, alas, for the rhyme with 'wait' and 'late' rather than as a description of what happened. When I was at Queen's I didn't have any very serious girlfriend until my final year, but once she arrived the relationship was very intense. I sat beside her in the library, I drove to dances in her home place during the holidays. But all along I felt I was more involved than she was – except, of course, when it came to the end. I met Marie and began the ever-painful business of disentangling: at that stage, the need shifted from me to her, so it would have been more to the point to say the 'mushroom love' ended in a certain amount of guilt rather than hate. But all this was in the age of innocence, when flirt was still the big f-word.

How much of a child of the sixties were you?

More a child of the fifties, really. I was well and truly formed by 1963, twenty-four years of age, college lecturer, up and coming, buying my first car so that I could drive round the country to inspect students on teaching practice. Still single, but not at large the way the next generation would be.

How do you mean, 'at large'?

I think there was far more sexual freedom, for a start. Ten years later, when I was teaching at Queen's, the students were on dope rather than drink, the parties involved magic mushrooms rather than home brew, the evenings involved what the Elizabethans called 'chambering' rather than chamber music.

One glimpse of you at large comes in the opening section of 'Red, White and Blue', where you are jiving at a Students' Union dance.

I was never what you'd call a good dancer. I was shy at hops in the university and never did manage to learn how to quickstep. None of that long loping and striding and swirling. I went a couple of times to lunchtime dancing lessons at a place called the Club Orchid in Belfast. It was full of young fellows like myself, trying to get over their wobbles and wavers, so it wasn't all that embarrassing. But I never got rightly in step, so never got fully into the pop-culture swim. In fact, one of the great releases that came when I began to take a drink in my early twenties was the shedding of inhibitions on the floor. Otherwise, I could 'pass myself' but not quite forget myself. That bit of 'Red, White and Blue' has me in fine fettle with Marie, who was a terrific jiver. But the hullabaloo of Irish dancing was another story. At home, you see, on Sunday nights, there were halls for big showbands and then there were other, smaller venues where they ran *céilís*. Apart from some GAA out-and-outers who were against 'foreign dances', there was no boycott of the show-band culture by the Catholics. On a different Sunday, you'd meet many of the *céilí*-goers in the ballroom in Clady, dancing to the strains of Mick Delahunty or the Capitol or the Polka Dots.

Weren't you an MC or fear a' tí *at* céilís? *That doesn't suggest any great shyness.*

The *fear a' tí* – the 'man of the house' – announced the dances from the stage and made sure that all the sets were full and ready to go. Every now and again you'd have to coax one or two couples off their backsides to fill up the set for a sixteen-hand reel – a *corr seisear déag* – but the task required no great expertise. It was a matter of getting up on your hind legs and making announcements. And you more or less knew everybody in the hall anyhow. You'd have to ask somebody to shift a car that was blocking somebody else's in the car park. Ask somebody known to have a good voice to come up and sing during the interval. Announce the raffle results.

Who sponsored those céilís? *Did the curate keep an eye on the proceedings?*

No priest on duty, no. I suppose it was a time when everybody was provided with their own inner priest. In most Catholic areas, the GAA had their hall and they sponsored the *céilís*. Parish events were in the smaller, separate 'parochial' hall, or else were held under 'parochial' sponsorship in the GAA hall. In the late fifties, early sixties, we're talking about small premises that would hold a hundred or two at the most. The box-office would be a cubbyhole, the refreshments would be soft drinks from a set-up table. Later on, there was a great expansion and nowadays some of the best equipped sports facilities and club amenities – bars included – are run by the GAA.

Was it after the céilís *that you'd have to face the RUC patrols mentioned in 'The Ministry of Fear'?*

Exactly. The police and the B-Specials were very active in those days because there had been an IRA campaign in the 1950s, and indeed many of the songs sung in the intervals of those *céilís* were crypto-IRA songs. Ones about contemporary events like 'The Patriot Game', and old reliables like 'Kevin Barry' and 'The Foggy Dew' – not the English one about the lovelorn bachelor but the 1916 vision of marching men heading into Dublin city on an Easter morn. One of the prose pieces in *Stations* is about those performances. It should be said we didn't come out of the hall inflamed with patriotism as the people are said to have come out after seeing Yeats's *Cathleen ni Houlihan* – we lived then, as I said in another poem, 'under the guardian angel of passivity'.

And you lived too, as you've said earlier, with your 'own inner priest'. Did you keep up regular attendance at Mass and the sacraments when you were at Queen's?

I did, and for a while I attended the sodality meetings. I remember, for example, the chaplain urging us as Catholic students to go beyond what was expected, to cross the boundaries and join societies that would have been regarded by us as the domain of the middle-class Protestant element – the Rowing Club, say. It wasn't so much ecumenism as an urge to get Catholics into the Ulster mainstream, to have a Catholic middle-class making their intervention. The first time I ever tasted a Sauternes wine, for example, was in the house of a Franciscan who taught Scholastic Philosophy at Queen's. He had been to Louvain and had a sense that cuisine had its place as well as Aquinas. Mind you, by that stage I was a graduate.

I gather from your earlier comments that you didn't drink as an undergraduate.

No drinking. I kept my confirmation pledge until I was twenty-one. There was an added temperance factor in that my aunt Sarah was secretary of the local Pioneer Total Abstinence Association and I was enrolled in that first as a 'probationer' at the age of fifteen or whatever, and as a full member later on. You said a prayer every day promising to abstain from drink for life – for the greater glory of God, in order 'to give good example, to practise self-denial and for the conversion of excessive drinkers'. It kept me off the streets, so to speak. Kept me in the library. I've never regretted missing the teenage drinking. But never regretted getting started in my twenties.

When did your smoking habit start?

I forced myself to start, against everything my body was telling me. It was at the beginning of my second or third year at Queen's. Late in the summer, there was this tragic death in a neighbouring family. One of their sons who had gone to England was drowned while swimming in the Bristol Channel. His body wasn't found for a day or two, and then it took a while to get it home, so there was this long period of mourning, a wake that lasted for four or five days, a wake with no corpse, but with all the traditional practices going on – people coming to the house to sit and sympathize, neighbours sitting up in the kitchen all night, tea being made and passed around constantly – and also cigarettes; that was the custom: cigarettes on plates, offered as part of the hospitality. I enjoyed sitting up throughout the night, being admitted into the adult circle, hearing the stories the elders had to tell in the small hours, learning some of the hushed-up things about people in the district, the outtakes, so to speak, and learning to smoke in the process. I forced myself to endure the cough and the cut of the smoke in my throat. Later on, when I went back to Belfast, I bought my own first packet, to produce and pass round and confirm my new membership of the *comitatus*.

When did you abandon smoking?

I gave it up on New Year's Day 1986. I didn't think I ever would, since it was so much part of my life at the desk: I more or less chain smoked when I was writing. A year earlier, on 31 December 1984, at midnight, I said, 'I'm going to give up smoking . . . one year from tonight.' So all through 1985 that boast was in my mind and the resolution grew strong enough for me to go through with it when the time came. Cold turkey, as they say.

*If I may disperse the smoke and return to Queen's, I'd like to ask
what university taught you – about literature or life – that you
couldn't have learned of your own accord? Has the reading you
undertook at that stage remained a bedrock resource for you ever
since?*

Definitely. In the first part of me there's still that student coming for
the first time on John Webster, Christopher Marlowe, Malory's
Morte d'Arthur, Gawain and the Green Knight, The Prelude.
Things that entered the system then have stayed with me: a feel
for Anglo-Saxon poetry, for Hardy, for Lawrence. What did I get
as student that I couldn't have got on my own? A sense of the
whole historical picture, I suppose, the layering of the language
from Anglo-Saxon to Hiberno-English, the Eliotesque sense of
'tradition'.

What extramural reading did you enjoy as a student?

I went through a phase of reading thrillers by John Dickson Carr.
Those old dark-green and white Penguin mysteries. And I was
always into P. G. Wodehouse. The odd novel by Maurice Walsh or
Canon Sheehan . . . I wasn't by any means a voracious reader, but
I did know the contents of the Belfast bookshops more or less by
heart, especially the poetry shelves. Mullan's in Donegall Place was
my cave of gazing, but even they didn't have a very extensive selec-
tion. A. P. Wavell's *Other Men's Flowers.* An early Yeats selected.
A collected MacNeice – the one that brought the work up to
the late 1940s. Moira O'Neill's *Songs of the Glens of Antrim.* Percy
French's *Prose, Poems and Parodies.* I actually bought more books
in the second-hand shops in Smithfield Market: Henry Hall's and
the U-Needa Book shop. Some of the volumes I still have at home –
my Tennyson collected and my Goldsmith, for example – were
picked up in those old places. They were also terrific for classical
texts – in those days there would be a big end-of-year trade in
school and university textbooks. I remember the smell of Jeyes
Fluid and musty old bindings, and a manageress who was like the
weird sister of the alcoves, in her brown shop coat and brown
horn-rimmed glasses.

*Was that where you redeemed the book token you won at
Queen's after your finals? You've written about opting for the*

book token rather than the medal you could have claimed because of your exam success.

I used the token in Mullan's, actually – Smithfield was for second-hand books and, on that occasion, I was after new ones.

Poetry books?

Not all of them. I got Wilde and Synge, for example, in the old Everyman series. And one poetry book, yes: Louis MacNeice's *Collected Poems*.

You once attended a poetry reading by Louis MacNeice. What effect did this have on you?

Not a great deal, I have to confess, because I just wasn't ready, didn't know the work, hadn't the ears to hear. It must have been in my final year at Queen's. I've a vague recollection of assembling in a big room off Elmwood Avenue with other students. There was a real sense of occasion – and somebody from the faculty, maybe Professor Butter, was there to introduce him. I seem to remember MacNeice's nose as the dominant feature of his appearance, but maybe that's because I've listened to recordings of him in the meantime and heard that strong nasal intonation.

And what happened when you did read MacNeice? You once said that the Collected Poems *kept you 'at a reader's distance' – what did you mean?*

Put it this way: some poets and poetry you admire in the way you admire produce in a market. Natural, beautiful stuff, delightfully there in front of you, thickening your sense of being alive. But you're still looking at it. You're savouring it but you can move on to the next display. Then there are other poets and poetry that turn out to be more like plants and growths inside you. It's not so much a case of inspecting the produce as of feeling a life coming into you and through you. You're Jack and at the same time you're the beanstalk. You're the ground and the growth all at once. There's no critical distance, as yet. Kavanagh and Hughes had the latter effect on me, but not MacNeice.

Even so, I was in thrall to MacNeice lines like 'The hard cold fire of this northerner' and 'The pier glittering with crystal lumps of salt'. I got his *Collected Poems* in 1961, in that first year out of Queen's when I was dabbling and fiddling but not really hitting the note. I did a poem called 'Newcastle', for example, after reading MacNeice's 'Birmingham' and 'Belfast' poems, and submitted it to the *Sunday Independent* in Dublin – in longhand, probably. In those days they printed a poem every week, but 'Newcastle' wasn't accepted. Newcastle, County Down, that was. I'd worked as a waiter in a café/restaurant there in the summer of 1961.

Robin Skelton's anthology Six Irish Poets *was published in 1962. Can you remember which of its poems made the biggest impression?*

I can remember a few. John Montague's 'The Water Carrier' was in it, and Austin Clarke's 'The Envy of Poor Lovers', Richard Murphy's 'The Poet on the Island', Thomas Kinsella's 'A Lady of Quality'. Michael McLaverty, by the way, knew the first stanza of that Kinsella poem by heart and often recited it. The Skelton anthology was an appetite-whetter, a first stirring. You had the western weather coming through in Murphy, something glummer and less attractive being registered in Clarke. There was promise of Ireland in the book; but, to tell the truth, A. Alvarez's *The New Poetry* gave me more of a charge. Probably the poets Skelton didn't include were the ones who'd have had a stronger purchase on a young reader from the North – Kavanagh and MacNeice and Hewitt, for example. But I did recognize the home ground – and the mysterious othering it can receive from poetry – in Montague's boy with his bucket and in those old people like dolmens round his childhood.

The Dolmen Miscellany of Irish Writing *was another major showcase for new Irish writing. Did you encounter it when it came out first in 1962?*

I got my hands on a copy of the *Miscellany* very early on. It was a marvellous thing to behold – and to hold – the paper so heavy, the printing so obviously letterpress, the sense of respect and achievement endorsed in the actual fabric of the volume. It marked a moment. It was the right treatment for the generation who came into their own in its pages – McGahern had an extract from *The Barracks*, Murphy had 'The Cleggan Disaster', Kinsella had 'A Country Walk', Montague a long essay on Goldsmith's 'Deserted

Village' – readable now as a premonition of *The Rough Field*. You also had Pearse Hutchinson, James Plunkett, and a strange, outsiderish piece by Brian Moore. I would say the *Miscellany* had a quality of guarantee about it. It changed the game, it secured the ground, and the fact that it was published in Ireland by the Dolmen Press was, of course, important. The work it carried told readers and young writers that cultural and artistic maturity had arrived in the land for good. It also got around. It opened a channel to the Dublin scene.

Was there anything one might describe as a 'Belfast scene' at that time?

The mid-sixties scene had still to happen: no Festival pamphlets yet, no Group, no sense of a younger crowd getting started. I was aware of some writers in the area, partly because I'd done a little research into the history of literary magazines in the North, partly because Michael McLaverty knew people like Roy McFadden and Padraic Fiacc (pseudonym of Joe O'Connor), but they were only names to me. I didn't get a book by McFadden until years later when I found a second-hand copy of *Flowers for a Lady*; and even though Michael arranged for me to visit Fiacc out in Glengormley, I didn't see his work until he had a second poetic birth later in the 1960s. The one writer I did meet in person early on was John McGahern. Michael marched into my classroom one morning with John at his side and introduced me. A strange, important moment. John told me afterwards he could see the panic in my eyes – I was still the young teacher, only recently appointed to McLaverty's school in Ballymurphy, and the arrival of the headmaster put me into a state of anxiety.

John McGahern in Ballymurphy?

He was a great admirer of McLaverty's stories and they had been writing to each other, so I think he simply came to Belfast to see Michael. But you could regard that in-and-out aspect of his visit as a symptom of the way things were in Belfast at the time – I certainly felt at a remove from the action. I associated Dublin with Dolmen Press, with Poetry Ireland, with the current affairs magazine *Hibernia*. Admittedly *Threshold* was being published in Belfast then, and the Lyric Theatre was doing great work, but there was a coterie element to the Lyric's work, which was part of its point. The presiding genius there was Yeats the dramatist, Yeats the man who wanted small audiences in small venues, and that was exactly what you got in the Lyric. It was a valiant endeavour in those days, managed by Pearse and Mary O'Malley. Visionary, even.

They put on Yeats's plays in a little theatre which they'd made out of the back end of their house on Derryvolgie Avenue. And other plays as well. I saw Robert Bolt's *A Man for All Seasons* there. But the lasting impression is of the Yeats cycles, especially the 'Four Plays for Dancers'. All that was thanks to Mary O'Malley, who came from Cork originally and had settled in Belfast after she married Pearse. Pearse worked as a doctor in the Mater Hospital. They were tremendously enterprising and creative. A leavening element: Yeats's plays, of all things, in bourgeois Britisher Belfast. I was very flattered in 1965 when the O'Malleys asked me write a poem to mark the laying of the foundation stone of the new Lyric at Ridgeway Street – I was on the programme with Thomas Kinsella and Austin Clarke.

Were you a regular theatregoer?

Not specially. But Marie and I did go to the Lyric and the old Arts Theatre. We were edging out from the college and university milieu, getting to know painters and singers. I first met the singer David Hammond, for example, after a performance he gave at the Lyric.

Hammond would, of course, later be the co-dedicatee with Michael Longley of Wintering Out.

David and Michael and I did an Arts Council tour round Northern Ireland in 1968, music and poetry, a programme called Room to Rhyme. Through David I eventually got to know a lot of people, north and south, who were involved with traditional music. He knew the Clancy Brothers early on, for example, and Tommy Makem's family, and the Dubliners. Marie and I had started to see each other just about the time of the folk revival. Marie was a very true singer so we moved about for a while with a crowd of other young teachers, scouring the parties. The singer Tony McAuley had done the St Joseph's postgraduate course with me, for example, and another free spirit called Donal Terrins. This Hammond name kept coming up with them, so I was glad to meet him. I once described David as a natural force masquerading as a human being. Halfway between a lord of misrule and a tuning fork. He grew up in Belfast and belongs in it but he's always had an extraordinary insouciance, as if he'd come through the sectarian fires and had the noxious stuff refined out of him.

Who else did you meet through the Lyric?

I actually met John Montague in the O'Malleys' home. But that was a bit later on, maybe in 1965. The painter T. P. Flanagan and his wife Sheelagh, for example, were very much connected with the theatre, although I first met Terry as a colleague in the training college.

He was at St Joseph's teacher-training college when you were on the staff there?

He was in the sister college, actually, the women's college, St Mary's. Michael McLaverty urged him to seek me out and the four of us were soon seeing a lot of each other. Terry's aunt had been in service with the Gore-Booths in Lissadell House and he had spent a lot of his time down there in Yeats country, so his landscapes not only featured the lakes and lowlands of his native Fermanagh, but Ben Bulben and the hills of Sligo as well. His work had a lovely combination of romantic vision and impeccable technique, but more than that, he talked as it were professionally about painting and painters. He and Sheelagh introduced us to new circles and made art and artists part of our life in a new way. They opened the path to Dublin and its galleries, since Terry showed with the David Hendriks Gallery, and a lot of our merriest times were on trips south to the openings of Terry's exhibitions. It was through the Flanagans, for example, that I first met the artist Derek Hill, and Gordon Lambert, the businessman, who was one of Ireland's first patrons of contemporary art and artists. So the Lyric was more than just theatre. It led to all kinds of contacts and enrichments.

You mentioned the coterie aspect to the Lyric. Was the same true of Threshold?

Threshold just seemed far away. It published a senior generation, and appeared to belong as much on the Liffey as the Lagan. The format was that of *The Bell*, and the general make-up of the magazine was much the same, part intellectual forum, part literary magazine:

a mixture of fiction, poetry and articles of an historical or politico-cultural nature. John Hewitt was poetry editor. It was a quarterly, but by the time I began to be aware of it, it was one of those quarterlies that appeared three times every couple of years. Mary O'Malley was editor, although towards the end of its history, the issues were mostly guest-edited. I eventually edited one of those myself, in 1969. And a good issue it was, come to think of it, including the first published poems by Paul Muldoon . . .

But in the early sixties I was closer to a student magazine in Queen's called *Interest*. Some of the poems I did in that first teaching year appeared in *Interest* in the spring of 1963. More a case of wobbling in verse than dabbling in it, I'm afraid. And for the next year or two, after The Group got going, I was still linked into the Queen's milieu. The Queen's Festival was getting started then, in a small way, by Michael Emmerson – another graduate who didn't or just couldn't leave the place. Philip Hobsbaum arrived around the same time, I guess, since the first meeting of The Group was in the autumn of 1963.

You are very precise about these dates. Do you have a diary to remind you of what was going on at that time?

Unfortunately, no. But I have definite markers for the different summers: summer of 1961 – graduation; summer of 1962 – St Thomas's appointment and work in London; summer of 1963 – appointment to St Joseph's College of Education; summer of 1964 – I wrote 'Digging'; and so on.

You once said that 'Digging' and those early poems began when your 'roots got crossed with your reading'. But it strikes me that your St Columb's and Queen's sojourns didn't alienate you from the life of your neighbours in the country. To what extent, during holiday periods, did you work around the farm?

I helped with the usual jobs. Moving cattle, for example. There was a good bit of droving to be done. Shifting the stock from farm to farm, from Mossbawn to Broagh, or sometimes as far as The Wood, three or four miles away. I had a certain confidence as a herder of cattle on the road, even prided myself on the way I could handle them in the face of oncoming traffic and all that. And when I began driving, I always got a certain pleasure when I encountered a herd of cows being brought in for milking, knowing how to drive through them without anxiety and without causing *them* anxiety – although the presence of cattle on the road is becoming rarer and rarer.

But the farm wasn't confined to pasture. Wasn't there arable land as well?

Hay, oats, grass seed, potatoes, turnips, kale – there was always a lot of field work going on, and bog business, of course, in the summer. Again, we're talking about the late fifties, very early sixties, when the farms weren't as mechanized as they'd soon become, so most of the haymaking was done by hand. You turned it with forks, shook it out, built it into 'lumps' and then into small haycocks. You were dependent on the weather and had to repeat one or other of those processes if it rained. With oats and grass seed, it was a matter of following the mowing machine, lifting and tying the sheaves; stooking and hutting. I did those jobs routinely, with siblings and with neighbours. I actually enjoyed work in the hay. There was a terrific rightness and lightness about the forks and rakes, a wonderful sense of the hand and the tool being made for each other. I loved to dress a ruck, comb it down, give it a nice firm set.

Was there any real prospect that – as the eldest son – you might follow in your father's footsteps as farmer or cattle dealer?

Once I went to St Columb's I suppose there was a presumption all round that whatever I did at the end of my time there, I wouldn't be back on the farm. I was being 'educated', and that meant being set a bit apart. And, in spite of what I've said about enjoying work on the farm during the summer, I never had a desire to get involved in any serious way in cattle dealing. I was familiar with the milieu of fair hills and cattle pens and I knew men in the trade and enjoyed the banter and the bidding and bargaining, slapping hands, throwing up the hands, walking away, pretending you were at your limit – it was terrific theatre and I didn't feel out of it; but, still, I didn't have an ambition to grow up and do it.

Was your father ambivalent about the educational path you had embarked on?

It's hard to know about that. There was a strong streak of fatalism in my father. For a start, he didn't talk much about our future – or about anything: the notion that there were options, that a future could be projected, that a change might be effected in the level of operations, I don't think he took that in. He was out on the road, earning a living. But in a different way from a wage earner. He would have regarded himself as more lord than labourer. There was a touch of the artist about him, I suppose. A certain pride, a certain freedom that came from being on the road, among the cattle people. He would have seen himself endowed with a definite position because of that, different from the neighbours who just farmed the land. To put it another way, he would have seen dealing as a calling and would have known that I hadn't been called. And – this is a wild guess, but maybe there's something in it – he might have unconsciously regarded me as belonging to the woman-world of the home rather than the man-world of the road. I was a great favourite with my aunt Mary, you see, and – as the first child – was a bit petted. When I was four or five, I went on holidays with Mary and Sarah to Portstewart. I don't remember any of the other children being brought away like that. So all in all, he may well have had an intuition from the start that some kind of divergence was built into the situation. As it turned out, none of us followed him into the trade because the trade itself changed.

What exactly did the dealer's trade involve? Do you mean your father would buy livestock from other farmers and quickly sell them again for profit, or that he would breed and raise cattle for eventual sale?

Both, but mostly the former. He would graze a few bullocks for sale for beef, and always we had cows for milk, but mostly it was a matter of ranging the country to people and places he had known for years, eyeing out saleable beasts, dealing for them and trying to get a profit on them at the next fair day when other farmers were on the lookout for cattle of their own. It meant there was always a lot of stock about the fields, in transit. And he also accepted commissions, he would supply cattle for people who were his regular customers. So he was a middle man; but when the middle man's area of operations dwindled and more or less disappeared in the early sixties, when auctioneers and farmers' marts and bidding at auction rings began to be the way business was done, he lost his calling. Instead of being the independent member of a guild, so to speak, he ended up as something of an employee. Instead of dealing in the country and selling at the fairs, he would go to an auction ring with a buyer and act as the adviser. He was a great judge of cattle, so people were always after him; but at that stage he wasn't so much exercising his calling as being called upon. It took the spring out of his step. I wrote about it in 'Ancestral Photograph'.

Did you ever know your father's uncle, the one you describe in that poem?

No, but I know he meant a lot to my father because he more or less taught him the trade. And at this stage of my life, I realize that when I was a youngster herding calves against the wall of the fair hill in Ballymena, say, my father probably saw something of his younger self in me, and something of his uncle Pat in himself.

W. H. Auden described Wordsworth as 'a person who early in life had an intense experience or series of experiences about inanimate nature, which he spent the rest of his poetical life trying to describe'. Can you identify with that Wordsworth?

The early-in-life experience has been central to me all right. But I'd say you aren't so much trying to describe it as trying to locate it. The amount of sensory material stored up or stored down in the brain's and the body's systems is inestimable. It's like a culture at the bottom of a jar, although it doesn't grow, I think, or help anything else to grow unless you find a way to reach it and touch it. But once you do, it's like putting your hand into a nest and finding something beginning to hatch out in your head.

II

ON THE BOOKS

3

'The hazel stirred'
Death of a Naturalist

~

Did the young poet who completed Death of a Naturalist *become a different person (more self-conscious, more confident or more bewildered) in the writing of it from the one who composed the earliest poems in the book?*

There was a new self-consciousness, yes, and probably some bewilderment when the book was published. But confidence, too, from the fact of having written the poems. In 1966 Marie and I were living on a housing estate on the outskirts of Belfast, a characterless sort of a place, and I remember getting my six free copies, probably in late April. The actual book looked very good: a lime-green and solid-pink dust jacket, and on the back a list of the Faber poets. Fabulous names: Auden, Eliot, Hughes, Larkin, Lowell, MacNeice, Spender. It was certainly strange.

Three years before, I was somebody who'd had one poem in the *Irish Times* and one in the *Kilkenny Magazine*. But it's probably the same for everybody, the moment of publication; it's always a moment of change, the start of the 'Borges and I' condition. The autobiographical creature begins to be implicated in the textual masquerade; you begin to read and hear about this composite who has written the books, and sounds very like yourself, although there's always going to be a certain stand-off between the pair of you.

But at the time there must have been a lot of sheer delight? A man who 'has published a new book' is one of Yeats's images for high excitement . . .

I was indeed excited. Mightily. But that afternoon, on my own in the new house, I was also very conscious of the mystery of what had happened – the ordinariness and, well, the election. I suppose I imagined that a poet published by Faber would be somebody in a realm apart, relieved of the usual botherations, acquainted with 'the shit in the shuttered château' and the bohemians in the pub. Not somebody with a job at a teacher-training college, with lectures to prepare and essays and exams to mark, taking his lunch at the staff table in the student dining room, listening to conversations about golf and life assurance.

Marie and I were very much the typical young marrieds of that period, with our teak furniture and our second-hand Volkswagen and, by that stage, Marie pregnant – or expectant, as the term was then. We had our own freedoms and revels, of course, but there was something beyond expectation in having a book out from Faber. That afternoon stands out, me in the house waiting for Marie to come home from school, waiting to give her her copy. *Death of a Naturalist* was dedicated to her. I can remember feeling elated and, maybe, OK, a bit bewildered. But not to the point of confusion. There was obviously great fortification in what had happened. Something had come to a head, it was 'take a deep breath and start again' time.

How large an element in the writing of the first collection was the fact that you and Marie were – in the terminology of the time – 'courting'?

I met her in October 1962 and the next month I published what I consider to be the first poem where I was in earnest. I'm not saying that one thing was a direct consequence of the other. In the beginning, the pump is primed as much by other poetry as by other people; but still, there was definitely a new charge, a quicker flow. I was sited that bit better in my life – and that bit more excited by it. But there was a poetry aspect to our first meeting, which was at a dinner to mark the retirement of the Queen's University chaplain. Marie was there as the guest of another graduate, but since we got on so well and she was in no particular relationship with him, I walked her back to the flat she shared with her sister. The road to her place, however, took us past my flat, so while we were en route I called in and came out with a copy of A. Alvarez's anthology, *The*

New Poetry, which I lent her – and which gave me an excuse to call back a day or two later to collect it. At St Mary's College, Marie had done extended essays on Louis MacNeice and Robert Graves; this meant that, from the start, poetry was one of the elements in the mix. So there was a muse energy in the air all right. 'The wood astir', as Graves says. A call to separateness, to some sort of extravagance, to be more yourself.

Did Marie have any inkling, when you became engaged, that you would offer her a very different kind of life compared with marriage to a non-poet?

Marie has always been a buoyant spirit. There's a terrific readiness about her. She has this great combination of spontaneity and staying power, so no doubt she'd have been a match for things no matter how they turned out. Even so, I think the possibility of an extra dimension helped to hold her interest. Our first brush with each other and with the arts gave our lives a hint of promise. Not long after we met, for example, her elder sister went off to teach in Madrid, and another younger sister upped and left for London at around the same time, and Marie herself certainly entertained notions of a similar move. But for one thing, she enjoyed the school where she was teaching in Crossgar in County Down and liked her colleagues. She was lucky, and different, I think, from many other young teachers starting out, because she was fulfilled by the job – which is to say she was good at it and felt good in herself as a result.

Everything happened quickly and at the same time – the development of our relationship, the entry into poetry, the marriage itself. Inside three years. One excitement quickening the other. And all the while I was what you might call professionally upwardly mobile. In the summer of 1963 I moved from schoolteaching to lecturing in St Joseph's College of Education; at Christmas in 1964 we got engaged – and the *New Statesman* published three of my poems, which led to Faber asking to see a manuscript; and their acceptance of a book in 1965 certainly helped my appointment as a lecturer in English in Queen's University in 1966. It sounds easy in retrospect and it was by no means an ordeal, but at the time nothing was predictable and there was the usual effort and anxiety.

And how did Marie respond to the poems?

She had a good sense of what rang true. No matter what she'd actually say, I always knew what she felt. It could be awkward enough, she being shown a poem for the first time, me full of the joys of having written it, she perhaps not just as joyful at having read it. Highs and huffs. Ho-hum. The usual see-saw.

You have mentioned A. Alvarez's The New Poetry *a couple of times. Clearly, it was an important anthology for you.*

Very. For one thing, it's where I got my first sense of R. S. Thomas. I'd encountered Ted Hughes earlier, in the pamphlets the BBC used to issue with their schools broadcasts – a series called *Listening and Writing*, edited by this marvellous literary producer called Moira Doolin. But *The New Poetry* was a big stimulus.

Did Alvarez's thesis about the over-genteel nature of contemporary English poetry ring true for you, or indeed influence the direction taken in your own writing?

The manifesto element in the introduction didn't matter all that much to me. On this side of the Irish Sea, and especially among the Northern Catholic minority, we had our own sense of distance and stand-off from English gentility. We didn't need Alvarez to instruct us in Albion's ways of averting the eyes and covering up. The Stormont Parliament was our particular version of 'negative feedback' . . . Still, the general sanctioning of a less-polished way with the words and a more head-on encounter with the subject was in tune with my own disposition and the Hopkins-handling in my student poems. And, by then I was under the sway of Lawrence, and there's something Lawrentian about that whole introduction; I think there's even a direct reference to a passage from *The Rainbow*.

Alvarez has been rather patronizing about your own work, inclined to see it as regressive and safe. That must have been a disappointment to you.

As a matter of fact, he assailed me before he became patronizing. When *Door into the Dark* came out in 1969, he did a hatchet job on it in the *Observer* where he was poetry critic. I suppose the good reception of *Death of a Naturalist* meant that some knives were going to be out for the second book, but Al ex-Alled himself. Yet in fairness it's as well to remember that Alvarez had been part of the action when Sylvia Plath and Ted Hughes were getting going a few years earlier; since my stuff came in the wake of all that, he probably felt that everybody needed to be reminded of it. Alvarez thinks of himself as a poet, of course, so I found being patronized by him hard to take. The attack was more in order. But it wasn't, as my mother used to say about pregnancy, a killing disease.

Your comment a short while ago about belonging to the Northern Catholic minority brought to mind Auden's remark that Yeats was 'hurt into poetry' by Ireland. Were the hurts you experienced, as an Ulster Catholic, among those which made a poet of you?

When I began to write in 1962, one of my first attempts was a poem about Loyalist emblems cut into the stone pier beside Carrickfergus Castle – including a little three-runged ladder of the sort you see on Orange sashes. And I think there was a carved-out hoof mark commemorating General Schomberg's landing there in 1689. The poem itself was a shaky item, although I believe it was eventually discussed at The Group. But what's interesting to me now is that I'd gone delving straight away into the sectarian seam of Northern life. At that stage I was a graduate with a job, a self-respecting adult of sorts, but I was still subject to the usual old Northern Ireland reminders that I'd better mind my Fenian manners. The B-Special Constabulary were on the roads at night. The anti-Catholic speeches were still being delivered by Unionist leaders on the Twelfth of July. The whole gerrymandered life of the place seemed set to continue.

So it probably doesn't overstate things to call that a hurt, although it wasn't one that set you apart. In fact, it bonded you, and the recognition and the consequences of that very bonding would eventually become something the poetry had to deal with also. But in the beginning, there was a battened-down spirit that wanted to walk taller. In other scholarship boys and girls from the Catholic side, it would find different expression – in politics, obviously, with John Hume and Bernadette Devlin. I'm certainly not saying that the simple fact of belonging to the minority made me a poet; but I am saying that, once a literary aspiration developed, it took account of the hurtful conditions. That would be true also for the generation ahead of me, people like John Montague and Brian Friel, as well as for contemporaries like Seamus Deane.

Were you consciously writing from a Catholic nationalist perspective? How was your work affected by the bonding you speak of?

I wasn't consciously writing from a Catholic perspective, but undoubtedly the work was affected by the bonding. If I were to say that I wrote consciously as a Catholic, it would imply that I saw myself as a representative, with some sort of agenda, yet there was no such thought and no such agenda. On the other hand, after I'd written 'Digging', I remember feeling that there must be hundreds of people of my generation who'd had a similar experience of exchanging spadework for pen work, and that they'd be bound to know what the poem was about. I suppose a majority of those scholarship people would have been Catholics, but by no means exclusively.

Your questions are hard to answer exactly. It would be untrue to say that I was without a Catholic self-awareness. You didn't grow up in Lord Brookeborough's Ulster without developing a them-and-us mindset. Even though there was no sectarian talk or prejudice at home, there was still an indignation at the political status quo. We knew and were given to know that Ulster wasn't meant for us, that the British connection was meant to displace us. No need to go into the list of complaints all over again, the discrimination in housing and in professions such as medicine, the paramilitary nature of the RUC and B-Special Constabulary – the main thing is that you shared what used to be called an 'anti-partitionist' stance. Now, truth to your feelings, acceptable or not, is one of the things that's not only required in poetry, it's often what drives you to poetry. So my early poems are true to my spots – maculate conceptions, if you like.

Did the publication by Faber of Death of a Naturalist *make you more alert to the political position you occupied?*

Undoubtedly. You know that old joke about the headline in the *Irish News* – 'Catholic Dog Wins Protestant Race'? Well, subliminally at least, there was some sense of that. The Ulster/Faber axis until then had been what you might call Liberal Unionist, with Robert Harbinson doing his travel books and, earlier, Forrest Reid doing his fiction, and Louis MacNeice in the background all along as some kind of presiding genius. MacNeice had no particular Unionist affiliation or animus; but his social position and religious denomination meant that he was, as he said himself, 'banned forever from the candles of the Irish poor' – which was not a ban I suffered from.

There was another Ulsterman, as he would have called himself, in Faber at the time: Charles Monteith, the chief editor, the man who had previously been T. S. Eliot's assistant, somebody centrally important in the firm and to me. The fact that Charles was a Northern Ireland Protestant with Unionist connections made for a certain understanding from the start, even if it was an understanding of difference. I remember when we first met in London in 1965, a month or two after he had accepted the manuscript, he remarked that I must have been in Belfast for the Twelfth of July and I admitted that I had been. 'Fine old folk festival,' said Charles, a bit disingenuously. 'To some people,' I replied, a bit uneasily.

The manuscript was accepted in 1965, and you recalled earlier that you published what you considered your first achieved poem in 1962. So Death of a Naturalist *contains no poems written while you were a student?*

No. The earliest ones are 'Turkeys Observed' and 'Docker'; 'An Advancement of Learning' and 'Mid-Term Break': the first two written in late 1962, the others in early 1963.

I'd like to hear about the places where you wrote those poems.

I shared a flat from 1961 until 1963 with two postgraduates in biochemistry. And I wrote 'Mid-Term Break' one evening there after a day's teaching in St Thomas's School, sitting in an armchair waiting for one of those guys to produce the evening meal. We had a rota: week by week, one did the shopping, one did the cooking and one did the dishes. It was my week for the dishes, so I had this free hour from five to six; and I remembered Christopher's accident because it was February, round about the time of his anniversary.

Anyhow, until I got married, I was living in flats – the one I've just mentioned on Wellington Park and another in Fitzroy Avenue near the university, a sitting room and bedroom, kitchen and bathroom, all on the ground floor – very desirable. I shared it for a while with Hugh Bredin, a friend from my time in St Columb's. Hugh was then in Belfast, finishing a master's degree, I think, and getting ready to proceed to Italy, where he did his doctorate on the aesthetics of Croce.

Once you started teaching, did you live in Belfast all the year round?

I stayed in Belfast during term time and would go home to Bellaghy at Christmas and sometimes at weekends and always for the summer holidays. 'Digging' I wrote at home in The Wood in August 1964, upstairs in the bedroom. 'Death of a Naturalist' I wrote in one of the flats on a Sunday afternoon, after lying out in the sun with Marie and her flatmates at the back of a place they had in Tate's Avenue. The dead heat in their little back garden and the reek of litter bins in the alley behind the houses reminded me of the stink of flax in the dam years before. 'Trout' I remember writing on a C&A carrier bag in Marie's flat, when they were all gabbling away together and the record player was going full blast. I couldn't manage that kind of concentration nowadays. I did a section of the famine poem, 'At a Potato Digging', sitting in the driver's seat of my VW Beetle in Botanic Avenue. I may have been waiting for somebody, or have parked on impulse to note the thing down.

Can you tell me about the jobs you were doing during those years?

In 1962, after a year of postgraduate teacher training at St Joseph's College, I worked in St Thomas's Secondary Intermediate School in Ballymurphy and then, in 1963, got appointed as a lecturer in English back in St Joseph's. I stayed there for three years, until 1966, which was the *annus mirabilis*: our first child, Michael, was born; *Death of a Naturalist* appeared; and I got a job in the English Department in Queen's.

Still, your life could have been very different had you taken up the studentship that was available when you graduated with a first-class degree. Is it true that you had the option of going to Oxford?

I believe I had, yes, although the whole thing happened so quickly it was over before it got right started. You know what it's like during that first day or two after the degree results are announced. Your status has changed but you're still a student and the professor is still an enormous authority figure. At any rate, when I went to see

Professor Butter, he let me know that a studentship would be available; and he indicated that, as an old Balliol man, he could smooth the path to Oxford – and he did indeed help other students in that direction in the years that followed. But I dithered and he didn't push. I suppose if I had anticipated a first and had known that I'd be invited to do a further degree, I might have readied myself and my family for new moves; but as things stood, there was an expectation at home that I'd go out and start earning, and there was my own unpreparedness for the research option. Not that there was any parental gun to my head to start working or contributing – it was just a general expectation, in myself and in them. There wasn't much advice they could give, and Butter was more or less leaving it to me, saying that of course I could always take the Oxford road a little later on, could do an MA part-time, while teaching in Belfast, and all that. Anyhow, I proceeded on the home front.

What sort of place was St Thomas's School?

St Thomas's was what they called in Britain a secondary modern and in Northern Ireland an intermediate school. Set up to provide secondary education for those who didn't make the grade to grammar schools via the eleven-plus exam. Set up for 'non-academic' pupils. No Latin, but woodwork and metalwork – at least for boys; and St Thomas's was all boys, and all Catholic and nearly all from a big desolate housing estate at the top of the Whiterock Road. Most of them from a poor background. The trimly turned-out ones were very noticeable in the classroom.

What happened was not what was supposed to happen. There was supposed to be a swerve away from the exam culture, a development of skills, an inculcation of self-respect by giving the non-academic pupils a prospect of fulfilment in other areas. But what actually happened was that the effort went into helping the top streams, the top fifth or quarter of the intake, say, to catch up in the academic race. In those days, the intermediate schools often turned out to be the place where the ones who failed the eleven-plus could get a second chance to clamber on to the academic conveyor belt by entering, for example, for the junior certificate or the GCE. So instead of a school where equal attention was paid to all abilities, there was this favoured upper stream and then the great non-academic flow-through. My job, for the year I was in the school, was to teach English at first-year and fourth-year levels, to two of the exam-oriented classes. And I had a PE class with a group of really low-ability first years, 1G, for God's sake, in a ranking that began with 1A.

I don't get the impression that you felt very fulfilled in this post. Did you have problems with discipline, for example?

To some extent, but not overwhelmingly. The problem was that the school was attempting to inculcate a regime of respectability and conformity, a kind of middle-class boarding-school style, but the home culture and street culture of working-class Belfast was very different. For example, the vice-principal made the rounds of the classrooms every day, examining the kids' shoes. They had to be polished. I remember seeing big lads of fifteen being given four slaps with a leather strap because their shoes hadn't been polished . . . Crazy. But the thinking behind it was this: if they got into the habit of rigging themselves out cleanly and acceptably, then they'd have more of a chance of bettering themselves, getting a job in the Corporation, things like that.

Was there a fear that you had ended up in the wrong place?

I was certainly unhappy. My main problem was inexperience in the classroom; but also lack of full commitment, a lingering feeling that I was now a bit off course, given that the Oxford option had come up. I don't mean that I was yearning or planning to get back to a university, just that I was quailing under the burden of marking class essays and working in an environment that was definitely non-literary. OK, Michael McLaverty, the headmaster, was a writer, and a congenial presence, and his friendship was a compensation. And there were a couple of other cultivated souls on the staff. But you had to contend as well with the oafs and gobshites. I just didn't enjoy the environment. I had no relish for getting up in the morning, getting on the bus in Shaftesbury Square and heading up to 'the plant'. It looked like an open prison, it had iron railings, steel window frames, tiled corridors – H-Block architecture, really. And all this when I was beginning to get a life, as they say.

Just when I should have been concentrating on preparing my classes and so on in the evenings, I was getting into very different activities – drinking and staying out late at parties and hullabaloos of all sorts. With all the usual penalties the next morning. But even so, I did have a good time with the fourth-year GCE students in particular. We studied *Twelfth Night* and a poetry anthology called *Rhyme and Reason*. I took them to Carrickfergus once to see where Louis MacNeice was born, the Norman Castle and the effigies of the Chichesters in church – all mentioned in MacNeice's poem 'Carrickfergus', which was included in the anthology.

Was there anything you did – or could have done – as a teacher to change the perspectives of those students and enlarge their prospects in life? Is art of any benefit in a context where the home life and community life are materially deprived and maybe, in some cases, emotionally arid too?

Put it this way: forty years on, I still remember five or six names and faces out of that fourth-year class – the more intelligent ones, admittedly, the ones with sensibility and personality. Which means that some sort of connection was made. Something was done by the book, as it were. It's a two-way process, after all, whether we're talking about art or education. What's on offer is one thing, what's picked up is another. The temperament and disposition of the ones on the receiving end are decisive, and so are the quality and suitability of the thing being offered. I think, for example, that the Louis MacNeice poem – plus the visit to Carrick – must have meant something to a number of them. They'd have got some kind of confirmation from finding a familiar name and place brought to book like that, some new grip on what they knew, some new freedom within it. So yes, I believe education can offer ampler prospects and a change of perspective or a reason for aspiration. And I'm sure that St Thomas's did that for a few of those boys.

But you're right to see disadvantaged homes and impoverished conditions generally as a barrier to growth and self-realization. The sectarian realities, the unemployment, the eventual presence of the British army, the IRA recruiting machine, the peer pressure – hard to see teenagers who were simply returned from the school to the street corner being able to transcend all that. Hard to have a Stephen Dedalus or a Paul Morel without some emotional and spiritual help in the home and outside it. One pupil, by the way, did triumph – the late Jack Holland, the novelist and writer on Northern Irish affairs, who eventually ended up in New York. Jack was in class 4B and his essays suggested he would make a path for himself. He had an appetite for language – and a sardonic sense of humour. If you have the words, there's always a chance that you'll find the way.

In Finders Keepers, *you recall how Michael McLaverty used to cajole the class into reading poetry. But he had an influence on your own reading too?*

Michael had his mantras: read Chekhov, read 'The Death of Ivan Ilych', read Friel's 'The Foundry House', read *Dubliners*, read John Clare, read Edward Thomas. Most of which I was reading anyway. But, for my own work, the most important thing he did was to lend me Patrick Kavanagh's *A Soul for Sale*, the book that included 'The Great Hunger'. I had encountered some of Kavanagh's Monaghan lyrics in *The Oxford Book of Irish Verse* and liked them, but 'The Great Hunger' took a deeper hold.

When did you meet Kavanagh himself?

Not until 1967. That summer I taught for a week or two at a summer course in Trinity College and was introduced to him by Richard Ryan, in the Bailey on Duke Street, standing at the bar. I didn't particularly want to meet him. I had some hunch he'd not want anything to do with a young one like me who'd had the luck – the neck – to be published by Faber. His own *Collected Poems* had come out just then – the book that begins with his saying that he'd never been much regarded by the English critics – and here was I, garlanded with sound bites from Christopher Ricks and C. B. Cox and so on. Could he not take his ease at his inn without this?

In fact, the whole thing went off very stylishly. At first I avoided the contact as unobtrusively as possible, kept my face to the counter when he stopped to speak to Richard, and waited for him to move on – he was coming back past our part of the counter on his way from the Gents. But the pause continued and what had begun as a reticence started to look like an ignorance; so I turned round and said, 'Mr Kavanagh, can I buy you a drink?' 'No', he replies, with the 'o' in the 'No' well lengthened out. So then Richard says something like, 'Paddy, this man's come down here from Belfast, and he's just published a book of poems. His name's Seamus Heaney.' And Kavanagh says to me, 'Are you Heaney?'

rhyming me with Rainey, as people did in the country at home. 'Well, I'll have a Scotch.' So I took that as a pass.

Was that all?

Well, no. After that I went over and joined him for a while, among the others in attendance. I remember I either commended Thomas Hardy or asked what he himself thought of Hardy, but he was on to me like a shot – suspected I was making too nifty a link between one 'country' poet and another, and replied ex cathedra, as obliquely and authoritatively as a Yeats, 'Pope's a good poet.' And that was me in my box.

You didn't see him again?

Once. A few days later, I went to a poetry reading by Brendan Kennelly in Hodges Figgis and Kavanagh was there with his wife Katherine, hawking and sighing at the back of the room. At that stage he wasn't in good health; so, at the end of the evening, I gave the pair of them a lift back to Pembroke Road, or wherever they were located at the time. They sat in the back seat of my Beetle and Katherine at one point said something like, 'There you are now, Paddy, you can be a poet and have a car after all.' You would always expect a bit of edge in those days.

Before Faber and Charles Monteith, there was The Group and Philip Hobsbaum. How did you get to know Hobsbaum?

In *Hibernia* in 1963, I reviewed the *Group Anthology* he edited with Edward Lucie-Smith, and we met after that. I'd ended the review by suggesting that some sort of poetic group work such as that described in the introduction to the anthology – a workshop, in effect – would be welcome in Belfast. Maybe I'd heard that Philip was thinking of starting something of that nature anyway. I'm not sure who made the link between us – maybe Stewart Parker, who was around the English Department then; maybe Alan Gabbey who was editing *Interest*. I went to his flat at 5 Fitzwilliam Street, and Marie – even though she wasn't writing poems of her own – came with me, and we met Philip and his wife Hannah. He was very intense, very much a teacher, full of strong opinion. A seminar leader as much as a poet. I suppose he was more or less conducting interviews with people who might be invited to come to the group he was about to start. On the lookout for local talent. Joan Watton, as she was then, before she married and became Joan Newmann, was picked out by Philip in a Workers Educational Association evening class and encouraged into poetry by him. Stewart Parker too he both admired and encouraged. And myself, every bit as much.

Was it through The Group that you met the Longleys?

I think it was at a party in the Hobsbaums' flat, maybe just before the first working meeting. I remember a singing session started and Michael shouted across the room that I was just another stage Irishman. There was a lot of banter and blather, and a definite connection was made. Then one evening Michael and I drove out to a pub on the Lisburn Road. I brought some of my poems – at his request – and he took them home. Edna and he were already doing what they'd continue to do, checking the talent, taking squarings. Edna at that stage was still Edna Broderick and had come to lecture in Queen's around the same time as Hobsbaum. Both she and Michael came to The Group early on and may indeed have been present at the first meeting.

Maybe you would describe a typical meeting of The Group: the room, the rules of engagement, the advice given, the criticism taken.

It began at eight o'clock on a Monday evening. People arrived five or ten minutes before that and sat around in the living room of the Hobsbaum flat, which was on the first floor. Philip would already be in the chairman's seat and other chairs would have been arranged in a big circle. People behaved as they do before a seminar – they looked at the poems on their sheets, spoke to the person next to them, and all the while the chairman didn't say much to relieve the air of formality and expectation. The poems by that week's poet would have been posted out or distributed at the previous meeting and everybody was meant to have read them, so that added to the classroom mood as well. Maybe I'm overemphasizing this aspect of the event; but it was important because it made for a certain seriousness and prepared everybody for the change of gear from chat to main business.

Once the meeting started, the critical loins were girded, Philip concentrated on the poem sheet and hunched forward like a man on a Harley Davidson coming down the road at ninety. For an hour to an hour and a half there'd be a reading of poems by the author, a statement about each by Philip and a general discussion by all present, wound up again by Philip. A pause then, coffee and biscuits served by Hannah, general across-the-room conversation, all of a literary nature, then after ten or fifteen minutes everybody was invited to read a poem and say why they had chosen it – not one of their own, usually, but something they admired, new or old, maybe a translation, maybe something just published. I remember different things that Philip read, a chunk out of *Piers Plowman*, a Lowell translation of Victor Hugo, poems by people who had attended the London Group, especially Martin Bell and Peter Redgrove.

What did you read?

You know, I cannot recollect. Probably Ted Hughes or Kavanagh. Maybe John Crowe Ransom. I was very devoted to 'Bells for John Whiteside's Daughter' and 'Dead Boy'. But that part of the evening was always an education. You'd hear people reading and talking about what meant most to them. What you were seeing in action was the effect of poetry stored up within an individual's memory and the way it functioned as a shared value. The Group gave the people who attended an audience and a motive for their own writing, but this other, more general toning up of the poetry muscles was equally important, maybe in the long run more important.

But what about the first part of the evening?

A different kind of engagement. Everything on each page was there to be tested or questioned. Now and again there would be a poem where all that needed to be said was 'Well done' – but you'd feel it was a dereliction of duty if that was all you did. You felt you had to workshop, as they say, whatever was put in front of you. That could be embarrassing if the work was useless, but then, fortunately or unfortunately, you can keep up a critical patter just as easily about junk verse as about the real thing – talk about line endings, focus on an image, compare the poem to known poems in the canon. In the end I suppose what the writer gets in these situations is a sense of the poem's madeness, its strangeness to others, and maybe, yes, its improvability. Some revisions were made as a result of those discussions, maybe even some improvements.

Was there rivalry in The Group?

Not exactly *in* The Group. It was more that the consequences of The Group ratings had to be lived with outside it. After a while, a *placement* of sorts was established and it persisted in an in-house kind of way. I think Philip's favourite was Stewart Parker, but Stewart went off to Cornell after the first or second meeting. Joan Watton he also held in high esteem, and rightly so. And I suppose I had a top-of-the-class rating as well. Michael Longley, on the other hand, was marked down because of his stylishness. Aesthetically too 'paleface' for Philip. 'Longley's a big man,' Philip used to say. 'Huge voice, huge chest. A rugby back. And he writes these polite little poems.' Longley felt that as a wrong but he had an inner sureness and a kind of detachment. At any rate, we worked out a modus vivendi among ourselves, almost like schoolkids coping with teacher's favouritism. You could even say that one of the big contributions of The Group was the counter-grouping and griping it entailed. Readjustments of the evening's judgements were required afterwards.

Young poets thrive on a mixture of affection and disaffection anyhow, they get involved in a kind of vying that's not quite rivalry, more an aspiration to outdo, pure and simple. But it would be disingenuous to imply that Michael and Edna didn't resent the Hobsbaum rating. On the other hand, they had a status drawn from their own examining board, so to speak, one that consisted of themselves and Derek Mahon and, at that time, Eavan Boland. They played and read the score by Trinity rules as opposed to Group rules.

Would you describe the rivalry as having been at all times healthy?

I don't think the rivalry, if that's the right word, was ever *un*healthy in the matter of writing, in the sheer aspiration to best yourself. The desire to have something terrific to pull out of your pocket when you met – that kind of trumping and self-trumping was enjoyed by all. No begrudging, in other words, of achievement per se. The awkwardness or resentment set in when one was promoted over the other by publication or praise or later by the award of a prize. More a matter of ratings than rivalry. But that kind of thing just cannot be helped. What's required all round in those situations is good behaviour – government of the tongue, so to speak, at least when face to face. And I believe we were well enough behaved. We managed to navigate the bad stretches without capsizing.

I always knew my reception and the favour I enjoyed brought out rivalry, not to say resentment, in others: Michael Longley has put on record a flare-up in drink one night at David Hammond's place where what was no doubt private dogma was shouted out as public challenge; the tongue was ungoverned and I was told that Mahon was the better poet. It didn't surprise me to know this was the verdict, but to have it expressed so aggressively was unexpected. For a long time I kept making inner allowances, telling myself to see it from their point of view, but at a certain stage I decided, *To hell with it, I'm not going round trying to get one up on anybody, it's live and let live from now on.* Michael told Jody Allen Randolph that 'we competed with each other more ferociously than perhaps we now remember', but I don't think I considered myself 'in competition' with anybody. Admittedly I may have been the cause of it in others, which only means, come to think of it, I was raising the standard without even trying.

But was there not a certain overt rivalry between Longley, Mahon and yourself, about who could do justice to Louis MacNeice's memory, on the occasion when you all visited MacNeice's grave in Carrowdore churchyard?

I had a go at doing a poem all right, but on an occasional rather than a rivalrous basis: I knew it was never going to be one I'd keep. Wasn't it Larkin who said there are poems you're given to write and poems you'd like to write? I'd have liked the MacNeice to have been given, but it wasn't. Anyhow. The trip was on a Saturday afternoon, at a time when I was the only one of us with a car. My job at St Joseph's involved supervising students on teaching practice, so I'd got a Volkswagen Beetle sometime around 1963 or so, and Marie and I often went out on drives with the Longleys after that.

We were all getting to know each other and getting to know the countryside around Belfast. A poem of mine, 'The Peninsula' – about the Ards peninsula in County Down – was written after one of those drives. And there was another one, not published in a book, about seeing a seal in the harbour in Ardglass. I suppose I'm saying that the context of the Mahon/MacNeice poem was a generative rather than a competitive one. You have to remember that there was a simple desire to get out there and enjoy ourselves. One St Patrick's Day, for example, we went and climbed Slemish. And drowned the shamrock at a pub in Carlisle Circus on the way back.

How early did you begin sending out to editors the poems published in Death of a Naturalist? *In the acknowledgements, you list familiar and prestigious outlets such as* The Listener *and* New Statesman, *but also* Interest – *the university magazine you mentioned earlier – and* Northern Review. *How did you decide where to send the poems?*

It was a matter of desire rather than decision. The lust of the unpublished. The thing progressed through three milieux, three successive phases. First there was Queen's and student magazines, plus the *Belfast Telegraph* and those other magazines you mention, *Interest* and *Northern Review. Interest* came out of Queen's for a couple or three years after I graduated, and *Northern Review* was sponsored by the Northern Ireland Arts Council but disappeared after a few issues.

So you published first and foremost in the North?

You know, my debut, if you'll excuse the expression, was in a national Irish magazine while I was still an undergraduate. But it wasn't poetry. There was a monthly called the *Irish Digest*, put out by the *Irish Independent* newspaper, I think. If you check out the files for April 1961 you'll find an article by me suggesting that the jive should be introduced into Irish dancing. I did it at Christmas the previous year. I'd hired a portable typewriter during the 1960 Christmas vacation and taught myself to touch-type and then did this winsome wee piece and sent it out. But it was also a case of sending out feelers to myself. Something was stirring. Something that wasn't being satisfied by the life of *céilís* and GAA and the local dramatic society. It would be a couple of years before the next publication in Dublin, but by then the poetry die had been cast.

In the meantime, you'd done a postgraduate teacher-training course in St Joseph's College and produced an extended essay on the history of literary magazines in Ulster. Did that research lead you to believe that to publish only locally would be something of a dead end?

It's hard to say what exactly the effect of that essay was. I definitely learned something. Got a grip on where I was. Which was in a situation bounded on one side by academic English Literature and on another by vernacular nationalist culture – Percy French and the Clancy Brothers and patriotic recitations like 'The Man from God Knows Where' – and on yet another by what these magazines stood for, a six-county Ulstery, Liberal-Unionisty brand of half-high literary culture. The one who would resolve it all into writerly action, of course, was Patrick Kavanagh, very much a man of the nine-county Ulster, but I just didn't know Kavanagh well enough in 1961 or early 1962. What I got from doing the essay was a demon-stration that the local was workable literary matter and a hint that I myself might be able to work *with* it.

When did you first publish poems beyond Belfast?

Quite soon after I was first published in the *Belfast Telegraph*. The second phase – which involved Dublin and Ireland – got started just three or four months after 'Turkeys Observed' appeared in the *Telegraph*. 'Turkeys', I think, is the earliest poem in *Death of a Naturalist*. Written in November or December 1962, partly as a result of reading Ted Hughes's 'View of a Pig', partly as a result of the butchers' window displays coming up to Christmas. At any rate, in the spring of 1963 the *Irish Times* took 'An Advancement of Learning' and later on one called 'Fisher'; and the *Kilkenny Magazine* took 'Mid-Term Break'. There was also an acceptance by the *Dubliner* of a sub R. S. Thomas poem about the death of an old farmer. So things hotted up that year – with the result that, when The Group started in the autumn, I'd already seen the light of print and had discovered a certain confidence.

The important thing was that literary editors had accepted the poems without knowing me personally, or anything about me. That was a big boost for the Incertus homunculus. In fact, just how unknown I was to the *Irish Times* became clear when they printed 'Fisher' on the books page and gave the author's name as 'James Heaney'.

You must have been even more of an outsider in Britain. How and when did your 'third phase' get under way?

I feel I've told this story several times already . . . I kept sending out work to the *New Statesman* and *The Listener*, especially in 1964, and kept getting it back. Then, in December 1964, Karl Miller accepted three poems out of the blue for the *New Statesman* and published them together in the pre-Christmas issue. Big moment, that was. And it came about because of intermediary work Philip Hobsbaum had done through his old Group connections in London. Edward Lucie-Smith came over to Queen's on one occasion: after that, Philip would send him the Belfast Group sheets and, as far as I understand, Lucie-Smith would then submit them to various magazines. I remember, at any rate, being sent for during a class in St Joseph's and talking to Karl Miller on the phone from the main college office. Heady stuff. And then not long after Christmas, early in 1965, a letter came from Faber, from Charles Monteith, asking to see a manuscript. So Teddy, as Philip called him, had an important hand in getting me published.

If I understand correctly, you had at this stage already submitted a manuscript to the Dolmen Press? Why Dolmen and not Faber?

Dolmen was 'where it was at' in Ireland. I was saying earlier that one effect of the publication of *The Dolmen Miscellany* was to make the home ground firm under our poetic feet. We were very conscious of Dolmen as the locus and the focus of poetry in the country. There was a cultural nationalist motive too, a first preference for the home pitch. Faber, as I've often remarked, was an elsewhere entirely; Russell Square spelled T. S. Eliot and an unenterable empyrean. Then too, like all young poets, I was in a hurry. Maybe overly so, thanks to the boosting I was getting from Philip at The Group. Anyway, I sent a manuscript to Dolmen late in 1964 and am lucky to have a copy of it still, so I know, for example, from the acknowledgements page, that it must have gone in some time before Karl Miller accepted 'Digging' and the other poems, since some of them are in the manuscript and yet there's no mention of the *New Statesman*. But I do conclude the acknowledgements by stating that 'some of the poems are still under consideration by various magazines'.

What exactly happened then?

I wish I had the letters in order to establish dates, if nothing else. The documentary evidence that exists is confined, as far as I know, to my copy of the manuscript and an entry in a Dolmen register recording either its receipt or its return.

Where is that register now?

I'm not sure. But I know it was exhibited in a display of Irish books and manuscripts arranged by the Grolier Club in New York in 2002. Dolmen had possession of the poems for at least two months. Maybe two and a half, or three. I remember very particularly worrying about the protocol, once Faber had written to me in January 1965. Monteith asked to see a manuscript and I may have sent him stuff before requesting a return of the poems from Dolmen. But I do recollect writing a letter to Dolmen saying that if they had not decided to accept the book, then I'd like to have it back. I didn't tell Dolmen that Faber was interested, so I'd left myself open to complications if Dolmen said they wanted to publish. But they didn't, they sent back the poems and I went on to a new track. As a matter of fact, Tim O'Keefe from MacGibbon and Kee wrote to me that spring also, suggesting that I might submit to them. I was steeped in luck.

Were the contents of the Dolmen manuscript more or less the same as those of Death of a Naturalist?

Very different. No 'Blackberry Picking', no 'Follower', no 'Barn', no 'Churning Day', no 'At a Potato Digging', no 'Personal Helicon' . . . On the other hand, it did include 'Digging' and 'End of a Naturalist' – the 'Death' bit would come later. The manuscript as a whole was entitled *Advancements of Learning* and was in three sections: 'Home Territory', 'MacKenna Country' and 'Portraits and Landscapes'. The MacKenna section came from reading R. S. Thomas's poems about Iago Prytherch. But equally he was a literary son of Kavanagh's Patrick Maguire, a thick-witted farm labourer reeking of sour pigmeal and parish piety, somebody who gave me a way of writing about the local subculture. And the third section had a number of things that also appear towards the end of *Death of a Naturalist* – 'The Folk Singers', 'Poor Women in a City Church', 'Storm on the Island'.

So those poems you've just mentioned – 'Blackberry Picking' and so on – belong to early 1965: a period when, according to your own account, you 'wrote a hell of a lot'. Was this writing an act of will, to ensure you'd have enough poems for the first collection, or were you writing with an extra surge of confidence because Faber and Faber was beckoning?

I was buoyed up and charged up and at the same time had a powerful will to deliver. Charles Monteith's letter picked out 'Death of a Naturalist' and 'Digging' as the poems that took his fancy, so that encouraged me to concentrate on subjects and settings around Mossbawn. And once I opened those channels, I got the surge, definitely.

Was it obvious from the beginning that 'Digging' would have to be the first poem in the book?

It was the first poem in the manuscript I sent to Dolmen and, from the moment I wrote it in August 1964, I knew it was a strength-giver. Where else could it be placed? It decided its position for itself.

Now that it's so famous, I should also ask if you remember how the gun/pen image occurred to you. And ask you too if there was any political significance in the fact that images of 'gun-barrel', 'bullet', ' armoury', 'salvo', 'pottery bombs' and so on appear in various pre-Troubles poems.

When Denis Donoghue reviewed the book, he suggested that I'd seen too many war films and cowboy films when I was a youngster. In fact, I saw very few films when I was a youngster, but have to admit to a partiality later on for *The Dam Busters* and *Reach for the Sky* and many of those old Second World War escape films – was there one called *The Wooden Horse*? So maybe Denis's guess is as good as mine. But the high-voltage diction of Ted Hughes's work had something to do with it too.

In the case of the pen 'between my finger and my thumb', 'snug as a gun', and all the rest of it, I was responding to an entirely phonetic prompt, a kind of sonic chain dictated by the inner ear. It's the connection between the 'uh' sounds in 'thumb' and 'snug' and 'gun' that are the heart of the poetic matter rather than any sociological or literary formation. On the other hand, there are those 'mud-grenades' in 'Death of a Naturalist' that seem to have a sexual pin in them just waiting to be pulled, so who's to say for definite about these things?

Can you remember sending off the final version of Death of a Naturalist?

Not really. I know that the book had been accepted by July because when I was in London that August – on my honeymoon, for God's sake – I went to the Faber offices to meet Charles Monteith. And, on that occasion I think, I brought another poem to add to it – 'The Diviner'. 'The Diviner' was the last one in.

Did you make many changes at proof stage?

As far as I remember, only one. I rewrote the last three or four stanzas of 'An Advancement of Learning'. I had a kind of superstitious loyalty to that poem because it was the first one accepted by the *Irish Times*. As a poem, it's fairly rickety – something I was aware of even then – but there are all kinds of irrational factors at work when you're dealing with poems. Superstitious loyalties that take precedence over your artistic better judgement.

Before the book appeared in 1966, a pamphlet of your poems issued from Festival Publications in Belfast. Who published Festival Publications and how did you come to their notice?

I was part of the Belfast Festival committee at that time. The Festival was just getting started, turning from being a set of student events into something bigger, with official support from the Queen's University administration. The man behind it was Michael Emmerson, whom I mentioned in passing earlier. Michael had come to Queen's as an undergraduate from Stratford-upon-Avon and then had stayed on and developed the programmes until the thing grew to be a fully fledged arts festival. And at that point a long and very productive relationship between Queen's and the Northern Ireland Arts Council and the BBC got under way. In 1965, however, there was still a touch of the ad hoc and the improvisatory about proceedings, so when I suggested a pamphlet series to Michael, it was a done deal in a minute and the booklets were brought out with very little fuss. The first three are collectors' items now, of course: Derek Mahon's *Twelve Poems*, my *Eleven* and Michael's *Ten*. They look as if they were just xeroxed and stapled; but they were the start of something.

Faber didn't mind those Eleven Poems *being published?*

Charles would have encouraged it because it worked as an announcement for the full collection. And in fact it got a very good review from John Carey in the *New Statesman*.

The reviews of Death of a Naturalist?

Christopher Ricks gave it a good send-off and that was important encouragement, coming in the *New Statesman* and coming as soon as the book was published. Then too John Hewitt welcomed it in the *Belfast Telegraph*, Michael Longley saluted me as an Ulster poet in the *Irish Times* 'Book of the Day', Brendan Kennelly raised his cap and Austin Clarke gave a nod. The fact that the poets included me in was good magic.

But in The Review, *Ian Hamilton's magazine, you were included out.*

'Mud-caked fingers in Russell Square.' And I also remember getting the brush-off in the *Observer* from one Peter Marsh, only to discover later that Marsh was one of Hamilton's pseudonyms. *The Review* was where you expected to get it in the neck anyhow. If they were hammering Ted Hughes and Geoffrey Hill, they were welcome to hammer me as well.

Christopher Ricks's review suggested that your love poems were influenced by Robert Graves. You both show a certain resistance to mainstream modernism, but I can't help thinking of his clipped diction as the polar opposite of your own 'vowels ploughed into other'.

It was typical of Ricks to pick up on that. I listened a good deal to Graves in the early sixties – I'd got my hands on an LP of him reading his poems and was a bit surprised by his officer-class accent and delivery. The actual voice and the clipped writing style were all of a piece. I liked in particular the soldierly address and imagery of 'Spoils': 'When all is over and you march for home, / The spoils of war are easily disposed of . . .' And that clipped way of handling matters got into some of those early love poems, ones like 'Scaffolding' and 'Twice Shy'. Michael Longley was a great Graves fan, and used to quote 'To Juan at the Winter Solstice'. And when I first met Marie, she knew 'Sick Love' by heart – the one that begins, 'O Love, be fed with apples while you may, / And feel the sun and go in royal array, / A smiling innocent on the heavenly causeway'. In fact, when we met Graves at a big eightieth birthday party for him, hosted by Garech Browne in Luggala, I asked him to write out that poem in longhand for Marie and he very kindly did so. He was wandering a little by then, but still straight as a rush, still the Roman profile and the old pukka idiom.

He divided the world into the 'all right' and the 'not all right'. He asked Marie, for example, what poets I liked; when she mentioned Theodore Roethke, he asked her to quote something. So she begins 'My Papa's Waltz': 'The whiskey on your breath / Could make a small boy dizzy . . .' and he interrupts to say 'I don't think it's all right to write poems about the smell of other people's breath.' And when Marie replies that Roethke's father was something of an alcoholic, Graves says, 'My father took the pledge.' Case closed.

So Roethke was important to you?

Not early on. But when *The Far Field* came out in 1964 and then the *Collected Poems* in 1968, he became one of the invoked spirits. I remember seeing 'Meditation at Oyster River' in the *Critical Quarterly*, and coming alive to the generosity and supply behind it. I loved his greenhouse poems, too, but something else that interested me about Roethke was the split in his poetic persona. He wrote those big Whitmanesque roller-coaster poems, and then, in a different vein, some very tightly rhymed metrical things, villanelles and so on. I suppose the interest sprang from my own experience of doing poems which were correspondingly open and closed, a trudging sort of poem like 'Digging', say, and then trimmer ones like 'Follower'.

When you reopen Death of a Naturalist *now, are you tempted to rewrite or revise or excise – or is it too late to think in those terms?*

As a matter of fact, I *have* done a bit of excising already. After Farrar, Straus and Giroux published *Field Work* in America, they put out the four earlier books in a single volume, and if you look in the *Death of a Naturalist* part of that collection – *Poems 1965–75* – you'll see I dropped seven of the poems. The *Naturalist* had been out for fourteen years at that stage and I felt free to exercise my judgement. But I would never interfere with the contents of the volume per se – the volume, I mean, reprinted under its own title. That stands and I have no problem about it. It is what it is. And what it was.

Another thing that stands is your acknowledgement of an anthology called Young Commonwealth Poets. *I would have thought you'd have been uncomfortable, even at the time, with the very title?*

Uncomfortable was about the height of it. As far as I remember, that anthology was organized from Cardiff for some festival or other in 1965 and Philip Hobsbaum – at his good work of promotion, as ever – sent our stuff to the editors. More uneasy for me was an inclusion in Jeremy Robson's *The Young British Poets* a few years later on. But you know, until Bloody Sunday, that nomenclature business didn't come all that strongly to the fore. Admittedly, it was always a worry in the background; but, as I keep saying, there was no very intense Republican motive operating in me or my family, more your typical nationalist minority stand-off from Unionists. The whole thing was warped by Little Ulsterism. In a contrary sort of a way, as a poet of nationalist background, I might even have enjoyed being included in those books. Croppy wasn't lying down any more . . .

  Then there's another thing: until I moved to Glanmore in 1972, my passport wasn't actually green, so there were all kinds of anomalies operating. My first passport was got in a hurry in the late 1950s, to go to Lourdes, of all places. Applying to Dublin wasn't even thought about. It was a sufficiently testing bureaucratic achievement for us to get the forms to Belfast. Convenience and unease were there in equal measure with the lion and the crown. And here's something else for the record: when I went to work in London in the summer of 1962, I got a job in the Passport Office in Petty France. I'd actually issued British passports, for God's sake, so I didn't think too much about carrying one. But, as the circumstances became more virulent and politicized in the 1970s, the need to establish new stays against confusion became more urgent.

Does it ever surprise – or indeed annoy – you that there are readers who still regard Death of a Naturalist *as their favourite collection?*

I can understand that easily. Readers who stay with you from the start are going to have a particular affection for early stuff. There's something self-charging about every good first-reading experience. If you asked me, I'd probably have to say that *Lupercal* is my own favourite Ted Hughes collection. It's not that I don't admire Ted's work all through. It's just that the original transmissions stay alive in a special way.

4

'Inwards and downwards'
Door into the Dark

∽

You must have felt burdened with high expectations after the reception of Death of a Naturalist. *How self-conscious and nervous were you when you embarked on* Door into the Dark?

I remember having this big hardbacked blue notebook, and starting in on it very deliberately one Saturday morning. That would have been in the autumn of 1965, not long after we'd come back from the honeymoon and moved into our first semi-detached on a housing estate on the edge of Belfast. I was like a pilot standing at the edge of an aerodrome, looking out at the plane he would have to fly. There was a terrific sense of having arrived somewhere, and at the same time a definite anxiety. Would you get off the ground again – and on course – and then get landed again safely?

The poem I did that morning came from a sort of professional drive, an order I gave myself on the lines of, 'OK, you're now a published poet and you should have a discipline, sit down at that desk and get on with the job in a more organized way.' The poem was one called 'The Salmon Fisher to the Salmon' and it appeared in due course in the second book. But I always had mixed feelings about it. It started where I always like to start, in the ground of memory and sensation, but I had a hunch that during the actual writing the impulse had got tied up rather than set free. There wasn't enough self-forgetfulness.

So, yes, there was definitely a new self-consciousness, at which point I realized that the one simple requirement – definition even – of lyric writing is self-forgetfulness. And luckily I was able to attain it when I hit on the first line of 'The Forge', 'All I know is a door into the dark', or when I got stuck into the matter and movement in 'Requiem for the Croppies'. I did those ones relatively soon after the publication of the first book and felt on course.

How high was your success rate at that time? Were you discarding many poems, or did most of what you wrote prove publishable?

A few of the poems that were published in magazines – and which I still like – didn't appear in *Door into the Dark*. The spring and early summer of 1966 had a strange freedom about them. Marie was pregnant and off school, so she came with me sometimes on long journeys through the country, when I was visiting students on teaching practice – away down on the shores of Lough Erne, for example, in County Fermanagh, or up in the Sperrins, in Glenelly. A poem I wrote about one of those trips eventually found a home in *Seeing Things* as the first section of a sequence called 'A Retrospect', and there's another pregnancy poem called 'Aubade' that I credit, although it isn't in any of the trade editions. I can't really remember what the general success rate was. I tend not to go on with a poem unless there's a fair chance of making something of it. But, even so, there were a good few discards.

Did you hold any poems over to get you started on a second book or did you begin again from scratch?

No poems were held over. As I mentioned earlier, the last poem to be added to *Death of a Naturalist* was 'The Diviner', in the summer of 1965. From then on, it was start-again time.

One difference between your first two collections, to which you yourself have drawn attention, is a deliberate shift from 'I' to 'we' in the poems. What prompted you to make this shift and in what sense – from what vantage point – do you feel you became a 'we' poet?

I suppose I could say, by writing wee poems . . . But no, this brings us back to the question of justifying the art. And to the question of the autobiographical and its status in poems.

But isn't it perfectly valid to retain an 'I' perspective and become in the process a truly representative poet? Might you have been developing a sense of poetry as a public art?

If you put it like that, I suppose I have to agree. When I made the remark about changing from 'I', I was thinking of poems like 'Requiem for the Croppies' and 'Bogland', and obviously the vantage point from which they were written was that of a Northern Irish Catholic with a nationalist background. Not many poets had come to the fore in that particular group: John Montague had published *Poisoned Lands* and *A Chosen Light* and that was about it. From the beginning, I was conscious of a need to voice something that hadn't got voiced, to tune the medium in order to do that particular job. It comes up as an explicit problem in the 'Singing School' part of *North*, in a sequence addressed to another literary-scholarship boy – Seamus Deane. 'Have our accents changed?' 'Ulster was British / But with no rights on the English lyric'.

What was needing to get expressed wasn't so much the political complaint of a minority being discriminated against – political protest and dissent had been there from the start in Northern Ireland. What I was after, even if I wasn't as clear about it at the time, was a way of making the central tradition of English poetry, which we'd absorbed in college and university, absorb our own particular eccentric experience. But I'm making heavy weather of the whole thing. Put it more simply: there was an element of transgression in celebrating the Croppies in official Ulster in 1966. And there was an implied alternative to the British connection in making the Bog of Allen the mythic centre. Yet I also have to say this: what pleased me most about 'Bogland' wasn't its theme or its first-person plural, but the fact that it had been given, had come freely, had arrived out of old layers of lore and language and felt completely trustworthy as a poem. It may have said 'we' but it was still all me.

It seems prescient that you placed 'Bogland' at the end of Door into the Dark *because the poem points forward to so many others where you use bog as a metaphor.*

From the moment I wrote it, I felt promise in 'Bogland'. Without having any clear notion of where it would lead or even whether I would go back to the subject, I realized that new co-ordinates had been established. Door jambs with an open sky behind them rather than the dark. I felt it in my muscles, nearly, when I was writing the poem.

An out-of-the-ordinary moment?

If ever there was, yes. Perfect self-forgetfulness, then coming to something different. The kind of thing you wish could happen all the time. It seemed the right poem to close with since it didn't seem to stop after the last line.

You mentioned elsewhere, if I remember correctly, that the poem came to you when you were dressing and about to go out for the evening.

All true. We were actually in London, in my sister-in-law's flat, and I was putting my right leg into the trousers when I got the first line. I've often speculated, only half in jest, about the relationship between the unimpeded passage of the leg into the open-ended trouser and the free progress of the poem to the 'bottomless' conclusion. It felt like its own yield. I revised a few words here and there but it had come as a matter of waft rather than word-choice. In the words of Kavanagh, 'some strange thing had happened'.

I'd like to move from the closing poem of Door into the Dark *to the title poem. Was the forge a real one or is it a composite picture of a place and a man?*

Somehow, any one forge is all the forges. But yes, I was thinking of Barney Devlin's forge at Hillhead, on the roadside, where you had the noise of myth in the anvil and the noise of the 1940s in the passing cars. As ordinary or archetypal as you cared to make it. Barney's in his late eighties now, but still capable of striking the epic out of the usual. For example, at midnight on the last day of 1999, he hit the anvil twelve times to ring in the millennium – and relayed the tune to his son in Edmonton by cellular phone. He's still going strong; the last time I was with him, he showed me two different anvils and played them for their two different musics: a sweet and carrying note from the one that had belonged to his grandfather – which is the one I would have heard a mile away when I was a youngster – and an abrupt unmelodious dint from a later industrial ingot, definitely not the one that rang in the year 2000.

Is it true you once acted as a blacksmith in a play?

Yes, that is true. It was performed in Bellaghy, probably 1959 or 1960, a melodrama based on a novel called *The Hearts of Down*, about Betsy Gray. Betsy Gray figures in the lore of the 1798 Rebellion in County Down as a kind of local Joan of Arc. There's this ballad where she appears in the last verse as the sister of the rebel leader, Harry Munro: 'Then up came Munro's sister, she was all dressed in green, / With a sword by her side that was well-sharped and keen. / She gave three ringing cheers and away she did go / Crying "I'll be revenged for my brother Munro" '. David Hammond used to sing it. In the play, I forged pikes for the United Irish insurgents on an anvil that Barney Devlin had supplied. Barney, in fact, had a part in that play too, although not, oddly enough, as a blacksmith. But he lent the anvil and rehearsed me in the gentle art of making it sing.

It has been suggested that E. Estyn Evans's Irish Folk Ways *influenced your early poetry. Would poems such as 'The Forge' and 'The Thatcher', say, have derived from reading his work?*

Not at all. Evans's work was nice to know, but those poems and others with similar concerns – the cornfield scene in 'The Wife's Tale', or the eel-fishing in 'A Lough Neagh Sequence' – they all came out of first-hand experience. Then, when I met Marie, I got to know about eels and eel fishing and even went out on the lough with the fishermen. One thing that did amplify my personal experience was a lecture on mumming by Alan Gailey of the Ulster Folk Museum. I'd actually encountered mumming in a vestigial form when I was a youngster. 'Christmas rhymers', we called them. 'Room, room, my gallant boys, and give us room to rhyme'. And my father had the rhyme for 'Doctor Brown' by heart and loved to repeat it. ' "Here comes I, old Doctor Brown, / The best old doctor in the town." / "And what can you cure, doctor?" / "The rout, the gout, the rainbow and the scurvy. / There was an old woman of fourscore and ten. / The knucklebone of her backside came out and I put it in again / With four turkey-hens' eggs four yards long, / A cat's blether and a guinea hen's feather / All stuck on in a plaster" '. Anyhow, it was a great thrill for me when Alan linked the carry-on of Doctor Brown and his health-giving powers to Indo-European fertility rites.

When you were growing up, did Lough Neagh hold any fascination for you?

Very much. It was right in the centre of a big map of Northern Ireland that hung at the front of the master's room in Anahorish School. And on the shelf of that room there was a piece of petrified wood, or at least wood that had gone through some process that rendered it silicate. It was a more or less scientific exhibit yet it seemed to confirm the more or less magical claim that you'd often hear about Lough Neagh, that it could turn wood to stone. In fact, there's a poem – 'Relic of Memory' – about that piece of wood in *Door into the Dark*. And we all knew the old legend about how the Irish giant, hunting the Scottish giant off the land, ripped up a sod that fell and became the Isle of Man, and how the sod had left a hole that became Lough Neagh. When I started to visit Ardboe in the sixties, I got introduced to the whole eel business and couldn't help being fascinated by the life cycle, the mysterious drift of elvers from the Sargasso and the programmed drive of the mature eel back to the original spawning grounds.

You mentioned a little earlier that you went out on Lough Neagh with the fishermen.

The first thing I ever caught was an eel. Nothing very big, but nevertheless there it was, alive alive-o, at the end of the line. I must have been eleven or twelve, fishing with a worm and a line on a bamboo rod, on a sand bed along the Moyola. Unforgettable, but not really 'eel fishing'. It was when I began to meet the fishermen in Devlin's public house, up in Ardboe, that I got to know about the actuality of the work. The digging of worms, the baiting of hundreds of yards of line, the early rising to lift the lines, the drag and drama of it all. I went out with two men one morning, Louis O'Neill and Pat Hagan, and the experience was so pristine I could hardly not have written about it. Louis O'Neill, alas, would eventually be killed in an explosion in another pub, on the night of the funerals after Bloody Sunday, and it was only then that I wrote about the actual dawn journey he took me on. The shine of morning light on the lough had an otherworldly quality, it reminded me of the dawn scene in *Hamlet*, when the ghost fades on the crowing of the cock – so in 'Casualty' Louis then turns into a 'dawn-sniffing revenant'.

I will 'question you again', as the poem says, about 'Casualty'; for the moment, I'm wondering about Ted Hughes's suggestion that you should work in the eel business. Was he serious?

He was serious enough, let's say. And there was just enough connection to Ardboe and the fish trade to make it an attractive fantasy. Marie's grandfather had been an eel shipper, buying from the local boats and selling to Billingsgate. And her father had kept it up for a while. The timing of this has to be kept in mind too – early seventies, just after we came back from Berkeley, in the academic year 1971/2. We were footloose: thinking of moving out of Belfast; looking at old places in County Tyrone; going up and down to County Kilkenny, to see Barrie Cooke and Sonja Landweer who kept encouraging us to get a house near them. Barrie Cooke and Ted had been friends for years, fishing buddies, hedgeback and riverbank boys, naturally gifted at making casts and planting lures. Then too there was an old barn behind the Devlin house at Ardboe that we considered renovating. So Ted's suggestion was just another part of that whole mix and moil of uncertainty and promise. When Glanmore Cottage hove into view, things very quickly found a more definite direction.

Fish – trout, tench, salmon, eels – and things connected with fishing – spoonbaits, 'slung gaff and net', 'flies well-dressed with tint and fleck' – and fishermen-artists such as Barrie Cooke, Seán Ó Riada, Norman MacCaig and Ted Hughes – are found in your poems. Are you a devoted fisherman yourself?

No. It may sound odd, given my attraction to it and the regularity of those references, but since my teens I've been on a riverbank hardly more than a dozen times. When I was ten, eleven, twelve, I had a wild longing to own a proper fishing rod, but it never transpired. I could still sorrow a bit about that. There was a real repining in me, having to make do with bamboo sticks and the simplest kind of reel and rod eyes and line and hooks with gut. Two or three wee trout were the height of it. But the depth of it was inestimable. The nibble on the worm, the tugs, the arc and strum of the line in the water, the moods of the water and the moods of the weather. I loved being on the riverbank. Part of the reason I didn't keep it up was our move from Mossbawn to The Wood.

Mossbawn was only half a mile from the Moyola and we had fields there that ran right to the bank. I was at home on the water in all kinds of ways.

Then, what with boarding school and the slightly more land-locked life of the new place, the opportunities dwindled and the habit slipped. I made an effort to get started in again and did eventually buy my own rod on a terrible day: I was down in High Street in Belfast, buying fishing tackle, on Bloody Friday in 1972. And on and off for a year or so, at that time when a move was in the air, I'd have a go in my old Moyola haunts or go out with Barrie Cooke on one of our weekends in Thomastown, where the mighty Nore was heaping past the back of his house. The trouble then was that I wanted to fish with a fly and just never stayed at it long enough to learn to cast, so that effort fizzled out too. But inside my sixty-eight-year-old arm there's a totally enlivened twelve-year-old one, feeling the bite. And that's enough for a lifetime of poems. That, and the memory of being out with Barrie on the Nore and once with Ted in Devon. Fleetness of water, stillness of air, stealthiness of action. Spots of time.

As a celebratory, affirmative poet in many respects, why did you choose to place an emphasis on death and darkness in the respective titles of your first two collections?

Death and darkness are there, I have to admit, in the titles, but I still want to object when you suggest I chose to emphasize them as negative factors . . . And why's that? Probably because I thought of 'the dark' in the second title as a conventionally positive element, related to what Eliot called 'the dark embryo' in which poetry originates. The phrase 'door into the dark' comes from the first line of a poem about a blacksmith, a shape maker, standing in the door of a forge; and, as a title, it picks up on the last line of *Death of a Naturalist,* where the neophyte sees a continuity between the effect he wants to achieve in his writing and the noise he made when he used to shout down a well shaft 'to set the darkness echoing'. There's also the usual old archetype of the dark as something you need to traverse in order to arrive at some kind of reliable light or sight of reality. The dark night of the soul. The dark wood. Even D. H. Lawrence's dark sexual gods. In those days Lawrence was something of a power in my imaginative land.

And the actual dark you knew as a child of the pre-electric age? I remember a Listener *article in which you remarked that the barn was a place where 'I was always afraid in its dark heart that something was going to jump out of its corners . . .'*

True enough. When I hear 'dark night', it's not just an echo of John of the Cross – it's the stars above south Derry, or the no stars and lash of wind in the beech trees along our lane. I did have my night fears as a youngster, on the road and even in the bedroom. The first poem in *Door into the Dark* is about hearing the horse in the stable, on the other side of the bedroom wall. The home horse turned night mare. But I imagine every child has experiences of this sort, they're part of the growing process of the species.

With a child of your own, as well as college work, essay-marking, travelling and earning a living generally, there was a lot more than poetry going on in your life in the late sixties. How did you contend with the different demands? Did you pine for a more bohemian existence?

I was never quite sure what I'd end up doing; so when the poetry suddenly arrived, just as I was starting out as a teacher, it was a redemptive grace but by no means an alternative way of life. At that stage, I never even considered the possibility that I could give up the day job. We were young marrieds, young teachers, starting out with lots of other young marrieds and young teachers. Round about this time, for example, we attended the Longleys' wedding and the Kennellys'. We all might have had a certain bohemian rascality in us but the weddings were formal affairs, clergymen and wedding dresses and carnations. And then came the mortgage and the kids. Come to think of it, it wasn't so long since Ted and Sylvia had gone through the same process in England . . .

Did you ever write the way Sylvia Plath did – getting up to attend to babies and then drafting poems in the early hours?

I'll never forget the first night Marie came home from hospital with Michael. We hardly slept at all. Listening for his breathing. Wondering what to do about any crying – whether to feed him or not, whether he needed to be changed. All kinds of protections seemed to have been peeled away, competence had deserted you.

But you gradually got used to it. We both tended to be awake for those feeds, waiting for water to heat in the bottle warmer, wondering if it was overheating, sterilizing the bottle, changing the nappies, dumping the dirties. I didn't actually write in those small hours, no; the waking-up did of course make us both a bit bleary eyed, but we were young and fit for it. If poetry can be written in the trenches, dammit, it can surely be managed between the day job and the night feed.

How much in earnest were you when you told an interviewer that you 'had terrific interest in [your] youngsters when they were in the womb'?

Was he perhaps asking me why there weren't more poems about the children once they came out? You know, that notebook I mentioned earlier, I was using it during Marie's first pregnancy and it's full of things where pregnancy is the theme or the preoccupation. Ones that were published, like 'Aubade' and 'Cana Revisited' and 'Elegy for a Stillborn Child' (lost by another couple who got married at the same time as us), other ones that weren't worth publishing. There was something beautifully generative about living with the new life between us. But when the child is born, the child is more than enough. Poetry's just not up to it.

When you published New Selected Poems, 1966–1987 *in 1990, you gave virtually equal space to work from* Death of a Naturalist *and* Door into the Dark. *Yet just eight years later, in* Opened Ground, *you allocated a good deal more space to* Door into the Dark *poems. Have you come to prefer the second collection to the first?*

There's no question of a preference. *Death of a Naturalist* is always going to have pride of place because a first book is a far more transformative event. You've been touched by the publication wand, you're on the *gradus ad Parnassum*, you've graduated, so the second book just can't be as magical. You're also that bit more self-aware, more alert to the facts of reception. I suppose some writers are on a steeper learning curve than others at that second-book stage. Obviously Robert Frost had enough poems on hand to plot a course from *A Boy's Will* to *North of Boston*. That certainly was a 'development' but it was very different from Sylvia Plath going from *The Colossus* to *Ariel,* from apprentice to oracle, in one unforeseen move – the poetic equivalent of breaking the sound barrier. I mean to say, I don't see all that much 'development' in *Door into the Dark*; it's more a matter of trying out and spreading out, trying out a sequence like 'A Lough Neagh Sequence', spreading out from Toner's Bog in Bellaghy parish to 'Bogland' in general. When I came to do the selection for *Opened Ground*, I believe I had a clearer sense of what was happening in the second book.

Neil Corcoran's critical book quotes a review in which Norman Nicholson suggests that the poet of Door into the Dark *is 'biding his time before the bigger gesture'. Was there a residual Incertus at work in the collection?*

There's a residual Incertus at work in every poem I write. Probably he's the one who keeps me going. But yes, there had to be a sense of biding time and taking stock during the writing of those *Door into the Dark* poems. I was blinking awake in a new situation.

How did your family in Derry – 'sceptical and exacting', as you once called them – take the fact that you were becoming serious about poetry? Was there any sense that you were getting above yourself and maybe above them?

No sense of that, but a strong sense of both the unlikeliness of the thing and the privilege of it, all handled in a way that was indeed 'sceptical and exacting'. It's probably fair to say that, from the morning I left our front street for St Columb's College in 1951, there was some understanding in the family that I was off to a different place. I'd guess that in their minds the poetry turn was consistent with a swerve that had begun far earlier. Think of it this way: when I was eleven, Master Murphy suggested to my parents that I come in to school early for tuition in Latin and algebra; when I was eighteen, I won a State Exhibition; when I was twenty-four, I ended up as a lecturer in a teacher-training college; so why wouldn't I publish a book of poems when I was twenty-seven? I don't want to make light of your question, but equally it would be wrong to go on about it too heavily.

Was there not concern that your poetry might tread on private family territory?

Probably there was, yes. But concerns of that nature wouldn't necessarily have been voiced explicitly. The method for dealing with them was already factored into the overall house style. Reticence and ribbing in equal measure, more reticence from the parents, more ribbing from local friends and neighbours. 'My father worked with a horse plough': a line like that would always come in for comment. 'Not a hell of a lot' was the sort of response you'd be likely to hear. On the other hand, I remember being worried about my father reading 'Follower', what he'd make of it, what I'd made of him. To this day, I don't know how all that went, whether he even read it. Years later he would hear it at poetry readings, but by then it had become more or less processed into a familiar tune. Things were more atremble in the beginning, when personal matters were being bared for the first time. It felt odder for everybody.

Is your father still alive and well in that part of you that is 'entirely unimpressed' by literary activity? You once said that your 'rural ancestors' had something to do with this: 'they, in me, or I through them, don't give a damn'. How would you distinguish that attitude from Philip Larkin's 'books are a load of crap' dismissal?

Larkin's remark was made in a poem, so to that extent it stands in quotation marks. And its coarseness makes it suspect. But it comes from the same impulse to blot the copybook, join the hecklers, stand up for bastards.

Does your innate scepticism intensify doubts about presuming to pursue a life in poetry?

You could say that every poem I write – or that anybody else writes, for that matter – is a way of overcoming those doubts. Anybody serious about poetry knows how hard it is to achieve anything worthwhile in it. I used to think that, if you came from a background like mine, your approach to the muse was shyer than if you came from a more bookish or artistic family, but now I'm not so sure. Yeats had an artist daddy, Eliot had a poetry-writing mammy, and that was a great help to them. But what about Elizabeth Bishop or Plath? Or Kavanagh? Or Pessoa? You could argue that scepticism about literature is what actually inspired Pessoa.

You have acknowledged that Kavanagh helped you to get going, as did Ted Hughes. Were you consciously reacting against British urban poets? Do you remember what Anthony Thwaite wrote in his review of Door into the Dark *– 'Turbines and pylons for the 1930s: bulls for the 1960s. It's an odd progression'?*

I do remember. But, at the time, I found myself pretty immune to that kind of jibe. In July 1969, soon after the book came out, Marie and I went with the kids for a long stay in the Bas Pyrénées district of France. This was thanks to the Somerset Maugham Award. We set off in a Volkswagen Beetle and took our time, driving from Le Havre right down to a village thirty miles inland from Bayonne. Making stops and digressions all over the place – to Blois, for example, where Wordsworth had met Annette Vallon. To rue Daguerre in Paris, on the way back, to see John Montague.

What struck me everywhere on that journey was the massive summer reality of the crops of the earth, the plains of wheat round Chartres, the high-ranking maize fields where we lived beside the *gaves* of the Béarn, the produce markets in every little town. There was an old sensational truth in those things. I got terrific strength throughout that summer from the sheer familiarity of the farmyard in Sorde l'Abbaye, the snarl of M. Puy's tractor at five in the morning, the spray of the irrigation pumps in the maize fields at all hours of the day, the cattle in the sheds . . . I was writing every day in an old barn in the *gîte* and felt guaranteed in my work. The pylons seemed more dated than the bull.

How did you regard the pop poetry of the sixties? The Beatles, Leonard Cohen, Bob Dylan – did you find any sort of poetry there?

Not really. It was more like background music or fairground music – I enjoyed the sound of it going on around me, but didn't regard it as having anything to do with the word-work. Poems that engaged me had a different kind of fetch and conviction about them; I underwent a strangeness when I wrote or read a good one. Whatever the Beats and the Liverpool Poets were doing, it didn't put me through the eye of my own needle the way 'The Bull Moses' or 'The Windhover' did. I had a feeling of being dispersed rather than concentrated. I still wanted pressure and density, wasn't susceptible to freewheeling rhythm and full-frontal statement. It's not that I didn't feel the salubriousness of Adrian Henri or the Orphic thing in Dylan. It's just that they belonged in a different mind-field or language-body.

Did you squirrel away many of their recordings?

I'm afraid not.

And what about Yevtushenko and Voznesensky? Did you pay any attention to them?

To Voznesensky, yes. *Antiworlds*, a book of translations of his poems, was published in the sixties and I thought it was marvellous. It gave me a real jolt; but it was so 'open', so clamorous, it couldn't and didn't affect my writing.

Michael Longley tried to interest you in jazz.

He did, and we used to go to live sessions now and again in Belfast pubs, with the painter Colin Middleton and his wife Kitty. And Solly Lipsitz, jazzman and record-shop owner. But I've very little to show for it. A Fats Waller LP. 'The shook the shake the sheikh of Araby', as Michael called him.

Michael Longley's first book, No Continuing City, *appeared in the same year as* Door into the Dark; *Derek Mahon's maiden voyage,* Night-Crossing, *had been launched the previous year. Did these publications increase your sense of Ulster camaraderie or did the fact that their preoccupations and styles were so different from yours confirm the need for all of you to proceed in your own individual directions?*

I wouldn't say the camaraderie was increased – or decreased. I would say rather that Michael and Derek felt themselves on a more even keel once they'd got their books out. Given their prior friendship and poetry life at Trinity, they thought the natural order of things had been reversed when my book was published before theirs. There may even have been a bit of lese-majesty involved, as far as they were concerned. Anyway, by 1969 the first fine careless rapture was over. When I came back from France that August, the British army was on the streets. And I think Derek had moved to Dublin. The probation period was over.

You had begun teaching in Queen's University in 1966. How did that appointment come about?

For some years, Queen's had had a poet in the English Department. Laurence Lerner had been there when I was a student in the late fifties, and Philip Hobsbaum succeeded him. Then Hobsbaum got a job in Glasgow and a space opened up at a time when a whole combination of factors were working in my favour. First of all, my book had been accepted by Faber; in those days, that almost constituted an official seal of approval. It signalled the approbation of 'the mainland'. Then too I was well known to Philip Hobsbaum and other members of the English Department, some of whom had even taught me. And, at The Group, I had met Professor John Harvey, the head of the department, and Professor Arthur Terry of the Spanish Department, which meant that in the senior common room I was a known quantity, even if I had no secondary degree. As well as that, it was the sixties, even in Belfast, and a new liberalism was stirring. But the main man in the whole business had to be John Harvey. W. J. Harvey, who had just arrived as a young professor and scholar-critic and who alas died just as suddenly, during my second year in Queen's. He told me, incidentally, that I needn't bother doing a thesis, that instead I should write essays, and in that way he set the pattern for whatever critical work I would eventually do. I still occasionally call to John's grave, in the churchyard at Drumbo.

What courses did you teach at Queen's?

I gave the First Arts poetry lectures, and taught Modern Literature seminars to the honours students in different years. Plus tutorials, sometimes to a couple of honours people, sometimes to larger groups of first years and general degree people. The great thing about the job was that it felt like a continuation of the extramural life I'd been discovering from the moment I got connected up with The Group. I'd begun to see Edna and Michael Longley, for example, in their flat and to be a late-night talker and drinker there – and at the same time Edna was a colleague in the English Department. And the poets we talked about in the late-night sessions were the ones on the different courses we were teaching – Edward Thomas, Thomas Hardy, W. B. Yeats, Wilfred Owen, Robert Frost, Louis

MacNeice. In other words, the foragings of the young poet paid into the duties of the young lecturer and vice versa.

As a Catholic member of the teaching staff in Queen's, did you feel discriminated against in any way?

No, not at all. Many of my colleagues were English anyhow, and had a kind of washed-hand attitude to local matters. At common-room level, the British Ulster element went on being themselves and I went on being myself and we all knew the rules of engagement or disengagement that were in play. I mean, there was something extremely bird-mouthed at the best of times in middle-class 'mixed company' in Northern Ireland, the Catholic/Protestant thing was more or less taboo except for jokes and banter; in Queen's, you had the added factor of a provincial British academic style that was halfway between briskness and prissiness. You narrowed and tightened yourself a bit in the Queen's common room. I didn't realize just how much this was the case until I came back from my year in Berkeley: a great university, with an altogether freer, opener style. Tom Flanagan, who had been a wonderful friend and mentor during that California year, came to give a lecture in Queen's in 1972. I took him to the common room for tea when the whole gang were assembled, around four in the afternoon; when we left, all he said was 'Jeez, Seamus! The sooner you get out of here the better.'

And you did get out at the end of that year.

Well, yes. A shift was in the offing and Tom knew that. I don't think we'd yet settled on Glanmore, but I was certainly thinking of making a move.

How comfortable did you feel about standing and delivering at the university lectern?

At St Joseph's College I'd had three years training in standing up and giving out, so when it came to engagement with the students, I was happy enough – as long as I was prepared enough. I do recall one panicky moment in 1968, during the Belfast Festival. Seán Ó Riada was 'composer of the year' and there were other free spirits roaming about the place – Garech Browne and John Montague, for example – which meant that there were liquid lunches and distractions of all sorts going on. So, at four o'clock one afternoon, I found myself in a state of high inebriation, having to give a lecture to a hundred or so first-year students. Since the subject was Wilfred Owen, the material was thoroughly familiar and I was able to coast and roll through it well enough.

The thing I should say, however, is that I am *always* nervous before a lecture. Even in my fifties, in Harvard, if I had a lecture, I'd be up early to try to get it squared out in my head – not that I could ever quite manage to do so. Lecturing week after week, as part of the pedagogic routine, is more of a test than people realize. In the end, the most important thing is to be in good physical and mental shape. You can prepare as much as you like and amass material galore, but unless you come in fresh, like an athlete on to the track, you aren't going to do the job required. At the end of a lecture, I tend to be as sweaty as a sprinter at the end of a race.

Ted Hughes suggested to you that the academy is acceptable 'as long as it doesn't change your language'. Was this a worry for you in the early years? Did you take precautions against creeping academicism – specialist jargon or dry allusion – in your writing?

D. H. Lawrence used to go on about 'sex in the head'. I'm tempted to answer by saying that my academic work involved poetry in the head, whereas my writing was actual poetry in the body. The writing of poetry used different muscles, almost physically. The words were dredged from different sources, through different systems. And to be truthful, I wasn't in any deep or trained sense 'academic'. I never even got as far as doing an MA degree. The way I talked in lectures and tutorials – and in various bits of reviewing and essay writing – was very far from the kind of lingo and professional theory-speak that a young academic has to master nowadays. I was amateur then and still am – although, like most literary people, I've been influenced over a lifetime by the Marxist and deconstructionist idiom that was just there, part of what 'the age demanded'.

Did you see your students 'off campus'?

I did have some students to the house, on and off – honours students, mostly. Larry Lerner and Professor Butter had done that kind of thing for us when we were undergraduates and I was just following their good example.

Some of your students were to become well-known writers:
Medbh McGuckian, Paul Muldoon, Ciaran Carson, Frank
Ormsby. What impression did you have of them? Did you see
their poems?

I *did* see their poems. It was all part of the energy and newness of
the time. The people you mention probably had a sense that some-
thing was coming awake for their generation. There was a general
change in the cultural and educational weather. For a student with
literary hopes, however secluded, there was more access available
and more energy flowing. You had published poets walking round
the university area at a time when 'creative writing' was gaining
new currency in the schools. Michael Longley was teaching at Inst.,
James Simmons was out at Friends' School in Lisburn. I remember
going to Paul Muldoon's college in Armagh and talking to Jerry
Hicks's English class – I'm not sure if Paul was still at St Patrick's
then, but Jerry was one of his teachers and had actually brought
Paul along and introduced us at a poetry reading in 1968 in the
Armagh Museum. So I knew Paul and his work a bit before he
came to Queen's.

I remember seeing poems by Frank Ormsby and Medbh
McGuckian when they were students, but I don't think I saw any
by Ciaran Carson, although Ciaran and Medbh were in a practical
criticism class I ran when I came back from Berkeley during the
1971/2 session. When I look back, the defining moment is a big St
Patrick's Day party I ran in our house in 1972 where they were all
in attendance. It was the last time I saw them together as a group:
that Easter, Marie and I would go to Wicklow and then I'd give
notice of my resignation from Queen's. So I think of that day as
marking a departure for me and my moment of recognition of them
as the next wave, as it were.

When you took over The Group from Philip Hobsbaum, did it
meet in your house at 16 Ashley Avenue? Did any of those
students participate?

I have to confess I don't have a very clear grip on the history of The
Group once it fell to me to run it. Certainly we didn't immediately
meet in Ashley Avenue, simply because I wasn't living in Ashley
Avenue when Philip left. There was a feeling among some people

that The Group had run its course, that it was a Hobsbaum thing and that with him gone, it should stop. At the same time, I felt I had inherited it as a responsibility and it clearly had become a poetry lifeline for others – for somebody like Norman Dugdale, for example, a senior civil servant who attended faithfully, or Joan Watton who'd got married and was now Joan Newmann, living on the outskirts. Unfortunately, when I was convener, the meetings were more sporadic and the locations varied.

Can you recall where you met?

We met a couple of times in a room in the English Department, then in a room in the Club Bar, also in another pub called the Four in Hand on the Lisburn Road. Philip's events had been seminars in essence; when he left, we were aiming for something different – not a salon, not a session in a snug, something somewhere in between. The format and strictness of the old meetings couldn't survive the randomness of the new premises, although there were indeed a couple or three meetings in my house after we moved from Beechill Park. Did Jimmy Simmons attend at that stage? Harry Chambers? I'm not sure. I remember Frank Ormsby and Michael Foley and Paul Muldoon showing up, possibly Ciaran Carson and Medbh McGuckian, but I'm not at all clear about the who and the what of it. The pretence of maintaining it as a living event stopped after I went for a year to Berkeley in the autumn of 1970.

Were you conscious, then or now, of a literary generation gap between you and those student writers?

Necessarily, yes. Apart from anything else, the gap was insisted on cheerily and cheekily by the *Honest Ulsterman* magazine under the editorship of Michael Foley. Michael was something of a protégé of James Simmons, but entirely his own man, smart as a tack. He once referred in print to Longley and Mahon and myself as the 'Tight Assed Trio' – so that was telling us. But if you have been a teacher and the other person has been your student, there's always going to be a demarcation, no matter how genial the relationship. The big difference between them and us, I'd say, is a simple one and it's this: the very fact that they had us present and talking to them. When we were starting out, we didn't have any equivalent elders or exemplars on the ground. John Hewitt did eventually come back to

Belfast, but he wasn't there at the formative stages. And Philip Hobsbaum would have been thought of more as an official pedagogic presence than one of the family.

There have been various accounts of your first meeting with Paul Muldoon. Could you say something about how that led to your publication of his work in Threshold *and eventually to a book from Faber and Faber?*

Jerry Hicks – the teacher I mentioned earlier and one of the three Paul has written about in his poem 'The Fridge' – Jerry brought Paul to this Arts Council recital of poems and songs being given by David Hammond, Michael Longley and myself. '*Rara avis*' was Hicks's verdict, after he had introduced him. Paul – as you would expect – was quiet, like any schoolboy being introduced by a master; but there was nothing schoolboyish in the poems he eventually sent me, written out in this terrific big bold black-ink calligraphic hand. The letter, as I remember it, said 'Perhaps you can tell me where I am going wrong'; I wrote back saying that I didn't think I could tell him anything he wouldn't find out for himself. There was such sureness of voice and distinctness of imagining, you were at home and away with the poems immediately. They belonged completely in the world of Armagh and in the world of the imagined. I considered myself lucky to have encountered them and had a real sense of occasion when I published them. Naturally I commended Paul to Karl Miller at *The Listener* and Charles Monteith at Faber, but there should be no imputation that I 'helped him to get published'. Editors are fighting to be first in the field with a talent like that.

Karl Miller was obviously important to you from the start. But, quite early on, you began to contribute to editors at other journals too – prose as well as poetry. Have you always thought of yourself as a poet-critic?

Not at all. Karl Miller kept urging me to do reviews – not necessarily connected with poetry. This was when he was still at the *New Statesman*. To begin with, I wrote about books on education, titles like *English for the Rejected* by David Holbrook, something called *How Children Fail* by John Holt. Among other things, it was a way of chalking up marks as a member of staff in the institutions where I worked. But I did write on poetry for *Hibernia* and very early on got stuck in like any newcomer, trying to take the established people down a peg or two. One of the first *Hibernia* pieces was a survey of contemporary Irish poetry and the opening sentence caused great bother in Dublin. The article began: 'There are no major poets at work in Ireland' – this being a very deliberate retort to an earlier declaration in James Liddy's magazine *Arena* that 'Clarke and Kavanagh are major poets'. So there was a bit of give and take in the correspondence columns about that.

You must have known you were going to stir things up.

Probably. I was full of T. S. Eliot and his distinctions between major and minor and all that. But I wasn't so much aiming at Clarke and Kavanagh as at a certain windiness in the rhetoric coming out of McDaid's and the Bailey. On my side, mind you, there was a certain English Lit. primness, but you have to start somewhere.

Can you say something about the contributions you made to Karl Miller at the New Statesman *and later at* The Listener?

Well, all along there were the poems. From the moment he first printed those three in 1964, Karl had taken poems regularly. Then I eventually got to know him and to meet his family in their house in Chelsea. He's a wonderful combination of strictness and merriment, intellectually fit as a fiddle, but with this really intuitive feel for poetry. I greatly cherish his friendship; there's a definite Scots edge to his intelligence and attitudes, a touch of outsiderishness. And he's fiercely interested in politics, so with the situation in Northern Ireland the way it was, he was always suggesting that I do more prose and indeed poetry on that subject. I'm very glad, for example, that he pushed me to do an article just after the batoning of the Civil Rights march in Derry on 5 October 1968. I owe a lot to him, not only for his support of the poetry but for his badgering me into all those bits of reviewing and reporting and commentary. From Berkeley, for example, and from Belfast, after I came back in 1971.

When you wrote about the Troubles in The Listener, *your sympathies must have been evident. What reaction was there from colleagues?*

I was saying earlier that the canteen culture of Queen's, if you can call it that, was very British; and the Civil Rights movement was of course appealing to overall British standards. The argument contended that, in Northern Ireland, Stormont presided over a state of affairs that would have been regarded as intolerable elsewhere within the United Kingdom. So, in that way, the early political dissidence was less inflected – or infected – with the Orange and Green-speak than it would be later on. All this activity I'm talking about came before the burnings of houses on the Falls and the shootings and the emergence of the Provos. For a while, there was a convergence of student radicals and fair-play academics. The Professor of Greek, for example, George Huxley – one of that great English Huxley family – attended those early gatherings in the Students' Union. So among the people I was meeting in the normal course of events, people who were mostly kindred spirits, there was no problem. Naturally, there would have been resentment in many a Unionist breast, but they governed their tongues.

Harry Chambers relocated Phoenix *to Belfast in 1967 – and would eventually publish your 'Lough Neagh Sequence' in his pamphlet series. Then James Simmons founded the* Honest Ulsterman *in 1968. How did you regard those local journals?*

Phoenix was more literary than the *Honest Ulsterman* and I tended to give more consideration to what I published there. Harry Chambers could never have used Wilfred Owen's 'Above all I am not interested in Poetry' as an epigraph, but Jimmy might well have. There was a lot of issue-based writing in the *Honest Ulsterman* from the start; but even though it was subtitled 'A Handbook for Revolution', I could never take it too seriously. It had the 'plague on both your houses' line, and by 1969 that old faults-on-both-sides stuff was wearing thin. My nationalist grudge was too strong. Simmons would eventually blame me for not scolding my own side, presumably implying that his castigation of aspects of Northern Ireland Protestant/Unionist culture was the example to be followed. But politically speaking, there was just a hell of a lot more to castigate on the Unionist side. I never felt any real weight in the *Ulsterman* proceedings. There were plenty of fireworks and plenty of wonderful spunky snook-cocking, especially when Michael Foley took over as editor.

How important was the magazine in keeping Ulster poetry from growing too complacent and introverted? Was it not, in certain respects at least, an Ulster equivalent of Ian Hamilton's The Review?

Maybe it had a similar corrective urge. But it suffered from a similar debility – the people who were its stalwarts early on weren't all that strong as poets. If by 'Ulster poetry' you mean Mahon and Longley and co., I can assure you the danger of complacency and introversion was taken care of by those people themselves. Belly laughs and Brecht were hardly unknown in that quarter. Eventually, of course, Muldoon and Carson and Ormsby and Medbh McGuckian would publish there quite a bit, but I don't believe they drew their aesthetic from it. They would never have demystified poetry to the rationalist extent that Simmons did.

What kind of relationship did you have with James Simmons? He never had any inhibition about belittling your work, and wanted you to be more humorous, more of a balladeer.

Personally, Jimmy was a very amicable and winning sort of man. A sweet smile, a note of reasonableness, always just as ready to take up the guitar and sing as to take up the cudgels and argue. We were always friends of sorts rather than sort of enemies. We didn't meet all that much after I moved from Belfast, but I saw a lot of him when he came back to Ireland in the 1960s. His house in Portrush, when he moved there to teach at the University of Ulster, was a definite out-post of bohemia. What bothered me in the end was a disjunction between his snotteriness in print and his pleasant ways when we'd meet, but it all arose from big temperamental and cultural differences. And deep down my irk was eased by the realization that Jimmy was just getting back at me. Without my ever having to tell him, he knew I didn't rate his poetry very highly. For all its discontents, it was extremely pleased with itself; it versified its positions and Jimmy's dispositions but it was all a bit trim. If he belittled, I disdained. Ever since I read Ezra Pound's injunction to pay no attention to the opinions of those who have not themselves 'produced notable work', I've had my own Star Wars defence system against certain attacks.

Does your lifelong habit of writing light verse pieces for the amusement of your friends, or to mark university commencements and so on, owe anything to the Honest Ulsterman *tradition?*

Not really. If there's any tradition involved, it's the common song-making, rural-bard tradition that I grew up with. Strong metres, strong rhymes, strong sentiments. 'Come all ye loyal Protestants and in full chorus join, / Think on the deeds of William and his conquest at the Boyne . . .' 'Come all you young rebels, come list while I sing' – that was where my first 'protest' song came from. And I was responding to a Gaeltacht-based Munsterman rather than an honest Ulsterman. Seán Ó Riada wrote to me after 5 October 1968 and asked if I couldn't do something, so I knocked out a few stanzas that were an ironical take on the Orange song 'Dolly's Brae' and the Percy French song, 'Clare's Dragoons'. William Craig was Minister of Home Affairs in Stormont at that time when the RUC cut loose in Derry, so I called it 'Craig's Dragoons', and meant it to be sung to the air of 'Dolly's Brae':

Come all ye loyal Protestants and in full chorus join,
Think on the deeds of Craig's Dragoons who strike below the
    groin . . .

That's how it started; then the last verse went:

O William Craig, you are our love, our lily and our sash,
You have the boys who fear no noise, who'll batter and who'll
    bash,
They'll cordon and they'll baton-charge, they'll silence protest
    tunes,
They are the hounds of Ulster, boys, sweet William Craig's
    dragoons.

Head-on stuff. I believe it was sung at the time on a Radio Éireann programme that Ó Riada and his musicians used to present, but it wasn't printed until Karl Miller cited it in *The Review*, of all places, in an essay on public poetry. I enjoyed the swagger of it, but always felt it was too coarse, linguistically and politically. On the other hand, I still like a set of Ulsterman-type verses that I contributed to the magazine in 1971, as an open letter to Michael Foley. There were rhymes like 'arts' and 'farts', 'action' and 'erection', and generally it did its best to learn the art of sinking to the approved level. I'd make the old Graham Greeney distinction, I suppose, between poems and entertainments.

To what extent then would you agree with Patrick Kavanagh's emphasis on the importance of the comic element in poetry or his assertion that 'Tragedy is underdeveloped Comedy'?

Every theory is said to be an autobiography of sorts, is it not? I think Kavanagh's notion of the comic was something broader, something closer to the French *comédie humaine* than to any notion that a poet's sense of humour be present in the verse. In that way I suppose there's as much, if not more, real comedy in Eliot's 'The Waste Land' as in his *Practical Cats*. On the other hand, if you look at Joyce's poems – a special case, I admit – there's a hell of a lot more poetry when the old ruthless humour is being let loose in 'Gas from a Burner' than when he's going all trembly about, say, Rahoon. It's a nice question, this. Would you guess from Dylan Thomas's *Deaths and Entrances* that he had an *Under Milk Wood* in him? Could you be sure from R. S. Thomas's work that he wasn't a bundle of laughs when you got to know him?

When you spoke at R. S. Thomas's memorial service in 2001, you said, 'There was something retained about the writing, as if the poet bore a grudge against his own lyric gift – and I liked that a lot.'

When I read him first, I enjoyed the self-conscious element in the writing – very artful versification, a slight affectation of diction, a touch of Crowe Ransom fastidiousness. But what made him especially attractive was the fact that a potential dandy was being suppressed by a very strict, very frugal censor. And then there was the sheer familiarity of his subject matter in those Welsh hill-farm poems. The one about doing a sick call, you know, the kettle boiling when he comes downstairs after attending to a farmer called Evans – it could have been about a curate in the Sperrins.

I read him first in Alvarez's *The New Poetry* and then got my hands on *Song at the Year's Turning*, and eventually wrote a short essay about him. Wrote poems influenced by him too – a few with a character called MacKenna as their subject. MacKenna, as I mentioned earlier, was my stand-in for Iago Prytherch. I got the early books as they appeared – *Poetry for Supper, Pietà, Not that He Brought Flowers* – but then, as Larkin said about his Yeats phase, the fever abated. When I came back to him, it was in the 1980s, and I was lecturing on contemporary British poetry at Harvard. What I loved then were those later poems about language, about God withdrawn and consciousness like a tilted satellite dish – full of potential to broadcast and receive, but still not quite operating. He got very far as a poet, a loner taking on the universe, a kind of Clint Eastwood of the spirit. Every bit as unsmiling as Clint, but in either case you couldn't be sure there wasn't a truly wild comedian lurking in there somewhere.

Another poet who was important for you in the late sixties was the Louis Simpson of books like At the End of the Open Road.

Simpson had a quality of openness; he was able to give the high cultural and the colloquial equal credence, able to get at life and still keep up a literary play. Able to do that maybe because he had been in combat during the Second World War, or because he was Jamaican – somebody who had internalized a traditional British-type curriculum and then broke free of it as if it had been a chrysalis. I was also interested in the way the closed form/open form debate played itself out in his work. In fact, the drifty, soft-edgy aspect of those quatrain poems at the end of *Door into the Dark* probably owes something to Louis Simpson. Nothing as direct as imitation, more a tuning, an inclination to make the line a feeler-out rather than a foot-by-foot advance. I felt even closer to Louis after I went to Berkeley. He'd taught there and been a friend of Tom Flanagan's; through Tom I eventually got to know him personally. When Tom went back east to teach in Stony Brook, they were colleagues again and I used to meet up with them in the late seventies and early eighties on Long Island. Karl Miller published a lot of Simpson's poems also.

Louis Simpson figures in one of your own poems.

In 'Making Strange', yes. It started from a chance meeting between my father, myself and Louis. He was being driven by me from Belfast to a poetry reading in the University of Ulster at Coleraine, so I took a detour through my part of the country and stopped at the pub next to our old Mossbawn house. Next thing, my father appears on the scene, and is being included as more or less part of the tour. So there I was between the pair of them, at home and not at home, between the Toome Road and the open road. It wasn't unlike those little poems Louis Simpson himself was writing in the 1960s, 'In the Suburbs', say, or 'After Midnight', where his own local American scene would also get itself defamiliarized.

You have anthologized Simpson's 'Carentan O Carentan' poem a couple of times. Is it a particular favourite?

All of his Second World War poems are good. 'Carentan' happened to be one that Ted Hughes also liked very much, so it ended up in both *The Rattle Bag* and *The School Bag*. It's a poem that tells and tolls all at once. It has soldiers going into battle in Normandy; but it also has this remote sweet melody and dreaminess, a bit like a Housman hymning his redcoats, except that Simpson's matter is far more deadly. It's not fifes but a fusillade that his soldiers march to.

When you were beginning to read Simpson, there were also the beginnings of a kind of internationalism in poetry. The Poetry International festival in London, the magazine Modern Poetry in Translation, *the Penguin Modern European Poets series and so on all date approximately from that time. But it wasn't until the mid-eighties that your readers became aware of your interest in poetry in translation. Had you been attending to those Russian and eastern-European voices before the eighties, before you wrote the essays collected in* The Government of the Tongue?

One of the bright spots on the wall of our little back kitchen in Ashley Avenue was a flier for a Poetry International festival where Miroslav Holub appeared. It had this brilliant chevron pattern of scarlets and lime greens and whites and azures, a very zippy design, and it carried the names of Holub and others in colour also. I had a definite interest in those people as the translations continued to appear from Penguin. Holub's 'The Fly' and Herbert's 'Elegy of Fortinbras' were as familiar as anything in Hughes or Larkin. I'd read the Penguin *Post-War Polish Poetry* anthology before I went to Berkeley in 1970 and, even though I didn't encounter Miłosz then, I did see a good bit of Peter Dale Scott who had been his co-editor, and Leonard Nathan, who would work as the co-translator of some of Miłosz's poems. I was totally alive to the Miłosz anthology material as a reader, but, you know, it takes a while for new work to enter you deeply enough so that you can talk and be convincing to yourself about it. That historically aware, hard-bitten eastern-European aesthetic meant more to me in the 1980s, as a precaution against the ahistorical, hedonistic aesthetic that I was encountering in America.

When did you actually meet Miroslav Holub?

I didn't meet Miroslav until I was in Harvard. Stratis Haviaris, who was in charge of the Poetry Room in the Lamont Library, introduced us and took us to lunch.

I thought your paths might have crossed at one of the early Poetry International festivals.

I wasn't present at any of those early Poetry Internationals, even though some memories of them have stayed with me to this day. A photo of Neruda in his cloth cap. Kavanagh, when I met him in the summer of 1967, telling me that he'd been over to London and had met Ted Hughes, 'a beautiful big tall fellow'. Then, come the early seventies, I did read at one, on a programme, as it happened, with Ted Hughes, and was actually introduced to Auden in the foyer of the hall. I'm not sure if that was the occasion when I heard Auden read, or rather recite from memory, his sad, terrific late poem, 'Lullaby'. Anyhow, it was a brief, even peremptory, encounter. He was jawing away to Charles Monteith and Eric White, and Charles called me over. 'Seamus! Seamus!' he cries, 'Have you met Wystan?' 'No.' 'Wystan, Seamus Heaney.' 'How d'you do, how d'you do?' And back they go to their chat. But I had the true Joycean epiphany at that moment, just as I left them. The fleeting, floating set of words that are everything and nothing. What I hear is this exchange between Auden and Monteith: 'What age are you, Charles?' 'Fifty-five.' 'Oh, [*chuckle, chuckle*], you're a chicken, you're a chicken, you're a chicken!'

If I may shatter the epiphany and return you Ulsterward for my final questions in this section . . . We mentioned Ashley Avenue earlier. How important was your house there to you as a 'place of writing'? Did you have your own working space, for example?

We moved to Ashley Avenue just before Christopher was born, so we were there for four years and more. It was a comfortable enough, big enough house, on the edge of a better-class area just across the Lisburn Road. We had older residents as neighbours, but there were artists and bohemian sorts mixed in with them. The sculptor Carolyn Mulholland had a flat about a hundred yards away. Andy Crockhart, a very congenial and not entirely conventional TV director, and his artist wife Doreen lived at the end of the terrace. We had started out in a housing estate on the edge of the city but now we felt we were in the right place, close to the university, near the centre of town and the centre of the action. The house was big enough for the kids to have a playroom downstairs and their own bedroom upstairs. I made myself a study of sorts in the upstairs return room, although I ended up doing most of my writing downstairs in the front sitting room on a makeshift desk: two tea chests supporting a big flush door that David Hammond had got at some stage when Burtons – the tailors – were renovating their premises in Royal Avenue. Such were the conditions. Ad hoc and all go.

We had very good times there. Late nights with a lot of music and singing. Painters and poets toing and froing. Terry and Sheelagh Flanagan. Colin and Kate Middleton. David and Eileen Hammond. John and Ruby Hewitt came to see us when they were in town. And various other writers, when they were over doing readings. I remember Marie and me sitting up with Ted Hughes and Assia Gutmann late in 1968, drinking poteen in that half-furnished front room. Marie singing Irish folk songs, Assia singing Israeli songs, Ted singing 'The Brown and the Yellow Ale', me probably singing too. So, yes, it was indeed a place of writing. When we went to Glanmore in 1972, we rented to students and it went out of our lives pretty quickly and never came back. I held on to it until 1976 and then sold to help raise a deposit for the house we were buying in Dublin.

In 'September Song', you mention 'Hammond, Gunn and McAloon / in full cry till the dawn chorus, / insouciant and purposeful'.

That was a big party we held in the summer of 1970, before setting out for Berkeley. Karl Miller was over at the time and several other editors and scribes assembled. Herbert McCabe of *New Blackfriars*, John Horgan of the *Irish Times*. 'Bliss was it' to be alive in that dawn chorus . . .

The Hammond of 'September Song' is presumably David Hammond – about whom you also wrote in 'The Singer's House'. Can you tell me something more about your friendship with him? Is he a literary man?

It's not how you would immediately think of him, although he's very much a reader and very much at home with writers. Our friendship started in that pre-Troubles, upbeat folk scene Belfast of the mid-sixties. Through David we met up with a lot of other singers and musicians, so the scope of social life widened and wakened that bit more. He's always been a free spirit, up to all kinds of pranks and carry-on, but in his professional life he's shown this powerful commitment to making life in Northern Ireland more salubrious and more fulfilling on all sides. It comes out in his work as an educational broadcaster and film-maker.

What I responded to immediately was a wonderful inner freedom, a quality of liberation, as if he had triumphed over the narrow-mindedness we'd all grown up with. He was as much at home with the Clancy Brothers as with the brethren of an Orange Lodge in Cregagh. And the fetch of that liberated thing was in his singing voice. So 'The Singer's House' ends, you remember, by suggesting that raising the voice like that is a way of raising the level of life generally. During the seventies, when Brian Friel and his family were spending summers in west Donegal also, we were often all together, away from the more noxious aspects of life in the North, and our sessions were conducted more, I'd say, as protest than as an escape. I guess I associate David with outbreak, a kicking over of traces, an impatience with the ordinary.

When you, David Hammond and Michael Longley embarked on the Room to Rhyme Arts Council tour in 1968, did you tailor the programme to take account of the religious/political sensitivities of the different communities you visited?

Well, to give you an Ulster sort of answer, we did and we didn't. There was a printed programme that we stuck to wherever we went. And wherever we went, it tended to be a mixed audience, people with an interest in hearing poems and songs, hence people with a certain ability to read not just the content but the codes in what was being presented. My 'Requiem for the Croppies', for example, has barley growing from seeds in the common graves where the 1798 rebels were buried, so it was placed in the 'Seasons' section of our little anthology, as if to say, this is an image of resurrection, of spring sowing and summer growing. Yet I'd guess there was nobody who didn't feel a frisson of transgression at the fact of a so-to-speak rebel poem surfacing in an official context, even though that particular context permitted it. And it was the same with Michael's 'Remembrance Day' whose very title inevitably endorses the British connection: it was placed in the 'Death' section and its political force was mitigated by personal circumstance since Michael's father had fought in the trenches.

It may be special pleading if I say that what we had was the beginnings of pluralism rather than the same old primness. The Ulster we were travelling through, after all, was one that was producing young candidates prepared to call themselves 'Liberal Unionists'. Because of the way things turned out a few months later – we did Room to Rhyme in May 1968 – my recollection of that moment may be too rosy, too subject to political as well as personal nostalgia. But the content and conduct of our programme were symptomatic of a change for the better.

Once the Troubles flared, 'Requiem for the Croppies' might have been read as a potential rallying cry for militant republicanism. If I'm not mistaken, you eventually stopped reading the poem in public.

When we were in Berkeley, sometime in 1971, there was an LP called *The Four Green Fields* that had various rebel songs on it and also a recitation of 'Requiem for the Croppies' – not, I should say, by me. Even so, at that early stage, I wasn't all that worried. The poem may have been appropriated but it hadn't been written as a recruiting song for the IRA. No way. In the Northern Ireland context, its purpose was to exercise the rights of nationalists to have freedom of cultural speech, as it were. To make space in the official Ulster lexicon for Vinegar Hill as well as the Boyne and the Somme. In 1970 and 1971 there was promise in the air as well as fury and danger, but soon enough it all went rancid. Internment was bad enough, but then you had Bloody Sunday in 1972, and Bloody Friday, dismaying hardness and ruthlessness in the violence all round, and at that stage a reading aloud of the poem would have been taken as overt support for the Provisionals' campaign. So that's when I stopped.

Were those the crucial consciousness-raising events for you –
Bloody Sunday, I mean, and Bloody Friday?

The stakes were being raised to deadlier levels all the time. There was the baton charge in Duke Street in Derry in October 1968 and the surge of protest marches after that. Then the pogroms into the Falls. The arrival of the British army. Internment. Bombings like the Abercorn restaurant. Shootings like the linen workers in Armagh. The shootings in the Pentecostal church at Darkley. People you knew getting killed either by accident or at random or by deliberate targeting. The combination in your thought and feeling of what Yeats would have called abstract passion and its opposite, what Owen would have called 'the eternal reciprocity of tears'. Nothing I can say about it seems to get it right.

To what extent were you involved with the Civil Rights
movement? Were you in any sense an activist?

I wasn't active, not an enrolled member, if indeed there was such a thing. The Civil Rights movement was operating and important even before October 1968 and I'd have known and met several of the moving spirits. Dr Conn McCluskey and his wife, who were founder members, even came to a Room to Rhyme performance, or maybe it was to a later poetry reading in Dungannon. Austin Currie, who took part in the first big sit-in in Fintona, had been at Queen's with us. I was all in favour of the Civil Rights people, but I've never been actively involved in politics. Too much fervour and certitude and point-scoring, even in the right cause, wears me out. Something in me just wants to appeal to a higher court and get it over with. I suppose that's what the big marches were, essentially, a gesture towards larger justice, a declaration that some things brought us to the threshold of the intolerable.

The Sunday after Bloody Sunday, for example, when British army helicopters were flying over the marchers assembling on the border, warning people over their amplifications that they were breaking the law, the helicopters and the armaments were completely irrelevant. The law itself had broken and morally the army was its broken arm. The same was true on the first big student marches in Belfast, after the RUC had run amok in Derry. When we were stopped by the police and Ian Paisley's supporters were out in force round City Hall, showing that their sectarian might was right, the big appeal was almost its own reward. But poetic justice isn't enough. That's why, the evening after the march, you had the founding of the People's Democracy.

Were you involved with them in any way?

No. But again, I was adjacent since I was lecturing at Queen's. I attended some of the early assemblies in the Students' Union, when people like John McGuffin and Bernadette Devlin and Michael Farrell were getting into their stride, and it was all very exhilarating. Michael Farrell – penetratingly intelligent, wonderfully cogent as a speaker, a kind of politicized Stephen Dedalus – was in my honours Literature seminar; and Bernadette was not only the muse of the movement but its furiously flexing muscle – again an exhilarating speaker: a pressure, as Hopkins might have put it, a principle and a proffer. But even so, well before those meetings had ended, I'd go home to Ashley Avenue and the essays and the nappies, while they'd proceed to student flatland and get going on plans for shaking and shaping the future.

5

'Vowels and history'
Wintering Out

~

Did you intend the title of Wintering Out *to suggest the wintering out of cattle as well as the 'winter of our discontent'? Does it hint at despair or is there a spring not far behind?*

No spring was being promised, but I still didn't think of the title as despairing. It came, as you recognize, from memories of cattle in winter fields. Beasts standing under a hedge, plastered in wet, looking at you with big patient eyes, just taking what came until something else came along. Times were bleak, the political climate was deteriorating. The year the book was published was the year of Bloody Sunday and Bloody Friday.

A recent academic article states that you had a draft of the book in manuscript when you returned from California in the summer of 1971 but that the realities of post-internment Northern Ireland compelled you 'to reassess the content and the shape of this new collection'. Do you remember anything about that?

Before I left Berkeley I did assemble a manuscript called *Winter Seeds* – named for the ones found in the stomach of the Tollund Man – but it was never submitted as a finished book. My reassessment of the contents derived from artistic instinct rather than any response to the conditions on the ground. Some things were dropped, some revised, but much of what is distinctive about the book – the place-name poems at the beginning, the new title poem, 'Servant Boy', 'The Other Side' in its final shape – was written that autumn and winter after I came back. Written in a little burst. You can see that much of the work in the first section is part of a single breath, a kind of exhalation from the 'lobe and larynx / of the mossy places'.

Was there any discussion with fellow poets like Michael Longley and Derek Mahon about how you should negotiate the artistic and political cross-currents of the Troubles? Was there a conscious sense among you of the poet as spokesman?

The role was available and to a certain extent inevitable, but the question was – and remains – to what extent the role of spokesman can or should be exercised in poetry. The visiting journalists were pressing for interviews and we all did our share of opining and explaining. I remember the phone ringing one evening in 1971 or 1972 and an American voice saying, 'Hey, I'm Jimmy Breslin of the *New York Post* and I'm out in Cultra and want to call over with you.' I knew there was a Jimmy Breslin who was famous as a columnist in New York, but I half thought it might be a joke call from David Hammond. But no, inside the hour there was Jimmy and his wife on the doorstep.

So it was mostly visiting journalists you spoke to?

Not just visitors. There was a significant rise in the number of pro-grammes on local radio and TV that involved 'talking heads', Unionists and nationalists, Protestants and Catholics, people who weren't necessarily spokespersons, but who could air the issues without getting into a fury with each other. On one occasion I took part in a radio programme on BBC Northern Ireland where the panel included the Dublin historian Liam de Paor and Aiken McLelland, the historian of the Orange Order. But the poets didn't meet like a war cabinet to discuss these things. Derek Mahon was off in London then anyhow, being theatre critic for *The Listener*. Generally, we were uneasy about claiming any special wisdom, so it was a case of Ulster downbeat rather than high talk, although we were certainly conscious that we were witnessing a decisive histor-ical moment. I remember John Montague wrote to me at the time, urging me to keep a diary of what was going on day by day in the ordinary life of the town as well as in the public arena, but I didn't do it and I regret it now. My reluctance was just one more symptom of the general wryness, the fear of inflating oneself or one's role.

You addressed this in your 'Place and Displacement' lecture when you said that your generation of writers felt it was not necessary to deal directly with political issues because 'the subtleties and tolerances of their art were precisely what they had to contribute to the coarseness and intolerances of public life'. Looking back, would you say that this approach continued to sustain you and the Ulster poets throughout the Troubles?

All of us, Protestant poets, Catholic poets – and don't those terms fairly put the wind up you? – all of us probably had some notion that a good poem was 'a paradigm of good politics', a site of energy and tension and possibility, a truth-telling arena but not a killing field. And without being explicit about it, either to ourselves or to one another, we probably felt that if we as poets couldn't do something transformative or creative with all that we were a part of, then it was a poor lookout for everybody. In the end, I believe what was envisaged and almost set up by the Good Friday Agreement was prefigured in what I called our subtleties and tolerances – allowances for different traditions and affiliations, in culture, religion and politics. It all seems simple enough. But here and now I sound far more civic and clarified than I ever was at the time.

'Whatever You Say Say Nothing' had appeared in The Listener *in 1971. Why, apart from the final section – used as a dedicatory poem in* Wintering Out – *did you hold it over until* North? *Did it seem too direct, too journalistic?*

What appeared in *The Listener* was a digest and carve-up of a set of verse letters I'd rattled out to friends shortly after I landed back from Berkeley in the late summer of 1971. To Tom Flanagan and our friends the Keefes in California. To Brian Friel and Maurice Leitch. Maybe to one or two others. They were done out of high spirits, with no view to publication, rickety, rackety quatrains, sheer hit-and-run stuff. Then Karl Miller at *The Listener* came after me to do a 'Views' piece about what it was like to return to Belfast and I got the notion of cutting and pasting the 'epistles'. Verse letters were in the air at the time, with Michael Longley writing to Derek Mahon, James Simmons and myself, in the months previous to the 'Views'. So the things were indeed journalistic, happily and I'd hope unpejoratively so, but they didn't fit the more inward, broody style of *Wintering Out*. The last section of the 'Views' digest, however, was more elegiac – mist and dew as well as motorway and the Maze prison – so it found its place musically and thematically as a prologue to the collection. Then three years later, when it came to putting together the poems in *North*, other bits of the sequence fitted the looser, more documentary style of the second half of that book, so in they went.

You have sometimes spoken of the first four collections as forming a single movement in your work. It seems to me, however, that Wintering Out *represented a significant shift in direction. The very notion of the phonetic as subject matter . . . How did this occur to you – the idea that the sounds of words ('My mouth holds round / the soft blastings, /* Toome, Toome'*) could be matter as well as means for poetry? Had you any precedent in mind?*

No precedent consciously in mind, but Joyce must have been at work downstairs. The first paragraph of 'The Sisters', maybe, where there's this dreamy caress of words like 'gnomon' and 'simony', or the little deliquescent hymn to the word 'suck' early on in *A Portrait of the Artist*.

Those languagey poems were all post-Berkeley, as far as I remember. Earlier on, in 1969 and 1970, I'd written the group of poems about women in distress – 'Shore Woman', 'Maighdean Mara', 'A Winter's Tale', 'Limbo'; and the first fruits of my P. V. Glob reading arrived around about the same time – I did 'The Tollund Man' in Ballydavid in Kerry at Easter in 1970. Marie and I had gone there for holidays regularly during the 1960s and the fishing scenario in 'Shore Woman' is in fact an amalgam of two Kerry occasions – one when we went out on Kenmare Bay with Seán Ó Riada and actually caught a heap of mackerel; another, reported to us by a man in Dingle, who told how his wife panicked when their boat was surrounded by porpoises. Anyhow, those narratives and monologues formed one segment of the contents.

The place poems came from a different source, etymological daydreams of sorts, playing with the fit between place and name, responses to having been born in what John Montague called the 'primal Gaeltacht'. They harked back to the Irish language underlay and were laying claim to a hidden Ulster, the Uladh of Doire Cholmcille rather than the Londonderry of the Plantation and the

Siege. But you're right to think of their energy as phonetic rather than political. '*Anahorish*, soft gradient / of consonant, vowel-meadow' and so on. What happened in them was a kind of melt-down of memory-stuff and Ulster myths of belonging. There was nothing civic about them, it was the ultimate Frostian sensation of the poem coming to itself like a piece of ice on a hot stove.

There was no question of sound poetry? Had you any interest in Kurt Schwitters or Ernst Jandl, or their English followers – Bob Cobbing, say?

No, I have nothing at all to declare in that area. I did hear Bob Cobbing at his antics a couple of times and enjoyed him, but had no desire to do likewise.

Adopting Dylan Thomas's distinction, do you think of yourself as someone who works 'from words' or 'towards them'?

Probably I do both. Prior to those place-name poems, for example, I wrote a poem in Berkeley called 'Gifts of Rain'. A strange, water-logged thing that went back to conversations I'd overheard as a youngster about a time in the 1920s when the Moyola had over-flowed and flooded some of the houses in Broagh. Older people would occasionally remember events and date them by asking, 'Was that before or after the flood?' So 'Gifts of Rain' came out of this sense of belonging to an antediluvian world, an Adam-clayman world, an original glottal, glarry ground. But I'm not sure how that rates in Thomas's scheme, whether it's from or towards words. I like the distinction but find it hard to distinguish which is which.

I wonder if your schoolboy fascination with the grammatical aspects of language might have been a harbinger of the more semantic and phonetic poems in Wintering Out.

Could be, but I'm reluctant to speculate too much about it. From parsing and analysis to poetry and phonetics . . . It's a crooked enough path. Maybe the link is to be sought in my first French class, when Mr Dunbar chalked up and belted out the sixteen vowel sounds on my first day in St Columb's College. I was suddenly very far from home. Talk about defamiliarization! It was a completely bewildering forty minutes, the whole class uttering the pure notes in concert: *ee, ay, eh, ah, aw, o, oo,* and so on into a climax of trumpetings and whinnies. But seriously, I don't know how to answer your question, except to say that the slight oddity and obsessiveness of the word-rutting in the book is what makes it interesting.

Were you conscious that you would be demanding more of your readers in this book and that you would perhaps be moving beyond what family and friends might feel comfortable with?

I would have thought that family and friends should have been completely at home with much of the book, since it begins with a poem about *fother* – not a mispronunciation of 'father' but the local way of saying 'fodder' – and then goes on to name and celebrate Anahorish and Toome and Broagh and Derrygarve and Castledawson and Upperlands. It even has a poem about our late neighbour Johnny Junkin, the man who'd originally observed that the ground in one particular field of ours was 'as poor as Lazarus'. I had no qualms about *Wintering Out*. I felt I was on the move, that I'd found a way in.

I take it that you had, by then, concluded that adherence to the 'common sense' principles of The Movement would retard your growth and development.

The thing is this: I had probably concluded nothing at that stage, and haven't concluded all that much yet. I never thought of myself as linked to The Movement and its principles, good or bad. Any relation I'm supposed to have had with movements comes from commentary by reviewers and critics, and from responses by myself to questions of the sort you've just asked: about the Northern poets and the well-made poem, the anti-modernism of the Belfast poets, etc., etc. . . . Just by answering, you contribute to the creation of a narrative.

In conversations, in drink even, I and others probably came out with remarks that can be construed and constructed as part of the literary historical picture. I remember, for example, a great night of boasting and flyting with John Montague and Mac Rosenthal somewhere in the States when the battle lines were drawn on the subject of Ezra Pound; I was doing him down in an exaggerated way, for scampishness and provocation. Those rogue remarks eventually began to circulate and to be taken as some kind of manifesto.

I'm devoted to Pound's early work. I love that first 'Canto'. He was important to me from the start as the author of the imagist principles and the breaker of the 'heave' of the pentameter. Nobody would want to deny his genius or his utter importance in the history of modern poetry. I just never studied *The Cantos*, could never get enough reward from them to motivate me to do the work. Eliot was the one whom I entered into and who entered into me. In some instances I just enjoyed harrying not so much Pound as the Poundians – although I still believe that there was something in my challenge that he is as much a great ventriloquist as anything else.

But to come back to The Movement and all that . . . Individual poets, individual poems were what mattered to me. Donald Davie, for example, would be considered your typical Movement bard, but the book of Davie's that meant most to me was *Essex Poems*, a Poundian swerve away from all that straight down the line *New Lines*-y ratiocination. By 1972, after all, I had roamed a bit, both geographically and poetically; travelled in the realms not only of Kavanagh and Hughes, but of Olson and Williams, Snyder and Bly. I was freed up and aware that, if I was going to take an individual step, now was the time.

In a similar vein, you told a BBC interviewer that around 1972 – having published two collections, and with Wintering Out *on the way – you still felt you 'hadn't broached whatever "poet" meant' and hadn't 'verified the word' within yourself sufficiently. What did you mean by that?*

I meant that I had passed the stage where just 'writing poems' was enough. I had passed the stage of probation and felt confident of vocation. To continue with the religious idiom, it was time to lose the nine-to-five life and to try to find a poetic life. I felt I had to try the experiment of becoming a freelance or full-time writer. So at that stage the move to Glanmore was already on the cards.

Wasn't there some remark made by the Minister of Community Relations in Northern Ireland that jolted you into a realization that poems could in fact be too appeasing? Did that realization contribute to the evolution of Wintering Out?

Not really. The remark was actually made after the book came out, probably in response to a poem like 'The Other Side'. But the minister would also have had in mind earlier ones such as 'Digging' and 'Thatcher'. The man was saying something perfectly true, namely that much of my work was immediately accessible to everybody in Northern Ireland, whatever their religious or political affiliations. So naturally he went on to observe that this proved how much common ground we shared and so on – perfectly harmless decent-speak on the part of a minister. But it rang a warning bell in me. I wasn't discommoded by English critics gabbling on about the out-of-dateness of bulls and bogs, but I was caught on the hop when I found those images being read as some kind of endorsement of the Northern status quo. I began to see what the political spin could be. So from that came a new readiness to print something like 'Whatever You Say Say Nothing', and later on to have a go at a sequence like 'Singing School'.

Your minister would have been pleased, no doubt, by the inclusion of dialect words, since they too would have bridged the sectarian gap in Ulster. But what about readers who would have felt excluded? There's a line in 'Nerthus', for example: 'Where kesh and loaning finger out to heather'. Did you expect non-Ulster readers to engage in some research or was it your hope that context and cadence would provide sufficient illumination of the meaning?

I didn't think at all of the reader's problem when I wrote the line. The joy was in solving my own writer's need. The word 'Nerthus', the Latin name of an earth goddess, was a big transmitter and through it I could broadcast my own signal from the Dirraghs. To my ear, the melody and cadence of the line had a rightness which banished any worries about the strange vocabulary. 'Kesh' and 'loaning' were of the language, and in the language, so *nihil obstat*, as it were, *imprimatur*. And if people thought there was a submerged reference to Long Kesh, 'the new camp for the refugees' mentioned in the dedicatory verse, well, that was all right too.

This, presumably, is the kind of thing you had in mind when you wrote in the Guardian *in 1972 that the secret of being a poet 'lies in the summoning and meshing of the subconscious and semantic energies of words'?*

Exactly. I was trying to prepare anybody who had ears to hear for the *Wintering Out* poems.

It seems that the classes relating to Ulster dialect which you took as a student at Queen's – rather than the old Gaelic tradition of place lore, the dinnseanchas – *gave you confidence in the use of local language and place names.*

Those few classes were seminal. In fact, one poem in the book, 'A Backward Look', derives from the inaugural lecture given by my former language teacher John Braidwood, when he was promoted to the rank of professor. His text was printed as 'The Ulster Dialect Lexicon' and many of the transliterations from the Irish that appear in the poem are lifted straight from the pamphlet. *Dinnseanchas* was a corroborating tradition, let's say, rather than an immediate influence.

Would you be reluctant to use dialect words which you know only from dictionaries?

I would. Other poets broach the dictionary hoard, and get great energy and exhibition from doing so, but for me the point about dialect or hearth language is its complete propriety to the speaker and his or her voice and place. What justifies it and gives it original juice and joy is intimacy and inevitability. I've always confined myself to words I myself could have heard spoken, words I'd be able to use with familiarity in certain companies. I've got this thick-witted obstinacy about doing otherwise. It's the corollary of my readiness to set down the name of a townland like Broagh as if it were as familiar as the town of Troy.

By the way, it is claimed in a book about place names that, by the 1990s, 'Broagh' was pronounced locally as 'Brox'. Could it be that the locals themselves can no longer manage 'that last gh'?

I'm afraid I have to say that that 'Brox' stuff is nothing but a load of ould boll*ogh*. On the other hand, the 'x' may be functioning there as the phonetic sign for the *och/oagh* sound rather than as the twenty-fourth letter of the alphabet.

Och, I stand corrected and will move swiftly on! Was the 'Servant Boy' of the poem in which the phrase 'wintering out' occurs somebody you knew personally? Or is he woven out of stories you heard about the hiring fairs?

He was based on an old man called Ned Thompson who used to visit our house once or twice a week. A small, stooped ancient with a droop moustache, a bit like a down-at-heel Thomas Hardy. He walked with his hands behind his back, wore a cap and smoked a clay pipe. The house he lived in had a clay floor and clay walls, a nineteenth-century cabin if ever there was one. And from him I *did* hear talk about different masters, about sleeping in the loft, about the ones who fed him well and the ones who didn't, about having to walk for miles home and back on a Sunday, and all that. He was at home in our kitchen, but he also belonged to the world of folk songs like 'The Rocks of Bawn' and 'Magherafelt May Fair'.

The servant boy in the poem, however, is also meant as a portrait of a minority consciousness, a minority artist's consciousness even: 'carrying the warm eggs' is what a servant boy would have had to do in the morning, check the nests and bring in what the laying hens had laid; but it's also an emblem of the human call to be more than just 'resentful and impenitent', even while injustices are being endured. In the poem, the servant boy 'kept his patience and his counsel' while he was wintering out: whatever he said, he said nothing; he knew the score, bore the brunt and bided his time. But by the time of the Civil Rights marches his stoop had begun to be straightened and his walk, I would like to think, was being braced by the poem in which he appeared.

There's another poem in the book which seems to be situated in that same shadowy area between folklore and politics: I'm thinking of 'The Last Mummer'. Is this an elegy for a traditional practice or is something else going on?

The last mummer is, like the servant boy, an alter ego of sorts. He too is resentful and impenitent. He carries a stone in his pocket. He beats the bars of a gate with his stick. He fires a stone up at the roof of the 'the little barons'. But he also controls his anger, fits in, his tongue goes 'whoring / among the civil tongues'. In a sense, he's the kind of guy who can be a spokesman, can go on a BBC panel without wrecking the decorum of the studio . . . The more I talk about those poems, the more I see that they were about the need to break out of the consensus that Ulster was 'a good wee place', the need to get on the road to Aarhus, to acknowledge the lostness and unhappiness of 'home'.

At the same time, you were drawing on childhood memories, were you not? You knew Alan Gailey's book, Irish Folk Drama, *but I presume it wasn't your primary inspiration.*

My inspiration was the 'Christmas rhymers'. I never heard the word 'mummer' until years later. But I realized that mumming was what I had witnessed in my early days when neighbours' young-sters would blacken their faces and dress up in old clothes and come into the house rattling a collection box and saying rhymes to suit their different characters: Beelzebub, Johnny Funny, Doctor Brown, Devil-me-Doubt. The practice was in its last gasp when I encountered it; but Alan Gailey's work sort of revived it, so now you have thriving troupes of mummers all over the place, dressed in straw masks, smacking their swords and dancing their jigs the length and breadth of Merrie Ulster.

Were the rhymes of the Christmas rhymers improvised?

Entirely traditional.

Were you ever tempted to write a mummer's play – in emulation of Patrick Kavanagh perhaps?

I once used the rhyming, self-dramatizing style of the mummers' plays in a BBC schools script called 'Everyman' – or maybe it was 'An Ulster Everyman' – but that was the height of it. I had one good notion, however, that went unrealized, which was to create some kind of dance drama that would involve mumming and tra-ditional music and would be set at a cockfight on the border between the North and the South. It was to show the violence and gambling and the factional element in cockfighting and would constitute a parallel universe, as it were, to the border country itself, ripped apart by the factions of the IRA and the UDA. Cockfighting and mumming, by the way, cut across the sectarian divide. All sides attended the fights. And because the fights were illegal, a special bond was created among the aficionados. My last mummer could have been a cockfighter too, 'picking a nice way through / the long toils of blood / and feuding'.

'The Other Side' presents a guarded but benign encounter between your family and your Protestant neighbour Johnny Junkin, whom you mentioned earlier. What were the factors that

*freed your household of 'sectarian energy'? Were you much
different in that regard from other families?*

Maybe not all that different, except, as I've said more than once
already, my father had a kind of trans-sectarian licence to roam,
through being in the cattle trade. Then too there were old friend-
ships going back between neighbours' families for generations.
And, if I may say so, there was a kind of natural grace in the
Heaney and McCann connections. Our house was happily open
and, until our last Protestant neighbour Billy Steele died, the visit-
ing continued without prejudice. It even feels slightly demeaning
for me to be talking in these terms.

*So relationships between your parents and those neighbours
didn't deteriorate during the Troubles?*

They did not. The Steeles and Junkins and McIntyres and
Mulhollands – who were both beside us and on the other side –
these were well-disposed and capable people. They had more than
enough inner freedom and confidence to retain friendships and dig-
nity, no matter what kind of overall tension and hurt everybody
had to endure.

Was there any intermarriage between Protestants and Catholics?

None that I remember.

*And what about the Orange Order? Would you have been aware
of their activities? Would you have taken care to be out of the way
when they were marching?*

It all depended on who you were dealing with. Obviously, there was
a bigoted element in the Orange Order, some of them rural families,
but mostly poorer ones from the villages. There would also have
been bitter Loyalist families whose menfolk served in the B-Special
Constabulary, and those we would have considered more or less
beyond the pale. A self-respecting Catholic dealt with such types
only with the greatest circumspection. It worked out, as you might
expect, largely on class lines. And the natural gumption and intelli-
gence of the individual came into it too. Generally, you wouldn't be
having anything much to do with the bigoted crowd at any time of
the year, so there was no particular need to avoid them around the

Twelfth of July. They might have thought *they* were avoiding *you*, which was more comic than cutting in the circumstances. Even so, I remember going out to the end of the lane at Mossbawn to watch an Orange band march and to wave at people we knew – including Alan and George Evans dressed up in their sashes. There was no problem at that personal level: if you were friends with the people, you conceded their right to their affiliations.

At the same time, you resented the overall shape of things because you also knew that the Orange arches erected in the villages and at various crossroads were what the Romans might have recognized as a form of *jugum* or yoke, and when you went under the arches you went *sub jugum*, you were being subjugated, being taught who was boss, being reminded that the old slogan, 'a Protestant parliament for a Protestant people', now had real constitutional force. So, resentful and impenitent, you carried the warm eggs of your smile to your marching neighbour and walked tall in defiance of the *jugum*.

Was there any equivalent of the Twelfth of July marches for nationalists? How did they display their emblems and assert their presence?

Illegally, a lot of the time. Political marches by Republicans carrying a tricolour would lead to confiscation of the flag or attempts to confiscate it by the RUC. And led as often as not to riots as well. One of the great triumphs – or transgressions, depending on where you stood – was to get a tricolour up overnight into the top of some tall tree and to have it visible all over the district. The police would then have to come and get it down – although on one occasion, I remember, some Orange guys came and actually cut down one such tree on the eve of the GAA sports day in Castledawson.

On the nationalist side, the sanctioned marches were by the Ancient Order of Hibernians, on St Patrick's Day and 15 August. The Hibernians were descendants of the Home Rulers and were consequently far less subversive than the Republicans or 'Shinners'. There was a religiose quality about their music and emblems: the banners showed St Patrick banishing the snakes, or maybe the Maid of Erin under a round tower, with inset medallions of St Brigid and Colmcille. And the tunes were often hymns: 'I'll Sing a Hymn to Mary' or 'Hail Glorious Saint Patrick'. Accordion bands, pipe bands, kilts, plaids, sporrans, the whole panoply. There was actually a small Hibernian hall beside our house in Mossbawn and the first music of yearning I knew was the sound of a piper practising in there after dark, in February or March . . . I suppose there was a certain melancholy attaching to the whole Hibernian phenomenon. They belonged to a Victorian ethos, and the movement had no great ideological force or passion to it. It was more Thomas Moore than Thomas Davis.

You witnessed those Hibernian marches yourself?

Many times. It was a great excitement for kids, to watch them assembling outside the hall, unfurling the banner, everybody getting into line, youngsters being allocated which 'strings' of the banner to carry, the pipes tuning up, the big drum being hefted, and then one, two, left, right, off they went and the skirl of the pipes began. I loved it. But it packed very little factional punch. I'd say the blood was stirred in an Orange child by those Orange processions far more than mine ever was by the Hibs, as we called them. 'Obedient strains like theirs tuned me first / And not that harp of unforgiving iron / The Fenians strung . . .' All true.

How did your mother's 'whatever you say, say nothing' attitude in sectarian Ulster square with some of the characteristics you ascribed to her earlier – her alertness to 'sectarian strains' and her readiness to be 'provoked by the hidden operations of the system'?

I suppose this should go on the record once and for all. My mother's attitude was not at all expressed by the phrase 'whatever you say, say nothing' – nor, I should say, was mine. Her use of it and my use of it put it very much in inverted commas. The phrase was a knowing acknowledgement of the power structure, a Catholic nod in answer to the Protestant wink that got the jobs and the houses. It was ironical rather than instructional. It was fundamentally an expression of anger rather than of acquiescence.

Did your family keep any 'flags or emblems', as I think they are termed in Northern Ireland legislation?

None. But we'd contrive to be out of the cinema before 'God Save the Queen' came on at the end. And we'd never call Derry

'Londonderry'. The only politically charged material I remember was acquired when my father went to Dublin for an All Ireland football final in the company of a bookish old bachelor cousin called Pat McGuckian. Two books appeared: *Guerrilla Days in Ireland* by Tom Barry, the IRA man who had led a flying column in Cork during the War of Independence, and a compendium of historical and Republican lore called *The Wolfe Tone Annual*. Images from the *Annual* eventually came up in a poem called 'The Old Icons' and the 'Stockinged corpses / Laid out in the farmyards' that appear in 'The Tollund Man' I saw first in a photograph in Barry's book. It was of a farmer's family who had been shot in reprisals by the Black and Tans, left lying on their backs beside their open door.

What about rebel songs?

My mother loved 'Boolavogue' and 'Who Fears to Speak of '98?' She was no singer, but she always made a shot at singing those ones. Mostly she went in for the old school songs, things like 'Loch Lomond', and others she remembered from barn dances in her younger days – 'Coming through the Rye', for example. Then we had our own local '98 man, Roddy McCorley, and Ethna Carbery's song about him being hanged on the bridge of Toome. And after the IRA campaign in the 1950s, there were ballads about the shooting of Seán South and Feargal O'Hanlon, although they were more listened to on radio than sung around the house.

Was Toome endowed with a patriotic aura for you because of McCorley?

Not really. For me, the aura at Toome was phenomenological rather than political. On the bridge, I was more conscious of the strong bright lumen and numen of the Bann river, the big lift of light over Lough Neagh, the wind, the strangeness of crossing wide water – for to me, in those days, the Bann seemed a wide river.

There was an archaeological dimension too.

Oh yes, the whole Bann valley had that. There was always a lot of talk at school about the Bann Drainage Scheme in the 1920s, about the flints and scrapers found in the mud of the banks. There were even flints in a cupboard in the master's classroom. When I started to visit the Ulster Museum as an undergraduate, I saw the name 'New Ferry' on label after label and was interested because New Ferry was at the end of the Ballyscullion Road, near where my father's Scullion cousins lived. The road ran right to the edge of the water – where the ferry had been – and just stopped. It was a plain yet mysterious place, the river just going along deep and steady and quiet and slow.

A scene-change now, from the Bann valley to Silicon Valley – or, at least, to the college campus at Berkeley. You went as a guest lecturer to Berkeley for a year from 1970. How did this come about?

Some time before that, I did a poetry reading at the University of York in England, where I met Tom Parkinson. Parkinson was a Yeats scholar, a member of the English Department at Berkeley, a friend of John Montague's, and I know he had heard something from Montague about me. He was on sabbatical just then and it was through him that the invitation came – to spend a year as a visiting lecturer. Exactly what I was ready for, so no hesitations whatsoever about accepting. I had a curiosity about the whole Beat scene, and at that time the Bay Area was as hot politically as it was poetically.

Had there been any history of emigration on either side of your family? Was a permanent move to America contemplated by you?

Nothing permanent was ever on the cards, although at the end of the year the chairman gave me an open invitation to come back some other time; a year later, his offer was a kind of safety net when I made the move from Queen's to Wicklow. There was no significant history of emigration in my background, however – except for one family of cousins on my mother's side who went to Philadelphia in the 1920s. Berkeley was a one-off adventure but a brilliant one. We loved it.

Were you challenged or changed by California?

Something changed, all right. It was the first time we'd lived for any length of time outside Northern Ireland. The first time we lived in the sun. The first time when the pay was enough for us not to be always thinking about money. I was taller and freer in myself at the end of the year than at the beginning. And it wasn't just the waft of the climate or the waiving of economic anxieties. It had to do with the intellectual distinction of the people around us, the nurture that came from new friendships and a vivid environment. There was genuine glamour and attainment about many people on the Berkeley faculty at that time. Mark Schorer with his bow ties and East Coast cool, cock of the walk at his own cocktail parties – I met Jessica Mitford and Lillian Hellman at the Schorers', and drank my first Martini. Tom and Jean Flanagan, who were our best friends about the place, and at whose house we met Conor Cruise O'Brien and Máire Mhac an tSaoi – on campus for a few weeks while Conor gave the Regents' Lectures. Lennie Michaels, the short-story writer, who had just published his first collection *Going Places*. Somehow, you were able to work yet feel *en fête*. I occasionally drove out with Marie and the kids to Marin County for breakfast, to Sam's Café, a hamburger joint in Tiburon. California champagne and hamburgers, for God's sake, at eight o'clock in the morning, and Dad back on campus for work at nine. Unimaginable around Queen's.

And the students?

Again, different from Queen's. And how. This was the time when freshmen would ask if you wanted to be called 'Seamus' or 'Professor'; the time of the loose garment and the long hair; of pot in the air and sex on the waterbed – which were the other side of the draft card and the water cannon. I couldn't altogether expel the Irish Catholic in me but he became a bit less uptight, and came home with a leather hat on his head and a short William Carlos Williamsy line in his ear.

How politicized were things generally at the time?

You could hardly eat a salad on campus because of solidarity with the Chicano lettuce pickers whom Cesar Chavez was organizing. You couldn't walk a hundred yards without encountering a couple of Black Panthers preaching power to the people. And there were taboos of all kinds that the campus liberal had to observe: no drinking of Coors Beer because the workers were non-unionized, no dealings with Bank of America or American Airlines because they were understood to be part of the war effort in Vietnam. Angela Davis was on the T-shirts, Bob Dylan and Pete Seeger were on the turntables, everything about the place was counter-cultural and anti-establishment. Hare Krishna and hard rockers singing from the one hymn sheet.

And your work in the English Department: was it much different from Queen's?

Some of it was: I taught Freshman Composition, for example, English 1A, and had a teaching assistant. That was different, for sure. But the main difference was the length of the courses, since Berkeley operated on the quarter system, four annual stints of ten or twelve weeks at a time. I taught two courses per quarter, and got to devise my own syllabus for each of them. Over the year, I gave lectures on contemporary poetry, a couple of survey courses on modern literature, prose and poetry, conducted a reading-in-order-to-write workshop, and did my duty with English 1A. Some of the classes had big enrolments, some small; but all were conducted to that lovely Californian student chorus of 'Hi-i-s' and 'Wow-w-w-s' and 'He-e-eys!' The hang-loose style was very attractive. Even though I was teaching a full load, it felt like a holiday. And Marie was having a different kind of Californian interlude – the company of other interesting women, and at home a certain amount of languor in the garden, the kids playing and Mammy enjoying the sunblock and the Gallo and the lawn sprinkler.

So the lotus-land image we have of the Bay Area fits with what you experienced?

It does. But we were very much visitors and lived just half a mile or so from campus, off Telegraph Avenue, so we missed a lot of the usual life. It was like living on a sixties film set. You walked to work along a street lined with craft stalls, selling home-made jewellery and leather goods, tie-dyed fabrics, aromatic candles, joss sticks, the *Kama Sutra*, the *Tibetan Book of the Dead*, you name it. You were also walking past the higher beggary. 'Any spare change?' was a constant mantra. There was grief on the pavements too, much of it drug-induced, but because it was mostly young grief, it was hard to distinguish from torpor or a trip.

There was an image of America as a table-top that had been tilted west, causing all that was loose or lost to roll towards California. Was there any validity in that somewhat disparaging image?

To an extent, yes, definitely. And the bad eggs rolled in with the good. One thing that happened on the streets of Berkeley shook us badly and shadowed Marie's life for a good while afterwards. She was mugged one evening as she walked the short distance between our apartment and the home of our friends the Tracys. Our kids had spent the afternoon with the Tracy kids and Marie was going round to fetch them. Next thing, she was out for the count, flat on the pavement. When she came to, she was being dragged towards the open back door of a van, with a man's voice telling her that if she opened her mouth he would kill her. But she fought and kicked and screamed and bit her way free, and arrived in great distress at the Tracys' door, almost unrecognizable.

Later on, she remembered that this guy had walked ahead of her, then turned to make some casual remark, and must have hit her an unmerciful blow in the eye. Her face was blackened and swollen and painful for weeks afterwards. Once she got away from him, he made off in the truck; but if Marie hadn't come to her senses in time, she'd have been in the truck with him. It was a huge trauma and gave us a glimpse of the darker side of hippy-land.

Was he ever found? Were the police involved?

The police were on the trail immediately and Marie was brought into hospital for emergency treatment. The worst outcome was the arrival of a squad car in front of our apartment a day or two later, with a suspect in the front seat. In come the police officers to Marie and suggest that she make a citizen's arrest. In other words, her accusation would be the only basis for taking the guy into custody. But there was no way she could be certain of the identification, so she let him go; once the police left, she found herself in a state of panic because the suspect, guilty or not, now knew where she lived. And a week or two later she saw the guy on the street. It was a nightmare for her.

All the same, even Marie had to laugh when our octogenarian landlord – no flower person he – heard the tale and displayed all the right prejudices. First, he tells her how sorry he is that this happened in California, and then asks immediately, 'Was he a hippy?' And when he's told 'no', he follows up with, 'Was he a black?' When the answer is again no, his upset is total: 'Gosh, Mrs Heaney, I *am* very sorry.' Next thing he arrives with a weapon for Marie to carry in her handbag – a deadly little three-sided file that had been honed razor-sharp by an inmate of San Quentin prison. The old fellow's son worked as a warden in San Quentin and had confiscated the thing; when he heard of Marie's situation, he sent it to her as a present.

The other shadow over the idyll was, of course, the Vietnam War. Did you attend rallies or marches? Did you follow the war news on TV?

Lieutenant Calley was tried for the My Lai massacre when we were there. The bombing of Cambodia happened. There was no way you could ignore the war. The whole lifestyle around you was a response to it. But I wasn't on any marches. I don't even know if there were any going on. By then the culture of the place added up to one long steady protest. The first weekend we were in Berkeley we went to a Pete Seeger concert, and later in the year I attended different anti-war readings – Robert Duncan rigged out in a Pierrot costume, Robert Bly in his poncho. There was a kind of revivalist cheer about all those events. Moral outrage and way-out gear. At another reading, by Bly and Gary Snyder in San Francisco, I suddenly realized that Bly's Lutheran background was coming through: what we had on stage was a poet-preacher. There was a lot of talk about the unconscious and the *vagina dentata* and so on, how the imperial male ego was responsible for the war, the cock and the 'copter somehow equally culpable – so for all the espousal of Zen, what we were listening to was a Midwestern minister haranguing a congregation.

Are you saying that you had a detached attitude to what was going on?

Not exactly. It's more that I was starting to learn what it meant to be American. There was a trust that things could be changed. The war machine and the capitalist pigs were held to be brutal and cynical, but the minds of the protesters were still infused with a belief in the reversibility of the situation. There was no tiredness, no real fear that the species was fallen, no European taking for granted that our understanding was dark and our will weak. To put it another way, I couldn't imagine a poetry reading in Belfast directed simply and solely against the Troubles. The poets and the audience were too clued-in to the complexity, we knew that we were all implicated. The nearest thing to that Bay Area mood happened in Northern Ireland with the Peace People, as they were called – Máiréad Corrigan and Betty Williams and Ciarán McKeown got a mass movement going that bore some relation to what we saw happening around Berkeley.

Did Robert Bly and Gary Snyder influence your writing?

There was an earnestness about them. There was a lyric core to their sensibilities, a certain religious disposition, if you like; with hindsight, I'd say those were the qualities that made them attractive to me. Bly's poems about old planks underfoot in a thaw, Snyder's about the rip-rap arrangement of paving stones on a path. The elements of their poetry were close to the elements of my own. Sequoias rather than sally trees, snowy fields rather than heather bogs; but still, the Gaia factor was definitely in operation. It was a very different aesthetic from the worldly irony of a poet like Zbigniew Herbert, and I was susceptible. It was partly under the influence of Bly's prose poems that I experimented with my own – the ones that appear early on in *Stations*. Also 'Gifts of Rain', 'Servant Boy', an early draft of the 'Mossbawn, Sunlight' poem – they were written around that time.

Did you meet many of the local writers?

Once Tom Parkinson had a big party and Snyder attended; but on that occasion the one I spoke to was Lawrence Ferlinghetti, a very courtly gentleman. He told me he'd been with the US Naval Reserve during the war and had put in at Belfast and Derry, which was a bit of a surprise. The poet I did see occasionally was Josephine Miles, by no means your sixties flower-power artist. A scholar-poet in the English Department. Occasionally also Leonard Nathan, who was in the Rhetoric Department; Leonard Michaels, the fiction writer, whom I've already mentioned; and Tom Flanagan – not yet the author of *The Year of the French*, but a terrific presence.

You didn't actually write much about California itself. You may recollect Patricia Beer's complaint – in her review of Wintering Out *in* The Listener *– that in the book's final poem, 'Westering', you couldn't wait to turn your gaze from California to Donegal.*

That poem began with Rand McNally's 'Official Map of the Moon'; and when I got that far, I suppose I thought I'd gone far enough . . . But Patricia Beer was right. What the Californian distance did was to lead me back into the Irish memory bank. And probably the fashion for Native American poetry, and Japanese and Chinese poetry, encouraged me to trust the 'nature' aspect of my own material. Meanwhile, you had James Wright doing his new tremulous thing, leaving the 'formal' for the 'naked' poetry camp, opening the praise channel, getting on the Rilkean wavelength, so that too disposed me towards origin and the inward path.

All the same, with your rural background, I wonder if you found the primitivism espoused by those writers a bit sentimental or naïve or just plain modish?

I did have those reservations, but I couldn't deny the fact that I responded to their work. Your critical head and your writing shoulders are often out of kilter like that.

Tom Flanagan seems to have been an important friend. Is it true that McCarthy – the poet character in The Year of the French *– is partly based on you?*

Tom said he was, at any rate. It's not that McCarthy's character or personality are anything like mine, just that he is a poet born into a violent Irish moment and shares concerns that Tom and I often talked about – not in the abstract, mind you, but in relation to the writing I was doing or not doing at the time: the conflict between detachment and solidarity, between being an activist and an artist, a poet and/or a propagandist, all that. But whatever about the original of McCarthy, the fact is that the Flanagans took great care of us when we first landed in California. Jean was our chauffeuse while we looked for an apartment and the Flanagan house was a home from home all that year.

Tom actually turned into a sort of literary foster father to me. It's no exaggeration to say that he reoriented my thinking. When I landed in California I was somebody who knew a certain amount of Irish literature and Irish history, but my head was still basically wired up to English Literature terminals. I was still a creature of my undergraduate degree. When I left, thanks mostly to Tom's brilliantly sardonic Hibernocentric thinking, I was in the process of establishing new co-ordinates and had a far more conscious, far more charged-up sense of Yeats and Joyce, for example, and of the whole Irish consequence. I was starting to see my own situation as a 'Northern poet' more in relation to the wound and the work of Ireland as a whole.

Tom had studied with Lionel Trilling at Columbia and won the Trilling Prize for his book on the nineteenth-century Irish novelists. He was the opposite of the New Critic kind of critic I was used to. Historical and political and biographical contexts always concerned him, and his talk was full of quotations. Not just literary, but historical – and comic. He had been a personal friend of Frank O'Connor, he had been at college with Truman Capote, he had written crime novels in New York in the fifties and won the Ellery Queen Prize for one of them. As well as all that, he seemed to have knowledge of every historical site in Ireland, since he had been coming to the country, summer by summer, for a decade and more. He was a brilliant raconteur with a sense of humour as pungent as his sense of history. And he was capable also of exhilarating anger. So it was thanks to Tom that my time by the Pacific was an education.

Was there any particular reason why you chose to dedicate the poem 'Traditions' to him?

It was Tom's poem because I lifted the conclusion of it from his book on the Irish novelists. The epigraph to that book juxtaposes Macmorris's question in *Henry V* – 'What ish my nation?' – with Bloom's answer in *Ulysses* to the Citizen's question, 'What is your nation?' 'Ireland', Bloom replies, definitely and unemphatically, 'I was born here. Ireland.' That seemed to cut through a lot of the identity crisis stuff that surrounded us in the early seventies so I stole it for the end of the poem.

Tom Flanagan wrote in the Harvard Review *about some trips you took together. He mentions, for instance, a journey to the battlefield at Ballinamuck and another to Ballylee.*

Ballinamuck was where the British put an end to the incursion of the French in 1798. The French troops surrendered and were let go up the Royal Canal to Dublin, but the Irish rebels who had followed them from Mayo to this godforsaken bog in Leitrim were cut down in their hundreds. Tom was writing *The Year of the French* at the time and we spent a day tramping around those sad old fields and hedges, trying to get the shape of the battle into our heads. It was a strange, grievous few hours. Very different from the Ballylee trip – a drive we took one St Patrick's Day from Dublin to Yeats's Tower, with a stop for oysters at Moran's of the Weir. David Hammond came with us too. The most notable moment was on the way back when I spied a notice at the gate of a house somewhere near Loughrea: '*Philip Larkin*', it said, '*Hurley Maker*'. Almost too good to be true, but true it proved to be, so we purchased hurleys apiece, stamped with the fabled name. I also got an extra one which I eventually delivered to Andrew Motion since he was at that time writing the other Philip's biography. I arranged to meet Andrew in the Pillars of Hercules pub in Soho and ceremonially placed the *camán* in his hands.

Tom Flanagan also referred to a visit to Carmel. Did you do much touring around with him when you were in Berkeley?

Not really. The Carmel trip happened later, when I went back in 1976. I spent the spring quarter that year as the Beckman Professor, teaching a couple of courses and giving the requisite public lecture. Tom and Jean took me to visit their friends the Dupees, who had then moved from New York to Carmel. F. W. Dupee, Fred Dupee, had been involved with the *Partisan Review* and had taught at Columbia. Well known in his time as one of the fabled New York intellectuals. And his wife Andy too was a great radical spirit. It turned out to be a memorable visit not only because Fred told me about the high jinks of John Ashbery and Kenneth Koch and Frank O'Hara – whom he had hung out with in New York – but because the other visitors that weekend were the Saids. I remember talking to Edward about what was going on in Beirut, and in Belfast, and recognizing his terrific intelligence and the way his indignation and compassion were so finely tuned and entangled. I think there was already some connection between the Saids and the Flanagans through their mutual friendship with the Cruise O'Briens.

There's a photograph in Geoffrey Summerfield's Worlds, *published in the mid-seventies, showing a large poster of Sitting Bull on your wall. Had you taken much interest in Native American art and culture while you were in California? Did you visit reservations, for example?*

No visits to reservations. But this was the moment when Native American history was being retrieved and rewritten in books like Dee Brown's *Bury My Heart at Wounded Knee*, and the bookshops were full of anthologies such as Jerome Rothenberg's *Technicians of the Sacred* and, a few years later, *Shaking the Pumpkin*. Coming from the minority in Northern Ireland, I couldn't not be in sympathy with the Civil Rights movement, the whole clamour for social justice that was resonating through the black American community, and starting up among the Native Americans. Paul Muldoon was on to this right away, in a poem like 'The Indians on Alcatraz': finding the correspondences, already in two places at the one time. I remember bringing him a copy of *Wounded Knee* when I came back from Berkeley in the summer of 1971. So I was aware, yes, of historical and political parallels between the Native American story and the Irish one; but I still couldn't take what Larkin described as the 'deliberate step backward' and go in for all that New Age stuff, the chant and the dance, whether as a rite in the commune or a style in the poem.

How much did California change your attitude towards the literary movements of the time – the Beats or the Black Mountain, say?

I bought and read – almost as if I were taking a course – books such as *A William Carlos Williams Reader* and *A Charles Olson Reader*. I devoted myself to Olson's essay on 'projective verse' and to some of his *Maximus Poems*; I had a determined go at the Orphic Duncan; I dabbled in Brautigan – and occasionally saw him in person at Enrico's café on Broadway – but in the end I held back. I just couldn't leave the gravitational pull of the poetry field I knew, couldn't slip the halter of the verse line and the stanza. I came to happy enough terms with Carlos Williams, whose ear is actually very delicate, but I couldn't spread out and let go projectively. At the same time, as I've often reported, I did learn how to hear and respect Gary Snyder, simply by listening to him read his own work.

I began to see the disposition of the verse on the page as a musical notation of sorts, so afterwards when I opened a book of his I had the sound of his voice in my ear.

The general assumption, then, that the short line of Wintering Out *is in the American, W. C. Williams grain is correct?*

I believe it to be so, although there was already a drift in that direction in the landscape poems at the end of *Door into the Dark*. If I couldn't altogether escape an Irishy/Britishy formality, I had an inclination from the start to dishevel it. I've always been subject to a perverse urge to galumph rather than glide. In the end, I suppose, it took me to *Beowulf* . . . But the free versus formal tension, Redskin versus Paleface, call it what you like, has always been there. It showed up in Belfast in our different prejudices and positions with regard to Larkin and Hughes, Lowell and Wilbur. It was part of my interest in Roethke. It gives added interest to the case of Thom Gunn.

Did you meet Thom Gunn?

During my later visit, yes, a couple of times. I don't think we encountered in 1971/2. But when I was Beckman Professor in 1976, Donald Davie organized a dinner in his house in Stanford and sent Alan Shapiro to collect me and drive me down. Alan was his graduate student at the time and had a car. Thom Gunn was a guest that evening also and the whole event went off with great brio; but what I remember most was the fact that Thom had hitch-hiked down from San Francisco. No pampering there – even the bus was too much for him. I think, by the way, that I still like the iambic, English side of Gunn better. *Fighting Terms* is a terrific first book; and there are poems like 'The Discovery of the Pacific' and those late Dantesque treatments of the pre-Aids gay scene in San Francisco. He can really build the pressure when his stanzas are working for him.

How did you feel about books like Robert Lowell's Life Studies *and W. D. Snodgrass's* Heart's Needle? *Isn't there a brief moment in* Wintering Out – *I'm thinking of 'Summer Home' – where the influence of confessional poetry might be discerned?*

I got powerful rewards as a reader of *Life Studies*, but never took to Snodgrass to the same extent. In fact, I only got my hands on *Heart's Needle* during my time in Berkeley – part of the huge pile of second-hand books I bought in the bookshops along Telegraph Avenue: Moe's and Shakespeare and Co. and Cody's. Those little poems in 'Summer Home' come more from pressure of personal experience than from any literary influence. Lowell didn't make his presence felt in the way I wrote until a couple of years later, after the blank-verse sonnets started to avalanche down upon us out of *History* and *The Dolphin* and the book *For Lizzie and Harriet*.

When Lowell was piling up the Notebook *pieces preceding those collections, you were experiencing a similar creative surge in Ireland. Can you still remember the week in May 1969 when – as you've reported in earlier interviews – you wrote 'about forty poems'? Were they just 'trial pieces' or did some of them survive into published collections?*

Several of them appeared in *Wintering Out*: 'Limbo', 'Serenades', 'Veteran's Dream', 'Midnight', 'Navvy', 'Dawn'. But a lot more saw the light of day just once, in spreads in *The Listener*. I don't know how to explain the dam-burst. It began with a hangover and continued with late nights and free days – this was in the month of May: Queen's University classes stopped around that time of year, or were about to stop. The day job, at any rate, wouldn't have been so pressing. It was a visitation, an onset, and as such, powerfully confirming. This, you felt, was 'it'. You had been initiated into the order of the inspired. Even though most of the poems didn't stand the critical test later on, the experience itself was crucial. From that point on, I felt different in myself as a writer.

But did it not disappoint you, even dent your confidence, to leave so many poems uncollected?

Not at all. The most important thing was sense of supply.

Did you personally decide what to include in the collection or did Charles Monteith – as the editor at Faber – exert influence? Would the fact of his Unionist background have inhibited you from including certain poems?

Charles never did interfere or exert that kind of influence or pressure. I would submit the manuscript and would then receive a very thorough and very supportive letter in response. And away it would go to the production department.

By the time Wintering Out *appeared, you had moved from Belfast to County Wicklow, whereas the book itself is deeply engaged with Ulster places and issues. Had you any hesitations about moving south? What clinched it for you?*

This story has been told before, but only because it's true. When we came back to Belfast from Berkeley, I had a different relation to the place. You can see a new devil-may-careness in those verse letters we were talking about earlier. The 'Whatever You Say Say Nothing' stuff. My confidence in my chances as a writer had firmed up – and I'm referring as much to chances of making a living as to the chance of writing decent poems. For the first time, I realized I had options – partly because of the open invitation I'd received from the department chairman at Berkeley to return some day, partly because of a feeling that the work being done was gaining purchase not just on myself but on the moment we were living through. I'd breathed and walked free in California, so when I got back I envied people here who'd managed to go it alone on the home ground.

At that stage, Marie and I began to think we should move out from the city. The autumn after we returned, we would take these long evening drives to look at 'for sale' signs along the roads in County Antrim, and go hunting around places we knew in Derry and Tyrone. At the same time, as I touched on earlier, we often went down to County Kilkenny to visit Barrie Cooke and Sonja Landweer, who were living then in Thomastown: artists, neither of them holding a job, making a self-sufficient life for themselves, fishing, gardening, painting, doing ceramics – they represented an ideal. So for a while we had a notion of moving to Kilkenny, since the area was full of arts-and-crafts people, musicians and so on, and seemed to offer a very conducive environment.

There was no element of fear or intimidation involved in your impulse to move?

None, even though Belfast in the early seventies was a pretty unpleasant place to be. But then, it had never been altogether beloved. It had been familiar, yes, but the Berkeley experience meant that I was seeing it – and the university – with new eyes. What Derek Mahon calls 'a perverse pride in being on the side / Of the fallen angels and refusing to get up' – that pride in the down-beat that eventually downgrades began to get to me.

I've heard stories of Ian Paisley's Protestant Telegraph *attacking you. Were there not threatening phone calls and all that?*

I did a TV programme – I believe in 1970 – called 'Heaney in Limboland' and it had footage of the B-Special Constabulary being passed out, but also of B-Specials at a firing range. As part of my voice-over commentary, I spoke one of those poems written in the poem-surge of 1969 that had a strong anti-B-Special animus. The evening the programme was shown there was a threatening phone call; it was actually taken by my mother-in-law and, for that rea-son, I suppose it was easier for me to play it down. Easy too because in those days threatening phone calls were all the rage, if you know what I mean. Any half-visible Catholic was liable to be rung up. The paragraph in Paisley's paper appeared after we had left Ashley Avenue and gone to Wicklow. It called me a well-known Papist propagandist and implied that I was corrupting the minds of the Ulster's Unionist youth and that I was a good riddance, having gone to my spiritual home in the Popish Republic. You could hardly quarrel with that.

You make light of it now, but at the time it must have given you pause?

But not much of a pause, truly. The motive for the move, as I've often said, was writerly. I knew I was at a turning point. And I was helped to make the turn by the encouragement of Barrie and Sonja, and also Ted Hughes. What clinched it finally was Ann Saddlemyer's offer of Glanmore Cottage early in 1972. Ann was in Toronto, but because of her research on Synge, she was back and forward to Ireland regu-larly. So when she heard that we were a bit footloose and looking for a place outside Belfast, she wrote to say that we could rent this gate lodge in Wicklow (and rent, I assure you, meant nominal rent). Down we went then, *en famille*, at Easter and loved the place, and when we came back I resigned my job.

You didn't agonize about the decision?

I was sleepwalking through those moves, and seemed to have a sleepwalker's remote control. Something in me had obviously been preparing for a change, and I was lucky that Marie was more than ready to go with the flow. In fact, she was very much in favour of leaving Belfast.

Arguments against the move must have been put forward by others?

Is it symptomatic that I can't remember any arguments being made against the move? There was a definite air of regret among people we knew, and Marie and I naturally shared it. But our sense of the timeliness and rightness of what we were doing was strong. I felt it was time to 'keep at a tangent'. In fact, the final section of 'Station Island', where that phrase occurs, repeats the injunctions I was obeying in 1972: 'You've listened long enough. Now strike your note.' 'When they make the circle wide, it's time to swim / out on your own'. I knew the apprenticeship was over. I had learned a lot in the ten years between November 1962, when I published my first poem in the *Belfast Telegraph*, and August 1972 when we hired a van and shifted a certain amount of our belongings to Glanmore.

I'd been blessed in the course of the decade with creative friend-ships, and the poems had been given a generous reception. But I still felt the required thing was to step away a bit. Only recently, for example, I discovered – in Heather Clark's *The Ulster Renaissance*, about those years – an extract from a verse letter to Jimmy Simmons: I was counting myself out of an 'Ulster poets' team that Bernard Miles was trying to assemble for a night at the Mermaid Theatre, diving for cover, really, withdrawing from the Ulster propa-ganda effort as much as anything else, uneasy about teaming up to bolster the good-news factor. There was a political reluctance in that particular stand-off, but the overall imperative was artistic. I said years ago that within our poetry collective we were writing almost out of a common mind, a too settled and circumscribed aes-thetic. Admittedly, it gave great energy and support, and continued to do so for the people who stayed on during the seventies and eighties. But for various reasons I needed a change.

Could your decision be seen as a sixties-influenced one – finding yourself, doing your own thing, rejecting 'the system'?

Maybe. All that was in the air. But rejecting the system? Not really. What system was I ever in favour of in Northern Ireland anyway?

At the time, sceptical consent was giving way among moderate nationalists to focused discontent. And unless I am greatly mistaken, there was even a sense in that pre-Bloody Sunday, pre-Bloody Friday period that the violence might be creative and a new order might emerge. We weren't going off in search of a different lifestyle. In fact, it was largely a case of more of the same, except that now there was no university job. I kept on doing schools radio scripts, doing reviews, doing readings, and in that first year the kids went to a convent school. It's not as if we had joined a commune . . .

Did you know you'd have sufficient freelance work before you took the plunge? Did Marie have plans to resume teaching?

Horace says: *vivitur parvo bene.* You can live well on a little. Our rent was a token rent and our outgoings were small. We did have a car, and we needed food and drink and heat and light; but, believe it or not, we had an appetite for the frugality. We'd both grown up in the country, so for us there was something rich and unstrange about bathing the kids by firelight, having them play around in the farmyard next door, giving them an experience of the dark country nights. It was more than nostalgic. It seemed right to supply them with memories of hedgebacks and hayfields and an open fire.

We had worries, right enough, about how the arrangement would work when they came to secondary school age; but, in the first years after we moved, the income from freelance radio and writing was fine, supplemented by occasional readings. Fees of around twenty-five pounds a time. One of those would pay the rent for a month. And you're right about the back-up I had from the start. David Hammond commissioned me to do a series for BBC Schools and then RTE gave me a weekly book-reviewing programme. I also inclined to do a bit more reviewing for print journals – Karl Miller was still at *The Listener.*

You worked during that first year in Glanmore on your translation of Buile Shuibhne, *the book that finally appeared a decade later as* Sweeney Astray. *Had you decided on that particular text before you left Belfast or was the choice a result of finding yourself 'astray' in the south?*

What got me interested in the Sweeney material were the short extracts that appear in Kenneth Hurlstone Jackson's *A Celtic*

Miscellany. Those prompted me to get my hands on the Early Irish Texts edition of the work, from which I got the idea that I should translate it in its entirety when I went to Glanmore.

I knew I'd still need a steady job, as it were, to ensure a sense of purpose in those first critical months, so I got stuck into it the minute we landed. But there was another motive, a very practical one, which had to do with a freelancer's forward planning: as well as book publication, I thought there could also be a radio dramatization and was encouraged in that direction when I spoke to the actor Jackie McGowran. I met Jackie around that time when he was recording Beckett material for Garech Browne at Claddagh Records. He said he would be interested in taking part in a recording of the Sweeney story when it was finished; sadly, Jackie had died before any of that could happen.

I'm wondering to what extent Thomas Kinsella's translation of The Táin *might have prompted your endeavour. You reviewed it in 1970 and saw it as 'clearly an effort to bring a literate Irish public into meaningful contact with its earliest literature; a conscious entry into the tradition of translators like Douglas Hyde and Lady Gregory'. Does that describe what you were doing with* Buile Shuibhne?

It wasn't in my head as a motto, but any translator of a big Irish-language work can't help but be aware of those predecessors. Kinsella's example was very important and I went so far as to report to him my intention of tackling Sweeney and got his encouragement – which felt as much like permission as encouragement, since he was and to a large extent remains the lord of the *ranns*.

Did you see much of Thomas Kinsella at that time?

Not a lot, and the visit I'm thinking of may even have pre-dated our move. But now and again Marie and I did call with himself and Eleanor in Percy Place and were thoroughly welcomed. It was Eleanor, indeed, who helped to get the boys into St Conleth's College when we left Glanmore for Dublin in 1976.

Were you making many new friends in literary Dublin then?

Not really. I felt at home with a group of people whom I'd known previously, writers and journalists and broadcasters associated with

RTE. When I went into the city, I'd often see John Horgan and Donal Foley in Bowes' public house on Fleet Street, opposite the *Irish Times*. Benedict Kiely, Máire de Paor, Seán MacRéamoinn, Dolly and Ciarán MacMahon. My entrée, if we can call it that, also came through people in the traditional music area. Garech Browne, for example, always had a lot of singers and players coming and going in his house in Luggala, which wasn't all that far from our place in Wicklow. And since Garech and his Claddagh Records company were then in full swing recording poets, you were as likely to meet Hugh MacDiarmid at his parties as Paddy Moloney. The one new poet friend I made in those days was Seán Ó Tuama, whom I got to know when I was appointed to the Arts Council in 1973. Seán and his wife Beití were in the first circle, as it were, from that time. Seán was somebody whom I could always talk to honestly and merrily and get honest and merry truths from in return. Sharp as a tack and full of knowledge. But he lived in Cork, so we didn't meet as often as either of us would have liked.

Did Seán Ó Tuama help with the Irish language in Buile Shuibhne?

He didn't. By the time I got to know him, I'd already come up with a first draft. And as I've explained elsewhere, my encounter first time round was more with the English on the right-hand page of O'Keeffe's edition than with the original on the left.

Was it a blow to your confidence when you found that your first version wasn't to your satisfaction and you put it away for years? Did you seek any second or third opinions to confirm your sense that it 'had become artistically broken-backed'?

I didn't seek second opinions and it would be wrong to say that my dissatisfaction with it constituted a blow to confidence. I always knew I'd come back to it. I was strengthened, if anything, just by having got through the job. Sixty pages in the drawer. What Beckett's *Molloy* would have called 'a little store'. That did me good.

Was there any carry-over from Sweeney Astray *into your own poetry?*

It was the other way round at first: the tentative quatrain that got developed in the writing of *Wintering Out* became a vehicle for most of the poems in the early version. But the pay-off for my own work came, a decade or so later, with a group of poems in *Station Island* called 'Sweeney Redivivus' where 'Sweeney' is rhymed with 'Heaney', autobiographically as well as phonetically.

Another name you played with in rhyme, I believe, as a game for children, was Conor Cruise O'Brien's. Did you see Conor and Máire when you came to Wicklow?

Mostly we'd meet the O'Briens in company with the Flanagans, since it was in Flanagan's house in Berkeley that we'd got to know them. Tom and Jean had spent the year 1971–2 in Dublin and I remember going down to see them there and attending a debate where Conor and Tomás Mac Ghiolla of Sinn Féin went head-on at each other over the Northern question. Conor had a very strong and salutary awareness of the position and disposition of Northern Protestants and refused to let people in the Republic forget that they had to be reckoned with in any future thinking about Irish unity. That was in the early seventies and it was his best contribution on the subject. It was forward looking and future seeking. But the more he identified himself with the 'no surrender' aspect of the Loyalist camp, the less sense he made.

Still, Conor and Máire will always be in my affections – not least because of the game you mention. It was on everybody's lips thirty and more years ago; and it was particularly good entertainment for youngsters on a long journey. You started with the appositional phrase, 'the well-known Irish travel agent, Conor Cruise O'Brien' and went on as long as you could with parallel inventions: the well-known Irish chimney sweep, Conor Flues O'Brien. The well-known Irish poet, Conor Muse O'Brien. And so on.

When I was in the Peacock Theatre, for the Dublin launch of Wintering Out, *I was struck by the presence there of some Labour Party politicians, Conor Cruise O'Brien and John Horgan among them. Maybe Kader Asmal of the anti-apartheid movement was there too. How did you get to know these people?*

I had met Conor first at a party given by Kader Asmal in 1967, when I was teaching in the Trinity College Summer School. Kader was a law professor at Trinity and a friend of Brendan Kennelly's, so it was probably through Brendan that I got into that particular swim. John Horgan was already by then a good friend and came up to Belfast regularly during the late sixties when he was working with the *Irish Times*. I wasn't a card-carrying member of the Labour Party, but I was at home in that company and would continue to do many readings over the years for the anti-apartheid movement.

Did you have any anxiety about the politics tainting the poetry?

No, although I was conscious that they involved what Conor Cruise once called 'a dangerous intersection'. But the roads I travelled landed me at that intersection and from there on I just took things as they came and tried to make the best of them.

6

'The bleb of the icicle'
North

~

In another interview you described North *as 'a very oblique and intense book' which had been 'fused at a very high pressure'. Looking back, do you think of your early years in Wicklow as the most intense phase of your writing life?*

Definitely. And not just of the writing life. We were at a turning point. Marie and I had moved from a semi-detached house in Belfast to a gate lodge in the country, from central heating to an open grate, from a university environment – and salary – to farmer neighbours and freelancing. We were exposed and ready in a new way; and the reality of the change was heightened that summer in 1972 when Marie got pregnant. So there was strong expectation in both of us: I remember feeling 'let joy be unconfined' that August when we drove down from Belfast with the first load of furniture and stuff for the cottage.

Later that afternoon, we went over to Garech Browne's house in Luggala. Garech wasn't at home but Paddy Moloney, the piper, was there, and so were two guests of Garech's, Mick and Bianca Jagger, just lazing around on their magic carpet. It was a heady moment but I still knew that a writer had to plough a different furrow from a performer. I might have stepped into a less-confined state, but I still had to deliver the goods. I'd got myself to a point where there were no alibis. That much was clear the first morning I took the children down to the school in Ashford and the headmaster wrote *'file'*, i.e. poet, in the column of the rollbook where he had to enter 'Occupation of Parent'. No more of your 'lecturer' or 'teacher'.

Does it surprise you that, rather than responding to the new life unfolding around you, you ventured so deeply into mythic terrain in North?

A line was crossed with 'The Tollund Man'. The minute I wrote 'Some day I will go to Aarhus' I was in a new field of force. It had to do with the aura surrounding that head – even in a photograph. It was uncanny, in the full technical sense. Opening P. V. Glob's book *The Bog People* was like opening a gate, the same as when I wrote 'Bogland'.

When you published 'Nerthus' and 'The Tollund Man' in Wintering Out, *you knew you weren't finished with Glob's book?*

There was a hiatus. I was treading earth, if you like. The archaeological drift I'd got into – via poems like 'Tollund Man' and 'Toome' – didn't just stop when I handed in the manuscript of *Wintering Out*. That summer of 1972, the month before we moved, well before the book came out in November, we did a lot of driving in the south-west of England, saw the white horses carved into the hills, visited Maiden Castle in Dorset and the old earthworks in Dorchester. When we were in Gloucestershire, staying in this lovely Tudor manor house where Marie's sister was then living, I wrote 'Bone Dreams' – the first of those loose-link, zigzaggy sequences that would eventually appear in *North*. I think 'Viking Dublin' was the next and then 'Kinship'.

The immediate stimulus was a deadline: I was supposed to deliver a prose piece on the work of Barrie Cooke for a new magazine – *Arts in Ireland* – and I was stuck. But Barrie at that time was doing a series of 'bone boxes'; thinking about them brought up memories of bones I used to find in the fields around Mossbawn, so next thing a frolic of free association got started and ended up taking in the whole of Romano-Celtic Britain, from Maiden Castle to Hadrian's Wall. The chalkiness of bone, the chalk downs, the amorousness and adventure of that summer are behind those particular 'dreams'.

But what brought you back to P. V. Glob? What, for that matter, drew you to his book in the first place?

It was, as Edward Thomas says, 'The name, only the name'. *The Bog People*. I bought it as a Christmas present for myself in 1969, the year it was published, but the minute I opened it and saw the photographs, and read the text, I knew there was going to be yield from it. I mean, even if there had been no Northern Troubles, no man-killing in the parishes, I would still have felt at home with that 'peat-brown head' – an utterly familiar countryman's face. I didn't really 'go back' to the book because it never left me. And still hasn't.

Did you ever consider a book-length sequence based on The Bog People?

No. Maybe if I'd bided my time and written more poems it would have been a possibility. Come to think of it, a limited edition, actually called *Bog Poems*, was published by Rainbow Press in the same month as *North* itself. But it didn't include 'Tollund Man' or 'Nerthus'.

Did you feel any pressure to take possession of the material before other poets began to draw on it?

No pressure, no, although there was indeed general awareness of the invitations of the material. But no big bog-rush ever occurred. Bogs anyhow are places where people work together. Richard Ryan, for example, was doing his Danish 'bog-fruit' poems around that same period. Louis Simpson also wrote a little Tollund tune that began, 'He was one of the consorts of the moon, / and went with the goddess in a cart'.

Can you remember the circumstances of writing any of the bog poems – did you write them with the photographs from the Glob book spread open in front of you?

There were a few of them – 'Bog Queen' and 'Punishment', in particular – where the information and speculation in the text were vital elements. There's no photo of the 'bog queen', only a quotation about a body being found on Lord Moira's estate in the late eighteenth century. I have an especially happy memory of writing 'Bog Queen' because it was the first time in my life, believe it or not, that I'd spent a whole uninterrupted workday on a poem. Before we moved to Wicklow, you know, my time wasn't particularly my own: there was always the Queen's job, or the school, or the training college, or grading papers, or having to go to see parents at the weekend, or whatever. But in Glanmore that day I learned to shift the emphasis, found myself free to regard poem work as the day job. It was a weekday in what I still thought of as term time; but I started in the morning and kept at it until after dark. 'The Tollund Man', on the other hand, was written a couple or three years before that, as I mentioned, when we'd gone to Kerry for an Easter break. It was done late at night when the kids were in bed.

Were poems like 'The Grauballe Man' and 'Punishment' difficult to write?

'The Grauballe Man' was done quickly. I had these notes scribbled on stray bits of paper that had been in my pockets in Aarhus, and one day I suddenly rallied them into a poem. But 'Punishment' was a much slower business.

Was the difficulty with 'Punishment' political more than literary?

That's not how I would put it, because that makes it sound as if I were 'addressing the situation in Northern Ireland'. Admittedly I 'addressed the situation' when I introduced different bog poems at readings and so on, although I now realize that it would have been better for the poems and for me and for everybody else if I had left them without that sort of commentary. What Anna Swir would have called the poems' 'biological right to life' was the point and remains the point and I never had the slightest doubt about them in that regard. The difficulty in getting 'Punishment' finished was expressive, as much a matter of sound and syntax as a matter of self-examination, as much to do with shaping the thing as telling about me. It involved discovering how to be true to my ear and true to the elements I was working with. How to take a stand between the tar-black face of the peat-bog girl and the tarred and feathered women in the news reports.

When you wrote the final lines of 'Punishment' and made reference in 'Kinship' to 'how we slaughter / for the common good', were you not proceeding more carefully, more cautiously than usual – to avoid being misunderstood and to avoid seeming to propagandize?

Is it too sophisticated to suggest that there's a difference between being alert to the situation and addressing it or addressing the reader about it? You're right to say I was proceeding carefully and cautiously, minding my mouth but minding it, I hope, for the right reasons.

Outside of Ulster, the reviews of North *were very enthusiastic, with critics as varied as Conor Cruise O'Brien, Michael Hartnett, Richard Murphy and Christopher Ricks all voicing their approval. Given that – as you put it in an interview – you expected* North *to be 'hammered', this must have been a pleasantly surprising reaction. Why did you feel the book would be negatively reviewed? Editors of journals and audiences weren't hostile to the poems, were they?*

No, but your instincts about the reception of a book tend to ignore that sort of evidence. When I spoke of the 'hammering' business, I wasn't thinking so much of so-called political reactions as of responses that the artistic doubleness of the thing might have provoked: a first section that has poems full of linguistic burr and clinker, and a second section full of more discursive, at times unbuttoned, things such as 'Whatever You Say Say Nothing'. I was very conscious of that double aspect of the collection. But I think I went on to say in that same interview that, whatever expectation I had with regard to the book's reception, I still felt safe. I had confidence in it – they could hammer to their hearts' content and the thing would hold.

The one place where North *did receive a 'hammering' was in your native province. Do you think the hostility of Ulster poets and critics towards* North, *in reviews and anthologies, was influenced by the fact that you had left Ulster?*

That's a question that would be better answered by them. I've said before that one of the reasons I had for moving was a need to get away from the consensus culture that had built up among us. The poetry crowd in Belfast in the sixties was very close knit and, for all the differences of temperament and taste, there was something like a party line on many things. At any rate, a party line was obviously developed on *North*. And there was one developing on me too, no doubt, the poetic equivalent of the *cordon sanitaire*. To be fair, what I had done by going to Glanmore was create a stand-off. I'd left the party and that complicates things for everybody, for the one who goes as well as for the ones who stay. You get my side of that in the last poem of the book, 'Exposure'.

Ciaran Carson's review in the Honest Ulsterman *was largely negative, although I imagine you might have found the tone more wounding than the content. And Edna Longley made her reservations known in the same* Honest Ulsterman *issue. Even the special Heaney issue of* Quarto, *the New University of Ulster magazine for which you provided worksheets from* North, *was partly negative.*

You know, there's this story, apocryphal maybe, but even so – about Auden getting an unexpectedly wounding review from an old admirer, Randall Jarrell. It was a bit of a *cause célèbre* at the time and some brave gossip asked Auden what he felt about it. 'Oh,' says Wystan, 'I think Jarrell must be in love with me.' But seriously . . . There was a kind of bitter drive to a lot of that stuff that you couldn't not be taken aback by, but it never made me doubt the book. And if I might just mention two other names: John Jordan and Helen Vendler. Jordan wasn't altogether a fan of mine but he wrote stirringly in praise of the volume in the *Irish Independent* and Helen's delight in the bog poems was palpable from the start. It wasn't as if I was assailed from all sides.

Your confidence wasn't rattled?

I don't want to imply that I was indifferent because I couldn't be: people I'd been close to in different degrees were serving notice that the terms of the relationship had changed. But to say my confidence was rattled would be a drastic overstatement. Let's just say a separation was achieved; from then on, I would be definitely and riskily on my own. The whole attitude derived from a submerged consensus, a feeling that I'd already got more than my due and therefore I had it coming to me. Edna Longley's 'Cliquey Clerihew' was a merry straw in that particular wind: 'Michael Longley / Is inclined to feel strongly / About being less famous / Than Seamus'.

In general, how do you react to negative criticism? Has your attitude to it changed over time?

Necessarily, yes, it has changed. I've been overwritten with praise and to a lesser extent with blame. I've had time to soak up the advantage of the former, and I've learned to inspect the latter to see if it's salutary objection or shitty backlash. But with regard to the negative stuff, there are times when it's a case of 'the redress of criticism', when you're being given penalties because the critic thinks you've had too much praise, and more and more there are occasions when the main purpose of it is to draw attention to the commentator or the columnist rather than to the work in question. Ted Hughes used to say, completely unfazed, 'The beginning of celebration is the beginning of execration.' And I've already quoted Pound's instruction to the neophyte – one of my favourites: pay no attention to the criticism of those who have not themselves 'produced notable work'.

On the topic of 'salutary objection', can you think of any instance where a negative or critical comment in a review has definitely proved helpful?

There was a prod in an anonymous *TLS* review of *Door into the Dark* that hit the spot and probably affected me for the better. The review was totally irreverent and said that I should loosen up, that there should be more wit, more lines like the ones in 'Bogland' about the skeleton of the Irish elk being 'an astounding crate / full of air'. I was delighted to find out years later that it had been written by Clive James.

Is it possible that the direction taken by your poetry immediately after North *– your deviation from the archaeological and mythological path – was influenced to some extent by negative criticism?*

A new direction is being followed already in *North*, in poems like 'Hercules and Antaeus' and 'Exposure'. The Hercules poem, for all its mythy content, is more like what Miłosz would call 'plain speech in the mother tongue'. And before *North* appeared, I was already writing the first of those 'Glanmore Sonnets' that would only come out five years later. I had started them in May or June 1974, a year before I saw any review of *North*. I'm sure about the date because in May 1974 I went to Grasmere to spend three or four days getting to know Wordsworth's Dove Cottage and the surrounding district for a TV programme; it was immediately afterwards that the first sonnet was written – the one beginning 'This evening the cuckoo and the corncrake . . .' I remember wondering, what the hell is all this iambic pentameter doing in my life? There's even a line mocking the too literary nature of the reality of

Wicklow that evening – cuckoos and corncrakes, you know, in the merry month of May: 'It was all crepuscular and iambic'.

You've mentioned visits to Maiden Castle and the Dorchester earthworks as among the inspirations for 'Bone Dreams'. How much of North *as a whole derived from actual tours of archaeological sites or exhibits?*

Quite a bit. There's a poem near the start of the book about visiting Belderg in County Mayo, the place that's known these days as Céide Fields. There's an interpretive centre there now, but when we were guided round by the archaeologist Seamus Caulfield in 1972, there was only bare heather bog. The actual visit to the Tollund Man – in Silkeborg, incidentally, rather than Aarhus – took place after the poem was written, but on that same visit in 1973 I saw the Grauballe Man in the museum at Aarhus. Then there was the Viking Dublin exhibit in the National Museum, based on the dig being done by Breandán Ó Ríordáin at the Wood Quay site.

At that same time, there was a campaign against plans to build Dublin's new civic offices on the site of Viking Dublin, culminating in the 1978 march on Wood Quay. Were you involved in any of that?

No, but I was very aware of it through people like Tom Delaney, a brilliant Dublin archaeologist who worked in the Ulster Museum. We'd become friends of Tom and his wife Máire before we moved to Wicklow. And Breandán Ó Ríordáin we would meet occasionally at the home of other friends, Bill and Diane Meek.

Thomas Kinsella was prominently involved in the Wood Quay protests. When did you first meet Kinsella – through the O'Malleys of the Lyric Theatre, perhaps?

A little earlier. Around, I'd say, 1963, when he did a reading of his poems for the English Society in Queen's. I remember he read from 'Old Harry' and 'Downstream' and made some typically sardonic remark about the latter, to the effect that it was good to have a couple of hundred lines of *terza rima* under your belt. I met him again briefly a year or two later, at the opening of the Lyric Theatre in Belfast and at the opening of Yeats's Tower in Ballylee. A great day that was: Padraic Colum in his eighties, trying to manage his script and the microphone, and the wind getting the better of all of them.

Were you surprised when Kinsella abandoned that early formal style which he had 'under his belt' for a freer, more Poundian one?

More enlivened, I'd say, than surprised. As a matter of fact, on the first books programme I presented on RTE radio – the series called *Imprint*, that began just before Christmas 1972 – I reviewed *Notes from the Land of the Dead*, the first of his Poundian books. I'd published one of the poems earlier when I guest-edited an issue of *Threshold*, but the impact of that Dolmen collection was powerful. I think I picked out 'Hen Woman' at the time, and maybe 'Ancestor'. I wasn't sure what to make of all the poems, but I was sure he was into a big mysterious stride.

How did you feel, poetically and politically, about 'Butcher's Dozen', Kinsella's scornful satire in response to the Widgery Tribunal on Bloody Sunday?

I had mixed feelings. The anger was salutary and justified, and the hurl of rage in the couplets never lets up. I admired, or better say I envied, that. It was blazing with hatred for the imperial cast of mind and that again was exhilarating, not just because of the cover-up by Widgery but primarily because of the shootings by the paratroopers. And yet, and yet – there were furious characterizations of the Unionist, Protestant collective in the North that seemed too stereotypical, a tilt towards the kind of bigotry the poem was scarifying. I found myself elated by the attack on the hypocrisy of the Widgery report and uneasy about the caricature of the Protestants. At the time, some of my best friends etc. . . . .

Soon after 'Butcher's Dozen' appeared in 1972, I remember John Montague and Tom Kinsella and myself assembled for a reading in a club in Clonard, up the Falls Road. John read 'A New Siege', his poem about the confrontations in Derry in 1969 that led to the establishment of the 'Free Derry' zone in the Bogside, and I read God knows what, but Tom certainly read from 'Butcher's Dozen'. No doubt Kinsella was right to scorn the criticism that his poem was 'unhelpful', true as the criticism may have been in some quarters. But it was more than unhelpful: there was danger in it, like a lick of flame.

I wonder if Kinsella's remark that the idea of a 'Northern Ireland Renaissance' in poetry was 'largely a journalistic entity' affected your relations at a personal level?

I don't think so. For one thing, we didn't see all that much of the Kinsellas, although they welcomed us when we first moved south and later on when we moved into Dublin in 1976. There was never any great closeness, more a kind of springy, cheery bluffness whenever we happened to meet – which meant that I was gratified indeed when Tom included a few of my poems and Derek Mahon's in his *Oxford Book of Irish Verse* . . . I always took his downgrading of the 'Ulster Renaissance' to be in part a payback for Edna Longley's attack on his early work, although that may be too petty an explanation. In fact, it should be said that nobody was more aware than the Northern poets themselves of any glamour the media were conferring on them. Their scepticism about their own importance in the scheme of things was always in good order.

As well as reading with Thomas Kinsella and John Montague at Clonard, you shared a platform with Montague in July 1973 for a public performance of his 'poem-cycle' The Rough Field. *Did you enjoy the experience of reading publicly from another poet's work?*

Very much. John clearly wanted the event to have a definite Northern flaunt to it. The first performance was in London, in the Roundhouse, with Beckett's friend the actor Patrick Magee as the star. And the support group included Ben Kiely, Tom McGurk and myself. Plus the Chieftains for music. It made a bit of a stir and was meant to. I think John saw himself and the rest of us as reincarnations of Shane O'Neill and the gallowglasses that he writes about in the poem, Gaels from Tyrone parading into the realms of the Sassenach. There's a roguish element in Montague that was playing itself for all it was worth in that production. And he kept harrying me with remarks to the effect that 1972 would be remembered as the year of *The Rough Field*, meaning that *Wintering Out* would simply drop from view.

Was a certain delicacy needed in dealing with an older poet like Montague who had already been writing about rural Ulster themes?

I had no awareness of such a problem when I began. At that stage, you think of all published poets as fixed stars, entities that have been translated beyond you, out there in a firmament of their own. It's the writings that concern you, you don't really think about the person except as the *fons et origo*. Some Montague poems were important to me from the start – 'The Water Carrier', for example, which I first read in the *Kilkenny Magazine*, and 'Like Dolmens Round My Childhood the Old People'. I also had bought his first book, *Poisoned Lands*, but the poetics of that work, I felt – and still feel – tended away from the kind of poetry I was tending towards. My words wanted to bed down and merge but John's were more in the business of stalking round and watching, like the light in his *ars poetica* poem, 'A Bright Day': 'The only way of saying something / Luminously as possible. / Not the accumulated richness / Of an old historical language – / That musk-deep odour!' When I started out, I was very much one of the musk-deep school, a rift loader rather than a window cleaner letting in the bright day. John and I certainly had many of the same childhood experiences but when it came to making them over into poetry, Ted Hughes's example was the vital one for me.

Still, his ragging you about Wintering Out *suggests that the perceived overlap had become an issue.*

It had, and it had to be handled lightly. Not, mind you, that it always was. During the years when I was writing *Wintering Out* and *North*, John came back from Paris and got set up in Cork. There was camaraderie and correspondence between us, a sense of the importance of the historical moment and a sense of answerability to it. That feeling of a shared Ulster destiny is just a given for us. What wasn't reckoned with was what you might call the ratings battle, Robert Lowell boosting me after *North* as 'the best Irish poet since W. B. Yeats', that kind of thing. That rankled all round, and probably, come to think of it, helped to sharpen the quills of the honest Ulstermen. At the time, I didn't take aboard just how badly Lowell had rocked the boat. But then, as Brian Friel used to say, everything's a test. And luckily also, everything flows.

To what extent has there been a tacit agreement between you and the other Ulster poets about respecting each other's artistic space?

Are there topics that are out of bounds for one poet because they are assumed to fall within the accepted ambit of another?

Well, not since Paul Muldoon started his texting and intertexting . . . By the late sixties, this was already something of a joke topic among us. There was one poem I wrote, for example, about a particularly sorrowful incident when a postman delivering Christmas mail around the islands of Lough Erne got trapped in the ice and froze to death. The poem was published in *The Listener* but never made it into a collection. Still, Michael Foley made hay with it in the *Honest Ulsterman*, complaining about trespass, affirming Frank Ormsby's territorial rights on Lough Erne and in County Fermanagh generally, since Frank had been born in Enniskillen. But, on the whole, we allowed each other rights of way, whether we went off on holidays to the Aran Islands or stayed about home. In latter years, everybody started ploughing up the common ground of the old school classics, Longley with his Homer, me with my Virgil, all of us with our Greek tragedies in translation. I might have huffed if somebody had got to Lough Derg ahead of me and staked a claim on Station Island; but, broadly speaking, there was plenty of come and go.

We'll sail towards Station Island *eventually, but for the moment I'd like to return to County Wicklow. I assume that most of the poems in* North *were written in Glanmore. Did you set aside part of the day for poetry and another part for freelance work?*

I started out resolutely, with regular morning sessions at work on the Sweeney translation. The early weeks were probably the most organized in that respect because, once Michael and Christopher were brought to school, the day was mine until they had to be collected. But soon the reviews were lining up and the BBC Schools scripts and the regular RTE radio broadcasts had to be prepared and delivered in the studio in Dublin, so before long that neatly timetabled day was gone and I was back where I'd always been and always will be: in a haphazard pattern of work and worry, fits and starts of highs and lows.

But did the extra time at your disposal not lead to changes in your approach to the writing itself?

It did, insofar as I was now far more conscious of myself being called upon to produce. Also, since the safety net of a job and a salary had been removed, I was readier to contemplate spin-off work: I always had the idea, for example, that the Sweeney translation could earn my keep in three or four different ways – as a book, of course, but also as a radio drama of some sort and maybe in a children's version, as an illustrated book for younger readers. Then too, I have to admit, when I stood up at poetry readings I was more conscious of standing up *for* poetry and for myself. Something bolder entered in.

Was all of your reading directed towards articles, lectures and broadcasts, or were you able to extend your range of interests and read more widely than you'd been doing?

In the main, it was directed towards those activities – which doesn't mean that it wasn't thereby extended. I did have plans to do a lot of more systematic, self-improving reading but they got pushed to the side. Even so, I got to grips with the Icelandic sagas and some general reading about the archaeology and mythology of Baltic Europe, as they called it. And before long I was plunged in Yeats's prose.

Despite young children running about, were you able to find a place to work in your small house?

The cottage had a sitting room upstairs and that's where I ensconced myself. There was a low tongue-and-groove ceiling, 'all hutch and hatch'. It was both a chain-smoker's den and a hermit's hut. But once you went downstairs, there was no escaping the cubs in the lair, so to speak. The best statement about that was Robert Lowell's understatement when he called with us en route from the Kilkenny Arts Week in 1975: 'You see a lot of your children.' He got it in one.

Your daughter Catherine Ann was born in 1973. Your poem 'A Pillowed Head' suggests that it was a somewhat different experience from the earlier two births.

It was. Marie and I had been parents for nearly seven years at that stage and we were that much more aware of the enormous meaning of a birth. And, since we already had two boys, we were hoping for a girl; so when a girl *did* come it was a special joy. The poem describes the circumstances – Marie felt the pangs early in the morning, an April morning, so we set off for the hospital just after dawn, when the country was quiet and there were pheasants down under trees all along the road. We both knew we'd never forget it . . . And the experience was different also because this time I went into the labour ward. I was there when the 'little slapped palpable girl' appeared.

At around this time, you published a sequence of four sonnets which must have been written about the birth.

'A New Life', yes, published in *The Listener*. The first sonnet was about feeling the baby moving in the womb. I was remembering my hand on Marie's pregnant stomach. But those four sonnets were actually a development from an earlier unpublished poem. In it, my hand was on the woman's shoulder and I said something to the effect that I had abandoned history for geology and that I was now like a climber on a mountainside, feeling out the terrain, and so on. Then it struck me – in a kind of Audenesque second thought – this just wasn't true, that abandoning history was a luxury that the times had disallowed: this was less than a year after Bloody Sunday and we were living through some pretty ferocious historical consequences, including the IRA's Bloody Friday.

Anyhow, my early meetings with Marie in her home in Tyrone and memories of our drives along the lough shore and our lovers' tiffs and so on, all got turned into an allegory involving the Elizabethan armies entering Gaelic Ulster and the ground being possessed by the planters – the whole *aisling* scenario – England being the male conqueror, Ireland the ruined maid and wee 'no surrender' Ulster the product of the union. Or Act of Union. Even so, in *The Listener* version, the thing ends with a sweet and hopeful cadence where the man/England envisages a time of restored order between woman/Ireland and himself and the 'new life', 'His hand in mine, us two hand in glove, / The triangle of forces solved in love'. Very nice as a concluding couplet, but much too pat to fit the reality. So that version was also eventually revised and became 'Act of Union', as it appears in *North*, the one that ends with 'the big pain / That leaves you raw, like opened ground, again'. A sterner, less plangent bit of work.

*More partition than parturition in that version, it seems. Some
critics have seen it as too macho.*

But the 'speaker in the poem', whoever he is, is deeply aware of his
implication in being 'imperially male'. He lies like the island of
Britain beside an expectant mother island who has her back turned
to him. He's experiencing a certain guilt at having caused the preg-
nancy and put the woman in the way of 'the big pain'. I seem to
remember that phrase being used almost as a technical term, cer-
tainly as colloquial shorthand, between women talking about the
different stages of a birth. I *did* appropriate the term, but at a time
when I was more preoccupied with the labour ward than the grad-
uate seminar.

*Has the representation of England as aggressive male and of
Ireland as passive or put-upon female run its course as a metaphor?*

It has a long Irish history, from the *aisling* to Yeats's Cathleen, the
daughter of Houlihan, but it's one that I wouldn't employ head-on
any more, the way I did in 'Ocean's Love to Ireland'. The trope has
been fully and fashionably deconstructed, but thirty years on, the
state of affairs pertaining between men and women has also shifted,
and so has the balance of power between England and Ireland.

The *aisling* understanding of history, let's face it, was based on the
facts of invasion, expropriation and defeat of the Gaelic order, so it
became part of the cultural nationalist mindset and continued to have
a more than subliminal appeal for Northern nationalists – we could
still romanticize ourselves as the ones in thrall to the foreigner, look-
ing forward to a moment of deliverance into some true, 'unoccupied'
condition. But the age of Blair and Brown is very different from the
age of Brookeborough. Catholics, men and women, were more than
metaphorically put upon when you had the likes of Brookeborough
telling his supporters not to employ Catholics. There has been
change, in other words, in the world that produced me, and change
has also been effected in me by what I've lived through in the
Republic and in America; and poetry is bound to manifest the reality
of change. For better or worse, it's a case of *quod scripsi, scripsi*.

*North opens with one of your best-loved poems, 'Mossbawn,
Sunlight', a tribute to your aunt Mary. Was she at ease with the
idea of your having become a poet?*

I'm not sure she ever entirely took it aboard. There was something in our relationship, whatever it was, that stood still. By which I don't mean that the relationship was immature or inconsiderable. For years she was crippled with arthritis and eventually had to have her bed brought downstairs into what had been our sitting room: before that, my brothers would carry her upstairs in her chair every night, but one by one they got married and left the house, so that arrangement just wasn't possible any longer.

My memories of those years in the 1970s, before she had to go into special care in the Mid-Ulster Hospital, are of arriving with Marie and the kids from Wicklow and greeting first of all my mother and father and sister Ann in the living room, then going in to sit with Mary. Not a lot getting said or needing to be said. Just a deep, unpathetic stillness and wordlessness. A mixture of *lacrimae rerum* and *Deo gratias*. Something in me reverted to the child I'd been in Mossbawn. Something in her just remained constant, like the past gazing at you calmly, without blame. She was a tower of emotional strength, unreflective in a way but undeceived about people or things. I suppose all I'm saying is that I loved her dearly.

You mentioned earlier that you began work on 'Mossbawn, Sunlight' in California. Can you remember how it evolved? Did you sense from the start that it was one of your best?

'Evolved' is a strong word for it. The first trace was a few lines trying to describe a straggle of fodder across our yard after a snowfall. When the hay was being carried in for the cows, there'd be a little trail of it left between the stack and the byre door. Mary used to milk the cows in that byre and, in my mind, she was the familiar spirit of the hay and the yard. Eventually that 'straggle of fodder / stiffened on snow' ended up in the 'Servant Boy' poem, and Mary would pass from the frost into the sunlight, from the yard to the kitchen. I can even remember the first time I read 'Mossbawn, Sunlight' in public, which must mean that I had a special feeling for it from the start. It was at a school concert in Orangefield School in Belfast, in honour of the headmaster, John Malone, and once again David Hammond and Michael Longley were sharing the programme.

Can you tell me more about the bread-baking which the poem describes?

It was as much a rite as a job, certain utensils being brought out, certain vessels being called for, certain ingredients being prepared, the stove stoked, the griddle heated. There was first the bakeboard, a special type of big clean wooden tray, and the roller pin – although I also remember a heavy glass bottle being used as a roller; there would be flour in a bowl, maybe also a bag of oatmeal, there would be baking soda and a jug of buttermilk. Next came the mixing of the dough and the patting of it into scone shapes, the dusting of the hot griddle with flour, the dusting of the pre-formed scones, the attending to the heat as the baking proceeded on the stove top, then the turning of the scones, the cooling of them on a little wire rack, even perhaps the cutting open and buttering and tasting of a fresh one as soon as it had cooled a bit . . .

Mary had white hair and a fair rosy face; she stood still and straight while her hands did all the work at the bakeboard and the kitchen filled with the fragrance of the baking bread. Sometimes too there was currant bread done in a baking tin in the oven, sometimes a cake, although mostly the cakes came from my McCann aunts, who had more of a gift – or maybe more of a taste – for 'sweet bread'.

Was there any tension between your mother and Mary – over boundary lines in the kitchen, say, or in competing for your father's or the children's affections?

Not that I was aware of. With the exception of the bread-baking, Mary was, as I say, the familiar of the yard. She did a bit of gardening too, put in sweet peas, brought in the cows, fed the hens, and so on. My mother tended to do the washing, the dishes, the cooking, the darning, the shopping. Each of them was a strong woman and, small as the space was, physically and emotionally, each made room for the other. But I wouldn't say there was any vying for my father's affection. In that culture, vying for it would have been a sure way of losing it . . . It was when they both got older and Mary was invalided that they were put to the test. And they both passed. Basically, they were givers rather than takers. In the early days, my mother tended to be overwhelmed with child-bearing and the unremitting business of child rearing. So you could think of Mary in those years as the necessary home help, the nanny, if you like – freer and indeed fitter than my mother. Later on, Mary was the invalid and my mother the nurse, even the matron.

As a 'great favourite' of your aunt, as you put it earlier, would you not have been suspected of disloyalty by your mother? You don't think that was a source of confusion or guilt for you?

The 'favourite' thing operated mostly when I was quite small. Like all first children and first grandchildren, I was something of a display item – and a focus for other aunts as well. No doubt Mary got the job of looking after me at a very early stage, my mother being so regularly pregnant, year after year for the best part of a decade. By the time I was going to St Columb's, however, I was closer to my mother. Mary was a simpler soul, in the sense of being less complicated – less experienced also, for that matter, being single and unreflective, an ancient rather than a modern. But let's face it, she was a kindness dispenser to every one of us.

An 'ancient'?

I'm thinking of Thomas Hardy's use of the word to mean an older country person formed within older, more reticent, more stoical rules and codes. There were many others like her when I was growing up, a neighbour called Annie Devlin, for example, who figures in a poem called 'A Drink of Water' – old vestals living beside an open hearth, with a dog that barked at you from behind the gate.

How old was your aunt Mary when she died?

In her late seventies.

And would you say she'd had a happy life?

For much of her adulthood, she was surrounded by the unconditional love of children and she gave it back without stint. She had a hard early life and a secure old age and both showed in her gaze. In the end, she could have sat for Rembrandt.

'Mossbawn, Sunlight' has more than once been compared to a Dutch interior, a Vermeer say. Were you deliberately seeking a painterly effect?

Not deliberately.

I ask because the companion poem, 'The Seed Cutters', makes a specific reference to Breughel. Do you feel a certain identification with him?

I always felt at home with his scenes – the hayfield, the peasant wedding, the hunters in the snow, children's games. Things looming large and at the same time being pinned down in the smallest detail. Birds on a winter tree. The stitching on a codpiece.

I'd like to now talk about somebody else you identified with in the 1970s: Osip Mandelstam. Were you already an admirer when you reviewed his work in 1974, or did you discover him when Hibernia *sent you that* Selected Poems *translated by Clarence Brown and W. S. Merwin?*

Karl Miller spoke to me about Nadezhda Mandelstam's *Hope against Hope* not so long after it was published and I have a hardback edition of it bought around 1973 or 1974. But it had to be the reviewing that focused my attention. Clarence Brown's biography came out at the same time as the *Selected Poems*, so you got text and context all at once. The agony and the Acmeists.

Which spoke to you first, Mandelstam's poetry or his life?

The poetry. A few utterly memorable poems, in the Merwin versions. Some from his first book, *Stone*, some from the late Voronezh notebooks. Early ones like 'Orioles in the woods . . .', or the one about Homer and sleeplessness, later ones like 'Black Earth' or the quatrain about 'quiet labour' silvering the ploughshare and the poet's song. Naturally, I wasn't just responding to Mandelstam but to something beguiling in Merwin's English and, in the review, I acknowledged as much. I remember Joseph Brodsky scolding about Merwin's free treatment of the poems – free in the sense of free verse, but also in the sense that some deviation from the literal sense had been allowed; and when I eventually read Bob Tracy's metrical translation of the whole of *Stone* and had the benefit of Tracy's notes and introduction, I could see what Joseph meant. What I got from Bob's book was an awareness of how important the architectural principle was for Mandelstam, not just in those poems about Notre Dame and the Admiralty building in St Petersburg, but in his whole aesthetic.

His prose seems to have impressed you no less than his poetry: his 'Conversation about Dante', for example, and his essays.

There was certainly a liberation in the prose. It was metaphorical, impressionistic, exultant even. Without realizing it, I'd been under the sway of T. S. Eliot and his repressive attitude towards 'appreciation' and 'impressionistic' criticism, but Mandelstam changed that. His comparison of the mind in the act of composition to a fugitive escaping across a river jammed with Chinese junks. That gave me permission, as they say, to do a bit of exulting on my own. Or his comparison of the word to a bundle with meaning sticking out of it in all directions. And some of his more enigmatic statements stuck in my mind because of an element of contrariness in them – a sentence like 'If I believe in the shadow of the oak and the steadfastness of speech articulation, how can I ever appreciate the present age?'

Would it be fair to link your admiration for that kind of contrariness to the exasperation you expressed in the 1974 review, when you spoke of commentators whose 'quest for poetry as a diagram of political attitudes' has 'all the fussy literalism of an official from the Ministry of Truth'?

That had to be prompted by Mandelstam's insouciance, definitely. Not that he was always insouciant or in possession of his 'inner freedom' and 'feeling of being right'. He called himself 'a sick son of the age', and in the late 1920s he was half in compliance with the new Soviet order; then towards the end he had a go at reinstating himself by writing an ode to Stalin. Which, to his credit, he couldn't bring off. What I found compelling was the conflict between his bent as a lyric writer nurtured on a pre-revolutionary, non-utilitarian aesthetic, and his discovery of himself in a Soviet world where there were indeed officials from the Ministry interrogating him in the Lubianka, asking him to give a political account of himself and his art. It was nightmarish for him and Nadezhda. I was entirely conscious of the inflation involved in thinking of Mandelstam's predicaments in relation to my own; but, insofar as I was being asked what bogs had to do with Bogside, there was a correspondence. He appears in 'Exposure', for example, which was being written at the end of 1973, as a David of poetry facing the Goliath of power.

So he was a role model during those early years of the Troubles?

More like a shadow presence. A reminder that the anchor of poetry had to be lifted off the bottom of the ear and should drag a certain amount of your inwardness up along with it. That it had to have phonetic purchase. That a politically correct purpose was neither here nor there when it came to saving your poetic soul.

Explaining your position on Horace's dulce et utile, *you once expressed the view that 'poetry just being useful is a bigger sin than just being pleasurable'. Do you still think that way?*

I do. Except that I'd want to tone down the either/or aspect of the antithesis. The 'usefulness' inheres in its 'pleasurableness' and vice versa. What 'use' is Yeats's 'Long-Legged Fly' unless you have an ear and a body and a mind that can take pleasure in the ratcheting and ranginess of the lines and the rhymes and the allusions?

Still on the topic of usefulness, were your views ever sought by the politicians you have known over the years? Would you have proffered advice to John Hume or Austin Currie, for example?

We would have talked about what was going on but there was never any sense of advice being sought or being given. They didn't need it anyhow and I didn't see them all that often. There was, however, one encounter that's probably worth mentioning. Just after we moved to Ashford, we discovered that Austin and Anita Currie were staying in a hotel nearby, under different names. It was immediately after their house had been attacked and Anita had suffered a mauling by a crowd of Loyalist louts, so they'd come south for a holiday. At any rate, we had a great reunion when they arrived with us in the cottage; but, even then, the talk would have been more about people than policy. We all operated from the same more or less 'constitutional nationalist' position.

I remember seeing some of the most prominent SDLP politicians, John Hume included, in the Abbey Theatre audience of Brian Friel's Volunteers *in 1975. Do you think they perceived writers like you and Friel (especially after his play* The Freedom of the City) *as significant allies in raising public consciousness of the nationalist viewpoint?*

No doubt they did. But it would be a mistake to infer too much from their attendance at first nights and such. You have to remember that John Hume was an old St Columb's boy, a former teacher in Derry city and somebody who would have known Brian personally all along. I myself knew John in much the same way, for although he was a day boy he used to come into the study hall with the boarders in the evening. The Derry/St Columb's context remains very important in those friendships, plus the fact that in the early and mid-seventies there was virtually a West Donegal Summer School in action. Marie and I would be up with the kids on holiday. Brian and Anne had a house in Mulladuff, near Kincasslagh. David Hammond and Eileen had their place down in Dooey, near Lettermacaward. John Hume used to hang out around Gweedore. Seamus Deane and his family would also be in the district occasionally. Everybody was highly conscious of the crisis over the border, but everybody was on holiday and ready for revels: public houses, the singing of songs, the reciting of poems, the raking over of all matters of current concern, literary and political.

Was the fact that Brian Friel had been a student in St Columb's of any significance when you first read his work? You mentioned earlier that Michael McLaverty had urged you to read 'The Foundry House'.

I bought his first book, *The Saucer of Larks*, soon after it came out and I believe the first Friel story I read was the title story. Then a couple of years later I drove with Marie to the German cemetery in Glencree in County Wicklow because it had figured in that story. The St Columb's factor meant little or nothing to me then. What caught the attention was the fact that Brian was a local writer getting books published and being hailed. I didn't get to know Brian until the late sixties, really. Certain moments stand out: receiving a letter from him about *Death of a Naturalist*, parking my Volkswagen beside the airport road up beyond Belfast and listening to a broadcast of *Philadelphia, Here I Come!* on the car radio. Meeting Brian in the crowd gathered in Guildhall Square in Derry the Saturday after the police had baton-charged the Civil Rights march in October 1968: he was there with a white hankie tied round the arm of his coat to indicate that he was one of the stewards. The great thing about him is his total grip on the home ground and his attentiveness to it, and at the same time his sense of intellectual and artistic responsibility drawn from the farthest horizons.

Friel had lived in the Irish Republic since 1967. Did this make you feel more secure about moving south?

Brian's domicile didn't impinge on that decision, but once I found myself in the full-time-writer situation – once I was more seriously at risk, more called upon to give an account of myself – I became particularly interested in how he managed. And grateful for his advice too. We had begun to see more of each other in the early seventies. All part of a reorientation everywhere. The shift from Belfast was one thing, but there was also the political urgency of those years and there was my own renewed interest in Irish writing per se, partly as a result of that year with Tom Flanagan in Berkeley. It was a swing of the pendulum, I suppose, from Belfast back to Derry. At that same time, I'd met up with Seamus Deane again in Dublin and he too became a vital part of the refresher course. Brian took a kind of mentor's interest in us, I think. We weren't protégés, but we were being watched.

When I say Brian had a sense of writerly responsibility drawn from far horizons, I'm thinking of his constant awareness of Chekhov and O'Neill, to name only two of the dramatists he would invoke. You could feel the inner devotion and couldn't help knowing that he had a calling as a writer and that equally he had a determination not to let the calling bloat into celebrity. He stayed clear of a lot of the razzmatazz of show business, possibly because he got a lot of success early on and had had his fill of the 'luvvy' scene. After *Philadelphia*, he came back from Broadway, built himself a house that was both a family home and a writer's bunker, and began his long campaign of staying put.

Were you tempted at all to follow his example in adopting a very low literary profile and remaining aloof from the artistic world? Did he ever suggest such a stance to you?

He didn't suggest it in so many words, no, but he was always asking about work and how I was getting on. Not that we exchanged manuscripts for comment or anything like that. We'd send each other the text of a completed book, and maybe write to each other about it, but there wasn't a literary correspondence as such. By the time we met, our habits were formed and although we both probably operated with the same kind of inner compass we were on different paths. His was to a large extent centripetal and mine centrifugal. The paradox is that at the moment when I pulled back from the academy and went to the cottage, I began to do more work on the podium. My first formally written-up lectures were done when I was in Glanmore, my readings increased in frequency, I did more freelance work on radio and in print and generally had my head above the parapet. But these things are as much a matter of temperament as of circumstance.

You have dedicated books to each other – Station Island *from you to him, and* Volunteers *from him to you. Are we to infer any special link between those books and their dedicatees?*

Brian was powerfully encouraging when I started on the Lough Derg poem. I sent him one of the early sections, maybe a bit about the meeting with the shade of either Joyce or Carleton, and I got this terrific letter back, almost by return, saying, go for it. But the *Volunteers* exchange was also significant. Brian sent me the manuscript in or around October 1974. I've talked about this somewhere else, but it's worth recording again. I had no idea that he'd been delving into the archaeological regions himself; but, when I read the play, I immediately started typing out all the bog poems and Viking Dublin poems that were to hand, plus the 'Singing School'/St Columb's poems and so on, and by the end of a weekend I found I had a manuscript that I could send to Faber as well as to Brian. That's how *North* got assembled; so, to that extent, there's a symbiotic link between it and *Volunteers*, which is why the dedication attaches to that play in particular.

Given the conspicuous stylistic division between Part I and Part II of North, *were you tempted to hold over the more conversational and personal poems of Part II for another collection?*

Not that I remember. For a start, there was a topicality about them. They were a second movement as much as they were a second section. Like an afterword. A kind of 'notes on the author' *by* the author. The thing to remember is the speed at which the book was assembled. Or better say the speed at which it crystallized. It wasn't a premeditated organization of the material but a more or less chance discovery of an order of contents. The poems in Part II may have been different in pitch but they weren't just occasional, they're integral to the book and help to underwrite its title. They come out of 'the matter of the North' of Ireland.

Were they written at different times? First, bog poems, then 'Singing School'-type verse?

Nothing as clear cut. 'Whatever You Say Say Nothing' pre-dates the bog poems. 'Funeral Rites' from Part I was written after 'Exposure' which ends Part II. And indeed the first part of 'Funeral Rites' was originally cast in blank verse of 'the more conversational and personal' kind and could well have found its way into the second section. It was all-through-other, as is usually the case with any collection until the final order is discovered.

In 1975, the same year as North, *you published* Stations – *a pamphlet of the prose poems you had begun to write when you were in America. I wonder if it makes sense to suggest that the conversational writing in Part II represents a compromise of sorts between the short-lined intensities of Part I and the looser conventions of the prose poem?*

I don't think it was a question of compromise. The prose poems started from a different impulse. Some of them were autobiographical, some emblematic. I believe it was after I handed in the manuscript of *North* that I took them up again and at that stage I went from dealing with the pre-reflective life of Mossbawn to pieces backlit by awareness of the historical moment or the political circumstances – there's one about the demobbed Evans brothers arriving on our doorstep with the rosary beads for my father, one about the German prisoner of war stationed at the local aerodrome, and one about encountering the Loyalists in the Gents of a Belfast hotel.

Judging by Stations *and by your subsequent prose poems, you seem to conceive of the form as a Joycean 'epiphany'.*

That's fair enough. It's a way to pounce on material that has been in my memory for so long it has almost become aware of me and has begun to be wary of being chosen for verse. It's not that the subjects treated aren't amenable to verse, more that they came into my sights at a time when I was in the prose habit. I'm not sure, by the way, that the things should be called 'prose poems': maybe it would be better to use David Jones's word 'writings' about them. Each is a making over into words that are more self-conscious than the usual prose record and yet not justified as verse.

Edna Longley reviewed Stations *without enthusiasm and based her response on what she termed her 'long-standing prejudice against the prose poem, as being a hybrid rather than a mongrel, as obliging practitioners to load every rift unnaturally with ore'.*

Well, that time at least she admitted her prejudice. And there's something in the objection. But there are prose poems – by Zbigniew Herbert, for example – which are ironical and, so to speak, oreless. Prejudice or no prejudice, the form is there and adds to the available registers.

One of the least characteristic and perhaps most Herbert-like of your 'writings' is 'The Unacknowledged Legislator's Dream' which opens Part II of North. *It seems to present the poet in a more ineffectual light than is customary in your work.*

It's a free-floating invention, that one. I remember writing it in a café in Bray as I waited for my Volkswagen Beetle to be serviced. There's a touch of the Herbert irony in it all right. It's a corrective to the more tragic-elegiac scenario in 'Exposure' at the end of the section, with the Mandelstam figure and 'His gift like a slingstone / Whirled for the desperate'. This particular unacknowledged legislator is fit as a fiddle, his spirit blithe, his audience in great fettle ('My wronged people cheer from their cages'), but he happens to be a kind of a joke in the eyes of his captor and he's aware that he has simply become a part of some new political spectator sport: 'Were those your eyes just now at the hatch?' I liked the flightiness of it.

Do you think there's a link from there to the parable-type poems you would publish later in The Haw Lantern?

I never thought of that. But, yes, they were conceived in much the same way, as translations of an imagined original.

Another poem – very different – in Part II which I'd like to ask about is 'Summer 1969', set in Madrid. Lorca figures in it, much as Mandelstam figures in 'Exposure', as a literary-political exemplar. Was he important to you as a poet, then or later?

For my generation, Lorca was on the horizon always. The Spanish poets were to anglophone readers in the forties and fifties what the eastern Europeans would become in the sixties and seventies – examples of writers 'under pressure', as A. Alvarez would express it, caught between the impulse to show solidarity with the people and a wariness of party lines. Lorca was a victim figure, I suppose, a figure of the poet as free spirit, committed to the cause of liberation; left-leaning but not propagandist, yet in the end enough of a taunt to the reactionary right to be conceived of as the enemy. The ins and outs of the lead-up to Lorca's murder are very complicated and very local – the whole thing was more Irish than Soviet, very clannish and very Catholic, as much a matter of homophobia as of ideology. Not that I was very clear about that in 1969: Ian Gibson's work on the death of Lorca had still to be published.

What I felt at the beginning of the Troubles was what any poet would have felt in the circumstances, a certain undefined accountability. Implicated in the politics, yes, but without any real appetite for the political role. Lorca, I imagined, felt much the same. But he was also on my mind in 1969 because the Madrid interlude was part of the journey I was making thanks to the Somerset Maugham Award. I'd brought a book of Lorca's poems to France and had been translating some of the short lyrics as a preparation for my trip to Castile. I also remember being lifted by the glamour and drive of his essay on the *duende*. I think Lorca was implying there that poetry requires an inner flamenco, that it must be excited into life by something peremptory, some initial strum or throb that gets you started and drives you farther than you realized you could go. That would certainly tally with my own experience.

In 'Summer 1969', you view the Goyas in the Prado while the Troubles are brewing back home. Was your interest in a painter like Goya given an additional impetus by the fact that he confronted political violence head-on?

To answer you in American, you're damned right it was. *The Shootings of the Third of May* is a picture with the force of a fusillade. It was Bloody Sunday *avant la lettre*. All the same, I went to the Prado as anybody would go, to delight and instruct myself – in fact, in those days Hieronymus Bosch's *The Garden of Earthly Delights* hung near the entrance. I wasn't there to study examples of art in a time of violence, I was there just to look, to be in the presence of masterworks that stood their ground and, in that way, steadied you and settled you. Goya's self-portraits, for example. But the so-called 'black paintings' had the force of terrible events. Visionary catastrophe – the scarlet blood in the picture of Saturn devouring his children, the levitation of the witches in the picture of the witches' sabbath. All that dread got mixed in with the slightly panicked, slightly exhilarated mood of the summer as things came to a head in Derry and Belfast.

You found Goya instructive?

I found him overwhelming. The scale of the *Shootings* picture, for one thing, is unexpected. It's big. You're up against it, in many ways. It can make you reel. And I suppose there was something about the whole torrid feel of those July days that was super-charged and ominous: we were staying in a small flat with Marie's sister and her husband and our two children. Toys on the floor, tortillas in the pan, toreadors on the television. Then, as I mention in the poem, there was a fish market down below with lorries starting to arrive from Galicia and wherever at three or four every morning, a whole hullabaloo of shouting and revving and banging and horn blowing. And then too, the bullfights, with all the dry mouth and dream danger that bullfights entail . . . When I look back on it, the Goyas were just another element in the phantasmagoria. The sun beat down on everything else, but the Prado was cool, so it was *sombre* to the *sol* of the rest of the holiday.

Did you take to the bullfights?

I had to go, just to find out what the word 'bullfight' meant. But it's still hard to know, even after you've been in attendance. I'm not sure what I'd feel about it nowadays, but half a lifetime ago the experience was mesmeric. I'm not saying it was without its cruelties, especially the goring of the bull by the picadors: a big iron-headed spear driving into the neck muscles and then the sweaty bleeding; that was brutal stuff. But gradually I would find myself in a kind of trance: the choreography in the ring and the surge and response of the crowd with the music going on and on just carried you away. And your focus stayed tight on the man and the bull. There was something hypnotic about the cloak-work, something even vaguely Satanic about that black crumpled-horn killing-cap on the matador's head – when it was over, you blinked and asked yourself 'Where was I?', then back you went like a sleepwalker for a second time. It's easy to understand the mystique of the *corrida*, and easy to understand the opposition to it also. It's a Roman experience. Once you've been there, you're implicated, you have some inkling of what it must have been like in the Colosseum.

Did you ultimately view the experience as an alien one?

I certainly felt that I'd been beyond my usual self, in an otherwhere. Alien isn't quite the word. You'd been taken up to a high mountain and shown things in yourself and the world, things you couldn't deny because – like Hemingway – you had been there.

Alien experience of a kind surfaces in 'Singing School'. In the first poem of the sequence, you talk about your six-year 'billet' as a boarder in St Columb's College in Derry. I wonder to what extent, in writing it, you were conscious of Joyce's A Portrait of the Artist. *Could Stephen Dedalus's experience in Clongowes be said to parallel your experience of St Columb's?*

It certainly could. When it comes to Catholic boarding schools of the late nineteenth and early to mid-twentieth century, it's very much a one-story-fits-all situation. I should emphasize, all the same, that St Columb's was mercifully free of sexual molestation from either staff or students. It was the usual monastic regime, Mass in the morning, masturbation at night, classroom in the day-time, the study-hall/scriptorium in the evening. Cold-water shaves, cold-weather playgrounds.

And what about the use of the strap for corporal punishment?

The doaker, we called it: stitched leather, deep in the soutane pocket like a sword in a scabbard. But corporal punishment wasn't general all over boarding school, it depended on the individual teacher. Some did have recourse to it frequently, but some hardly used the strap at all. The one teacher we dreaded more than the rest prac-tised a form of mental rather than corporal punishment. The 'What's your name, Heaney?' man. He actually gets a chapter to himself in Seamus Deane's *Reading in the Dark*.

How did your friendship with Seamus Deane begin?

We were in the same class at St Columb's but the friendship really started during our sixth year, when we came back to do a repeat A-level year. We'd both done well enough at A-levels in our fifth year, but were considered a bit young to go on to university, so we ended up in an English class that consisted of Seamus and myself and two other boys, Michael Cassoni and Paddy Mullarkey. After that, we proceeded to Queen's where the St Columb's clique held together at certain tables in the Students' Union, and during our second year Seamus stayed in the same digs as me. Just for part of that year, since he went into a flat with a crowd of Derry city fellows after that – day boys, as they'd been in St Columb's, where I'd been a boarder. That country/city, day boy/boarder distinction operated between Seamus and me, humorously and pretty definitively, well into adult life. But the friendship was already strong in our student days, full and free, term time and vacation time. We wrote letters, exchanged poems and, since I was occasionally able to get the loan of our car, I would visit him now and again in his home in Derry.

In 'The Ministry of Fear', you mention poem-filled 'bulky envelopes arriving / In vacation time'. Were you aware of yourselves all along as potential poets?

Certainly not at St Columb's. At Queen's, Seamus would have been seen as the poet in waiting. He wore the mantle. He had a terrific imaginative flair, a great opulent flourish of language. His *hommage* to Wallace Stevens, for example, began 'Of the svelte diction, master!' – a line I inveigled into 'The Ministry of Fear': ' "Svelte dictions" in a very florid hand'. I think Seamus *did* have a sense of a calling at that stage. I on the other hand was far from confident.

What 'bewildered' you – to use your own word from 'The Ministry of Fear' – about Seamus Deane's 'poems in longhand, ripped from the wire spine / Of [his] exercise book'?

Their sheer panache, the sumptuousness of the words and movement, the high style of the utterance. OK, the sense may have been hard to make out at times, but the bewilderment was more because of the level of the performance. He had got beyond himself and us in the writing.

Would it be fair to say that Seamus Deane has always been more at ease with abstract thought, and more politically minded than you?

Certainly. And that side of him got great reinforcement when he went to Cambridge University to do his PhD. He'd done a 'literary' MA on the novels of E. M. Forster, part-time, in the years after he'd left Queen's and gone back to teach in Derry. Next thing, he was married and was off to Cambridge and had a son and was doing a thesis on the reputation and influence of the French *philosophes* in England in the last decades of the eighteenth century and the opening decades of the nineteenth. He turned into a learned man and ended up teaching in universities on the West Coast of America, in Reed College and Berkeley. So in those years we were hardly in touch at all. It's not that we parted company, just that our lives took us to different places and found different directions.

And those were the years when you began to publish and receive more than a little attention as a poet?

Indeed. Between 1962 and 1972, between the end of our undergraduate life and the time when we met up again, I had gradually moved from *incertus* to *file*. I had also commingled more with 'the other side' in Belfast and was more at home in 'official' Ulster – the Arts Council, Examiners' Boards, the Northern Ireland BBC – than Seamus ever was or would have wanted to be. In the years before he came back to teach at University College Dublin, he kept in touch with Derry city and the people he'd grown up with in the Bogside. Despite his travels he continued to be far more at home 'at home', if you know what I mean, than I did.

  His sense of the political rigging in Northern Ireland was always far more exacerbated than mine. From the age of twelve, I was that bit detached from the place where I'd grown up, whereas Seamus lived on his home ground and kept his ear to it. His Ulster had always been politically more melodramatic than mine anyhow, more Manichaean even, more hard-edged Republican and Loyalist. He never had Protestant neighbours in and out of the house, no day-to-day experience of come and go between the two communities. In the Bogside, the RUC were bigoted bastards and that was that. And while it may have been true as a matter of fact, it was true for the people he knew as a matter of hard and gemlike prejudice as well. So it's no wonder Seamus wrote about the North in what Yeats might have called 'a fiery shorthand'.

After you'd moved south, and Seamus Deane was teaching in Dublin, did you feel pressured by him to be more political in your poetry?

To say 'yes' to that would be to overstate, but to say 'no' would be to misrepresent the reality of the situation. A friendship, you know, especially one that involves writers with similar backgrounds and preoccupations, is a field of force. There's mutuality, a happy shadowing and colouring of minds. You wake to different things in yourself and the world just by coming alive in the company of different friends. At the time, I was as susceptible to the mythic Ted Hughes as to the mordant Seamus Deane. I didn't feel pressured by him, I felt extended, awakened, called upon to take in more of the Northern experience we both shared. We discovered that we were poets together again, and for a few years the careless rapture was actually recaptured.

What memories stand out from the years when you were both more or less resident in Dublin?

The Deanes' car running out of petrol on Glenshane Pass the night of the Bloody Sunday funerals in Derry. They were driving back from Derry late: Seamus and Marion to their in-laws in Maghera, me to Belfast when I came upon them parked on the mountain road. We left Marion and the kids in the Deane car and Seamus and I drove back to Dungiven to rouse the owner of a petrol pump. In truth, we banged the door of his pub where there was still a crowd of after-hours, post-funeral drinkers on the premises ... Another thing I always associate with those days is Seamus singing 'The Coolin' at any of the hundred and one parties in Donegal or Dublin. Then too, the long drives from Dublin to Derry and back for meetings and first nights during the Field Day years.

How did you regard Seamus Deane's New Yorker *article in March 2000, about your time together in St Columb's? Did it take you by surprise or were you given a chance to comment on it in advance?*

It didn't take me by surprise because it had been due to appear earlier. Seamus wrote most of it in 1995, at the time of the Nobel Prize, and I believe it was meant to be published to coincide with the ceremony that December – which explains, by the way, why there was so much about the prize in an article that came out five years after the event. Anyhow, for one reason or another it wasn't printed in 1995; so it was still on file when the *Beowulf* translation came into the news in the millennium year and Seamus was then asked to bring it up to date. I didn't have a chance to comment except about the accuracy of the reported facts: the *New Yorker* fact-checkers were on to me day and night and that meant I had a fair notion of what was going to appear.

What does it feel like to read about yourself in an article by an old friend?

I said to somebody at the time – it may even have been to Seamus Deane himself – that it was like going into the private room inside your head and finding somebody else sitting there.

Did you recognize yourself in the portrait he painted?

Well enough, but there were people who thought it didn't come out right. They kept bringing up his word 'cunning', which isn't one I'd apply to myself – even in my best *mea culpa* mood.

He said you were 'well in' with those in power and also capable of holding them at arm's length. Do you recognize yourself there?

Insofar as it is a portrait of up-frontnesss and independence, yes. Once he took on the job, he was cornered between winging and wounding. I mean, as a friend, he may have felt constrained to keep the daimon's mouth muffled, if not gagged; but, as a writer with a brilliant turn of phrase and a furious intelligence, he needed to take the hand from the mouth, do the transgressive thing and hope for the best.

Presumably the friendship had lost a certain intensity after you both began to go your separate ways again: you to Harvard, he to Notre Dame?

I'd put the marker down in the early nineties, just after the appearance of *The Field Day Anthology of Irish Writing*. Seamus's own focus changed a bit then, and the general camaraderie that had been the driving force of the Field Day venture began to get dispersed. Then too he began his American stints, and I kept going to Harvard; all in all, there was a general sense of the end of youth. Something had passed, not just between Seamus and me, but between all of us who had been cresting on each other's company since those Donegal summers in the 1970s.

You have posited a contrast between 'mythic' Ted Hughes and
'mordant' Seamus Deane. Could you say a bit more about that?

I'm not sure. I've probably overstated the contrast. Neither of them
ever was insensitive to poetry itself, so there was nothing pre-
dictable. It's possible that for all his Derryness and political drive,
Seamus would have preferred 'The Grauballe Man' or 'Funeral
Rites' to 'The Ministry of Fear'.

As for the 'mythic' Ted Hughes, did he encourage you to publish
Bog Poems *with his sister Olwyn's Rainbow Press? Did he*
encourage you, for that matter, with the poems themselves?

He encouraged me with the poems in one very particular way.
There was a Poetry International event in London, 1974 or there-
abouts, and the Dutch poet Judith Herzberg was present. Judith
was a friend of Sonja Landweer and Barrie Cooke, so she had spo-
ken to me in the course of the evening when we read together. But
at the end of the evening she told me that Ted had instructed her to
pay special attention to my reading and to listen in particular to the
bog poems – that information, as you can imagine, did me a lot of
good. I knew Ted liked the poems but his commendation of them
behind backs, as it were, sealed the thing. I imagine that's how Ted
and Olwyn regarded the publication with Rainbow – a seal of
approval. It's certainly how I regarded it. We all got along easily.
Olwyn had a house on Chetwynd Road, and on several occasions
in those years I'd be invited there after readings. Everything and
everybody got a good sifting on those occasions, but the bog poems
passed.

Were you and Ted Hughes close friends by the mid-seventies?
Would you have exchanged work?

I could hardly say we 'exchanged' work. I would send Ted a poem
or two if I was writing to him and he might enclose one of his when
he wrote back. Nor could I say we were close friends at that stage.
I felt free in his company, felt trusted and on the right wavelength
with him. And that to me was a privilege – a sort of change of life:
Ted's work had had an almost magic effect on me in the beginning
and to get to know the man responsible was a big thing. And to feel
his approval was a precious thing. You don't always need to have

your poems 'workshopped', if you know what I mean, in order to get help as a poet. Just being treated as an equal by the poets you especially honour can affect you inestimably. It feeds your confidence and makes you feel that bit more creative.

You often refer to Seferis's search for poetry that is 'strong enough to help'. Am I correct in thinking that the writing of 'Exposure', your closing poem, was a 'help' at a time of personal uncertainty and public disorder?

I'll answer you with two other bits of wisdom that I like to quote, from poems by Miłosz: one where he says 'What is articulated strengthens itself'; another, where he says 'One clear stanza can take more weight / Than a whole wagon of elaborate prose'.

7

'The life we're shown'
Field Work

~

Would you agree that Field Work *is more concerned than the earlier collections with the shaping of the verse?*

Probably, yes. You have sonnets in there. You have quatrains that rhyme and many more that don't. There's a poem in an irregular five-line stanza at the beginning and one in a blunted form of *terza rima* at the end. One of the first things I wrote after the publication of *North* was 'The Harvest Bow', and in that case you would say the stanza form was what made the poem. I remember discovering a shape and then realizing that it could be built on, and relishing the whole gradual cumulative effect. But the texture of 'The Harvest Bow' is richer than many of the others in the book.

More Keatsian, even, whereas the general tendency is Yeatsian. In fact, I'd like to touch generally on your relations with the 'arch-poet', as Roy Foster calls him. The received wisdom is that all Irish poets work in his shadow and that he is therefore a stifling presence as well as a stimulating one.

He was never stifling for me. It may seem odd to say it, but for a good while Yeats wasn't really part of the air I breathed. The English Lit. stalwarts were more pervasive early on. Wordsworth, Keats, Hopkins, Eliot and then, to a lesser extent, Frost. After that, Kavanagh and Hughes, the War Poets, contemporary Irish poets. I didn't, as we used to say, 'do' Yeats when I was an undergraduate. And when I began to read him in earnest, it was in order to teach him, first in the training college and then at Queen's.

So until I was thirty or so, he wasn't so much a point of reference as part of my self-improvement, almost a part of my curriculum. I remember Philip Larkin, in his *Paris Review* interview, pooh-poohing the idea that you *study* a poet (outside of a classroom, that is), but in the case of Yeats something like study seems to be required. It cost me time and effort, at any rate, to get my head round a poem like 'The Tower'. And the same was true of the big sequences, 'Nineteen Hundred and Nineteen' and 'Meditations in Time of Civil War'. I said earlier that I did my serious reading of Yeats in the 1970s, which was when I needed him most, and it then involved his autobiographies and essays as well as the poems.

You mention Kavanagh – indeed, you always mention him as part of your Irish genealogy. Do you consider him more important than Yeats as a literary forebear?

Kavanagh was more important when I was getting started, Yeats more important when I had to keep going. Mind you, as you get older, there are twin dangers when you're reporting on these early influences: you tend to either overstate or understate their effect. But there's no doubt that, during the mid-1960s, I was more *in medias* the *res* of Inniskeen than of Coole Park and Ballylee. In those days 'The Great Hunger' was to me the equivalent of wrap-around sound in one of today's cineplexes. It had the wham of big-screen cinematic close-up, an amplified language that could knock you sideways. Head-on, as cold-breathed and substantial as the stuff the potato digger was kicking up from the drills. Kavanagh walked into my ear like an old-style farmer walking a field. He had that kind of ignorant entitlement, his confidence contained a mix-ture of defiance and challenge. You were being told that you would never hit your stride if you didn't step your own ground, and would never hit the right note if you didn't sound as thick as your own first speech.

Yeats had nothing of that sort to tell you?

I once used the term 'art speech' in relation to what Robert Burns achieved in his *Poems, Chiefly in the Scottish Dialect*. I was wanting to remind myself as much as anybody else that sounding natural is a stylistic achievement. Just because you have an idiom and an accent when you open your mouth doesn't mean you have style when you put pen to paper. On the other hand, you may believe, in Yeats's words, that style is 'found by sedentary toil / And by the imitation of great masters'. Your art, in other words, may want to sound artful rather than artless. So let's just say that I was susceptible early on to the illusion of artlessness, or at least of spontaneous direct address, as in 'The Great Hunger' or Hughes's 'The Bull Moses'. It's what I was mostly after in the beginning in my own writing.

Your interest in Yeats began to deepen in the 1970s?

I'm not saying that I wasn't exhilarated by the work before that. When I was half tight I enjoyed baying out the famous lines as much as the next one, 'Sailing to Byzantium' and 'Irish poets, learn your trade', 'Turning and turning in the widening gyre' and all the rest of it. But there came a moment when I wakened up to what Donald Davie called the 'articulate energy' of poetry, poems that packed their punch because of syntactical stamina, the distribution of argument over the line-ends and stanzas; the poem, if you'll excuse the expression, more a matter of vertebrae than plasm. It was when I began to teach in Carysfort College, lecturing on the metaphysical poets for the first time, and discovering that element of 'tough reasonableness' that Eliot spoke of in Marvell. I had this sudden powerful admiration for Marvell's 'Horatian Ode' and his very strange piece 'The Nymph Complaining for the Death of her Fawn'. At the same time, I began to hear and value in a new way poems in that three-beat, pressure-raising line you find in 'middle Yeats' – 'Easter 1916', 'The Fisherman', 'Men Improve with the Years'.

It was all happening, I think, because of what had been happening in my own writing and in the North of Ireland. In a sequence like 'Singing School', I'd been working out a position or a stance in relation to the place and the times we were inhabiting. There was a reach for statement – in 'Exposure', for example. And that turn made me alert to the big integration and vigour in Yeats, the way his affections and disaffections as a citizen and controversialist could get included and transformed. He had this marvellous gift for beating the scrap metal of the day-to-day life into a ringing bell.

So you 'trod with a lighter tread' when you heard that bell-beat?

Spoke with a plainer tongue, at any rate. In 1976, when we moved from Glanmore to the new house in Dublin, I was worried about it as a 'place of writing'. I wasn't going to be happy there until I had produced work. So very soon I sat down and deliberately took the hammer to my own scrap and tried to beat sense and shape out of the loss of friends like Sean Armstrong and Louis O'Neill. That was the one time when Yeats was an actual tuning fork for a poem I was writing. 'Casualty' commemorates the eel fisherman Louis O'Neill – whom I've mentioned – and I was counting out the metre to keep in step with 'The freckled man who goes / To a grey place on a hill / In grey Connemara clothes'.

Were you not running the risk of yielding too much to Yeats's influence?

I don't think so. Yeats's music was so other and so detectable that I would have been conscious of it as an intrusive element. At the time, I was more conscious that I was ventriloquizing for Robert Lowell.

You cite Lowell at the very beginning of 'Yeats as an Example?' – an essay based on a lecture you gave in 1978, the year before Field Work *appeared. Were you looking consciously to Yeats and Lowell as role models at that time?*

Again, 'role model' may not be the right word. Sometime in the mid- to late seventies, I gave a lecture at the Yeats Summer School on *The Wind Among the Reeds*, one that I plundered for 'Yeats as an Example?' In the course of preparing it, I realized that that collection was the culmination of one kind of poetry and that – after its publication – the plainer, 'walking naked' Yeats had taken over. And although I was well aware of the dangers of inflation, I couldn't help noticing that a similar turn was occurring in my own work after *North* – even, indeed, before *North* was finished . . . And it was occurring at round about the same age as it had occurred for Yeats, between thirty and thirty-five. Insofar as I could see a parallel between the master's work and my own, he was an example – or perhaps, since the turn that arrived between *North* and *Field Work* happened independently, better say there was a corroboration. I didn't set out to imitate Yeats, and that's why I'd hesitate to call him a model.

Yet, living through the Troubles, you must have been conscious that Yeats had lived through his own period of 'Troubles', the

1916 Rising and the Irish civil war included. Did the example of those tragic-elegiac sequences responding to his times loom large for you?

Of course it did. But great work like that cannot be emulated. You lift your eyes to it as to the hills, but thence cometh no help.

So whence came it?

From the writing of the poems themselves, ones like 'Oysters': 'the clear light, like poetry or freedom / Leaning in from sea . . .' From living up to my neck in complication, resident in Dublin but feeling called upon by what was happening in the North. From a renewed sense of the value of poetry itself as a consolidating element. The writing of certain poems took me to the bottom of something inside myself, something inchoate but troubled. The 'Oysters' poem, for example, that I've just quoted from. 'The Singer's House'. 'The Harvest Bow'. 'The Guttural Muse'. The Troubles, you might say, had muddied the waters but I felt those poems arrived from an older, deeper, cleaner spring. There's something unoppressed about them. I can see that more clearly now, of course, than I could have at the time.

You've mentioned your admiration for the oracular, prophetic quality in Yeats; yet you have also said that, in Field Work, *you wanted the note of the poetry to sound more like your 'social self'.*

I should have said 'include my current circumstances' rather than 'sound like my social self'. At the time I was glad that something of the actual life I was living in Glanmore was getting into the poems, that the silage smell came from the farm next door and not from the flax dam in Broagh. At this distance, however, 'Death of a Naturalist' or 'The Tollund Man' or 'The Grauballe Man' seem to have as 'social' a voice as anything in *Field Work*.

Would it be fair to say that there's a certain inclination to the 'prophetic' voice in Field Work *also – in the second section of 'Triptych', for example. What is your view of poetry as prophecy?*

I'd say I'm more susceptible to the didactic voice – to Miłosz, for example. It's probably a matter of the tuning of your ear, even perhaps of the posture you were trained to adopt towards godhead. If you were tuned to Gregorian chant rather than the surge of Old Testament prose and poetry, if you began within the magisterium of Roman Catholicism rather than in the arena of individual conscience, you're probably less likely to aspire to the voice of one crying in the wilderness. Even so, poetry always reserves its right to reach for the stars. The question is whether the poet can rise to that challenge.

How difficult is it for contemporary poetry to accommodate language which is not essentially plainspoken?

Maybe the plainspoken poetry that's truly poetry, not just chopped prose, is presuming to be heard in dialogue or in contrast with some older unheard 'poetic' note. Ashbery, for example, is sporting with all kinds of traditional sublimities. Alternatively, you have the case of a colloquialist like Christopher Logue seeking the upthrust of Homer. American poetry is generally readier to elevate the proceedings: when I think of Louise Glück, say, or Jorie Graham, not to mention Lowell, I think of voices not embarrassed to try for higher scales and dictions. But still, on this side of the ocean, you have Derek Mahon, who can rise to a magniloquence that has high canonical sanction. As does Philip Larkin at the end of 'Church Going', and 'The Whitsun Weddings'. Then there's Les Murray: for all his Aussie demotic, Murray puts torsions and tractions on his language that ratchet it up as often as they rein it in. The same with Tom Paulin – again somebody who espouses the vernacular but who rises with it, whose downbeat is a like a hunched run towards lift-off.

Would you grant some credence therefore to the view of Naguib Mahfouz that the colloquial is 'one of the diseases from which the people are suffering . . . one of the failings of our society, exactly like ignorance, poverty and disease'?

I *would* grant credence to that. The world is reduced by the reduced power of speech in somebody like George W. Bush. In a severely impoverished speech world, what Auden once called 'the mass and majesty' of the reality we inhabit and should be measuring up to – 'all / That carries weight and always weighs the same' – all that is slighted. Which is not to say that the use of a plainer speech necessarily prevents a poem from attaining nobility. Think of Yeats's 'Long-Legged Fly'. Or indeed Auden's 'The Shield of

Achilles'. Cadence with a head of intelligence and strong shoulders of syntax still has a lot of carrying power.

You have frequently quoted Yeats's statement, 'Even when the poet seems most himself, he is never the bundle of accident and incoherence that sits down to breakfast; he has been reborn as an idea, something intended, complete.' Do you return to this remark because you sense a chasm between your person and your persona, between Seamus Heaney the man and Seamus Heaney the poet?

'Chasm' is a bit drastic. I keep coming back to the statement because it gets at the truth. It's another way of accounting for the fact that, if a poem is any good, you can repeat it to yourself as if it were written by somebody else. The completedness frees you from it and it from you. You can read and reread it without feeling self-indulgent: whatever it was in you that started the writing has got beyond you. The unwritten poem is always going to be entangled with your own business, part of your accident and incoherence – which is what drives you to write. But once the poem gets written, it is, in a manner of speaking, none of your business.

I'm still interested, nevertheless, in the bundle of accident and incoherence that sat down to breakfast in Glanmore: the person who had moved from city to country, drove the children to school every morning in his Volkswagen Beetle and then climbed the stairs to write; who was trying to devote himself to his own work but was earning his keep by freelance work. I suppose I want to know more about what led to the 'intended, complete' feel of poems like 'Glanmore Sonnets'.

Two important things about Glanmore: I knew it was the right place because, when I was there, I always felt what Wordsworth might have called that 'blessed mood, / In which the affections gently lead us on'. Glanmore led me on to new confidence and new work, so I never had any doubts about the move. Never thought, 'Oh God, I wish I were back in Ashley Avenue.' At the same time, there was an element of anxiety because I knew that living there couldn't be a permanent arrangement. During those years, Ann Saddlemyer had every intention of retiring to Wicklow, so she wasn't going to sell the place, and it was too small anyhow for three kids and two adults to inhabit indefinitely. Our furniture, for example, was back in the house in Belfast, which we still owned. Even so, everything in me felt connected up to an energy source. Maybe it was because of certain physical aspects of the house – cold cement floor in the living room, latches slapping up and down on the doors, a fire in the grate – things that connected back to the Mossbawn house.

I found myself, if you'll excuse the expression, sensationally unalienated, living in the Republic of Ur-land. There was no heating, apart from the open grate and those miserable little two-bar electric fires, but the very bleakness had its attractions. And there were the compensations of watching leaves sprout and weeds flourish and birds build. Even though I mostly looked out at all this through a fug of cigarette smoke, it was still a sustenance. And the stand-off of our situation – the distance from Dublin, never mind from Belfast – produced a kind of empowerment. You were determined to have something to show for it. So when the cuckoo and the corncrake 'consorted at twilight', almost two years after we had landed, I gave in. I wrote at that moment, involuntarily, in 'smooth numbers' – iambic lines that were out of key with the more constrained stuff I was doing at the time, the poems that would appear in *North*. But that musical shift meant that I had a definite stake in the Glanmore ground.

In what sense?

Glanmore was the first place where my immediate experience got into my work. Almost all the poems before that had arisen from memories of older haunts; but after a couple of years in the cottage, it changed from being just living quarters to a locus that was being written into poems. 'Exposure' – which we've discussed – was the start of it; then, the following May, just after I'd gone to do that BBC programme on Dove Cottage, the sonnets announced themselves. There was even a sonnet about a place in Grasmere called the White Moss where Wordsworth used to walk – his moss *bán*; but in the end I didn't think it worked, probably because it was overworking that kind of wordplay. Glanmore truly was what I called it, a 'hedge-school' in the literal sense. I gathered blackberries off the briars and ate them, as if I were back on the road to school. I even found a blackbird nest in the hedge at our gable.

On the jacket of the first Faber edition of Field Work, *there's an old map indicating a heavily wooded area. And there's a drawing of Glanmore Castle with a little dot that says 'Lodge'. Is that where you were situated?*

'Lodge' marks the spot all right. Glanmore Castle was built by Francis Synge in 1804, on lands – thousands of acres of 'lands' – that he had bought in and around the Devil's Glen, a famous beauty spot then and now. The castle's there still, 'a castellated mansion', but at this stage it's in apartments and the estate has been broken up and sold and resold, so that you have an equestrian village and various 'desirable residences' hidden in the environs. But you cannot miss that old landlordy feel. Estate walls for miles along the road, big rolling fields, planted slopes, and the remains of magnificent farm buildings, as big as a military barracks. I say 'remains' because the roof came off these outbuildings in the 1920s, and what you have now is a wallstead, but a mighty one, as extensive as many a ruined abbey.

That's what I looked out at from the upstairs window of the room where I worked. A big field sweeping up to this hill-topping stone wall, the wall inset at regular intervals with oval windows, and each window picked out with a surround of beautifully pointed brickwork. And around and overtopping all that, the Devil's Glen woods. When the place was a working farm, deer from those same woods were a constant nuisance. Anyhow, that's where we landed in August 1972 – a far cry from Ashley Avenue and the Ashley Arms at the corner where the landlord, Mr Lavery, had been blown up as he tried to carry a parcel bomb out of the lounge bar.

What size was the gate lodge itself?

Pretty small, but the confinement of the quarters was made up for by the general attractiveness. There was a lot of 'there' there. Pillars and gates. Stone house, slate roof, and again those lovely red-brick surrounds on all the windows. Roses. Wallflowers. Dormer windows in the upstairs rooms. A low tongue-and-groove ceiling in the upstairs sitting room – the room I took over for a study – furnished with a glass-topped walnut burr table and whatnots and pink armchairs, like something out of a Mrs Gaskell novel. The original house had a hall and two rooms downstairs, comprising a living room with open fireplace and a bedroom where the two boys slept. Upstairs, there was the sitting room and two more bedrooms, one of them very tiny, just big enough for Catherine's cot. In the 1950s a little outshot had been added, so we also had this stark, concrete-floored bathroom and a galley-sized kitchen with a cooker that ran on cylinder gas. Water pumped in by electric pump from a well outside the front door – although the pump was forever breaking down. You had to get coal and logs for the fire and bathe the kids in front of it, since there was no central heating. But we were young enough to enjoy it as an adventure.

Did you feel isolated? You mentioned earlier that you visited Garech Browne in his house at Luggala. Were there other people that you knew in the vicinity?

Not at the beginning. And it has to be said that our visits to Luggala were mostly at times when Garech was holding a party or entertaining a poet. He was a marvellous host, very active in the early seventies as head of Claddagh Records, so Luggala was often full of musicians and writers and revellers of all sorts. There would be the painters and artists in the company too, Louis le Brocquy and Anne Madden; Barrie Cooke and Sonja Landweer; the sculptor Eddie Delaney and his wife Nancy; the piper Paddy Moloney and his wife Rita; Dolly MacMahon, the singer, and her husband Ciarán, the broadcaster and authority of Irish folk music. And John Boorman had bought a place nearby in Annamoe, so he would turn up with his family. In fact, one of the big treats for our kids in those days was to go to Boorman's because John had a mini-cinema in the house and showed them movies in the proper dark picture-house conditions.

You weren't exactly out of the social loop, therefore.

Not at all. Although it should be said that those parties were very much the high points. Mostly we were battened down in the cottage, and my social centre wouldn't be an eighteenth-century lodge in the hills but the counter of the pub in Ashford, a mile and half or so down the road. We were lucky, all the same, in our neighbours: the Johnsons on one side, who had a dairy herd, and the Chapmans on the other, who did more arable farming. I remember very soon after we landed, coming up the road from the village and being faced with about ten or twelve cattle galloping down the hill towards me, with Mrs Johnson well back behind them. I realized they had broken out and had to be turned, so I spread my arms and let a shout out of me the same as I would have done at home on our own land, and the beasts halted. I got them turned and, from that moment, I think I was regarded as OK. Later on, Marie taught in the Ashford school and – thanks to her work there – we were even more integrated into the local life. In the shop and on the road, I'd meet the schoolkids' parents, and our babysitters' parents, and some of the customers in the pub would have heard the radio programme I used to present every week, so all that helped to settle us in.

Did the ephemeral nature of those radio programmes trouble you: a great deal of work done, but no written trace left?

Just then, the cheque was the important written trace. I was anxious to have some kind of regular money coming in, so the weekly fee was reassuring. I've always liked radio work, and by then I'd had a fair amount of experience in BBC studios, in various arts programmes and in the schools broadcasts I'd done with David Hammond. I also enjoyed the different books that came my way – not just poetry and novels, but biography and non-fiction, books on distilling whiskey, for example, travel books, stuff I wouldn't otherwise have taken much notice of. Reading the week's book, preparing the script and travelling into Dublin to make the broadcast – often on the bus – gave me a feeling that I was now well and truly in the freelance life. I wrote a five- or six-minute review for each programme and had two or three other contributors deliver pieces on other books. It was a simple formula, but well worth doing.

How would you regard Les Murray's view that 'any employee's a child, in the farmer's opinion' and that 'any job is a comedown where I was bred'?

I know, as they say, where Murray is coming from. My father would certainly have felt smaller if he'd had to work for somebody in order to earn a wage. In fact, as I was mentioning earlier, when the cattle trade changed from being a matter of individual enterprise by dealers and ended up in the hands of auctioneers, he was suddenly in the position of consultant rather than kingpin and didn't relish it at all. But the kind of job that accrued from being educated was regarded as a step up rather than a comedown. My father's sister Sarah, for example, was a schoolteacher and for that reason would have been regarded as more of a lady than a child. The question that was with us all from the beginning was 'What are you going to be when you grow up?'; once I got my scholarship, there was always a sense that I'd have to get a position. That was just the economic shape of things. And the moral shape.

With reference to Matthew Arnold, you once said, 'You can sin against your own gift by not remembering always to keep it ready; and you can sin against it by being moral in another way . . . looking after a job.' Do you still think that?

What I've always been interested to find is the right balance between insouciance and application. For years I had a dread of turning out conscientious verse and had a rather negative attitude towards industriousness; it didn't seem to produce great artistic results – in others, at any rate. Poetry had come into my life suddenly and I'd experienced a change that felt almost magical at the time. So that old-fashioned understanding of poetry as a visitation has been a determining one for me; and, for better or worse, I never set up my writing life on what you might call a professional basis. For most of the years when I was teaching and breadwinning, there was no daily time set aside for the composition of poems, no routine. I'd even say that deep down there was a superstitious fear that such a procedure might drive the poems away. I had this contrariness, a kind of perverse drive not to trade, even in my own eyes, on the safe conduct that the word 'poet' might provide in the academy. Does that make any sense to you?

It certainly ties in with something else you once said, in an interview with the Christian Science Monitor: *'Reading your poetry as a breadwinning activity . . . commits some sin against the freedom of poetry. I do believe that poetry is in the realm of the gift and in the realm of the sacred.' Do you still stand by those sentiments?*

I do – although it doesn't mean that I won't accept a fee for a poetry reading. That particular declaration came from the experience of going on a tour sometime in the late seventies or early eighties. It was a breadwinning outing, undertaken as such, and organized by an agent. Two or three weeks of tough going. Night after night in different universities all over the States. It happened shortly after Tom Flanagan moved from Berkeley to SUNY at Stony Brook, where he was once again a colleague of Louis Simpson's. Louis recommended me to this lady who was his lecture agent at the time and had also been Auden's agent. She lived close by on Long Island, so I met her when I was visiting the Flanagans. Before long, she had produced a flier telling all about me and my work – including the news that I had been taught at St Columb's College by Gerard Manley Hopkins; in the biographical note I supplied to her, I said that I'd been influenced early on by Hopkins.

Anyhow, the upshot of it was this big sweep around: flights every day, interviews, dinners with students and faculties, receptions with donors, then the readings, more receptions with audiences afterwards, parties at somebody's house after that again and finally, of course, the need to have a drink on your own in the hotel – just to celebrate the fact of being on your own. Not that you hadn't had a drink already . . . I was a wreck at the end of it. But worse, my pleasure in presenting what was more or less the same programme gradually waned: I started the day weary, although I could manage to work myself up to scratch by the time I reached the podium in the evening. As far as each new audience was concerned, I was doing OK, but for me the whole event began to lose spring and spirit. I realized that the ideal poetry reading would be the one you could preface with Yeats's line, 'Speech after long silence. It is right . . .' What began to disappear in the repetition was what I call the gift aspect, the genuineness of your pleasure in sharing the poem, in rediscovering it for yourself. In a good poetry reading – good for you, the poet, that is – you retrieve some of the quickening that you got when you first wrote the thing. The surprise and gratitude are with you again for a moment – the old sense of having been supplied with the words you needed to summon. You have an obligation as a poet not to betray the reality of that. You have been mysteriously recompensed by the words and you owe some fidelity to the mystery.

How does such a conviction square with your having continued to do readings year after year all over the world?

First of all, after that big tour, I never again let myself in for such sustained night-after-night work. And I have developed a habit of deep preparation for every event, no matter how routine or low-key. Whether it's in Athens or in Anahorish School, unless I have had at least a couple or three hours to daydream about which poems to read and have had time to fiddle with the links and the order and the general shape of the programme, I can hardly proceed. So nowadays, every time I stand up I have been to the inside of what I hope to turn out, and feel both prepared and protected. Perhaps it's meditation by another name, but at this stage it's become a necessity. It means that each reading attains a sense of its own occasion. You may be speaking the same poems, but they are part of something intended, they aren't just inclusions in some accidental or incoherent bundle of things. It means you can give out and keep to yourself at the same time.

That notion of giving out something and yet keeping it to yourself is touched on too in your remark about poetic technique as a means by which an intimate experience can become transformed into 'an object to be inspected. It calls you close and the intimacy is not embarrassing.' Does this apply to 'The Skunk', and indeed do you feel that the remark reflects your expectation of art generally?

Definitely. The truth of it comes home to you when you happen to be served with the untransformed material. I was once present at a small academic gathering when the speaker became emboldened enough to read one of his love poems. He had been giving a paper on love songs and the good reception, not to speak of the presence of his wife in the front row, encouraged him to go that bit further. Anyway, we braced ourselves and out came the first line: 'I like you in your underwear . . .' End of story. The poem continued, but we had stopped listening and the whole effort went into keeping a straight face. Lowell used to maintain that you could say anything in a poem as long as you placed it right, and one thing this man had definitely not learned was how to do the placing. If ever you wanted an illustration of the fact that what's true in life isn't necessarily automatically true in art, there you had it.

Could you say something in this context about 'The Skunk'? Were you nervous about showing it to Marie?

I don't think there was any nervousness. There was a playful element in the poem, after all, and a definite serious engagement. It was about a skunk, fair enough, but it was also about the transatlantic cable that connected us. I was in California when I saw the creature out on a verandah; there was no stink – all that had been obliterated by the eucalyptus on those fragrant hillsides in North Berkeley. I had a whole house to myself for the term, house-sitting for Mark and Ruth Schorer. They'd told me to look out for this skunk and her family and, if they appeared, to keep very still and all would be well: no fright would equal no spray. What I saw close up was the slink and shimmer of her tail, the waving plume of black and white stripes. To this day I associate that visitation with the erotic.

How important a force in the writing of poetry is eros? Do you feel that an oeuvre without love poetry or erotic poetry – however sublimated – is almost certain to be a deficient one?

Maybe eros is the sine qua non. The force that through the green fuse drives the flower. Driving through Shakespeare and the Bible, even. Dante and Yeats. Sappho. Anna Swir. D. H. Lawrence. Derek Mahon. The list is as long as poetry. Unfulfilled desire, sexual repletion, impotence, infatuation, sublimation – there's no end to it. And in poetry a recollection is as potent as an erection. Think of Wyatt. Memory allows what Lowell called the body's thousand rivulets of joy to flow to the roots of words. But what sprouts from the roots isn't necessarily sexual material in any obvious sense. Eros can disguise himself and turn into a seedling in a greenhouse or into the sinuousness in the movement of a villanelle. But still, it's hard to pronounce upon the deficiency or otherwise of an oeuvre without love poetry. Love poetry, I suspect, is not in itself a necessary element. I can't think of it forming a significant part of Zbigniew Herbert's work, for example, although I'm probably just ignorant of the full range of his poems. But George Herbert is worth remembering here too. Hopkins even. No sonnets to a mistress, but the rivulets are sweetly rilling everywhere in their relish for 'versing' as such; there had to be sexual juice and joy behind all the budding and 'bright shoots'. In my own case, eros eventually got curled into the crook of a poem called 'Fiddleheads' in *District and Circle*.

I even wonder if the white washing spread on the whins – in the title poem of *Field Work* – wasn't something that had been unconsciously eroticized by Autolycus's song in *The Winter's Tale*: 'The white sheet bleaching on the hedge / Doth set my pugging tooth on edge'. It's not that there's anything particularly sexy about the lines, but the open-air love life in many Shakespeare songs, that vista of a countryside where 'Between the acres of the rye . . . / These pretty country folks would lie', that may well have cast a venereal gleam on nests in the cornfields and hay barns where Rosy Donnell or Teresa McCloskey would have come and gone with never a thought of Shakespeare.

Did you sometimes feel frustrated that your life as a writer deprived you of the freedom to 'lean and loaf' at your ease or spend more time with your family? The woman in 'An Afterwards' wants the poet to 'come down laughing from your room / And [walk] the twilight with me and your children'.

Obviously, there were many times when I was under pressure to finish stuff for a deadline, and there were absences from home when I was doing broadcasts or readings, and there were the withdrawals and impatiences that are part and parcel of writing. But you're espoused to poetry too, after all, and other poets, dead and alive, attain the status of in-laws. So in a sense you're living a double life, with two families. Yet, given goodwill and good stamina – and humour – this particular bigamy is manageable. The humour, I'd have thought, is central to 'An Afterwards'. Virgil's wife – an entirely imaginary one – and the poet's wife, there on the infernal ledges, looking down at the spouses in the ice of the ninth circle . . . The fiction of the poem makes my actual family sound jealous of my relationship with poetry; but, in fact, the thing is really about jealousy within the poetry family itself, 'the sulphurous news of poets and poetry', as the woman says.

That 'she', whoever she may be, is not exactly enamoured of the poetry profession. Does Marie have anything in common with her in this respect?

Marie used to joke – joke in earnest – that the stock market wasn't nearly as bullish as the poetry market, that the financial markets were clean compared with the insider dealing of the salons. Dear as many a poet has been to her, she has always had her detachments.

You've said that you and Marie 'started again' in Glanmore. What did the new beginning entail? Had something ended in Belfast?

Belfast is where we grew up, in Glanmore we were grown-ups when we arrived. It was a new stage, probably the foundation of my belief that the secret of life and art is the threefold: getting started, keeping going and getting started again. We were at the end of a decade of extraordinary richness, whether you look at it in terms of creative life or professional career or personal loves and friendships. In 1962, I'd started teaching, met Marie and started writing. In 1972, I resigned from Queen's, withdrew from a thriving poetry scene and went full-time as a writer in the more solitary conditions of Wicklow. Yet Glanmore was a retreat in more senses than one. It was like the spiritual retreat we'd always do at the beginning of the school year: on the last evening there would be a formal renewal of your baptismal vows. I'd say that the move we made required something similar, a renewed espousal. I think that sense of two people committing, or recommitting, is present in 'Glanmore Sonnets': 'our separateness; / The respite in our dewy dreaming faces'. As is the other commitment: 'Vowels ploughed into other, opened ground, / Each verse returning like the plough turned round'.

Was there a sense that Marie had been displaced from her working life by the move to Wicklow? You mentioned that 'later on' she taught at the school in Ashford. What was the position when you first moved?

Marie had already stopped teaching so as to be with the two boys as they grew up. That was a very conscious decision on her part. Then too we'd had that year in Berkeley, when there was never a question of her becoming the working wife; and a year later, when we went to Wicklow, she was expecting Catherine. So there was a deliberateness about her being at home during those years, and a fulfilment that she recognizes more and more as the years go on. Later, yes, an opportunity would come for her to teach in the school at Ashford, and that was both a boost to our budget and a chance for her to shine in the classroom; she was greatly cherished by the parents in the district and that, as I was saying, definitely helped to settle us in.

Did you go back much to the North?

More to County Derry and County Tyrone, to our families, than to Belfast. My work for the BBC Schools Service with David Hammond meant that I was more in touch with him, and David's summer house in Donegal was also becoming a regular destination in the summer. In those years, you were contending with the whole drag-down of Troubles Belfast – not just the army and police, but the polarization and the lurking sectarianism. One motive that some writers had for staying on was to redeem the place, perhaps even redeem the State, but I had no such motive. It was a time of 'shifts in the camp', as I said years later in 'The First Flight', realignments that became clear, for example, with the responses to the publication of *North*.

Are you saying therefore that you deliberately detached yourself from the Belfast camp?

To a certain extent, yes. When I came back from Berkeley, I had a sixth sense that some shift or shake-up had to happen; otherwise the whiff of freedom and promise I was feeling might pass for ever. I knew it was a turning point, although I didn't necessarily know we'd end up in Glanmore. The move south came by chance – even if it was a happy one. To quote 'The First Flight' again, 'It was more sleepwalk than spasm / yet that was a time when the times / were also in spasm'. Also, to repeat something I was telling you earlier, we had friends' voices – Barrie Cooke's and Ted Hughes's – urging us to think about making a move, and their encouragement was significant.

Did the Synge connection to Glanmore mean much to you?

It was a richness, but it didn't have any effect on what I was doing. Grasmere, with the Wordsworths' cottage, probably meant more to me at the time than the Synges' castle in Glanmore. John Synge wasn't all that much connected to the castle, anyhow. He had grown up in Glenageary and spent more time around Annamoe than in Glanmore. I eventually put Synge into an eclogue, where he appears as Meliboeus and Ann Saddlemyer becomes Augusta – Ann having been a feminine Augustus to me, as well as a class of a Lady Gregory.

And what about the literary scene in Dublin? Austin Clarke?
Thomas Kinsella? Eavan Boland?

We did see a bit of the Kinsellas, as I was saying earlier. And Eavan
and her husband Kevin Casey visited us once in Glanmore. Austin
Clarke I had met in Belfast a couple of times with Nora, and they
had been good company, but that was the extent of the contact.
Eavan I had known through Derek Mahon and the Longleys; in
those days, we talked regularly on the telephone, and would
encounter each other here and there in Dublin – in RTE studios,
for example – but at that time I was in withdrawal from any scene.

Were you aware of any resentment towards you among Southern
Irish writers – any sense that you were trespassing on their
territory? Or some feeling that you possessed, in the Troubles,
a purchase on a 'big subject' which they lacked?

Only an idiot would think the writing environment is ever free of
resentment. I didn't give much thought to such things because I
would have taken them for granted. But I also took for granted that,
in the republic of letters, there were rights of way everywhere for
everybody. I didn't perceive myself as a trespasser. If anything, I
would have felt more like a homecomer. Given my own political and
cultural background, I thought of the 'Southern' dimension as some-
thing that I myself belonged to and that belonged to me. The only
obvious resentment I experienced was the usual sort, occasioned by
a couple of lightly negative reviews I'd done on *Imprint*. On the
other hand, I do believe that the novelist John Broderick went ape for
a while after he got a very Leavisite scolding on that same pro-
gramme from Frank Ormsby. Ormsby being from Fermanagh and
yours truly from Derry, Broderick probably thought it was some
kind of Northern conspiracy to do him down; but I had no idea what
Frank was going to say and even if I'd wanted to restrain him, it
wouldn't have been my place to do so.

Despite being 'in withdrawal from any scene', you were editing
the anthologies of new Irish poetry called Soundings, *the first in*
1972, the second in 1974. How did Soundings *come about?*

James Gracey was assistant librarian at the Linenhall Library in
Belfast in the early seventies and had started the Blackstaff Press.

The idea for the anthologies must have come from the usual give-and-take between him and me and Michael Longley, who was by then at work with the Arts Council. Again, I envisaged the editing job as useful journeywork, but I was also interested in ending the North/South poetry stand-off. Eventually, for example, I included people like Peter Fallon, Gerard Fanning, Harry Clifton, Dermot Healy, Gregory O'Donoghue, Patrick King, as well as Northerners such as Ciaran Carson and Frank Ormsby.

Did you encourage any of those younger poets from the South to show you their work? Did you ever consider setting up a 'Group' in Dublin?

The one writer I met and talked to a bit about his poems was Dermot Healy. He sent a pile of material that was sprouting talent in all directions and I remember meeting him in some pub just off Henry Street, not far from RTE's old studios in the GPO. I also remember very clearly that the pair of us were eyed on that occasion by Anthony Cronin, whom I don't think I had then met in person. But Dermot was the exception. Generally, I was just interested in giving an outlet to people, and had no desire to enter into any further workshop negotiations. I'd had enough of that. For a short while after we moved back into Dublin in 1976, I toyed with the idea of having a kind of literary open house one evening per week – for my own sake, really, just to keep the young poet in me alive. But it seemed more like a latecomerly imitation of the 'evenings' that the old poets used to hold, Yeats and AE and co., and the moment passed.

To come back again to the 'big subject': Field Work *contains accounts of sectarian killings as well as several elegies. Yet, when it was published, you depicted the book as a quest for 'a door into the light'.*

Synge's remark about style being the shock of new subject matter comes to mind. And Lowell's line, 'Why not say what happened?' And Miłosz's respect for 'one clear stanza'. The dark matter of the news headlines needed to get into *Field Work*, but the light I was hoping for is the kind that derives from clarity of expression, from plainer speaking, as in those middle Yeats poems – 'the clear light, like poetry or freedom / Leaning in from sea' that you get in 'Oysters'.

The first section of 'Triptych', which immediately follows
'Oysters', alludes to the assassination in 1976 of the UK
ambassador to Ireland, Christopher Ewart-Biggs. Had you
actually met the ambassador during his posting in Dublin?

I had not. It wasn't so much personal grief as shock at the assassina-
tion that knocked me and everybody else sideways. Killing an
ambassador was more like the breaking of an ancient taboo than a
breach of international protocol. The news that morning on the
radio mentioned two men with rifles running up the hill from the site
of the explosion. Whether or not this was ever confirmed, I'm not
sure, but it stayed with me as a kind of dream image: it was as if the
ghosts of those Old IRA men of the West Cork Flying Column – 'the
unquiet founders', the ones who'd fought and ambushed the Black
and Tans – it's as if they were coming back to haunt the state they'd
fought to establish.

Was there hostility among Republicans because you were openly
critical of the killing of a British representative?

No hostility that I encountered at first hand, at any rate. What I got
obliquely, from closer quarters, was retro-criticism, if I can call it
that, after I presented the Ewart-Biggs Prize. This was given for a
book that helped Anglo-Irish understanding, or some such rubric.
John Bowman's book on de Valera was the first winner, and – if I'm
not mistaken – Conor Cruise O'Brien was one of the judges. The
retro, Republican line on all this was that Ewart-Biggs had been in
MI5 – or is it MI6? – and therefore was fair game, since he'd been
part of the British imperial war machine, and that the prize was
therefore little more than British propaganda. I could see there was
something in the propaganda allegation, but in my old-fashioned
way, I thought the honour of the Irish nation had been compro-
mised by the killing and whatever qualms I might have had were
minor compared with the recompense due.

'The Toome Road', the poem after 'Triptych', is resentful that the
British army is patrolling your home ground. Was the placing of it
an attempt to present a balanced picture of your feelings at this
time, a 'plague on both your houses' approach?

That wasn't the intention and was never how I saw it. I soon dis-
covered, all the same, that 'The Toome Road' had annoyed some

very fair-minded people. They wanted to know what my alternative to army patrols would have been, given the IRA campaign. And at the academical, theoretical level, there was probably an objection to the essentialism in my invocation of the 'invisible, untoppled omphalos'. Essentialism or not, however, there was still an affront to *dúchas* in being questioned about my name and address by these uninformed cubs in uniform at the end of my own loaning.

But the main thing about the poem, as far as I'm concerned, is the way it was sanctioned by a dream I'd had long before the Troubles. I dreamt I was running across fields to tell about an invasion. In the dream, I'd seen these Asian soldiers in tanks, coming in convoy down along the Antrim Coast Road, and I was the only one there to raise the alarm. It was eerie and it stayed with me for years, partly because I connected it with a famous old prophecy of Nostradamus's that the Russians would water their horses by the shores of Lough Neagh. That prophecy, incidentally, turned up years later as the title of a famous Troubles painting by Dermot Seymour, where you have a British army helicopter doing surveillance and, down below, you see this young fellow in a kind of anxious, haunted state, crossing a field full of big black cattle.

Helicopters and roadblocks have appeared regularly in your poems. Were you especially aggrieved by British army patrols of that sort?

One half of me would be saying, 'They're only a bunch of squaddies doing their job; as individuals, they'd sooner be at home in Leeds or wherever – they're here because of the IRA's threat to life and limb.' But another half rebelled when I'd turn a corner and there were the armoured cars blocking the road, marksmen in the hedge, soldiers in warpaint manning the checkpoint. A lot depended on the manners of the individuals you were dealing with. But the truth of the matter was that they were deployed to keep you in your place, their comrades had shot down people in Derry and they could basically do what they liked. The disgrace of the army comes from the way the higher-ups protected the low-downs. Leaving aside the scandal of Bloody Sunday, there were those cases where soldiers who'd shot innocent people and were found guilty of it got a token sentence and then were readmitted, smirking, to the ranks. In cases like that, the contempt for the nationalist people, the contempt for justice, told you what you were dealing with.

At that point you just wanted to say, 'To hell with them.' And it wasn't the squaddies from Leeds you'd be thinking about, but the Loyalist element in the Scottish regiments and the blond-voiced top brass in the officers' mess. For twenty years and more, every time I drove up from Dublin into Tyrone and Derry, I always felt a kind of generalized menace on the lonelier bits of the roads: you knew the countryside was full of clandestine activity, not just by the paramilitaries on both sides, but by the undercover operations of groups like the SAS. I remember doing a haiku about it: 'Springtime in Ulster: / Aerials in hedges, squawk / of walkie-talkies'.

After Bloody Sunday, you actually wrote a song, 'The Road to Derry'.

I did it after I attended the funerals of the people who had been shot. Luke Kelly, the singer with the Dubliners, asked me to write something and said he'd perform it. So I came up with this traditional ballad, starting off with the words 'On a Wednesday morning early I took the road to Derry, / Along Glenshane and Foreglen and the cold woods of Hillhead' – which echoes one of my favourite songs in the Irish tradition, 'The Boys of Mullaghbawn':

On a Monday morning early as my wandering steps did lead me
Down by a farmer's station of meadow and green lawn,
I heard great lamentation that the wee birds they were making,
Saying, 'We'll have no more engagements with the boys of
    Mullaghbawn.'

The air of the song is beautifully slowed and grief-stricken and I thought it would suit the words and the mood of what I was doing; but it didn't seem to work for Luke, he didn't sing it, and the moment passed. Most of the words hold up all right, but there's one verse and a couple of lines that are pretty ropey, artistically speaking, even within the convention, so when I reprinted it on the thirtieth anniversary of Bloody Sunday, I did a bit of cutting and revision. But the core images and statements were there from the start: 'And in the dirt lay justice like an acorn in the winter . . . where the thirteen men lay dead'.

You weren't tempted to include it in any of your collections?

No. It belonged to the moment that produced it. It was what Wordsworth called 'a timely utterance' that gave relief. Like any song, it was made for the communal voice. If it had been sung by Luke Kelly, it would have functioned immediately and rightly as an expression of shared grief and outrage. If, on the other hand, I had reprinted it later in a book, I'd have felt I was currying favour with a certain constituency, writing propaganda and basically letting myself down. Doing the kind of thing Brodsky used to mock with the phrase, 'Here come the good guys.'

You returned to the Bloody Sunday theme a few years later by writing 'Casualty', which tells of a drinking friend who was 'blown to bits' for failing to maintain a paramilitary curfew. You have already mentioned this man and I'd like to learn more about him.

Louis O'Neill was a regular customer in my father-in-law's public house in Ardboe: a small farmer and eel fisherman. The kind of level-headed, low-key, humorous countryman I always feel at home with. Sometimes I'd be on the outside of the counter with him and his friends, as a customer, and sometimes, as the publican's son-in-law, I'd be on the inside, doing barman. My friendship with Louis was special because of that unforgettable summer morning when I went out on Lough Neagh with him and another companion to lift the eel lines. So when he was killed in that explosion, I knew I would have to write something, but wasn't sure how it could be done. My father-in-law had closed his premises on the night of the curfew to mark the Bloody Sunday funerals, but Louis had gone to another place that was admitting people by the back door and continuing to do business. In the beginning, incidentally, we thought that the bomb might have been placed by the Provisional IRA as a reprisal for the publican's defiance of the curfew, but that's not the opinion of the journalists who compiled *Lost Lives*, a book that reports the facts surrounding every death resulting from the Troubles. They believe it could have been a UVF operation. But whoever did it, they left Louis O'Neill 'blown to bits'.

'Casualty' seems to have been a difficult poem to complete, since it appeared in different versions before its final inclusion in Field

Work. *What was the nub of the difficulty? Were you wary,*
because of the misreadings of 'Punishment' by some reviewers of
North, *of exploring aspects of 'our tribe's complicity'?*

There was no such wariness, and I cannot at this stage remember
why it took so long to get the thing right. Even at the time, I proba-
bly couldn't have told you. I did have one big uncertainty to explore,
a dilemma that many people in the North were then experiencing
very acutely, stretched as they often were between the impulse to
maintain political solidarity and their experience of a spiritual con-
dition of complete solitude. I saw in Louis O'Neill's transgression
of the curfew – which was basically a call for solidarity – an image of
the Joycean *non serviam*. 'Casualty' was a new kind of poem for
me, a plotted shape, and the narrative and metrical built-upness of
it meant that bits of it could be shifted from one position to another,
in a way that wouldn't be possible with free verse. The sixth sense is
what you're depending on at times like that, the hunch that the job's
not finished, the need to put feelers out around it and into it to see
where the problem lies.

You mentioned earlier that you had engaged in some
'ventriloquizing for Robert Lowell'. Presumably therefore it
made sense to you that the Lowell influence was emphasized by
some critics, including Donald Davie (in verse!).

Oh yes, that made sense all right. In fact, you can see the influence
in the second half of *North*, in the blank verse, 'why not say what
happened' bits of the 'Singing School' sequence, and in particu-
lar in the 'Fosterage' section. That one is an unrhymed sonnet,
modelled on those unrhymed sonnet-portraits of writers in *Note-*
book and *History* – 'Robert Frost', for example. 'Fosterage' could
equally well have been called 'Michael McLaverty'. And that same
pitch and head-on approach to portraiture – if we can call it that –
is definitely present in *Field Work*, in the memorial poem for Seán
Ó Riada, and of course, in the one for Lowell himself.

With regard to *North*, I should probably mention Lowell's break-
out from his private hospital to present me with the Duff Cooper
Award in London in early 1976: he had agreed to do the presenta-
tion, but when the time came he was in one of his 'high' periods
and confined to a nursing home. Then – on the afternoon of the day

in question – he disappeared, much to the distress of his wife and friends, who eventually found him in the room in London University where the award ceremony was to take place. It was a sad, mad event, Lowell going about with a jacket over his pyjama tops; Diana Cooper with a chihuahua on her arm, telling him at some point that the prize was to be presented by some mad American; Lowell wild-eyed and nodding, 'I know, I know.' In the end, his speech consisted of a reading, with commentary upon – and questions to me about – the 'Summer 1969' section of 'Singing School', a section which also shows a debt to his *Notebook* approach.

Did those later Lowell sonnets influence your own 'Glanmore Sonnets'?

Not that I'm aware of. I remember sending some of them to him after we'd spent time at the Kilkenny Arts Week in the summer of 1975. I was very conscious of how correctly iambic they were in comparison to his own much lumpier ingots, and indeed he implied in a letter to me that they could do with a bit of knocking about, but I was delighted when he said of them in general that they 'seemed to have come through a grief'. He had a wonderful way of coming close, personally and critically.

How did you manage to draw Lowell for the entire week of that festival in Kilkenny?

I invited him to do one poetry reading in the middle of the week, but he landed at Dublin Airport on a Sunday and stayed through until the next weekend, when he went on, via Glanmore, to stay with Garech Browne in Luggala. I met him at the airport at the start of the trip and brought him as far as Glanmore at the end. When he was in the cottage, Michael – who'd just turned nine – said to him, 'I know you are a famous poet, but it's my ambition to meet a famous footballer.' And that was also the occasion when Lowell said to me, 'You see a lot of your children.' He went on to stay with Garech because he liked the touch of bohemia and the touch of Anglo-Irish class that Luggala provided; and he knew Garech from London, as a relation of Caroline Blackwood's. In fact, I first met Lowell in 1972 at a party given by Sonia Orwell to celebrate Cal and Caroline's wedding. Not that I was invited: I was staying with Karl and Jane Miller and they were on the guest list and brought me along. It was a very starry affair – Cyril Connolly, the Spenders, Sonia Orwell herself, not to mention the happy couple.

I actually got into a corner with Lowell for about half an hour and did the laundry list, as Brodsky used to say – checking out what was to be said about which poets. George Mackay Brown, for example, whom Lowell had visited with Garech when the Claddagh Records people went to Orkney to make a Mackay Brown recording: 'He's a good poet, but he's not a great poet.' The antennae were always out. He knew Michael Longley's work and Derek Mahon's, and what with Caroline having grown up in Clandeboye in North Down, he was well clued into the Northern Ireland situation. It was a genuine enough meeting, and he was immensely charming and even more immensely intelligent; but I'd read Norman Mailer's account of him in *Armies of the Night*, where his powers of flattery are very accurately set down, so in spite of my delight at how well we got on, I was still a bit on my guard. Then a year or two later, after I'd done a review on *Imprint* of *The Dolphin* and the rejigged *Notebook* that appeared as *History* and *For Lizzie and Harriet*, he wrote to thank me. So at that point, I invited him to the Kilkenny Arts Week.

You would have known the poems long before you came to know the man.

'The Quaker Graveyard at Nantucket' I had known since I was an undergraduate, so for me that poem and its author were the real canonical goods. All through the sixties I was reading him, constantly – *Life Studies, Imitations, For the Union Dead* – books that were just part of the air we breathed. And Lowell was often favoured at The Group: Philip Hobsbaum inclined in particular to *Life Studies* and *Imitations*: I remember his reading of the Victor Hugo piece from the latter, and Arthur Terry's reading – from that book – of Leopardi's 'Saturday Night in the Village'.

Did Imitations *influence your own attitude towards translation? You've said, in recent years, that 'the older I get the more obedient I tend to become', which suggests a repudiation of the Lowell position.*

At the time, and in the context of The Group, Lowell was implicated in the Paleface versus Redskin version of American literary history. It was a simplification but it was a way of lining up. I was generally in the Redskin/Lowell camp, whereas the Longleys would have been more for the Paleface Wilbur. And they would have held up Derek Mahon's translation of Villon, in his first book, as a superior job to Lowell's – which it probably is. And they would have forwarded the claims of Larkin over Hughes. And so on. These were the currents we were creating and navigating among ourselves. So, yes, I was influenced in my attitude to translation by Lowell, but not particularly influenced by his style – not then, at any rate.

The bit of Lowell translation that had most impact on me was his version of the Brunetto Latini canto in *Near the Ocean*. If I hadn't encountered that, there would have been no 'Ugolino' in *Field Work*. On the other hand, if I were doing 'Ugolino' today, I mightn't allow myself the supernumerary extravagance of an image such as 'a spattered, carnal melon'. That definitely came with my Lowellizing. It's hard to generalize in relation to this obedience/divergence question. On different occasions you have a different covenant with the original. I couldn't imagine doing Ó Rathaille's 'Gile na Gile', for example, without trying to suggest something of the metrical drive; but with an Irish bardic poem, I wouldn't necessarily feel an obligation to keep to the patterns of assonance and syllable count and all the rest of it.

Introducing Lowell's Kilkenny reading, you said that 'to master the meaning of your art and to master the meaning of the word "poet" is the poet's task'. Wouldn't many poets prefer not to become too self-conscious about these matters and to discover the answers simply through performing the poetic act itself?

Maybe so, although I still think those high terms about mastering the meaning of the art and the task were justified. Lowell was a poet who took public stances and in that way followed the Horatian injunction to be 'utile' and the Philip Sidney injunction 'to instruct'. On the other hand, epoch-making poems like 'For the Union Dead' and 'Near the Ocean' did not arrive from a programme of instruction, they came from where he was cornered, in himself and his times, and were the equivalent of escapes, surges of inner life vaulting up and away. Every true poem arrives like that, with self-consciousness giving way to self-forgetfulness in the glee of finding the words. It is, as you say, a discovered answer. Still, to go back to your question, I do believe that the more you think between times about those 'meanings' I referred to, the better your chances will be of doing worthwhile work. In the end, it's probably a sweetly vicious circle: until you have had the experience of genuinely 'performing the poetic act', you won't have any reason to think about what it means.

Did you see much of Lowell after Kilkenny?

There wasn't all that much time after that. I saw him a few months later at that Duff Cooper event, and in the next year and a half, which were his last, he and Caroline called on us on two or three occasions in Dublin. They'd get bored out in Castletown House – a vast Georgian pile near Dublin, where Caroline had rented an apartment from her cousin, Desmond Guinness – and they would hit town and the vodka and us in one single swoop. Their life was pretty turbulent, wherever they were, and they probably regarded Marie and me as freakishly domesticated; but there was always a lot of gumption and gossip in the air when they landed.

Your 'Elegy' was begun within days of the last of those visits by the Lowells. Did he seem like a dying man to you then?

He seemed just that bit flaccid, but only in the body, and I certainly had no sense that he was near the end. He left a copy of the American edition of *Day by Day*; when we heard the news of his death, it was still lying there on the coffee table where he'd put it. What I did sense, however, with the aid of the gossip then going the rounds, was that the relationship with Caroline was about to end. In 'Pit Stop Near Castletown', I conflated two things that happened that evening. One was the stop we made near the gates of the demesne so that he and I could relieve ourselves by the side of the car; and the other was a quick coded exchange between us in the hallway before I drove them home, when Marie and Caroline were getting their coats. 'Will I be seeing you soon again?' I asked and he replied, with that high neigh that sometimes came into his voice, and one of his lightning-flicker looks over the glasses, 'I don't think so.'

In that same poem, you mention that Mary McCarthy depicted – or disparaged – your address at the London memorial service as

*the 'biggest cover-up since Watergate'. Why do you think you
were selected to deliver that address?*

I cannot say why I was chosen to do the address, but it had to be a
very deliberate decision on the part of Caroline and, probably,
Jonathan Raban, who had been close to the Lowells during their
last years in London. It probably galled some people who had
known him over there – Alvarez, for example, who was in the con-
gregation, and Ian Hamilton. Again, as usual, anxiety about speak-
ing on such an occasion made for a certain elevation. I stuck to his
calling as a poet and his conduct of it, and made reference neither
to his madnesses nor to his marriages. In the end, I heard the
McCarthy remark from Tom Flanagan who heard it from Conor
Cruise O'Brien to whom the lady herself had hissed it on her way
out of the church early, in order to catch a plane for Paris.

*To go back for a moment to the Kilkenny Arts Week in 1975:
while there, you received news that your second cousin Colum
McCartney had been killed by Loyalist paramilitaries in a random
sectarian assassination. This must have presented you with an
awkward dilemma – if you went north to the family funeral, you'd
be abandoning your post with Lowell and the other poets; if you
stayed, you'd feel you had 'failed an obligation' (to borrow a
phrase from 'Station Island').*

At the time, the alternatives weren't as stark as that. Colum
McCartney was the son of a cousin of my father's, a Scullion mar-
ried to a McCartney. But Colum wasn't personally known to me,
and I wasn't close enough to the family to feel obligated in any
immediate way. I'd been living in Belfast since the early sixties,
and then in Wicklow. My brothers and sisters and parents would
have been at the wake and the funeral and I would not have been
expected. Still, the circumstances of his death were so brutal you
couldn't not feel that your presence was called for, in protest as
much as in sympathy.

So you felt some guilt?

Guilt might be too strong a word, unease might be too weak.
Protocol was at issue, and protocol was being observed by the
Heaneys in County Derry.

1 Patrick Heaney and dog Nora.

2 SH, age about three, in Tullyroan, outside a relative's pub.

3 Heaney children and mother, c.1950. Left to right: (*front*) Hugh, Patrick, Colm; (*back*) Sheena, Charles, Margaret Heaney (holding Christopher), Ann, SH.

4 SH with Aunt Mary and brother Colm.

5 Heaney children, *c.*1950. Left to right: (*front*) Seamus, Ann, Sheena; (*back*) Patrick, Hugh.

6 Anahorish primary school football team, 1951. SH is in the back row, fourth from left.

7 Scholarship winners, St Columb's College, Derry, 1957. Left to right: Robert McLaughlin, SH, Seamus McGrotty, Patrick Deery.

8 SH and Marie on their wedding day, August 1965.

9 SH – as lecturer at St Joseph's College of Education, Belfast – and Marie, attending staff dinner with SH's colleague T. P. Flanagan and his wife, Sheelagh.

10 Michael Longley, SH and David Hammond on the Room to Rhyme tour, 1968.

11 SH, Marie, Michael and Christopher at Broagh, near Mossbawn, 1972.
(Photo: Larry Herman)

12 SH and son Michael at The Wood, Bellaghy, *c*.1973. (Photo: Jim Bennett)

13 SH with daughter Catherine Ann, 1983. (Photo: Fergus Bourke)

14 SH's parents, Margaret and Patrick, 1973. (Photo: David Hammond)

Yet, when you returned to the subject in 'Station Island', you allowed your cousin to allege that, in 'The Strand at Lough Beg', you 'confused evasion and artistic tact'. Did you really feel you had been guilty of over-aestheticizing his death, or was this a dramatic dialogue set up to explore the whole idea of public poetry?

It was set up, exactly as you say. It was another of those instances where the intertwining of the 'creative' and the 'responsible' is, as they say, interrogated. I had not at that stage heard Joseph Brodsky's dictum that 'if art teaches us anything, it is that the human condition is private', but that's what's being said in 'The Strand at Lough Beg'. In the opening stanza, there's probably enough hard information about the context of the killing to offset the healing landscape passage at the end.

Why, in the poem, do you call Colum McCartney's people – and your own – 'slow arbitrators of the burial ground'?

The McCartneys lived near Lough Beg, so that was the proper place to encounter Colum's shade. The strand there is remote and rushy and misty, and there's an island called Church Island out in the middle of the water. The spire on the old church was erected in the eighteenth century by the Earl Bishop of Derry and the whole area has a kind of melancholy, Gray's elegy feel to it. But it had special memories for me because I often went there in the evenings with my father to check on cattle. He rented the strand for grazing, so sometimes at 'parting day' we'd walk out in the long grass and sedge, and feel the loneliness of the place and the stillness of it. We were on a practical errand but at the same time it was like a bath for the soul.

When I read the passage at the start of Dante's *Purgatorio*, describing that little lake and rushy shore where Virgil and Dante find themselves once they emerge from the murk of hell, I couldn't not connect it with my own strand, so that last bit of the poem was the first bit to be written. The beginning and middle were done later – including the reference to the 'arbitrators of the burial ground'. The phrase is there, I suppose, to summon up the talk of those Scullion elders – Colum's antecedents as well as mine: slow, ruminative discussions at gables and in byres about cattle and crops and dead ancestors, who was buried where in the graveyard, and so on and so forth. Those people were not in any sense politicized, the march of events might be occurring at the end of their lanes, but they weren't ever going to 'crack the whip or seize the day': I just wanted to suggest that Colum and I had been born into that same quietist, fatalistic tribe.

Were the details of his murder ever established?

The consensus is that he was flagged down by a group of Loyalist paramilitaries rigged out in Ulster Defence Regiment uniforms. The UDR had its 'bad apples', of course, and the *Lost Lives* book opts for that explanation.

Was Colum McCartney your only relative to die in the Troubles?

The only relative, yes, but other friends – and friends of friends – were lost. Louis O'Neill, of course. Willie Strathearn, the shop owner in Ahoghill. Sean Armstrong, a friend from university days who ended up as a social worker and was shot on the landing of his flat. Francis Hughes, the hunger striker, whom I didn't know personally, but his parents and elder sisters were well known to me. Martin McBurney, the barrister in Belfast, about whom Michael Longley wrote. Sean Brown – very well known to me – the secretary of the Bellaghy GAA Club, shot by a Loyalist killer gang as late as 1997. And there would have been others. One or two, at least, of the kids I'd taught in St Thomas's School in Ballymurphy.

'A Postcard from North Antrim', which also recounts your first meeting with Marie, was written in memory of Sean Armstrong.

Sean was at Queen's when I was there and edited the rag magazine, *PTQ* – the initials of Belfast's motto, '*Pro Tanto Quid Retribuamus*'. I don't remember how we first met, but in October 1962 he was giving a party and had asked me. I'd actually met Marie a couple of nights before, on the Tuesday of that week, and had arranged for her to drop back the book she borrowed on the Thursday. So when she arrived to deliver it, I suggested we go down to Sean's jamboree; she agreed, and the thing took off from there. Sean then disappeared from the scene and turned up again in the early seventies. He had spent time in communes of one sort or another in California, and turned into a wonderful, colourful, original man, half hippy, half artist, wholly committed to trying to do some good in Belfast. He became active as a social worker, and was moving between the factions, crossing the peace line from Shankill to Falls; for that reason, we have to presume, he began to be regarded by the hard men as some kind of spy and was shot.

In the poem, Sean is asking you for 'the raw bar' . . .

'The raw bar' was an Ulsterism we'd heard from, I think, Sean O'Boyle, the song collector. It just meant a song sung without accompaniment.

And did you actually sing?

Chanted. Growled in recitative. I never had a singing voice, but there were things I did as party pieces – 'A sailor courted a farmer's daughter / Who lived contagious to the town of Strabane; / With loving melodies he did besought her / That she'd marry him before she'd marry any other class or classification of a man'. And then 'The Cruise of the *Calabar*', that's mentioned in the poem: 'Come all ye dry land sail-y-ors and listen to my song, / It's only got forty verses, it won't detain ye long, / It's all about the advent-y-ures of this ould Lisburn tar, / And how sailed this man before the mast / On the good ship *Calabar*'.

Were you a regular at the 'ballad sessions' in the sixties?

I didn't go to many concert performances, but am one of the generation who felt the full blast of the Clancy Brothers' breakthrough and listened a lot to their early records. Many songs were learned that way: 'Brennan on the Moor', 'The Bonnie Maid of Fife-ee-o', 'The Holy Ground', and suchlike. Marie was a good singer and had lovely songs from Ardboe, and I loved in particular to hear her do 'Slieve Gallon's Brae', one of the most beautiful Northern airs, named after our own local mountain. Tony McAuley was often with us and Tony too was a wonderful singer; and after we became friendly with David Hammond, the repertoire was extended further and the roguery and revelry got still more unconstrained. But most of that activity was in our own houses and flats, late at night, after a meal or after the pubs shut. I don't remember going to all that many public concerts. One concert I *do* remember was on our first Saturday in Berkeley in 1970: Marie and I, with the kids, and Pete

Seeger chorusing to us, 'This land is your land, this land is my land . . .' Stirring times.

How did you regard Seán Ó Riada's music?

The score for *Mise Éire* was a big thrill in the sixties. The 'Slievenamon' theme. The 'Róisín Dubh' theme. And then there was the work he did with Ceoltóirí Chualann, as arranger and conductor and player of the harpsichord. His contributions *did* rectify things greatly in the world of traditional music. Ó Riada definitely had a touch of genius, and he left the traditional music world in better order, and the entire music culture of the country to some extent retuned. You couldn't be young in sixties Ireland and not feel some of the Ó Riada effect, either on radio programmes or in the arrangements of tunes he popularized: Carolan's Concerto, 'An Ghaoth Aneas', planxties and polkas and that whole outburst of *bodhráns* and fiddles and drones and chanters and concertinas and whatever you're having yourself.

You've referred earlier to Seán Ó Riada's broadcast of 'Craig's Dragoons'.

I didn't actually hear the programme. It was in 1968, as I mentioned, just after the Civil Rights march had been baton-charged in Derry. He wrote to me in early October, a short note asking for something he might use on his programme on Radio Éireann, and I provided the words of 'Craig's Dragoons'. I'd met Ó Riada that summer in Ballydavid, in Kerry, when Marie and I were down on our holidays. He occasionally turned up in Begley's public house, and I remember him dancing Kerry sets, going at it for all he was worth. His wife Ruth was there too and that summer they invited us over to visit them in Coolea, in the Cork Gaeltacht.

They'd moved from Dublin, some years before, and Seán at that time was constantly on the go with the musicians, hitting the road and hitting the bottle, striding out like a prince among his people, but at the same time in hiding from his vocation as a composer. There was a histrionic streak in him, he swanked a bit, but at the same time there was piercing intelligence and a readiness to probe and provoke. I remember that morning, when he took me into his workroom, he came on not so much as a musician as a grey-Connemara-cloth type of Yeatsian man, drawing attention to his guns and his fishing rods.

At the same time, there was sudden, naked honesty, when he as much as said he wasn't working as he should be. I put one little part of our exchange, word for word, into the poem in memory of him: 'How do you work? / Sometimes I just lie out / like ballast in the bottom of the boat / listening to the cuckoo'.

You also capture him conducting the Ulster Orchestra 'like a drover with an ashplant'. When did that occur?

Later in that same year, 1968, when he was 'composer of the year' at the Queen's University festival. Soon after the first attack on the Civil Rights march. I remember getting a terrific charge when he and his musicians appeared on the stage of the Sir William Whitla Hall, lashing into all those Irish jigs and reels and marches. The Whitla Hall was such a temple of official Ulster, the sanctum of posh, potato-in-the-mouth, British-not-Irish types, a lot closer to Britten than to Erin, and here was the *fíor-Ghael* on the rampage, one night in *báinín* with his own session men, and the next in black tie and in charge of his own baton, conducting the province's finest. I couldn't deny, then or now, the cultural boost that Ó Riada gave me at that time. Although he was only one among many, since the festival was also attended that year by John Montague, Tom Kinsella and John McGahern, and we were all involved on one occasion in a symposium chaired by Tyrone Guthrie, who was then vice-chancellor of the university. If William Craig had paid more attention to intelligence from members of that symposium than from members of the RUC Special Branch, the next thirty years might have turned out better.

Did you get on well with Ó Riada?

Well, yes, but I have to say his posturing irked me. Swirling the snifter of brandy and brandishing the cigar. Setting himself up as commissar, interrogating rather than conversing. I remember walking into the Club Bar that week and being asked rather grandly – in front of Kinsella and Montague – 'And where do you stand on the North?' I should have said that, unlike the company I was in, I'd stood on it for thirty years, but I just let it go. I admired him even if I didn't get too close. But I have to say he treated me gallantly when we were down in Kerry, and made me feel welcome in his company, part of the action.

Would you think of him in any way as a mentor?

No. But the romance – and commitment – of his change of life, from Dublin bohemia to Gaeltacht *dúchas*, was an example that was there to be followed. If he had lived, I might have got to know him better. Certainly I was as shaken as the next person when he died in 1971.

Your own next move was into, rather than out of, Dublin. Had you become weary of the freelance life? Was it just too precarious to be sustained?

It was neither a case of weariness nor precariousness. More like prudence. By 1975 we had three children, two boys and a baby girl. The boys had grown to a point where they were about to step into the system, on to an escalator that would carry them from primary school through secondary school and on to wherever. If we stayed out in the country, I saw years of travel for them in the backs of school buses, summers and winters of delivering and collecting them at the nearest bus stop, overcrowding in the gate lodge, Marie being left isolated in the country with all that on her hands when I went off to do lectures or readings, and so on.

It seemed the best thing would be to move into Dublin, get the boys into a school where they could finish up the primary stage of their education and then move up to the secondary stage without having to transfer to another place. But to do so we would have to get a mortgage, and to pay the mortgage I would have to get a job. The freelance earnings were good enough as long as we were paying Ann Saddlemyer's nominal rent in Glanmore, but for a more sustained commitment – and a far more expensive one – something settled and secure was called for. That was the thinking behind the move, obvious and logical; and for once I followed the logic. As soon as the decision was taken, we looked for a house in Dublin, on the south side of the bay, on a direct bus route into town, and we were lucky to get a very good one.

You had already taken on a teaching job, in the English Department of Carysfort College, where teachers were trained.

I got an invitation to apply for a post that was becoming vacant. In the summer of 1975, we'd been in Wicklow for three years, *North* had come out, the first movement was complete and there was a good deal of uncertainty about the next: we still had our Belfast house rented to students, and decision time was again upon us. I loved Glanmore, the actual house, greatly. I had no desire to leave. I knew I was in absolutely the right place for writing. Every time I lifted the latch on the door into our little scullery, the sound and slack fall of it passed through me like gratitude. Or certitude. Theseus had his thread, I had my latch and it opened for me. Or rather, it opened *me*. But I also had four other people in my care.

So the invitation to apply came at the right moment?

And from the right kind of place. My notion was that I should take a job, not in a university but in some less high-profile institution, where I could slip in and out of the city, earning a salary while continuing to live in my head – and in the country. I'd already taught in a teacher-training college in Belfast, so when a delegation from Carysfort landed to the cottage one Sunday afternoon, I was susceptible. All the more so because the workload at that stage was light. So that was the start of it, and it suited very well just then. I travelled up and down, three or four days a week, sometimes on the bus, sometimes in the car, and the college authorities were very accommodating, allowing me, for example, to go to Berkeley in the spring of 1976, to do duty as that year's Beckman Professor.

Was there a sense that you had failed to sustain yourself in the freelance life?

I don't think I felt that. In the first place, the freelance life wasn't what I had opted for. What I'd been after was a separate domain for myself as a poet, a surer sense of a destiny. And the three years in 'the hedge school' had given me that. Still, I did feel I was betraying something when we shifted ground to the suburbs; I'd reneged on something I loved, but it was for the sake of other loves. I also felt I was setting up good foundations for the next decade, marking a space within which and out of which I could operate as a poet. There was an attic in the new house which was safe and sound, a place where I could immediately be self-bound. There was even a Yeatsian 'narrow winding stair'.

In The Place of Writing, *you speak of the various dwellings in which Yeats lived, most of them fairly anonymous, as against the very deliberate flourish and symbolism of Thoor Ballylee. In buying your house on Strand Road, Dublin, were you determined not to suggest that it was an artist's dwelling but rather – to quote you on the topic of Hardy's Max Gate – a place which 'both embraces and embodies ordinariness, if only as a camouflage or a retreat'? Was your Strand Road house Hardyesque or Yeatsian?*

If those are the alternatives, it had to be Hardyesque. But it wasn't until I wrote several poems in the new place that I began to feel safe again and gather moss. I remember, for example, starting in on 'Casualty', downstairs, at the end of a long refectory table we had picked up when the Carysfort dining hall was being refurbished, and feeling surer of myself and of the house when I managed to finish the poem. After that, the anxiety abated and the sense of purpose steadied.

Were you ever tempted to move again?

Never. In fact, in the very first moment of my tenure a soothsayer told me I'd be in the place for ever. The evening I got the key from the estate agent, in November 1976, John McGahern was in town to attend the presentation of that year's Hennessy Awards for contributors to 'New Irish Writing'. He had been a judge, as had Alan Sillitoe, who was in John's company when I met him. Anyhow, my sense of occasion prompted the two of them to come out to Strand Road with me and cross the threshold ceremoniously with a candle for light and a bottle of Bushmills for libation. But just before we went into the house, we stood at the gate, looking up at the bulk of roof and chimney against the winter sky, and John said, 'Well, you've bought the coffin.' Deep down, I knew it already, but that particular McGahernism sealed my knowledge.

How did the new abode work out for the rest of the family?

Very well. The boys, as I was saying earlier, were accepted in St Conleth's College, thanks to the advice and support of Eleanor Kinsella. Catherine got started in kindergarten and then attended the local primary school in Booterstown. For the next few years, Marie was in a very real sense what they call in the States 'a homemaker'.

And you were a lecturer in a college run by the Sisters of Mercy. Perhaps you'd elaborate a bit on why you chose that academically unambitious role rather than, say, working alongside Seamus Deane in University College Dublin?

For one thing, I was not academically ambitious. In the decade after I'd graduated, I'd had enough academic upward mobility to be going on with – starting as a schoolteacher, being appointed a college lecturer, then a university lecturer in Queen's, then a visiting lecturer at the University of California. All this with only a BA to my name. I wasn't interested in proving myself as a scholar. I wasn't a researcher or a literary historian, I hung halfway between literary journalism and the lecture hall. Meanwhile, poetry had come and changed me and my sense of myself, so my need at that moment, at the age of thirty-six or thirty-seven, was to consolidate the poet part of me: my instinct was that a university would be far too public a milieu, that Carysfort would offer a better chance of keeping the head down and following the sixth sense. And anyhow, nobody was asking me to join the UCD faculty.

Were you expected to bring a Catholic emphasis to your courses at Carysfort College? Did you have to affect a certain piety?

I didn't have to affect piety, nor did anybody else. And I certainly didn't give any different emphasis to my teaching than I had done at Queen's or for that matter at Berkeley. The place was owned and managed and to a certain extent staffed by the Sisters of Mercy, and since they'd been doing the job for the best part of a hundred years, the ethos of the place was certainly Catholic. The principal was a nun with an admirable breadth of mind and sympathy, Sister Regina Durkan, and until I took over a year or so after I was first appointed, the head of the English Department was also a member of the order. The wimple and the veil were much in evidence in the corridors, but the place was in transition.

Part of the reason I was attractive to them was my history of bilocation, if you like, between my experience in St Joseph's College of Education in Belfast, which was largely professionally oriented, and my experience in the university proper. Carysfort was just then beginning to award the BEd degree, needing new confidence as an institution within the national university system. It was laicizing itself, and inside a couple of years after I arrived, the composition and academic standing of the faculty altered swiftly. And anyhow, as a student at Queen's University and then later on as a lecturer, I was well used to withholding 'ratification' from some of the forms and presuppositions of the institution where I found myself. Wherever you happen to end up, there are protocols and courtesies to be observed. In the sixties in Queen's, it had involved things like the RUC band and 'God Save the Queen' on Graduation Day; in the seventies in Carysfort, it was 'Faith of our Fathers' and a College Mass to start the year. Your private life was still your own. Indeed, to my certain knowledge, I was a hell of a lot more emancipated from Catholic practice at the time than many a star in the UCD firmament.

Was there not still a certain convent atmosphere, as opposed to a secular feel, at Carysfort?

There was, yes. For one thing you had the occasional statue in a niche and holy pictures on the walls, and you had, I think, the angelus. And the elder nuns tended to infantilize the students. But all that, as I say, was in the process of change. In the six years I worked there, I witnessed the regimentation disappearing and a far more independently minded student body establishing itself. I have to say that Regina Durkan was a positive influence on this development. And I should further say that I was positively glad of the opportunity to play a part in that movement for change. I had something to contribute, both in the matter of content of courses and of contact with people in university departments. I was in a position to show my students and my colleagues that they shouldn't think of themselves as second-class academic citizens. I came and went between various third-level institutions and felt no need to apologize for my work address, so why should they? I believed and still believe there was educational meaning to what I was doing.

You've mentioned the acquisition of a refectory table from Carysfort; and I know you furnished your attic with a makeshift desk, using two planks from the old classroom benches. Why were you satisfied with this rudimentary arrangement?

The narrow winding stair was a factor: very hard to get anything other than boards to the top floor. In fact, it was a colleague in the English Department, John O'Doherty, who put up the first bookshelves. But apart from the physical difficulties, there was a superstitious fear of making a designer study, a film set rather than a bolt-hole. I didn't want to feel self-conscious when I went up there. I also wanted to keep faith with the frugal circumstances of Glanmore. The workplace was in conscious resistance to the expectations of suburbia. It was a dis-place, if you like. Like most places of writing. And it has served me well ever since.

It appears in 'Weeping', your act of poetic thanksgiving, in Electric Light.

It does. What I do there is recount a dream I had, not long after we moved into Strand Road, and which I took as a good omen. I dreamt I opened the doorway to the attic and down the stairwell there came this immense flood of crystal clear water full of green roses, washing over me but not in any way panicking or threatening to drown me. A downpour that seemed to me to bode well. That too was an important moment.

8

'To the edge of the water'
Station Island

~

As an undergraduate, you made the Station Island pilgrimage on no fewer than three occasions. I'd like to hear why you went, with whom and to what effect.

Curiosity had a lot to do with it. I'd been hearing about Lough Derg since I was a youngster, about people in earlier generations doing 'the black fast'. Apparently they would walk the whole way to Donegal, keeping going on black tea and dry bread. So that scenario was with me from the start and, when the time eventually came, I set off in a spirit that Chaucer would have recognized – for the company and the outing, just to see what was entailed. The first time was after the summer exams at Queen's; we travelled by special bus from the Catholic chaplaincy, in a party that included a fair number of the people I used to knock around with. A couple of years before, we'd all been college boys and convent girls, but now we were beginning to take the measure of ourselves and our freedom, so there was a flirtatious aspect to the trip. But there was a religious dimension too. The fasting and the all-night vigil had the attraction of the unknown. The first couple of times I went were basically end-of-term expeditions, although it's possible at this stage to see them as rites of passage. A 'been there, done that' sort of thing.

Was there any family tradition of making the pilgrimage?

None.

When you say it was basically a student outing, are you implying that you didn't take it all that seriously?

This was the late 1950s, when religion was still a pervasive element, so a cheery atmosphere didn't mean an unserious engagement. Lough Derg was a ritual, it entailed the fulfilment of set exercises, the repetition of prayers, keeping a fast, going round the basilica and 'the beds' in your bare feet. While you were engaged in all that, you were necessarily concentrated on getting through it but not necessarily absorbed in sacred reverie. Nor were you required to be. Technically speaking, there was a plenary indulgence to be gained by completing the pilgrimage, but the real motivation was in pitting yourself against the conditions – the fasting, your bare feet on hard ground, rain or shine, keeping awake during the first night and the second day. At the end of it all, there was a definite catharsis. As you sailed away from the island, you'd sing the Lough Derg hymn, 'Hail, glorious Saint Patrick'; but, deep inside, your body and soul were singing 'Look, we have come through!'

You have mentioned St Patrick's association with Slemish mountain in County Antrim, so I wonder if you thought of him as a local presence. Was he the object of special devotion?

Not at all. He was basically a life-size statue cast in plaster, a bishop in a green chasuble, with a mitre on his head and a crozier in his hand, staking down a cluster of snakes at his feet. Slemish, where he was said to have worked as a slave boy herding sheep, did have a certain aura; even so, Patrick wasn't ever a spiritual figure for me. He was a creature of legend, the man who lit the fire on the Hill of Slane and challenged the Druids, the man who banished the snakes, a figure who appeared on banners on St Patrick's Day.

What mental image did you have of God when you were young? As just another plaster statue?

I had a stronger image of my guardian angel, a tall winged strider at my elbow, like something out of a Renaissance painting. That was a real imagined presence; but God the Father, no, there was never a likeness in my mind's eye. I did imagine a realm of light up there, a world-ceiling that was a heaven-floor, a loft full of distance and translucence where He had absconded. And all that must have had some connection, synaesthetically, with the shine inside the ciborium, the reflection of the packed communion wafers on the gold plate lining. There was definite mana in the chill and sheen and ring of those holy vessels.

Did you have to wrestle with concepts (or words!) like 'transubstantiation' and 'real presence'?

Not in the beginning. Like everybody else, I bowed my head at Mass during the consecration of the bread and wine, lifted my eyes to the raised host and the raised chalice. I believed (whatever it means) that a change occurred: I went to the altar rails and received the mystery on my tongue, returned to my place, shut my eyes fast, made an act of thanksgiving, opened my eyes and felt time starting up again. It was phenomenally refreshing and, when I began to admit to myself that I was losing faith in it, I was very sorry. Intellectually speaking, the loss of faith occurred offstage, there was never a scene where I had it out with myself or with another. But the potency of those words remains for me, they retain an undying tremor and draw; I cannot disavow them. Nor can I make the act of faith. In 'Station Island', I arranged for John of the Cross to help my unbelief by translating his 'Song of the Soul that Knows God by Faith'.

Do you think of Station Island *as a confessional book?*

I think it was more like an examination of conscience than a confession. A kind of inner courtroom, as dramatic as it was confessional. It was written, sure enough, to release an inner pressure. But it was also set up so that different voices could speak and different weights get lifted.

Would it be going too far to say that the Dantean idea of having lost one's way in mid-life – as person or as writer – was among the things which prompted the writing of 'Station Island'?

Dante was the first mover of the sequence, no doubt about that. The experience of reading him in the 1970s was mighty, and translating the Ugolino episode was like doing press-ups, getting ready for something bigger. I had the shape of it in my head when I came back from Harvard in 1979. We'd spent the spring semester there and then gone down for a few summer weeks to the Flanagans' house on Long Island. But in the month of June I came home to mark the Carysfort exams; and, while I was back in Ireland, I went north to see my parents and to visit Tom Delaney, our archaeologist friend who was in hospital at the time with a serious heart complaint. A fatal complaint, alas. When the exams were marked, I went back to Long Island and Tom Delaney died sometime during the weeks that followed. So the first bit of 'Station Island' to be written was the section about Tom, begun that September, after we all came back from Cambridge. There was a story about a rook flying into the church during his funeral and that's what got me going – since there was a rook-look about Tom himself, with his black hair and narrow face and forehead.

You'd had a long poem in mind for some time?

Lough Derg had been in and out of my head for years. As early as 1966 I'd written a short piece called 'Lenten Stuff' that began, 'Now I can only find myself in one place, / Lowbacked island on an inland lough. / A cold chapel takes up half the island'. I'd been skipping through an anthology of Elizabethan prose and got the title from Thomas Nashe; I know it was done in May 1966, because of where it appears in a notebook. My body was packed with memories of the pilgrimage and I had a sixth sense that it was my subject, but nothing in the material really moved that first time.

Robert Pinsky contends that 'at some point Heaney decided not to write an epic, decided that this work ["Station Island"] was not going to be as large as that'.

Talk of 'epic' goes a bit far. I never did think on those lines or that scale. Possibly I'd read too much C. S. Lewis as an undergraduate, on primary and secondary epic, all that discussion of the genre in *A Preface to Paradise Lost*. What I conceived of was a poem-cycle, with a central protagonist on his fixed route through the pilgrimage. The three-part Dantean journey scaled down into the three-day station, no hell, no paradise, just 'Patrick's Purgatory', which is how the place is known to this day.

Paul Breslin described 'Station Island' as 'one of those crisis poems that poets sometimes have to write in order to break an impasse'.

Paul Breslin gets it right. I needed to butt my way through a blockage, a pile-up of hampering stuff, everything that had gathered up inside me because of the way I was both in and out of the Northern

Ireland situation. I wasn't actively involved, yet I felt dragged upon and put upon by it. You know the opening of that Berryman 'Dream Song' where he addresses the shade of Yeats: 'I have moved to Dublin to have it out with you, / majestic Shade'? 'Station Island' was taken on in a similar mood, in order to have it out with myself, to clear the head, if not the decks.

I always had a hope that I'd get as free as Sweeney, and that I could inhabit his voice or have his voice inhabit me. Sweeney's flight had a similar purgatorial element, but in the end it carried him to where he could tell his story freely and thoroughly. When I started 'Station Island' I was after that kind of freedom and thoroughness. For a long time, in fact, I had the idea that Sweeney would figure in the last section of the poem, but the bit I wrote for him eventually ended up in a cycle he got to himself, the 'Sweeney Redivivus' poems that conclude the book.

In the end, it was James Joyce who gave you absolution and, as they say, 'permission'. I wonder if you ever thought of invoking Joyce earlier on the journey? I know you toyed with the idea of a guide, the way Dante enlisted Virgil.

William Carleton was the one who auditioned for that part. Joyce would never have walked those nineteenth-century Catholic roads or put up with the murmurs and the *mea culpa*s of the island. Carleton, on the other hand, had all the qualifications: he was a cradle Catholic, a Northern Catholic, a man who had lived with and witnessed the uglier side of sectarianism, but still a man who converted to the Established Church and broke with 'our tribe's complicity'. He had a wide-angle understanding of the whole Irish picture and a close-up intimacy with the vicious Northern side of it. When I read the reissued *Autobiography* in the sixties, I felt I knew him inside out, and that feeling was immensely strengthened when Marie and I drove into the yard of the farmhouse in County Tyrone where he was born. It was like driving into our own yard at home, a whitewashed house, a door opening directly on to the street, a life that could have been your own going on inside.

Had you read a lot of Carleton when you were younger? Did he mean as much to you, for example, as nineteenth-century Northern poets like Samuel Ferguson and William Allingham?

I didn't read any Carleton when I was younger. I was teaching at Queen's before I encountered his work. The first impression – and the strongest, because it *was* the first – came from that reading of the *Autobiography*, an edition introduced by Patrick Kavanagh. I reviewed it for the *Guardian*. Different paperback selections from *Traits and Stories of the Irish Peasantry* were coming on the market then and, in due course, I read the Carleton chapter in Tom Flanagan's book on the Irish novelists. So he turned into someone very strongly imagined, as much a *shuler* as a writer, far more present to me than either Ferguson or Allingham. As gaunt in the mind's eye as Aodhagán Ó Rathaille, with maybe a touch of Blind Pew. So I was delighted when I found Carleton appearing in the rear-view mirror – although strictly speaking he should not have been visible in a mirror since he had to be a ghost. But it was a good way for him to arrive from his other dimension.

Did you read James Clarence Mangan?

Mangan was definitely a stronger voice in my ear than Allingham or Ferguson, if only because of 'Dark Rosaleen'. Over the years I've got more and more affection and respect for the range and strangeness of Mangan's poetry. But he doesn't loom. Not that he loomed for anybody, even when he was alive. Mangan was more of a shimmerer than a loomer, what Eliot might have called 'a face still forming'.

Eliot's 'Little Gidding' and Keats's 'Ode to a Nightingale' were cited by you, in an essay, as examples of poems which escape 'the local trappings of the historical moment' and are 'suspended in the ether of a contemplative mind'. Was it your hope that 'Station Island' would effect a similar escape or were you content that it should be a creature of its time and place?

Maybe I shouldn't have talked about poetry escaping the historical moment, but rather about its surviving it or cohabiting with it. Obviously, I wanted readers to open the book and walk into a world they knew behind and beyond the book, but with a feeling of being clearer about their place in it than they would be in real life, a feeling of being stayed against confusion. That has to be one of the great joys of reading and a sign of success in writing. I wanted the journey to be as matter of fact as a train journey, but to produce the sensation a train journey also produces, a sense that the whole thing is a dream taking place behind glass, so that arriving at the station is indeed like arriving at the end of Keats's 'Ode' and being tolled back to your sole self.

Did Chaucer, whom you mentioned earlier, figure in any way as a model? Does he figure in your mind at all?

I can still recite bits of the 'Prologue' to *The Canterbury Tales* that we learned by heart in our A-level year at St Columb's College, and I love the voice of the Pardoner in the prologue to his tale, so yes, there's a Chaucer soundtrack that means something to me. But it doesn't lead in very deep. He's remote. I could cite the Canterbury pilgrimage as a precedent in a general literary historical way, but it was in no way a model.

And Thomas Kinsella's 'Downstream'? You've written of that poem as an exploration of the quest 'for coherence and integrity in a world of constant disintegration and slippage'. That sounds like a fair description of what you were seeking in mid-life and mid-Troubles Station Island.

It sounds that way because it was written after *Station Island* was written. Kinsella hove into view when I began to prepare an essay on Dante and the modern poet. Luckily, 'Downstream' wasn't on my mind when I worked on the Lough Derg sequence. I say luckily, because consciousness of it as a *terza rima* performance would have been more of a hindrance than a help. Oddly enough, the pilgrimage poems by Patrick Kavanagh and Denis Devlin didn't give that sort of bother, probably because the Dantean motif was absent from them.

Or because you don't rate them as highly?

That's also a part of it. The Devlin poem seems to me too rigged, not enough inner binding in the sound of it, too much striving. The Kavanagh has more going for it, slack strung as it is – slack to the point of unravelling. There's a lot of old blather; but at least you're in the company of flesh and blood, and everywhere there's this mixture of grim truth to life and gleeful language. Especially in those four or five sonnets which function as pilgrims' prayers. They're brilliant things.

*Critics often credit Denis Devlin with having introduced a
welcome modernist strain into Irish poetry.*

I'm more conscious of *signs* of strain. What I hear in him is the
expression of anxiety – a sense of artistic strain, a misfit between
means and matter and sensibility. In Joyce, in Flann O'Brien, in
Beckett, you immediately recognize the rightness of the fit – at least
most of the time in Beckett, because I'd exclude 'Whoroscope'. In
fact it was a single partisan review from the Beckett of 'Whoroscope'
that foisted this fantasy of a 'tradition' of Irish 'modernist' poetry on
us. It seems to me that in the final uptoss, as Kavanagh might have
said, those thirties modernists get marks for effort, and effort in the
right direction, but the stuff they actually wrote is generally of per-
iod interest.

*Does your own 'Station Island' still please you? In previous
interviews, you depicted the sequence as something of a solemn
and even sullen poem, looking back on twenty years of the
Troubles in Ulster. Does this mean you'd begun to regard it
the way Kavanagh came to regard 'The Great Hunger' – as
insufficiently open to the comic dimension?*

That would be going a bit far; it would also be a bit inflationary.
And maybe those remarks were ill judged in the first place.
Sometimes you test the work you've done by hitting it a few cracks,
just to see how it stands up to the abuse. At different times, I've
enjoyed calling the poem 'a big barge full of subject matter' and
suchlike, but you can be attached to your barge, especially if
you're a landsman by birth. Michael McLaverty used to repeat an
anecdote about Somerset Maugham that was meant as a warning
against this kind of self-deprecation. Maugham was apparently
asked by a journalist if he felt his work had any particular defi-
ciency and he replied, 'I lack lyrical quality.' 'And you know,'
McLaverty would crow, 'every time he was reviewed after that,
they were saying he lacked lyrical quality.'

*You've actually taken the Maugham route, referring to 'Station
Island' as refusing 'lyrical sweetness' and punishing the lyric
side of yourself. Why would you have wanted to, as it were,
punish the innocent party – the lyric – rather than stretch it to
fit the changing demands?*

I didn't begin, as you know, by writing at the head of my page, 'Now I shall punish lyric.' After the poem was published, I was trying to characterize it from the outside – and doing so, I suppose, in order to give a new reader some orientation. There's a very earnest note to the thing, but I don't think I could have done it any other way. The literary critic in me might have fun with what eventually came out, but the poet in me just had to work through the material that was lying piled up in the middle of his road. Then, if you'll excuse the expression, he lightened up and got a bit of lift-off in 'Sweeney Redivivus'.

On the pilgrimage, you encounter friends and relatives – as well as other, more anonymous, characters such as the missionary priest and the murdered shopkeeper. In portraying these people, did you take many liberties?

I took very few liberties, although the first character to appear happens to be something of a composite. He was named for a traveller called Simon Sweeney, but I also bring in a memory of an old neighbour called Charlie Griffin who used to be forever roaming the hedges with a bowsaw, cutting branches and dragging them home for firewood. Still, as I was saying before, the first section was not the first to be written. The earliest was the encounter with the shade of Tom Delaney, and that section pleased Tom's widow, Máire, because she felt it was drawn truly from life. As far as she was concerned, there was something new or different about the writing, which I took to be her response to the narrative element. It had a certain daylit, documentary quality.

You came back to the world of Simon Sweeney – the world of the travelling people, or 'tinkers', as they were known in your childhood – much later, when translating the Janáček lyrics of Diary of One Who Vanished.

I always hear the tinkle of a whitesmith's hammer in the word 'tinker', the rim of a tin can being beaten trim. In our house, the word didn't imply disapprobation. In fact, Simon Sweeney always came up in talk as a respected figure, always referred to fondly, somebody trusted. I didn't actually know him, even though he was the paterfamilias of a troop who would pitch camp a couple of times a year on the little byroad we took to school, the Lagans Road.

But, for all the acceptance that Simon had at home, there would be a slight apprehension in me every time I approached the caravan and tent. Often at that time of the morning the place would be in complete stillness, and if it happened to be raining, you'd have the water in puddles under the caravan and in little catchments in the folds and hollows of the tarpaulin covering the tent. But there would still be a fire, smoking and smouldering if it was wet, hot and attractive if it was dry. And that old familiar smell of woodsmoke. And fresh horse dung on the road. And ponies hobbled on either side of camp. What was it John Clare called them? 'A quiet, pilfering, unprotected race.' I'd say our crowd were more pestering than pilfering.

The real trouble was on the doorstep, with the women who were there to sell stuff – tins, cans, pot-menders; but also, I remember, artificial flowers with big heads made of dyed woodshavings. I was always hoping my mother would deal for one of the flowers; mostly, though, she was getting fed up with the women for keeping on asking for more after she's given them eggs and a poke of tea or whatever. 'Ah, Missus', they'd say, 'you're very hard.' Big hefty dames with ropes of red hair, an infant hoisted in a shawl in the crook of one arm, a broad basket of goods on the other.

The men tended to have a reputation for wildness.

They belonged in the wild, for sure. Usually I'd meet the men singly, out in the open, out on their own. 'Did you see an ould hoss, boss, down the road anywhere?' That would be the extent of my contact. But I do remember a scaresome fight at the end of Broagh Road, just a couple of hundred yards from our house in Mossbawn. In the middle of the day, grown men howling and battling and bleeding. I wasn't close enough to see anything in detail, but I'll never forget the fear and danger. It was the unprepared nature of the fight and the fury of it that was so scaresome. Battle fury, I suppose. The kind of thing you tend only to see nowadays in close-up special effects in the cinema. Ever since I saw Goya's 'black painting' of the two berserks beating hell out of each other, clubs and coat-tails flying, I've associated it with that afternoon. It's like a dream to me still. The descent of the angel of violence. And nowadays I associate it in my head with something that happened to Marie when she was a youngster. She felt the same fear when a tinker who was raving drunk hurled a bicycle through the window of their pub. Her father had refused to serve any more drink to the man and had put him off the premises. So, yes, there was wildness there too.

Could we now follow up the earlier glimpse of you on the wild Lagans Road, being taken to school for the first time, with a more detailed look?

The Lagans Road ran for about three-quarters of a mile across an area of wetlands. It was one of those narrow cobblestoned country roads, with a grass crown in the middle, grass verges and high hedges on either side of it, and – behind the hedges – marsh and bog and little shrubs and birch trees. For a minute or two every day, therefore, you were in the wilderness. But on the first morning I went to school it was as if the queen of Elfland was leading me away. The McNicholls, as I was saying in that earlier account, were neighbours; and Philomena McNicholl – by then one of 'the big girls' – had been put in charge of me during those first days. Ginger hair, freckled face, green gymfrock: a fey, if ever there was one.

I remember my first sight of the school, a couple of low-set Nissen huts raising their corrugated backs above the hedges. From about a quarter of a mile away, I could see youngsters running about in the road in front of the buildings and hear shouting in the playground. Years later, when I read an account of how the Indians of the Pacific Northwest foresaw their arrival in the land of the dead – coming along a forest path where other travellers' cast-offs lay scattered on the bushes, hearing voices laughing and calling, knowing there was a life in the clearing up ahead that would be familiar, but feeling at the same time lost and homesick – it struck me I had already experienced that kind of arrival. Next thing, in the porch, I was faced with rows of coathooks nailed up at different heights along the wall, so that everyone in the different classes could reach them, everyone had a place to hang overcoat or scarf and proceed to the strange room, where our names were new in the rollbook and would soon be called.

How many rooms were in the school?

Four rooms, four teachers, all of whom arrived at the place each morning on bicycles. Master Murphy and Mrs Murphy together, Miss Walls and Miss Gribbin separately and from different directions. There were two Nissen huts, each divided in two, boys in one hut, girls in the other. The Nissen huts would have been erected by the Ministry of Defence in 1942, after the land where the old schoolhouse stood had been requisitioned for an aerodrome.

When did you begin attending?

In 1944. In the month of May, just after my fifth birthday. The building might have been new, but to us it felt like eternal school. And still does. Master Murphy's room retained the traditional layout. A tall desk at the front, the master like a helmsman behind it in blue serge suit and waistcoat, poplin shirt and starched winged collar, a big loose knot on his tie. A round iron stove to one side of the desk, on the master's right, with an iron chimney-pipe straight up to the roof; on the other side and slightly to the front, a big blackboard on pegs set at adjustable heights in the legs of an easel. Then, directly in front of the master's desk, there were our desks: each with the traditional heavy plank top, maybe eight feet long, a solid, slightly sloped surface with inkwells at intervals along the top where you also had those little carved-out grooves for pens and pencils. The bench part of the thing was narrow and hard, but you could fit in six or seven pupils, elbow to elbow. We weren't all that far away from a time when 'form' would have meant the one you sat on, in the first or second or third row. In fact, in Master Murphy's room third class sat on the first form and so on up to sixth, maybe even seventh. In the late forties, before the eleven-plus examination started to cull the scholarship winners, the back of the classroom was full of fourteen-year-olds – ideal members of the gardening class, of course.

You're talking solely about boys?

Yes. Miss Walls was in charge of the infant classes for boys. The senior girls were with Mrs Murphy, junior girls with Miss Gribbin. The senior girls would have had cooking and sewing classes instead of the gardening.

In the Master Murphy section of 'Station Island', you mention the soil of the school garden, so I presume you took part in the gardening.

I did, on a couple of occasions. It wasn't a regular exercise, by no means part of the weekly timetable. I suppose there had to be some instructional aspect to it, but I remember it mostly as recreational, vernal even. The little clinks of spades and rakes and hoes on the occasional pebble, the silence and the intentness, everybody tilling and breathing in his little plot of earth. And there was the added strangeness of seeing the master in his shirtsleeves. I loved the pile-up of those gardening tools in the storeroom at the end of the porch: every now and again the door would be open and you'd see this lean-to of seasoned shafts that could have been spear shafts stacked against the wall.

'There are charts', you wrote in 'Alphabets', 'there are headlines, there is a right / Way to hold the pen and a wrong way'.

All of the above, yes. Mostly, however, the charts were in Miss Walls's room, ones with pictures and – in big black letters – the names of things that appeared in the illustrations. And the headlines were those strips of lined paper inscribed with sentences in Vere Foster copperplate which you then had to copy out and learn to do correctly, making the right kind of loop on the 'l's and the 'h's, not blotting the eye of the 'e', keeping the small letters within the narrow-gauge blue lines, and the big ones looping at a tangent to the lines done in red.

I can hardly believe what I'm telling you here, it's so long ago, and in such different circumstances. The ink in the inkwells, for example, was made up from ink powder that used to be kept in that same storeroom with the gardening tools. And here and now it strikes me that there was no running water in the school, because one of my clearest memories is of being sent out with a can or big beaker of some sort down to the stream that flowed at the end of the playground in order to collect water for the mixing of the ink. What was odd and memorable was the otherness of the school at that moment: you were only a few yards away from life in the classroom you'd just left, but you felt a world away. You were outside, you had the whole sky and land to yourself, yet there it was in front of you, the silent building. You saw it in all its uncanniness and had a taste of yourself in all of your own solitude and singularity.

You have written about the map on the school wall. Was that in Master Murphy's classroom?

It was. In Miss Walls's room, the infants' part of the boys' school, you were allowed the things of a child – plasticine, a counting-frame with coloured beads, coloured charts, catkins in vases, and so on. But the master's room seemed furnished with reminders of an adult world: a map, a big wall clock with a pendulum going behind glass, a cupboard with scales and all kinds of glass utensils for science lessons that never, as far as I recollect, took place.

Were all of the pupils Catholics?

Not at all. Anahorish School was under Catholic management, but it was still attended by the children of the local Protestant families. My next door neighbour Tommy Evans, for example, went there. Also the Booths, the Dixons, the Ewarts, the Kirkwoods, the Ellises, the Clarkes, the Bowles ... They got out early before lunchtime, when the rest of us did the catechism and said whatever prayers were said. I'm not very clear how we felt about it, nor, I suspect, would the Booths or the Kirkwoods have been very clear either. We'd all have been aware of the lines of division, although maybe I should say instead, aware of the difference. 'Division' is probably a hindsighted exaggeration of what we felt at that stage. This wasn't urban ghetto life, but cheek-by-jowl, lane-by-field, country-neighbour life. And that, I believe, is sociological fact rather than sentimental fantasy.

What songs were you taught – local songs, such as 'Roddy McCorley', for example?

We were taught 'Slieve Gallon's Brae', but not 'Roddy McCorley', because it would have been regarded, quite rightly, as a 'party tune', a rebel song, and hence immediately divisive. I suspect the songs we learned had been part of the school's repertoire since before partition in 1922 – when Master Murphy and Miss Walls would have started teaching: 'Loch Lomond', 'My Singing Bird', 'My Grandfather's Clock', 'Marching through Georgia' – in Atlanta, it might have been a party tune, but not in Anahorish. Also, I'm afraid, Stephen Foster's 'Poor Old Joe'. After independence, schools in the Irish Free State changed the song repertoire to something more nationalist; but much of the old British system stayed in place north of the border.

The minute I say 'north of the border', I realize again how deep an imprint that wall map was making – a large-scale one of the six counties of Northern Ireland, what the BBC news announcers used to call, and often still *do* call, 'the province'. The six partitioned counties were marked off from the rest of the traditional province of Ulster and the rest of Ireland by a thick red selvedge that ran from below Newry, right along the border with Louth, Monaghan, Cavan, and Donegal. The bottom of the map was attached to a black horizontal rod that simply cut off the rest of the island, relegated it to a political and geographic nowhere. So the map was meant to imprint an official Northern Ireland and establish a six-county-centric point of view from the start. I can still see the little boats sailing on their dotted routes across the North Channel from Larne to Stranraer, from Derry to Glasgow, from Belfast to Heysham – all happily bound for 'the mainland'.

Did the mixed attendance at the school influence your relations with the other children? Would it, for instance, have been acceptable for a Catholic child to have had a Protestant child as 'best friend'?

It was a bit early for the 'best friends' syndrome to have got going. There was a kind of herd life in the playground. The religious difference didn't matter much at that stage, personal fondness was more important than family faith. The people I'd see in the evenings after school, the nearest thing to 'best friends', would have been people who lived nearby: Eamon Gribbin, Henry Gribbin, the Hurls and the Shivers.

In 'Alphabets', you call St Columb's College 'a stricter school', which implies that the Anahorish regime was relatively benign.

Miss Walls had a rod, which she rarely used; more of a switch, really. The rod of correction, 'the stick' as we called it, belonged to the master: about two to three feet long; a bit of ash or sally, cut from a tree in the hedge; as thick as a man's index finger. It sat on a ledge under the window and came down every now and again. Master Murphy wasn't a slasher but he was stern and could 'slap' without compunction. I only saw him lose his temper once and that, oddly – almost dementedly – was because a boy persisted in pronouncing the word 'geography' with a stress on the last syllable, so that it rhymed with 'fie'.

How then was he regarded in the local community?

With respect. He must have been in his sixties when he taught me – and so he would have taught local people of my parents' generation. He had given extra coaching to my aunt Sarah in the early 1920s, when she was studying for a King's Scholarship. The older, unschooled people would come to him with forms to sign – if they were applying for the pension, say, or some farming subsidy. When they needed help with official correspondence, they'd turn to him.

I'd like to ask about the 'seaside trinket' in the third section of 'Station Island'. Why did it affect you so deeply?

It had the status of relic in the house. It was kept deep in a sideboard in my parents' bedroom, wrapped up in white tissue paper, a little grotto shaped like a sentry box, clad in tiny iridescent seashells. One of our transgressions was to get down into those deeps and salvage everything out on to the floor, and you soon learned from the reactions of the grown-ups that in their eyes the little grotto – I don't really know what else to call it – had a touch of the sacred. Then I learned, also at a fairly early stage, that it had belonged to Agnes, Aunt Agnes as she was called, who died from TB in her teens. Her name has always been synonymous with tenderness. Her relic is one of my first and last things.

Agnes notwithstanding, there has been some critical resistance to the poem on the grounds that it is essentially a male pilgrimage, with the women as silent partners.

The maleness of the thing may give offence and can be taken up as an issue, in much the same way as you could take issue with the Catholic setting and characters, but those objections, it seems to me, are often based on the particular critic's agenda. I'd say, at any rate, that the feminine principle is strongly at work in those three sonnets in Section VI that trace the pilgrim's progress in the shedding of sexual guilt. But it's also true to say that there's more politics than erotics in the sequence as a whole. The predominant hauntings, the things that stirred behind the sequence and got it going, were generally to do with Northern Ireland politics. The examination of conscience was conducted mostly within that arena and those terms of reference.

Returning to that arena, and in particular to the murdered shopkeeper in Section VII, I'd be interested to hear whether his

family responded to what you wrote. Had you spoken to them
before you published the section, to check certain details or to
ensure that they raised no objections to the poem?

I didn't speak to the family beforehand. Obviously, 'the murdered
shopkeeper' is exactly how the man appears in the poem, anony-
mous and representative, yet it would have been clear to people in
the Bann Valley area that he was based on a known figure. I relied
on the general word of mouth about what had happened to
William Strathearn, how he had been called down in the middle of
the night from his bedroom above the lock-up shop by two RUC
men and shot on his own doorstep. These were members of the
police force all right, but they were also active Loyalist parami-
litaries. My anxiety in the writing, I admit, had more to do with rep-
resenting the RUC as sectarian killers than with the sensibilities of
the family. I took for granted that the family would see the writ-
ing as being in total sympathy with their loss, an attempt to hon-
our Willie's memory. But while I wanted to 'say what happened' I
didn't want the thing to turn into a general *'j'accuse'* of the RUC.
I wasn't out to provide ammunition in the propaganda war.

I've heard you say that audiences at poetry readings often
assumed the killers on the doorstep to be IRA men. Did you
regret not having made the facts more explicit?

It didn't delight me; but, twenty years on, I'm still happy with the
way the facts were handled. And even happier to be able to report
that one day, after I'd read the poem to a class in Magherafelt, one
of Willie's children came up and told me how much it had meant to
his mother and the rest of the family.

What of the families of other 'Station Island' figures? Colum
McCartney; the young priest; the hunger striker . . .

No response. But none would have been expected. The clerical stu-
dent on his rounds, the young priest from a local family saying his
first Mass in the home and blessing the neighbours, all that was
typical. In the case of the others you mention, there would have
been a natural reticence. The families lived close to us, physically,
and were close also in terms of friendship – and there would have
been an understanding anyhow that writing about these sorrows is

what poets do. One of the things said when I came into company around home in County Derry would always be, 'Watch yourself, this fellow might write a poem about you.' It was a joke, but it acknowledged a reality.

The second priest figure introduced towards the end of 'Station Island' seems a mouthpiece for mystical vision more than a character in his own right.

He was based on a Carmelite who gave a retreat during my last year in St Columb's. He didn't actually suggest I translate John of the Cross as penance, but he had indeed just come back from Spain and seemed to shine with inner light. And he *did* say to me, 'Read poems as prayers.' He probably would have explained what he meant by quoting Hopkins, 'The world is charged with the grandeur of God', and by saying that God's grandeur shines out in the 'shook foil' of poetry. I could and can see the sense of that, and the point of reading poems in that spirit. It's in line with something Miłosz once wrote: 'He felt gratitude so he couldn't not believe in God.'

Why did you choose to finish 'Station Island' with Joyce rather than, say, Yeats?

One reason why Joyce is there is to help my unbelief. Yeats couldn't have been a member of the cast because, to put it crudely, the pilgrimage was for Papists.

But why assign the advisory role to a prose writer rather than a poet?

Because Joyce qualifies as a poet more than most writers of verse. He enters and explores and exceeds himself by entering and exploring and exceeding the language. My intention always was to have the pilgrim leave the island renewed, with liberating experience behind him and more ahead. The pattern always was the simple one of setting out, encountering tests and getting through to a new degree of independence; on such matters, Joyce is our chief consultant.

All the same, might you not have resisted him as mentor because he would have scorned a 'bullockbefriending' family such as yours? Wouldn't he have associated it with 'the nets of nationality, language, religion'?

He certainly would. And because I was a member of such a family his work was an essential aid to self-awareness. But the scene in *A Portrait of the Artist* where Joyce imagines Stephen Dedalus wrestling with the old man of the land ends with Stephen relenting, releasing his grip on the 'sinewy throat' and saying, 'I mean no harm.' And the same attitude comes out in the portrait of Stephen's hurling-playing friend Davin. So there's a limit to the enmity for the rural. Joyce wasn't Brendan Behan. There's also the fact that, by the 1960s – at an imaginative level, if not entirely at the legislative level – Joyce's battles had been pretty much fought and won. He had left, as Lowell says, a loophole for the soul which others had found and followed through.

I've wondered about the advice which, speaking through Joyce, you gave yourself: 'it's time to swim / out on your own and fill the element / with signatures on your own frequency'. Hadn't you been doing that from the very start?

The advice itself is unexceptional: 'Tell the truth. Do not be afraid.' A bit like the maxims given out later in the book in that poem called 'The Master'. But, in the fiction of the poem, the advice is given to somebody who has been 'in the swim' of Lough Derg, as it were, rather than out on his own. He's being told to flee the nets.

Brian Moore is dedicatee of your poem 'Remembering Malibu'. Did you regard Moore as somebody who had swum out?

Definitely. Much of his fiction is about disengagement from middle-class Catholic Belfast. *The Emperor of Ice-Cream* is your essential Ulster *Bildungsroman*.

In remarks made immediately after Moore's death, you stressed how much his 'writerly solidarity' meant to you. What had you in mind?

His kindness, for a start. He invited Marie and myself and the kids to visit him and Jean in Malibu during that year we spent in California. It was a boost for somebody with only two slim volumes to his name to be accepted as a member of the guild by somebody as established as Moore. And from that time onwards we would see Jean and himself, regularly if briefly, when they came to Ireland in the summertime. But the solidarity came out in more decided ways when he reviewed *Station Island* for the *Los Angeles Times* – and when he objected to some patronizing remarks about me by A. Alvarez.

You might have been expected to identify with a rural writer like John McGahern, rather than the urban Brian Moore. You once wrote that the real 'end' of McGahern's 'social realism' is 'to get in close to an inner space of feeling' – you could have been describing yourself.

I'd be very happy to be so described. In McGahern's case, the defining statement was one he made at that symposium in Belfast which I mentioned previously: 'I'm only interested,' he said, 'in poetry, which occurs more often in verse than in prose.' I felt closer to McGahern not because of the rural background and subject matter but because of his register, his distinctive rhythm. The undertone is important, the melancholy of his music. Cadence was as important to his sentences as content, maybe more important.

Are you wary of work that is too comfortably embedded in the everyday, which settles for social realism alone?

I am, yes. Unless there's some evidence of a sensibility I can't get all that interested. The sine qua non is a binding element between the words, something that gives them psychic and musical weight. If Yeats left out the word 'now' in the first line of 'The Lake Isle of Innisfree', you'd have the same everyday truth about a moment of homesickness but you'd be missing the *in saecula saeculorum* pivot that the line turns on. It's not that I'm against content or subject matter as such. Far from it. It's just that I like it to be dreamt through, as it were, rather than dumped down. Edward Thomas's 'As the Team's Head-Brass', for example, or Elizabeth Bishop's 'At the Fishhouses'. Wordsworth's 'Resolution and Independence'.

Wordsworth is one of the poets in whose footsteps you have followed as a literary pilgrim. It strikes me that Station Island was only one of your pilgrimage places, since you must have visited more dead writers' houses than any poet alive – Yeats's Tower, for example, Hardy's birthplace . . .

. . . and Carleton's birthplace, Tennyson's birthplace, Dylan Thomas's Fern Hill, Alphonse Daudet's mill, Hopkins's grave in Dublin, Joyce's grave in Zurich, Wilde's grave in Paris, Emily Dickinson's house in Amherst, the Keats House in Hampstead, Akhmatova's 'House on the Fontanka' in Petersburg, Brodsky's 'room and a half' in the same city, not to mention Stratford and Abbotsford, Coole Park and Spenser's castle, Lissoy and Langholm . . . I'd have thought the urge to go to those places was common enough. A matter of dedicating, as Yeats says in one of his Coole Park poems, 'a moment's memory to [a] laurelled head'.

You don't go in hope of inspiration?

Not in that spirit, no. The one poem that came from such a visit appears in *Station Island*: 'The Birthplace', about the Hardy home in Upper Bockhampton. The trees around the place, the thatched roof, the small rooms, all reminded me of Mossbawn. But that wasn't the only reason I wrote it, there was also the fact that Hardy's novels and poems were so much part of me by the time I got there. In fact, the grave in Stinsford churchyard and the house in Upper Bockhampton are literary 'stations' I keep going back to. On 31 December 2000, for example, a hundred years after Hardy wrote and dated 'The Darkling Thrush', Marie and I went to Dorset and I read the poem in the Stinsford graveyard. And read 'A Church Romance' in the church.

Did you ever – as a young writer, or indeed later – snatch (or sneak) a look at the locale of a living writer in the hope of getting a glimpse of that author?

In the mid-sixties, when I was down from Belfast, I used to drop into the Bailey pub in South Anne Street in Dublin, to take a peep at Kavanagh and company. Once, before we were married, when Marie and I were in the west of Ireland, we went to O'Malley's bar in Cleggan. We knew Richard Murphy's poems about 'The Cleggan Disaster' and 'The Last Galway Hooker' and knew also that he sailed that hooker out from Cleggan to Inishbofin. And next thing Richard Murphy himself arrives in his Aran sweater and seaman's boots. I recognized him from his photographs but didn't speak to him. Too shy, and anyhow, he was with his own party.

*Are there places around Dublin to which you habitually bring
literary visitors?*

There are a couple or three obvious sites: Hopkins's grave in the
Jesuit burial plot in Glasnevin Cemetery – and while we're there,
Parnell's grave and John O'Leary's, where Yeats says romantic
Ireland is also buried. Joyce's Tower in Sandycove, Patrick
Kavanagh's memorial seat on the banks of the Grand Canal. St
Patrick's Cathedral where Swift was Dean and where you can see
his epitaph on the wall. There's no shortage of destinations.
Charles Wright, by the way, wrote a wonderful poem about his
visit to Hopkins's grave. 'Father Bird-of-Paradise' he calls him.

The first poem in Station Island *is literally set in a station – an
underground railway station in London – rather than in a place
of literary or spiritual pilgrimage. Is there any reason why 'The
Underground' was chosen to be the opening poem?*

The last poem in *Field Work*, 'Ugolino', was an underground poem
of a very different sort, so we're into this next book at a run, head-
ing up and away. I liked it because it seemed to have both truth to
life and truth to love. It starts with a memory of running through a
tunnel from the South Kensington tube station towards the Albert
Hall, late for a BBC Promenade Concert. We were on our honey-
moon and Marie was wearing her going-away coat. In the course
of her sprint, the buttons started popping off. But in the end, the
'damned if I look back' line takes us well beyond the honeymoon.
In this version of the story, Eurydice and much else gets saved by
the sheer cussedness of the poet up ahead just keeping going.

I assume that the 'Wedding Day' poem in Wintering Out *recreates
your mood on the day you and Marie were married. There's a
hallucinatory quality about the images in it – that face, for example,
full of 'wild grief'. You make it sound a pretty grievous experience.*

On the day, of course, it was a party. Even though it was the first
wedding in either family, even though there was necessarily a rare
newness about the whole occasion, it was still an unmysterious,
ordinary get-together. Everybody in good form and in full cry. The
families being themselves, even more themselves than usual, our
friends enjoying the fling. My father refused to get into the hired

gear; nor would he make a speech, since speech was never his thing anyhow. But, for all that, he and my mother enjoyed themselves. Everybody was, as they say, out for the day.

Yet, in the poem, Marie is singing 'behind the tall cake / Like a deserted bride'.

A wedding always has its moments of strangeness, sudden lancings or fissures in the fun when parent and child have these intense intimations that the first circle is broken. It is in the literal sense *unheimlich*, an unhoming. I tried to catch some of that in 'Mother of the Groom' also. You have to be pretty immature not to feel the life-change at such a time. That moment in the taxi, for example, when you both drive away and the faces and places vanish, 'to be renewed, transfigured, in another pattern'. It's hallucinatory all right, and that's why it stays with you.

Your children, as they grew up, presumably continued to reconnect you with aspects of your own childhood. Might poems like 'The Railway Children' and 'An Ulster Twilight' have resulted from comparing your childhood with theirs?

'The Railway Children' was written very quickly one afternoon in my room in Carysfort College, before a tutorial. But you could be right about its having some connection with the children, because a few years earlier a photographer called Larry Herman came to County Derry and took pictures of them and Marie and myself roaming about in some of my old haunts. Several of these eventually appeared in a Penguin anthology called *Worlds*, edited by Geoffrey Summerfield. There could well be a connection between 'The Railway Children' and a photograph in that book of the four of us – no Catherine Ann on the scene yet – up to our waist in grass on the slopes of the railway cutting in Broagh.

I was definitely remembering my own childhood when I wrote 'A Kite for Michael and Christopher' – an afternoon when my father came out to a field at the back of the house and launched a kite. What was surprising and what I still remember most vividly was the powerful drag in the kite string: partly because the kite itself was a heavy big job, made of lath and pasted newspaper; and partly because the haulage got more and more powerful as the kite lifted. The more string you could pay out, of course, the higher and more spectacular your flight; although often and often, because of that mighty strain, the string would break and you would lose the kite and even if you eventually found it, it would have been wrecked by the fall.

Did you actually make a kite for Michael and Christopher?

I bought one for them made of nylon. We were well and truly into the consumer age by that time. In 'An Ulster Twilight', for example, the toy battleship that I'm to get for Christmas is being made by the local carpenter, but when it came to Michael and Christopher's turn for toys, it was Action Man out of the shop.

Was Santa Claus an annual visitor?

Definitely. Christmas mornings were as simple and delightful as ever. Marie and I were reliving our own childhoods then too.

Had Santa figured strongly in your childhood fantasy?

Not all that strongly, but I did expect him to deliver and did believe in him for a while – even though, from very early on, there was a provisional edge to my faith. On Christmas Eve my father would tell us, 'He's on his way now, coming round Slieve Gallon, and if you listen hard you'll maybe hear the sleigh bells.' I remember one time climbing the beech tree at the end of our lane, looking and listening through the frosty air. But of course my father would also warn that, if we didn't behave, there'd be no Santa at all that particular year.

'Changes', apparently addressed to one of your children, ends with an injunction to remember a bird nesting in a pump 'when you have grown away and stand at last / at the very centre of the empty city'. Did it sadden you that, by moving from Wicklow to Dublin, your children would experience an urban upbringing rather than the rural one which had been so enriching for you?

It did sadden me a bit, but there were compensations. And as a matter of fact, that reference to the empty city didn't come from my own sense of what their future was going to be like. It's an image from the *I Ching*, 'the book of changes' – hence the title of the poem; in that context, it could signify the illusory nature of conquest or triumph: you take the citadel or the town only to find there's nothing there.

As well as 'The Sandpit' in Station Island, *there are poems in other collections – 'Damson' and 'Alphabets' among them – where there's a fascination with building and bricklaying, trowelling and plastering. Anything to declare about this?*

Two things. First, vis-à-vis sand, and sandpits in fields, and sandbeds and gravel beds by the river. During the war, the construction of the aerodrome at Creagh, with its new runways and outbuildings and so on, created a demand for sand, a demand that did not lessen once the housing schemes got started after the war. It meant that some people made a fortune from having sandpits on their land, with the result that sand became a golden resource, and not only because of its colour. But there was also the fact that my uncle Mick, the one who turns up in a poem in *District and Circle*, was a bricklayer – Mick Joyce, a Corkman who had been in the army and had married my father's sister, Susan. I always remember him arriving at Mossbawn in his khaki outfit, coming up the field from the railway, either when he was on leave or had been demobbed. Mick was tall and exotic to us because of his accent and his tales of having been in England and in the North African desert as a medical orderly. And he had this big canvas bag full of bricklayer's tools – mortar board and trowel and skimmer and plumb line and what have you. All of them heavier than you'd have expected, Achillean gear of sorts, really. You had to be a hero to wield it.

You are also fascinated by trains. They are everywhere in your work. You play trains on the family sofa, lie with your ear to the railway line, see the fireman riding the firestep as if he were Pluto in his chariot.

T. S. Eliot called the river that ran through his home city 'a strong brown god'. On my home ground, the steam train was a black iron god, whether it was clanking along as a goods or firing past as a passenger service. The London, Midland and Scottish Railway divided the farm, iron gates had to be opened and closed at a crossing that led from the field behind the house to fields on the other side. Our floor shook every time an express train passed. Steam billowed and faded, coal smoke darkened and reeked. The shunting at Castledawson station was like the grunting of a giant.

Did you travel by train when you were young?

A very few times. I loved the upholstered seats, the compartments, the heavy reliability of the engineering. The first time was with my aunt Mary and aunt Sarah, on a day trip to the seaside, and it marked me for ever. Somehow or other I managed to let the carriage door fall shut on my hand. No broken fingers, luckily, but unforgettable pain. That's probably why I have this indelible impression of the bulk and solidity of those carriages.

And later on? What were your most memorable journeys?

A pilgrimage to Lourdes in 1958, by train the whole way from Derry to Dun Laoghaire, then ferry to Holyhead, train to Dover, ferry again, then train from Calais on down south. My first time in France, first time to hear French spoken by French people, the waiters mocking the constant requests for 'Teeteeteeteetee . . .' A trip to my first rugby game with Michael Longley on the Belfast–Dublin 'Enterprise Express', sometime in the mid-sixties. An Ulster rite of passage, that was. Drinking in the bar, howling in the stands at Lansdowne Road, standing in the bar again all the way back. And then, a couple of years ago, the overnight sleeper from St Petersburg to Moscow, watching pine forests hurl past and the moonlit lines reel away and away from the back window of the last carriage.

Another memorable journey, clearly, was the one you memorialized in 'The Flight Path', where you're hectored by the Republican spokesman about not writing something for the Republican cause. The poem is stated to be 'for the record', so I assume you described the encounter as it happened.

The account of what went on in the train is as it happened, yes. I make the speaker a bit more aggressive than he was at the time, but the presumption of entitlement on his part, which was the main and amazing aspect of that meeting, is rendered faithfully.

How public was the confrontation?

It was all done pretty discreetly, actually. My interlocutor was the Sinn Féin spokesman Danny Morrison, whom I didn't particularly know at the time. He came down from his place in the carriage and sat into the seat in front of me for maybe eight or ten minutes. There was nothing loud or noticeable about it; it was as if two people who discovered themselves on the same train by coincidence were getting reacquainted. I didn't feel menaced. It was a straightforward face-to-face test of will or steadiness. I simply rebelled at being commanded. If anybody was going to pull rank, it wasn't going to be a party spokesman. This was in pre-hunger-strike times, during 'the dirty protest' by Republican prisoners in the H-Blocks. The whole business was weighing on me greatly already and I had toyed with the idea of dedicating the Ugolino translation to the prisoners. But our friend's intervention put paid to any such gesture. After that, I wouldn't give and wasn't so much free to refuse as unfree to accept.

In the poem, you say that the man in the train had appeared in a dream.

That's not strictly 'for the record'. I did have a dream in which a school friend who'd been interned in Long Kesh appeared to me and asked me to deliver a proxy bomb in much the same way as the thing is described in 'The Flight Path'. My interlocutor that morning, however, was not a friend, although he did represent the reality of the situation which was producing the dreams and anxieties.

In 1988, nine years after that encounter, four years after the publication of Station Island, *the anxieties lingered. Accepting the* Sunday Times *Literary Award, you spoke out more strongly than was your custom against British government policy in Northern Ireland, saying that 'the caution rightly induced by detachment has its limits'. How was that speech received at the newspaper banquet?*

There was a certain amount of growling from the back of the room and a certain tension at the table, but nothing drastic. This was happening after the abduction and killing of those two British soldiers who had driven into a funeral crowd on the Falls Road. Barbaric IRA stuff, but not my fault, nor the fault of Irish people in general, although the *Sunday Times* and the British press in general had come out with the usual anti-Irish slabber. I just didn't think I could stand up and receive their award without making clear my attitude to that kind of xenophobia. This was my own protest and I knew I would be failing if I didn't proceed with it. Earlier that day, I'd had lunch with Karl Miller and he encouraged me to go ahead and say something.

The Sunday Times *award speech seems to have been something of a one-off. Did you feel it would be dangerous to make interventions of this kind more often?*

I did not feel that. I never held back because of such apprehensions. The thought of repercussions of a personal sort wouldn't have crossed my mind. But neither did I ever feel much like being a member of the chorus or a cheerleader. If I was quiet, it was from inner unease rather than outward compulsion. When I did *An Open Letter,* for example, after I was included in *The Penguin Book of Contemporary British Poetry*, I felt more awkward than indignant. I felt honour-bound to break silence about the whole British/Irish nomenclature, but I still didn't like putting a spring into the nationalistic step of either side.

During the H-Block hunger strikes, it must have been impossible not to feel something like guilt at not being able to help alleviate the situation or contribute to its resolution.

It was impossible, yes. This was during the time when 'Station Island' was being written, and the self-accusation of those days is everywhere in the sequence. Also in individual poems such as 'Chekhov on Sakhalin' and 'Sandstone Keepsake' and 'Away From It All'. Because of my earlier brush with Mr Morrison on the train, during 'the dirty protests', I was highly aware of the propaganda aspect of the hunger strikes and cautious about being enlisted. There was realpolitik at work; but, at the same time, you knew you were witnessing something like a sacred drama. If I had followed the logic of the Chekhov poem, I'd have gone to the prison, seen what was happening to the people on the hunger strike and written an account of it, 'not tract, not thesis'. In truth, I was 'away from it all' during those months: at a physical remove, living in Dublin, going on holiday in France.

In 'Frontiers of Writing', you touch on the evening when the body of Francis Hughes – a neighbour's son and the second hunger striker to die – was being waked in his home in County Derry.

You were not only in Oxford when he died, but staying – of all places – in a British cabinet minister's rooms.

It was bewildering. Charles Monteith had brought me as his guest to that year's Chiceley dinner in All Souls College. The Fellow's room I was assigned for the night was one that belonged to Sir Keith Joseph, the then Minister of Education in the Thatcher government. It took me ten years to come back to that occasion and see it as emblematic of the general stalemate. Francis Hughes was a neighbour's child, yes, but he was also a hit man and his Protestant neighbours would have considered him involved in something like a war of genocide against them rather than a war of liberation against the occupying forces of the crown. At that stage, the IRA's self-image as liberators didn't work much magic with me. But neither did the too-brutal simplicity of Margaret Thatcher's 'A crime is a crime is a crime. It is not political.' My own mantra in those days was the remark by Miłosz that I quote in 'Away From It All': 'I was stretched between contemplation of a motionless point and the command to participate actively in history.'

Whatever your proper doubts about the 'propaganda aspect' of the hunger strikes, had you some sympathy for the men, even some admiration for their courage?

Of course I had. That was part of the cruelty of the predicament. At the same time, I was wary of ennobling their sacrifice beyond its specific historic and political context. Uneasy, for example, about seeing it in the light of Yeats's *The King's Threshold*, his play about a hunger strike in the heroic age, in the other country of the legendary past. Anthropology didn't get you out of the moral corner you were backed into. One thing that had some point, if no great resolution to it, was when I attended the wake of Thomas McElwee, the eighth man to die. He was a cousin of Francis Hughes and lived adjacent. It happened that I was up in County Derry when his remains were returned to his home. I remember the sunny August afternoon when I walked across their yard, into the room where the corpse was laid out. The usual ritual of paying last respects. It gave some relief, to me at least. The family would have known that I wasn't an IRA supporter, but they would also have known that this crossing of their threshold was above or beyond the politics that were distressing everybody.

Did they, or the Hughes family, seek your intervention or intercession?

Never. By that time, I'd been away from the Bellaghy area for twenty years and probably didn't figure much in their minds as a local who could be appealed to.

Did literary friends like Seamus Deane and the Australian poet Vincent Buckley encourage an overt pro-hunger-strike stance?

I don't recall being pressed by them to change my ways but equally they left me in no doubt that they took a different view. I realized that Vincent Buckley had an unflinching loyalty to the hunger strikers when he began a sequence of poems about them, even naming them individually. As far as I was concerned, Vincent was romanticizing the situation that pertained by then. He was caught in a time loop and was holding on to a late-1960s, early-1970s vision of 'the struggle'. He'd been involved early on in Australia, I think, in fundraising for the internees' families, and had retained contacts with various Republican sympathizers in Ireland. I don't mean IRA volunteers, although Vincent was closer to being a political activist than I could ever have been.

He was a passionate man and I saw a good bit of him during the early eighties, when he was spending as much time as he could in Ireland. I'd known him since our days in Glanmore; we always spoke frankly and fondly, and not just about politics. He was an honest reader of any new work I was doing and I remember in particular showing him the 'Sweeney Redivivus' poems, which must have been in or around 1983. He didn't altogether like them, although that didn't bother me because I was certain of them from the start. He probably didn't approve of the clean pair of heels Heaney/Sweeney was showing in poems like 'The First Flight' and 'Drifting Off'.

So were people right to detect a strong autobiographical element in the Sweeney poems?

'Autobiographical' isn't quite the word. They're strictly dramatic monologues. I felt relieved of myself when I was writing them.

They belong to what you have called 'the sprint mode' of writing poetry. Do you tend to place special trust in the sprint poem – because it is more likely to be 'inspired'?

I do trust it for that reason. If I might invoke another home-grown critical term, I'd say the sprint mode is more likely to produce lines that have a 'bare wire' quality.

The tone adopted in the Sweeney poems is far more confident and unapologetic than in the 'Station Island' sequence. Did you find them especially satisfying to write?

I did. I felt 'up and away', as one of the poems has it. At full tilt. Reckless and accurate and entirely Sweenified, as capable of muck-raking as of self-mockery. The poetry was in the persona.

There's certainly a sense of rebellion, of somebody lashing out. Several of the poems contain remarks and reminiscences that might have been more difficult to represent in your personal voice.

All true. There's more than a whiff of 'the sulphurous news of poets and poetry' in the air. I got a lot out of my system, for instance, in relation to the northern response to *North*. And the resentment of my 'runner-in' status in the south is there in 'The Scribes'. But there's positive stuff secluded in the poems as well, stuff that would have been equally hard to present directly. 'The Master', for example, is a transmogrified account of meeting Czesław Miłosz. A meal with him in a Berkeley restaurant, in the company of Bob Hass and Robert Pinsky, gets turned into an episode where Sweeney stops to consult a 'master' in an old tower.

I'd assumed – probably because of the tower – that the poem was a homage to W. B. Yeats.

There's a windswept, wing-beaty atmosphere in the poem that has to come from Yeats; and he was certainly a composite element in the figure of the master. But the character as I imagine him – unhistrionic, unmysterious, clear spoken, his authority deriving from veteran rather than visionary experience – all that came from the meeting with Miłosz.

Another master, Cézanne, appears to be the subject of 'An Artist'. Why Cézanne?

'I love the thought of his anger,' as I say in the poem. Sitting there *sur le motif*, his grumpy contrary old back turned on us as he faces the humpy countervailing mountain. The first time I went to London I came back with a Cézanne print of Mont Sainte-Victoire. The first art book I bought for myself was about Cézanne. When I wrote 'An Artist', I was reading Rilke's letters about his infatuation with Cézanne and some of Rilke's words are included. What I love is the doggedness, the courage to face into the job, the generation of what Hopkins would have called 'self-yeast' – but in a positive sense: the miller gristing his own mill. This may or may not be the Cézanne known to the art critics and historians, but he's the one I've lived with, the one rewarded with those incontrovertible paintings, so steady in themselves they steady you and the world – and you in the world.

Has he been more important to you, more instructive maybe, than the other Impressionist and post-Impressionist painters?

I could enter all kinds of qualifications but still the answer is yes. I'll never get over the first eye-burn of a room full of Van Goghs in their former Jeu de Paume home, nor the grief of his crows above the cornfield in the Van Gogh museum in Amsterdam, and who would want to be without Matisse or Monet or any of them? But the fact of the matter is, when I go to a new gallery I head for the Cézannes and could spend whatever time there is to spend in front of them.

Does part of his appeal for you lie in his country landscapes?

Not so. The appeal is more in his character than in his subjects. Corot would be my country landscape man. Riverbanks, old tree-roots, just the willow-world of the Moyola. Or Emil Nolde. Or Constable, for that matter, as muddy as he's cloudy. But in painting I'm susceptible to things far from the Moyola. I like Puvis de Chavannes. Richard Diebenkorn. Jacques-Louis David. Philip Guston, for God's sake.

Guston might have responded to the cockpit rivets in another of your Sweeney poems, 'In the Beech'. Were those soldiers in tanks and that pilot in his plane actually witnessed by you?

They were. For a while in late 1943 and early 1944 there was a lot of activity in the air and on the ground as the Americans got ready for D-Day. The planes would come in low on a course that crossed our front garden and I could occasionally see an image that's now an indelible part of Second World War iconography, the pilot with his leather football helmet-head and his goggles and his corrugated mouth-mask – all very fleeting but unforgettable. And I *did* sit hidden in the fork of the beech tree at the head of our lane as the tanks and armoured cars and marching soldiers passed below.

You are also hiding in a tree – a willow – in the poem 'Oracle'. Were you a loner?

I remember much of my childhood as a trance of loneliness, and in those places something in me was utterly at peace. Probably I was slipping back an evolutionary era or two, into some stage of the process where I was sheltering in savannah or living in the branches. No wonder the 'Sweeney Redivivus' cycle ends in a cave in the Dordogne.

When Sweeney Astray *and* Station Island *were being launched, there was much talk of your own Sweeney-like flight by helicopter. A promotional helicopter tour by you and Craig Raine is still spoken of as if it had actually taken place.*

Craig's book, *Rich*, was being published by Faber at the same time as *Station Island* and *Sweeney Astray*, in early October 1984. The itinerary was being arranged months ahead, in May I guess, when I was in Harvard. At any rate, I agreed on the phone that we could do Oxford and somewhere in the north of England on the same day, if we took a helicopter rather than a train. The mode of transport, as far as I was concerned, was entirely instrumental. But during the summer it became a feature, as they say, an element in the firm's PR that was being handled then by Desmond Clarke.

I just ended up getting more and more irked. I remember writing to Matthew Evans who was managing director at the time, and saying that by going in pursuit of the market in this gimmicky way, Faber was in danger of losing its mystique. At any rate, the helicopter was eventually cancelled; but since the schedule still demanded a quick transfer of the bards, we ended up travelling on a small aeroplane. In this case, however, PR stood very definitely for privately reserved: it wasn't part of the promotion.

9

'The books stood open and the gates unbarred'
Harvard

~

Some years before Station Island *was published, you began working in Harvard College on a contract that required you to teach one term each year.*

The initial contract, starting in spring semester of 1981/2, was for three years, but I'd already spent the spring of 1979 in Harvard as a guest lecturer in the English Department. Robert Lowell died suddenly, you remember, in 1977 and Elizabeth Bishop was compulsorily retired that same year on grounds of her age, of all things. I arrived on a one-off basis in 1979. That was how my Harvard life began.

In other words, you'd been back in Dublin for a couple of years before you received the invitation to take up a more permanent position?

Exactly. That came sometime in the spring or early summer of 1981. By then, people in the Harvard English Department had known me as a colleague, had heard me talk and read, and would have had a chance to read the students' reports on the workshops I'd conducted. But there was no formal interview. What was being offered at that time was a part-time contract, not a tenured position.

Did you regard this as an honour?

I did regard it as an honour. And also as a release. By that time, the Carysfort job had become a big drag. We were operating a full three-year course and there was now a graduate component; I was head of department, doing lectures and seminars, marking essays and exams, but also taking on tutors, involved with curriculum matters and college board meetings and all the rest of it. It was mid-July by the time I got myself clear in the summer; by early September I was back on duty for the repeat exams. The Harvard offer basically said: here you can be yourself as a poet all the year round, except that you'll have to teach poetry workshops in the springtime. On the other hand, this entailed my going away on my own, leaving Marie with the family; not a simple thing to decide, although the fact that we had lived *en famille* in Cambridge for that half year meant that everybody had some idea of the life and the friends I'd be going back to.

Marie was ready and willing for the change, but two things decided us. The first was an offer by her sister Claire to step in for a couple of weeks every year to let Marie over to Harvard for a holiday. But the second was equally important – a dream I had on the night before I was to give my decision to the department chairman: I was in the desert, it was getting dark; suddenly in front of me, there's this cliff with a sort of lean-to constructed against the face of it, somewhere to shelter during the night. Next thing then, next dream-frame, it's a sunlit morning, the cliff has gone, and I'm standing on the banks of the Suez Canal. What I'd taken for a cliff was a docked liner that had moved on during the night . . . And this in turn I took to be a counsel of boldness, a reminder that what looks safe and settled isn't necessarily so, that you shouldn't rely on the status quo. So I decided to move before the Carysfort liner moved.

You've said somewhere that Tomas Tranströmer gave you good advice at this juncture.

He certainly did. We met Tomas during the summer of 1981, when a lot of things were happening. We'd had that long holiday in France when I visited Rocamadour and the caves in the Dordogne, and all the while the hunger strikes were keeping on and on at home. Then later in the summer, in July, maybe, I went with Marie to a poetry festival in Morelia, in Mexico, the best I ever attended. It was arranged by Homero Aridjis who'd been Mexico's poet-ambassador in The Hague. Homero got the idea of an international festival from the Rotterdam festival and had his contacts from Rotterdam also, so when he was called back home, he went into action and everybody he invited turned up: Tomas, Vasko Popa,

Tadeusz Różewicz, Borges, Günter Grass, Allen Ginsberg, Marin Sorescu, Michael Hamburger, Octavio Paz . . . It was an intoxicating event, not least because it included my first sustained encounter with mesquite, the Mexican moonshine. But for other reasons too. The timing of the thing, for example, couldn't have been better: there I was, 'free at last' to be a poet, on a roster with the heroic names. There was still a slight niggle as to whether we had taken the right decision about Harvard – and Tomas banished it. For years, he and his wife Monica had lived a life where he was much on the road, away from home; in his wisdom, as poet and psychologist, he advised us that all would be well provided we never let six weeks pass without seeing each other. And we never did.

Did you and Marie ever seriously consider moving the whole family to Cambridge?

Never. I often said I was more like a lighthouse keeper than an emigrant. Four months on, eight ashore.

Does this imply a lonely, maybe even cold, experience?

Far from it. Already in 1979, on my very first tour of duty, so to speak, I'd arrived to a welcome from people I knew. There was Helen Vendler; and even though Helen wasn't officially at Harvard, we'd known her from the days of the Yeats Summer School in Sligo and that famous Kilkenny Arts Week in 1975, so she was very much a guide and guardian to us, bringing us to dinner in Brookline, introducing us to legendary figures like John Malcolm Brinnin. Then too there were the Alcorns, an American family who'd lived in Wicklow during our days in Glanmore, but who'd gone back to the States some time before we set off in 1979. Alfie Alcorn was a graduate of Harvard who'd resigned from his job as a newspaperman and moved with his wife Sally and their two daughters to a rented house in Wicklow in order to write a novel. We'd become good friends with them and spent a lot of time in their company, and it was the Alcorns who met us at Logan Airport on our first foray into Massachusetts, and drove us to an apartment they'd found and rented for us ahead of our arrival.

I'll always remember driving along the Charles river in the Alcorns' car, looking across at the Harvard houses on the other side of the water – Eliot House and Lowell House and Winthrop and Adams – with their domes and their belfries. The apartment they'd got for us was just a few blocks from The Yard – Harvard doesn't call it the campus; on my way to the English Department during that first visit, I'd walk through the Law School and past many of the Harvard landmarks, such as Massachusetts Hall and the Widener Library.

Did you know anybody in the English Department when you arrived in 1979?

I didn't. But the day after I arrived Monroe Engel, the professor in charge of the Creative Writing section, took me to lunch in Mr Bartley's Burger Cottage – another Cambridge landmark – and very quickly settled me in. Monroe was a novelist and former publisher, a friend of Bellow and Berryman, a man of great kindness and constancy, and in the months to come he'd mark my card, as it were, about the department. The race of giants was still in residence, in the autumn of their reign: Walter Jackson Bate in the English Department; Harry Levin in Comparative Literature; and Robert Fitzgerald, who had a sabbatical that year and who gave me the use of his study in the new Pusey Library. Even so, many of my friends and contacts that year and in the years that followed were not Harvard people but writers and revellers from the environs.

Such as?

Well, Frank Bidart, Lowell's former student who'd gone on to become his friend and literary confidant, and would eventually be his literary executor and editor of the *Collected Poems*. I'd met Frank first in Dublin, when he made a quick visit to see Caroline Blackwood, not long after Cal's death. Frank's best friend was Robert Pinsky; in no time at all, I was meeting the pair of them and another Lowell aficionado, Alan Williamson, the poet who was Briggs Copeland Poetry Fellow in the English Department. Then, since Frank was a great pal of Elizabeth Bishop, Marie and I frequently ended up at dinner parties in the Cambridge apartment Elizabeth often shared with Alice Methfessel, and sometimes in Elizabeth Bishop's own residence on one of the old wharves in Boston Harbour. And all the while, we were being spirited across the river to Brookline, into Boston University territory, for our dinners at Helen Vendler's house. All of those people, and many more, entered our lives during that first 1979 stint. Just five months, but a lifetime's friendships established.

And how about Bernard and Jane McCabe? Stratis Haviaris? Sven Birkerts? I've heard you talk about them and others: William Corbett, for example, Askold Melnyczuk, Dimitri and Cynthia Hadzi . . .

. . . and Adele Dalsimer, Ellen Wilbur, Peter and Padraig O'Malley, Shaun O'Connell, Lucie Brock-Broido, Henri Cole, Michael Blumenthal, Stanisław and Anna Barańczak, Catherine Shannon . . . Over the years, our Massachusetts friends came from three different worlds: Harvard and other universities in the area, the writing community and the Irish or Irish Studies community. It was an expanding universe of acquaintances. Peter and Padraig O'Malley, for example, had run a famous Cambridge pub called the Plough and the Stars and Peter had founded *Ploughshares* magazine. Peter was then married to Ellen Wilbur and was a friend of the McCabes, the McCabes had a wonderful big house that they would allow Peter to use for fundraising parties for *Ploughshares*. Bernard McCabe was a brother of Herbert McCabe, the Oxford Dominican and editor of *New Blackfriars*, and I met Bernard and Jane first at a party run by friends of the poet Desmond O'Grady, who was also around Harvard during that spring of 1979. Bernard and Jane were to become fast and lasting friends, and their house would eventually be a home from home for me in Cambridge, but we didn't see all that much of them until I began my annual stints. And the same could be said of Stratis and Sven and the other people you mention. I find it hard to believe, indeed, that I was on the Harvard faculty for fourteen years, from 1982 until 1996.

Are you not still on the faculty?

When, in 1996, I resigned from the Boylston Professorship, President Rudenstine and Dean Knowles urged me to keep some connection with the university, so I was designated the Ralph Waldo Emerson Poet-in-Residence, although the residency requirements were not too demanding – a few weeks every second year, during which time I gave lectures and a reading and had meetings with students. In 2007 I resigned from that post also.

Can you say something about the Boylston Professorship? I have the impression that it is regarded as a special position at Harvard.

It was created for John Adams, after he came back to Boston from Washington, so it's one of the most venerable chairs in the university. It's a Professorship of Rhetoric and Oratory, and the oratory aspect survives in that the Professor must organize the annual Boylston Speaking Contest. This was endowed in 1829 and, according to Nicholas Boylston's original rubric for the competition, the judges are urged to pay special attention to 'everything that adds beauty to written discourses when spoken aloud'. In the nineteenth century, of course, those written discourses would have been in Greek and Latin and Hebrew, but it was mostly English when I was in charge – poems, prose extracts, excerpts from speeches by Martin Luther King and John F. Kennedy, for example – although you still did get the occasional chunk of Cicero. In the past fifty years or so, the chair has been occupied by writers, Archibald MacLeish before Robert Fitzgerald, and at present it's held by Jorie Graham, the first woman incumbent.

Did you always feel like a visitor in Cambridge?

How does a migrant feel? I was both home and away. I was an insider of sorts and at the same time situated at an angle to the place. In later years, I recognized the same placement and displacement in Derek Walcott and Joseph Brodsky, both of whom were also in and out of the Massachusetts scene. I may only have been a visitor, but from the start, I had my own American domicile, since I stayed every year in the same rooms in Adams House. This was thanks to Robert Kiely, a colleague in the English Department, who was Master of Adams House where his wife Jana was Assistant Master.

Year after year, I'd arrive and unpack the suitcases, set up books on the shelves, wander out to the bookshops, and after that to the bar-counter of the local restaurant, 'One Potato Two Potato'. In the course of the first week, I'd receive some sixty to eighty sets of poetry manuscripts from people wanting to take one of the two workshops, coded English Sbr and English Rbr, the former being for the more capable or 'advanced' students. In fact, that first weekend of adjudication was the most testing moment of the semester, because the selection of people for the workshops was of crucial importance to oneself and to the people selected – to say nothing of the ones not selected.

Did you interview prospective students?

No interviews, and no essays about who they were and why they hoped to take the workshop. I wanted only five or six poems from each applicant. Their writings alone were what I decided on. Almost everyone intelligent becomes interesting once you talk to them. What I wanted was evidence of their artistic doings. I didn't want to be constantly exposed to the disparity between the poverty of most of the poems you'd receive and the plenitude of those essays of self-introduction that American students are so good at. The consequence of this, of course, was the need to get your judgement right from the start. If you put a dud into the advanced class, you did the dud and the rest of the class and yourself a disservice. If you turned away a real talent, you delivered a wound and rattled a confidence. You were fallible, but had to act infallible, there was so much store set by the acceptances and rejections.

Any 'goof-ups'?

Only once, I think, did I make a real mistake. The most disturbing thing in those cases is the falsity at the heart of the negotiation. You cannot say to a student at the end of the third or fourth week of term, 'Look, I'm sorry, I made a mistake, you don't have the talent I thought you had, so you better get out of the class.' By the time you realize you have misjudged, a covenant has been established so you just work on as a teacher, keeping faith with each member of the course. The unnerving truth is that you can easily enough find 'interesting' comments to make on middling or bad work. In the Harvard situation, however, these workshops were undergraduate courses, mostly one-off, one-semester engagements. It wasn't as if the students were enlisted for a year or two in a master's degree programme.

How well-read were your Harvard students? Was there a fundamental clash between their personal canon and yours?

Clash would be too strong a word. But there certainly was a divergence. For a start, there was no consistency in the schooling they'd had in poetry in their pre-university days. Students from the gilded

New England academies would have had an intense literary training and be as well prepared as good sixth formers on this side of the Atlantic, probably better prepared, and with more developed individual tastes . . . If you've read Tobias Wolff's novel *Old School*, you'll have a true picture of that kind of student. On the other hand, somebody from a high school in California or New York City might know a smattering of contemporary work from the American anthologies and not know one canonical English poem. In general, I saw it as part of my job to introduce them to poems from the fifteenth century onwards: sonnets, carols, songs, odes, elegies, the lot. William Dunbar, William Wordsworth, Wystan Auden. Irish poems too, of course, Yeats especially. I quoted things to them from memory; not too many, I hope, but enough to suggest that they themselves ought to stock up. I made *The Norton Anthology of Poetry* a set text.

Did you require them to learn poems by heart?

I urged but did not require . . . Joseph Brodsky had single-handedly, or perhaps I should say univocally, reintroduced the practice of memorizing poems as a writing-course requirement. My guess is that for most students it was an exotic challenge rather than a formative exercise. If you begin belting out poems in primary school and continue learning chunks of Shakespeare and Chaucer until you're eighteen or nineteen, your ear has a fair chance of getting tuned; but if you only start memorizing after that I'm not sure it has much effect.

Did the new life affect your own writing habits?

Not to begin with. I was slogging away at 'Station Island' when I made the move, and was much concerned with the matters of Ireland. What happened was a kind of separation of powers: in Harvard I tended to teach, do readings, put my executive self in charge, then come home and in the summer months attempt again to 'relish versing'. It usually worked. I'd always experience an immediate physical joy on those mornings in late May when the Aer Lingus plane came down over the midlands and the whole country was a flourish of hawthorn, green and white, hill-surge and surf-bloom. Summer was 'i-cumen in' and I was back home with no students for another eight months.

You weren't afraid that the professing might drive out the poetry?

I didn't worry too much about that. The way poetry had crept up on me early on, or I had crept up on it, meant that I tended to regard a full-time writing life as something of a luxury. But when the Boylston chair came up, Robert Fitzgerald urged me to think very carefully. Robert, I believe, had found the professorship a bigger drain or constraint than he'd bargained for. Previously, he'd been in journalism and then had worked full-time in Italy on his translation of the *Odyssey*, so for him Harvard may have come to represent the shades of the prison house. He was genuinely concerned, at any rate, about whether or not it would be good for me to take the job – afraid it might interfere with the poetry work. Which is why I called him my 'Harvard Nestor' in one of those sonnets in *Electric Light*. But I still think that, in my case, the four-month/eight-month arrangement was a definite saving grace.

The great majority of American poets now earn a living in universities as teachers of creative writing. Has this irretrievably changed the role of the poet in society?

Nothing is irretrievable in poetry; but yes, until another seismic talent shows up, some Grendel from beyond the pale, some Ginsberg or Whitman to flutter the L-A-N-G-U-A-G-E dovecotes and upset the mead-benches, poets and poetry will tend to be heard on short wave, as it were. Robert Frost was one of the first to enter the academy, but you could say that he conquered it rather than entered it. He had established himself on the open market and – son of a schoolteacher mother, and himself a schoolteacher early on – was qualified in all sorts of ways for the classroom.

Maybe Lowell was the last American to be a dual citizen of the university and the world beyond it, at home in Harvard, but also at home among the metropolitan set, a figure to be photographed at cocktail parties and on marches to the Pentagon. He had authority as well as celebrity. I cannot think of any poet in the States at the moment who occupies that kind of cultural space – Adrienne Rich or Gary Snyder might fit, although there's something sectional about their appeal. The professionalized academic condition is typically American, but it increasingly applies in Britain and Ireland. It was different for my generation, we had the example of Auden and

MacNeice, Patrick Kavanagh and R. S. Thomas, Ted Hughes, Philip Larkin, Stevie Smith, all kinds of individual talents broadcasting outside the academy and finding an audience beyond it. Not to mention Dylan Thomas and Hugh MacDiarmid. None of them had a roost in the writing schools. But nowadays, most poets perch in some department or other. Even so, and happily so, in Ireland there are still a few independents like Paul Durcan and yourself. Not to mention the singing school maintained by the bounty of Aosdána.

You seem to be implying that a career-based life in the creative writing schools undermines poetry as a vocational activity.

For some people, certainly. In the States, during those sessions of questions from the audience when the visiting poet is asked about other poets he or she admires, the names given are rarely those of the great dead. Usually you hear about people at other writing schools, people who are at the centre of webs, good enough representatives of the contemporary scene, but proof of what Donald Davie once termed – in another context – 'lowered sights and diminished expectations'. There are times when you realize that the guild now consists as much of networkers as dreamworkers.

Without a network, what chance does a gifted new twenty-first-century poet have of being selected from the teeming slush-piles and in-trays?

Hardly any, I agree, so the care of teachers and the network of writing schools is the new reality. A necessary ecology, in fact. Apart from anything else, there's the size of the place. When Irish or British writers start to get haughty about the literary culture that pertains in America, they forget the sheer populousness of the scene, the physical extent of it, university writing centres everywhere from Seattle to Southern California, Harvard to Houston, Arkansas to Utah, Princeton to Stanford, NYU to North Carolina, BU to Iowa.

On our side of the ocean, the borders are more or less sealed, the acoustic is more sensitive, the chances of being heard that much better. But the universities here have also cottoned on to the fact that creative writing can be an earner: there's a convergence between the general, New-Agey, self-realization industries and the entrepreneurial turn in the university faculties, and one result is a burgeoning number of people seeking not just realization but ratification as well. The workshop and the poetry biz are all part of the one phenomenon. More and more poets in Britain and Ireland are employed as writing fellows in universities and with regional arts organizations, so the vocational and the professional are becoming more and more implicated.

You once remarked that, after a term spent in poetry workshops, a poet can end up exhausted and hating the activity.

When I said that, I was simply acknowledging the wear and tear your spirit undergoes when you work intensely and closely with other people's hopes and inwardness. What wears you down is, on the one hand, a constant expectation of response, honest response presumably, an effort at truthful judgement, and on the other, a consciousness that nurture is called for also, and praise is being sought.

In my own case, I could be seeing as many as thirty students over the course of a twelve-week semester. Having personal, one-on-one interviews on at least two occasions, being further available during office hours to them and whoever else wanted to turn up with a fistful of manuscript. As your relationship with each student developed, and the portfolios thickened, it was as if your head was getting attached to thirty different terminals all around Harvard. The image I had was of Gulliver with his big head roped down in Lilliput, pegged to the ground by strands of his own hair. It was a full-time, demanding job, and all your poetry-speak, if you'll excuse the expression, was called upon. And since this was a class and grades had to be given out and the students were there for instruction, you talked – necessarily, I suppose – as if improvement were in all cases possible, as if even success were possible.

So as well as the exhaustion that comes naturally in any teaching situation, there was a further, deeper attrition, because the can-do ethos of the workshop was at odds with your sense of the fated – and chancy – nature of artistic achievement. At the beginning of term each year, I would say the same thing to all the classes, almost as if it were a grace before teaching. I would tell them that I was going to be involved with their capacities as writers, but that their destinies as writers would be their own business.

Meaning?

I meant I'd have more to do with their choice of words than their life choices, that our activities in the classroom and our negotiations over submitted work would be pointed, technical, advisory, and, well, professional. Implying thereby that there is another aspect to the art which is, as you say, vocational. I suppose I was also talking from a deep assumption that the growth of a poet's mind is a solitary affair, in spite of all the help it can receive from context and company. Wordsworth and Coleridge, Owen and Sassoon, Moore and Bishop, Hughes and Plath were part of each other's destinies, but it would be crazy for students to expect that kind of phenomenal experience from a workshop. Having said that, it should also be added that, over the years, a teacher-poet is bound to develop special relations with some students.

To what extent did this happen in your case?

There have been a few people who became friends, a few whose work I kept up with afterwards. But that kind of thing is not part of the contract, nor should it be part of anybody's expectation from a class. Usually the people you stick with are those who have a tacit understanding that – for all the democratic openness of the workshop situation, for all the rights it confers on its members to think of themselves as equally entitled in practice and aspiration – the reality in the end is much more hierarchical. And what's true of students is also true of poets. Some are just better at the work than others, and deserving of a different kind of respect.

How great a part do poetry readings – in America or anywhere else – play in developing a poet's audience?

Readings definitely have an effect upon audience. Or perhaps better say 'audiences'. You can, in other words, get to the people there in front of you, but you can never be sure how big or how dependable the carryover is going to be from the ones in the auditorium to the ones buying and reading the book. What's more, a poet in the United States can have a relatively big reputation in the relatively hermetic world of writing programmes. He or she can live sustained by the regard of peers in the guild, without ever stirring reaction or attracting attention beyond that particular circle of aficionados. Yet, even within that circle, readings and personal appearances are important.

In my own case, the thing built gradually. My first four books were published in America to considerable silence. *North* did admittedly get an enthusiastic salute from Helen Vendler, and Robert Fitzgerald wrote a laudatory overview in the *New Republic*, so by the mid-seventies I was on the go here and there in the States, chiefly as the result of sponsorship by friends in different universities: Bert Hornback and Donald Hall at Ann Arbor; Tom Flanagan in Berkeley; Donald Davie and Bill Chace at Stanford; Frank McShane at Columbia; friends in two different colleges in the Philadelphia area. What had come first with these people, and others who helped me at the time, was a reading of the books – the live appearance was subsequent to the silent reception.

Then the publication of *Field Work* in 1979 changed the game considerably: Harold Bloom and Denis Donoghue gave that collection a lift in the *TLS* and the Sunday *New York Times* respectively, and the effect began to be noticeable not only in the number of invitations to read, but in the requests for specific poems to be included in the readings. Bloom, for instance, had paid particular attention to 'The Harvest Bow' and often that poem would be asked for. Which suggests that star critics and reviewers also have a considerable effect upon the development of an audience.

Elizabeth Bishop's name has cropped up several times here and I'd like to learn more about your meetings with her. In 1980, in the TLS, *you published a poem dedicated to her. That poem, 'A Hank of Wool', was never reprinted.*

I didn't feel I'd got it right. I had a first go at it in the summer of 1979, when we were staying at the Flanagans' house on Long Island. I was writing poems with titles like 'A Kite for Michael and Christopher', 'A Hazel Stick for Catherine Ann', 'A Cart for Edward Gallagher' (which became 'Last Look'), and had a shot at one called 'A Hank of Wool' for Elizabeth. In the course of that spring in Harvard, we'd got to know her and Alice Methfessel, as I mentioned earlier; at the end of term, they invited Marie and myself and the kids to come up to their holiday place in Maine. By then, we were very much at ease with both of them, but we had already made plans to house-sit for the Flanagans on Long

Island – so instead of going to Maine, I sent Elizabeth some poems. And along with them, 'A Hank of Wool', for herself. It was just a little flutter, a note of acknowledgement of the invitation and an apology for not being able to take it up. The poem began with me as a child holding out a hank of wool on my arms – so that my aunt Mary could wind it into a ball – and ended with me standing with arms still stretched out, empty, facing Maine, in a gesture of homage to Elizabeth.

I then got a letter from her saying she liked this and that in the poems, and telling how her grandmother in Nova Scotia had taught her to knit during the First World War, little coloured squares that would be stitched together into patchworky items to send to soldiers. But the typical Elizabeth bit came at the end, where she reported that, once she had dutifully knit the squares, she would proceed to rip them out . . .

The saddest thing was that she died suddenly at the end of that summer, one evening in October, as she was dressing for dinner in her Boston apartment. She was getting ready to come across to Cambridge, to do a reading with Mary Lavin. Some time after that, at any rate, I revised and extended the little Maine greeting and printed it as an 'in memoriam'. It was OK as a personal salute, maybe, but I just didn't think it got a proper purchase.

You said, in a radio interview, that you felt Bishop 'didn't utterly disapprove of what I wrote'. Did that negative construction imply a certain backhandedness in her compliments?

Not at all. I'm afraid I was being a bit too coy about her comments. In fact, Elizabeth's letter said how she liked specific bits of the poems, such as a line about 'the deer of poetry' standing 'in pools of lucent sound'. What I meant to suggest in the interview was Elizabeth's characteristic manner, the very attractive, very dry yet merry intelligence that was always at work, a wonderful combination of propriety and transgressiveness. A capacity for humour and strictness, in equal measure.

Both Marie and I felt completely at home with her, and it had to do, I think, with a strain of Scottishness that we were both familiar with. We'd grown up among the Ulster Scots and there in Cambridge we'd come across a Nova Scot: the life that Elizabeth knew early on in Nova Scotia had actually a lot in common with the life we'd known in Ulster. Just take her story 'In the Village': a country dressmaker, a blacksmith, a forge, a child being sent on an errand . . . It could have been Ardboe or Bellaghy. Or take that bus in 'The Moose', and the people on it.

When you met her, did you already know her work well?

I did. I'd had the old *Selected Poems* that Chatto published in the 1960s. For years I'd loved 'Roosters', 'At the Fishhouses' and several others. 'Florida', for example, and 'The Sandpiper'. I put her poem 'The Map' on a handout for a practical criticism seminar in Queen's: it was for a group that included on that particular day, I remember, Ciaran Carson; so Medbh McGuckian and Paul Muldoon may have been there as well – unless, of course, it was a day when they were cutting class. *Geography III* had appeared a while before we went to Harvard and people were talking a lot about those poems. When I arrived, Elizabeth was very much the 'in' figure.

Did the fact that you were her Harvard replacement taint your relationship?

Before my arrival, I *did* worry about that. I knew that Elizabeth had been told unexpectedly and, according to rumour, insensitively that her tenure in the department was coming to an end – simply because she was reaching the age of sixty-five. I felt she was therefore bound to resent the young whippersnapper from Ireland, the cuckoo flying in to occupy her nest; but happily it didn't turn out like that at all. We all became the best of friends. At her birthday party that year, after I'd given her a present, she gave me one in return – a bottle of Rebel Yell bourbon that had been sent to her from Texas. At another party in New York, after a reading I'd done at the Poetry Center in the Y, she even sang a song for Marie and me – the Vassar College laundry list, to the air of 'Yankee Doodle'.

Bishop had her demons – among them her drinking, and the loss by suicide of two people who had been very close to her. Did she strike you as hurt or troubled or at odds with the world?

I could quote again that remark of Lowell's and say that she seemed to have 'come through a grief'. Which is not to say there was any element of glumness or grieving in her manner. I never saw her on the rampage with drink or in withdrawal because of it, and there certainly was never any opening of the heart about her personal life. There was a true and tempered quality to her, a terrific alertness of perception, both moral and physical. If there was a fly on the wall, she'd be the first to have her eye on it. And obviously, her vigilance, her even gaze at everybody and everything must have come from the sorrows she had known and lived with, early and late. Still, the saddest thing about our friendship with Elizabeth was its untimely end. When we parted in June 1979, there was every reason to believe this was the start rather than the finish of something. I felt there was plenty of time. I never even asked her to sign one of her books.

Does it surprise you that our age greatly prefers Elizabeth Bishop to Robert Lowell?

Lowell is taking the punishment that's always handed out to the big guy eventually; so no, I'm not surprised. Lowell was a white Anglo-Saxon Protestant male, a Eurocentric, egotistical sublime, writing as if he intended to be heard in a high wind. He was on the winning side from the start: Boston Brahmin, friend of Eliot, part of the literary establishment on both sides of the Atlantic – although he was, of course, ever-conscious about these advantages, and forever making his courtly bows, in public and in private, to Elizabeth and her achievement. But then the fashion shifted, the culture favoured a less imperious style, the gender balance needed adjusting, the age of Merrill and Ashbery arrived, chamber music and cabaret rather than orchestral crash were in favour, and the time was propitious for the perfect pitch of Bishop.

And yet Elizabeth Bishop had strong loyalties to people in the traditional canon, to George Herbert, for example. I remember, indeed, that you compared her place in American poetry to that of Larkin in England.

I think her kind of formality does come, yes, from a grounding in English poetry.

Did that make it easier for you to hear her?

Maybe, yes. But she had her own way of fastening her lines to the page and into the ear.

*Interesting that you should speak about fastening lines to the
page, since you have, in the past, spoken of a kind of 'floating'
quality in American poetry, words with 'less specific gravity' than
in Ireland and Britain, poems with less 'relationship to the actual'.*

It was Frank Bidart who once used that image of fastening the
words to the page or the ear, and Frank was obviously picking up
on Robert Frost's notion of the fundamental importance of 'tones'
and 'sentence sounds' and 'the sound of sense'. Bishop is an artful
stylist, a maker if ever there was one, a text-weaver, a very self-
conscious writer, but in the old orality/textuality debate, she can be
cited by both sides. Her lines have what Tom Paulin once called
'the now of utterance' about them. 'I caught a tremendous fish . . .'
'Now can you see the monument?' 'The state with the prettiest
name . . .' 'Awful but cheerful' . . .

My original preference would have been for poetry with that sort
of connectedness to whatever was there and then. Poetry, as Bishop
might have put it, from 'a cold spring' – in the indicative mood, in
some relation to the historical. When I said those things about
American poetry, I was a bit on the defensive, or perhaps better say
I was defending my patch. In the Irish/Northern Irish context, there
was a constant pressure for gives or takes on 'the situation', so you
were forever looking at how other poets made their imaginative
way in the world. The work that meant most to me was stuff born
out of more stressful conditions, stuff that had a knottier origin
and a tighter grain than the school of Ashbery or, for that matter,
Merrill. I got more of a charge from Zbigniew Herbert and
Miroslav Holub and that whole eastern-European school. Not that
I cannot go where a different kind of poetry wants to take me.
Poetry, I mean, that is more at large in its subjectivity, more musi-
cally relaxed, hedonistic, wily, ready to riff or drift into reverie. As
a reader I can of course go with that, especially when it's well done,
as in O'Hara and Schuyler and Koch and company.

*Over twenty years ago, you described John Ashbery's work as 'a
centrally heated daydream', adding that 'it's also sorrowful, it
knows that it's inadequate'. Since then, however, you have
spoken more positively about his poetry. Did you have to struggle
particularly hard with Ashbery's work, if only because your
students admired him greatly?*

When I looked at *The Tennis Court Oath* in Berkeley, over thirty-five years ago, I confess I could make nothing of it, nor did I make much of an effort. Olson and Duncan were a steep enough learning curve to be going on with. But when I open a magazine nowadays and see an Ashbery poem, I can, so to speak, hear it. It's partly that I know a hell of a lot more about what it feels like to live the American life in America, partly that Ashbery has hypnotic gifts and has indeed created the taste by which he is enjoyed. But now that we are in the post-9/11 world, I think my reference to the 'centrally heated daydream' and my feeling that Ashbery knew it was 'inadequate' make more sense. I wasn't trying to demean him, just pointing out that he wasn't prepared to deliver jeremiads about the corporate Goliath his country had turned into.

Basically, I was trying to express my sense that a certain American age had passed, the age when America could be spoken for or spoken to, in a Lowellesque kind of way. America in the eighties seemed like an immense hovercraft, buoyant on its own prosperity and trust in the future. It was as if Americans had lived for years inside a geodesic dome of continental proportions – communally, sumptuously insulated from the cold blast of world poverty, not prone to anxiety about dangers in the civic and political realm. It was their pride and their luck. They lived the American dream, which is certainly 'centrally heated'. And that was a way of saying that Ashbery's poetry matched the uncannily insulated, materially comfortable, volubly docile condition of a middle-class population on the move between its shopping malls and its missile silos. Ashbery would have been as aware as anybody of the immense power of the military machine, but his gifts and equipment did not fit him for the minatory role. He was no Ginsberg. He was closer to the Feste of 'Hey, ho, the wind and the rain', sorrowful in that kind of way.

Did your Harvard years deepen your ability to 'hear' American poetry, while leaving you somewhat indifferent towards the results?

I could answer by making a distinction that Christopher Ricks makes: instead of saying, that's true, I could say, there's truth in that . . . But when I think of people like Tom Sleigh and Henri Cole, to mention only a couple of the younger poets I got to know in Cambridge, I feel I've been making far too much of a poetical 'them and us' out of what is basically one big earful of voices. I'm in communion, as it were, with poets who have an aesthetic far different from mine. Jorie Graham and Lucie Brock-Broido. William Corbett and James Tate.

Might there even be some of that American-style 'open-weave talkiness' you once remarked upon creeping into your own poetry? You've referred to some of the Electric Light *poems as 'loose-weave' works.*

This time, I suppose, I have to quote not Ricks but King Lear: 'And that's true too.' There's certainly more free associating going on, and the whole thing is a bit more unmoored. But I find it hard to locate direct American influence in the style or substance of the poems. I got a taste for a looser kind of movement after writing 'Keeping Going', which appeared in *The Spirit Level*. And that poem, I'd guess, came from reading those big open sequences by Miłosz. But then, by the middle eighties, Miłosz more or less counted as an American poet.

American landscapes and responses to American culture certainly feature in Miłosz's work to an extent that they never have in yours. Could it be that you were more migrant worker than artist-in-residence?

I think you've hit the nail on the head there. When I was asked to do a poem for the 350th anniversary of the founding of Harvard College, for example, what got me started was the discovery that John Harvard's father had been in the cattle trade in Stratford before he came to be a successful butcher in Southwark – that, and the knowledge that the original college building was near the cattle sheds and yards of the new town that would henceforth be called Cambridge. There I was, travelling back to where I started – 'the housed beasts, the listening bedroom' – in order to celebrate a different Yard, one where 'The books stood open and the gates unbarred.'

But did the distance from Ireland you gained by being in America allow you a new perspective – even a certain crucial objectivity – vis-à-vis Ireland and the Troubles?

Hard to say . . . My feeling is that the time spent at Harvard meant little enough in that regard. The year in California at the beginning of the seventies was much more important. I came back from Berkeley to Belfast in a more detached frame of mind and more change followed as a result.

Are there dangers inherent in so many Irish poets gravitating towards America as a place to earn a living and seek a reputation?

'Dangers' is a big word. I think the two cultures are by now fairly pervious to each other, so that the coming and going serves to gratify curiosity rather than constitute danger. The main danger for Irish poets in America is ghettoization within Irish Studies programmes, networking along the lines of ethnicity. I don't think there's any real danger in being able to earn a lump sum or a bonus from a residency or a few readings or a year or two in an exchange. It tends to be good for people. The danger – anywhere – is to be unaware of critical standards or to live in a scene where critical standards are in suspension. It happens in the United States, of course, but don't tell me it doesn't happen in Ireland. Loose, open-weave, centrally heated – maybe those words should be called home to roost at the top of our own review columns.

10

'A river in the trees'
The Haw Lantern

~

Do you have any particular preconceptions about how many pages a collection of poetry should contain? I ask because you followed Station Island, *your longest collection, with* The Haw Lantern, *one of your shortest.*

There's probably a lower limit of about forty pages although, when it comes to collections of lyrics, shortness isn't necessarily a fault: *The Less Deceived, Lupercal, Geography III* – none of those goes in for the long haul. I thought, in fact, of doing the 'Station Island' sequence as a single volume, and the same thought occurred later on with the forty-eight 'Squarings' in *Seeing Things*. At any rate, when it came to *The Haw Lantern*, I was after something trim. There was an even shorter selection of the poems, *Hailstones*, published in a limited edition with Peter Fallon's Gallery Press in Ireland.

You've published a number of special editions with Gallery Press – some, like Hailstones, *as interim collections, but others as unique books, such as the Ovid and Brian Merriman translations in* The Midnight Verdict.

My relationship with Peter Fallon goes back a long way. I'll always remember him arriving at our door in Belfast just before Christmas in 1971, a long-haired youth with John Lennon glasses, carrying a set of broadsheets that had been done on a hand press in Trinity College: a limited edition of a poem of mine which he'd brought from Dublin for signing. Already he was operating on two fronts, writing his own poems and publishing other people's, low-key and resolute, very much his own man. Over the years the friendship just grew because of confidences exchanged and trusts maintained, because of humour about things in general and an earnest particular interest in poetry. In 1995 Peter was a guest at the Nobel ceremonies on two counts – as personal friend and my Irish publisher. The books I've done with him may be short but our connection is a long one.

Did you feel you were pushing out the boundaries of your work in The Haw Lantern? *You remarked in your Oxford lectures that 'to find its true measure, creative talent must exert itself beyond the limit'.*

It didn't feel so much like pushing boundaries, more like sliding open partitions, or Japanese screen doors. Like trespassing in strange rooms, in a new light, especially in the parable-type poems.

Is it possible The Haw Lantern *was relatively short because you could take those parable-type poems no further?*

The length of the book hadn't to do with the supply or otherwise of the parables. They were unexpected and odd and a big excitement for a relatively short time, but then the excitement just went. I remember presenting the finished manuscript to Bernard and Jane McCabe one morning in the summer of 1986. We were on a drive though England, had stayed the night in a hotel in Lincoln, and later on that day would visit Tennyson's house in Somersby. The book was dedicated to the McCabes; the two-line dedicatory verse is about a moment Marie and I enjoyed with them on another holiday, when we stopped at a little Saxon church in Gregoryminster in Yorkshire.

Are many of the other poems similarly associated with particular locations, or with the places where they were written?

Most of them would have been written at home, in the attic of the Strand Road house. But a good bit of 'Parable Island' was done in Iceland, in 1985, and 'Alphabets' was composed over a couple of weeks in Adams House, in Harvard – in response to a commission to do the Phi Beta Kappa poem for 1984. The other poem I associate with a particular place is 'The Mud Vision': it's set in the Irish midlands, but the actual memory behind it was of thronged roads and gardens around a housing estate in County Tyrone in the late 1950s, when the Virgin Mary was supposed to have appeared to a woman in Ardboe.

Wasn't there also some linkage with the Guinness Hop Store's exhibition space in Dublin?

There certainly was. The image that got me going was by the artist Richard Long, a huge circle of muddy handprints that he'd made on a high wall of the Hop Store. It was part of a big exhibition of his work in Dublin. A kind of *boue* window. Mud in the eye, at any rate, for the rose window.

A whole underlife or otherlife of religious devotion, known from childhood, seems to inspire 'The Mud Vision'.

There are a couple of lines in another *Haw Lantern* poem that refer to 'the melt of the real thing / smarting into its absence'. They're about the sensation of holding a ball of hailstones in your tightly closed fist. But they also point to one of the main concerns of the book: call it loss of faith – or rather loss of faiths, of all kinds. Religious faith, as in 'The Mud Vision' or in the one called 'The Spoonbait'. Faith in patriotism in 'Wolfe Tone' and 'The Disappearing Island'. Loss of faith, to a certain extent, in language itself, or at least doubts about the 'real presence' behind it, as in 'The Riddle'. I didn't see this as clearly at the time, but now I can see also that there's a counter-vailing impulse at work, a refusal to discredit 'the real thing', however much it may be melting. There's a contest going on between Derry and Derrida. Not that I had read Derrida, but in the eighties, back in the milieu of the Harvard English Department, it was impossible not to be aware of the challenge he was offering. The words in the word-hoard were in danger of being dematerialized and every-thing in me was protesting silently – which is why, in 'The Stone Verdict', my father's silence is placed in the scales as a kind of counterweight to all speechifying and theory-speak, why I favour 'the land of the unspoken', and why the population of the demystified country in 'The Mud Vision' experience disappointment once 'experts / begin their *post-factum* jabber'. What was at stake for the population in that poem was also at stake for the poet who wrote it.

How do you mean?

They've been sprung from the world of the awestruck gaze, where there was belief in miracle, in the sun standing still and the sun changing colour – just as it was said to have done at Fatima: they have entered the world of media-speak and postmodernity. They've been displaced from a culture not unlike that of de Valera's Ireland – frugal, nativist and inward looking, but still tuned to a supernatural dimension; and they find themselves in a universe that is global, desacralized, consumerist and devoid of any real sense of place or pastness. They have moved from a world where the young were once sent to serve as stretcher-bearers at the shrine in Lourdes to a world where the young have shares invested for them at birth by their Celtic Tigerish parents. And in all this, that fictional population is like myself.

I know from your earlier remarks, and indeed from your 'Brancardier' poem in District and Circle, *that you actually visited Lourdes.*

I did: with my cousin Michael Joyce, on the Derry Diocesan Pilgrimage in 1958, fares paid by our aunt Jane. For four or five days in Lourdes we acted as *brancardiers*, stretcher-bearers and wheelchair-pushers. I was often on duty too as altar boy and thurifer, since I had recently finished up at St Columb's College, and was therefore known to many of the priests officially in charge of the pilgrimage.

How harrowing – or consoling – an experience did it prove to be?

I took it for granted, with the blitheness of somebody in his late teens. I kind of foreknew it. At the time, the image of that grotto was omnipresent in Catholic houses and houses of worship: Bernadette kneeling with her beads in her hand and her shawl on her head, Mary with her blue sash and her pale hands stretching out. By then, we were even familiar with photographs of the shrine itself, the banks of candles and the rampart of crutches, reputedly cast away by people who had been cured. So, when I arrived, it was neither harrowing nor consoling, more a combination of expectancy and wariness.

I believed utterly in doing the good work, I believed that a cure was possible, although I had no trust in the inevitability of cure or in the necessarily divine cause of it. But still, I assisted at special Masses and blessings in front of the grotto where the disabled and infirm were given access. It was both routine and eerie, and I was susceptible, of course, to the surge of crowd emotions, the big choral responses to the rosary, the hymns, and the druggy fragrance off flowers and candles in the grotto itself. You could think of it as either 'utterly empty' or 'utterly a source'.

Did you end The Haw Lantern *with 'The Riddle' because you were unsure which way to turn next? Had Incertus returned or were you in fact aware that you were about to embark on the new* Seeing Things *phase?*

Incertus, as I've said before, never really left. At that time he was living through the eighties, which was a decade of considerable dismay in Ireland – and in myself. It began with the hunger strikes; and, as it proceeded, the stalemate in the North showed no signs of being broken, nor did the violence show any signs of abating. People in the nationalist camp were caught between the Provisional killers and the revisionist historians. In some respectable quarters, 'green' became a term of abuse. Romantic Ireland died again. Or rather it was put to death because of the crimes of the Provos and the crimes of the patriarchy. I felt unmoored from much that I had grown up with.

Intellectually, I could sympathize with the vehemence of the women's movement, with the critiques of the cult of Ireland as the suffering maiden, with the need for diversity and pluralism. I too came to realize that much of what we accepted as natural in our feelings and attitudes was a cultural construction, yet I was slow to begin the deconstruction. The second last poem in the book, for example, 'The Disappearing Island', is still a form of *aisling*, a vision poem about Ireland, even though it is an *aisling* inflected with irony: 'All I believe that happened there was vision'. So there may indeed be something in your suggestion that I had got to the point of *Seeing Things*. In fact, the dedicatory poem to *The Haw Lantern* would work equally well as a prologue to the later collection: 'The riverbed, dried up, half-full of leaves. / Us, listening to a river in the trees'.

Is an allusion intended to Emily Dickinson's letter where she remarks 'I hear to-day for the first time the river in the tree'?

No allusion. I didn't know the sentence until now. And I don't know whether to be happy or unhappy about it.

I wonder if the image of the dried-up riverbed arose from a feeling – or a fear – that you might be entering a dry patch as a poet. Or do you see it as purely a poem of 'replenishment' (your own word)?

A better word might be 'reprise'. I believe it was the last thing in the collection to get written. Small as it is on the page, it was an important little gift. I even toyed with the idea of calling the book *A River in the Trees*, but that seemed a bit too soothing at the time. Still, the two lines *did* encompass an idea that would get expressed in different ways in *Seeing Things*: the growing realization that poetry shouldn't allow itself to become 'sluggish in the doldrums of what happens'; that it should proceed in the belief 'that whatever is given / Can always be reimagined, however four-square, / Plank-thick, hull-stupid and out of its time / It happens to be'. Deep down, the question about obligation in relation to the Troubles persisted. The old Miłoszian challenge was unavoidable: 'What is poetry which does not save / Nations or people?'

And what you offered the troubled times was an image of the haw as 'a small light for small people'. Why did you want 'The Haw Lantern' to be the title poem? Were there other possibilities besides A River in the Trees?

The Stone Verdict was a definite favourite for a while, but then Richard Murphy brought out *The Price of Stone* and that was that. The haw is wintry, wee, often wet from the rain, sweetened by the frost, an image of subsistence, and it contains within itself its own little stone verdict. I liked those associations, but I also liked the poem because it was requiring strict self-examination from everybody, be they poets, pundits, priests, party political jabberwocks, whatever. It discovered a bedrock disappointment; it couldn't not admit the stuntedness and small-mindedness that prevailed in Northern Ireland, but at the same time it allowed for a flicker of light. And it was also, happily, a bit odd.

The idea of being scrutinized and tested runs through the poem and could be regarded as the leitmotif of the whole collection. It's there in 'From the Frontier of Writing', for example, and 'From the Republic of Conscience'.

I'd say it's *a*, but not *the* leitmotif. There are those sonnets in memory of my mother, for example, and several forays into the occasional and the elegiac.

Given that mixture, was it a particularly awkward book to organize? I wonder if it strikes you now as something of a stand-alone volume, a singular collection of trial pieces without very much connection to your other books?

It's a light craft, I agree, and tacks and veers along, but I think of it as a recovery book – recovery of writing 'for the joy of it', as instructed in 'Station Island' by the old artificer himself. I remember getting a real lift when I was doing the stanzas of 'Alphabets', for example, and feeling happily off the beaten track when I started 'From the Republic of Conscience'. And, for all the loss in the 'Clearances' sonnets, they were actually a pleasure to write.

The first two poems you mention were commissions: one from Harvard, the other from your local branch of Amnesty International. You clearly don't regard commissions as inhibiting. Would you go so far as to say they are a stimulus?

I *would* go that far, but in a viciously circling way, because there can be no stimulus unless you discover a way of responding to them that brings you to life. The Phi Beta Kappa poem, for instance, is meant to concern itself with 'learning', usually learning with a capital L. But when I got the idea of keeping it lower case, and writing about my progress from the desks of Anahorish School to the podium of Sanders Theatre in Harvard, I was up and away. The first stanzas came to me one morning in Adams House, while I was still in bed; they had clearly been prompted by Miłosz's poem, 'The World'. 'The World' is written from the point of view of a child who's just beginning to handle his pencil and open his primer. That agogness was exactly what I needed – if I hadn't heard that note, I don't know what would have happened.

And the Amnesty International commission which resulted in 'From the Republic of Conscience'?

Again, I remembered a poem by another writer that helped me to get started, in this case by Richard Wilbur. I'd actually used Wilbur's poem 'Shame' to do a bit of commissioning myself: Wilbur makes an allegory of shame by turning it into a small cramped country, and during the previous term I'd asked the Harvard students in my workshop to write a poem based on it. So it occurred to me that I could ask myself to do the same thing: make up an imaginary country to represent a particular state of mind or feeling. Once the job was presented in those terms, the element of play entered and I was able to cross the frontier of writing, able to shift out of the 'doldrums of what happens' (or, in this case, the actual cruelty of the conditions). Amnesty had sent me some reports about the injustice and suffering endured by prisoners of conscience in different parts of the world and all I could do at first was quail before that evidence. No cry I could have made in verse could have matched what was crying out in the dossiers. I had to recover and 'by indirection find direction out'.

I understand there was an Orkney connection at work also.

I imagined the Republic of Conscience as a place of silence and solitude where a person would find it hard to avoid self-awareness and self-examination, which is what made me think of Orkney. I'll never forget the silence there, on the airstrip, the first time I landed. I was on a small propeller plane: when it taxied to a halt and the engines were shut off, we had to sit and wait for the ground crew; and all the while you could feel the plane shaking slightly in the wind. Then the door was opened, the steps were let down with a clunk and, as I walked across the grass to a little arrivals hut, I heard the cry of a curlew. It was like the curlew in 'Paudeen', that poem of Yeats's where he talks about 'the lonely height where all are in God's eye' and where 'There cannot be, confusion of our sound forgot, / A single soul that lacks a sweet crystalline cry'.

Might 'The Republic of Conscience' and other allegorical poems in The Haw Lantern *have been influenced by the Gaelic voyage literature, the* immrams?

Not that I'm aware of. But when you're dealing with these archetypal quest stories, everything from the *Odyssey* to 'The Ancient Mariner' echoes everything else. I'd say, however, my experience of immigration control and customs checks was more important than any reading of the *immrams*.

And your reading of the eastern Europeans? Or perhaps Borges's fables?

All of that did point generally in the direction of the parable mode. I don't think there was any one poem or poet or fable that set me off, but there's a plainspoken, translated feel to those 'From the . . .' poems that tells me and you and everybody else that their provenance is likely to be found in the Penguin Modern European Poets series – and, conceivably, in Borges.

Did the writing of the allegorical poems require a different mindset from your other poems?

Not all that different from, say, the 'Sweeney Redivivus' series. You adopted a posture of the voice, or a posture of the voice adopted you, and you went with it. But you're right to sense difference in that particular group. There was a lightheadedness to the writing of them, they got nicely free of subjectivity. The usual old pull of documentary gravity was suspended.

By introducing Diogenes, Penelope, Socrates and so on, The Haw Lantern *is a collection which – like its successors – readily alludes to classical literature and myth. Was there any special reason for the greater prevalence of this classical material?*

It had always been there at the back of the mind, but I came round to it again when I met up with Robert Fitzgerald and started to reread his *Odyssey* and *Iliad*. The general availability of the classics in translation in the Cambridge bookshops also had its effect. I was reacquainting myself with the material, and with a part of myself. One book, for example, that I bought by chance – just because it was on the shelf – turned out to be of great and permanent interest: William K. Guthrie's *The Greeks and Their Gods*. That's where I read about the relationship between herm and Hermes. A herm was a standing stone – in many senses: a stylized representation of Hermes erect; and Hermes, as god of travellers and marketplaces and suchlike, was connected with cairns at crossroads and stone-heaps of all sorts. Through all that, I began to connect him with my father, and so you got 'The Stone Verdict'.

Considering that Latin had been your school subject, it is surprising how frequently you draw on Greek literature and myth.

With the Greeks, you're hand to hand with the world: much of the Roman stuff was texted to them, whereas the Greeks turfed it all out on their own. There's a clannish energy about the classical and pre-classical Greeks that feels familiar. I've a notion that the Irish word *fleadh* would cover what happened on many of their calendar days better than the word 'festival'. Epidauros wasn't exactly Glyndebourne: there was a touch of Knock Shrine about it, maybe even Puck Fair. And the frisson of the cave at Eleusis, for instance, must have been something like the frisson of the 'cave' that pilgrims used to enter on a Lough Derg pilgrimage. I sense a far greater closeness between the lived life and the official pomps in Greece than in Rome. It's the vitality of that ritual and romance at ground level that attracts me as much as the big earth-moving machinery of the literature and the myths.

Did you approach the study of Greek texts methodically?
You must have had access to the complete range of the Loeb
Classics – which are of course published by Harvard.

Indeed they are, green volumes for the Greek, red ones for the Latin. It would take a braver man than me to face into the study of that series. My reading was very much piecemeal, unsystematic.

In 1998, at a Miłosz conference in California, you spoke of a
visit to Hadrian's Wall in Northumberland, during which you
discovered that you were standing on ground sacred to the
Romano-Celtic goddess Coventina. This, presumably, is the
background to 'Grotus and Coventina'.

In a museum on the Wall, I saw a couple of images of this lovely little creature, recumbent on her elbow; under the other elbow, she had a pitcher that poured out a steady stream of water. More of a mud maiden than a marble nymph. Or maybe I remember her like that because I visited her shrine. This was only a couple of hundred yards from the Wall itself, in the soggy, rushy corner of a field that could have been the corner of a field at home, one of those mucky old sanctuaries down overgrown lanes, far from the road and the house. Back in the museum, I saw what the display card called an 'altar' dedicated to Coventina by one of the legionaries – a little stunted brickbat of a thing, with the name 'Grotus' cut into it in very crude letters. OK, it was a 'votive object', but it was also like a girl's name cut into a desk or written on a wall. As Patrick Kavanagh says, 'This is what love does to things.' So Grotus and Coventina and the little altar eventually ended up in a poem about Marie and myself and our difficulties with the water pump in Glanmore.

In embarking on a poem like 'Grotus and Coventina', or the poems containing classical references, do you ever hesitate about using allusions which your readers might regard as esoteric or 'elitist'?

'Grotus and Coventina' was written for its own sake, for Coventina's sake, for the sake of our Glanmore life. It wasn't a matter of 'reference' but of *res*, of the things themselves. Not so much elitism, therefore, as a *res*-ing of the stakes. Anyhow, when you say the words 'Grotus and Coventina', you get immediate aural and oral pleasure, the consonants and vowels melt in your mouth like hard-boiled soft-centred sweets, and that should compensate for any whiff of high culture off the names.

The classical references in the poems aren't there to show whose side I'm on in the 'culture wars'. In fact, I don't think there's anything highly cultured about them. Poetry inheres in other poetry, and to that extent it is literary; I have nothing against the literary per se: it is a category of knowledge, of reality, of human understanding, of durable value. We have lost the overall, ordering Christian myth of 'down there, up there, us in between'. It's been lost as a living myth. But its place in Western culture has been taken by general awareness of classical myths. In my case, it's mostly that – a general awareness: I don't think of my cultural baggage as 'learned'. I just happen to belong to the last generation that learned Latin, that read Virgil, that knew about the descent into the underworld.

In 'Alphabets', you mention your schoolboy study of Elementa Latina, *and evoke the sing-song recitation of declensions. Did you always enjoy Latin?*

Yes, from the beginning. I enjoyed it even before I went to St Columb's, in those early-morning lessons that Master Murphy provided after I'd won the scholarship. It was so workable and predictable, once you got the hang of the declensions and conjugations and genders and all that. So when I started in college, I started at an advantage and never looked back. I was lucky too in the teacher I had during my senior years: Father Michael McGlinchey, who loved the language and had a feel for the literary qualities of the texts – especially Virgil. One of our set books was Book Nine of the *Aeneid*, but I always remember him repeating at different times, 'Och, boys, I wish it were Book Six' – which gave me an interest in that book long before I ever read it.

Your daughter Catherine published an article in which she recalled jokes you made in Latin for her amusement.

For her education too, of course. When she started college I used to introduce crazy transliterations. If the gates came down unexpectedly at the level crossing in Sydney Parade, I'd cry out '*Sanctos fumos!*' or maybe '*Sanctum Jesum!*' and then exclaim, 'Exclamatory accusative!' Sometimes I'd use the macaronic method, in Irish and Latin, to ask if she had the key to the house: '*Eochar habesne?*' Or even, to emphasize that accusative case, '*Eocharum habesne?*' And, as mentioned already, when I myself was a youngster I'd had etymological negotiations with my mother: rhymes about prefixes and suffixes and Latin roots, of which, I'm afraid, I can't remember a single one. But that first introduction to the historical dimension of language readied me for something. It was an intimation of the different strains and registers that go to make up the whole keyboard.

Your translations, in The Midnight Verdict, *of two passages from* Metamorphoses *displayed much more fidelity to Ovid's originals than one finds in Ted Hughes's* Tales from Ovid.

Ted was fired up by the Ovid. He was a natural storyteller and was right to go for it in his own idiom, flat out. Ovid got an engine going inside him that simply refused to stop. You often have the feeling in those tales that he's watching himself go over the top, that Ovid's glee has given him permission to out-Hughes his own Hughesiness. He had the right subject and it exhilarated him. It was free and far out, but it was also, to use a phrase of Montale's, 'a great untrammelled event'.

Would you say the same of his Oresteia?

I admired the head-on clash with that material also, the way he just pitched in with his Yorkshire attack, 'the gutturals of dialects', using the short, stressed line to keep jabbing and jabbing, gradually getting on to an incantational roll. There was a sense too of big, world-wrenching issues being plied; even better than that, you could feel a big, world-coursing energy right there in the language. Ted was excessive, so he couldn't and didn't need to be obedient. You can legislate to your heart's content about how translation should be done, but the practice is going to ignore or outflank the theories.

In your essay 'The Impact of Translation', dating from the year before The Haw Lantern, *you remarked that poets in English 'felt compelled to turn their gaze East and have been encouraged to concede that the locus of greatness is shifting away from their language'. Do you still subscribe to this view or does it, in retrospect, seem too strongly slanted in favour of a few east Europeans, too carried away by its own enthusiasms?*

It's certainly slanted in favour of the eastern Europeans – and the Russians – but I still believe there was something in what I was saying. I did have my enthusiasms, but I don't think I was deluded by them. That clued-in, undaunted poetry of post-war Poland, for example, was a pointer to the kind of thing I wished someone could have written in the admassed USA. It was certainly a tonic to somebody who had grown up in Northern Ireland, where the quiet surface covered up profound faults and disturbances. It suited the mood and attitudes of the minority population I belonged to. It said, 'Maybe you can't expect much from life, but never forget that you deserve more. Just because you put up with demeaning conditions doesn't mean you're not made for relish and fulfilment.' Eastern-European poetry – or rather what I knew of it from the Penguin Modern European Poets series – was at one and the same time a *viaticum* and a *vade mecum*. It was nurture, but it was also injunction: it enjoined you to be true to poetry as a solitary calling, not to desert the post, to hold on at the crossroads where truth and beauty intersect.

Would you have been a different poet without those east-European exemplars?

Probably not all that different in what I'd have written, but not as convinced about the worthwhileness of writing itself. Apart from that flutter of allegory, there's not much direct influence. My way with words was very different. I would tend to 'colour in' whereas they were very much for the black-and-white line-drawing.

Did Ted Hughes deepen your interest in foreign-language poetry? He had, after all, helped to initiate the Poetry International festivals in London; and he was a friend of Daniel Weissbort – the poet, editor and translator with whom he co-edited the journal Modern Poetry in Translation.

I met Danny first, I think, in Iowa, and the fact that we were both friends of Ted's just made us that much readier to be friends with each other. And the same was true when I met Ted's great Irish friend Terence McCaughey. Terence had introduced Ted to *Buile Shuibhne* when they were undergraduates at Pembroke College in Cambridge, so poetry in translation was always important and a two-way exchange from the start. Ted's conversation was full of poets from every time and place, all very real to him, and whoever he talked about would attain a terrific new solidity. He had a sort of one-to-one relationship with everything he'd ever read: *Gilgamesh, Sir Gawain and the Green Knight*, Vasko Popa, Janos Pilinszky, Emily Dickinson, 'Donal Óg' . . .

Ted was a chip off the Old English block, for sure, but in his own view of himself, he was a relict of Elmet, the old Romano-Celtic kingdom of the north-east; and he also had what John Donne called an hydroptical immoderate desire for learning. He hunted and gathered knowledge and notions of all sorts. And he did believe in the good force of poetry. His programme note for the first Poetry International was a manifesto of sorts, all about the way poetry might create a spirit that would help nations to make what he called 'a working synthesis of their ferocious contradictions' – a creation of the spirit that might presage some new political reality. But Ted was no Vaclav Havel; he was more mythic than civic. When it came to remedying the ills of society, he was liable to think of the shaman rather than the senate.

You met Vaclav Havel on a couple of occasions: most publicly in 2003, in the Abbey Theatre in Dublin, when he received an Amnesty International award named after your 'Republic of Conscience' poem. You had an earlier meeting when he was on a

presidential visit to Ireland in June 1996 – what sort of
impression did he make on that occasion?

He had made his impression long before we met, through the
clarity and cogency of his various essays and interviews. Not to
speak of his record as a man of principle, whether prisoner or
president. I also admired the distinction he insisted on between
hope and optimism and had often quoted it. So we talked a
bit about that. And about Kundera. But it was more of a formal
occasion than a real exchange. There was limited English on
his side, and a certain shyness on mine, as well as the presence
in the room of different presidential aides and friends. But the
compactness and integrity of the person in front of you were
unmistakable.

Did your interest in eastern-European poetry ever bring you into
contact with the literary dissidents of the time? Were you ever
asked, for instance, to smuggle in a forbidden book or smuggle
out a banned manuscript?

I'm no Cold War hero, I'm afraid. My visits to the Eastern Bloc
were almost non-existent before the early 1990s, when I began to
know some people in Krakow. I was at a conference in Macedonia
in 1978, then at a big Festival of Youth and Students in Moscow in
1985, when Yevtushenko organized a series of poetry readings.
That was the height of it. But it was enough to make me familiar
with the Soviet way, the ideological lock on the media, for exam-
ple, and the glum weight of the Party people in charge. I have to
admit that something in me responded positively to the frugality of
the fare, the absence of marketing, the bare reality of loaves and
lard and apples on the counter top. At the same time, I remember
how glad I was when I landed back in Shannon for the mere fact of
colour, the flim-flam of display in airport shops.

Can you tell me a bit more about your visits to Poland, which
seem to have meant more to you as a writer than your American
forays?

At different times American poets – Frost, Lowell, maybe even
Bishop – influenced my way with words, which is not something
I could ever say about the poets of Poland. But by now I do feel

a special relationship with the Poles, partly because I've met and am friendly with a good few of the poets, and partly because, historically and culturally, the Poles and the Irish have a lot in common. The first time I met Miłosz, for example, was in the company of Robert Pinsky and Robert Hass, and Hass and Miłosz and I spent a good part of the evening going on about our experience as Catholics – the sense of the sacred, the sense of sin and so on.

When did you first go to Poland?

November 1994, with Stanisław Barańczak, his wife Anna and their daughter, for the launch of a selection of poems that Stanisław had translated. The book was published in Krakow by Znak, a small literary house run by Jerzy Illg, so it was in Krakow that I got my first sense of the intensity and camaraderie of the poetry scene. At a party in Jerzy's house, after the reading, I first met, for example, Wisława Szymborska and Bronisław Maj. The mixture of close-knit friendships and commitment to poetry reminded me very much of Belfast in the 1960s.

Wasn't there a phone call from Czesław Miłosz during that party?

There was, and what he said to me, from six thousand miles away in Berkeley, was this: 'You are with some very good people there.'

Did you know Miłosz well by then?

I couldn't say that I ever knew Miłosz well. I was always a bit in awe of him. The first time I felt free with him, or rather made free, was in 1987. This was at an event in Iowa to celebrate the founding of the International Writers' Workshop, on a day when the Nobel Prize was due to be announced, and he had some notion – correct, as it turned out – that Brodsky was in line for it that year. At any rate, he had agreed to do an interview with some Swedish newspaper, should Joseph indeed prove to be the winner, and he was obviously on tenterhooks when I met him. 'I am puzzled,' he said, with that long, slow, Slavic enunciation that made 'puzzled' rhyme with 'sozzled': 'I am puzzled; I have not heard from Stockholm.' I just couldn't help the words that came out of me: 'Czesław,' I said, 'as far as I know, you can only be awarded that prize once.' Anyhow, to my relief, the great shoulders shook with laughter, and I felt I had gone beyond stage one of our relationship.

Many years later, he and Carol, his second wife, came to dinner in our house in Dublin, and after that Marie and I visited him in his own place up on Grizzly Peak Boulevard, where he had the view of San Francisco Bay which appears in his poem 'Gift'. He was very happy at that stage, and I think a lot of it came from life with Carol. But Carol, alas, died from a sudden, cruel cancer, and the last time I saw him, in 2003, in his apartment in Krakow, the most memorable thing was the presence in the room of a life-size bronze torso of her. He was a little deaf in the latter years so he tended to talk and entertain you from the moment you came in.

Can you recall a decisive moment when you realized he was going to be an essential poet for you?

From the moment I got my hands on that first Ecco Press *Selected Poems*, the one that begins with 'Encounter' and contains 'Child of Europe' and '*Oeconomia Divina*', I was in thrall. I'd known about him, as editor of the *Post-War Polish Poetry* anthology, as far back as 1970, but it took longer for me to get to know him as a poet. Next thing I remember reading, at the library of Carysfort College, his Nobel Lecture in the *New York Review of Books*, and finding myself hugely attracted by what he had to say there. In 1982 I started my Harvard life, and was able to get my hands on every new volume of his as it appeared in English. Also at Harvard I attended his Norton Lectures, the ones that were eventually published as *The Witness of Poetry*, and I introduced him at a poetry reading in 1992. I remember him saying to me at breakfast the next morning that, in his poetry, he often felt just like a little boy playing on the bank of a river – which was very endearing, and connected up with the last lines of 'What Once Was Great', one of his shortest poems but still one of my favourites: 'Stretched on the grass by the bank of a river, / As long, long ago, I launch my boats of bark'.

Am I right in thinking that the example of Miłosz's life is as important to you as his books?

It would be hard to separate them. His intellect wasn't forced to choose between 'perfection of the life or of the work' – it was forced to meld them. When you think of Yeats's life, for example, you have a strong sense of what he did, the way he actively impinged and imposed himself on Irish life and Irish history; he cut a figure and made a spectacle of himself, very deliberately. There was the thirty-odd-year engagement with the Abbey Theatre, his controversies and interventions, his need to make marks in the cultural landscape with the tower at Ballylee and the headstone at Drumcliff.

But when you think of Miłosz you think of the mark made on him by event rather than any need on his part to make an event of himself. He undergoes things which turn into memories and then into origins. He is a child in Russia when the Revolution breaks out, there with his engineer father who's engaged in bridge-building for the Czar's army; he's at university in Vilnius when Poland regains its independence; he's in Warsaw during the Nazi occupation, when he witnesses the destruction of the ghetto and the tragedy of the uprising; he's in France during the ideological civil wars of the 1950s, siding in the end with Camus rather than Sartre; he's in Berkeley during the era of the Beats and the flower children and anti-Vietnam protests; and he's present in spirit – omnipresent, you might even say – in the era of Solidarity in Poland.

All this is formative; yet, apart from the writing, there is nothing performative in Miłosz's response to it. It would be hard, on the other hand, to think of Yeats moving along that same trajectory without trying at some point to cut a figure. Yeats inclined to believe that 'honour is flashed off exploit' – a line that Hopkins finishes with a qualifying 'so they say', but Hopkins is unqualified in his admiration of those who, like Miłosz, endure the war within, those whose exploits are moral and spiritual. Miłosz I hold in high regard because of the way he followed conscience into solitude; one of the most revealing books in this regard being his correspondence with the Trappist monk Thomas Merton. I'm not saying that he was a saint or a hero – nor did he ever cast himself in those roles. No doubt he always remained conscious of the fact that he had not borne arms in the Warsaw uprising and had served for a while with the new Communist regime, but he made his soul, to coin a phrase, by writing his way out of that state of affairs – not only in the poems, but in *The Captive Mind*, and in essays and letters. Keats says somewhere that there's always an allegorical element about the life of a genius, and in the case of Miłosz, what you're witnessing is indeed a kind of twentieth-century pilgrim's progress.

Did he consciously influence how you conducted yourself during the Troubles or as a writer in general?

I don't think so, no.

But you mentioned earlier that, in the darkest days of the Troubles, your 'mantra' was Miłosz's remark about being 'stretched between contemplation of a motionless point and the command to participate actively in history'.

Doctor Johnson speaks about reposing in the stability of truth, and something of that nature happened when I first read those words and every time I encountered or repeated them afterwards. They weren't a solution but they described exactly the nature of the assignment. So they were a help.

Miłosz's comment that 'the Devil is social' suggests that he didn't waste much time at dinner parties.

Jane Hirshfield reports that remark. Jane was in his Dostoevsky class in Berkeley in 1980 on the day he got news of the Nobel Prize, and he told them there and then how he dreaded the public dimension that would accompany the award. So that was the context. Before that, his life in the States had been relatively quiet: in California he had silence, exile and sunning, and was able, day in, day out, to get on with his writing; but he rightly foresaw that the world was going to start beating a path to his door, and he didn't like it. Yet no writer managed to handle the public role and the private vocation better. There was something extremely gregarious in him, after all. He was as capable of revelry as retreat. He could manage to go around, 'pretending to be himself', as Larkin called it, doing his readings and his lectures without suffering the injurious consequences that Larkin seemed to believe were inevitable. You've only to look at a poem like 'Capri' to see how self-aware and resourceful he was on that front.

You sometimes cite the closing lines of Miłosz's 'Blacksmith Shop': 'It seems I was called for this: / To glorify things just because they are'. But how far is it possible for a poet of the twenty-first century – who is not in denial at some level about the world and human nature – to 'glorify things just because they are'?

The line is from a poem, so it has the free-floating status of poetic utterance, and you have to take it in relation to Miłosz's philosophic convictions, his observation, for example, that the ideal occupation for a poet is the contemplation of the word *is*. It's all of a piece with his impulse to contemplate the 'motionless point'. But it obviously represents only one side of what he knows and feels, and states the position of only one side in the quarrel with himself that gives rise to the poetry. The other side is expressed in a different set of formulations, such as the more famous 'What is poetry which does not save / Nations or people?' You might illustrate the case by thinking of Isaac Rosenberg's 'Break of Day in the Trenches'. In that poem, Rosenberg celebrates the poppy in his ear 'just because it is', but nobody is going to say that the celebration shows he is in denial about the world or human nature. In defiance maybe, but not denial. And the same would be true of Miłosz.

Did you admire Miłosz for continuing – unlike many other prominent east Europeans – to draw on the full resources of language after the war and refusing to implicate language itself in the guilt for Auschwitz (as Tadeusz Różewicz has done)?

Poetry comes from a temperament as much as from the times, even more than from the times. To caricature the case, you could say that Miłosz would be inclined to respond to atrocity with the 'Dies Irae' from Verdi's *Requiem*, whereas Różewicz would be more likely to seek out a performance of something utterly bleak and minimal by Beckett. I find it hard to take sides in those Polish culture wars. But I certainly don't blame Miłosz for sticking with the Christian humanist wager. It was neither a symptom of denial nor an artistic mistake. It was the necessary agon of 'a child of Europe'. If Miłosz continued to hew to the symphonic possibilities of his language, it was because of visionary obstinacy rather than arrested development. It might be pushing it to compare his case with Wordsworth's, but you could argue that there's something analogous to Miłosz's deployment of the full orchestra after Auschwitz in Wordsworth's response to the loss of visionary gleam in his great 'Ode': it was only when the gleam had fled that Wordsworth opened all the gorgeous stops. There's nothing else in his work as deliberately orchestral and linguistically plenary as the Immortality Ode.

*How soon after Miłosz's death did you write the lengthy tribute
which appeared in the* New Republic *and the* Guardian?

Almost immediately. After I got the news, I was lucky to have a few
days to myself and could respond to Jerzy Illg's request that I do
something for one of the Polish newspapers. For a good while I'd
been aware that Czesław was lining up in the queue for Charon's
barge, and I knew from the poems he was writing that his point of
view was that of a man who'd already made the crossing. In fact, he
was in my mind a few months previously when I translated that
speech by the Messenger in *Oedipus at Colonus*, the one that tells
how the old king was called to the other world by a voice out of the
earth, and how – in response to the call – he disappeared into the
earth. Sophocles himself was an old man when he wrote the play,
and it shows in his tenderness towards Oedipus' longevity and readi-
ness. The whole scenario just seemed right for Miłosz, since he, like
Oedipus, had found a resting place after years of hardship and wan-
dering and was due to become a hero. I mean a hero in the full tech-
nical sense, which is to say a genius of his place, one who would have
a cult and be honoured as a kind of guardian spirit.

*And the funeral in Krakow was, in that same technical sense, a
hero's funeral?*

Indeed. One of the greatest ceremonies I ever attended. I arrived at
the Mariacki church in the main square forty minutes before the
Mass was due to begin; even then, nearly all the pews were full.
Right at the entrance to the sanctuary you had the coffin, a mighty
timber box with the inscription 'Czesław Miłosz, 1911–2004' on
the end that faced the congregation. Soldiers at attention at each of
the four corners. The flanks of the catafalque covered with flowers,
wreaths as big as waggon wheels, candles as tall as the soldiers.
Poets, politicians, public figures from all over the country waiting in
silence: Wisława Szymborska, Julia Hartwig, Adam Zagajewski,
Adam Michnik, Lech Wałęsa, the film director Andrej Wajda.
Robert Hass had come from America, Tomas Venclova also. Then
the concelebrated High Mass begins, cardinal and bishops and
priests in full vestments, the choir in full Gregorian voice, the altar
agleam with mitres and croziers. Afterwards, we walked in a
cordoned-off procession through crowds surging up against barriers

that lined the route for the best part of a mile to the Skalka monastery. There again the coffin lay in state on steps in front of the main door, more liturgical ceremonies took place, and different people read poems. Finally, the entombment occurred in the crypt of the church, among the tombs of other Polish patriots and writers.

Did you read a poem?

Not at that point. It was mostly Polish people, although Robert Hass, as his longtime friend and translator, did join the service. My turn came in the evening, when between twenty and thirty poets met on the altar of another church, St Catherine's, I think, with Jerzy Illg as master of ceremonies. Each of us read a single poem, then lit a candle in memory, then sat down. It was simple, reverent and potent, and was attended by a large, silent congregation. I was honoured to be a part of it.

Wisława Szymborska remained to the end?

She did. And Julia Hartwig and all the others I mentioned. Zbigniew Herbert's widow also. Tony Miłosz, the son. Tony's wife Joanna. An entire hosting of the clans.

Very little is known in the English-speaking world of Wisława Szymborska as a person.

She's vivid and humorous in company, very subversive and very intelligent, but unfortunately she hardly speaks English, so – even though I've been with her and shared laughs and been in the swim of conversations at dinner tables and so on – the communication has been mostly through eyes and animation and interpreters, yet none the less real for that. She is, as they say, a very private person. She'll turn up at events all right; but the minute the ceremony is over, she just skims away like a sylph. One thing I especially like about her is the way she smokes: really stylish, almost as if she were a 1940s film star with a cigarette-holder, tilting it at a high angle between drags.

You were in Poland in 1996 when the news of her Nobel Prize came through.

I was. By sheer coincidence, Jerzy Illg had arranged a reading to celebrate the Polish publication of Stanisław Barańczak's translation of *The Spirit Level*.

Any views on the award of the prize to Szymborska rather than to Zbigniew Herbert? I suspect Herbert had been more important to you.

He had been, yes. I'd known his work for more than a quarter of a century and had written about it. Herbert stood in my mind like a classical arch, needless of honour, really. Noble rather than Nobel material. I would have expected him to win all right, but there was still something happy about the choice of Szymborska. With Herbert, it would have been ratification, with her it was revivification. It was as if the Swedish Academy had decided on an Elizabeth Bishop rather than a Robert Lowell. Arguable, but energizing.

You never met Zbigniew Herbert, I know, but you did meet other eastern Europeans, including Marin Sorescu and Yevgeny Yevtushenko – two poets with an anti-establishment image under repressive regimes, but with an unusual degree of freedom to travel also.

I met Sorescu in Mexico in 1981, at that festival – the one I've already spoken about – which was attended by Vasko Popa, Tadeusz Różewicz and Günter Grass, among others. He seemed to have the friendship of those people; that circumstance, combined with his sad face and drooping Balkan moustache, not to mention the melancholy and humour of the poems, meant that I took him as I found him – a bit separate, a bit networky, but equally a bit hangdoggy. He did travel around more in the years that followed, and turned up in Ireland a couple of times, but I never got to see much of him or to know him any better. Nor do I know enough about his situation in Ceauşescu's Romania to speak about his political conduct. But I was glad to do a short introduction to a volume of his poems published in America; more recently I contributed another introduction, this time in Irish, to a selection of Irish translations.

And Yevtushenko?

Nothing hangdoggy about Yevtushenko. I met him three times, first and most memorably in Moscow in 1985; then fleetingly in Las Vegas, of all places – at the University of Nevada, where he had a visiting professorship in the 1990s; and, when I visited Russia again a few years ago, at his home in Peredelkino. In that summer of 1985, the Russians held the 'Festival of Youth and Students' which I've mentioned – a kind of Soviet Olympics, in Moscow. As a sideshow to that event, Yevtushenko organized an international poetry festival and invited several of his pals, including Robert Bly and Ernesto Cardenal and, believe it or not, Bob Dylan. Somehow Marie and I got included also as 'the Irish delegation' and I had my poem 'Digging' translated by Yevgeny and belted out by him in the basketball stadium where we all read. But the typical Yevtushenko event happened when he brought Marie and me and Bly and Bly's wife out to his *dacha* in Peredelkino. He seemed to be able to summon chauffeurs at all hours, because it was late in the evening, long after the end of a reading, when we set out, and it was well into the small hours when we got back. In between, we were the privileged ones, drinking Georgian wine, being treated to stories about Pasternak and Zabolotsky, spun along in a torrent of energy and ego.

Towards the end of the night, I was grateful for Bly's flat refusal to go out with candles and vodka to the cemetery nearby, where Pasternak is buried. We, the visitors, were a bit wary, not sure about how far the long arm of totalitarian law could reach. Dylan was meant to turn up that night also, but the bus never arrived – although he did show a night or two later, a few yards down the road at a party in Voznesensky's place; showed, but stayed almost entirely shut up the whole time.

Come to think of it, Voznesensky had spent a night in our house in Dublin a while before that, when he was over doing a reading at the Project Arts Centre ... And in fact I preferred his poetry to Yevtushenko's. When *Antiworlds* came out in English translation, with a preface by Auden, it was – as I've mentioned – a big excitement. But that moment passed and the shelves began to fill up with a set of very different Russian and east-European names: Nadezhda and Osip Mandelstam, Akhmatova, Tsvetaeva, the aforesaid Poles, the Czechs, the Hungarians, and then, of course, the Brodsky.

I imagine 'the Brodsky' had something to say about the aforesaid Voznesensky and Yevtushenko?

He was scornful, but didn't go on about it. His actions spoke louder than his words. He resigned from the American Academy of

Arts and Letters when Yevtushenko was elected a member. When he talked about them, it was like Virgil talking to Dante about the damned in their circles: he instructed you to observe and pass on quickly.

I'd like to pass now to an east European of a different sort: Mircea Eliade. In another interview, you linked him, and his writings on sacred and profane space, with your notion in 'Clearances' and elsewhere of 'walking round and round a space / Utterly empty, utterly a source'. How did you discover Eliade and how important has he been for you?

I may have heard of him first from Barrie Cooke or Ted Hughes, both of whom talked a lot about his work on shamanism. But I discovered his book on sacred and profane space in the early eighties. I'd read it, at any rate, by the time I was writing the 'Station Island' sequence, where walking round and round constituted the whole action of the pilgrimage. The phrase you quote first occurs in Section III of 'Station Island', where the pilgrim remembers where he 'found the bad carcass and scrags of hair / of our dog that had disappeared weeks before', a place that felt half sacred and half profaned.

The desacralizing of space is something that my generation experienced in all kinds of ways: faith decaying and the *turas* – the turn around the holy well or the Stations of the Cross – losing its supernatural dimension; 'fairy rings' being archaeologized into 'hilltop forts'; grates being removed from living rooms and kitchens, hearths blocked up, central heating installed, with the consequent loss of *focus*. At the same time, I have memories of the world-marking power of a dividing line, such as the first furrow ploughed in a field, or the laying out of house foundations, or even the marking of a pitch for football. Not to mention a deeply ingrained notion of 'sanctuary' in the space behind the altar rails; always conscious too of the boundary between the graveyard and the road; and so on. Eliade's book gave all those disparate awarenesses a credible frame of reference; he helped you to see the accidentals of your autobiography and environment as symptomatic of spiritual changes in your world. So that gives him a definite importance.

With 'Clearances' as backdrop, I'd like to hear more about your mother. You mentioned earlier that she was 'readier to be provoked' than your father by sectarian injustices. And in your Paris Review *interview you characterized her family, the McCanns, as strict adherents of dress codes and table manners; also as 'great argufiers'. How did these characteristics transmit themselves through your mother and to what extent were they passed on to her children?*

She had a capacity for endurance and defiance, and when that got combined in her children with the Heaney gift for solemnity and disdain, it produced different results in different people. There was a lot of humour in the McCanns as well. With one or two exceptions, her sisters and brothers were nimble-minded and volatile in a way the Heaneys were not. They were great ones for conundrums and puzzles. My mother also had a strong devotional element in her makeup, and I have the impression that her father was both strict and ardent in the practice of his own and his family's religion. Prayer, at any rate, was an important part of her habit and her equipment.

Her 'equipment'?

The longer I live the more I'm aware of the siege she must have experienced in body and spirit for the first two decades of her marriage – a child arriving almost every year to begin with, then being cooped in a small house, the family crowding in and growing up around her, living in a farm kitchen, her body thickening – some reinforcement was required and I believe it came from prayer and religious understanding. Religion in some sense 'equipped' her. Identification of a mother's suffering with the suffering mother of Christ. Praying for strength to bear up. As she recited the rosary, you could almost hear a defiance in the strength of her voice announcing the mysteries and leading the Hail Marys, as if she knelt to give challenge to the conditions. And then the invocation of the names of the Virgin in the litany – 'Tower of Ivory, House of Gold, Refuge of Sinners, Health of the Sick, Morning Star, Star of the Sea' – it now seems to me to have been the redress of praying.

The image I have of her in 'The Swing' in *The Spirit Level* is literally, almost transgressively true. It's 'photography' but also, I hope, heart-mystery. Often, in the evening, when she'd bathed her swollen feet in hot water in an enamel basin, 'she took / Each rolled elastic stocking and drew it on / Like the life she would not fail and was not / Meant for'. There was real dignity and endurance in her at that time.

And later in life?

When the child-rearing was over and the family began to branch up and out and over her, she got great reward and pride from them. And I believe she settled into a far easier life of faith, sceptical but not disaffected, still 'practising' but not, I think, believing in the afterlife as she might have to begin with. She was heavy and physically encumbered in her latter days, but there was a definite inner glow to her and real confidence. She had more freedom as the house got cleared of us, more of a sense of being her own woman.

Did she administer the punishments to the children as you were growing up?

No punishments were administered. She never raised a hand to one of us. What loomed, when the situation was grave, was the authority of my father, although this was never exercised as corporal punishment. I'm not sure who was the stronger of the two: their personalities and address to the world were so antithetical, or should I say complementary? She would affirm herself by articulating her position defiantly, he would counter by holding fire and embracing silence, but in such a way that the silence seemed like comeback rather than withdrawal. But I shouldn't overstate the potato-potatto aspect of things. Most of the time they bore out Antoine de Saint-Exupéry's idea that 'love does not consist in gazing at each other but in looking together in the same direction'.

The third sonnet of 'Clearances' is one of your most popular poems. Did that poem stand out from the others during the actual writing of the sequence?

As a matter of fact, it – or a poem like it, one in couplets – was begun a few years before my mother died. It had the potato-peeling scene in it, and there was also a memory of my lifting, from under the kneeling board in the church, Mass cards that had fallen from between the pages of her missal. I never got it finished and no doubt the writing was hampered by the same considerations that kept me from publishing another parental poem, 'Boy Driving His

Father to Confession'. This reminds me, you know, of a conversation I had away back in the 1960s with the poet Tony Connor. He shared an OUP paperback in those days with Austin Clarke and Charles Tomlinson, and he had a poem in it called 'Elegy for Alfred Hubbard' that began 'Hubbard is dead, the old plumber: / who will mend our burst pipes now . . .?' I was very fond of it and told him so and he said, 'Oh, well, you know, Hubbard is alive and well, but it's hard to write a true poem about somebody who's still knocking around, so my solution was to make the elegy.' When my mother died, my own thing was easier to complete. I actually enjoyed writing those sonnets, and did them quickly. And quickest of all was the one about folding sheets, which also turns out to be the most intricate and most playful.

Which one do you think she herself would have most enjoyed?

Maybe the one about her shade returning to her first home in New Row, to that shining, spick-and-span kitchen and to her bespectacled, shining-pated father. She would have enjoyed the evocation of that old McCann house-style, the domestic cleanliness and correctness, the well-set table, the well-polished linoleum and sink taps, returning from the farm to the finesse her aunts had brought from their days of service in The Lodge, the residence of the mill-owning Clarkes in Broagh.

There is tenderness towards your mother in those poems, and indeed tenderness and empathy towards women in general in many areas of your work. But some critics have preferred to emphasize what they claim is a certain sexual swagger, arguing that the women in your poems are stereotypical and picturesque rather than living creatures. Are there any of those poems which you would now want to revise?

My education in this regard came from living with a woman of independent spirit. There are certainly one or two poems I'd like to revise, or better still lose, as much for artistic as ideological reasons – 'Rite of Spring', for instance, in *Door into the Dark*, is a crude bit of work. But in that same volume I'd still stand by 'Undine', farm drainage and burgeoning sexuality yoked by violence – literary violence, that is – together. And I believe that 'The Wife's Tale', picturesque as it may be, gets something right about

man/woman companionship and contesting. Again, there's a pic-
turesque setting, if you want to call it that, in poems like
'Maighdean Mara' and 'Shore Woman' in *Wintering Out*, but, you
know, they happen to be set in what is now Nuala Ní Dhomhnaill
territory, both psychologically and geographically.

Still, the poems I've written are by no means immune to doctrinal
criticism. The ideological feminist approach has been transformative,
even if in some cases the methods have been applied pretty crudely.
And, naturally enough, like everybody else I too have changed
because of the shift in consciousness that feminism effected. But as in
the case of other political pressure – the Sinn Féin case, for example,
that's recorded in 'The Flight Path' – the poet in you has to resist being
told what to do. It's not so much correctness as rightness that we're
after, and I think poems like 'The Underground' and 'The Otter' and
'The Skunk' and 'An Afterwards' and 'Red, White and Blue' were and
are right enough to be going on with.

*Some of your translations from the early nineties seem to be
salvoes in the gender wars. I'm thinking especially of* The
Midnight Verdict – *not just the Ovid but the portion of Brian
Merriman's* The Midnight Court *which you included too.*

I've always liked what Thomas More said about Tyndale's trans-
lation of the Bible, that he had 'a naughty intention'; so I admit
there was a naughty intention at work in *The Midnight Verdict*.
I'd been asked by Michael Hofmann and James Lasdun to do a
version of the Orpheus and Eurydice story for their Ovid book;
when I finished it, I thought why not go on and do the death of
Orpheus, far more grievous material, and more sombre in the tell-
ing. But then, once I got started, the merry man in me couldn't
help seeing the beleaguered Orpheus as a General Editor figure,
being attacked not so much on the ground of a field as on the
grounds of the Field Day Anthology. The episode begins with
the women catching sight of Orpheus playing his lyre and then
'One of them whose hair streamed in the breeze / Began to shout,
"Look, look, it's Orpheus, / Orpheus the misogynist" ', and off
we go into the pursuit and dismemberment of the bard, until in
the end the god proves unwilling to forget the atrocities commit-
ted against Orpheus and turns the women into trees. Since the
general tenor of the Ovid fitted in with the women versus men

theme in *The Midnight Court*, and since I had other specifically literary reasons for linking the classical and the Irish material, I thought it would make sense to juxtapose the versions in a short book.

Did The Midnight Court *form part of your Irish-language curriculum at St Columb's College?*

The opening passage, the scene-setting bit, was included in an anthology called *Filíocht na nGael*, but we never got to grips with even that much of the poem – simply because the Irish was too difficult for us at that stage. We were fit for 'An Bonnán Buí' or an *aisling* like 'Úr-Chill an Chreagáin' or a song by Séamus Dall MacCuarta – stuff with an Ulster turn to it – but the big Munster orchestra was beyond us.

How was Irish presented in the college? Was it part of the nationalist formation? To what extent were you conscious of it as a subject with counter-cultural implications?

First, it has to be said that Irish was not taught in any deliberate or structured way as a 'formation'. But given that official Northern Ireland was resolutely British in its orientation, there didn't need to be any force feeding of the nationalist line for the subject to have, as you say, counter-cultural implications. It was other. At the same time, it was part of the curriculum and was a subject in the Ministry of Education's exams. Basically, it came over as 'heritage'; it linked you into Gaelic pastoral rather than nationalist politics. The prescribed texts by Seosamh Mac Grianna and Máire and the like were all set in West Donegal, you had hiring fairs and fishing boats and *seanchas* and gombeen men; and if it wasn't Tyrconnell folklife, it was Kerry fantasy, with Father Peadar Ó Laoghaire's *Séadna*, the devil at the fair and all the rest of it.

Can you still speak Irish?

Not adequately. But I wouldn't be scared off by material printed in Irish. Now and again I listen to talk on Radio na Gaeltachta and occasionally I begin to pick my way through an Irish-language column in a newspaper, or face a parallel text of poetry. But that's the height of it.

*Do you see any justification for the view that Irish people, in
speaking English, are somehow out of step or out of sync with
their experiences?*

It's a viewpoint has been lived through and I've come through to an
un-anxious state. But that's not to say that those old concerns were
vacuous or in vain. They arose from drastic historical experience,
and there was something magnificent and redemptive about the
whole effort to reverse the Anglicization of Ireland and regain
respect for indigenous literature and traditions. For generations –
and I belonged to one of the last of those generations – it seemed
that there was always going to be a conflict between pietas and
modernity, but there's more composure and self-confidence around
nowadays. I still believe that my English is inflected, perhaps better
say by Ireland than by Irish, but at this stage that's neither a cause
for swank nor for shyness.

*Much of what you have written about the Irish language is
elegiac, so I wonder if you think it is (as the final stanza of
'A Shooting Script' suggests) mere writing in the sand?*

But that stanza also suggests that the writing in the sand will go on,
'just when it looks as if it is all over'. 'A Shooting Script' belongs in
a cluster of poems towards the end of *The Haw Lantern*, all of
them about the doubleness of Irish experience at any moment: on
the one hand there is the sensation, as in 'Wolfe Tone', that Ireland
is 'dwindling', that 'what might have been origin', as the people say
in 'The Mud Vision', gets 'dissipated in news'; on the other hand
there is the constant possibility of renewal, as in the stanza you
mention and in the last line of 'The Disappearing Island': 'All I
believe that happened there was vision.'

I don't believe that faith in Irish as a language and a value is
misplaced; the evidence suggests that it now inheres in the cultural
imagination of anglophone Ireland as a vital element. The TV
slogan about it may sound trite, but it does express a common
enough attitude: it's 'part of what we are'. This isn't to say that
the demographics are about to change in its favour; but a line
will be held, I am sure, and there will continue to be a small, small
Irish-speaking population. Paul Muldoon, by the way, must share

315

this belief, since he translates the title of Nuala Ní Dhomhnaill's 'Ceist na Teangan' not as 'The Language Question', which would have returned us to the old problematics, but as 'The Language Issue', which bears us forward into parturition and the prospect of new life.

11

'Time to be dazzled'
Seeing Things

~

How important was Yeats in leading you towards the poems in
Seeing Things *that 'credit marvels'?*

I'm not sure. It all started from 'Fosterling', from that image of 'the
tree-clock of tin cans / The tinkers made'. Not a very clear image, not
even to me. I'd heard a story years before, in Wicklow, about people
in a certain district who'd made a pact with the devil. I can't remem-
ber what boon they were granted, but in exchange they agreed that
the devil would come at a certain time on a certain day to collect
their souls. And of course as the hour neared the panic heightened
until, at the last minute, this band of tinsmiths – tinkers – landed and
proposed to build a fantastic tin clock in a tree and set the time
wrong. Then once that's done, the devil arrives and discovers he has
made a mistake, has arrived too late and broken the agreement, so
the people are released.

What stayed with me was the image of that strange flashing tin-
flanged tree, just asking to be written about. It was the opposite of
Lawrence's Bavarian gentians. The gentians appeared in order to
lead the spirit down to the halls of Dis, but the tree-clock pointed
an Orphic hand up towards the light. And as I'm telling you this, it
strikes me that Patrick Kavanagh may be the one we should be
talking about rather than Yeats. . .

In what sense?

You know that early poem of Kavanagh's, 'The Long Garden'? I've
a feeling there's something in the airiness and scatter and sheer ordi-
nariness of that Kavanagh poem which connects it to the tree-clock.

Do you find more visionary gleam in Kavanagh's Monaghan than in Yeats's 'Byzantium'?

Not as a reader, no. The carrying power of the 'Byzantium' stanzas is phenomenal. There's no Kavanagh music to match them. Yeats's quest is conducted in burnished armour, the lance rings on the door, he's like William Blake as he appears in 'An Acre of Grass', the Blake 'Who beat upon the wall / Till Truth obeyed his call'. There's something out of this world about Yeats's imagining, but the poetry itself still bears the brunt of the physical. Even in those two short lines I've quoted, you can feel the full blast of Blake's spirit-force, but you can also feel his fist meeting the solid wall. Still, you're right to imply that I'm much closer to the fundamentally Catholic mysticism in Kavanagh. My starlight came in over the half-door of a house with a clay floor, not over the dome of a Byzantine palace; and, in a hollowed-out part of the floor, there was a cat licking up the starlit milk.

Do you take any interest in Yeats's A Vision? *Would you care to undertake some similarly synoptic work?*

All of that began for Yeats – according to his own account – because, deprived of religion in his youth, he proceeded to put together a do-it-yourself religion out of 'a fardel of old stories'. I realize this is much too neat a reduction of his account of what happened, but it suggests a neat answer to your question – which is this: far from being deprived of religion in my youth, I was oversupplied. I lived with, and to some extent lived by, divine mysteries: the sacrifice of the Mass, the transubstantiation of bread and wine into the body and blood of Christ, the forgiveness of sin, the resurrection of the body and the life of the world to come, the whole disposition of the cosmos from celestial to infernal, the whole supernatural population, the taxonomy of virtues and vices and so on.

No doubt Yeats would cite Blake and say that I was enslaved by another man's system and was failing to create my own. But I suppose – like many Catholics, lapsed or not – I am of the Stephen Dedalus frame of mind: if you desert this system, you're deserting the best there is, and there's no point in exchanging one great coherence for some other ad hoc arrangement. Having said that, however, it must also be said that Yeats's construction, bare-handed, of a cosmology and a psychology, if not a theophany, was first of all another proof of intellectual power and secondly, as is universally acknowledged, a great scaffolding, a kind of theatre of memory which provided him with a sense of psychic and historic back-up. He was proud of his unchristened heart, as he calls it, but at the same time he wanted the equivalent of apostolic succession, he wanted endorsement and access to the wisdom of the ages. When he had constructed his system, he was satisfied that he had achieved this.

Would you see some connection between 'Squarings' and your 'fardel' of Catholic beliefs?

Undoubtedly.

Even if the very first poem is firm in its conviction that there is no afterlife?

But it's also firmly grounded in a sensation of 'scope', of a human relation to the 'shifting brilliancies' and the roaming 'cloud-life'. It's still susceptible to the numinous.

Writing the sequence must have been a great boost to your artistic morale.

It was. I felt free as a kid skimming stones, and in fact the relationship between individual poems in the different sections has something of the splish-splash, one-after-anotherness of stones skittering and frittering across water.

You employed similar terms in your lecture at Wolfson College in 2002: 'I thought of them in terms of speed and chance . . . I tried to make myself wide open to whim.' Did it trouble you at all that, in being spontaneous, you might also be unintentionally private, that many readers might not know, for instance, what a 'particular judgement' is?

I didn't worry about that at the time, nor have I worried since. When I was writing the twelve-liners, I experienced something halfway between a stiffening of linguistic resolve and a dissolution of it. Many of the lines just wafted themselves up out of a kind of poetic divine right. 'The music of the arbitrary'. 'Where accident got tricked to accuracy'. 'Do not waver / Into language. Do not waver in it'. 'Particular judgement' may be an archaic technical term, even for Catholics, but there's a strict phonetic clip to it and I'd rely on that to suggest a moment of final spiritual reckoning.

Given their spontaneity, did you subject the 'Squarings' poems to fewer revisions than normal?

It was a case of fewer revisions being required. I may exaggerate but I don't misrepresent if I say that, in general, I was subject to the poems and not the other way round.

Did you learn things from writing them which you can draw on to this day?

I learned the difference between *les vers donnés* and *les vers calculés*. I learned what inspiration feels like but not how to summon it. Which is to say that I learned that waiting is part of the work.

How long did the inspiration last?

About sixteen to eighteen months, from September 1988 until the end of the next year. After that it was a matter of ordering and discarding.

You had more than the forty-eight poems which now form the sequence?

A few more, maybe six or eight. I got into the habit of swooping on anything that stimulated memory or association. One of the unpublished sections was about making jam, another about sweet-pea seedlings under the bed in Mossbawn. You could think of every poem in 'Squarings' as the peg at the end of a tent-rope reaching up into the airy structure, but still with purchase on something earth-ier and more obscure.

When did you decide on the twelve-line form for individual poems and twelve-poem units for each of the four sections?

The first poem more or less wrote itself one afternoon in the National Library of Ireland. I was working very hard on an anno-tation of a selection of W. B. Yeats's poems. I'd been in the library for about six weeks and, the day I finished, I was sitting in this most beautiful reading room with the rain coming down on the glass dome. Suddenly I wrote a few lines and it became a twelve-line, four three-lines, thing. It felt given, strange and unexpected; I didn't quite know where it came from, but I knew immediately it was there to stay. It seemed as solid as an iron bar. So I began to treat it as a different kind of *barre*, a stimulus to repeating the exercise, and in a couple of days I'd written the first three poems – in the order in which they eventually appeared in the book. The form operated for me as a generator of poetry.

What got me going in earnest was the gloss in the third poem on the word 'squarings', which had appeared in the second. In that case I felt the private meaning had to be explicated, so I did my best to describe how a player took 'squarings' when he positioned himself to shoot a marble in the school playground. How the preparation involved 'anglings, aimings, feints and squints', 'test-outs and pull-backs, re-envisagings' – all of which terms suggested ways of proceeding with more poems. Then too, as I kept to the twelve-line form, the word 'squarings' suggested that I might aim for a total of 144, but in the end I settled for 48, a four-square pattern, each square twelve twelve-liners.

Did you conceive of each of the four sections being different in some way from the other three?

Not initially. The overall shape discovered itself gradually. The title of the first section, 'Lightenings', arrived by accident, when I found a dictionary entry that gives it to mean a flaring of the spirit at the moment before death. And there were also the attendant meanings of being unburdened and being illuminated, all of which fitted what was going on as the first poems got written. The one about the boat in the air above Clonmacnoise, for example. Or the ones about Thomas Hardy as a child, on his back among a flock of sheep, gazing up at the heavens.

That Clonmacnoise poem has become the best known in the sequence.

The story was unforgettable: it's there in Kenneth Hurlstone Jackson's *A Celtic Miscellany*, but the version I have is a bit different because I misremembered some of the details. In the original, the boat's anchor 'came right down on to the floor of the church', whereas I have it hooking on to the altar rails – somehow it enters miraculously through the roof and the crewman shins down a rope into the sanctuary. That wasn't a deliberate alteration, although

I'm sure the image in the first 'Lightenings' poem of an unroofed wallstead and an unroofed world must have prompted it.

The story has the 'there-you-are and where-are-you' of poetry. A boat in the air, its crewman on the ground, the abbot saying he will drown, the monks assisting him, the man climbing back, the boat sailing on. The narrative rises and sets, the magic casement opens for a moment only and the marvellous occurs in a sequence that sounds entirely like a matter of fact. The crewman is a successful Orpheus, one who goes down and comes back with the prize, which is probably what gives the whole episode its archetypal appeal.

There's an unhampered freedom and fullness and fluency about Seeing Things *that suggests a second wind, a fresh start.*

My father's death in October 1986 was the final 'unroofing' of the world and I'm certain it affected me in ways that were hidden from me then and now. But the freedom of a sabbatical year and a renewed access to Glanmore also had a mighty positive effect. For once, I'd taught the full academic year at Harvard, from September 1987 until June 1988, so when we got back I had a clear space of eighteen months, since I wasn't needed back in Harvard until the spring term of 1990.

Meanwhile, the formal purchase we'd arranged with Ann Saddlemyer restored us to the 'beloved vale' in Wicklow. Glanmore Cottage was available from then on as a completely silent place of writing, close to Dublin, no phone, no interruptions whatsoever. In fact, the second poem of the 'Squarings' sequence is an immediate act of thanksgiving for the cottage as a 'bastion of sensation'. 'Batten down', it says. 'Dig in. / Drink out of tin. Know the scullery cold' – this was before we'd got the central heating installed. All that naturally sent a powerful surge through the system, as did the writing of 'Fosterling', which ended by stating that it was 'Time to be dazzled and the heart to lighten'. And it also mentioned the approach of the fiftieth birthday, another factor in the whole subliminal mix.

Those years also saw some of the most atrocious incidents in Northern Ireland, including the Remembrance Day bomb in Enniskillen and the vicious murders of two British army corporals in West Belfast. Did you feel any inclination to return to Troubles themes?

I was in America at the time of those incidents, but visited London shortly after the murder of the soldiers in West Belfast to receive the *Sunday Times* Literary Award I mentioned before – the one at which I protested about the way the incident had been handled in the British press. I was still involved with 'the most distressful country that ever yet was seen', but as a subject it had just gone flat. I hadn't at that stage discovered the phrase 'the redress of poetry', but my sixth sense was already telling me that I had to come back at conditions rather than cave in to them. Not that anything was very clear at the time. There's an interesting passage, all the same, in a poem called 'A Royal Prospect', about a couple who 'are borne downstream unscathed, / Between mud banks where the wounded rave all night / At flameless blasts and echoless gunfire': those lines clearly register a disjunction between the unscathed life I was living in Harvard and Dublin and the conditions being experienced on the ground in Northern Ireland.

Yet 'A Royal Prospect' is by no means a Troubles poem. Like Part II of 'A Retrospect', it looks back through a long-distance lens at courtship and the early days of marriage. I find something uncharacteristic about those poems – perhaps it's the distancing device of the third-person narrative . . .

For me, there was a feeling of touching on a taboo subject, especially in 'A Royal Prospect', conducting my own 'particular judgement', maybe even the general one. That probably accounts for the strangeness, but then strangeness is good.

In a television interview, to mark your fiftieth birthday, you spoke of three phases in a writer's life – the starting out, the taking stock (at around thirty), and the new freedom of later life. Does this still seem valid to you as an analysis – or has your perspective changed, now that you are approaching seventy? Is there a fourth phase?

If there is, I haven't got to it yet. But I can imagine it – a phase of solitary wandering at the edge of the mighty waters. What I said in that interview I have repeated often since, but in a somewhat different way. I believe the three phases turn out to be cyclic, that there are renewed surges of endeavour in your life and art, and that, in every case, the movement involves a pattern of getting started, keeping going and getting started again. Some books are a matter of keeping going; some – if you're lucky – get you started again. *Seeing Things* was a new start. There, for once, the old saw came true: life began, or began again, at fifty.

How did you mark the occasion?

Marie and I went to Rome for a holiday with Bernard and Jane McCabe. And the *Irish Times* published a selection of the twelve-liners as a celebration.

You must have written that 'Squarings' poem about climbing the steps of the Capitol around that time?

Shortly after I came home. I was pouncing for twelve lines on all kinds of occasions, chance sentences from my reading, chance sightings of dictionary entries, such as the words 'lightening' and 'offing', chance visits to places that unlocked the word hoard. I wanted, if possible, something nonchalant yet definite. 'Unfussy and believable', as I say in the section about Han-shan's Cold Mountain poems.

There's even a twelve-liner about a Vietnam-bound soldier; it begins with a Yeats quotation which I don't recognize: 'To those who see spirits, human skin for a long time afterwards appears most coarse.'

It's from one of his letters to Lady Dorothy Wellesley. The quotation isn't exactly word for word, but it's very close. It reminded me of a young soldier I'd once seen on an airport bus when I was coming across from San Francisco to Berkeley – the only other passenger. He was around nineteen or twenty, obviously lonely and no doubt afraid, en route to Treasure Island military base, which was the embarkation point for Vietnam. He looked doomed and there was a pallor on his brow, probably the result of a hangover from a party the previous night in Arkansas or wherever; it gave him that ghost-who-walks look. I'll never forget it. A crossing, for sure. The airport bus as death coach.

One of the 'Glanmore Revisited' sonnets reports that the first time you were 'really angry' at your children was when they stripped away the bark of an ash tree where a friend had carved his name. Had you been hoping to begin an autograph tree like the one at Lady Gregory's Coole Park?

Coole was the last thing on my mind, and the carved names recalled a very un-cool event – Michael's first communion. Brian Friel and David Hammond were down in Wicklow that day and – to mark the occasion – I got them to cut their initials into the tree. Michael and Christopher may well have picked up the example of tree-vandalism at that very moment; but, for whatever reason, they did strip off the bark a few months later.

When John Haffenden interviewed you in the early 1980s, you told him, 'My temperament doesn't incline to anger very much.' Yet isn't there a suggestion in the 'Weighing In' poem in The Spirit Level *that it is salutary to let anger rip sometimes?*

There certainly is. But that poem, in fact, isn't so much about my anger as about my failure to do precisely that, let it rip. In the end, my concern with 'redress' probably means that I'm temperamentally more inclined to weigh up than weigh in. The poem started with the physical fact of a weighbridge, and its roots lie in the different sensations of hefting two fifty-six-pound weights on to a weighbridge and balancing a hundredweight bag of potatoes against them on the other side, adding or throwing out potatoes until, as the poem says, 'everything trembled, flowed with give and take'. And then that discovery of buoyancy in burden sent the writing veering into further thoughts on bearing, bearing up and bearing out, passive suffering, turning the other cheek and then, wham, yet another turn, against tolerating hurt, against returning good for evil and so on.

After you became the owner of Glanmore Cottage, how did you regard it: country retreat, escape, workspace?

Workspace, first and foremost. Which meant that it was also a retreat. It remained what it always had been, the poetry house. It's a silence bunker, a listening post, a holding, in every sense of that word. It holds meaning and things, and even adds meaning. In my life, Glanmore Cottage stands for what Wallace Stevens said poetry stands for, the imagination pressing back against the pressures of reality. Glanmore is a contested zone – Marie thinks it's a weekend cottage, I think it's a studio for writing in, though we find ways of balancing that out. I always found the place conducive to writing and it saved my writing life, because I was able to disappear from home in Dublin – which was becoming like a cross between a travel agency and a telephone exchange – and bury myself down there.

I used to very much like claustrophobic conditions – facing the wall with a low-set ceiling. In the cottage, we had this lovely old low ceiling and one of the things that Marie and I disagreed about was a skylight. She liked the idea and I said, 'No, keep the place a hutch, keep the hatch battened down.' I came back from Harvard one time and went upstairs in the cottage – there was a skylight! Actually, it was a tremendous change for me; again something to do with getting near fifty: I lifted up my eyes to the heavens . . .

Returning to earthly things, the settle bed described in Seeing Things *is kept in Glanmore Cottage?*

It belonged to a distant cousin of my father's, an old *cailleach* in County Derry, Biddy Carmichael, who left it to me in her will. A big, high-backed, fold-out, wooden box-bed, as heavy as a piano: vernacular furniture with a capital V. There would have been no room for it in Strand Road and it would have been out of place there anyhow. But it belonged in the cottage. When you contemplated it in its corner, you could have been Miłosz contemplating the golden house of 'is'. It was, as the poem says, the given that can always be reimagined, and I don't believe it could have attained that state outside of the cottage. Although I've never actually slept in it, I do consider the settle bed 'a fine and private place'. Like the cottage itself.

'The Settle Bed' is preceded by an intriguing poem called 'The Biretta'.

The odd thing about 'The Biretta' is that, in spite of its title, it began with a soft hat – specifically the hat worn by the priest in Matthew Lawless's painting *The Sick Call*, which hangs in the National Gallery of Ireland. I was asked to write something for a festschrift in honour of James White, the former director of the gallery, and had a hunch that the Lawless painting had a poem hidden in it somewhere. It's a nineteenth-century genre piece, a solidly realistic rendering of a rowboat on a river. In the boat, you have a priest, and the priest is clearly thinking of the sick parishioner who's waiting for him and for the holy viaticum. It's an unspectacular, very sympathetic study, nicely successful in conveying the priest as somebody halfway between a man of sorrows and a man of service. And the hat is so ordinary, so unstylish, it seems like an objective correlative of all that. It's certainly the opposite of what the hard-edged tricorn biretta stood for: the hard line, the pulpit bark, the articulated and decided authority of *unam sanctam catholicam et apostolicam Ecclesiam.*

But it's the biretta that is the focus of the poem . . .

. . . because the memory of holding a biretta by its central fin is still there between my finger and my thumb. As an altar boy, I was always fascinated by the materiality and weight of it and, as a child, I tended to be frightened of priests with birettas on their heads. At the same time there was something trim and shipshape, almost airborne, about the feel of the thing. When you took it into your hand from the priest's hand, there was a momentary temptation to launch it into the sanctuary like a paper dart or a little black-winged stealth bomber. In the end I let that impulse stand for poetry's impulse to outstrip the given, and turned it instead into the boat of imagination that Dante launches in the opening lines of the *Purgatorio . . .*

. . . and into the little gold boat from the Broighter Hoard in the National Museum.

Yes, I've always loved that piece, found in County Derry, a Bronze Age treasure, extraordinarily delicate – 'Refined beyond the dross into sheer image'. There was a photograph of it on the jacket of the American edition of *Seeing Things.*

The jacket of North *included the portrait of you by Edward McGuire.*

As far as I remember, that was the first time Faber broke with the old house style, which had never featured author photographs or jacket art, but used hand-cut lettering for the title and the poet's name on the front, with an alphabetical list of Faber poets printed on the back. I suspect Charles Monteith saw the McGuire picture at some book launch or other in the Ulster Museum and decided to reproduce it. It was and remains a terrific painting.

In a Seeing Things *poem, 'A Basket of Chestnuts', you mention
that Edward McGuire visited your house in 1973. Did he paint
you at home? How did the portrait end up in the Ulster Museum?*

It was actually commissioned by Ted Hickey, who was then Keeper
of Art in the museum. It was a bold stroke to choose a sitter as
young as I was then, but Edward McGuire was noted for his
portraits of poets; he'd done magnificent paintings of Pearse
Hutchinson and Michael Hartnett, and Ted was eager to have one
for the collection. So as soon as the commission was confirmed,
Edward arrived at our house, on the lookout for any props that
might add a bit of character to the background or the foreground,
and settled on this basket of chestnuts that I'd gathered, 'golden-
bowelled as a moneybag'.

But they don't actually appear in the portrait.

No. My notion is that he concentrated all the light he might have
glossed over the skin of the chestnuts into the toes of my boots. If
you look at the painting, you'll see that the footwear is positively
lustrous.

*You are shown at a table, holding an old book open. Did you
actually adopt that pose for him?*

I did, yes. His studio, in a room in his home, was quite small. This
meant that my chair was backed tight into a corner and I was more
or less barricaded behind the little table. The way I look in the por-
trait, slightly at bay, penned in, staring out, that's partly a result of
the physical constriction. But there was something else that pro-
duced tension in me and consequently in the portrait, which was
my inability to relax totally in Edward's presence. He was unfail-
ingly friendly and fiercely funny; but even in the mornings, which
was when the sittings occurred, he would be hard at the Guinness,
and since he had a reputation for being a dangerous drinker, I was
constantly watchful. And that is what Edward faithfully painted,
the poet vigilant.

The painting was true to what Edward detected in me and a
strong likeness of what he saw in front of him – which is why I like
and admire it. I remember Derek Hill, who did a softer-edged por-
trait some fifteen or sixteen years later, saying that Edward's was

more like a wood carving than a painting, that I smiled more than the figure in the picture, and so on. But in fact, the gathered-up, pent-up, head-on quality is what I admire: Edward saw that I was a keep of tensions and kept what he saw. When it came to seeing things, he was very good indeed.

The McGuire portrait proved to be the first of many. How did sitting for him compare with your experiences with Derek Hill, Barrie Cooke, Peter Edwards, Louis le Brocquy and – most recently – Tai-Shan Schierenberg?

Maybe because it was the first, because it involved the most protracted series of studio visits, and because of the element of anxiety that I've just described, the McGuire sitting left the deepest mark. I never actually sat for Louis le Brocquy and I guess he would call his work 'images' rather than 'portraits'. On all of the other occasions, however, I was more relaxed than I had been with Edward and the process was considerably shorter. With Derek Hill there was a lot of cheery talk, with Barrie a more intent silence, but with Peter Edwards and Tai-Shan Schierenberg, I only had to pose for a couple or three hours. They did quick drawings, maybe a little preliminary sketch in oils, took many photographs and then released me.

Did those subsequent likenesses catch things which McGuire had missed?

The artists who followed were faced with an older face and a sitter more used to being inspected, so they had the harder task. But they've conferred their own strengths and increases on me and I'm in their debt for that. There's a line in Hopkins which is an address to the godhead, but it could also work as a sitter's address to his artist. When you look at different versions of yourself by different painters you could say, 'Over again I feel thy finger and find thee' – although the line could equally well read 'and find *me*'.

One man who gave ample space in his life to both poetry and painting was John Hewitt. Where did you first meet him?

I think in the company of Terry and Sheelagh Flanagan, probably sometime in 1965 or 1966, when the Hewitts were back in Belfast on holiday. They'd gone to Coventry in 1957, after John was denied promotion to the directorship of the Ulster Museum, a great scandal at the time and one that left him permanently embittered. John Hewitt figured a lot in the Flanagans' conversation: they were devoted to him but always enjoyed mimicking his abrupt speech and readiness to cut the boots off people in conversation. When Terry was starting out as a painter, Hewitt had been an important mentor. In fact, in the Ulster of the forties and fifties, he was something of a cultural and intellectual standard-bearer, combative and authentic, left wing and puritan, but still somebody the Flanagans had remained very fond of.

Were you also fond of him?

I was. He and Roberta came to see us in Belfast and I also met them in their place in Coventry. In the late sixties, early seventies John and I exchanged the occasional letter. He had done a favourable review of *Death of a Naturalist* for the *Belfast Telegraph* and would eventually organize a poetry reading for me at the Herbert Art Gallery, where he had gone as director. He also arranged an exhibition of work by Terry Flanagan and Colin Middleton; I remember travelling over with them to Coventry for the opening. So we were friendly long before he came back to Belfast as the grand old man of Ulster letters.

He was encouraging towards your work?

He was. I was never close enough to feel like a protégé. At the same time there was support in the way he kept in touch, both by letter and in person. Before MacGibbon and Kee brought out his first *Collected Poems* in 1968, his stuff was hard to get and he'd given me several privately printed pamphlets. I'd read some of his poems early on, in a Faber anthology of contemporary Irish poetry done in the 1950s – one of the few poetry books in the Magherafelt library. Then, in 1962, when I was writing an extended essay on literary magazines in Ulster, I encountered not only his poems, but his ideas about regionalism, his desire to foster an Ulster literature for an Ulster people.

Would it be fair to say that you have tended to see Hewitt as a poet whose politics – the socialism and regionalism – were not ultimately able to transcend Unionism? I'm thinking of your remark in The Redress of Poetry *that his concept of regionalism*

*'suited the feeling of possession and independence of the
empowered Protestants . . . more than it could ever suit the sense
of dispossession and political marginalization of the Catholics'.*

The first thing to be said is that Hewitt was a poet to be grateful
for, whether you were a Protestant or a Catholic. He tilted the
lenses a fraction. The Northern Ireland situation was allowed its
historical dimension: he recognized that it was a colonial predica-
ment and hence 'The Colony' remains an important intervention
by a poet. Politically, he was gruffly the democrat, committed to
equality and civil rights for everybody. It would seem, in fact, that
he suffered because of that probity, in that his liberal convictions
and associations probably led to his being denied promotion at the
Ulster Museum – which is how he ended up spending fifteen years
in Coventry.

But for all that, in John Hewitt's imagining, the Catholics in the
North, and the Irish south of the border, remained definitively
'other'. He had a principled regard for them and would have
fought for their rights, but nothing in him could altogether flow
towards them. He was laureate of the reformed conscience, the
embattled Ulsterman in stand-off from both England and Ireland. I
find him most convincing as a poet when he realizes the emotional
cost of the stand-off, in poems as different as 'The King's Horses'
and 'A Local Poet'. He's at his best when he gets away from his cut-
and-dried, man-of-the-left decidedness and finds himself talking to
no one but himself. Most of the time, when he seems to be talking
to himself, Hewitt is really instructing the reader, wanting to let
you know what you should be thinking and feeling. He's pretty
short on negative capability.

It's best to read him in the *Selected Poems* which Michael Longley
and Frank Ormsby edited. Every time I open the *Collected*, I'm in
awe of his industriousness, his drive as a maker of verse; but his
vision of himself as the decent craftsman, his sense of the poet as
tradesman, results in a lot of the poems ending up too efficient for
their own imaginative good. I close the book feeling mean because
of my response; but the *Selected* – which I read from start to finish
when it appeared – moved and convinced me in a new way.

*Did you see much of Hewitt when, after retirement, he returned
to Belfast?*

Very little, less than when he was in England. He came back in 1972, the year I went to Wicklow, and from then on he was more and more integrated into the local scene. He even wrote a poem entitled '1957–1972', about the period he was forced to spend in Coventry, as if it were a lost life. But the regionalism he'd been promoting in the forties was very different from the parochialism that prevailed in Belfast in the seventies. Kavanagh's influence had proved stronger than Hewitt's, for me and for everybody else.

Hewitt had a vision of a cultural canton where 'we' would speak an English inflected by Tudor pronunciation and Lowland Scots vocabulary, and the ambition of the writing would be to reflect and consolidate the terms of an Ulster culture more Glens of Antrim than Sperrin, more Belfast's shipyard than Derry's Bogside. But that vision had been supplanted by one that was bolder and more border-breaking and owed more to the artistic triumph of Kavanagh's poem 'Epic' than to Hewitt's sociocultural programme. Although he was a fondly regarded father figure, Hewitt couldn't be a formative influence on the Muldoons or McGuckians of the place.

To what extent was he a formative influence on your own work?

I don't think there is any stylistic influence. I never felt susceptible to his idiom. I simply didn't know his work well enough early on. What I felt was some kind of corroboration from the fact that he was a local poet with a sense of standards and a fidelity to the home ground. My self-confidence was helped by his interest and approval, but reading him left no genetic trace on the way I wrote.

You dedicated 'The Schoolbag' to John Hewitt's memory, and use the word 'handsel' in the poem – a nod in the regional direction, if I am right in thinking that the word was used years ago in transactions at the old hiring fairs.

That is so. Once an agreement was made on the street between the master and the girl or boy he was hiring for the next quarter, a shilling or two changed hands as a guarantee, and this was the handsel. But if that was a nod in the regional direction, it was no more than that. I actually revised the final couplet of the sonnet in order to lessen the folk-museum element that had been present in the first version. In its earlier form, the poem ended with a vision of Hewitt falling into step with an ancestral line of men and girls on

their way to the hiring fair, walking away with them into the world
of the local ballad, really. But in the end I thought the image was
too pious, too 'trig', too like his own pastoral vision of himself, so
I changed to an image that conjured up instead the lonely child in
him, the *animula* who's in there at the heart of the Hewitt poems I
like best. I made him 'step out trig and look back all at once / Like
a child on his first morning leaving parents'.

Did he play any part in your visual education?

Not directly, but during his years as the Keeper of Art in the Ulster
Museum, he was responsible for the purchases, so some of the stuff
I was looking at in the early sixties would have been his choosing.
Mostly work by British painters of the generation just ahead of
him, including Ben Nicholson and Victor Pasmore; also the work
of local artists such as John Luke and William Conor, and younger
ones like T. P. Flanagan and Basil Blackshaw.

*Works by many of these artists were included in a 'personal
selection' from the museum's holdings made by you for an
exhibition in 1982. You chose very few abstract paintings, so I
wonder if abstract work has less appeal for you in general than
more representational painting?*

Probably. I find it hard to love the late, hard-edged Mondrian, for
example. Yet it's equally hard to resist the antics of a Klee or a
Miró. But then, wham, you think of Picasso and he overwhelms all
this finessing, all this distinguishing between abstract and represen-
tational. I made my first visit to the Picasso Museum in Paris a few
years ago and, in one long afternoon, got over a lifelong resistance.
Until then I had a prejudice against the sheer unremittingness of his
progress. I also resisted the priapic element. In galleries I tended to
note the Picassos but to linger with the Cézannes, but that journey
through the rooms in the Marais was like a journey through a
wonderland. I was overwhelmed by the plenitude of what he had
done. There was more benignity in it than I had realized. It was
bountiful as well as brutal. As if Hephaestus and Lewis Carroll and
Hieronymus Bosch and the cave artists of the Dordogne had all
decided to pool their talents in one pair of eyes and one pair of
hands and set them free to decorate the twentieth century. And
dismay it too, of course.

Did Pound's warning to go 'in fear of abstraction' affect your attitude?

Not with regard to painting or sculpture, nor was it meant to, although it certainly did influence me when it came to poetry. Early on, it was like a thread-end I held on to in order to approach the mystery for myself. But the mystery proved bigger and less rule-bound than Pound's do's and don'ts allowed for. I remember, for example, Michael Longley arguing – rightly – that there was nothing 'abstract' about a rhythm, that vocabulary and image weren't the be-all and end-all of poetry.

And you must have come round to that position again when you found yourself admiring Miłosz's 'Incantation'.

I did, yes, gratefully. Although Miłosz's parable about his own conflict when it comes to poetry is like a parable for the conflict between the abstract and the representational: on the one hand, he'd like an overall view, as if viewing the earth and its predicaments from a great height, and on the other hand he doesn't want to desert the particular plights of breathing, suffering individuals down there at eye level.

Returning to the topic of visual art, I'd like to hear more about your favourite painters. You listed several of them during our discussion of your Cézanne-inspired poem, 'An Artist'.

I'm more at home in front of a Breughel cornfield than a Tintoretto Assumption. But anything can happen in a gallery: that's the joy of it. Being *surprised* by joy: Giorgione's *Tempest*, for instance. I'd seen reproductions of it for years and was familiar with the content, the woman and baby, the big overcast sky, the unconsoling space at the centre. But when I saw it in the gallery in Venice I was moved in a completely unexpected way. The picture was smaller than I'd imagined, the physicality of the pigment made the menace and mystery of the scene more palpable, so that there was this sudden 'making strange'.

That same unpredictable deepening of purchase, a feeling of being dropped through some trapdoor of perception, happened to me one day in the Museum of Modern Art in San Francisco. I turned the corner past a lovely lyrical Diebenkorn and came face to face with a Magritte. Not so much surreal as photo-real or super-real – a close-up, an almost primitivist view of a man's toilet table. Great solitude, great sorrow even, implicit in the rendering of a comb and a shaving brush, in the grain of the wood of the table. There was something grievous about the dark greens and plum blues. Woeful without being pathetic. *Lacrimae rerum* in the teeth of a comb.

Which painter, given a choice, would you like to have been?

No way of answering that one. There's the desire to pick somebody whom you consider a kindred spirit and equally there's the desire to pick somebody completely different. Forget Breughel, therefore, and think of the Piero who did the picture of the scourging of Christ. I'd like to be him, as Euclidean as he is dreambound. But then too I'd like to be the Douanier Rousseau who did that painting of the poet and his muse as a shabby old couple standing in their ordinary old doorway. A worn-out image of themselves as bride and groom. It's a wonderful game and you could play it till the cows come home – till you'd even want to be Cuyp! – but there'd be no real conclusion.

Barrie Cooke appears in one of your 'Squarings' as a 'walking weathercock'. Elsewhere you compare him to a Ben Gunn. You make him sound as much hunter-gatherer as painter.

Well, he is. His passion for fishing is at least equal to his passion for painting, and it shows in the work. There are sensational links between the rodman and the brushman. Water and ground and river run into woman and groin and eros, the flood is made flesh and dwells amudst us. His art is as much bushman as brushman. No wonder he and Ted Hughes were such good friends.

Did the three of you often meet when Ted was in Ireland to fish?

No – Ted would go directly, often with his son Nicholas, to meet up with Barrie somewhere in the midlands for the pike fishing. Or farther west, for trout and salmon. They would occasionally call with us on their way back, but fishing was fishing, a different sodality, and Barrie would head to his own place once the expedition was over. Still, you'll remember being with Barrie and me on New Year's Day 1985 when you took a photograph of us holding up a banner in front of a bicycle shop in Blackrock owned by one – perhaps I should say *another* – Ted Hughes. I'd often wanted to take our Ted to see his name on that shop front, but instead Barrie prepared this big paper scroll with one of Ted's famous lines misquoted on it, 'Bike, perfect bike in all parts . . .', and we posed with it between us. We sent your photograph off to him anonymously but he knew immediately where it had come from.

To what extent did Barrie and Ted influence your awareness of what would now be called environmental issues? 'Augury' in Wintering Out *indicates that you were alert to these matters quite early.*

Pollution, especially the pollution of rivers, was an obsession with the pair of them, and it was something I myself knew about from childhood. There was always a dread of allowing 'lint water' to get into the Moyola, since it was deadly for the fish – lint water being the water left in a flax dam after the flax had been retted. And I also remembered the sight of the first white froth floating down the Moyola after Nestlé opened their factory at Castledawson. So I was an apt pupil.

Back on dry land, your poem 'The Pitchfork' suggests that you were very much in your element when it came to making hay.

Well, yes, I was. I loved handling the fork and the rake, their lightness and rightness in the hand, their perfect suitedness to the jobs they had to do. It meant that the work of turning a swathe, for example, was its own reward; angling the shaft and the tines so that the hay turned over like a woven fabric – that was an intrinsically artistic challenge. Tasty work, as they say. Using the pitchfork was like playing an instrument. So much so that when you clipped and trimmed the head of a ruck, the strike of the fork on the hay made it a kind of tuning fork.

You didn't have mechanical turners and rakes in your part of the country?

They were around, but they didn't come into general use on small farms like ours until the early sixties. My heyday in the hay was just before that, when I was in my mid- to late teens, home from college, enjoying the camaraderie of neighbours, the freedom of the holiday. And it would always be happening in sunshine, because you couldn't work at hay unless you had good weather. The smell of hay still opens a path to the farthest and fondest places in me. Even a word like 'hayshed'. I'm riding on the back of a horse-drawn ruck-shifter, leaning into the ruck that had been winched tight, my upper leg cold against the smooth steel tail of the float, the load tilting and jolting as the rubber wheels bump along the old cart road. Bring on John Constable! But what came on instead was silage, which had its own potent smell, especially at twilight, early winter twilight, when the electric lights came on in the milking parlour and the whole mechanized orchestra began to rattle and hum.

'The Journey Back', the opening poem in Part I of Seeing Things, *is about Philip Larkin: a man whose labours were – as the poem itself notes – of the nine-to-five kind.*

What prompted the poem in the first place was an invitation to contribute to a memorial volume being edited by George Hartley of the Marvell Press. I didn't know Larkin well enough to write a personal reminiscence, and I'd done my *hommage* in a sixtieth-birthday tribute, so a poem seemed the way to go. Dante was at the back of my mind since I'd introduced his name in the conclusion of my tribute, saying that if Larkin were to write an *Inferno*, it would begin not in a dark wood but in a railway tunnel, that his Mount Purgatory would be a hospital tower block and so on. Larkin died in 1985, before Christmas, in the season of Advent, the season when the magi were traditionally believed to have set out on their journey, so I make his shade set out for the land of the dead on a bus in a pre-Christmas rush hour. It's as if he's going home from work one more time, and being allowed his own epiphany of himself – 'A nine-to-five man who had seen poetry.'

Although you felt you didn't know Larkin well enough to write about him as a person, you did meet him on a few occasions.

First, in Charles Monteith's office in Faber's, on 6 August 1965. I know the date because it was the first day of our honeymoon and I'd made an appointment with Monteith at the earliest possible moment. Larkin was coming in as we were being ushered out, so we shook hands, but that was about it. Then, some years later, I caught his eye in the quad at Queen's – he may have come to Belfast on library business – but we didn't speak because we were past each other before we knew, and anyway, I wasn't going to be the one to speak first. The time I saw most of him was when we were judging the Arvon Poetry Competition in 1980; even that was fleeting, and mostly bantering, in company with our fellow judges, Ted Hughes and Charles Causley.

And his references to you in the published correspondence?

I suppose I was lucky to get off as lightly as I did. Once you came within his orbit, you became part of the comic apparatus, an item that had to be included in the show. I couldn't not be in the show but was glad not to be entirely in the shit. 'The Gombeen Man', he called me. I suspect he didn't exactly know the meaning of the term, except that it was meant to inflate and demean at the same time. Ted, of course, was 'The Incredible Hulk'. Not bad. A lot of the time in the letters, he was writing a script for himself, lines to be spoken by his inner Steptoe, the Thersites of Toad Lane.

How much of all that was persona and how much actual man?

I think he instinctively set about confounding that distinction. Larkin probably wouldn't have had much time for John Berryman's *Dream Songs*, but there's something about his whole masquerade that reminds me of Berryman. It would be too forgiving to call the viciousness of the correspondence carnivalesque, yet there's something like that going on – it's just that Larkin's masks allow for something a lot more brutal and unlikeable than Berryman's. Substitute a Mr Bollocks for Mr Bones, a National Front man for the frontman Henry, and you have the team and the permission. He had such a horror of being holier than thou that he went to the other extreme.

Is it possible that – for all his small output – Larkin was more successful than Hughes in producing enduring individual poems and that his oeuvre as a whole may prove more permanent?

One part of me is inclined to say yes to those questions, because Larkin's poems inhere so sweetly and ineradicably in the memory and in the language – as serene as they are sorrowful. Once upon a time I compared the mood of 'At Grass' to the mood of Gray's 'Elegy', and I've always thought that in a century or two Larkin's work will survive the way Gray's survives, as an ongoing perfect pitch. Although it might be better and more testing to compare him to Marvell, and not just because of the Hull connection.

On the other hand, when I think of Hughes, I think of a 'bright and battering sandal' that has more power than pitch, more effulgence than finish, and generally more mana. There's Blakean recklessness in Hughes, the poetry of the living present, the shimmer of the gene pool and the galaxies. When I was starting out, I got more from Hughes, I knew his poems in the joints of my body and just felt he had a bigger transmitter – so that makes for endurance too. He doesn't plod home at twilight with Gray's ploughman but mucks into the yard work with Caedmon and then starts to sing creation with him in the cowshed.

In your Irish Times *obituary for Larkin, you note that his poetry 'is full of a yearning to repose in the transcendent'. Is this the aspect of it you admire most?*

It's the aspect that makes for the quarrel with himself, the grain he has to work against and, in doing so, a grain he polishes until it shines.

Immediately after your Philip Larkin poem comes an evocation of childhood football.

It was what we all played – Gaelic football, that is. I was by no means a natural, but I ran with the pack: always more in backs than in forwards, sometimes in goal. The 'Markings' poem you refer to is set in one of our own fields at Mossbawn where a crowd of us would gather up in the summer evenings and play until the light died – but what I remember is the way we kept going and even kept seeing the ball after it had got dark. That became an analogy for the extra-vision and extra-timeness of poetry, 'a game that never need / Be played out', a game played with improvised markings but with unlimited possibilities. Folded-up jackets for goalposts, imagined touchlines, the fantasy of starring . . . 'Some limit had been passed' and we entered a state that was 'unforeseen and free'.

Seamus Deane in his New Yorker *memoir presents you as having been less than enthusiastic about football later, not playing at St Columb's 'except when required'. Is that how you remember it too?*

It is. Gaelic football was compulsory if you were a boarder; there were inner college leagues and teams, and every weekend we'd get togged out and go for it, willy-nilly. The football Seamus played was soccer and it would have been during the week with other day boys, at lunchtime – unofficially, as it were. On those Saturday and Sunday afternoons, I would have preferred to be in the library. I didn't have the right physically aggressive attitude to enjoy the game or excel at it.

But you were skilful enough to play for the Castledawson minors, and you even received a trial for the Derry county team.

I could hold my own in the half-back line all right; and a combination of peer pressure and local loyalties meant that I stayed with the Castledawson team until I went to Queen's. Then, since I was spending so much time in Belfast, I gradually got separated from the players and the place.

Your uncle Sonny McCann was a local hero – a member of the Castledawson senior team and a star player at county level.

Sonny's name and fame were as much a bother as a benefit. He was always being held up as proof that I was bound to have it in me to be as good as he was. For once, I knew what it must be like to have an older brother who has excelled before you came trailing along behind him.

In March 1991, some months before the publication of Seeing Things, *a highly critical article about you – by Desmond Fennell, a lecturer and essayist – appeared in the review pages of the* Irish Times *with the subtitle 'A disparity between the work and the reputation'. It can't have been pleasant to get up one Saturday morning and find this attack staring you in the face.*

John Banville, the paper's literary editor, had given me a hint that something of the sort was going to be printed. I was in Harvard when it eventually appeared, so for the time being I was at a third remove. Even so, while it wasn't pleasant, it was hardly devastating. What dismayed me was the complacency of it, the tone of condescension. I may be thinking more about Fennell's pamphlet, for which the article was a kind of trailer, but I couldn't understand how he managed to get himself to a level where he felt entitled to speak *de haut en bas* on the subject of poetry. But at least he did speak, he didn't just keep mewling and muttering behind backs, although I realize he was encouraged by many who did.

Had you known Fennell – a fellow Northerner, after all – already?

Oh yes. We'd met on quite a few occasions; in fact, I'd once driven him to Derry to attend the first night of a Field Day play in the Guildhall. He'd even telephoned me a couple of times at home to invite me out for a drink. Maybe I should have accepted.

You were among friends at the 1988 Writers' Conference in Dun Laoghaire. This is reputed to have been the only time that you, Joseph Brodsky, Les Murray and Derek Walcott – writers often cited as evidence of the ascent of non-metropolitan poetry – were all gathered together.

It *was* the one and only time, yes, so we were lucky to have been photographed for the record outside the RTE studios, after we'd done a broadcast for BBC Radio 3, chaired by Michael Schmidt. Everybody was at ease, as I recollect – free to agree or disagree, because we enjoyed one another's company and one another's work. Everyone was downbeat and humorous, but capable of high talk when it came to poetry. And low talk too, of course. You'll remember that Les and Valerie Murray had spent a couple of nights in our house in Dublin in 1977. Les endeared himself to me then by telling me he'd heard in Australia that I too wore elastic-sided boots – this after he had taken off his own in the sitting room prior to going upstairs to bed.

So there was no shyness or games-playing with him, or with the other two, whom I was then seeing every spring in Massachusetts. Each came to the table with his own argot from his own outback, each had a foot in a home camp and an away camp, each knew the kinds of cultural and political cross-currents the others were negotiating, so the conversation was more like ribbing than rivalry. There was great glee in being quick on the uptake, weaving past the clichés and the *idées réçues*. When things go well like that you just feel you've recouped something. You remember what it was like when you were a young poet.

You went to Australia a few years later for the Melbourne Festival. Did you meet Les Murray at that time?

I didn't, no. I believe he was then on his travels in Europe and the States. But even if I didn't meet him at that particular time, and have seen him only rarely since, he's very much a presence. He's one of the 'ironic points of light'.

On the Radio 3 programme, you described Murray's work as 'both democratic and learned'. Are those, to your mind, still the essential components?

They are. And you could add words like original, obstinate, word-hoarding, wild-ranging, regenerate . . . I once heard him say he was 'against relegation' and I thought that was almost a password to his system of values. And he has also said he's against 'tightness', all for a bit of 'sprawl'.

Is Derek Walcott another of your 'ironic points of light'?

As a writer, Derek is more an amicable than an ironic figure – which is not to say that he's without irony in person. From the time I began to read his poems, in the early sixties, I found myself not only admiring the amplitude of the art, but feeling at home with it. I recognized the nature of the conflicts it arose from. There were obvious parallels between the cultural and political situation in St Lucia in the second half of the twentieth century and the situation in Ireland in the first half. In both places the writers were furnished with two languages, the vernacular of the home and the idiom of the school, and the choice between them had political implications.

In Ireland in the 1920s, for example, you had a cultural nation-alist critic like Daniel Corkery promoting the nativist line, saying that you weren't a truly Irish writer if you couldn't find the heart of the matter in the crowd attending a Munster hurling final; the post-independence requirement therefore was to practise the govern-ment of the tongue and deny the imperial modes and matter. And in the 1960s these pressures were in operation elsewhere, with a poet like Edward Kamau Brathwaite turning from 'the voices of his education' in English literature to the voicing of the Afro-English of the Caribbean, tuning his lines to the African drum rather than the iambic metronome. It was a playing out in a different time and place of the conflict Joyce had designated in Ireland between the 'full stoppers and semi-colonials'. I was interested, at any rate, in Walcott's refusal to renege on the inherited English strain and admired him for trying to let the whole problem play out in his work, and pay into it. I'd known his poems for fifteen or sixteen years, so I was familiar with him before I actually met him.

How did you meet? In a BBC radio programme at the time of your sixtieth birthday, Walcott recalled that his first contact with you was a letter he sent to express 'anger' at a review of your work.

Derek isn't one of nature's correspondents, so 'letter' would be a strong word for it; but he did send a note via the people at Farrar, Straus and Giroux – it was when I was in New York for a couple of days in 1980. He was objecting to something A. Alvarez had written in the *New York Review of Books*, to the effect that the English literary establishment always reserved a place for one Irish poet and I was currently flavour of the month. As I remember, Brian Moore actually wrote to the magazine about the same review. By then I'd been given Derek's phone number so I rang him and arranged to meet in Pete's Tavern, just off Gramercy Park. At that stage, I had reviewed *The Star-Apple Kingdom*.

You rated that book highly?

I did, and still do. I don't think I'd want to change a word of what I wrote about it at the time. 'The Schooner *Flight*' is one of the milestones.

In that same BBC broadcast, Walcott mentioned how much he'd enjoyed being driven by you through County Derry.

It was at the time of the Field Day production of *The Cure at Troy*. Derek and his partner Sigrid Nama were in London and came over to see the play in Derry, so I drove them round Mossbawn and Broagh and many of the old haunts. We even met my brother, by sheer coincidence, on the road in Broagh. That clinched something in the relationship. And I believe it made Derek eager to get me over to see his own home ground in Castries and Gros Islet.

And what was that like?

Rich and rare. I love the island, green and small, easy to get to know the length and breadth of it. Lush valleys with banana plants, rainforest on the higher ground, coconut palms on the shore, cows and ibis in the marshes, roosters in the streets. Roads full of minivans flogging along at full speed, the people in full cry, the patois fast and furious. I love also the *en bas gorge* music, fiddle and shak-shak and bongos, and the rum shops and the roadside stalls. It's like walking into a Walcott poem. Like walking into Broagh, for that matter. You have to be able to hold your own in the banter at ground level. You're up to your neck in familiarity. Of course, if I'd gone on a package deal to one of the big tourist hotels, things would have been different. More a matter of bikinis and Martinis in a theme-park than beer and barbecues on the beach. But we were lucky to be a part of the rabblement. It helped me to understand Derek's creative confidence, his alternation between anger and insouciance about the whole colonial consequence. It made me think of something Bob Dylan once said about Tommy Makem's singing. When Tommy sang, according to Dylan, there was an elsewhere in his eyes where the singing came from. In St Lucia, I felt that bit closer to the elsewhere behind Derek's vision.

12

'Keeping going'
The Spirit Level

~

'Listen now again' is how the first poem in The Spirit Level *ends. Did you feel that there was some reprising of earlier themes in this book, albeit from a different perspective?*

I didn't. That first poem is as much about middle age as about a rain stick. The instruction to listen was directed more to myself than to the reader, a reminder to keep the lyric faith, to trust in what you might call the George Herbert syndrome – 'And now in age I bud again . . . / I once more smell the dew and rain, / And relish versing'. 'The Rain Stick' is about being irrigated by delicious sound, about water music being created by the driest of elements – desiccated seeds falling through a cactus stalk. I'd occasionally seen and heard rain sticks in shops that specialized in ethnic goods, but I'd never heard anything like the one in the Brandes home in North Carolina. It was so lush and I was so entranced that Rand and Beth made me a gift of it – which is why the poem is dedicated to them.

So the poem is really about 'keeping going'?

Exactly.

But how do you keep going over a long period and ensure that you aren't just repeating yourself or going round in circles?

Ask me an easier one! You want, naturally, to be led by what Lowell called 'the incomparable wandering voice' and you try to wait for a given note, but inevitably there are times when you go into overdrive. Personally, I don't think that's the end of the artistic world. It can be a way of riding the current until the next surge comes along.

Some years ago, you spoke with admiration of Patrick Kavanagh's capacity 'to retain the abundant carelessness of lyric action into his bleaker later life', something you say Eliot lost. Can a poet take any steps to insure against suffering Eliot's fate?

Again, I can't pretend to be Sir Oracle. When you write, the main thing is to feel you are rising to your own occasion. And different poets will aspire to that in different ways. The remarks you quote 'privilege', as they say, Kavanagh's carelessness over Eliot's costiveness, but I'm not so sure about that any more. I can accept, or nearly accept, dodgy doggerelly stuff from later Kavanagh because there was always a who-cares, what-the-hell kind of energy in his best work – in 'The Great Hunger' and the canal bank sonnets, for example. But Eliot's genius was much greater and very different, his critical superego a lot more vigilant, so it was natural for him, early and late, to write poetry that was more strictly conceived and fastidious than anything Kavanagh would ever have produced or wanted to produce. Whatever about the middle stretch, stamina seems to be what counts in the final stretch. Stevens, Yeats, R. S. Thomas, Miłosz – they all kept rising to their own occasions. But even when your poet seems to have settled for the run of his own mill, the unforeseen can arrive. Wordsworth's 'Extempore Effusion', for example. Frost's 'Directive'.

In your lecture on Robert Lowell, you quoted – with a hint of approval – a statement by the Polish poet Anna Swir: 'We could say in a paradoxical abbreviation that a writer has two tasks. The first – to create one's own style. The second – to destroy one's own style.' Why, having – often with great difficulty – found his/her voice, should the poet then lose it again?

I'm not so sure. Swir's thesis chimed with what Lowell was doing in *Notebook*, so it made good sense to quote it in the lecture. And it seems to apply also to what Geoffrey Hill has been doing since *The Triumph of Love*. But it's over-emphatic, over-dogmatic. It doesn't apply to Elizabeth Bishop, for example, or to any of the strong finishers I've just mentioned. You could say they have a late style – but you could hardly say they 'destroyed' their earlier style in the process.

Helen Vendler, who wrote The Breaking of Style, *is dedicatee of* The Spirit Level. *Could you outline how your friendship with her developed to the point where she was one of your guests at the 1995 Nobel Prize ceremony? I take it you are by now friends in the social – and not just literary – sense.*

Definitely. 'The soul selects her own society.' I've known Helen since my early thirties, and have no more truthful or more cherished friend. We met, OK, because she liked my poems; but she's dear to Marie and me because of who and what she is in life. Her integrity and her kindness make her a standard in matters far beyond the literary. A mighty fortress is our Helen. But it was literary matters that brought us together. She was in that audience at the Yeats Summer School in Sligo in the early 1970s when I read some of the bog poems; she focused on them with the kind of avidity you expect only from a fellow poet, maybe only from a rival poet. She has intensity, intelligence, perfect pitch – a uniquely gifted listener-in to poems.

You were colleagues at Harvard.

Eventually, yes. When I met her first, she was teaching full-time at Boston University, in a department that included John Malcolm Brinnin – the man who had brought Dylan Thomas to America, almost as legendary to me as Thomas himself. Next thing, Helen got a half-year appointment at Harvard and before long she was there full-time and moved from Brookline to Cambridge; so at that stage, in the mid 1980s, we saw a lot more of each other. And we continued to meet in Dublin and Sligo every time she did her stint at the Yeats School. She has been a close companion as well as a close reader. She's a great giver of presents, for example, always mindful of her friends, especially when they suffer a hurt or a setback, and mindful too of their children. Intensely loyal and fond. Marie and I have had some of our happiest times in her company.

In 1988 – in the context of a reference to another very supportive critic, John Carey – you spoke of the danger of 'a too perfect collusion' between critics and poets. Are you conscious of that danger with Helen Vendler?

My relationship with Helen is more like that with a fellow poet. Obviously, I'm hugely in her debt because of her advocacy – nobody realizes it more. But whatever it adds up to, I don't believe it can be called 'collusion'. Maybe I should have said 'sympathy' in the first place. 'Collusion' suggests that there's something afoot that needs investigation, but in the case of John Carey or Helen, there's no need to investigate what's out in the open. That's why I dedicated *The Spirit Level* to her. To some people, it might have looked as if I were courting favour, but for years her favour had been bestowed and basically I wanted to signal that she was as much a generating force as a critical champion.

Do you show her work in progress?

Sooner or later. I value the immediate raking and combing she can't help giving to words on a page. When she responds on the spot, it's practical criticism, swift, intuitive, nuts-and-boltsy, the reaction of somebody who talks like a practitioner. What she writes in more formal and public accounts of individual books is different from what you get off the record. She *is* a writer, let's face it, invigorated by her own language as much as by the language she reads, and once she puts pen to paper she goes wherever she's led by insight and excitement. Everybody benefits because of this ability to articulate what a poem is intimating, but obviously I've been especially lucky.

Do you accept her advice about poems in progress?

Most of the time, yes, because she is a natural assayer: she can put her finger on something problematical, the word or phrase or rhythm that has you worried already.

And her critical judgements generally?

She has more decided views than I have, there are poets I admire whom she resists, and vice versa – all entirely natural. She doesn't get as much from Robert Frost, for example, as I do, whereas I have learned from her to pay a lot more attention to Wallace Stevens. But the main thing, the common denominator, is that we both came to poetry in the age of close-reading, the age when 'discrimination' was not only practised but taught, and memorization was still common. So there's a shared attitude, a belief in poetry as something substantial and sustaining, and a belief in literary criticism per se. Helen's as aware as the next one of the instability of the subject and all the deconstructed rest of it, but she shares the poet's

15 Left to right: Charles Monteith, Ted Hughes, Stephen Spender, and SH, at the Auden memorial reading, University of London, 1973.

16 Robert Lowell and SH at the presentation of the Duff Cooper Memorial Award for *North*, 1976.

17 SH visits Hugh MacDiarmid at his home in Biggar, Scotland, 1977.

(Photo: David Hammond)

18 SH with Ted Hughes and Charles Causley, judging the Arvon Foundation poetry competition, 1981.

19 Members of the board of the Field Day Theatre Company. Left to right: (*back*) Seamus Deane, Brian Friel, Stephen Rea; (*front*) SH, David Hammond, Tom Paulin.

20 Left to right: (*back*) Michael Longley, James Simmons, Brian Friel; (*front*) SH, John Hewitt and David Hammond, after the conferral of an Honorary Degree on SH by Queen's University, Belfast, 1982.

21 Thomas Flanagan, 1982.

22 Peter Maxwell Davies, SH, George Mackay Brown, Stromness, Orkney, in 1982.

23 SH and Paul Muldoon (as Professor of Poetry), Oxford, 23 January 2001.
(Photo: Norman McBeath)

24 Peter Fallon's wedding, January 1986, at which SH was best man. Left to right: Paul Muldoon, Brian Friel, Derek Mahon, Peter Fallon, Dillon Johnston, SH, Michael Longley.
(Photo: Courtesy of Peter Fallon)

25 SH with Czesław Miłosz.

26 SH receives Honorary Degree at Queen's University, Belfast, 1982.

27 SH and Seamus Deane, Dublin, 1994. (Photo: Alen MacWeeney)

28 SH receiving Nobel medal from King Carl XVI Gustaf, Stockholm, 10 December 1995.

29 Stamp (2004) commemorating SH's Nobel Prize in Literature.

30 Helen Vendler, Harvard, 1996.

31 Winners of the Nobel Prize in Literature at the centenary celebrations of the Nobel Prize, Stockholm, 2001. Left to right: Kenzaburo Oe, Derek Walcott, Nadine Gordimer, Günter Grass, SH.

paradoxical desire to make the medium stay itself long enough for a provisional rightness to form and be felt. Her readiness to make value judgements does alienate people in the poetry world and creates definite enmity in some factions, yet I can't think of anybody in the last forty years whose writings have created a better 'attendance', as Yeats would have called it, for the art.

Do you share what you once called 'her unorthodox wariness of the Ezra Pound / William Carlos Williams inheritance – especially the poets of Black Mountain lineage'?

I wouldn't say I'm wary of the Williams inheritance; but, as I explained earlier, my efforts to understand and become an aficionado of Charles Olson were not successful. I gave myself as good a schooling as I could in his work when I was in Berkeley in my early thirties, and that was well before I knew Helen. Charles Olson and Robert Duncan were serious, completely dedicated poets, with an elevated concept of their role, but when I think of them the image that comes to mind is of two life-size figures waving and creating this larger-than-life shadow play. There was too much gesture for my taste, and too little gist. More poetics than poetry. William Carlos Williams was a different case, since I liked the clarity and articulation very much, even though I would sometimes wonder, 'Is this all?' I loved, for example, the 'Pictures from Breughel' sequence, but was almost afraid to concede that the so-called 'poetry of a grown man' could be so open faced and child-arty.

In a radio programme to mark your sixtieth birthday, Helen Vendler said that she found 'Mycenae Lookout' – one of the central poems in The Spirit Level *– 'shocking' when she first read it. Had you shown it to her, or to others, in manuscript? Were there reactions that prompted rewriting or greater caution?*

No rewriting, no greater caution occurred. I can't remember when exactly Helen first saw it; it could have been at the manuscript stage. The shock element was in the crudity of the language in the 'Cassandra' section, the 'fuck' and the 'cunt', and in the rendering of the cruelty of that Mycenaean world. But I always had confidence in the sequence, and whatever revision I did was done without advice. Even though the poem was written after the 1994 cessation, the impulse was to give a snarl rather than sing a hymn.

Did any specific person or event provoke that mood?

Not really. It wasn't a matter of what was happening just then, more a rage at what had gone on in the previous twenty-five years. 'That killing-fest', as the poem calls it. What brought it back and crystallized it was the situation of the watchman at the beginning of the *Agamemnon*. He says he cannot speak because there's 'an ox on his tongue'. Sometime in the 1970s I'd heard the writer Alan Garner give a lecture with that same title to a conference of English teachers, and it stayed in my mind. Then, when I was reading different translations of Aeschylus, wondering if I mightn't have a go at the whole trilogy, the phrase kept developing a stronger and stronger magnetic field around itself.

Who's to say where a poem begins? There was a certain amount of book learning involved; more important was the sensory depth charge contained in the phrase itself. The splatter of cow's feet on the floor of a byre in Mossbawn, the charge of bullocks up the 'tripper' of a cattle lorry, the child's register of the weight and danger of those clattering beasts. Slaughterhouse panic. It all added the necessary irrational charge and kick-started a couplet attack on the subject. I remember coming back from the Melbourne Writers' Festival in October 1994, going upstairs to the attic a few days later and starting in with the couplets the way a construction worker starts in with a pneumatic drill. Call it a rage for order.

'Tollund', another post-IRA-ceasefire poem, is dated the previous month, September 1994. Were you actually in Jutland at that time?

The coincidence was extraordinary. The IRA announced the ceasefire on a Wednesday, the last Wednesday in August, if I'm not mistaken, and I was asked to write about it for the next weekend's *Sunday Tribune*. That same weekend I was also bound for Denmark, to do a reading in Copenhagen University, and inevitably I was remembering the visit I'd made to Jutland twenty-one years earlier, to see the Tollund Man. What happened, at any rate, was an unexpected trip to the actual bog in Tollund where the body had been found in the 1950s. My host in the English Department, Nick Rosenmeir, took this sudden notion on the Saturday afternoon, bundled his wife and Marie and myself into his car, crossed to

Jutland that evening on a ferry, put us up that night at their holiday house near Silkeborg and on the Sunday morning brought us to the actual spot where the turf cutters had dug him out.

'Hallucinatory and familiar', you called it.

That's exactly how it felt – as familiar as Toner's Bog in the townlands of Mulhollandstown and Scribe, all named in the poem. It was like a world restored, the world of the second chance, and that's why there's an echo of that Shakespearean line, 'Richard's himself again', in the last stanza. I also wanted to get in something of the dawn promise you find in that beautiful little speech at the end of the first scene of *Hamlet*: Marcellus talks about a hallowed moment in the dark of the year when 'the bird of dawning singeth all night long'. On our Sunday morning in Tollund, I felt a similar lightening of mood and opening of possibility. We were like 'ghosts who'd walked abroad / Unfazed by light, to make a new beginning / . . . Ourselves again, free-willed again, not bad'. What we were experiencing, you could say, was hope rather than optimism, and that's why I liked the complicating echo of the words 'Sinn Féin' in the phrase 'ourselves again'.

You were still sceptical?

Cautious, certainly. I knew it would be crazy to expect a great change of heart on either side.

You weren't all that surprised presumably when the IRA bombed Canary Wharf in 1996?

I was disappointed if not entirely dismayed, but I still didn't believe it was the beginning of the end. More the end of the beginning. I couldn't see things being rolled back to their pre-ceasefire state. Too many adjustments, small but significant, had been made, not just in the public arena but at the core of most people's consciousness. The collective resolution had firmed up – again, not optimistically, just more or less obstinately.

You believed, therefore, in the 'peace process'? From the start?

I was chary, from the start, of the use of the term 'process'. Peace in Northern Ireland – to begin with, at any rate – was always going to be a rigged-up, slightly rickety affair: something ad hoc and precariously in the balance, depending at once on great stealth and great boldness by individuals on both sides. There's something too foreclosed about calling it a 'process', as if all you had to do was to initiate certain movements or exchanges and the whole thing would work itself out in theory and in practice.

The fact that the Good Friday Agreement of 1998 resulted in a power-sharing executive that included both Unionists and Republicans – David Trimble and Gerry Adams – as well as constitutional nationalists must have been beyond anything foreseeable in your childhood?

Definitely. And the fact that the first executive bickered and faltered and fell was less important than the change it effected in the overall mindset. Loyalists were enraged to see Republicans holding ministries at Stormont; but, because of the long, slow, painful turn of events that had led to that eventuality, they lived with it and were very slightly changed by the experience – just as Republicans and nationalists were changed by being included, however reluctantly, in the affairs of the Northern Irish state. They became participants and created an Irish dimension in a political culture that was officially British. In the end, we arrived at a point where Sinn Féin and the DUP could, as they say, do business in the devolved assembly, which meant that Ian Paisley had to actually speak to Gerry Adams and Martin McGuinness, with unexpectedly good initial results. The population as a whole has allowed itself more hope and trust in the future, but the sectarian underlife is still there, of course.

At times of great hope or tragedy – the Ulster ceasefires, the Good Friday Agreement, the Nobel Peace Prizes for Hume and Trimble, the Omagh bombing – you have written newspaper commentaries. These were always prominently published (sometimes on the front page), so I presume they were commissioned by the editors. Did you welcome such commissions?

Short notice is the crucial factor on those occasions. You're giving an immediate response, at a moment when the adrenalin is running. I couldn't say I welcomed the commissions, but I do feel some obligation at moments like that. It's hard to find the right language, of course. You want a note of seriousness, but at the same time you don't just want orotundity. I think, however, that a poet does have a role and a responsibility. You're allowed, for example, to quote poetry – probably *expected* to quote it; in the wake of the Omagh bombing, I remember how grateful I was to invoke Wilfred Owen's line about 'the eternal reciprocity of tears'. At times like that, you realize Philip Larkin got it right when he said that 'someone will forever be surprising / A hunger in himself to be more serious'.

Your 1998 Irish Times *article about John Hume and David Trimble, after their joint Nobel Peace Prize, recalled Hume at St Columb's College in the 1950s as somebody who 'already displayed the qualities that have led him to this new eminence'. I'm wondering to what extent you kept up contact with him over the decades.*

We didn't seek each other out, although ever since the days at St Columb's there was friendship. In the sixties, John was in Derry and I was in Belfast; even then, well before he came to notice as a political leader, he was recognized as a figure of some mark and likelihood. He was involved with the credit-union movement and had started a smoked-salmon business, some sort of co-operative. Then, after things hotted up in 1968, he and I would occasionally find ourselves in the same company once again, in private and in public.

We had mutual friends in Brian and Anne Friel, so in the seventies we'd often meet in Donegal during the summer holidays. Then too, we might find ourselves at the same dinners and receptions in Dublin, and occasionally also in the States. John had been a fellow at the Kennedy School in Harvard a year or two before I first went there in 1979, so I tended to be included whenever he came to town. And he'd always be in the audience on the first night of Field Day productions in the Guildhall in Derry. I believe the last big do we attended was in the White House in 2000, on Bill Clinton's last St Patrick's Day as president.

Was that your first time in the White House?

It wasn't, no. In 1996, Hillary Clinton had hosted a lunch there for Marie and me, a small group of twelve or so people, very relaxed and personal.

But the president was not included?

Presidents are busy men. Marie and I had met him and Hillary when they visited Ireland in December 1995. Jean Kennedy Smith was American ambassador at the time and she arranged it – a private audience for about fifteen minutes in the ambassador's residence, before they all went off to a farewell dinner in Dublin Castle. It was a heady moment for everybody, the Clintons had been the darlings of the crowd in Derry and Dublin, and we were just about to go off to the ceremonies in Stockholm. Earlier in the day, the president quoted that line from *The Cure at Troy* about hope and history rhyming, so I'd brought along a handwritten copy of the stanza for him, and a copy of the published play for Hillary, inscribed with lines from the final chorus – 'Now it's high watermark / And floodtide in the heart / And time to go', and so on. So Marie and I go home and are watching the speeches from Dublin Castle on the television when suddenly Bill uses those same lines as his own peroration and farewell.

What impression did the Clintons make on you then? Did the president talk poetry or politics?

On that occasion, we talked more about people and places. I'd been to his home state of Arkansas a number of times. In fact, one of my favourite places in America happens to be a hardware shop in the town of Conway, just north of Little Rock. It turned out that he too knew the store and seemed to rate it as highly as I did. I was also able to tell him that I'd had three 'firsts' in the first half hour after I landed in Arkansas – I drove through a paddy field, I drove past a dead armadillo on the roadside, and I drove through a 'dry county'. 'Fast, I'm sure,' he retorted to this last bit of intelligence.

He's very quick, very articulate, and he talked impromptu – and well – about the themes of *The Cure at Troy* on that White House occasion. I had read the 'hope and history' chorus, and in his formal remarks the president took up the discussion with more ease and insight than you'd get from many a professor of literature. His mind and his mouth went together, if you'll excuse the expression, with the result that you came alive in his company.

Clinton was a good one, as far as I'm concerned. He was genuinely involved in the give and take of negotiations that led up to the Good Friday Agreement. Those phone calls in the middle of the night helped to screw courage to the sticking point in the principal players, and his contributions in that area were sustained and dispassionately motivated. It may have helped him with the Irish-American voter but his involvement, I believe, was not primarily a matter of vote-seeking. So it was a great pity when he entered into the Monica Lewinsky affair and gave his enemies the opportunity to ruin his second term in office. And it was also a disappointment when he issued that slew of pardons to all kinds of shady characters at the end of his presidency. Still, all in all, I'm definitely for Bill. And for his wife as well.

Nearer home, have you made many visits to the Irish presidential residence in the Phoenix Park? Would you number Mary McAleese and Mary Robinson among your friends?

I knew them both quite well before they were elected to the office and each did me the honour of inviting me to the residence. I attended Mary Robinson's inauguration in Dublin Castle and was at the reception later that day in the Phoenix Park, as were Eavan Boland and Paul Durcan. Then, on the night when I came home from Greece, after getting news of the Nobel Prize, President Robinson arranged for Marie and me and the family to come directly from the hullabaloo at the airport to a more personal welcome in the residence. But I had known Mary long before she became president. Her brother-in-law, Peter Robinson, used to have a restaurant near where we lived in Wicklow, and we were acquainted with each other at that stage. She was a barrister and a law professor and quite soon a senator representing Trinity College, so in the come and go of Dublin life we kept meeting. It was a very heartsome, cheerful, bantering kind of relationship. And still is. I really admire her gumption and her commitments.

And President McAleese? Had you known her in Belfast?

Not while I was living there, only in the 1990s, when she was prominent at Queen's University. She's a truly ardent spirit, again a law professor, with great verve and generosity – as I know from the way she talked about me in some of her speeches. During her first term of office I heard her give an address at the Kennedy School in Harvard. The formal presentation was substantial and her way with questions from the floor very swift and very certain. I'm extremely fond of her as a person, but I don't want to give the impression that I'm in and out of the Phoenix Park every other day. Over the years, I've been there on four or five occasions.

You celebrated the achievements of two other women, artists both, in The Spirit Level: *Carolyn Mulholland and someone you've mentioned earlier, Sonja Landweer, the Dutch-born ceramicist and sculptor.*

We knew Carolyn when she was an art student in Belfast; in 1967 or 1968 she did a head of me, a straightforward classical bust that has stood the test of time and has been in the house ever since. I've written the occasional note on her work and opened a couple of exhibitions. To begin with, she was best known for her portrait heads, but then the commissions started to come in for public pieces. The poem ' "Poet's Chair" ' is a response to one of them, a bronze chair with sprouting leaves she made for a little courtyard at the foot of George's Street in Dublin. Unfortunately, the leaves proved too easy to pluck, too vulnerable to the vandals, so the sculpture had to be removed. Still, it was a lovely conception. I don't believe Carolyn was thinking of Derek Mahon's poem 'Nostalgias', although she could well have been: 'The chair squeaks in a high wind, / Rain falls from its branches'.

Were you yourself thinking of 'Nostalgias' when you wrote ' "Poet's Chair" '?

No way. If I had been, I couldn't have written anything. As it was, I did the first version of ' "Poet's Chair" ' quickly, to be read out at an exhibition of Carolyn's work that I had agreed to launch. I was thinking about sculpture in a public setting, how it might centre the world for you, so the poem started from there. And from something in Leonardo's notebooks that's quoted in the opening lines: 'The sun has never seen a shadow.'

Any memories, by the way, of sitting for the head she made?

The sound of the clay being slapped, the shine of it, the dampening of it with water every now and again. I loved looking and listening as she worked. It made you want to regress to the puddle-and-plasticine stage of childhood. This was before any moulding of the features began. She rolled these little sausage shapes of clay in her hands and plumped and patted them round the armature to build up the bulk of the head. I also enjoyed having my measure taken by the calipers, the sharp steel points of the instrument just tipping your temples or your cheeks or your chin. There was something surprising about those cold, strict touches, a reminder that you weren't all inwardness, that your head was shape as well as source.

'To a Dutch Potter in Ireland', the poem dedicated to Sonja Landweer, incorporates images from the Second World War. Are they connected to her life and art?

Sonja's father was actually shot by the Nazis as they retreated from the Netherlands at the end of the war. One night, years ago in Thomastown, when we were visiting her and Barrie Cooke, she talked about the savagery of that moment. But she also talked about a marvellous thing that used to happen in her childhood, when the waters of the North Sea sometimes got luminous with plankton: she would go swimming and then come splashing out along the shore with the gleam of the stuff all over her body. 'A nymph of phosphor by the Norder Zee', as the poem calls her.

Sonja was marked by the cruelty and evil of what happened to her father, but also by the beauty and marvel of what happened to her on that shore, so she has a profound sense of what is at stake in the making of art. She could repeat with Coleridge that the artistic act is a repetition in the temporal sphere of the eternal 'I am'. She has fierce conviction about the value and necessity of good and beautiful work – as well as a horror of work where she detects the spirit of nihilism. She lives at a high spiritual pitch, so I tend to connect that personal strength and integrity with the steadiness and rightness of the forms she fires. That's why there's a line about 'the gates of horn behind the gates of clay' – in the myth of the gates, true dreams come through the horn and false ones through the ivory. Virgil tells us that.

The war imagery in the poem seems influenced also by wars in our own time.

Very strongly influenced. I was writing just after the first Gulf War, when the oil wells were burning in the desert, like an infernal contradiction to all that Sonja understood herself to be doing. She once called the work of glazing 'bringing down the sun' – because the silicates in the grass and glass and ash have been derived originally from the solar light. The phrase gave a slightly angelic aspect to her ceramics, and suggested 'bringing up the earth' as a complementary description of her modelling in clay. And the diabolic opposite of bringing up the earth is bringing it down, which is how I regarded the firing of the wells. That's the kind of association that was going on. Around about that same time, I'd done a version of J. C. Bloem's 'After Liberation', a poem which is partly his act of thanksgiving for the ending of the war in Europe and partly an act of faith in the ultimate prevalence of life over death. And since all this was getting written and published just as movement towards an IRA ceasefire was becoming perceptible, there was a sense that our own 'liberation' was imminent.

You have increasingly returned to the period of the Second World War – most recently in several poems in District and Circle. *It had already been recalled in your Nobel lecture and in* The Spirit Level – *not just in the Dutch potter poem, but indirectly also in* 'A Sofa in the Forties'.

It's a matter of coming to terms with reality. A matter of things once taken for granted being granted too casually their sombre significance. When I was a youngster, for example, there would be gas masks lying around in sheds and cupboards – not at Mossbawn, I should say, but in my grandparents' place in Castledawson – and we'd often put them on, to act the monster and scare ourselves. There were also blackout blinds, always pulled down at night. There were the ration books. There were the aeroplanes and the aerodrome and the soldiers stationed there. There were also eventually German prisoners on the aerodrome who were let out to visit local homes on Sunday afternoons – although that may have been after the armistice.

Do you remember the armistice?

Not at all. But I remember the aerodrome, because it was a sort of forbidden zone, fenced off with barbed wire and built over with runways and hangars and Nissen huts; at the same time there was a touch of wonderland about it, what with the planes coming in and rising up and the pilots and ground staff all in uniform. Menace and marvel equally in the air.

Would there have been a marked difference of attitude to the war among local Protestant and Catholic communities?

It would have varied from family to family, I have no doubt. Among the Protestants, I'd assume there was total solidarity and support for the Allies, because of a staunch loyalty to the Union Jack. Many of them would have joined up, like the Evans brothers from our own district. But on the Catholic side it would have depended on the degree of education in the household, or perhaps better say on the degree of ignorance and political disaffection. Families with strong Republican or IRA connections would not have been in favour of Churchill; my own memories suggest that Lord Haw Haw wasn't altogether demonized among some people I knew – and they were by no means rabid Republicans. Even if Haw Haw provided a lot of clandestine amusement, the dread was of the Germans; they were the enemy in earnest, and all over the country there were evacuees from the blitz in Belfast to prove it.

In an essay on Seeing Things, *Darcy O'Brien recalls a visit to your family in Derry, during which 'I met an aunt who had loved a German prisoner of war'. Was Mary the aunt in question?*

No, it was my aunt Jenny, a sister of my mother's who lived with her aged aunt in Broagh. She was younger than my mother and single, so I suppose she welcomed the visits of the POWs. Towards the end of the war, as I said, some of them would be let out on Sunday afternoons to call on local houses. They used to bring presents, things they'd made in their spare time, maybe as part of some occupational therapy regime, little Alpine scenes modelled in plaster, fitted into bulbs ... After the war, you'd find them on mantelpieces all over the country. Anyhow, one or two of these guys came to Jenny's place a few times, and I used to see them passing as they walked along the railway lines – which is why that POW appears in the 'Visitant' section of *Stations*. But Darcy was going too far with 'loved'. It would have been more a case of romantic giggles and flutters than a fully fledged affair of the heart.

When you write about your wartime childhood in your Nobel speech and in 'A Sofa in the Forties', the radio seems absolutely central. Can you describe the family wireless?

We were dependent on batteries, a dry dispensable one and a wet one that was forever being taken to Castledawson for recharging. Our set was a Cossor and relatively small in comparison with some others in the district: baize fabric covering the speaker; a white dial with black and red lettering showing the stations; and a single ominous dial hand, delicately fitted, sharp and sweeping. There was a thrill of omnipotence almost when you twirled the knob and watched the hand roam over Düsseldorf and Warsaw and Stockholm and Stuttgart and all the rest.

You spent a long time staring at that dial?

I was entranced by it. But just as often I had my ear to the baize, since there was a lot of competing noise in our kitchen and you had to get close to the speaker, especially when the batteries were running down. Mostly I'd be glued to the Dick Barton detective serial on BBC. There also used to be a 'Children's Hour' at five o'clock, where they'd have dramatizations of Captain W. E. Johns's Biggles stories. I hadn't much interest in the other Children's Hour stuff – apart from the voice of Larry the Lamb in *Toytown*.

Which programmes held the adults' interest?

The news, from both BBC and Athlone (as they called Radio Éireann in those days). Mícheál O'Hehir's commentaries on football matches in Croke Park. The Grand National. *The Billy Cotton Bandshow* on BBC's Light Programme, so-called to distinguish it from the heavyweight Third and the middleweight Home Service. There was also a feature called *The Family Doctor* and a midday outside broadcast called *Workers' Playtime*, with smutty comedians doing their thing in factory canteens the length and breadth of middle England. *Workers' Playtime* either preceded or followed the midday news, so it was overheard rather than listened to, there to be deplored really, an example of how low the Sassenachs would sink.

A radio announcer is heard in 'A Sofa in the Forties'. Any chance of a description of the sofa itself?

It had the air of something that had been in place from the beginning: a case of *in principio erat sofa*. It was big, it was solid and elegantly shaped, and seemed immovable. Upholstered very simply in black leatherette, but there was still a touch of grandeur about it.

The main thing was the size: about six feet from one curved arm to the other, so we could all fit on to it side by side. Sometimes we'd be lined up, our legs dangling over the edge, for 'question time'. The grown-ups would proceed to ask us questions in turn – one each per round, and not very testing: 'What colour is grass?' 'What do you call our dog?' 'Where does Granny McCann live?' At other times we'd pretend we were on a train or a bus, and kneel up on the seat with our backs to one end and our faces to the other, imitating the sounds of a steam engine or the gear changes on a bus. The 'children's house of make believe', as Frost says.

Why does 'Directive', the Frost poem you cite, speak so profoundly to you? When you discuss it in the introduction to The Redress of Poetry, *it becomes a kind of* ars poetica.

It's a quest poem and what the speaker finds at the end is something that used to be found in the yard or garden of any house where there were children: an imitation kitchen, with an old board for a dresser, and broken bits of delft for a tea set, and a block of timber for a chair, and so on, and you'd have a little girl miming the boiling of a kettle on a stove or the pouring out of tea into a cup. 'Playing wee house', we used to call it. Frost suggests that playing wee house is a form of art, insofar as it answers and redresses the goings on in 'the house in earnest' on the other side of the yard.

For me, the poem has two kinds of appeal, one entirely irrational, to do with the memories it conjures up of those secret, fetid corners full of shards and junk where we'd congregate in a little half-sexual huddle and scrum; but there's also an invitation to make a fable of the story, as Edwin Muir might have said, to attend to the abstracting, allegorical strain in the presentation of the material. As a matter of fact, my one unease about 'Directive' is the ending, where Frost has such a palpable design on you he pushes past allegory into uplift. I want to love the last line, but something tells me to resist it: 'Drink and be whole again beyond confusion.'

'Two Lorries' is the only sestina you have produced, I believe. Does that mean you found the form restrictive?

On the contrary, it got me on the move. I'd started off as usual with an image that had been with me a lifetime – a coalman delivering bags of coal in our back yard at Mossbawn. So I set down the description of that scene in six lines, and then just stalled. The material was still exerting pressure, but the signal had jammed. I remember sitting at the end of the table in Glanmore, big with the poem but at the same time balked of it, and then suddenly thinking of Elizabeth Bishop's 'Sestina', whipping her book down off the shelf and going for it head-on, letting the repeated end-words take me wherever they wanted. Ultimately, they brought me forward from the 1940s to the 1980s, from a lorry delivering coal to one delivering a proxy bomb in Magherafelt.

In the poem, you tell how the bus station in Magherafelt was blown to dust and ashes by the bomb. Had the building strong emotional associations for you?

Magherafelt was only four miles or so from home in those days, but my mother occasionally did a special shopping there, and going on the bus was a bit of an adventure – the Magherafelt via Toomebridge one that's mentioned in the poem. I spent a good bit of time with her in that waiting room, a stark cell that was hard to forget, nothing but a concrete floor and benches round the four walls. The time I remember most, however, was a little later on, at Hallowe'en in 1951, when I was on my way home from St Columb's for my first mid-term break. There was a private bus that took the south Derry boarders as far as Magherafelt; when I arrived, I found my mother in the waiting room, there for the 'service bus' that I too had to catch for the last bit of the journey. At the time, I thought it was just a coincidence, but in later years I realized she must have planned it, in order to be first to see me and to have that little while on our own together.

There is a clear link between 'An Invocation', your poem to Hugh MacDiarmid, and your Oxford Professor of Poetry lecture on his work.

When I was reading for the MacDiarmid lecture, I found myself admiring the man most when he was *in extremis*, emotionally and creatively and financially, during the short period he spent on the Shetlands in the early thirties. The poem is really a gloss on the prose, done in those four-by-three units that became a habit when I was writing 'Squarings'. The core image was of MacDiarmid's big round brow, like the earth-globe sloping away up north of him towards the Arctic. And there are various allusions to his work – to 'Stony Limits', 'On a Raised Beach', 'The Stormcock' – and even an allusion to something I'd written about him twenty years earlier in a review, where I said there was a touch of MacGonagall about his verbosity.

A 'blathering genius', you called him. Is he a poet you return to?

More one who looms in the background. He's the least read, least acknowledged of the twentieth-century modernists. Or maybe it would be better to say 'moderns', since there's so much that's traditional and romantic about him – the cultural nationalism, the scorn of the metropolitan culture and so on. Even there you have contradiction, what with his admiration for the Joycean in language and the Marxian in politics, the hankering after worldwide liberations and discourses and intercourses, all seemingly at odds with his devotion to what is recalcitrantly local in vernacular Scots and Scots Gaelic, the working class of Glasgow and the fishermen of the Shetlands. That urge to be 'whaur extremes meet', as he puts it, appeals to me. He too 'grew up in between'. I often think the warning issued by one of the characters in Brian Friel's *Translations* applies to MacDiarmid: 'To remember everything', Hugh O'Donnell tells his son, 'is a form of madness.' But it's a form of madness that Friel's play implicitly endorses and that Joyce too endorses, all part of the imagination's *odi et amo*. And it's what produced a masterpiece like *A Drunk Man Looks at the Thistle*.

In your Oxford lecture you said, 'He prepared the ground for a Scottish literature that would be self-critical and experimental in relation to its own inherited forms and idioms, but one that would also be stimulated by developments elsewhere in world literature.'

MacDiarmid's ambitions are still the right ones. What was great about his effort in Scotland was the inclusiveness of it. He was as formative of present-day literary culture in his country as Yeats and Joyce were in ours, but he paid far more heed to the Gaelic element than either of our geniuses ever bothered to. You could argue, in fact, that Sorley Maclean, the saviour of Scots Gaelic poetry in modern times, owed a lot of his conviction to MacDiarmid's personal encouragement and example.

Is it true that MacDiarmid, when you first met him, told you your poems were too short?

True, yes. At a party in Kader Asmal's house in December 1967, before a big anti-apartheid reading he'd organized in Liberty Hall to mark Human Rights Day. MacDiarmid was the chief reader and was in very sprightly form altogether: Marie remembers him more or less hunting her round the table, telling her how good she looked in her condition (she was pregnant at the time), and I remember him telling me not that my poems were 'too short' but that they were 'very short'. I suppose the odds is the difference.

After that first meeting, I saw him and Valda occasionally in Garech Browne's house at Luggala, during the time when he was recording his poems for Claddagh – the Claddagh company, incidentally, issued the whole of *A Drunk Man* on two long-playing discs. The most memorable occasion was in 1977 when David Hammond and I visited Valda and him in the cottage in Biggar. We went out on the bus with Trevor Royle, who was working for the Scottish Arts Council at the time, and spent the afternoon discussing poetry and drinking whiskey. He was still recognizably the man who had written the poems and produced the polemic, you could hear the old dynamo throbbing away, although by then he was well into his eighties, 'the old vigilante / Of the chimney corner', as he's called in the poem. I loved the fact that I was talking to a great poet who spoke what they'd call in Ulster Scots 'the hamely tongue'. There he was beside the hob, smoking his pipe and saying 'aye, aye, aye' to himself, for all the world like one of my father's cousins in Ballyscullion.

But in spite of that personal contact, I grew into a far greater awareness of his importance after he died, through my friendship with Patrick Crotty, whose doctoral work was on MacDiarmid. He actually spent a lot of his research time in Edinburgh in the 1970s and was friends with Chris, as he tends to call MacDiarmid, and has many stories of the Scottish milieu – or perhaps I should say mêlée. He likes to quote Edwin Muir, for example, who once described himself as a man 'acquainted with Grieve' – MacDiarmid's prepseudonymous family name. Patrick is his best advocate and understands his strictly poetic importance as well as his significance for Scottish politics and culture. He can read MacDiarmid as an event in language, because he is one of those rare people who is passionately devoted to poetry in and for itself. Somebody whose response I value to my own work in progress.

Were you ever tempted to try writing something entirely in Derry dialect, synthetic Ulsterese, as it were, in imitation of MacDiarmid's synthetic Scots?

Never. On the other hand, I'd say that a lot of my poems, from 'Digging' in my first book to 'Anahorish 1944' in *District and Circle*, are tuned to an Ulsterese register. And there's certainly a hidden Scotland at the back of my ear, the Ulster Scots idiom I used to hear from County Antrim farmers at the cattle fairs in Ballymena.

You once mentioned a personal connection with MacDiarmid's work through his use of 'jing-bang' – a term which you had learned from your mother. Did you inherit more dialect vocabulary from her than from your father?

Not really. What I got from my father was the idiom of the cattlemen. He would call a worthless character a 'guinea-hunter', and say he could 'cut a better man out of the hedge'. But two terms of abuse that used to be applied to him by a wild old neighbour called George Shivers have a definite historical interest. Old Shivers was forever giving my father hell in a good-natured sort of way, calling him names, calling him among other things 'a gull' and 'a kerne'. Pure Elizabethan. Still there, three centuries and more after the Planters landed. But truth to tell, that kind of exoticism was scarce enough and I can't really remember where the different Ulsterisms and Irishisms came from. 'Jing-bang' is an exception. And 'lachtar', which my aunt Mary used in its original Irish sense of a setting of eggs or a flock of day-old chicks.

'Forcibleness' is a quality you have attributed to Hugh MacDiarmid and also to Christopher Marlowe. Do you see 'forcibleness' – Sir Philip Sidney's translation of the Greek energeia – as a litmus test of true poetry?

It's certainly what sets the seal of inevitability on much of the best writing. It's 'the force that through the green fuse drives the flower'. The attribute that makes you feel the lines have been decreed, that there has been no fussy picking and choosing of words but instead a surge of utterance.

'Postscript', the final poem in The Spirit Level, *strikes me as just such a 'surge of utterance', a single burst of inspiration. Was that how it seemed at the time?*

It was written quickly, yes, and I believe I sent it off almost immediately to the *Irish Times*. It could have been given a long Wordsworthian title, something like, 'Memorial of a Tour by Motorcar with Friends in the West of Ireland', but that would misrepresent the sudden, speedy feel of it. Now and again a poem comes like that, like a ball kicked in from nowhere: in this case, I was completely absorbed in writing one of the last of the Oxford lectures when I had this quick sidelong glimpse of something flying past; before I knew where I was, I went after it. It came from remembering a windy Saturday afternoon when Marie and I drove with Brian and Anne Friel along the south coast of Galway Bay. We had stopped to look at Mount Vernon, Lady Gregory's summer house – still there, facing the waters and the wild; then we drove on into this glorious exultation of air and sea and swans. There are some poems that feel like guarantees of your work to yourself. They leave you with a sensation of having been visited, and this was one of them. It excited me, and yet publishing it in the *Irish Times* was, as much as anything else, a way of sending a holiday postcard – a PS of sorts – to the Friels.

'Ballynahinch Lake' in Electric Light *seems to have been conceived as a companion piece to 'Postscript'. The lines declaring 'that this time, yes, it had indeed / Been useful to stop' seem in dialogue with the earlier poem's 'Useless to think you'll park and capture it / More thoroughly'.*

All true. Again, the second poem was written very soon after the experience it records – a Sunday morning in Connemara when we parked beside 'the utter mountain mirrored in the lake'. I suppose the poem is saying 'find the mortal world enough' – something that 'Postscript' would find difficult to agree with.

A blind musician, Rosie Keenan, is mentioned in 'At the Wellhead'. What made this neighbour so special to you?

The blindness itself was the wonder. The Keenans lived only a couple of fields away from us, in the country equivalent of 'the next block'. Rosie would often be out on the road, sometimes on her own, sometimes with her sister. This was the Broagh Road, a side road, and in those days the traffic amounted to no more than a few locals on bicycles and the occasional horse and cart, so she was safe enough, walking tall and straight, her white stick in hand, her pale face looking straight ahead, unwavering and unseeing. She came home for the school holidays – she worked in Belfast, in some capacity in a school for the blind. When I first knew her she would have been in her late thirties or early forties, a contemporary of my mother's, who had been at school with her. So there was great ease between them and always a special sweet atmosphere when she came to the house.

Were you and your siblings pressed into service as her guides?

We were not. The pressure was to perform for her, to sing a school song or say a school poem. She would often bring her violin because my mother loved her to play and sing: Irish dance tunes mostly, jigs and reels. Thomas Moore songs. So her visit would turn into a little home concert. She made that musical dimension a living thing for us. She also had a piano at home and, in the middle of the day, we'd often hear her playing as we passed by Keenans' house – which I always found strange, because in our experience the daytime was when grown-ups were out working. But as the years have gone by, I've begun to think of her as the one who first made time and space in our lives for art. Our Blind Rosie, like Blind Raftery, '*ag seinm ceoil do phócaí folamh*' – 'playing music to empty pockets'.

You had no musical instruments in your own house?

Not in Mossbawn. When the new house was built in Bellaghy, a second-hand piano arrived in the sitting room and I made a shot at teaching myself a couple of old-time waltzes, but never managed to get very far. At that stage I was at St Columb's, and then at Queen's, so no lessons were ever contemplated. I think the piano would have been mostly regarded as significant furniture in the new house, something that would come into play when people assembled for a party.

367

Is it true you had a yearning for a harmonica when you were young?

True, and happily I did acquire one relatively early: a mouth organ. They used to be commonly available in newsagents' shops in country towns, most of them made by a firm called Hohner. Different makes and registers, with names like 'Echo' and 'Regulation Band'. Eventually I graduated to the higher class of instrument, the one with the little device that you worked with your thumb in order to vamp and get the half notes.

Does music remain an important part of your life?

Not as much as I'd wish it to. If I had life to live over again, I'd make more time for concerts. Early on at Queen's, I did have an entrée to that culture of chamber concerts and symphony concerts, and kept up attendance for some years afterwards. I lapsed, I'm afraid, when the focus changed to poetry and the locus to pubs.

You've said that the interludes of orchestral music and song gave the Nobel ceremony in Stockholm in 1995 a special elevation.

On the Sunday morning of the awards ceremony, I had to see a doctor for a prescription to rid me of flu symptoms. I was throbbing with anxiety as well as excitement that day. Dry mouthed and hot browed. The one time I gathered myself was during those intervals for music, between the citations for prizewinners in the different categories: Medicine, Chemistry, Physics, Economics, Literature. We were all there on the stage of the concert hall, with the king and queen and the young princess downstage. Every fifteen minutes or so – after the litanies of praise had been recited in those low-key, slightly mournful Swedish voices, after the tumult of applause when the king handed over the medal and the parchment – there would be a moment's silence, then the transport of a Mozart aria or a Handel fanfare. The sense of occasion was already high but the orchestra and the sopranos bore it even further aloft. I was in a strange state that day; the music made sense of it, trans-sensed it, if you like.

At the time of the Nobel announcement in October 1995, President Mary Robinson said, 'I hope this prize will be a joy to you and will not become a burden.' How did it work out: how much joy, how much burden?

368

Joy to start with, certainly, then a gradual burdening. The mail, for example, hasn't lightened and the requests to help good causes are probably on the increase. But when the news came there was as much shock as anything else. We were already on a high of sorts, halfway through a holiday in Greece, set up in a little hotel just a couple of hundred yards from the harbour in Pylos, away down in the south-west corner of the Peloponnese. Marie and myself and Cynthia and Dimitri Hadzi.

Your first trip to Greece, I think.

It was. Long promised, long deferred, but finally it had become inevitable. I'd done the first Sophocles translation five years before and had just published a limited edition that included the 'Mycenae Lookout' sequence, with art work by Dimitri. I'd got to know the Hadzis in Harvard, where they were both attached to the Carpenter Center for the Arts. Being Greek-American, Dimitri spoke some modern Greek; and being a sculptor in stone and bronze, he was an ideal guide to the sites. Cynthia had travelled the route with Dimitri several times before – Ancient Corinth, Mycenae, Epidauros, Arcadia, Sparta – so she was our driver. At any rate, after the news reached us, we had a crucial half-day to ourselves, in a place where nobody knew us. One of the happiest moments of the whole affair was a celebration that night – squid and chips at an outside table on the harbour front. Between trawlers and tavernas. Starlight and electric light reflecting in the water. I felt as strange there as Telemachus must have felt. But Telemachus was about to get some guidance from wise old Nestor whereas there's no instructor to tell you how to handle the bounty of Sweden.

You didn't plan to be out of media reach, just in case the Swedish Academy decided it was your turn? The annual announcement is made in early October.

The announcement is made in early October, right enough, and a couple of times in previous years my name had turned up in the annual gossip, but that only made me try to banish the whole thing from my mind. Our kids, for example, used to wince if anybody made the slightest reference to the topic. I couldn't miss hearing the rumours, but I did my best not to allow myself even to think about it. Consider, for a start, all the writers who did not get the Nobel Prize: you would have to be pretty self-satisfied to list yourself in that company, never mind the company of ones who *did* get it. Nobody in their right mind would ever start casting themselves for a walk-on part in Stockholm. The Greek holiday was never planned to coincide with the announcement. If it had been, I wouldn't, for God's sake, have waited a day and a half to ring home. The news conference takes place at noon on the Thursday and it was Friday afternoon before I heard.

Your son Christopher was the one who broke the news to you. Did he assume you knew already?

He did. With all the hullabaloo going on around him in the house, he would have found it difficult to imagine the remoteness of Pylos. I'd spent the Friday morning on the small whitewashed balcony of our hotel room, writing a letter to a former student of mine: Sarah Ruden had studied classics at Harvard and been in one of my poetry workshops; she published a small book of poems dedicated to me, but – as usual – my acknowledgement and response were long overdue. Afterwards, I went with the letter to the post office and then had lunch with the others, as arranged, at the restaurant we would return to that evening. Sat totally relaxed on the quay, watching the little barbounia fish scooting about in the water.

Eventually we went back up to the hotel. I had a bath and a change of clothes; at that point, I thought I should ring Dublin, since Christopher might have got in from the language school where he was teaching. Sure enough, he answered the phone and immediately said, 'Dad, we're so proud of you.' And because he realized the greeting puzzled me, he said next, 'Have you heard the news?' 'What news?' 'You've won the Nobel Prize.' So I say to him, 'You'd better tell your mother,' and get Marie to the phone.

The Harvard Review *published a photograph of you on the phone, taken that afternoon by Dimitri Hadzi.*

That's how the shock affected me: after I spoke to Christopher, I spent hours on the phone, trying to contact people at home and friends all over the place, in Ireland and America. I was in a sweat, literally and figuratively. I couldn't think clearly, because suddenly there were a dozen things to be done. Dimitri took another photo of me, for example, out on the little whitewashed balcony, writing out a statement that Faber needed for the press. And the Swedish Academy had to be contacted. And champagne had to be drunk. It wasn't all bad.

Can you tell me something about your flight back, the welcome you received on arrival in Dublin, the receptions, official and unofficial?

It was all quite public and there was no time to think. The Taoiseach on the tarmac at the airport, family and friends hustled to the VIP lounge, then the limo to the president's house. Everything just happened, hurry, hurry, hurry, one thing after another. For weeks you woke up with the pressure of things to do and went to bed exhausted. You had a feeling the world was pressing its nose to your window. From the minute I phoned that Friday afternoon, it was a matter of decision, decision, decision: which interview you should or should not give, whom to invite to what event, how to get time to write the Nobel lecture, how to answer the hundreds of letters. I promised, for example, to do the first interview with RTE; but that evening on the quayside a television crew came sidling up, just as we were finishing our coffee – a local Greek station that I couldn't very well send packing.

So they were the first you spoke to?

Yes, but I asked them not to use the footage, such as it was, until later the next day, when I'd have talked to Irish television, and they honoured that. One of the first things I'd had to do was contact the Irish embassy in Athens. I had the presence of mind not to give the hotel name or phone number to anybody except the family, but Christopher had a string of people I was meant to ring, including Tommy Gorman, RTE's man in Europe. Tommy was by then on the spot in Athens, ready to fly anywhere in a hired helicopter, so I told him that we'd be at Kalamata airport the next morning, the Saturday, at nine o'clock, packed and ready to go back to Athens in time for the Olympic Airlines flight.

And that's what happened. Not much sleep that night, of course, some reporters from the Greek newspapers already in the hotel dining room at breakfast. Tommy was at Kalamata, the helicopter was on the tarmac and – after I'd done the interview at an outdoor café in the town – all five of us were airlifted to Athens. I was in front, in the glass bubble, too close for comfort to those razor-edged mountains of the Peloponnese, not enjoying it at all until we got to the east coast and the pilot dipped down and circled a couple of times above the theatre at Epidauros – where we'd visited a few days earlier. It was an unforgettable end to a journey that had started with another marvellous omen the previous Wednesday. That day, up in the mountains between Argos and Sparta, we turned a corner and found the road covered with apples that we couldn't help driving over. One or two crates must have fallen off a lorry, but at the time they appeared like the bounty of Ceres.

Samuel Beckett's wife regarded her husband's Nobel Prize as a catastrophic intrusion into a very private life. I'm wondering how drastically – if not catastrophically – your own privacy has been affected by your rising fame since 1995.

What I've said before, only half in joke, is that everybody in Ireland is famous. Or, maybe better say everybody is familiar. Since I was a schoolboy, I've been used to being recognized on the road by old and young, and being bantered with and indeed being taunted. And since I published my first book I've been used not only to a certain amount of recognition but also to a certain amount of resentment. You just conduct yourself as best you can in the circumstances. I've always taken people as they come, tried to be courteous but to keep my distance from shits and sycophants. I can only hope that the carriage I've learned stood me in good stead when the spotlight turned on me.

Speaking of resentment, there were some dissenting voices and some begrudging ones at the time of the Nobel announcement, although it must be said that they were vastly outnumbered by laudatory voices.

Only an idiot would expect to receive the Nobel Prize and not take stick of some sort. Every choice is going to be contested, and I was familiar enough with the literary ground to know the kind of objection that would be raised and where it would come from. Still, I count myself lucky that the most notorious attack came at home, from somebody who was guaranteed to wreck the consensus: Eamon Dunphy, a *Sunday Independent* columnist with a reputation for stirring things up, who would have been funking his role if he hadn't targeted me. Even at the time, however, I realized he was unwittingly doing me a service. He queered the pitch for stealthier people capable of more informed criticism. It was unwelcome stuff but not difficult to live with. It even gave me extra status with the barber and the barmen, to have featured like that. In the land of taunt and banter, it's always better to take a few hits.

Nobel Prize laureates sometimes fear they will never write another word. What in fact was your first post-Nobel poem?

A very short one, but no less important for that reason. I was asked to do a tribute to Norman MacCaig, and all of a sudden I remembered an image from the Norman writer Giraldus Cambrensis and came up with 'A Norman Simile': 'To be marvellously yourself, like the river water / Gerald of Wales says runs in Arklow harbour / Even at high tide when you'd expect salt water'. The muses were instructing me, I thought, to be myself, not to go with public expectations of something oceanic and tidal and super-Nobelish, but to stay fresh and true to the old channels.

A few years after receiving the prize, you said to an interviewer: 'You need access to a complete attic life of stillness and concentrated solitude but equal access to an energized social life.' A famous writer will find it much easier to gain access to the social life than to the solitude. Is it a source of great frustration that your work is continually interrupted by book launches and dinner parties and interviews and readings?

What frustrates me most is the gall of people who press you to do a book launch or go to a dinner party or give a reading – and then tell you that you ought not do so many book launches or dinners or whatever. You quickly realize that almost everyone considers himself or herself the exception. Your real friends leave you alone, so you end up doing less for them than for others. On the other hand, my job as a teacher in schools and colleges and universities has always involved things like references and conferences and readings and schools visits. For better or worse, I was never a person who preserved myself for my writing. In fact, I do believe that your vocation puts you in line for a certain amount of community service, so to speak.

But there's a limit; and, in the past fifteen or twenty years, even before the whole upping of the pressure caused by the Nobel Prize, I've had to decline and avoid and weave my way past an increasing number of requests. Which is why our cottage in Wicklow became the absolute haven. Once I get down there, it's as if I'm connected up to all the old terminals, and disconnected from every messaging device the executive and professional world has ever invented.

Do you think the 'celebrity' culture we inhabit saps the energy of a poet, so that the capacity to engage in multiple cultural activities, such as Yeats managed, no longer exists?

What's required, in Yeats's time or at any time, is scepticism and stamina. There's no guarantee that husbandry of the private self is going to be all that productive either – Larkin was hardly a socialite, even if he enjoyed huge celebrity, but he still ground to a poetic halt in his sixties. Yeats, on the other hand, was no slouch when it came to the dinner-party scene or the lecture circuit or even – late in life – the broadcasting studio; but the old boy kept the mills grinding to the end. Four women at his deathbed. And two poems in the last two weeks.

'So deeper into it'
Electric Light, District and Circle

∼

*I understand that 'Audenesque', in memory of Joseph Brodsky,
was among the first poems you wrote after your Nobel Prize. I'd
be interested to know the wheres, whens and hows of that poem.*

When I started going *tumti, tumti, tumti, tum*, I was relying on
Joseph's sense of humour as well as his reverence for W. H. Auden.
The best-known section of Auden's elegy for Yeats begins 'Earth,
receive an honoured guest; / William Yeats is laid to rest'. I just
took up the tune: 'Joseph, yes, you know the beat. / Wystan
Auden's metric feet / Marched to it, unstressed and stressed, /
Laying William Yeats to rest'.

Joseph was a stickler for form and had echoed that Auden metre
in his elegy for T. S. Eliot; but even *he* might have balked at my
'Trochee, trochee, falling: thus . . .' The fact that Joseph died on
28 January, the same date as Yeats, was a powerful prompt,
although the poem was begun only after I got stuck on a prose trib-
ute for the *New York Times*. Eugenio Montale once said that a per-
son might face the gallows whistling a few bars of 'Funiculi,
funicula', so the jaunty metre was that sort of gallows whistle.

I'd actually seen Joseph in America three weeks earlier. Marie and I
were over for the New York opening of Brian Friel's *Molly Sweeney*,
during what turned out to be one of the worst blizzards in years.
Manhattan came to a standstill on the night, drifts of snow in the
avenues, no traffic, not even a taxi. The next day, when things had
eased a bit, Joseph made the trek in from Brooklyn to the Union
Square Café, where we were having lunch with Roger Straus and
Jonathan Galassi. He looked awful, stooped, pale, out of breath, still

smoking, and we knew, of course, that his heart condition was very bad: he couldn't settle at the table, just kept coming in and out between cigarettes. It was valiant and typical of him to turn up to greet us, and it was the last time we were to see him.

So the news of his death wasn't unexpected?

I couldn't say that. Even though I knew he was living under a threat, even though I knew he'd had several bypass operations and had seen with my own eyes the state he was in, something in me just refused to consider his death an imminent possibility. I felt suddenly bereft when the phone call came that Sunday. Knocked about to the extent that I began writing those stanzas immediately. Until then, I would have had a resistance to 'extempore effusion', would have tended to regard such a prompt verse tribute as a form of bad taste. But in Joseph's case, something just needed to get into words. I felt I owed him.

Owed him?

Joseph was a kind of poetry samurai, totally alert, totally trained in his art, a bit of a dazzler and a bit of a danger. Before he arrived in the West, we'd heard of his trial and his defiance of the Soviet authorities, and regarded these things as the boy-deeds of a poetry hero. Then he comes among us, sponsored by W. H. Auden, considered by Akhmatova a worthy successor to her own great Russian generation, full of a trust in poetry and an unashamedness about it that was Delphic and not a little dismaying to the ironists and dandies of Anglophonia. Yet my first impression of him, at the Poetry International festival in London in 1972, was of a slight, somewhat nervous fellow about my own age, shooting the half-tentative, half-suspicious glances that any young poet shoots at a big-deal poetry reading – the kind of glances I was probably shooting myself. We took note of each other, I know, since at that time a Belfast address gave any traveller a certain radical chic; then the following spring we met properly and talked very eagerly at a poetry event in Massachusetts. Joseph had a combination of obliquity and strictness and humour that was very Ulster, so we got on immediately. Soon after that we saw each other again a couple of times in Ann Arbor and the fondness turned into friendship, a friendship that fortified poetry for me, and me for poetry. Which is why I felt a bigger than usual debt. And loss.

Did anything he said to you personally, or which you discovered
in his writings, serve you – the way Czesław Miłosz served
you – with a principle or precept to live by?

I don't think so. Miłosz was a sage as well as an artist, his presence
and his poetry had a soothsaying effect. Joseph tended to be more
like a star, an exhilaration, a transformer. The pace quickened
when he entered a company, the bar was raised, the daring
increased, the feats became more spectacular. He was a tonic, an
'upper' for the poet part of you.

Did you never find him overwhelming or overbearing? Miłosz
spoke of a 'towering arrogance to which I have been witness on
many occasions'.

He was indeed arrogant, but often – not always, I admit – it was on
behalf of ideas or standards. His 'plane of regard', as he would
have called it, was truly elevated. To a large extent his conduct was
regulated by his belief in a hierarchy of mind and spirit, something
that Miłosz also remarked upon and admired. Stupidity made him
angry, with the result that he didn't suffer fools gladly. I suppose all
of us rebuke ourselves now and again for doing just that, but hav-
ing seen Joseph in action I'm persuaded that it's better just to keep
on suffering them.

Was your friendship with him a friendship of equals, or was he
too arrogant to accommodate that?

Friendship creates equals. His arrogance was reserved for combat,
whereas what came out with friends was merriment and mockery
and indeed tenderness. Joseph liked to lay down the law; certainly.
Even among friends, he would act the boss poet; but if you had his
respect, he would take what you had to give. He couldn't help
speaking ex cathedra, trampolining off his own brilliance, and
there was something ungainsayable about those performances, but
he also enjoyed backchat. On the subject of Auden, for example,
when I stated a preference for the strangeness and intensity of the
young poet over the ambling Auden of later years, the connoisseur
of metres and dictions, Joseph retorted, 'But intensity isn't every-
thing.' And when I in my turn retorted, 'You don't believe that for
a moment,' he just gave a kind of mad smile.

Did you show him work in progress?

Oddly enough, not until very late, not in fact until the second last time we met, which was in Finland in September 1994. We were both at a festival in Helsinki and had the good fortune to travel together on a train to Tampere – the journey that's referred to in 'Audenesque', 'Swapping manuscripts and quips. / Both of us like cracking whips'. I remember showing him some of the things that would eventually appear in *The Spirit Level* and his special liking for the poem, 'Mint', and also, I think, for 'The Gravel Walks'. Those ones rhymed and were in regular quatrains, so that would have inclined him to favour them.

Did you discuss issues of form, on which he was so dogmatic?
Did you ever encourage him to take a less doctrinaire view?

Joseph once told me that he thought Yeats's rhymes weren't always up to scratch; and he resisted all my instruction in off-rhyme and the virtue of a slight dissonance – 'A stricken rabbit is crying out / And its cry distracts my thought' – so I left it at that. He had settled the matter to his own satisfaction. But I did take the plunge on one occasion and pointed out enjambements in some of his own translations which I thought were far too abrupt. It was a Saturday morning, in my apartment in Adams House, after he had driven in from Mount Holyoke; all of a sudden I was worried because his breath began to shorten and he was putting his hand into his jacket, over his heart, yet still urging me, 'OK, OK, go on, go on.' Then he could just stand it no longer, and began reading the lines as he heard them, beating out the metre with this fierce Russian emphasis, taking no account of the velleities and different voicings that certain runs of sense and rhythm entail in English, so I let it go. I felt honour-bound to raise the matter with him; but having raised it, I felt absolved of further responsibility.

What you say accords with something many readers found hard to accept about his poetry in English: he declaimed it with total bardic assurance, yet on the page it could be linguistically clotted, syntactically confused, tonally misjudged, not to mention rhythmically unconvincing.

To be fair, when Joseph declaimed, it was usually in Russian, although naturally enough he would carry over the conventions and cadences of his native tongue into his English readings. He certainly had a tendency to accelerate and modulate. The first part of the poem would often be spoken in a kind of tenor drone, as if it were a plane headed down a runway, then you would have lift-off and a climbing note, and then a higher pitch again, until things settled down at cruising altitude. I have to admit it never bothered me. I took the Slavic style for granted and even enjoyed the melody and oddity of it.

But the words on the page were another matter, and I can't believe the translations Joseph made of his own work did it justice, especially in the case of those chunky, long-lined stanzas. You still get some sense of the forked-lightning speed and range of association, but in English it's all a bit off, a bit anxious. You miss what has to be there in the Russian: phonetic glee, a sense of words doing breathless but apparently effortless trapeze work. Akhmatova wouldn't have been one to rejoice in poetry that was simply out of tune. And when you read the poems which are unquestionably in tune in English, those early translations by Richard Wilbur and Anthony Hecht, for example, you don't need a special pleader to tell you this is the real thing.

In February 1988 you took part in 'An Evening for Joseph Brodsky' at the American Repertory Theatre in Cambridge, and even wrote a verse introduction to the occasion. Do you remember any of the lines?

I remember ones that Joseph especially liked, which refer back to a graduation address he gave at Ann Arbor. In it, he talked about how he had once defied the labour-camp authorities in Siberia by refusing to stop when they deemed one of his punishments had gone on long enough. He'd been given a task of splitting logs, but when they indicated that he'd done his bit, Joseph refused to lay down the axe, and went on and on, splitting and splitting, furious at the absurdity, exposing it by his excessiveness. In my mind, that axe got mixed up with Kafka's remark that 'a book must be the axe for the frozen sea inside us', so one of the stanzas went like this:

> Yet Joseph's tool is not the spade.
> The axe with ice upon its blade
> Is more his thing
> And then, you lied, you lied, you lied,
> The echoes ring.

Brodsky was reportedly an unreconstructed macho male.

Certainly not in his dealings with Maria, the woman he eventually married. I'll never forget his arrival with her one evening in Harvard Square; when she shivered a little at a coolness in the air, he was off like the most obeisant Petrarchan lover to buy her a shawl. Maria was very beautiful and very intellectually distinguished, and he clearly adored her; but yes, with other dames – as he might have called them – he could be bloody brusque. Part of the old comrade culture, perhaps, although once again all kinds of caveats have to be entered, because he had bewitching kindness and attentiveness in him too – as Marie would very fervently attest.

How do you respond to Joseph Brodsky's contention that 'a reader who has a great experience of poetry is less likely to fall prey to demagoguery on the part of the politician'? There is also Yves Bonnefoy's somewhat similar view that 'poetry is a cure for ideology'.

Joseph was right to contend that a person sensitized to language by poetry is less likely to sway in the mass-media breeze; and I agree with Bonnefoy if he means that successful poetry will launch itself beyond the pull of the contingent and get into its own self-sustaining linguistic and imaginative orbit. Take a poem like 'Leda and the Swan'. It begins with what Bonnefoy might call ideology: Yeats starts thinking of the Russian Revolution, which represents the rule of the many, the arrival of power from below, from down to up, and to that he opposes the rule of the few, the rule from above, from up to down, so the violent descent of Zeus upon Leda comes to mind as analogous to all this – but then, as Yeats himself has told us, bird and girl took over his imagining, and the poem, powerful and problematical as it is, took off. Thinking about rhymes became as important as thinking about revolution.

But poems can be political insofar as they discover the paradigmatic. Think of Cavafy. Cavafy's cameos of the ambitions and victories and defeats among various tyrannies and dynasties and satrapies during the Hellenistic age have a wonderful, clarified political wisdom, but they're free – or, if you prefer, *cured* – of ideology. It's hard to talk about this without citing examples, probably because examples tell us that the only real answers to the general problem are specific poems in specific situations. Whitman's hospital poems during the American civil war.

Poems by Auden and MacNeice in the 1930s – 'Look, Stranger', 'The Sunlight on the Garden'. Derek Mahon's 'Lives'.

How should we regard a question like Czesław Miłosz's 'What is poetry that does not save / Nations or people?'

It's a cry wrung from him *in extremis, de profundis,* the cry of the responsible human. But it's one he answers in different ways in his work – in the witness of poems like 'Campo dei Fiori' and 'Song on Porcelain', and in the obstinate espousal of beauty and order – the calligraphy, as he once called it – of poems like 'The World', or 'Encounter', or 'Gift'. These latter ones, incidentally, could have as their motto Brodsky's equally challenging declaration that 'if art teaches anything, it's that the human condition is private'.

Where do you stand between those two positions?

Betwixt and between them – which is, in effect, where Czesław Miłosz and Joseph Brodsky also stood. Joseph was out to save people when he suggested during his time as Poet Laureate of the United States that poetry should, like the Gideon Bible, be available in hotel rooms and should be distributed like handouts at supermarket checkouts. And Czesław writes about loving herring and strawberry jam as well as beauty and truth.

How seriously did you take that suggestion of Brodsky's about disseminating poetry in hotels and supermarkets?

I took it to be a fantasy and enjoyed it as such, but now that you ask the question, I'm inclined to think it wasn't all that over the top. It was probably some kind of carryover from the big centralized Soviet system; it was also of a piece with his war on what he called 'the vulgarity of the human heart'. A populace that is chloroformed day and night by TV stations like Fox News could do with inoculation by poetry. Obviously, poetry can't be administered like an injection, but it does constitute a boost to the capacity for discrimination and resistance. The proposal was another instance of what I call his tonic effect.

To what extent would you accept Brodsky's contention 'the only thing politics and poetry have in common is the letter "p" and the letter "o" '?

I'm always tempted to agree with it, but I cannot entirely. First of all, it takes the word 'politics' at its lowest evaluation. Secondly, it ignores the political reality of poems such as Alexander Blok's 'The Twelve' or Wilfred Owen's 'Strange Meeting' or Elizabeth Bishop's 'Roosters' or Allen Ginsberg's 'Howl'. It ignores, indeed, whatever truth there is in the Brodsky statement you just quoted about a poetry reader being 'less likely to fall prey to demagoguery on the part of the politician'. I take it to be Joseph's typical overstatement of the truth that a political poem has to outstrip the condition of tract or propaganda. Joseph would probably say that a poem like 'The Fall of Rome' by his adored Auden is cured of politics by being masterful poetry, but I don't think that's the whole story. To transmogrify Wilfred Owen's famous line, I'd say that the politics are there in the poetry. 'Altogether elsewhere, vast / Herds of reindeer move across / Miles and miles of golden moss, / Silently and very fast' – when Auden conjures up that vision of freedom and at oneness, it surely entails some refusal of the given conditions, some revolutionary promise. Some intimation of menace also.

When Brodsky's fellow countryman Osip Mandelstam remarked of Russia that 'poetry is respected only in this country – people are killed for it', was he right to imply that a political reading of even the most lyrical poem is always possible?

I do believe he was right. Lyric poets always feel a bit on guard when the big crises arrive, a bit defensive when war is declared or disaster strikes, but even so, they usually hold out against herd-speak. They know that the integrity of the polis is guarded as much by the solitariness of their enterprise as by other people's solidarities, although it's hard to proclaim that truth when closed ranks and consensus are the things most in demand.

At the time of the first production of The Cure at Troy, *you told an interviewer, 'I'm not a political writer and I don't see literature as a way of solving political problems.' But if poetry doesn't solve political problems, can it inform them in some way?*

That's a nice distinction, and a real one. When I was young, the spiritual directors used to talk about the necessity of 'an informed conscience' – as opposed to culpable ignorance. And I think your terms imply something similar. The detached, disinterested quality of poetry is what's formative of both understanding and stand-off. I could go back here to the analogy I used years ago and say that poetry is like the line Christ drew in the sand, it creates a pause in the action, a freeze-frame moment of concentration, a focus where our power to concentrate is concentrated back upon ourselves.

Taking stock now, can you say what contribution poetry made to the situation in Ulster during the Troubles?

It's easier to say something about the contribution the Troubles made to poetry. During those years, poets found they needed to be answerable, and debated within themselves and among themselves what that entailed. They also found recognition and respect, including self-respect, because they and everybody else had to take life more seriously than heretofore. Those hoary old chestnuts about the relationship of literature to life lost their hoar and were all of a sudden new again. But it's also worth remembering that in the plain, day-to-day reality, poetry born from our predicament in Northern Ireland was being taught during the Troubles to schoolchildren and students born on both sides of the divide. Poets came to the fore in the media. Poetry publishing flourished and in general the practice of poetry thrived, so you could say that the cultural self-respect of the region was strengthened as a result. And that's a real enough 'contribution to the situation'.

When, in 1970, Derek Mahon wrote that 'a good poem is a paradigm of good politics', what do you think he meant?

I think Derek meant that a good poem holds as much of the truth as possible in one gaze. Can a good untrue poem be written? If you are an Israeli or Palestinian poet at this moment, what poetry ideally requires of you is a disinterested gaze at how you are situated, whereas your people will require passionate solidarity, and opposition to the Other. The same situation prevailed in Northern Ireland in a diminished way: Protestants, Catholics, nationalists, Unionists, are you with us or against us? But what Mahon meant, and what I would mean, is that we in Northern Ireland *qua* poets were subject to that larger call to 'hold in a single thought reality and justice'.

Is it always a mistake to be upfront and explicit in a political poem?

There's no reason why a poet shouldn't be upfront and explicit in a poem about any political position or issue. All that's required is that the position or issue should suffer some little bit of a sea change. A poem like Zbigniew Herbert's 'The Power of Taste' is a case in point. It is explicitly against the Soviet way of life and language, yet its rhetorical stance keeps it equidistant from rant and whimper. And Auden's 'Spain', notwithstanding the author's qualms concerning 'the necessary murder', is not harmed by its frank espousal of the Republican cause. Nor is 'Easter 1916' by the wearing of the green.

How legitimate would it have been, on the other hand, for a poet living in Belfast not to have made any reference to the Troubles, and to have insisted on the autonomy of art by ignoring the social and anthropological reality outside the walls?

'Legitimate' is an unnerving word there. Art may claim a certain kind of autonomy; but, in the artist, we require what Miłosz calls 'a certain level of awareness'. The question is, how much awareness is there in this poetry that insists on avoiding contact with the social and anthropological reality? If there's a genuine deficiency on that front, the work is unlikely to have much staying power. Deliberate flouting of an expectation of 'relevance', on the other hand, could be a sign of very high awareness indeed. Need I yet again cite Miłosz's 'The World'?

So who or what is an 'aesthete'? Is the term necessarily pejorative?

The true aesthete would perceive himself – 'aesthete' seems to me to parse as masculine – as a subversive, and in artistic circles there's nothing derogatory about that. I'd keep the pejoratives for idiots and show-offs. The apologia for the aesthetic position is in the collected works of Wallace Stevens.

And you approve of Stevens? Of his fidelity to the imagination as the great good?

The Stevens achievement is as big and solid as the man was himself – as the Hartford Accident and Indemnity Company, for that matter. Approval or disapproval doesn't come into it. Nor does the old antithesis between intellect and imagination, reason and feeling. Stevens's combination of gorgeous display and a bottom-line awareness of the 'plain sense of things' has an intellectual hardness at the centre of it, an uncompromising attitude to all kinds of illusion and collusion. He's the artistic equivalent of a tycoon. There's an excessive, ostentatious, unapologetic quality about the writing, prose and verse. Deep down, he's as bleak as the Larkin of 'Aubade', except that he's determined to replace the 'moth-eaten brocade' of religion with the heavy embroidery of his own songs of earth. But I do admit that I find some of the longer swatches of that fabric heavy in the pejorative sense.

In your Paris Review *interview you associated political poetry with a writer like Pablo Neruda. Yeats, you said, was a public poet, interested in the polis – but you saw him essentially as a visionary poet. Auden you categorized as a civic poet. Can you elaborate a bit on those distinctions and maybe say which category you would place your own work in?*

The distinctions were ad hoc, made on the wing, but I still think there's something to them. Adrienne Rich turned herself into a political poet of the Neruda kind; her work at a certain stage became more issue-based, important in the United States as a driving, activist feminist force. Whereas Lowell, when he wrote 'For the Union Dead' and 'Waking Early Sunday Morning', became more public, rose to the occasion of the *res publica*. With him, it was more a case of anxiety than issue. And civic? Is it crazy to adduce Philip Larkin? His work espouses a certain kind of civic order, with its show Saturdays, its Whitsun weddings, its large, cool stores and housing estates and hospital wards. He's all in favour of the old 'toad' – work – the late-night drink and the small-hours piss. Yet where to include myself in all this? Not, at any rate, in the first category. It would be nice to have oneself nominated for the 'public' slot, but I'd leave that to other people.

Which of your poems do you think of as being pitched in a public voice rather than a private one?

We've got to watch out here: as far as I'm concerned, public poetry of the sort I value springs from the poet's inner state and gives vent and voice to a predicament as well as addressing the state of the poet's world. Admittedly, there are writings of mine I'd think of as public in the megaphone sense of the term – things like the song I wrote after Bloody Sunday and the 'Human beings suffer' chorus of *The Cure at Troy*. 'Casualty', on the other hand, is a public poem of the sort that I'd aspire to.

Are you suspicious of the kind of poet who can automatically turn out a poem in the aftermath of an atrocity like the September 11 2001 attacks?

When you say 'automatically', of course I'm a bit suspicious. But there's nothing intrinsically wrong with 'extempore effusion'. I remember the impact of James Simmons's song 'Claudy', written after people had died in an IRA explosion in that village. And we'd all be poorer without Thomas Hardy's 'The Convergence of the Twain'. And Yeats's 'Easter 1916'. And Wordsworth's 'Loud is the Vale!' – composed, as the subtitle tells us, when the author had 'just read in a newspaper that the dissolution of Mr Fox was hourly expected'. Anyhow, it would ill become me to deplore that kind of early response since I myself produced 'Anything Can Happen' – even if it was an adaptation of a Horace ode – in the aftermath of the September 11 attacks.

You once wrote of the post-war east-European poets that 'there is something in their situation that makes them attractive to a reader whose formative experience has been largely Irish', and you went on to mention their capacity to 'survive amphibiously, in the realm of "the times" and the realm of their moral and artistic self-respect'. How far did these parallels take you?

What attracts you to a poet? A sense that you're in safe hands, artistically speaking, and that the work embodies knowledge of life. That's what I felt, at any rate, about those eastern Europeans. They were a standard. I don't mean that their styles or strategies were to be imitated or emulated, just that I recognized the double bind they were in, between the out-of-joint times and the necessary inwardness of poetry. I recognized their predicament as an extreme stage of a discomfort I was experiencing myself.

Miroslav Holub, the subject of one of your essays, held an important research job in communist Czechoslovakia and was not an active dissident. How do you regard poets like Holub and Tadeusz Różewicz, who reached varying degrees of accommodation with officialdom?

What I'd say about them is what I'd say about any poet: the task was to take the strain of being themselves in their own time and place, to survive without compromising their moral and artistic self-respect; the ones you mention seem to have managed that. I find it hard to adjudicate in these areas. Presumptuous, even.

Let me push you, nevertheless, with a hugely hypothetical question: had you been a poet in, say, post-war Romania or Poland, how do you think you would have dealt with the demands of the Communist Party for socialist realism and conformity to the party line?

Whatever answer I give to that is going to sound either too self-deprecatory or too self-inflatory. Still, going on how I worked in my own political circumstances, I believe I might have found a way to maintain a hygienic distance, found some non-confrontational but still contrarian stance. I risk saying this because I began as the lad who wrote 'Requiem for the Croppies' in 'official' Northern Ireland in 1966, and over the years have had to keep parrying demands for poetry that would fall into line with one or other party – or para-party.

Does contemporary poetry in translation still play a large part in your reading life?

Not as much as it did. I get to see *Modern Poetry in Translation*, and the things that are published in magazines like *PN Review*. But it's fairly casual. I still come on stuff that makes the needles tremble a bit, although it's often of earlier vintage: Zabolotsky, late Amichai . . .

Rilke, Cavafy and Seferis made appearances in District and Circle. *What stirred your interest in those poets?*

Chance, in the case of Rilke. I had one of those sudden reimmersions, started off by opening Edward Snow's big volume of *New Poems* in translation. Coincidence, in the case of Cavafy, since I'd just recently written a preface to a volume of translations of his poems by Stratis Haviaris, and was wakened up all over again to the nonpareil combination of 'grief and reason', to use a Brodsky phrase, in his tone and his understanding. I take it that my first response to Cavafy was like everybody else's: immediate suscepti-bility to the clear steady gaze at the world and himself, at the stealth in passion and power politics.

With Seferis it was the result of an ongoing effort. In 2000, his centenary year, I did a presentation about him for the Greek Department at Harvard and got a better grip on 'Mythistorema' and poems like 'Helen' and 'The King of Asini'. Then I read Roger Beaton's biography and was particularly fascinated by the account of what he went through during the time of the Colonels: under huge pressure to speak out against the regime, but reluctant – tem-peramentally and as a former diplomat – to join a chorus on the left. In the end he did issue a statement deploring the state of affairs that pertained, and wrote a late poem about the fate of tyrants that became one of his most popular in Greece.

After all that talk of politics and poetry, I'm reminded of the fact that, near the beginning of Electric Light *– in 'Out of the Bag' – you place coercion in a distinctly non-political context: 'the cure / By poetry that cannot be coerced'. Could you elaborate on that?*

Some cures can in a certain sense be 'coerced' – by operations, by antibiotics and the like, but there are others that occur slightly mysteriously – through the intervention of a healer or a doctor or a prayer. The good that poetry does is akin to that kind of intervention.

Has it ever done such good in your own life?

It has, because it has proved itself something more than a placebo. Has proved true, you might say. A while after I wrote 'Out of the Bag', for instance, I did a lecture in the Royal College of Surgeons in Dublin called 'The Whole Thing'. I played with the etymological connections between 'whole' and 'heal' and 'health' and argued that 'the whole thing' could function as a definition of poetry itself, so the phrase you quote – 'the cure by poetry' – was already grop-ing in that same direction. What I like about it, and about the poem where it occurs, is the feeling of being on the edge of something not quite revealed. Like watching the horizon just before sun-up. A true thing felt out by free association. Loose-weave stuff.

Electric Light *found you in eclogue – as well as loose-weave – form.*

David Ferry did a new translation of Virgil's *Eclogues*, published with the parallel Latin text, and for a while I was captivated entirely. I still have enough Latin to be susceptible to the mesmerism of the hexameters. You have *melopoeia* aplenty there; but it also struck me that there was something implacable in the way Virgil hewed to the artificiality of the convention. Here was a young poet coming back with an almost vindictive artistry against the actual conditions of the times. There was something recognizable at work, a kind of Muldoonish resistance. Virgil's eclogues proved an effective way for a poet to answer whatever the world was hurling at him, so I had a go at writing a couple of my own.

In his citation for your 2005 Irish PEN Award, Tom Paulin suggested that Virgil's Aeneid *has been 'a seminal and founding text' for you, and that your oeuvre has been a Virgilian epic journey. Are you conscious of having undertaken such a journey?*

Not conscious. Tom's likely to have been picking up on Brian Friel's allusions to the *Aeneid* in *Translations*. *Urbs antiqua fuit*, 'there was an ancient city' – Jimmy Jack's reference to the defeat of the old civilization of Carthage by the military power of Rome is one of the perspectives the play offers on the British–Irish relationship, and that has added a Virgilian dimension to the general discourse. But there's one Virgilian journey that has indeed been a constant presence and that is Aeneas's venture into the underworld. The motifs of Book VI have been in my head for years – the golden bough, Charon's barge, the quest to meet the shade of the father.

Why, by the way, did you nominate Tom Paulin as the writer from whom you would receive the PEN Award?

Tom and Giti have been friends of ours for years, very kind to us when we were coming and going to Oxford. And for all Tom's combativeness and outrageousness when he was a panellist on the BBC's *Late Night Review*, he still has a very tender side. But he hasn't been all that integrated into the Irish scene, and this was a good opportunity to widen the circle for him – especially since the PEN people were interested in a presenter with his kind of media appeal.

*Tom Paulin has always been much readier than you to become
involved in controversy, much more combative, as you've suggested.
He adopted – to say the very least – an uncompromising stance on
American Jewish settlers in the Palestinian territories, for example,
and on T. S. Eliot's anti-Semitism.*

Giti Paulin is Indian by birth and the Paulin children have had
to put up with their share of racist abuse, so Tom is more than usu-
ally sensitive and easily provoked when it comes to issues of race.
And once he's provoked, he's not one to finesse his language. It's
very much a case of character as fate; but since I know his charac-
ter to be governed by a passion for justice, I was greatly in sympa-
thy with the plight he found himself in, after he made those
remarks about the West Bank settlers. 'Wild and whirling words'
they certainly were, and he didn't help matters by showing no
immediate signs of regretting them, so he found himself both
shunned and assailed. But there's moral courage mixed in with
Tom's recklessness. He's fond of quoting William Blake on indig-
nation: 'The voice of honest indignation is the voice of God.' It
could be the Paulin motto.

*Your mention of a quotation that could be a motto prompts me to
ask about a statement by Ted Hughes that seems to have enormous
resonance for you, his contention that a true poem must be 'a
statement from the powers in control of our life, the ultimate
suffering and decision in us'. To what extent does this coincide
with your own view?*

It coincides with it entirely.

How do you interpret the word 'decision' there?

I believe he's talking about the limit of your tolerance, the point
beyond which there's no compromise, the last moral ditch, wher-
ever you screw your courage to the sticking point.

*You dedicated 'On His Work in the English Tongue' to the
memory of Ted Hughes, but it was written while he was still alive.*

I was given a manuscript copy of *Birthday Letters* a month or two
before the book appeared, given it in confidence by somebody at
Faber. I was on my way to Oxford, intending to do a couple of days'

work in Magdalen College; but when I got there, I spent most of the time on top of the bed, reading through this material and having a strong sense that I was stealing a literary march. I wrote most of what would eventually become the poem there and then, in the intensity of the moment. I actually sent it to Ted sometime in 1998. I even sent it to the *New Yorker*: they'd asked me to review *Birthday Letters* and I had declined, but offered them 'On His Work . . .' as a substitute. Almost immediately, however, I reneged on the offer.

Did you feel convinced by Birthday Letters? *Might it not be said that the writing is banal in places and that the attempts at self-exculpation through mythologization are less than convincing?*

All right, that might be said. It's a big slab of material; there's much in it that's being set down for the record and much of it does have a palpable design. Ted himself was well aware that it operated at a different level from what he considered his 'right' stuff in the creative/symbolic mode. He said so explicitly, in a letter to me after I sent him the 'English Tongue' poem: 'I always had some idea that my dealings with Sylvia would have to emerge inadvertently, in some oblique fashion, through some piece only symbolically related to it – the authentic creative way. But there they are.' Overall, however, there's huge emotional pressure behind the data. If you compare it with other big late-career sequences – Wordsworth's 'Ecclesiastical Sonnets', say, or Lowell's 'Notebook' – it more than holds its own. Put it this way: if it hadn't been written, something necessary would have been missing from Hughes's oeuvre.

In the long run, won't Birthday Letters *be regarded as of biographical more than literary interest?*

That's not how I see it. Many poems in the book will retain their force because they have definitive things to tell about poetic vocation. Off the top of my head, I'd list 'Chaucer' and 'The Earthenware Head', 'Flounders' and 'Epiphany' and 'Freedom of Speech'. You're dealing here, after all, with a book by a poet of genius. He may not have overborne artistic demands as cavalierly as Hugh MacDiarmid – who likened himself, you remember, to a volcano 'emitting not only flames, but a load of rubbish' – but he had the same kind of readiness to wreak havoc in the salon.

Were you surprised at how well the poems were received?

How well were they received? The surge of media attention was unsurprising, as was the immediate reaction of reviewers. There was a general, understandable recognition that here was a poet whose long silence simply had to be broken, who had earned the right to release himself finally from the pincer jaws of an emotional and artistic dilemma. For years he was going to be damned as an exploiter of Sylvia Plath's life and death if he wrote about their relationship, and if he didn't write about it he was damned for covering up or suspected of having something to cover up. But in fact the popular vote which the book received prompted a critical backlash from some stricter parties.

To what extent was his decision to release the Birthday Letters *poems influenced by the fact that he felt close to death?*

Hard to say. The book came out on 29 January 1998. A cancer had been discovered early in the previous summer: I remember standing with Christopher Reid and Matthew Evans one evening that May, on the steps of the Faber offices, waiting for him to turn up to accompany us to Brighton. He and I were to do a reading at the Brighton Festival: *The School Bag* had just been published and this was to be the last of the promotional events. A phone call came to say he was ill and couldn't make it, although there was also a request that no mention of illness should be made to explain his absence. I forget how we handled that, but we proceeded to the festival and Christopher Reid stood in for him at the reading.

To be truthful, I felt at the time that Ted might just have got fed up with the touring and decided to go to ground. Then, not long after, I spoke to him on the phone and he reported the facts with characteristic directness, saying he'd had 'a lump of [his] gut cut out' – an operation for cancer of the colon. But I'm almost certain he had decided on the publication before that. He'd occasionally talked about the possibility of his doing the book – as far back as 1980, the year when he gave me 'You Hated Spain' for a special issue of *Ploughshares* I edited; also the year when he'd published 'An Earthenware Head' in the *London Review of Books*. His illness just happened to coincide – very cruelly – with a huge cresting of his confidence. But then he got through the chemotherapy successfully and when we saw him and Carol in Dublin the follow-ing June, his hair had grown back and he was in powerful fettle.

Was that the last time you saw him?

It was. I went to Harvard in late September, unaware that the can-cer had suddenly come back and attacked the liver. I got a terrible shock when news of his death came at the end of October. We were able to go back in time for the funeral in North Tawton.

Had you any sense that the June meeting would be the last one?

Ted and Carol just appeared at the door, without notice, one Sunday afternoon. They were full of good cheer and looked the picture of health. They'd decided to take a quick refresher trip to Dublin, and were also going to meet Terence McCaughey – Ted's old friend from his days in Cambridge, who would eventually be minister at the memorial service in Westminster Abbey. But the moment I saw the pair of them, I had this sudden superstitious feel-ing that Ted was 'taking the last look'. It was banished, more or less, by the evidence there in front of me of the man's strength and recovery, but I couldn't rid myself of it entirely.

Did he say anything to suggest that he shared your intuition?

Not at all. Marie and I were having an extension added to the house, and the whole place was in a mess. We talked a lot about clearing out books and papers, making a new start in a new space – partly because Ted had just let go a big consignment of his papers to Emory University. I do remember one typical Ted remark after he saw the shape of the room we were adding: it was an odd four-sided outshot to the main building, so he says, 'Anything that tends towards the octagonal makes your house a tower.' I still find that somehow fortifying. It has a kind of soothsaying quality that was often in his words.

Any other especially memorable remarks?

Many about writers. I've put his description of meeting Eliot into the 'Stern' poem: he said it was like standing on the quay watching the prow of the *Queen Mary* come towards you, 'very slowly'. He once told me that Robert Frost looked like a chimpanzee: short body, long arms, big hands. He said Shakespeare was crippled with a limp, that the Arden family had had his stick for generations. And I always remember his quoting and laughing at J. B. Priestley's advice to young writers: 'Never do anything for anybody' – meaning you should avoid piecemeal jobs and do only your own proper writerly work.

How damaged do you think Hughes and his work were by the public perception of him – however wrongheaded – as having contributed to Sylvia Plath's suicide? Would he have been a different, maybe better, poet had he been able to fully detach himself from her shadow?

I'm reluctant to speculate about that. 'Damaged' is a strong word to apply either to the man or the work. If you take some of his definitive early poems – 'An Otter', for example, or 'The Bull Moses' – you have portraits of poetic consciousness that suggest the young Hughes believed in seclusion and endurance as the proper response to the conditions of existence. And as is often the case, the young poet wasn't just reading the world, he was also intuiting a destiny and readying for it. The obsession with the First World War, with the trauma his father suffered in the trenches, his notion that his home district in Yorkshire was 'in mourning' for that lost generation – it all seems to signify a place of suffering and decision in him that was prepared for something fatal to happen.

I'm not saying that his life and his poetry weren't knocked askew, or that he didn't suffer badly from woundings within himself and houndings without. You might argue that *Crow* and *Gaudete* were evidence of damage to the artistic system, but equally you could argue they were evidence of valiant damage control. They showed the extravagant side of Hughes that came out early on in the rhetoric of a line like 'Hearing the horizons endure', they showed that side of him running with the wounded side, and producing work that had an inexorable wildness about it. A mixture of the psalmist's *de profundis* and Yeats's old pensioner: 'I spit into the face of Time / That has transfigured me'.

Still, damaged or not, Hughes had his flaws – among which was a reputed shrewdness and parsimony in money matters.

No parsimony was evident to me. On the contrary, there was a largesse about him, an unstintedness when he was among friends, an attitude of 'giving though free to refuse'. If you want to call the ingrained habits of a freelance full-time writer 'shrewdness', I suppose you might say that in his professional dealings Ted was shrewd. But there's a demeaning edge to the word that's just wrong. Ted and Sylvia started life together without a penny and, for years, earned every penny from fees and royalties, all of them minimal. Ted never went in for residencies, or lucrative American tours.

In the eighties, when he had a chance to be paid a decent one-off sum for doing what he had always done – educational work, readings to sixth formers and so on – he took the chance and was right to do so. A man in his fifties, still dependent on literary earnings – it was completely in order, and near time it had happened. I remember Donald Davie once made some remark about Ted's 'greed' for money which I considered unworthy of him. This was in relation to expensive limited editions which Ted occasionally produced, but again, those were breadwinning projects. It ill became a professor in a highly paid position in the States to sneer at another member of the guild of writers doing his best to make a few extra shillings.

Did you feel utterly at ease with Hughes or did some of your youthful awe remain? Was he your closest friend among poets?

He was the one who fortified me most, the most intuitive about what I worked from and how I worked. In the latter years, I did feel completely at ease with him; but yes, to begin with, I was certainly that bit shyer. Even so, right up until the end I still experienced a sense of privilege in his company. There was something foundational about my relationship with him. I felt secured by his work and his way of being in the world, and that gave the friendship a dimension that was in some sense supra-personal.

You mentioned The School Bag *earlier, but I'd like to ask you also about* The Rattle Bag, *the first anthology you edited with Ted Hughes. Was it a commission or was the idea your own?*

Charles Monteith had an idea away back in the 1970s that Marie and I should do an anthology called *The Faber Book of Verse for Younger People*. In those days I was still in the English Department at Carysfort College of Education and Marie was working part-time as a teacher, so the pair of us must have seemed like a good bet for the job. Years went by without anything happening, and Marie wasn't particularly keen, so Charles then proposed a collaboration with Ted. This would have been around 1978, because I remember doing a good bit of systematic reading for the book in the Poetry Room of the Lamont Library, when I was in Harvard in the spring of 1979.

You and Hughes worked independently?

In the beginning, yes. Each made his own heap of poems, his own list, each worked independently to start with; it then took us a good while to get together to finish the job. In the end, the work on it came as a pleasant follow-up to the task of judging the Arvon Poetry Competition in 1980. In the course of that year, we'd got into the habit of meeting and reading and sifting and making selections and shortlists, so all of that stood to us when we started compiling the final contents.

What about omissions from The Rattle Bag? *There's no George Herbert . . .*

. . . and no Milton, no Dryden, no Pope, no Gray, no Wyatt . . . We took it for granted that these would be to some extent familiar to 'younger people' because of their inclusion in the schools' syllabi, and decided therefore that our brief was to branch off into other areas. As I said in the introduction to *The School Bag, The Rattle Bag* was never intended as a checklist of canonical names, rather as something of a poetry carnival. It was meant to be a come-hither, the kind of book that says to kids – and grown-ups, for that matter – 'Poetry isn't so daunting, you shouldn't be shy of it, you too have a right of way into it and can enjoy it.' But it was saying this without patronizing the readership; the poems had artistic integrity and were from all ages. If we had Yoruba songs, we also had Yeats. If we had Ogden Nash, we also had Shakespeare. If we had Betjeman, we also had Blake.

Even if it was a book that kicked its heels, it was still more deeply devoted to educating people in poetry than many a textbook meant for the classroom. Too many of those take the pupils' supposed interests rather than poetry itself as the guiding principle. They fill the pages with lots of contemporary material that is presumed to engage students because it 'reflects their experience'. But one of the gifts of poetry is to extend and bewilder, and another is to deepen and give purchase. The canonical stuff shouldn't be ignored, it's like the hoops on the contemporary barrel.

Whatever happened to The Faber Book of Verse for Younger People *as a title?*

It was dropped at the last minute, after we'd made out the contents list. And even though that decision came late, it was made swiftly and certainly. We always felt the original title was a bit staid and half knew we'd find another one. Faber was happy to accept it.

And The School Bag?

That was my idea. From the moment *The Rattle Bag* was published, I was all for a second anthology, with a different purpose and with that title. I wanted to supplement the random, whimsical method of the first book with something more decidedly literary-historical. *The Rattle Bag* granted poetry its ad hoc, one-off, poem-by-poem life, but I also wanted to affirm it as a whole thing, a tradition, if you like. I said later, quoting Robert Frost, that the first book treated poems as 'the playthings in the playhouse', whereas the second treated them more as Yeatsian 'monuments of [the soul's] magnificence'. Ted was in favour of this too, although his idea was to call the second volume *The Kit Bag*, since a kit bag contains all that is fundamentally necessary for the journey. But I told him, more than half in earnest, that I couldn't go with the imperial associations of the kit bag. It reminded me of Brits in cork helmets and shorts, wielding their swagger sticks.

You eventually limited your chosen poets to a single poem apiece. Deciding which poem was to be the representative choice was a tough assignment.

Of course. In fact, that proved to be the big reward of the job – digging down and digging up and rediscovering the work of each poet. It was great, for example, to set Pope's 'Epistle to Arbuthnot' like a cat among the writing workshop pigeons. To put a poem by Thomas Moore beside Betjeman's poem about Moore's grave in Wiltshire. To remind the world of 'Tam o' Shanter' and introduce it to Alasdair MacMhaighstir Alasdair. I could go on, but I've written about the whole purpose and process in the foreword.

You also talked about it in 2002, in a lecture to the Prince of Wales Summer School. I'd like to ask about your relationship with the prince. After Ted Hughes's death, were you approached by him or anybody else to allow your name to go forward as a possible Poet Laureate?

The Prince of Wales didn't approach me, although I met him briefly after Ted's memorial service – in the porch of Westminster Abbey, in the company of other members of the Hughes family. I met the Queen Mother on that occasion too, again briefly. Ted was a great favourite of hers, and apparently he also got on well with Prince Charles's boys. He'd spent a good bit of time fishing the rivers round Balmoral, so there was ample opportunity for everybody to get to know one another.

There was a suggestion in the press at one stage that you had some kind of rapport with the Prince of Wales. Any truth in that?

He wrote me a letter after my memorial address in Westminster Abbey, then later on I met him at a dinner in the British embassy in Dublin, and ended up doing a couple of lectures at his summer school for teachers of English and History. During one of those summer schools I met him briefly again, in 2002, at a reception. He was a big pal of the painter Derek Hill, and I think he got some sense from Derek and Ted that I was an approachable sort. And yes, he himself was affable and smart in company.

Were no approaches made about the laureateship?

Some. I'd been on a committee that Ted appointed to help with the nomination of people for the Queen's Gold Medal for Poetry; so, over the years, there had been a certain amount of contact with the man in charge of that business at Buckingham Palace. I can't remember how exactly the laureateship was mooted, but I do remember writing a letter to that official, including a longish short-list, ranked in order, of poets whom I thought would be suitable.

Was there, at any time, an explicit request that you allow your own name to be put forward as a possible laureate?

Some people, whom I presumed to be enquiring on behalf of whoever makes the decision, asked me straight if I would be interested – Matthew Evans, for example, who was head of Faber and Faber at the time. I presumed from the way he approached the subject that there could have been a line from him to the palace. And while we're on the subject of the palace, I can tell you something else: around the time when all this was in the air, I was invited to lunch there, and went. Apparently – during six or eight months of the year – the Queen and the Duke of Edinburgh organize one lunch every month to which various individuals are invited for various reasons. I presumed that I was asked because I'd been a friend of Ted's, and the laureateship was in the air, maybe also because there was a desire to include an Irish dimension, since we were then in the wake of the Good Friday Agreement. Anyhow, for those reasons I was glad enough to accept.

Were you the only guest?

God, no. There were a dozen people. A woman who had a high position in the British prison service. Sir Christopher Bland, who was Chairman of the Board of Governors of the BBC. An engineer from Cardiff University who had developed some new technology for motor-car engines – the man the duke was interested to meet. But I was placed on Her Majesty's left. She spent the first half of the meal talking to the BBC chairman on her right, then came round to me.

What did you talk about?

About our former president, Mary Robinson, and our new one, Mary McAleese. About Ted. About the dogs she was constantly feeding and befriending under the table. About Billy Connolly's performance in the film *Mrs Brown*. Things like that.

She didn't bring up the subject of the laureateship?

She didn't, but I suppose it was lurking somewhere behind the other subjects. Even so, I couldn't have taken the job, the most obvious reason being that I could never have written the kind of poems it requires.

Did she make any reference to An Open Letter: *'My passport's green. / No glass of ours was ever raised / To toast* The Queen*'?*

No. She disappointed me there.

*If I can now switch from the English queen to the Queen's
English, I'd like to ask how important in your discovery of poetry
were the school performances of Shakespeare you describe in 'The
Real Names'?*

The full dress performances in the darkened hall, with the charac-
ters in costume, made up and made different, under the stage lights,
those were rare moments of genuine strangeness. But I'm not sure
I could separate the effect of the verse from the overall theatrical
impact. In fact, I got a stronger sense of the magic of Shakespeare's
poetry in the daylight conditions of the classroom, listening to play
readings in the course of English lessons – the kind of thing
described in 'The Real Names' where the teacher calls out Cassoni
to play Lorenzo in the love scene that opens Act V of *The Merchant
of Venice*. That was in my third year at St Columb's, when I was
fourteen or fifteen, just beginning to be susceptible. 'In such a night
/ Stood Dido with a willow in her hand / Upon the wild sea banks,
and waft her love / To come again to Carthage'.

Did you yourself ever take part in the Shakespeare plays?

I didn't. I was in the audience for the two productions – at
Christmas, I think, during my second and third year in the school.
The first year there was operetta – *The Maid of the Mountains*;
later on, there was *The Arcadians*. I had a small part – a speaking
part, since I was a complete crow – in *The Arcadians*.

My stage debut was in *The Sport of Kings* – a West End farce,
involving a butler who was also an undercover bookie. I played the
butler – named in that case Bates. A year later I played an irate
Indian-army colonel in another such production, a farce called *The
Private Secretary*. At one point I rehearsed for weeks as the lead
part in *The Admirable Crichton* – but for some reason that pro-
duction never got as far as the stage.

*Was it at St Columb's that you first had contact with acting and
actors?*

As a matter of fact, my first contact was more with people whom
Shakespeare – and, for that matter, Yeats – would have called 'play-
ers'. There used to be a travelling company, a fit-up company,
called Sparks who would arrive every year to the little Ancient

Order of Hibernians hall at the foot of our front garden, basically a galvanized iron shed where the local Hibernian band used to do its practising for the 'walking days'. 'The tin hut', it was called locally. And accurately. It probably held sixty or seventy people on benches. But the benches would fill for Sparks. Posters would appear on telegraph poles and gateposts and barn doors advertising 'plays and sketches, spot prizes and variety acts' and a buzz would run through the whole country.

They did melodramas like *The Murders in the Red Barn* or dramatizations of tragic ballads like *Noreen Bawn, or The Curse of Emigration* or historical pageants based on the rebellion and capture and execution of Robert Emmet. But the main thing was the raffishness they brought to the townlands, the glamour of flesh and the flash of colour. Head of the company was Old Lynch, or Old Sparks as he was known to us – MC and generally in charge, making the announcements in his purple jacket and green bow tie, all grease paint and elocution. And then at the end of the play, the variety act – a Lynch daughter or daughter-in-law, fishnetted and full throated, all cleavage and piano accordion, would come on to howls of glee. And this in the pre-electric age – closer, as I say, to what happened in *Hamlet* than what was happening in Hollywood.

Did the experience of the 'tin hut' imbue you with ambition to perform?

Not at all. It sort of scared me. I remember one of the sketches involved a haunted house, a ghost in a sheet with extended arms, able to wave the garment out over the front row. That really haunted me. Although we lived beside the hall, we still had to negotiate a hundred yards or so of pitch darkness.

Was exposure to the stage in St Columb's beneficial to you in any broader ways?

It certainly helped my confidence. I came out of myself and enjoyed getting the laughs. I had a new kind of status in the school after that, was seen to be less staid than I appeared.

And it must have assisted you as a public speaker and poetry reader?

As a speaker, perhaps, in that I'd had the experience of being up there in front of an audience and surviving it. But as a reader, no. I think it wasn't until the 1970s that I began to read convincingly, with some kind of personal rightness. The one who helped me in that regard was Ted Hughes. Ted held fast to the pitch of his first voice, stayed generally faithful to his first accent. Obviously, the accent was less Yorkshire than it would have been had he not gone south to Cambridge and London, but it still kept close to the cadencing of the Danelaw. He managed to sound out his inwardness without crossing the line towards ingratiation. When he spoke his poems, it was as if he was retrieving them rather than reciting them. Hearing him made me want to do likewise.

Was there much 'recitation' in your own family?

At home, I heard ballads and 'recitations' as such, and was expected to deliver on occasion myself. My father always liked me to say 'The Four Farrellys' by Percy French, and a comic piece about an agricultural inspector, in the voice of a Northern Ireland farmer. In later life, the whole family loved me to say this, partly because of the heavy-handed humour of it, but mostly because I had learned it from my father's old cousin, Pat McGuckian, a man with a lisp, and I would also mimic the lisp and Pat's dramatic stance on the floor as he recited the inspector's instructions to the farmer: ' "Your hens, sir, should be fed on glue, / A splendid thing to make them sit; / Your goslings should have gaiters too / To keep their ankles from being wet. / Your milking cows, I'm very sure, / Are not being treated right," says he, / "Your yield of milk is very poor / Compared with what it ought to be –" ' and so on. Family fun.

What about family words, or at least Ulster dialect words? In District and Circle, *for instance, there's 'braird', 'hagging', 'súgán', 'snedder'. Back in* North, *you used the word 'coomb'; and I remember hearing you say that this was a word with a meaning specific to a small area of Ulster. Does this imply that, in a sense, your first and ideal reader is a local one?*

The ideal reader is one who would feel a strangeness – but also an attraction – in the sheer phonetic substance of those things. The local reader would feel something different: the surprise of at-homeness rather than strangeness.

*How is the average, as opposed to ideal, reader to proceed? Treat
the words as exotic obscurities, or hope to find the word in a
specialized Ulster dictionary?*

It's up to the reader. I believe people can live quite happily with one
or two pebbles in their vocabulary shoe. I don't have a policy on
usage – there's no official linguistic regulator inside me applying a
consistent set of rules. It's an on-the-spot business, all depending on
whether a word seems to belong or not to belong in a specific con-
text. When I balked at using 'wrought' for 'worked' in 'Follower' –
'My father worked with a horse-plough' – I probably felt, at an
unconscious level, that it would be read willy-nilly in a more or less
politicized way, not so much a dumbing down of language as a suck-
ing up. The message would have been, 'See me, I say "wrought", I
belong with the ploughing classes, I know their language': political
correctness, old style.

In the title poem of Electric Light, *it's your turn to be
disconcerted by an unfamiliar usage – your grandmother's 'ails'.*

I never did forget the experience of being unhomed, as it were, the
moment my grandmother asked me 'What ails you, child?' 'Electric
Light' began with the gash in her thumbnail, which was said to be
the result of a severe case of whitlow in her girlhood. From the
beginning, I was in awe of it. If the poem were to be filmed, you'd
have to begin by filling the screen with a close-up of that 'puckered
pearl'. Then, when I began thinking about the granny, up came
'ails' in its otherness and oddity – full, to my adult ear, of an *echt*-
Englishness, so that led on to memories of my first trip to England,
going to London by ferry and train, that summer when I lived with
other graduates in a flat on West Cromwell Road.

The same summer that's recalled in 'The Real Names'?

Exactly. In 'The Real Names', I wrote about an open-air perfor-
mance of *Twelfth Night* in Regent's Park, but in 'Electric Light' I
was remembering visits to the Southwark area – because the
Canterbury pilgrims had set off from there, from the Tabard Inn,
and of course the Globe Theatre was there also. My English classes
were having their effect. So you get these different London echoes
and re-echoes. T. S. Eliot was quoting St Augustine when he wrote

in *The Waste Land*, 'To Carthage then I came', and I was more or less quoting Eliot at the end of that 'English' section when I wrote, 'To Southwark too I came, / From tube-mouth into sunlight, / Moyola-breath by Thames's "straunge stronde" '.

How did it come about, by the way, that there were only four pupils in your final-year English class in St Columb's?

I'm not sure. It was an A-level class, taught by Sean B. O'Kelly, who was a great influence on us at that stage. The four of us were back to repeat the Senior Certificate examination. I believe we'd all done English at Advanced level already the previous year, but since we were deemed too young to proceed to university, we had our scholarships deferred. Maybe the syllabus changed that year, maybe the president decided we were a bright bunch and deserved a class to ourselves; but for whatever reason Seamus Deane, Paddy Mullarkey, Michael Cassoni and myself had the privilege of sharing what was in effect a tutorial for the whole of that sixth-form year.

That class oriented me towards English as an academic subject. It deepened my feel for poetry and my knowledge of it, and certainly helped me to start 'dabbling in verse'. All of us, for example, had got large swatches of canonical verse by heart. Partly because Sean B. assigned passages for memorization, partly because our engagement with the set texts was so intense we couldn't not get to know them by rote. At the end of that year, I could have repeated almost every scene in *Hamlet* without looking at the book. And portrait after portrait of the pilgrims described in Chaucer's 'Prologue' to *The Canterbury Tales*. And a whole lot of Wordsworth and Keats. The Wordsworth part of the course had a definite long-term influence on me. The grip I got on poems like 'Michael' and 'Resolution and Independence', the deep familiarity with the preface to *Lyrical Ballads*, stood to me for the rest of my life.

Can you say something of O'Kelly himself?

He'd done an MA at University College Dublin. He had a literary sensibility, a refinement and detachment that was different from most of the other teachers. He was involved and disinterested. He actually relished the stuff he was teaching, there was spontaneity as well as strictness in the way he handled the class, and he had personal oddities that we fastened on. One of his nicknames, for example, was 'Honk' – which was more or less what he did when he asked a question. He'd add this interrogative honk, something like a broadened version of the French *hein:* 'And what exactly is "an antic disposition", honk?' He loped up and down the college walks, backwards and forwards across the front of the classroom, and usually he'd be playing pocket-billiards, as the term was then. But the main thing about him was the passion and focus, focus on what he was teaching and who he was teaching.

In 'Bodies and Souls', you are seen practising nightly on the school lawn. This was obviously school exercise – of the non-academic kind – for the day.

In the summer term, for a couple of weeks before sports day, the senior classes were allowed to practise for half an hour or so after night prayers. It's one of my abiding memories of the college, the cool air, the smell of newly cut grass, the breath and labour of the other runners glimmering along in their white pants and football jerseys. Those were our white nights, there was midsummer magic in the air – all the more so because, at that stage, we would soon be getting home for the summer holidays.

I wonder, however, if there weren't black nights of the soul as well as 'white nights' of the body in St Columb's? Did you suffer much, for example, from the whole Irish Catholic regimen, with its emphasis on the sinfulness of lust and 'impurity'?

I went through agonies. Of desire, of guilt, of dread at confessing, the usual Catholic adolescent griefs. It was all so secret and private. As far as I can remember, there was no banter among us about masturbation, no acknowledgement of it as a common bother, no bringing of the taboo into the talk, and so no way of defusing the anxiety with humour or obscenity. We were cowed because we weren't clued in. Once you can joke about wanking, you have won a certain independence from the catechism and the confessional. But I didn't get that kind of perspective until I arrived in Queen's. And then, believe it or not, my education came from sharing digs with two Jesuit-schooled medical students from Clongowes. They were a lot more suave than the St Columb's product, their attitudes more adult and somehow their accents too.

And what about your relationships with girls?

There was calf-love, you might say, while I was still at St Columb's: letters exchanged, longings on summer evenings, chance meetings; but nothing like trysts, no frank closeness or contact. Early on at Queen's, during the summer vacations, I had demure bicycle rides to grassy riverbank locations along the Bann, but nothing more. She was 'a nice girl', a 'good girl', desirable but approvable. At Queen's itself, a lot of us lived a flirtatious but rigorously unfleshy boy–girl social life, with crushes and occasional partnerings to formal dances, that kind of thing. Gradually I got through that stage and there would be 'necking', for the want of a better word, after *céilís* at home in County Derry, and in the end the more sustained, infatuated relationship mentioned earlier with a student girlfriend. What the Scots would call 'a serious attachment'.

Your Japanese friend in 'Fiddleheads' believes that the erotic belongs in poetry.

He's right, but the problem is, how to get it in. It's present – again in an abstinent kind of way – in a *District and Circle* poem like 'Tate's Avenue'. And more obliquely, maybe more vividly, in 'Moyulla'. 'Moyulla' is about a polluted river, but there's a river nymph on the scene too, aswim in the words and the water. There's erotic glee as well as ecological gloom.

Readers will know the River Moyola in County Derry from 'Gifts of Rain' in Wintering Out, *where 'the tawny guttural water / spells itself'. How does 'Moyulla' relate to 'Moyola'?*

I wanted the darkening of the vowel from 'ola' to 'ulla' to suggest the darkening of the ecological climate, the pollution of the river over time – the release of poisoned water from flax dams years ago, for example, the discharges that began in the 1950s when Nestlés built a milk-powdering factory at Castledawson, and the general ongoing release of agricultural waste. 'Moyulla' is a praise poem but it's keenly aware of 'green' issues; and, to that degree, its drift is also political. If the poem were to have an epigraph, it could be Hopkins's 'There lives the dearest freshness deep down things'.

Do you think poetry can play any practical or meaningful role in changing minds and hearts on environmental issues? In the past

*you have conceded that no poem is strong enough to stop a tank,
so my question is: can a poem stop an SUV?*

I think that one answers itself. What has happened, however, is
that environmental issues have to a large extent changed the mind
of poetry. Again, it's a question of the level of awareness, the hori-
zon of consciousness within which poet and audience operate.
There are those like Gary Snyder and Alice Oswald for whom these
matters are an explicit concern, but at this stage nobody can have
an uncomplicated Hopkinsian trust in the self-refreshing powers of
nature. Yet if Philip Larkin were writing his poem on water nowa-
days, it would still be in order for him to end on a note of rever-
ence, and 'raise in the east / A glass of water / Where any-angled
light / Would congregate endlessly'. I suppose I'm saying that defi-
ance is actually part of the lyric job.

Was District and Circle *a pleasure to write compared with* Electric
Light? *I have a sense that you were returning to something
vaguely resembling normal working conditions: time
having passed since the Nobel Prize, your foreign travel
commitments having lessened and Glanmore Cottage having
been reclaimed?*

That's right. I associate *District and Circle* with a time of *pouncing*
on poems; being more focused, more alone, more at work in
Glanmore Cottage. There are different kinds of engagement always
with the material. For me, there has to be a bleeper going off – a
subject, a memory, an image, a word. Even a photograph. 'The
Turnip Snedder' – about a machine for mangling and slicing
turnips – is dedicated to the artist Hughie O'Donoghue. In the cat-
alogue for an exhibition, he included a photograph of this old
implement surrounded by a pile of sugar beet. The minute I saw the
photograph, I felt the iron, the grip, the haft of the handle. So I was
up and away.

*Do you ever deliberately try to set off the bleeper by looking
through a family photograph album, listening to evocative music,
handling some redolent artefact?*

Never deliberately. It wouldn't work. The accident factor, the sur-
prise factor, the *oops* factor is important. On the other hand, there

are certain things that are in your memory for years: the poem 'In Iowa', for instance. It started as a recollection of a sight I saw once on a snowy afternoon as I drove along a highway in the state of Iowa, among the cornfields, in a part of the state where there was a colony of Mennonites, a Christian sect who reject, among other things, infant baptism. The last poem in the book, 'The Blackbird of Glanmore', contains a memory of my young brother Christopher. The first time I came home from St Columb's College, when he was just about two or three, he actually frolicked and rolled around the yard for pleasure. That stayed with me forever and came up more than fifty years later in the poem.

One of the most distinctive features of District and Circle *is the prose poetry – some of it adapted from this book. It's a form we have already discussed in the context of* Stations. *What is it you are still looking for in the prose poem, so many decades after* Stations, *that is not to be found in the more conventional poem?*

The early French prose poetry depends a lot on posture; it's highly literary, highly self-conscious. I went a bit in that direction in *Stations*. I enjoyed the posturing, but I also distrusted it. Then a few years ago I did a sequence called 'Private Excursions'. There are a couple of samples in *District and Circle* – one called 'Boarders' and another called 'One Christmas Day in the Morning'. And there were other 'spots of time' – about twelve or fourteen of them – that might have made a little pamphlet. But my trust in them failed. The ones in *District and Circle* are samples, I suppose, or you could call them experiments.

How important is experiment to you?

Each poem is an experiment. The experimental poetry thing is not *my* thing. It's a programme of the avant-garde; basically a refusal of the kind of poetry I write. The experiment of poetry, as far as I am concerned, happens when the poem carries you beyond where you could have reasonably expected to go. The image I have is from the old cartoons: Donald Duck or Mickey Mouse coming hell for leather to the edge of a cliff, skidding to a stop but unable to halt, and shooting out over the edge. A good poem is the same, it goes that bit further and leaves you walking on air.

In all our talk of memory poems, of 'spots of time', I don't want to overlook the fact that District and Circle *also includes many poems – including 'Anything Can Happen', mentioned earlier – which arise from contemporary political events. Clearly, you have not allowed the Ulster ceasefires to exonerate you from further jury service as a poet of political or war-related subjects.*

Many years ago, in the early seventies, I read *The Temptation to Exist* by the Romanian aphorist, essayist, philosopher, E. M. Cioran. There's a passage in that book – a beautiful observation, which I know by heart and will quote by way of answer to your question. It's from an essay called 'A Little Theory of Destiny' in *The Temptation to Exist* and it goes: 'Routine of the sigh and of calamity, jeremiads of minor peoples before the bestiality of the great! Yet let us be careful not to complain too much: is it not comforting to oppose to the world's disorders the coherence of our miseries and our defeats? And have we not, in the face of universal dilettantism, the consolation of possessing, with regard to pain, a professional competence?'

Well, Northern Ireland did have its coherent miseries, but what we have to deal with now are the disorders of the world. 'From the Republic of Conscience' is a little parable about the answerability of each and every one of us. We are all citizens of the Republic of Conscience; the last line of the poem says that 'no ambassador would ever be relieved'. To quote 'Mycenae Lookout', there is 'No such thing / as innocent / bystanding'. During fourteen years in Harvard, I learned about being in America, how different it felt and they felt; and two occurrences particularly registered as a result: firstly the attack on the Twin Towers and secondly the Afghanistan and Iraq crackdowns. You cannot distinguish between your condition as a creature of the times and your action as a scribbler.

'The Tollund Man in Springtime', too, seems to relate to contemporary conditions.

A quarter-century after I had written 'The Tollund Man', 'The Tollund Man in Springtime' imagines the Iron Age man who had been found preserved in a bog in Jutland coming-to in his display case in the museum and coming out to walk like 'a stranger among us' in the new world of virtual reality and real pollution, a world of violence and polluted public speech.

Then, after I resurrected him and set him on his way through the 'virtual city', I had the idea of sending him down into a London tube station, and that eventually produced two sections where he was back underground, going into the tunnels and then riding along in the hurtling train. But I came to feel that in these bits – especially in the episode where he meets the busker – there was something more specific and autobiographically weighted than in the other sections, so my instinct was to detach them and make them a separate unit. I was encouraged by you, if you remember, to follow that instinct.

Was any thematic link intended between the title poem of District and Circle, *the 'separate unit' to which you refer, and the London Underground bombings of 7 July 2005?*

The figure who speaks in the five sonnets that make up 'District and Circle' is at a remove from the people among whom he finds himself. This is partly because I'm remembering the other, younger person I was when I first journeyed on a London tube train; somebody who was much less at home, more anxious and 'out of it' than I would come to be later on. But the feeling of unease is also there because the figure in question is haunted by all kinds of new awarenesses: awareness of the potential danger of a journey nowadays on a London tube train and awareness of the mythical dimensions of all such journeys underground, into the earth, into the dark.

The double sonnet was there in May 2005; but after the July bombings, a poem called 'District and Circle' was going to have to bear additional scrutiny. So I added one section, then another, then a third. Not particularly to do with the atrocity, more an attempt to convey the actual experience of an ordinary journey by tube, which almost always has something oneiric about it. When I had the Tollund Man meet the coin-collecting busker at the entrance to the station, it wasn't intended to suggest a mythic parallel. In the first instance it was a direct reportage, a recollection of something that happened and keeps happening – not just to me, but to everybody who travels by tube in London. Inevitably, however, the classical echoes were going to be heard, and the underground/underworld/otherworld parallels come into play.

Is the sequence where you resuscitate the Tollund Man primarily an environmentalist protest or lament?

I think it has more to do with what's implied in your use of the verb 'resuscitate'. Naturally, when the Iron Age bog man awakes and walks abroad in the world of the twenty-first century, he senses that all is not well in the earth and the air – 'larks quietened in the sun, / Clear alteration in the bog-pooled rain'. So 'environmental lament' is a very good way of describing it, but the charge in the actual writing came from identifying with the man as somebody who had 'gathered . . . [his] staying powers'. He gets out of the display case and back into the living world by an act of will that is equally an act of imagination. He told his 'old uncallused hands to be young sward, / The spade-cut skin to heal, and got restored . . .' Basically, he's the voice of a poet repossessing himself and his subject. At the same time, he's still the Tollund Man who was put down in the bog in order that new life would spring up. A principle of regeneration. A proffer, as Hopkins might have said, made in the name of pollen and Tollund.

'Höfn' too, with its melting glacier, could be included among the environmentally aware poems in District and Circle.

Liam O'Flynn and I were in Iceland for a performance of our 'Poet and Piper' programme, flying in a small propeller plane from Reykjavik to Höfn in the south-east, and we crossed over this stony grey scar of ice. The original 'cold star' couldn't have been more scaresomely neuter. I felt a wild primitive fear that the plane would go down and we'd perish in the absolute *frigor* of the place. But then, when we landed at our destination, we learned that the ice is actually melting. As a 'child of earth', I've rarely felt more exposed.

Does a moment like that provoke practical changes of a 'green' nature in your own life?

I go on driving my car, I'm afraid, and flying in the aeroplanes. Not much changes except my awareness of what has happened. That 'we are here as on a darkling plain', or better say a flooding plain, unignorant and unremitting. In terms of the distinction you made earlier between 'environmental protest' and 'ecological lament', I incline temperamentally to the latter. The poems are more like elegies for water and air than calls to action. Liam O'Flynn would have to accompany them with a slow air rather than a marching tune.

How did your partnership with Liam O'Flynn begin?

At a reading organized in the Gate Theatre in 1989 to mark John Montague's sixtieth birthday and my fiftieth, Liam O'Flynn was invited to join us. Some time after that, Liam and I were asked to appear together at a traditional music festival in Kenmare. It was in a small church on a Sunday evening, and we met only half an hour or so before the proceedings were due to start. But there and then, in the vestry, we mapped out a poetry/music, poetry/music, poetry/ music running order and found that it worked and that we were greatly at ease together on stage – or, in that particular case, on the altar. So that was the start of it.

Does your programme still follow a similar pattern?

The way we do it is simple: I read a couple of poems, Liam plays a couple of tunes, some of our contributions are short, some longer, and it's all over in an hour and a half or an hour and three-quarters. It creates ideal listening conditions in the audience. The Irish pipes produce a big sound, not as martial as the Scottish bagpipes, more suited to slow airs and grace notes, but capable of all the registers from mourning to merriment to majesty. Liam is a master of the instrument, so you get something like orchestral force and complexity in the sound, yet his presence is as affecting as his musicianship: there's something absorbing about his own absorption in the business of playing, working the bellows with his elbow, the chanter with his fingers, the drones and regulators with hands and arms. When he stops, the ear itself has been deeply ploughed; it's more than usually open and awake and ready to hear the spoken word.

There's music too in one of the District and Circle *poems, 'The Birch Grove', where 'a CD of Bach is making the rounds / Of the common or garden air'.*

'The Birch Grove' is really a portrait of Bernard McCabe and his wife Jane in a little grove they planted at the bottom of their garden in Ludlow, in earshot of the Teme river. Bernard luckily saw the poem before it appeared in the book: he died at the end of March 2006, and the book came out at the beginning of April. He was

English, or perhaps better say Hiberno-English, since his grandfather had been an Irish speaker from Cork who settled in Yorkshire – although Bernard, when we met him, was teaching at Tufts University. He and Jane lived in a big old family house close to Harvard Square, a place where the rooms were always full of music, the fridge full of Heineken, and the porch like a raft of rocking chairs. It was a haven for somebody like myself, living in single quarters, so I spent many evenings with them during those first migrant semesters. After Bernard retired, they came back to England, so in latter years Marie and I would take the car on the Holyhead ferry and drive across north Wales to Housman country, the blue remembered hills and the birch grove. Idyllic but for real. 'Above them a jet trail / Tapers and wavers like a willow wand or a taper'. Or to put it more liturgically, perpetual light shone upon us.

14

'In a wooden O'
Field Day, Oxford Professor of
Poetry, Translation

~

*At what point did you first become aware of the proposal to
found Field Day?*

By the time I was aware of it, it had already been founded. It began as
a theatre activity, and was designated as such, Field Day Theatre
Company. When Brian Friel and Stephen Rea formed the company in
1980, to put on Brian's *Translations*, they probably regarded it as a
one-off venture, a kind of do-it-yourself experiment, since Brian had
become increasingly dissatisfied with the way his work was being
served and received in Dublin. *Volunteers*, for example, had been so
resisted and downgraded by local reviewers that Seamus Deane and
Tom Kilroy and myself ended up doing a post-performance discussion
in the Abbey, in order to counter the negative reception. Even so, I
don't think the company was conceived of as a great long-term affair.
I've a feeling too that the name was snatched out of the air just as the
programme was about to go to press.

When did you become a director?

After the success of *Translations*. The tour of that first production
sent a wave of energy through the country. What happened on the
stage woke something in the collective consciousness. The play is
peopled with stereotypical characters – hedge-schoolmaster, poor
scholars, redcoats, colleens; but the art of the thing is in the way
Friel subverts the response that all those stereotypes invite. He's
shadow boxing with nineteenth-century historical sentiment as well
as nineteenth-century melodrama, and in the drunken scene at the
end between Hugh O'Donnell and Jimmy Jack, he's even having a

bit of intertextual fun with the 'state of chassis' scene at the end of Sean O'Casey's *Juno and the Paycock*. *Translations*, you could say, was both a crowd-pleaser and a critique, there was something in it both for the general theatre audience and the political intelligentsia, with the result that it stirred things up.

It invited you to see parallels between the dramatic action and the present moment, what with the British army's presence among an Irish community, the assimilationist versus the separatist response to the English language and modernity, and so on; at the same time, it was a work that held you at bay. It wasn't agitprop, yet it agitated the spirit and worked at a level beyond and below showbiz. It was a unique kind of success, so we urged Brian not to let the excitement pass but to ride it and do something more. At which point he said, OK, if you're as enthusiastic as all that, why don't you pitch in yourselves and then let's see what we can make of it together? I think that's a fair account of how the first 'directorate' was formed: friends who had been meeting and talking together for years eventually arrived at a formal meeting in a room in the Gresham Hotel in early 1981 and sketched out a few activities that were designed to produce work from themselves and responses from their contemporaries.

Still, being a director must have absorbed considerable time. Were you at all reluctant to get involved?

I was glad. The time commitment would have been significantly greater if I'd been on the theatrical side of things, but at first I was involved in only three or four meetings a year. The word 'director' may be a bit too imposing here: basically it was a case of people who knew each other being party to an ongoing conversation.

But you held formal meetings?

Formal meetings with minutes. Eventually, there was an office with an administrator and Arts Council funding.

Field Day also set out to interrogate aspects of Irish culture and identity: was this what drew you to it?

The programme of interrogation evolved and the articulation of the programme developed in the course of the next few years. We began to be interviewed and had to give an account of what we were up to and why. I got involved out of solidarity with the effort Brian and Stephen had put into the initial enterprise, and because of the surge of excitement produced by *Translations*. And there was also a hope from the start that the poets on the board might branch out and do something for the theatre.

In her book Acting Between the Lines *Marilynn J. Richtarik writes: 'One suspects that much of the appeal of the Field Day enterprise for Heaney was its Northern slant. Involvement in the company would be a focus for his thoughts on the continuing crisis of his birthplace and a way for him to affirm his identity as a Northerner.'*

That's generally true, but it was true in a general way about everybody involved. It has been pointed out many times, for example, that of the six directors who teamed up in 1981, only David Hammond actually lived in Northern Ireland. Brian Friel was over the border in Donegal, Stephen Rea was then based in London, Tom Paulin was in Nottingham, Seamus Deane and myself were in Dublin. But we were indeed all Northerners and shared a particular edge and unease, being not quite in place north or south.

And you looked east – towards England – in An Open Letter, *your Field Day verse letter. In challenging the publishing practice whereby Irish poets were usually categorized as 'British' in English-published poetry anthologies, you confessed to being conscious of biting 'hands that led me to the limelight'.*

It was an awkward moment, personally and every other way. *The Penguin Book of Contemporary British Poetry*, edited by Blake Morrison and Andrew Motion, had been published in 1982, giving pride of place to my poems. Blake was already the author of a short introductory book on my work. Nevertheless, it was a moment when I felt I had to address the issue of the British nomenclature, and in that way I ended up biting his hand – although not very drastically.

Was there pressure from the Field Day team to go ahead and bite?

None whatsoever. If there was pressure, it was simply the pressure being felt by all the non-theatre people on the team, the need to do something other than sit at a table and pontificate about plays and policy. Very early on, a decision had been taken to do a pamphlet series, the understanding being that the poets on the board would start it off. This was around the time of the hunger strikes and just after, when the Thatcher crowd were in charge in Britain. So that was the immediate context for Seamus Deane's *Civilians and Barbarians*, which basically traced the history and consequences of English attitudes to Ireland and the Irish. And Tom Paulin set out to complicate the usual understanding of what 'the language question' meant in Ireland, giving it a definite Northern spin.

How would you respond to Eavan Boland's objection – which Marilynn J. Richtarik quotes – that, because you had been included in British anthologies for years, the fact that the 'British' tag was used by Blake Morrison and Andrew Motion can scarcely have come as much of a shock to you?

She's right in saying the 'British' tag didn't come as a shock, and I don't think I ever implied that it did. It had been an imposition long before I ever published a poem. I've written about all this in a piece called 'Through-Other Places, Through-Other Times' in *Finders Keepers*, so I don't want to go on about it here. People from the minority in Northern Ireland always felt there was an element of coercion when the 'British' word was applied to them. OK, Yeats might be included in a British Literature course in the United States, I myself might have been included in such a course; in that context, the term would have been a mere convenience. In Ulster, it was an imposition and intended as such, although on the other side of the Irish Sea the Brits themselves hardly gave it a thought.

By the early eighties, however, *I* had to think about it. It's perfectly true that I was at home, personally and poetically, in what you might call the British collective. Published by Faber, friends with Blake Morrison and Craig Raine, my poems appearing in *The Listener*, the *London Review of Books*, and so on. But would I go, say, on a British Council tour as a representative of British literature? I wouldn't. I didn't want to fly Margaret Thatcher's Union Jack for her. As far as I was concerned, there was a political as well as a cultural context to be taken into account. Things had changed since the sixties, when my work did indeed appear in an anthology called *The Young British Poets*, although even then 'silent things' were accumulating within me – as the Gaston Bachelard epigraph to *An Open Letter* suggested: 'What is the source of our first suffering? It lies in the fact that we hesitated to speak . . . It was born in the moment when we accumulated silent things within us.' By 1983, I badly needed to serve notice that the British term was a misnomer.

'He has either changed his mind', Eavan Boland wrote about your decision to publish the letter, 'or changed his friends, and neither process is completely safe for poets.'

Times had changed, I had changed, everybody had changed. But working with Brian Friel and Seamus Deane and David Hammond in no way entailed change of friends. People were killing and being killed because of matters related to the British and Irish words. It was hardly out of order, in the circumstances, for a poet to do something not completely safe. In those days in the North, well-disposed individuals on both sides were caught between conciliation and polarization. You'll understand I didn't write the letter as part of a 'Brits Out' campaign. As a character says in *Translations*, confusion is not a dishonourable condition. I'd even say there was an element of the 'confessional' involved. I may have been involved with Field Day, but what I felt when I published *An Open Letter* was more like solitude than solidarity.

'My passport's green', the poem proclaims. Yet you revealed, in an early section of this book, that you'd had a summer job in the Passport Office in London and, until you moved south in 1972, held a British passport. Under the constitution of the Irish Republic, you could have applied for an Irish passport much earlier.

A number of Republican families in Northern Ireland made that effort, but most people on the nationalist side just filed their application with the Passport Office in Belfast or wherever: it was all part of the confusion or, if you like, the coercion. As I mentioned earlier, I applied at short notice for my first one when I was going on the Derry Diocesan Pilgrimage to Lourdes in 1958.

My holiday job in the British Passport Office in London was for six weeks or so in the summer after I got my teaching diploma, taking the Green Line every day from Earls Court to St James's Park. My job was to write addresses on envelopes and collate information on the application forms with data on the issued passport. It was tedious in the office; overall, though, those few weeks were some of the richest in my life. I went to the Proms for the first time, I attended performances of Shakespeare in Regent's Park, I got the feel of London as the sixties were starting to swing.

Do you have any regrets at this stage about An Open Letter *as a poem?*

I'm sorry it's not shorter and punchier. For once, 'considerations of space' meant that the text had to be longer rather than shorter. Even so, I'm still glad I published it. I had to put up with the accusation that I was having my British cake and eating it, which couldn't really be denied; at the same time, I had cleared something in myself, and felt I was addressing a subject that needed addressing. Anthologies nowadays, for example, are a lot more aware of the Irish dimension within the British jurisdiction. But then, in the meantime, we've also had the Anglo-Irish Agreement and the Good Friday Agreement and the slow, messy advance to a power-sharing assembly and full acknowledgement of an Irish dimension in Northern Ireland affairs.

Were you uneasy, nevertheless, about aspects of the Field Day commitment – the need to speak communally rather than individually, the pressure to toe a certain cultural line?

There was plenty of give and take at the board meetings. The truth of the matter is that Seamus Deane was the most passionate and eloquent in the articulation of a Field Day agenda, and we were all grateful for his brilliance and provocations, if not always for his excessiveness. I wasn't happy early on with dismissive remarks he made about the Lyric Theatre in Belfast, although on that and on other occasions the cabinet responsibility factor did apply. But Field Day wasn't anybody's whole life. I don't think it ever had much to do with me *qua* poet, for example. Without being very clear about it, I probably regarded it as belonging more in the sphere of cultural service than in my creative life: the years of meetings and openings and planning for the *Field Day Anthology* and so on; doing the Yeats selection for the anthology; even doing *An Open Letter.*

And The Cure at Troy, *your version of Sophocles'* Philoctetes?

The Cure at Troy was not occasional in the way *An Open Letter* was. It may have been slow to arrive – ten years after *Translations*, six years after Tom Paulin's version of *Antigone* and Derek Mahon's version of Molière's *School for Husbands* – but it was nevertheless a partial fulfilment of Brian Friel's hope that Field Day would induce the poets to have a go at work for the stage.

Did you choose that play or was it suggested to you?

I chose it. I'd read about it, years before, in Edmund Wilson's *The Wound and the Bow*, and then it was brought to my attention again by a colleague in the Creative Writing Department at Harvard. Michael Blumenthal was a poet who'd begun life as a lawyer in Washington and he showed me the script of a lecture he'd given on the operation of justice in *Philoctetes*. But the main attraction was the material itself, in particular the way Sophocles explores the conflict experienced by the character Neoptolemus – the crunch that comes when the political solidarity required from him by the Greeks is at odds with the conduct he requires from himself if he's to maintain his self-respect. That kind of dilemma was familiar to people on both sides of the political fence in Northern Ireland. People living in a situation where to speak freely and truly on certain occasions would be regarded as letting down the side.

Did you encounter difficulties in the move from lyric poetry to poetic drama? How hampered were you, for example, by your lack of Greek?

I'll never know just how hampered. I had three main translations to help me. There was an old-fashioned Loeb version, full of pseudo-Shakespearean diction, but at least it was a parallel text, done in verse, and it followed the metrical shifts of the original Greek, so that was very useful. I was also lucky to come upon a late-nineteenth-century crib, a literal translation obviously prepared for use in grammar schools; stylistically it was a hash, but it was also a godsend in that it gave the word order and the word-for-word meaning. My third check was a modern translation by David Grene. I worked line by line, in blank verse – except for the choruses, and a couple of prose paragraphs for a change of pitch. I got through it relatively fast. I started in Harvard at the beginning of 1990 and handed in a first draft in July; by September, we were into rehearsals.

The choruses, it seems to me, were where you felt most at home as a poet. You even went so far as to add a chorus of your own devising, one that contains the lines for which the play is now best known: 'once in a lifetime / The longed-for tidal wave / Of justice can rise up, / And hope and history rhyme'. Did you feel free to make public utterances of that nature because the angle of address in a play is very different from the one-to-one relationship you strike with the reader of a lyric poem?

That's it exactly. The choral ode, the choral mode, allows for and almost requires a homiletic note that you would tend to exclude from personal lyric. So the quotable element in the lines comes in part from that unrestrained rhetoric. 'Human beings suffer, / They torture one another', and so on.

You went further in the next stanza, introducing a contemporary element and referring to hunger strikers and police widows and 'the innocent in gaols'. Was there not a case for letting the timelessness of the play make its own mark?

There certainly was, and once the performances started I came to realize that the topical references were a mistake. Spelling things out like that is almost like patronizing the audience. But luckily it was the more quotable 'hope and history' line that caught on. Even Gerry Adams went for the uplift factor . . .

. . . as did many others, including Bill Clinton – who, like Adams and Nadine Gordimer – drew on 'hope and history' for a book title.

I was grateful to see the lines enter the language of the peace process, but very aware that they belonged in the realm of pious aspiration. So when I came to do the *Antigone*, I kept much more strictly to the original.

But you still changed the title, as you did with Philoctetes. *Was there any particular reason for that?*

We were going to be touring *Philoctetes* to audiences who wouldn't have much historical sense of the play or its place in Sophocles' oeuvre, so I believed a new title could work as a pointer, a kind of subliminal orientation. And this led to *The Cure at Troy*, since in Ireland, north and south, the idea of a miraculous cure is deeply lodged in the religious subculture, whether it involves faith healing or the Lourdes pilgrimage. With *Antigone*, on the other hand, the problem was different: a lot of people were going to be overfamiliar with that play rather than underfamiliar, so I was glad when the phrase *The Burial at Thebes* came to mind, quite early on in the process. The word 'burial' pointed directly to one big anthropological concern that's central to the action, and the whole title was a nice parallel to *The Cure at Troy*.

Did the experience you'd gained from the earlier play prompt a different approach to the actual writing of The Burial at Thebes?

For one thing, I had a different purchase on the actual line-by-line writing, and more pleasure in it. The blank verse in *The Cure* came to feel like a container for the paraphrasable meaning. There wasn't any great job of fashioning being done – whereas, in *The Burial*, I started with the idea of making different metrical provisions for different characters and different phases of the action, which gave me a far greater sense of mining a verbal face. There was an ongoing line-by-line, hand-to-hand engagement with the material. At the beginning, there's a three-stress line for the exchanges between the sisters, then comes a surge into more or less Anglo-Saxon metre with the choruses, then on again into blank verse, but blank verse that was dramatic and suited to the character of Creon rather than simply a metronome – and all that made the day-to-day work far more rewarding.

The Abbey Theatre commissioned your version of Antigone *for their centenary programme in 2004. Was it a play you'd always wanted to translate?*

It was not. I'd have preferred to go with *Oedipus at Colonus*, but Yeats had done his version for the Abbey in the 1930s – and of *Oedipus the King* also – so there was that constraint. On the other hand, there was a certain satisfaction in being invited by his theatre to complete the trilogy. George Bush's 'war on terror' was on my mind when I started. And the Guantánamo Bay prisoners, a couple of whom were Americans and whom Bush would have regarded much as Creon regarded Polyneices, 'an anti-Theban Theban' etc. Creon's lines got inflected with at least one Bushism, where he says of subversive elements, 'I'll flush 'em out.' And here and there the word 'patriot' is employed with a definite neo-conservative righteousness.

So, despite your greater textual strictness with this play, you were still mindful of its contemporary significance?

There's always a balance to be struck. The question is, just how much contemporary allusion should be allowed into a text? In *The Burial*, I felt that on the whole I was keeping to the 'less is more' rule. The problem is that you end up serving not only the text but the publicity machine which the theatre requires. You respond to questions about the play's contemporary relevance, you do programme notes and interviews and the like, so you end up mediating between the otherness of the thing itself and the mood of the moment.

That seems to describe exactly what you did in 'Anything Can Happen', the Horace ode you produced after the attacks of September 11, 2001. It appeared first in the Irish Times; *then you introduced it in a lecture to the Royal College of Surgeons and published it in* Translation Ireland; *finally, you republished it, with several translations of your translation, in a booklet in support of Amnesty International. Why did you proceed in that way?*

Ongoing civic service, I suppose. The requests for contributions to different series and different causes is unending and that material suited each of the occasions, but the reassuring thing was that the adaptation had a genuine 'biological right to life'. The year before the 9/11 attacks, I'd been brought to my senses when I read the thirty-fourth *Ode* in Horace's first book. I'd come across it in David Ferry's translation of the complete *Odes*. In that autumn of 2000, I'd talked about the poem in a lecture at Harvard and had juxtaposed it with Robert Graves's poem 'The White Goddess', because both Horace and Graves were writing about transformations caused by the 'bright bolt' of terror.

In Graves, it was a psychosomatic frisson, which he associated with the presence of the goddess; in Horace, it came from the tremendous force of unexpected thunder and lightning which announced the power and presence of Jupiter. I even called the lecture 'Bright Bolts'. When the World Trade Center attacks happened, I suddenly found that the shock-and-awe factor in the Horace poem matched what I and everybody else was feeling. The Latin words that mean something like 'for sure the god has power' I translated – fairly enough, I thought – as 'anything can happen'. My version was partly an elegy – but, to quote Wilfred Owen's 'Preface', it was also meant 'to warn'.

About what?

About retaliation that was bound to come – and *did* come.

What were you hoping to say to the post-9/11 reader through Horace?

It was more a case of trying to register the impact of the attack than of commenting on its significance. Miłosz talks somewhere about how a scream, as he calls it, a scream made in poetry, could not equal the scream of reality during the days of the destruction of the ghetto and the uprising in Warsaw. What was called for, he said, was something like a calligraphic stroke that responded truly but in a different register. Turning to Horace was a bit like that.

Did you feel compelled to make some kind of response to the attacks?

For better or worse, you can't be liberated from consciousness. What happened on September 11 meant that the whole condition of the world was altered henceforth, the spirit of the age had darkened. I didn't feel compelled to respond; but as somebody who'd worked regularly in the States for years and had benefited from the connection, I couldn't ignore what had happened – and was going to happen. I knew a crackdown was bound to come; but I also foreknew it would exhibit a moral arrogance and military mercilessness that would be scaresome. In fact, the poem is born as much out of dismay at what lies ahead as out of distress at what has occurred. 'Stropped-beak Fortune / Swoops, making the air gasp, tearing the crest off one, / Setting it down bleeding on the next'.

You were still dealing with that dismay when you published your translation of the 'wonders of man' chorus in the New Yorker *at*

*the time of the invasion of Iraq. Introducing it at a reading, you
said that the chorus could be regarded as a kind of open letter to
George Bush. But can't this text, like many great works, be read
in contrasting (indeed contradictory) ways?*

Within the context of the play, it certainly can. It's about human
overbearing and its deadly consequences, and it's spoken after
Creon has announced his intention not to allow the burial of
Polyneices, so it can be seen to apply to Creon. But read from
another perspective it can apply equally to the unremitting
Antigone. Even so, I don't feel that the publication of the chorus at
that particular moment was opportunistic or distorting: if I might
be permitted an elevated analogy, I'd say it was as Tiresian as it was
topical.

And would you say the same about your translation, in Field
Work, *of Dante's 'Ugolino' episode from* The Inferno?

That was probably closer to being a 'black painting'. Yet it was still
done as a response. I like the way Nadine Gordimer sees all this.
The writer, she maintains, cannot remain in what she calls 'the
Eden of creativity'. The creative act is witnessed by history, and the
writer writes to be read. In that sense, I translated 'Ugolino' in
order for it to be read in the context of the 'dirty protests' in the
Maze prison. But the contemporary parallel is not at all necessary;
the sine qua non is personal rapport and writerly excitement. For
example, for a while I was so exhilarated by the whole marvel of
Dante that I was tempted to have a go at doing the complete
Inferno – simply for its own imaginative splendour.

Why did you abandon the idea?

Because I didn't know Italian, because I couldn't gauge tone,
because I was at a loss about all the little particles strewn around the
big nouns and verbs. That was what I told myself, at any rate. I sol-
diered on for four hundred lines or so, consulting my Sinclair and
my Singleton; but after I'd done three cantos, there was a realization
that I couldn't achieve what I wanted, which was to get a style going
that would be right for me and for the material. I couldn't establish
a measure that combined plain speaking with fluent movement. I
just couldn't match the shapes that the bright container of the *terza*

rima contained. For a big job like that, you need a note that pays you back, if you know what I mean: you need to be making a music that doesn't just match the original but verifies something in yourself as well.

Something like the Scullion voice you found for Beowulf?

Exactly. Or what I called my 'hidden Scotland' when I was talking about turning Robert Henryson's *Testament of Cresseid* into common English. Henryson's language was animating because it brought me back to an underlying Scottish strain in my own first speech. The mid-Ulster vernacular retains traces of the language spoken by the Lowlanders and Londoners who came over during the Plantation in the early seventeenth century.

In translating 'Hallaig' by Sorley Maclean [Somhairle MacGill-Eain], you made contact with yet another 'hidden Scotland'. Would you place 'Hallaig' in a different class from the rest of Maclean's work?

I take the word of Gaelic-speaking poets and critics that *Dàin do Eimhir* is an epoch-making book, but in order to know what's going on in the sequence I'm nearly entirely dependent on translations by Sorley himself and by Iain Crichton Smith. 'Hallaig', on the other hand, I have been able to enter gradually on my own, partly because I have enough Irish to go word for word into the sense of the Gaelic, partly because I have the cadences of it in my ear from hearing the poet read it, and partly because I know the kind of place the poem evokes – a setting of deserted wallsteads, houses with roofs fallen in and gardens and outgoings all overgrown with shrubs and nettles, the kind of thing you used to see everywhere in Ireland, in the south and west especially, although there was just such a ruined dwelling on land very close to our own place in Derry.

Maclean's homesteads were cleared by a landlord, so there was a tragic dimension to their solitude; yet the Hallaig scenario is still a familiar one, and when I read the first couple of lines, 'Tha bùird is tàirnean air an uinneig / troimh 'm faca mi an Aird an Iar . . .', I'm both home and away. Everything stands clear again in the uncanny light of poetry: 'There's a board nailed across the window / through which I saw the west . . .' It wasn't too hard to find a tune for the words because I had Sorley's voice in my ear from the start. More recently, I thought I would do some Irish-language translations – one-off poems that I'd known and loved – for pleasure and joy. I now actually like translation because it's a form of writing by proxy: you get the high of finishing something you don't have to start.

A more extensive foray into translation – in collaboration with Stanisław Barańczak – resulted in a collection of poetry by Jan Kochanowski, a Renaissance Polish poet of the late sixteenth century.

Kochanowski's *Laments* are as well known and loved in Polish as Shakespeare's sonnets are in English, a sequence that commemorates the death of the poet's four-year-old daughter, Ursula. I was actually introduced to the poems twice, but only paid attention the second time, when Stanisław Barańczak presented me with an almost complete version of the book, done in couplets that matched the originals line for line and rhyme for rhyme.

One afternoon, in April or May of 1992, I was in the Barańczaks' house to meet the scholar and translator Clare Cavanagh. I was saying how susceptible I'd always been to poems about dead children, such as those by Ben Jonson and John Crowe Ransom, and was putting this down to the accidental death of my own young brother, Christopher. At that point I remembered a set of Polish poems about a dead child that had been sent to me some six or seven years earlier by the poet and translator Adam Czerniawski; and the minute I mentioned them, Clare and Stanisław began to talk about how good they were and how central to the Polish canon and so on. So next thing, as I say, there arrives in the university mail this bundle of translations, accompanied by a suggestion that I might look them over and team up to produce the complete sequence in a book.

I was so busy and tied up with other jobs that I did little more than acknowledge receipt of the things. For months they just lay in a desk drawer, but eventually, during the following spring and summer, I began to address myself to them while Stanisław delivered versions of the remaining poems. We had some face-to-face sessions in the Widener Library before I went back to Dublin in the summer of 1994, kept in touch by fax that autumn and had on-the-spot dealings again in Krakow in November, when we were there to launch a selection of my poems in his translation.

How did you actually contribute to the Kochanowski translation?

Obviously I was in no position either to aid or dispute the construing of the Polish. The delivery of equivalent meanings was all Stanisław's doing, as was the first shaping of the verse. He's famous for his technical genius in Polish, his gift for poems in every conceivable shape and size, and his English translations had an uncanny finish to them, delivered with the rhyme and metre and syntax in perfect running order. What I did was to listen for points where, to my ear, the note sounded either too literary or strained or old-fashioned or whatever. Sometimes I'd suggest the toning down of a full and heavily stressed rhyme, sometimes I'd suggest a change of diction, sometimes I'd just want to transpose a perfectly good line into a register that was more personal, less Standard Englishy. And mostly we were able to come to an agreement.

You can see my hand in a locution like 'slow airs', at line 3 of the opening poem. But before that, in the very first couplet, you get the unmistakable Barańczak signature with the rhyming of 'threnodies' and 'Simonides': Stanisław was a demon for what Ben Jonson would have called keeping the accent, never abandoning his unapologetic fidelity to the metre of the original. My contribution, in the case of the opening couplet, was to decide that he got away with it – although at other times I'd adjudicate against him and we'd work towards new solutions. I was doing, in other words, that most luxurious of all jobs, revising another person's work.

Barańczak, in a Harvard Review *essay, recalled the immediate rapport (including a shared interest in Hopkins's prosody) between you, from the time you first met in 1987. Was he one of the people you were closest to in your Harvard years?*

He was one of those I was fondest of. We didn't meet up all that often, partly because he lived with his family out in Newton, partly because he wasn't a regular on the local poetry scene. But I was excited to get to know him and Anna, there was so much principle and passion and political awareness in them, and so much personal kindness. Their friendship meant much to me during the latter part of my time in Cambridge.

Does your preference for faithful translations over 'creative' renderings or versions cause any significant problems for your translators?

The way translations get done is generally ad hoc and on the hoof. You just have to trust the people involved and hope for the best. When my own work is involved, I *do* prefer the 'faithful' to the 'creative' approach. On the whole, I like a rhymed sonnet to be rhymed in the other language. But then you have to worry about the translator's ability to do rhyme without making it sound laboured or corny: better to get an equivalent of the sense in some decent cadence than a rhymed and metred job that goes Humpetee-Dumpetee, tumptettee-tumptettee, hickory dickory dock . . . For all their 'creativity', it's probably safer to have poets doing the work; I've been lucky in that regard in places as different as Finland, France, Greece, Italy, Russia, Catalonia, Mexico. In Finland, I even had the experience of being taken aside and told the translation was very good. Usually it's the other way round.

As if you weren't already busy enough, you held the Oxford Professorship of Poetry from 1989 to 1994 – a topic to which I'd now like to turn. Why did you let your name go forward as a candidate?

I'd been approached on two previous occasions, to see if I'd stand: Charles Monteith was already urging me to think about it in 1979, and he renewed the proposal in 1984; but I felt neither up to doing the lectures nor ready for the exposure. But by 1989 I had seven years of Harvard teaching behind me, had delivered the T. S. Eliot Memorial Lectures at the University of Kent and the Richard Ellmann Lectures in Emory University, so I was that much more experienced and confident about taking on a big series.

Is it true, by the way, that Richard Ellmann himself suggested you for those lectures before he died?

That's what I heard from Ron Schuchard, who was his colleague at Emory during his years there as a visiting professor. Dick Ellmann knew before he died that there was going to be a series of memorial lectures and Ron, who by the late 1980s was a friend of mine, had the job of organizing them. I first met Ron when I went to Emory to do a reading and he ran a party in his house afterwards – the high point of the evening being a performance by a blind postgrad-uate student. This man's research was on the music and methods Yeats employed when he did those incantatory readings with

Florence Farr, and he had managed to get a replica of the Dolmetsch psaltery constructed for himself. He had also a haunting, high-pitched voice and delivered Yeats's words to the accompaniment found on the original sheet music. Anyhow, that's how the Emory connection started. On that first visit I also met a graduate student called Rand Brandes who was to devote himself to my work over the years and would end up doing my bibliography. In fact, in the course of my Ellmann lectures visit, he interviewed me for a special issue of *Salmagundi* . . .

. . . *published to celebrate your impending fiftieth birthday, if I remember correctly.*

It was. And that's another reason why I was ready to let my name go forward for the Oxford post. I felt a bit more grown up, having entered the sixth decade, but I had also got a certain restoration in the course of a sabbatical year. I was, for instance, writing the 'Squarings' sequence of poems and had reached a point where the preparation of statements about poets and poetry was helping to clarify and consolidate what the whole thing meant in my own life. Most importantly, I believed that, if I stood, I'd have a good chance of being elected.

You weren't afraid of overload? You still had your poems, Harvard teaching, correspondence, readings and the rest of it to cope with.

One way you keep yourself up to the mark is by raising the bar. I suppose by then I thought I'd be funking something if I didn't have a go at the Oxford job. It would have been different if nobody had been wanting me to put my name forward; but as it was, there had been encouragement going back ten years and being put on your mettle is no bad thing. Never once did I think of the professorship as either a distraction from poetry or in conflict with the Harvard appointment. It's an honorific post, requiring the holder to deliver three public lectures a year, but the residency requirements are minimal. And the fact that Matthew Arnold and Robert Graves and W. H. Auden have held the office endows it with extra meaning and seriousness.

Were there subjects you were burning to explore in the Oxford lectures, or did the topics emerge only gradually?

There was no preconceived plan of campaign. It took me a good while to settle on a topic for the first lecture, which is where you want to give some idea of the shape of things to come. It's also one you can't help being anxious about, since you're up there under scrutiny, strutting and fretting your hour upon the podium. I remember thinking at first that I'd call it 'Doing English', and talk in a more or less autobiographical, more or less post-colonial way about how a farmer's son from Derry ended up behind the lectern in the Examination Schools. The interesting case of Heaney and hegemony, as it were. But very soon that approach struck me as entirely expected, too pat for a Paddy, and not really the kind of thing I either did well enough or believed in sufficiently. I didn't have the theoretical grounding for it and my natural bent was to celebrate rather than deconstruct the art of individual poems and poets.

So when the phrase 'the redress of poetry' swam up, I myself was aswim with intimations of possibility. I suddenly realized that I could talk about poetry as something hung out on the imaginative arm of the scales to balance or redress the burden of the actual and the endured. I don't mean as compensation or as consolation, more as comprehension, a comprehension which has to be its own reward. There was still no clearly worked-out programme or argument, but all of a sudden the lecture, indeed the whole series, had discovered an orientation.

How did you actually go about drafting the lectures? Did you make a lot of random notes or did you start with a blank page and then develop your thoughts, paragraph by paragraph, as you went along?

Blank page, paragraph by paragraph, with pen and ink, no word processor – and usually no typescript until after the thing had been delivered. One development that helped inestimably, however – and not just with the lectures but with the poems I'd been writing during that 1988/9 sabbatical year – was the fact that we were back in possession of Glanmore Cottage. I'd gone to give a lecture in the University of Toronto in January 1988; while there, having lunch with Ann Saddlemyer, she told me she was ready to sell the place. I nearly fainted at the table. She was prepared to give me access for a second time to the *locus amoenus*. Nothing that had happened since we left Wicklow was more important in my writing life; when I got back to Ireland that summer and back down to the old grounds, I was like a fugitive in a safe house. So it was in the cottage, in the early autumn of 1989, that the first lecture was written.

I presume there were one or two false starts – subjects adopted and then abandoned? And there are the lectures you delivered but did not include in The Redress of Poetry.

I can't remember false starts, other than that first thought about 'Doing English'. But it still took me a while to get my bearings in Oxford and set a steady course for the series. To begin with, all my energy and anxiety went into preparing the inaugural – after which I was off to Harvard for the spring semester of 1990, with the Field Day *Philoctetes* assignment on my hands, as well as the need to get two more public lectures ready. One of these, about Robert Frost, followed the redress theme quite systematically and the other, on Louis MacNeice, was a bit last-minutey, and floundered rather than focused. Then the following year there were three more, a diptych and an extra, as it were, all under the general title 'Talking Shop': the first part of the diptych was called 'The Playthings in the Playhouse' and the second 'The Weight of Hours', the first saying that poems were basically part of the whole extra dimension that *Homo ludens* had created for himself, the better to enjoy life, and the second saying that within the playground of the poem there could be a coming to terms with 'the weight of hours', 'the thorns of life', whatever. The third lecture, 'Above the Brim', on younger Irish poets, suggested basically that the generation of Muldoon and McGuckian, Ní Dhomhnaill and Durcan had a less earnest relationship with the historical moment than the poets of my own or the previous generation; they had a more absolved relationship to politics and were happy to redress or resist the gravity of the times by going 'above the brim' (a phrase from Robert Frost's 'Birches').

In your inaugural Oxford lecture, you quoted with approval Wallace Stevens's view that the nobility of poetry consists of a 'violence from within that protects us from a violence without'. Although, a little earlier in this book, you remarked that Stevens's achievement was 'as big and solid as the man was himself', I nevertheless wonder if his work was too abstract and detached – too 'ivory towered' – to effectively counter 'the pressure of reality'. Would you say something more about how you regard him?

A bit like one of those mighty decorated cruise liners that sail the Spanish main and dwarf the Caribbean quays. There's a discursive, abstracting tendency all right, but there's also a huge buoyancy, a post-Impressionist appetite for colour and flourish. He made his living, let's not forget, in what we'd now call the corporate sector. What went on in the boardroom didn't enter the poetry as content, but the hard stare of the executive, the cutting through fudge to get to a bottom line – that kind of unremitting need to reach an unblinkered view of the real state of affairs – is where the poetry starts from.

He knows, in other words, how the liner was built and the cost of it before he goes on to decorate it. He's not just the Mallarmé of Hartford. He's what the headhunters once called 'the right stuff'. God is gone, he says, the world runs down the ringing grooves of change, the imagination is necessary if the human is to stay on track and not be run over. Frost famously told Stevens that his poems were full of bric-a-brac, but the opulence and flim-flam of Stevens cover up a stark vision of unaccommodated man and his need to accommodate himself as best he can to this 'old wilderness of the sun'. The poetry, in other words, is a very deliberately constructed defence, the equivalent of a camouflaged stockade or an ozone layer. It allows for stand-off and resistance – the violence from within.

Could Stevens ever rival Frost in your personal canon?

His poems are not nearly as deeply lodged as Frost's. I'm not possessed by them to the same extent, although every time I look at 'The River of Rivers in Connecticut' or 'The Plain Sense of Things' or any number of those late poems, I'm in thrall to their plain mystery, the way thinginess and concept are plied together. It's a very hard, very clean poetic alloy. But I grew into this appreciation late, so Stevens hasn't figured much in my 'keyboard of reference', as Mandelstam might call it.

While praising your Oxford lectures highly, Andrew Motion, in his review of The Redress of Poetry, *said that the lecture on Yeats and Larkin 'raised questions'. Do you, Motion asks, 'believe so absolutely in the poet's duty to show an affirming flame that moods which simply refuse to be transfigured are intrinsically inferior? And if they are, what is the poet to do about them? Suppress them? Ignore them?'*

It's overstating things, I believe, to suggest that I made it 'the poet's duty to show an affirming flame'. I certainly stated a preference for such poetry and set Yeats's 'The Man and the Echo' against Larkin's 'Aubade' in order to contest the latter's line that 'Death is no different whined at than withstood'. It's the poet's duty to make, *tout court*, and make what he can of what Andrew calls the 'moods', whatever they happen to be. I certainly did not do down Larkin's poem *qua* poem, nor did I decry or question the feelings he was expressing. On the other hand, I stated a preference for the different feelings that Yeats was expressing and I also knew that I would raise eyebrows as well as questions.

Did you have much contact with the Irish community in Oxford?

In those years, there were quite a few postgraduate students at work in the Irish Studies area with John Kelly at St John's College, and I met several of them through my friendship with John and Christine Kelly: John Redmond, for example, and James McCabe. Geraldine Higgins. You had a very active music scene as well, with the singer Mick Henry at the centre of it, and late sessions in the Bullingdon Arms.

All that was wonderfully enjoyable, but I should also say that the English dimension was every bit as enriching as the Irish. There were the rites of college life, but also the rewards of drives in the Oxford countryside on Saturdays with Bernard and Heather O'Donoghue, and Sunday lunches at a lovely old inn with Jon and Jill Stallworthy. I remember, in particular, being brought by Bernard to the Rollright Stones. I'd wanted to see them because John Hewitt had alluded to them movingly in his poem 'The Search' as 'a broken circle of stones on a rough hillside', an emblem equally of homelessness and at-homeness. But we also did the rounds of Matthew Arnold's Thames, Ottoline Morrell's Garsington, John Masefield's Boar's Hill and C. S. Lewis's house at Headington Quarry. I was being spoiled.

You mentioned the 'rites of college life'. Did you take easily to high table and High Church evensong and all the rest of it?

434

Evensong, and for that matter, morning song, was pure joy. During the five years of my tenure, Tony Smith, the president of Magdalen, made an entire suite available to Marie and me in the President's Lodgings. The bonus was the location of the rooms, just above where the college choir did its practice, so we'd waken in the mornings to the sound of these angel sopranos practising their scales. *O ces voix d'enfants, chantant dans la coupole*! I did greatly enjoy some aspects of college life, especially walks in the grounds at Magdalen, around the deer park, following the path established by Addison, Addison's Walk. But I was happily bilocated during those years, since I'd been made an honorary fellow of St John's College as well, thanks to the good offices of the Kellys and President Bill Hayes and his wife Judy. One thing I greatly liked about St John's was the line-up of their poets in the senior common room – a portrait of A. E. Housman on the wall, and bronze heads of Graves and Larkin and John Wain on the shelves. It gave me the idea of donating a bronze head of Oscar Wilde to Magdalen in gratitude for my years in residence. Oscar, who had been a student there, now gazes across the hall at another old Magdalen man, the famous law lord and Master of the Rolls, Lord Denning. If I did nothing else at Oxford, I at least managed to change the balance of sculptural power.

After your time there as Professor of Poetry, you gave a lecture in Oxford, to the Friends of the Bodleian Library, on translating Beowulf. *Tellingly, you called the lecture 'Fretwork'; and it coincided with the debate about whether Anglo-Saxon should remain a compulsory part of the undergraduate degree course in English.*

There was no connection – none intended, at any rate – between the title and the argument about the Oxford English syllabus. The 'fret' was meant to echo Stephen Dedalus's description in *A Portrait of the Artist as a Young Man* of his sense of difference and alienation as an Irish speaker of English: when he hears the accent and pronunciation of the English-born Dean of Studies, he famously declares, 'My soul frets in the shadow of his language.' So my first point was that Joyce's linguistic achievement cleared 'fret' of that negative charge and allowed Irish writers to say what I make Joyce's shade say in 'Station Island', 'The English language belongs to us.'

My second point was that this stake in the language entailed a different kind of fretwork for the Irish translator of Old English verse – work, that is, where 'fret' means 'to adorn with interlaced work'. I was just stating the obvious, saying that the attempt to keep the metrical, interlacing, alliterative patterns of the Anglo-Saxon verse line was a fret, but in that second, positive sense.

Presumably you favoured the retention of Beowulf *as a prescribed text?*

I was in favour of some Anglo-Saxon component in the course, some encounter with the beginnings in order to give students a sense of the physical brunt of the old tongue and the etymological foundations of modern English. You couldn't be absolutely in favour of everybody having to go the whole Anglo-Saxon hog, nor could you be absolutely against an historico-linguistic requirement of some sort.

Were you attracted to translating Beowulf *by your admiration for the poem per se, or was your love of the Anglo-Saxon language itself the deciding factor?*

More the latter. I didn't, in truth, have any special fondness for *Beowulf* before I started work on it. The heroic poem I knew as a student and liked better was the shorter, incomplete 'Battle of Maldon'. The more elegiac poems, 'The Wanderer' and 'The Seafarer', were the ones that gave me a feel for the language, voices shaken by the North Sea wind, as it were, voices crying under the ness. I'm still not sure whether Anglo-Saxon was a heard melody for me or an unheard one, a music I imagined for myself.

You've written about your immersion in the Anglo-Saxon of Beowulf *as a sort of antidote to the American English of your Harvard years. Work on the translation, you implied, was an anchoring influence, an exercise that worked against the 'untethered music' of American poetry. Was this something you realized at a later stage, or was it a conscious motivation all along?*

More like a half-conscious one. When I got into a passage with lines like 'Men climbed eagerly up the gangplank, / sand churned in surf, warriors loaded / a cargo of weapons', I was brought to my writing senses in an old familiar way. Theoretical anxieties fell away. I was like an oarsman on the rowing benches, getting on with the job. I hadn't to think of navigation, hadn't to calculate or keep an eye on the stars. The experience was physical and the result different from the generally frictionless idiom of transatlantic poetry. I felt the encounter was restorative and salutary.

Did John Braidwood, the Queen's University lecturer mentioned in your introduction to Beowulf, *invest Anglo-Saxon with excitement when you were an undergraduate?*

Not really. He was a Scotsman who'd been in the army during the war, a professor who was still in large part a major. He had a brusqueness and tart humour that I liked, but had no special feel for the literature as such. We went through the first half of *Beowulf* with him routinely and reluctantly, even in some cases resentfully, because it was prescribed for the final exam.

Thirty years later, as translator of the entire poem, were you able to work directly from the original text, or were you dependent on cribs and other translations?

Very dependent on glossaries in the different editions, and on cribs as well – mostly in fact on the literal prose version by E. T. Donaldson in *The Norton Anthology of English Literature,* the one my translation was due to replace. But I also used a translation I'd used as a student, again in prose, by Clark Hall, revised by C. L. Wrenn. Wrenn had been the external examiner when I did my finals at Queen's, so I had a special relationship with that particular edition. And every now and again I checked with Bill Alfred's version in The Modern Library series, not least because Bill was a friend and a colleague at Harvard.

Michael Alexander's verse translation had been the standard Penguin Classics edition for years. For that very reason, I tended not to consult it – or any other verse translation, for that matter. Occasionally, after I'd got through one of the set pieces, I'd take a look at how Michael handled it, but never as an aid to construing. The better the literary translation the worse it is to see it before you've done your own. There was, mind you, another translator in America who sent me his book when I was halfway through, asking to see some of the stuff I was doing. It was a bit much; but, since we're all supposed to be part of this great big commonwealth of letters, I sent a few samples. He was an Anglo-Saxon specialist who'd had a fine fat paperback of text and commentary on the market for years, so no doubt he was touchy about an amateur shouldering his way into the field. I probably enjoyed his discomfiture as much as he enjoyed his superior knowledge.

Speaking of superior knowledge, how inhibiting or irritating was it that Norton appointed a kind of academic 'minder' to ensure you didn't stray too far from scholarly orthodoxy?

I was glad to be minded. Alfred David was one of the general editors of the Norton anthology and it would have been remiss of him not to have exercised some kind of quality control. The translation, let's face it, was a product that was going be promoted by an educational publisher with a high reputation and high standards. Even so, Al mostly gave me my head: I'd done a few hundred lines before I sent him anything for inspection, and his commentaries from the start were firm and clear but also friendly. He wasn't your pedantic literalist, he knew there were literary considerations involved and he'd often suggest rephrasings and rewordings that took account of metre as well as meaning. Naturally he was at pains to indicate where I had strayed – sometimes knowingly – from the sense of the original, but overall he was the good policeman and I was only too happy to co-operate.

We conducted a lot of our business by mail or by fax. I would send off a wad of typescript, he would annotate the pages, add his comments wherever there was a problem, maybe also where he considered something well handled, and then he'd return the revised draft with a letter. Usually that was the end of it, although sometimes there would be follow-ups and small refinements. That part of the business was actually very pleasant, since rewriting is a lot easier, especially when you have a sympathetic collaborator. Generally speaking, I was allowed the final say, but I was never in a position to disregard Al's comments.

Never?

I *did* override the literal once and Al gave in to my special pleading. This was in the famous description of what's conventionally known as 'the haunted mere', the mountain lake where Grendel's mother has her underwater hideout. The place is so sinister, King

438

Hrothgar tells Beowulf, that a hunted deer will stop short on the bank and allow itself to be killed rather than enter the water. The kenning used by the poet when he's talking about the deer is 'heath-stepper', which is strong and springy and dry and delicate, but in spite of all that I wanted 'heather-stepper'. I wanted my fingerprint on the diction, wanted access to my own boggy heather rather than exposure on the Brontëan heath, and wrote a long explanation of my preference, or prejudice, to Al. And he accommodated. But there was some tit for tat involved, since I had made an earlier sacrifice on the altar of accuracy. This was in the description of Shield Sheafson's funeral boat as it strained at its moorings in the frozen harbour, a line which is faithfully translated in the Norton volume as 'ice-clad, outbound, a craft for a prince'; in typescript (and in 'A Ship of Death' in *The Haw Lantern*), it had been rendered more freely as 'clad with ice, its cables tightening'. Although not a word-for-word equivalent, it nevertheless seemed to me to have more physical and linguistic strain and strictness.

Did Professor David, or others on the Norton editorial team, need persuasion that your many Hiberno-English usages were justified?

No persuasion, they probably just decided to indulge me. I'd hit upon what I called the 'Scullionspeak' register years before Al became involved. The first approach by Norton had come around 1984 or 1985, when an editor called John Benedict approached me with the idea of a commissioned translation. I therefore prepared a draft of the first hundred lines or so, up to the point where the minstrel sings in the hall, and they seemed to like it all right, although they understandably wanted a bit more – something from the action sequences, from Beowulf's fight with Grendel, for example. But at that point I had no appetite to proceed further. It was slow, hard going, I wasn't sure if I'd be fit for the long haul . . . For various reasons, it was the spring of 1995 before I started on the job for a second time. By then, however, the idiom had long been established – first time round I'd got my 'So' for a starter and my 'thole' for a seconder; by line 13, I'd turned young Prince Beow into a 'cub', which is what he'd have been called in south Derry in the 1940s; I also had Shield Sheafson laying down the law and the great Halfdane holding sway, and in general had launched the

Anglo-Saxon keel on my own vernacular. So it was natural enough to proceed eventually to a 'bawn' and a 'graith' and an eagle 'hoking' through the corpses on a battlefield. I went too far, I now realize, when I called King Hrothgar's spokesman a 'brehon', but Al was prepared to let it stand.

It seems, therefore, that Terry Eagleton was justified in asserting that you ('an erstwhile outsider') had made your Beowulf *translation 'the final, triumphant reversal of (your) cultural dispossession'.*

It's a grand statement of the case, but it makes the right point. Instead of putting 'The End' on the last page, I could have finished by rewriting a line from the conclusion of 'Lycidas': 'Fret no more, woeful Seamus, in the shadow of his language.'

Another reviewer, Nicholas Howe, remarked: 'Heaney's Beowulf *would have been far more exciting if it had followed the practice of Derek Walcott's* Omeros, *and travelled the full and exhilarating distance from translation to poetic remaking. Why didn't Heaney do so?' Is this a question you would care to answer?*

The answer is simple: I didn't know or love *Beowulf* enough to remake it. If it had been a poem I'd internalized and lived with long and dreamily there might have been a chance of doing what I'd done with *Buile Shuibhne* in 'Sweeney Redivivus' or have done, more recently, with *Aeneid VI* in 'Route 110'. I like that book of the *Aeneid* so much I'm inclined to translate it as a separate unit, as Sir John Harrington did in the seventeenth century. But in the case of *Beowulf*, I only really got to know and love it page by laborious page as I translated.

Did you eventually come to enjoy the task or did it remain a chore to the end?

It was unusual for me to manage any more than twenty lines a day, or to work at it for more than five or ten days at a time. I did it in sheer concentrated bursts like that, in longhand, on big lined notebooks, looking up the meanings of words, co-ordinating with the cribs, prospecting for alliteration and so on, but every so often I would indeed warm, as they say, to the task. Each morning I was like a man sentenced to hard labour, rolling up his sleeves, spitting on his hands and taking hold of the shaft of a sledgehammer. This was especially so when I was doing the first half. It was less of a chore – I had more relish and momentum – when it came to Beowulf in old age and the slow, inexorable movement towards the last scene with the funeral pyre.

Which parts proved the most enjoyable to translate?

Beowulf's sea journeys to and from Denmark, with all the rituals of arrival and departure. The two great funeral scenes – the ship of death at the beginning, the construction of the pyre and the barrow at the end. The descriptions of the dragon, of Beowulf as he addresses his thanes and makes ready for his last stand. I tended to enjoy what was most mournful or most majestic.

As you worked on the poem, did you form any sense of the character of the poet who originally wrote Beowulf?

In the introduction, I talked about his undeluded understanding of what people have to face in a violent world – very attractive because it gives weight and emotional credibility to the *sententiae* he keeps delivering about *wyrd* and so on, the *swa sceal* factor in the writing: the 'so shall a man who does this be that' formula comes across as something more than a mere proverbial QED, more like wisdom possessed at some personal level. I got the sense of a personal voice, of somebody with a special sympathy for the older characters – grey-haired Hrothgar under attack in Heorot, depending on the young Beowulf, then the old Beowulf depending on himself alone as he goes out to face the dragon.

There's a marked gravity and composure in the voice which I found attractive, an attention, for example, to the details of protocol and correct behaviour: he's always happy describing good conduct at feasts or funerals or on the field of battle. He even feels a kind of sympathy for the old dragon, who's only, after all, doing what an old dragon is meant to do: going on the rampage after somebody breaks and enters his gold hoard.

Grendel and his mother?

They have strong parts and the poet must see to it that they play those parts for all they are worth; but when he's dealing with them, I think he's more like a director in a director's chair, very aware of himself as the professional scop, the ringmaster in charge of an epic show, less 'shut-eyed' in his imagining. To use the language of TV listings, you file Beowulf's fights with Grendel and his dam under 'Action', the fight with the dragon under 'Drama'.

Even though you did not produce a TV version of Beowulf – *or, for that matter, contribute to the recent film – you seem to have had a wider public in mind than would be usual for an Anglo-Saxon poem. When you first published the translation with Faber and Faber in London and Farrar, Straus and Giroux in New York, you added marginal glosses – a bit like voice-overs – as if to signal that this was more than a text for academic study, that it could also be approached by a general readership.*

Norton had commissioned the translation for a teaching anthology, meant for use in the classroom. But the president of the firm was extremely decent and allowed Faber and Farrar, Straus, my regular literary publishers, to go first and market the book as if it were work I had done on my own initiative. That was why I wrote the introduction and got the idea of adding those little sidebars as guides for the non-student, non-academic audience.

As things turned out, you did *attract an enormous general readership. How do you account for the best-seller status* Beowulf *achieved on both sides of the Atlantic?*

Your guess about that is as good as mine. Sometimes I think it may have had to do with the name *Beowulf*. There's terrific phonetic strength to it; it has a slight air of ancient mystery and – in the 'wolf' bit – a slight hint of danger. There's the fact that the poem is widely taught in high schools in America – which means that, for a great number of people over there, it has an appeal that is half nostalgic and half familiar. And there's also the mystery of the best-seller phenomenon itself, the mass buy-up of a book that possesses a certain cultural cachet and takes the general fancy but isn't necessarily going to be read.

Were you surprised that the poem was shortlisted for the Whitbread Prize? Did you expect a translation to be eligible?

I was surprised, because *The Spirit Level* had won the Whitbread Book of the Year for 1996 – which alone suggested that the translation would not be nominated. When it *was*, however, I don't remember any worry on my part about its eligibility in the poetry category. Once the question was raised, I could see that there was something debatable, but at that stage it wasn't my job to debate it.

Much was made by the press of the fact that the judges who chose your Beowulf *included a model (Jerry Hall) and a comedienne (Sandi Toksvig) . . . What do you recall of the Whitbread dinner and of meeting the judges?*

The only judge I met was Jerry Hall, and that was very briefly, in the big surge of people round our table once I came down from the stage. She was there among the rest to offer congratulations and I was in the act of moving into one of those luvvie kisses when I remembered the press cameras and braked or swerved in the nick of time. But the near-miss was still recorded and was run the next day on at least one front page. Marie also saw the same Jerry interviewed on TV about her part in the business; when asked if she had voted for the Harry Potter book, she answered in her calm Texan drawl, 'I did not, but my children would have.' In fact, in the lead-up to that final stage of adjudication when judges – no matter who they are – are faced with the impossible task of deciding between fiction and poetry and biography and children's literature, what was nice was the way J. K. Rowling and myself featured much less in the discussion than the subjects of our books. It was Beowulf versus Harry Potter, not me versus her. I found that a relief.

15

'An ear to the line'
Writing and Reading

~

Some years ago, you told an English journalist: 'My notion was always that, if the poems were good, they would force their way through.' Is this still your experience?

Eagerness, excitement, a sense of change came over me when I began to write poetry in earnest in 1962. So I've always associated the moment of writing with a moment of lift, of joy, of unexpected reward. For better or worse, I arrived at the notion that labour wouldn't help. From Catholicism, I acquired the notion of grace; and I do believe that, unless there is a certain unforeseen energy to begin with, you can't proceed. I always believed that whatever had to be written would somehow get itself written. That was in the early days, when there was plenty of charge in the battery. But I still can't get away from that; I don't know how to write a poem unless there's something to write a poem with. You can't get started without a first line that goes musically – by which I don't mean melodiously, just that it needs phonetic purchase or rhythmical promise.

Over the years, you have often quoted Keats's observation, 'If poetry comes not as naturally as leaves to a tree, it better not come at all.' Is that just a young poet's perspective?

Well, it doesn't mean – and it didn't mean for Keats – that the actual labour of composition or the working on the poem is an involuntary natural function like sneezing. You have to work. One of the best books I discovered early on, just when I'd begun to write, was Jon Stallworthy's *Between the Lines*, about Yeats's manuscripts. A poem like 'Coole Park, 1929', thirty-two lines long – a middle-range

Yeats poem; a cruising-altitude poem where he's not breaking any sound barriers – takes thirty-eight pages of drafts and yet he had only a few of the lines to begin with. If you have a stanza form, whatever the stanza form is, whether it's a sonnet or couplets or quatrains or whatever, you can work at that – and work with it – because the stanza form immediately calls up all other stanzas in the language. To some extent, you're playing variations or singing in chorus. The quick free-verse poem sometimes happens; but, oddly enough, my experience is that the poem comes more quickly if there is a form.

Does this mean that a poem essentially begins for you when you find a form?

Sometimes it begins with a theme, at other times with a form. Generally speaking, my poems come from things remembered, quite often from away back, or things I see that remind me of something else. Sometimes the thing has an aura and an invitation and some kind of blocked significance hanging around it. I'm a great hoarder, of course; I once did a little sequence of poems called 'Shelf Life': things that are kept, picked up, like bits of stone, an iron spike, an old smoothing iron that belonged in our house, and so on.

Is there a poetry time of day and a prose time of day?

Well, it used to be that – whatever I did – I wrote at night. That was in my twenties, thirties, forties, partly because I was teaching and busy all day and living a full life with the thrilling Heaney house-hold. The house, you see, quietened later at night. Now that the house is quiet all day, I tend to work in the mornings if poems are coming. But I don't have a time of day for poems and a time of day for essays. In fact, my experience is that prose usually equals duty – last minute, overdue-deadline stuff or a panic lecture to be written. Some of the poems I like best were written in the lay-bys of a lecture I was preparing; you forget yourself when you get into a hurry like that.

I remember Anne Yeats saying that her father mumbled to himself when he started to write. Would the Heaney household know that a poem was coming on?

Not so much in the house, because I would withdraw a bit in order to be on my own. One of the best times for me, for incubating and counting out the beats of a poem, is on long drives. Marie always knows, because she sees my fingers on the steering wheel beating out the thing. Many, many poems were conceived of and started out in that shut-eyed manner – well not *literally* shut-eyed! As well as car journeys, long aeroplane journeys and seclusions in hotel rooms are good. Escapes like that, displacements from your normal life, are useful for making lists and for allowing images to come up.

Do you ever feel burdened by the sheer amount of work you know it will require to do justice to a particular inspiration?

One of the difficulties is to know whether a little, quick flash of lyric is sufficient. You have the invitation and the inspiration, for want of a better word, but the question that I can never answer is this: to what extent the will should do the work of the imagination, as Yeats said; how far you should push a thing. A lot of poems I have a fondness for came smartly through. On the other hand, the poems in *North* were grimly executed, and I really like them because they're odd and hard and contrary.

When you're starting out as a young poet, you love the high of finishing. So you do the lyric quickly and that's a joy. As you go on, the joy of actually doing it, of beating the gold out further, of making more of it, of wondering can I take it further, is what you ideally want. But then the doubt comes in: Am I killing it? Am I deadening it? Coleridge said, 'Poetry, like schoolboys, by too frequent and severe correction, may be cowed into dullness.' But there are poems that ask to have more poems attached to them, to grow. Another question to which there are different attitudes is whether imperfection hasn't got its imperatives also, or whether you should make the poem as trim and as perfect as possible. I remember Craig Raine saying, 'A poem should be as tightly shut as an oyster.' Well, D. H. Lawrence might have said it should be loose as a big hibiscus.

How can you tell a poem is finished?

Hard to talk about that. It's an intuition. You see it physically in painters: prowling round a canvas; the body is distressed and stressed and then, when it's finished, the body relaxes. You know when it's *not* finished at least . . .

Do you keep a notebook of phrases and images for later use?

I haven't kept a notebook regularly and what I depend upon is mood. I remember seeing, in the early seventies, Theodore Roethke's *Straw for the Fire*, a book of lines that didn't get into poems. I thought, God, I could never do that at all, there's no straw, just old brick. I do have *some* notes, little lists of things, subjects and so on.

You mentioned earlier that the poem will come more quickly if there is a form. Would you be offended to be called a formalist?

I wouldn't be offended but I think it would be a mistake. 'Formalist' to me sounds like a kind of doctrinaire position. I totally believe in form; but quite often, when people use the term, they mean shape rather than form. There's the sonnet shape, fair enough, but it's not just a matter of rhyming the eight lines and the other six; they happen to be set one on top of each other like two boxes, but they're more like a torso and pelvis. There has to be a little bit of muscle movement, it has to be alive in some sort of way. A moving poem doesn't just mean that it touches you, it means it has to move itself along as a going linguistic concern. Form is not like a pastry cutter – the dough has to move and discover its own shape. I love to feel that my own voice is on track; that can happen within a metrical shape where you're stepping out to a set tune or it can happen in a less regulated way within a free shape.

The poem I began with as a writer, 'Digging', was truer to my phonetic grunting from south Derry than to any kind of iambic correctness from the books. Every writer lives between the vernacular given – whether it be the vernacular of Oxford or of the Caribbean – and some received idiom from the tradition. Ted Hughes had a marvellous little parable about this. Imagine, he said, a flock of gazelles grazing. One gazelle flicks its tail and all the gazelles flick their tails as if to say, 'We are eternal gazelle.' Most writers, Hughes says, have a first speech of that sort – a dialect of the tribe or the class or whatever. Suppose they are in a foreign city and they hear a familiar accent, it's like a gazelle tail flicking, so then the other gazelle flicks and thinks, 'Ah, I'm at home here, I'm strong here.' For every writer, there's that first language and then there's the lingua franca. Joseph Brodsky believed we must keep to the lingua franca of the forms, but I am equally inclined to the gazelle-speak of south Derry.

The book of mine that came most intensely out of the first shock of the Troubles was *North*. The first section of the book is gnarled and fossilized; the writing comes at great pressure but it's not in any traditional cast. It has forms all right, but they're like clinkers inside a stove or like cinders. The second half of the book has a certain amount of iambic pentameter for opener, less intense stuff. So I would say that the place where I was most intensely engaged with the Troubles is least connected with traditional form. The second wave of my writing was a lesson to myself and a reaction to the lecturing I was doing. In the mid-seventies I had begun teaching again: poets like Sir Thomas Wyatt and Andrew Marvell, whom I hadn't studied since I was an undergraduate. And I had been reading Yeats more intensely at that stage, middle Yeats especially. In Wyatt, Marvell and Yeats, I was very attracted to a plain style. My first impulse when writing had been to make the language as rich as possible and to have a stained-glass effect. But in my forties, I wanted plain clear glass, and soon realized that if the first appeal of a poem isn't going to be in the texture of its language, then it must have some other means of taking hold, and traditional metre and a syntax that runs over and plays against the lines can do the job.

Do you have a preference for pararhymes and half rhymes over full rhymes?

On the whole, I'd go for something less than the full rhyme, 'melt' and 'milt', 'talkback' and 'goldbeak', that kind of near-miss; but every now and again it's great to do the unapologetic thing and sound the full chime. I've even indulged in the luxury of feminine rhyme. 'Brighten' and 'lighten'. 'Between us', '*amoenus*'. I improvise on the hoof, or maybe better say in the hope. Once or twice I've left a gap, but not very often. That kind of waiting for the right word to fill the space is something I associate more with translation. If you're writing your own poem, you're after something just at the edge of your knowledge, so you're in a much more improvisatory frame of mind. But when you're translating, you tend to know the effect you're after, the space is there at the centre like an empty space in a jigsaw, and what you need most is the one piece of language that fits exactly. Often the way to find it is to wait, think about it when you waken at night, or when you're trying to get to sleep, for that matter.

You are a poet for whom the sound the words make is crucial.

Completely. It's the key to getting started. In saying that, a poem must have the right sound – I don't mean sound as decoration or elaboration, as 'verbal magic'; I mean something to do with what might be called the musculature of your speech, the actual cadencing of the thing as it moves along. When, for example, I wrote the opening of the first poem in my first book – 'Between my finger and my thumb / The squat pen rests; snug as a gun' – I just knew I had got stuck in in earnest.

Would you accept Eliot's contention that the subject matter is simply a device to keep the reader distracted while the poem performs its real work subliminally?

It's hard to separate subject matter from action. Synge asked, 'Is not style born out of the shock of new material?' I can't conceive of a poetry that hasn't a subject to deal with. The subject may be secluded or it may be seen constantly in the process of dematerializing, as in the case of John Ashbery; but actually his subject is the nature of contemporary reality shifting away from you. In my own case, I like to have matter as well as subject and the heftier it is the more interesting.

Frost is a great master of subject matter. In 'Out, Out –', he writes about a child having his hand cut off by accident by a circular saw in a yard in Vermont. You could tell it as an anecdote. The suddenness, the shock, the unpreparedness are prepared for as he establishes a calm sense of the ordinariness and the solidity of this world. But the poem isn't just what Ezra Pound would have called 'photography'. At the end, there's the line 'And they' – the people left afterwards – 'since they / Were not the one dead, turned to their affairs'. This leaves it up to the reader to make what he can of it: is this a callous dismissal or is it a fatalistic and sorrowful proceeding with things as they are in the world? Frost has made a thing that imitates, Aristotle might have said, that re-presents the first thing. It's all done there in language. You have that also in

D. H. Lawrence, in a completely different way: poems about bats or a mountain lion, but not just documentary, full of word-energy and action.

What role does humour play in your poetry?

There's a good deal of humour in me, I hope; and I have a kind of sardonic attitude to a lot of things. But for better or worse, when I sit opposite the desk, it's like being an altar boy in the sacristy getting ready to go out on to the main altar. There's a gravitas comes over me. 'Gravitas' may be the wrong word – it's a matter of depth of engagement and musical register, a matter of what is at stake for yourself in a poem. If I'm writing light verse, it doesn't matter a damn to me whether it's good or bad; nothing is being tested or verified – there's simply a performance going on. Nothing is at stake, nothing is being won or lost. Occasional poems are 'entertainments', as Graham Greene might say. I don't demean them, I enjoy writing them: poems for people getting married, retirement poems, birthday poems . . . Lately, mind you, I've been fiddling with the 'moral fables' of the medieval Scots poet Robert Henryson. And the humour is a big part of their attraction, a dry insinuating Scottish humour, very close to the kind I grew up with.

What are your thoughts about accessibility and obscurity in poetry?

At the moment, certainly in younger British poets, on the example of somebody like Paul Muldoon, there is a genre of poetry which exults in its far-fetchedness and in which privacy of reference is not an anxiety. Oblique in a way that collapses the distinction between the elusive and the allusive. The Internet quality of the information that is pulled into the poem is part of the poem's self-fashioning. So, there is a dandyish, show-off and stand-off quality to some of that writing. There's a touch of the late-metaphysical swanky-fancy mode there. I am a slower reader myself and have to be convinced that there's a chance a payload is going to be delivered.

If you take a brilliant performer in prose, like Italo Calvino: he is a pastry chef of a high order who can do wonderful things; but, because of the quality of intelligence and an eagerness of attention, what is indicated to you – in spite of the fluency and elegance of the whole thing – is a strength of mind, a sense that we are performing on the high wires here but there's no safety net. This is serious stuff.

And how is that transmitted? By the writing, by the tone, even, one might say, by the muscle-tone. If I encounter difficult poems, I listen – that's the only way I can read – for an indication of somebody who knows the score poetically, who's after something beyond all this fiddle.

And the avant-garde?

It's an old-fashioned term by now. In literature, nobody can cause bother any more. John Ashbery was a kind of avant-garde poet certainly and now he's become a mainstream voice. The work of the 'Language Poets' and of the alternative poetries in Britain – associated with people in Cambridge University like J. H. Prynne – is not the charlatan work some perceive it to be; however, these poets form a kind of cult that shuns general engagement, regarding it as a vulgarity and a decadence. There's a phrase I heard as a criticism of W. H. Auden and I like the sound of it: somebody said that he didn't have the rooted normality of the major talent. I'm not sure the criticism applies to Auden, but the gist of it is generally worth considering. Even in T. S. Eliot, the big, normal world comes flowing around you. Robert Lowell went head-on at the times – there was no more literary poet around but at the same time he was like a great cement mixer: he just shovelled the world in and it delivered. Now that's what I yearn for – the cement mixer rather than the chopstick.

What about your own critics and reviewers?

The main disadvantage of being a poet anywhere at the minute is that there is no strong sense of a critical response which has lived and loved that which it is responding to. Reviewing has turned into something more piecemeal and, in the main, lightweight. What I depend upon are friends who know poetry well and who can quote from it, people for whom poetry is a value lived for and lived out.

You told Seamus Deane, in an interview in 1977: 'If you live as an author, your reward is authority. But of course the trouble is how to be sure you are living properly.'

The essential for doing a poem is either entrancement or focus, which equals enjoyment. When you're truly absorbed, everything else is forgotten – you aren't asking 'How well am I behaving?' or whatever. What is important for the doer is the quality of attention, the 'habits of meditation' Wordsworth spoke about. In his preface to the *Lyrical Ballads* – a document still full of wisdom about how the thing works – Wordsworth says, 'I believe that my habits of meditation have so formed my feelings, as that my descriptions of such objects as strongly excite those feelings, will be found to carry along with them a *purpose*.' That would be my feeling: agonizing over those things – how to live properly, I mean – is worthwhile because it forms your 'habits of meditation', your frame of mind, your disposition, your temperament. When it comes to the actual doing, all you really have is your temperament, your disposition, your impulse. But you can affect your temperament by thinking in certain ways.

Is there a sorrow quotient in all works of art?

The deeper register of your understanding, which includes that sense that 'we're going to have to pay for it', has to be there somehow – even in a celebratory poem. The grieving register is one that better not be shut off: it surely is something poetry has to take cognizance of.

I wonder how you would react to this statement from Paul Celan: 'Poetry can no longer speak the language which many a willing ear still seems to expect from it. Its language has become more austere and factual; it distrusts the beautiful and it attempts to be true. It is thus . . . a "greyer" language.'

Paul Celan's biography and historical conditions are deeply implicated in his statement. I would veer more towards the 'rooted normality' remark. It's not impossible to write a poetry of tragic recognition, which recognizes the whole weight and burden of the suffering of the world and at the same time doesn't either fly into bits or go into enigma. Robert Frost's late poem 'Directive' almost has it. A poem about getting lost and encountering a hard landscape. It ends with a religiose release; but there's enough in evidence in Yeats and in Frost and Elizabeth Bishop to prove that the poem itself can stand clear as public architecture and can be there for the contemplation, available to the understanding, without betraying you into simplicity, deception or fake consolation. Think of Zbigniew Herbert.

Robert Frost is among the poets most quoted in your talks, readings and essays. He seems to have provided you with an entire philosophy of poetry.

I felt at home in the world of his poetry – the New England farm world, the people, the idiom that was used. I now realize that Frost is a highly literary poet but he allows the world as it is to have its say. There is a description in 'The Code' of how you have to build a stack in a certain way, so that it can be unbuilt – which I knew very well from building hay myself. There was exhilaration for me in that accuracy, and in his inwardness with a way of life that I was familiar with. Frost was at home in the high cultural context of the university courses, but he still gave you a link back down into what you stored in your own intimate child-body, the tramping of hay. So I responded immediately to that primal reach into the physical.

Also there was a covenant with the reader, an openness, an availability which I liked. I liked his sense of 'this-worldness', the subject matter, the dead-on and the head-on-ness. But, as I read more, I began to relish the wizardry in Frost. I came to appreciate more and more the sophistication of his art, what he made of what he was given. I also admire – and this is why I continue to quote him – his teacherly quality. He was a schoolmaster – a farmer, of course, too; when he worked in schools and universities, he found ways of not betraying the complexity or seriousness of poetry but was able, with real pedagogical originality, to simplify things, to give people a way in. In his readings, he spoke archly but also artfully about what poetry was and what it entailed.

So there's a seriousness, an inner core of high, hard intelligence, in Frost. There's a sorrowing core also – in Robert Lowell's words, 'not avoiding injury to others, / not avoiding injury to myself'. He was a highly cultivated, highly literate man; but he kept a hell of a lot secret. There is that little poem called 'The Secret Sits': 'We dance round in a ring and suppose, / But the Secret sits in the middle and knows'. Anybody who tried to find a way into Frost met charm, intelligence, decoy – and I think that's very good equipment for a poet to have.

Have you deliberately limited your exposure to Frost's work, so as not to be over-influenced by him?

No. I can see Frost in one poem clearly: in *Door into the Dark*, 'The Wife's Tale' is practically a Frost pastiche. A woman brings tea to the field where the men are working. A man–woman balance, marriage, vigilance, rural setting, work customs in the field and so on; the cadence too is Frostian and I'm conscious of it. But I don't think of him as genetically important to my voice – Hopkins was far more important.

Does the fact that Frost writes in an American idiom present any barrier for you? Does Edward Thomas provide similar pleasures to those of Frost?

For a couple of years, Edward Thomas was very important to me. How quickly these things happen when you are starting to write – your companionships, the intensity with which you talk poetry into the night, with which you read it and exchange books ... Edna Longley was writing on Edward Thomas at that stage and he was somebody I taught as a young teacher at Queen's. *He* was influenced by Frost; but the poetry is less crisp, it's warmer. Edward Thomas has the slight temperature of English summer about his writing, whereas Frost has a New England fall, with a nip of winter coming on. Now that I think of it, there's a softer movement in *Wintering Out* – 'Oracle' is more Thomasy than Frosty, more English-naturey than Frost. The writers you mightn't be conscious of as influences may be the ones who are entering.

Frost received some bad biographical press – is the character of the poet relevant to the quality of his work?

It *is* relevant. Frost was manipulative and many of the things they say about him are true. He was hard on people, hurtful to them. But he probably knew this and the capacity for self-knowledge is called for in a writer and is part of 'character'. 'Home Burial' is a great twentieth-century poem about a husband and wife after the death of their child, a wounded and wounding couple. There was a deep conjugal connection – and war – in Frost's life: hurts, sorrows, losses, children dying and committing suicide. The inner black box, recording Frost's flight, would be an interesting one to get. But what we mostly hear is the pilot saying, 'Everything's OK, just settle down.'

In poems and essays from around the time of Wintering Out, *you made reference to the roles played by Sir John Davies, Sir Walter Ralegh and Edmund Spenser in the conquest and plantation of Elizabethan Ireland. Did you ever find their colonizing role coming between you and enjoyment of their poetry or, at least, complicating the way you respond to their work?*

I read them first as textbook poetry; they were part of my learning process: finding where I was in the world of culture. These ideological issues came up more urgently and explicitly in the last twenty-five years, with post-colonial criticism, and I was forced to think about them. But you can live with so many truths at once. You can take pleasure in their verse yet understand that they were racist theorists, contributors to a nascent English imperialism. Edmund Spenser writes a treatise for the elimination of the native Irish: either they can be made English or they can be done away with. Incidentally, when I was teaching in Harvard, I'd say, 'This Spenserian attitude towards the native population worked better in New England.'

Christopher Marlowe has great stride to his blank verse, great energy, great heady excitement; and arguably it's a martial excitement, the excitement of a culture that's going to defeat the armada, stride the world, go over to Ireland and clean *them* up. I have this fancy about the quality of decisiveness, the clean beheading stroke you get in Walter Ralegh's poetry, that it's related to the professional English captain who cut the heads off Spanish soldiers at the Smerwick massacre in Ireland. That Renaissance *sprezzatura* gives you style in the line, but it also gives you a ruthlessness with the sword. Ralegh is a soldier-poet in the full sense – it's not the 'pity of war' but the exultation of swordsmanship that you feel in his work.

It's entirely important to change the plane of regard and relocate ourselves in the world of culture – in other words, not to respect the imperial drive, to come forward and say expropriation and brutality and force are evil and we understand that now. So it would be an instructive, self-educational thing at this minute to read Edmund Spenser in relation to Iraq, for example. You wouldn't have to accuse Spenser of writing bad poetry, but you'd have to understand him historically, in the full and present realization that civilized people can do wrong things . . .

*. . . which inevitably brings to mind the Nazi commandants
listening to Mozart at night and gassing Jews by day. How can we
still claim that art has moral force?*

It is possible for the poet to be better than himself in the poem he
writes. That is one of the functions of the doing of any art and one
of the benefits of putting yourself into the contemplative, receptive
and transporting presence of art. It makes you a bit better than
yourself for the moment; it doesn't mean that you won't relapse or
fail yourself.

*Do you think the traditional notion of a literary canon comprising
the best works, judged on the basis of artistic merit alone, can
survive in the era of literary theory and political correctness?*

The canon was under assault because of a world change over the
last forty or fifty years. The assault comes from two quarters. First,
the women's movement. The place of woman within the whole of
world culture and politics is re-situated. The intervention of femi-
nist criticism and ideology necessarily calls into question the male
power structure which determined the canon and the way it was
utilized. Then there are the deconstructive readings and the post-
colonial readings, which see hegemony and imperium at work in
the construction of a canon which sidelines not only women but
native populations, minority languages and so on. All of that
rereading is absolutely in order. It's the work of justice, of renewal
and reordering. The battering ram has to be taken to the castle in
order to shake it up; but the old castle is usually rebuilt.

When I say 'canon', I'm thinking Homer, Virgil, Dante,
Shakespeare . . . These are nuclear deterrent words almost! But they
can all be reread in terms of new idioms. Which is to say they are
classics, secure because of their human and foundational quality.
Another voice will cry out that that's a Eurocentric attitude to things.
It certainly is – that's where they come from and where I live and it's
part of my equipment for locating myself in time and consciousness.
You don't have to abandon values which you have created yourself
in order to be open in the world to other values.

*With so many thousands of professional poets writing in our own
time alone, is it really feasible that the 'test of time' will apply?
Who can possibly sift through all those books?*

I think the test is becoming a decade-by-decade thing now. There were a hell of a lot of books published in the 1980s and 1990s, a hell of a lot of names that are gone already.

Justly or unjustly?

Mostly justly. It's a matter of word of mouth between practitioners. It starts small, with the inner circle of contenders. Who's the good one out there? In poetry in particular, an ancient and sacred art, the word 'poet' still has an aura – that's why people want it so much. Maybe I'm talking idealistically; but I do believe that published poets have a responsibility to the unpublished poets in a way that novelists don't. It's a sacred charge; and that's why the selection process is independent almost of the marketing process or the rep-utation game. Those who have got it – whatever 'it' is – watch out for other people with it. In general, it is poets who look out for other poets. If you meet poets, who do they talk about? – the ones that they respect.

There is the extra problem which is created in the vast conditions of the United States of America. There are plenty of poets in Ireland – too many – but there's a sense of what's what among practitioners; the acoustic is very sensitive because it is small. The same would be true in Sweden or Poland: always contentious, always fighting, always jealousies; that's part of the energy of the thing. In the United States there's a great crop of ripe, waving poetry – but there's no monster hogweed sticking up out of it. And that creates a problem, so that there are separate listening systems. When you ask people in the United States what poets they admire, usually they mention some of their own literary group. Very rarely do people name anybody from the canon.

Is there still some kind of general or non-specialized audience for poetry?

There is a nice question here to do with readership versus audience. Audience – 'audio' – has to do with the ear. I don't know what quo-tient of an audience in a venue where poetry is being read to them goes to get the book not *after* the reading but before it. It may be true that the audience for poetry which seeks out the book remains more or less constant, and is relatively small. But there are certain poets, of whom I am lucky to be one, who transmit, first of all, through the good reception of a book or books; then that first group of readers is succeeded and extended by other culturally clued-in, generally well-disposed types. Then again, if something extra happens, if you get a prize maybe and get to be known to a larger public, a third gang kick in: the people who buy the books at Christmas and keep them, or who buy them as presents for other people.

Can a larger audience for poetry be encouraged?

You can say, on the one hand, that poetry is an ad hoc reality: you can log-on, log-off; you don't need to know very much, just enter where you like, take what you want and go. But it's also a coherent inner system or order of understanding. So there's work to be done in creating an audience for poetry understood in that second way, and this, speaking in the largest sense, is the work of education, which takes place first in the schools but continues later on through all kinds of dissemination, institutional and accidental.

We have actually moved from talking about the poet, in the solitude box writing, to the relationship between the work and the audience. And that's another reason why Frost was very important in American culture – he was a great teacher who flew the flag for poetry. I suppose in the end there are two kinds of critic who help to create an audience: there's the appreciator (who says 'You really must have this, it's terrific') and there's the adjudicator (who says 'I really wonder if this is worth having at all'). They are both necessary.

III

CODA

16

In Conclusion

~

You suffered a serious illness – a stroke – in August 2006.

I woke up unable to move my left leg or left arm. Marie and I were in Donegal, at a birthday party for Anne Friel, and had stayed the night in a guesthouse. Several other friends had booked into the same place, so from the moment the problem arose I had wonderful support from all of them. Desmond Kavanagh alerted the medical services, and his wife Mary, who is a physiotherapist, helped Marie and me to stay calm; strong-armed Peter Fallon helped the ambulance people to get me down the stairs and helped me to laugh while they were doing so. I was very lucky not to have suffered any impairment to speech or memory or vision or humour.

Humour? There can't have been a lot to laugh about.

Well, Tom Kilroy was at the foot of the stairs and, as I was carried past, I remarked to him that it was 'the curse of Field Day' – since Brian Friel had had a stroke a year or so before. When Brian came to visit me in the hospital, his first words were 'Different strokes for different folks'.

How long did the paralysis continue?

After thirty-six hours in hospital, just before I was brought by ambulance from Letterkenny to Dublin, messages began to get through from the part of the brain that had clotted, and I was able to twiddle the big toe of my left foot; so there and then I knew that the improvement had begun. For the next three or four weeks I was shaky on my pins; but soon enough I was getting strength back into my leg and hand and arm, to the extent that I felt slightly embarrassed when I transferred to the stroke unit of a rehab hospital – the Royal in Donnybrook.

Inside a relatively short time, I was able to move around: first on a frame, then on a tripod-type support, then on one of those standard-issue adjustable aluminium sticks. Soon too I was able to use both hands at mealtimes, could butter bread, cut up food on a plate: things that none of my five fellow patients in the ward could manage. For the most part, they were in a far worse state – one man virtually speechless, the majority of them in wheelchairs, all of them admitted long before I arrived and all but one still there when I left five weeks later. In fact, hospital turned out to be a rest cure and I was never more grateful for thrillers: Henning Mankell, Robert Harris, Donna Leon, Andrea Camilleri – I'd go at them day and night. Although I was out of commission for a good while, my stay was relatively short compared with those others. At the end I had suffered no pain, had read more than I had read in years, had lost a bit of weight and was well and truly rehabilitated.

A former president of the United States must have been your most unexpected visitor to the stroke unit?

Bill Clinton called in one morning at breakfast time and stayed for half an hour. Caused consternation . . . He was in Ireland for a variety of reasons – to attend the Ryder Cup golfing competition, to meet the Taoiseach and receive a donation to his Foundation from the Irish government and also, if possible, to enjoy some kind of a holiday. Anyway, he'd heard about my 'episode' and on the Friday morning, when he was due to leave the country, a message came through that he was on his way to the Royal Hospital. And sure enough, inside half an hour, he strode into the ward, all aglow, like one of those gods who came down to visit old Philemon and Baucis.

Did he remain with you in the ward?

He shook hands with my fellow patients; then we moved out to a private room farther down the corridor. Marie had arrived and, by that stage, the place was buzzing, so we had to take cover.

Did the visit feel strained or uneasy in any way?

Not at all. I didn't take in the extraordinariness of it at the time because it felt so natural. It was a great honour but there was an easy friendly atmosphere to it. He's a marvellous talker, exceptionally well informed with facts and figures, and great recall of everything he's ever read. You soon realize that you're meeting a former Rhodes scholar as well as a former president. In the end, of course, his minders got him out, but only after he'd done a tour of the other wards and corridors. His visit was a tonic for everybody in the hospital and did the whole place a lot of good.

You've used the phrase 'rest cure' to describe your stay in the stroke unit. Have you ever thought of taking a permanent rest from poetry readings, lectures, book launches, festivals, honorary degrees, exhibition openings and all the time-devouring travel and distraction which such activities entail?

I often thought like that. And lately I was becoming more successful at staying clear, although I never found it easy to refuse friends or good causes or honours and degrees and suchlike.

But isn't there a point at which honours and honorary degrees, well intentioned though they unquestionably are, can become a burden for a famous writer hoping to get on with some writing?

That point is soon reached, I agree.

Have you ever actually declined an honorary degree?

Several times – at moments I was either exhausted or overloaded. But mostly I've said yes, for a whole variety of reasons: because my proposer has been working for months to get my name through various panels and committees; because a personal friend happens to be the university president; or in order to acknowledge a university's commitment to Irish Studies. Or maybe the place is just generally admirable (as in the case of The Open University) or is of such majesty that refusal would amount to outright lese-majesty. But now, after my stroke, it's more likely to be doctor's orders for me than doctorates.

Any regrets about that?

None, really. I was at the end of my honorary-degree tether. In the beginning, the sense of occasion was real; but I grew too familiar with the rites and insufficiently responsive to the honour.

Do you have much secretarial assistance with your correspondence and phone calls?

By the early 1990s I'd had the privilege of a secretary – or the quarter of one secretary's time – at Harvard, so at that point I finally started to have somebody come into the house in Dublin one or two mornings a week, just to do typing. I began by dictating answers into one of those little battery-driven tape recorders, but realized very soon that I did a better job and a quicker one if I scribbled a reply on the bottom or the back of the letter. Then I had the good fortune to employ – if that's not too grand a word for such a fleeting job – somebody who had the ability to be my 'minder': a woman with excellent judgement, lively personality, perfect manners and enough nous to manage a corporation. We reached a terrific modus operandi, if only for those couple of mornings a week, and might have proceeded to something more like a full-time engagement, when, wham, her husband got a job in Hong Kong and I was back to square one.

There and then I should have gone professional, as it were, and found a personal assistant who'd be on the spot two or three days a week; instead I continued for the past few years to keep up these half-day arrangements with a succession of different people. But my luck holds, and my 'minder' and her family are now back from Hong Kong, so it's full steam ahead.

Richard Murphy, in his memoir The Kick, *recounts the advice of Ted Hughes that he should begin writing poetry early in the morning, 'while the door to the dream world was not yet closed by the day's activity'. Did you receive similar advice?*

I did not, though I've come to behave as if I had. For the past few years I've been able to grope from the bed to the desk without intervening worries about preparing for classes, or reading manuscripts to be ready for scheduled interviews with students during the day, or grading student papers, or writing recommendations, or whatever ... Ted was undoubtedly right about early morning being the time when the gates are still unbarred.

Occasionally, I waken during the night with the start of a poem in my head, and have learned to scribble down whatever phrase or image is being broadcast from the bunker. Those messages are usually trustworthy and you should act on them as soon as possible – not only write down the encrypted code but get up and get started on the actual decoding. The middle of the night is one of the best times. Because I don't have to rise to go to work, I can pad about at four in the morning knowing that, if need be, I can sleep late. At times like that, in fact, I'm more than happy to be a 'bundle of accident and incoherence' at breakfast because the 'intended, complete' thing has happened in the small hours.

Do you feel anxiety, as well as excitement, about your more ambitious poetic promptings?

I surely do. It's why I stalked around the watchman in 'Mycenae Lookout' for so long, and around the Station Island idea, and the idea of kidnapping Mad Sweeney into my own time and place. When I finally pounced, both Sweeney and the watchman started singing like stool pigeons.

Any hypothesis about how Yeats remained so productive to the end?

Roy Foster's biography of him and Ann Saddlemyer's biography of his wife George contain enough evidence to buttress Yeats's own conviction that sexual excitement and creative excitement are near allied. There was something manic about the amours of the last years, but it was so transgressive and barefaced that you can't help admiring – and admiring as well, of course, his wife George's permissiveness or compliance. In its crazy way, the whole spectacle is another contradiction of the notion that the life and the work are at odds: the recklessness and 'caroling', as Hardy might have called it, of those last poems, the extravagant success of them, have to do with the extravagance and carry-on of the wild wicked old man.

The lesson must be that staying alive in the body is a sure-fire way of not becoming a dead-head. But the great thing is that – as ever with Yeats – you could argue the counter-truth and say that, body or no body, this poet was deeply concerned with 'making his soul'. Unchristened his heart may have been, but his effort towards the end – and the nearer he got to his end, the more obvious it becomes – was to prepare himself to meet his unmaker and confront him with made things. The very deliberately chosen and executed *terza rima* of 'Cuchulain Comforted', for example, is like a passport he issued for himself just before he had to cross the dark water. It says that this particular body is ready to board the barge as a shade.

Every good poem a poet writes could conceivably be an epitaph. 'The Lake Isle of Innisfree', even. But in certain great poets – Yeats, Shakespeare, Stevens, Miłosz – you sense an ongoing opening of consciousness as they age, a deepening and clarifying and even a simplifying of receptivity to what might be awaiting on the farther shore. It's like those rare summer evenings when the sky clears rather than darkens. No poet can avoid hoping for that kind of old age. But equally no poet can forget Wordsworth's loss of grip or Eliot's alibis in the theatre. Still, everybody should also remember Wordsworth's marvellous rally in a poem like 'Extempore Effusion', the one in memory of James Hogg, the Ettrick Shepherd. There's no rule.

How secure is Yeats's reputation?

Is it fair to make a distinction between the reputation and the achievement? There will always be attacks on the reputation, but the achievement is rock-sure.

You don't think his stand against modernity, his 'big house' snobbery, his anti-democratic tendencies will tell against him in the longer run?

If I'd met him, I might well have found the whole masquerade hard to take – affected and carried away – although there's ample evidence of gumption and humour and what Lady Dorothy Wellesley called 'his splendid laugh'. And there's also that impression of him in his prime, recorded by Virginia Woolf, that he was 'like a solid wedge of oak'. But we aren't talking here about the figure he cut, we're talking about the 'something to perfection brought' in his writing: as a whole, it has an inner thought-outness, a personal truthfulness, a clear-headedness about consequence in the personal and historical life, and none of that is ever going to fade. The artistic structure is sound as a bell. Individual poems will drop from view – 'The Phases of the Moon' isn't going to be on every curriculum in a hundred years' time, but you never know.

Even in a Dublin of financial centres and restaurant critics and mobile phones, those old towers and wild swans and cold heavens will probably hold their own. They were always conceived of as outposts rather than as 'in' places: better think of the poems as a *clachán* of hermit huts rather than an amusement arcade. I'm talking here about how the work will survive among readers passionate about poetry. What they will always find and value is solid evidence of the makings of a soul as well as the makings of music. Of course, he and the work will be assailed, but they're ready for it. If ever there was an oeuvre that can take a hammering, that's even daring you to have a go at it, it's Yeats's. 'What's the use of a held note or held line / That cannot be assailed for reassurance?' The rereadings and reactions haven't knocked him askew, they've just helped us to know ourselves and him better.

What has poetry taught you?

That there's such a thing as truth and it can be told – slant; that subjectivity is not to be theorized away and is worth defending; that poetry itself has virtue, in the first sense of possessing a quality of moral excellence and in the sense also of possessing inherent strength by reason of its sheer made-upness, its *integritas, consonantia* and *claritas.*

Have you ever felt you had failed poetry in some way?

Yes, because there were times when I should have disregarded Miłosz's injunction and my own censor and let bad spirits rather than good spirits choose me, as he says, 'for their instrument'.

Can you be more specific?

If poetry itself couldn't get me to open up on those fronts, I don't know that I can start now.

How do you deal with envy and personal resentment on the part of other writers?

That kind of thing rarely manifests itself face to face. When it's there, it's usually under the surface, as irrational and undeniable as sexual attraction. So when you're dealing with it, it's like a kind of reverse flirtation. The magnets are repelling rather than attracting. One way of proceeding was recommended to me years ago by John McGahern: 'implacable courtesy'. Another is an unspoken 'Well, fuck you too, buddy.'

Never actually spoken?

That would spoil everything – it would be like smashing the hot-house glass and killing the plants. Still, living with that kind of thing doesn't require any great fortitude. And you can understand easily enough what causes it.

To what extent do you embrace modern technology? Do you send text messages on your cellphone?

Since I've learned to use 'predictive text', I do. But I don't use e-mail, because I want to keep the messaging at bay as much as possible. I do have an iBook and enjoy the inspiration of a screen aglow and the immaculate conception of letters.

Do you always use pen and ink for writing poetry?

Not always. But a clean sheet and a good pen still give me the sensation of being ready and able. It's partly the tonic of what the old Irish scribe called 'the beetle-sparkle of ink', partly the fact that when you're bent to a desk with a pen in your hand, you feel a bit of gathered force. More and more, though, I warm myself up by gazing at whatever's already there on the screen and sometimes, before I know where I am, I'm fiddling with the keyboard. That screen-gaze does undoubtedly help to induce the self-forgetful trance.

Is the thinning of language which results from media-speak and globalization a problem for poetry? Can such a diluted idiom possibly produce work on a par with the masterworks of the past?

Genius will find a way. Some cyberspace Dante may well be at his keyboard already. But you're right to suggest that I myself couldn't broadcast on that wavelength: before I can believe there's anything worthwhile on the line, I need to feel that the line is trawling and taking the strain deep down in the undertow. Language, like so much else in the world, has been dematerialized. The word is no longer Mandelstam's bundle with meaning sticking out of it in all directions, it's more a sift and a waft in the galactic wind. But poetry will say *'humani nil a me alienum puto'*, and find a way to be a makeweight in the unweighing of things.

Recently, for example, I read a poem by the Welsh poet Robert Minhinnick: it starts off from sand in an hourglass, then proceeds into a fantasia of association, a whiteout of sand images that end up being suggestive of the kind of desiccation and dematerialization you're talking about. And yet, because of the sheer sandiness of the writing and the sheer extravagance of the invention, credibility and palpability end up being saved – by the poem, that is, and within it. But beyond the poem, things are still far from safe.

Has popular culture – of the kind which has been dominant since the sixties – exerted a baneful influence on intellectual life and the arts, including poetry?

Maybe it's going too far to call it baneful: it's probably just inevitable that, in the early twenty-first century, a pop-inflected idiom is going to have more emotional density for a younger generation who have absorbed it and internalized it than it ever will have for me. The invocation of film titles and album titles and brand names can open the path inward for a majority of people nowadays. I see this in the case of my own family. For them, there's a substantial element in such things, a specific cultural and emotional gravity that I miss entirely. So while I agree that there's a baneful reality to the wrap-around vulgarity and vacuity of the muzak and media we're all made to suffer, discrimination may still be every bit as possible – and dare we say as rare – as it ever was.

Phrases like 'pop poetry' or 'pop art' put me off. They're that bit too coercive, meant to rub your nose in something, to tell you to come off your snooty preferences. I've no doubt that good poetry can be made from the billboards of pop, just as plenty of bad poetry was made from the hoardings of high culture, but if it's good *qua* poetry it will be capable of making its way without the 'pop' placebo.

In your lecture 'Eclogues In Extremis' you quoted approvingly from the theatre director Peter Brook, who declared, 'The responsibility of anyone in the arts is to look . . . for the other side of every coin. The moment you see a black side, your obligation is to look for a luminous side.' Aren't there fundamental problems with the Brook philosophy? I am thinking in particular of his viewpoint – also cited in your lecture – that writers should confront 'the pitiless nature of human experience in a way that makes you, at the end, very positive, full of courage, in a sense stronger than when you came in'. An obvious difficulty with this viewpoint is that it foresees the ultimate outcome of a work of art, rather than discovering its dynamic in the course of the creative act.

Brook's statement was made in a press interview, so there's a free-wheeling, off the cuff aspect to it. And the remark about being made 'stronger than when you came in' is a reminder that he's speaking very much as a theatre person who uses theatre as his measure of the arts: the work he deals with has already been worked through, as it were, plays being there to be re-enacted constantly on stage. His statement has more to do with his director's take on *King Lear* or *Waiting for Godot* than with the toils involved in Shakespeare's or Beckett's creative process. A director probably needs to approach his task with a plan or interpretation of some sort already in mind. His job is more like the translator's than the original writer's.

Obviously, a knowing or voulu approach is against the creative law. But having said that, I still believe that once a literary work has been totally imagined – no matter how authentically negative its reading of life may be – it will be capable of having a 'strength-ening' effect on a reader or an audience member. Deep down, most people's reserved position is much the same as Thomas Hardy's: 'If way to the Better there be, it exacts a full look at the Worst.' I'd argue, for instance, that the desire to sit on quietly, after the curtain has come down on some powerful performance of a tragedy, has more to do with steadying and reorienting – gathering strength, if you like – than with being dispirited.

Would you agree with Wallace Stevens's remarks that poetry is 'a means of redemption' and that 'God is a symbol for something that can as well take other forms, as, for example, the form of high poetry'?

I've no doubt about the second statement. Poetry is a ratification of the impulse towards transcendence. You can lose your belief in the afterlife, in the particular judgement at the moment of death, in the eternal separation of the good from the evil ones in the Valley of Jehoshaphat, but it's harder to lose the sense of an ordained structure, beyond all this fuddle. Poetry represents the need for an ultimate court of appeal. The infinite spaces may be silent, but the human response is to say that this is not good enough, that there has to be more to it than neuter absence. Admittedly we now know that the spaces are far from silent, that they are continuously alive and fluent in their own wordless language, but if you stand out in the country under a starry sky, you can still feel a primitive awe at the muteness of the vault.

In 'The Stone Verdict', I imagined this uncommunicativeness as a sort of divine corrective to human protestation. I was thinking of my father and his 'old disdain of sweet talk and excuses': 'He will expect more than words in the ultimate court / He relied on through a lifetime's speechlessness'. So, to the extent that poetry is a pay-off for all the duplicities of language and disappointments of reality, it can also be said to be 'a form of redemption'. Which is probably why Czesław Miłosz called it 'a dividend from what you know and what you are'.

You once described yourself as 'Jungian in religion'.

When I was young, from first awareness until at least my early teens, I dwelt entirely in the womb of religion. My consciousness was dominated by Catholic conceptions, formulations, pedagogies, prayers and practices. Salvation, damnation, heaven above, hell below, grace and guilt, all were for real. So the drama of last things, the melodrama and even the terror of them were present from the start. You'd hardly got out of the cot before you were envisaging the deathbed. Soon, too, you would learn about the sacrament of extreme unction, able to answer knowledgeably about holy viaticum and the final anointing of the organs of sense with chrism and so on. You had your puny south Derry being within the great echoing acoustic of a universe of light and dark, death and ever-lasting life, divine praises and prayers for the dead: as in 'Grant them eternal rest, O Lord, and let perpetual light shine upon them. May their souls and the souls of all the faithful departed rest in peace. Amen.'

'Once a Catholic, always a Catholic'?

I suppose so, because Catholicism provided a totally structured reading of the mortal condition which I've never quite decon-structed. I might have talked differently, certainly more diffidently, if you'd asked me about these matters thirty years ago, since I even-tually did my best to change from catechized youth into secular adult. The study of literature, the discovery of wine, women and song, the arrival of poetry, then marriage and family, plus a general, generational assent to the proposition that God is dead: all that screened out the first visionary world. But, in maturity, the myths of the classical world and Dante's *Commedia* (where my Irish Catholic subculture received high cultural ratification) and the myths of other cultures matched and mixed and provided a cosmology that corresponded well enough to the original: you learned that, from the human beginnings, poetic imagination had proffered a world of light and a world of dark, a shadow region – not so much an afterlife as an afterimage of life.

Getting older has therefore been a matter of dwelling with and imagining in terms of those archetypal patterns – which is why I called myself 'Jungian'. For years I've been writing poems where I meet ghosts and shades; they are among the ones I like and value most: 'Casualty', 'Station Island', 'The Tollund Man in Springtime', 'District and Circle' (where I more or less ghostify myself). Then too, one of the things I've done with most relish is a version of the Messenger's speech in *Oedipus at Colonus*, where he tells of the end of the old king, how he simply disappeared, assumed into earth rather than into heaven.

Could it be said that you don't fear death?

Certainly not in the way I'd have feared it sixty years ago, fearful of dying in the state of mortal sin and suffering the consequences for all eternity. It's more grief than fear, grief at having to leave 'what thou lovest well' and whom thou lovest well.

Despite your Catholic observances having lapsed, do you still approve of the ceremonial aspect of church obsequies?

I do. I think it's the right moment for ceremony. The funeral pyre is one thing, the crematorium something else. At that stage you want a stand taken against nothingness and a word spoken, rather like the one in Miłosz's poem 'Meaning', a word that 'runs ... / Through interstellar fields, through the revolving galaxies, / And calls out, protests, screams'. At Miłosz's own funeral, of course, it was a sung mass rather than a galactic screech, and that suited him since he was a practising Catholic, if a very sceptical one.

CODA

Why did you travel all the way to Krakow for his funeral?

Because he was a great poet who gave the art a noble profile. Because I loved and was strengthened by his work. Because I had come to know him better personally in the years before his death. Because I knew that, when I got to Krakow, I'd be among friends who were dear friends of his. Because going to funerals is so much a part of the culture that formed me, part of the ethic of respect. The experience meant so much to me that I jotted down an account of it. I don't usually keep a diary, but this was something I didn't want to let pass.

What about writers who, unlike Miłosz, did not practise religious beliefs and yet were given church funerals?

Even when I've attended religious obsequies for such writers – the 'non-practising' ones, if you like – I've not felt unease or incongruity.

Ted Hughes? John McGahern?

Two very different talents, obviously, although each funeral was conducted with a similar quiet propriety. In each case, the individual talent was being absorbed, or reabsorbed, into his tradition. They had come to the end of their work and the religious service functioned like a properly placed punctuation mark. Ted Hughes's in the small church in North Tawton, just down the lane from his house in Court Green: family and friends, writers and publishers and public figures all packed in together, the Church of England service raised to the power of the literary by the Book of Common Prayer. John McGahern's in a local country church, also with a congregation of family and neighbours and writers and publishers and public figures, although without the Book of Common Prayer. And no Latin either, just the vernacular parish mass – a low mass, as they used to call it – during which a tribute was spoken by the celebrant. No music, no addresses by friends or writers, the coffin carried down the aisle the same as at the funeral last week and last year and last century, the rosary said at the graveside and then local men shovelling in the mould.

Would you like your own final mould to be that of Derry rather than Dublin: in Bellaghy where generations of Scullions and Heaneys have trod, rather than Glasnevin where Gerard Manley

473

Hopkins 'bleared, smeared with toil' lies? Preceded by a Latin Mass of course – especially now that it has the papal imprimatur!

It's a nice question. But when I consider it, I'm inclined to consider a couple of other places as well – the little Church of Ireland grave-yard at Nun's Cross, not far from our house in Wicklow, associated with the Synge family, or a very beautiful burial ground on the shore of Lough Neagh, behind the high cross at Ardboe, where Marie's parents and ancestors are laid. Except that in the first case it's the wrong faith and in the second it's the wrong family, so we're back to square (or should I say plot?) one. Maybe the solution is the Thomas Hardy one: divide yourself between the home ground and the official address, be in two places at the one time. But the Hardy arrangement would involve taking the cor from the corpse, so maybe not. Perhaps just have two ceremonies. How about that?

Well, Ted Hughes certainly went that way. As well as the village ceremony, he was also honoured at the memorial service in Westminster Abbey, with royalty in attendance and Hughes's national role as Poet Laureate celebrated with great pomp.

That is so. But memorial services are different from funerals. Funerals are closer to the bones, as it were; they have to deal with the rent in the fabric. The memorial service has more to do with the recompense of reputation, sometimes maybe with its retrieval. It's closer to the obituary notice than to the eternal questions, so a secular memorial service with music and musings and all the rest is going to work perfectly well. Still, Ted's did have an extra dimension, what with Westminster Abbey, the clergy in full dress, the organ at full blast, Biblical readings in the language of the Authorized Version, Ted's own recorded voice speaking Shakespeare's 'Fear no more the heat of the sun', his poems read by Lord Gowrie and Michael Baldwin and Caroline Tisdall and myself, Alfred Brendel playing Schubert, the Tallis Scholars singing 'Spem in alium'. That too amounted to a proper punctuation for Ted as English poet and English patriot, the myth-minder with a feel for the monarchical. What was marvellous and reliable about the event was the way Ted's language worked in the same register as the language of the liturgy, the extent to which the scope of his imagining had accommodated the idea of the divine.

At the end of his book of interviews, Czesław Miłosz remarks:
'It's possible to detect a single refrain in everything I've said here –
namely, the desire not to appear other than I am. I have to admit
this has bothered me my whole life, and still does.' So – at the end
of this book of interviews – I wonder whether Miłosz's concern
not 'to be taken as other than I am' (which, he said, was especially
acute after his Nobel Prize) is something you can identify with?

Talking about oneself in the same breath as Miłosz is a bit much, but
still: to answer 'yes' to the question sounds like a boast, and to answer
'no' would be untrue. I don't believe I'm a self-concealing person:
admittedly, I incline to discretion, which I think is different from a
desire to appear 'other than I am'. But what goes on in self-presentation,
even in the case of Miłosz, is no simple matter and one's analysis of
one's own case can never be the whole story. That said, however,
Miłosz's statement is one I could make without anxiety.

Since you have endured this sustained interrogation so patiently, it
seems fitting that the final two questions should be your own.
First, a question adapted from 'Known World': 'Were we . . .
made for summer, shade and coolness / And gazing through an
open door at sunlight?'

I think so, yes. Often when I'm on my own in the car, driving down
from Dublin to Wicklow in spring or early summer – or indeed at
any time of the year – I get this sudden joy from the sheer fact of
the mountains to my right and the sea to my left, the flow of the
farmland, the sweep of the road, the lift of the sky. There's a double
sensation of here-and-nowness in the familiar place and far-and-
awayness in something immense. When I experience things like
that, I'm inclined to credit the prelapsarian in me. It seems, at any
rate, a greater mistake to deny him than to admit him.

And finally, from 'Keeping Going': 'Is this all? As it was / In the
beginning, is now and shall be?'

If those questions had to be translated into Latin, they'd begin with
the word 'Nonne', which indicates that the answer they expect is
'yes'. Fundamentally they're saying what William Wordsworth said
long ago: that it is on this earth 'we find our happiness, or not at
all'. Which is one reason for keeping going.

Seamus Heaney
Books and Interviews

SELECT BIBLIOGRAPHY

POETRY

Eleven Poems, Belfast: Festival Publications, 1965

Death of a Naturalist, London: Faber and Faber, 1966; New York: Oxford University Press (USA), 1966

Door into the Dark, Faber and Faber, 1969; Oxford University Press (USA), 1969

Wintering Out, Faber and Faber, 1972; Oxford University Press (USA), 1973

Stations, Belfast: Ulsterman Publications, 1975

North, Faber and Faber, 1975; Oxford University Press (USA), 1976

Field Work, Faber and Faber, 1979; New York: Farrar, Straus and Giroux, 1979

Selected Poems 1965–1975, Faber and Faber, 1980

Poems 1965–1975, Farrar, Straus and Giroux, 1980

An Open Letter, Derry: Field Day Theatre Company, 1983

Station Island, Faber and Faber, 1984; Farrar, Straus and Giroux, 1985

The Haw Lantern, Faber and Faber, 1987; Farrar, Straus and Giroux, 1987

New Selected Poems 1966–1987, Faber and Faber, 1990

Selected Poems 1966–1987, Farrar, Straus and Giroux, 1990

Seeing Things, Faber and Faber, 1991; Farrar, Straus and Giroux, 1991

The Spirit Level, Faber and Faber, 1996; Farrar, Straus and Giroux, 1996

Opened Ground: Poems 1966–1996, Faber and Faber, 1998

Opened Ground: Selected Poems 1966–1996, Farrar, Straus and Giroux, 1998

Electric Light, Faber and Faber, 2001; Farrar, Straus and Giroux, 2001

District and Circle, Faber and Faber, 2006; Farrar, Straus and Giroux, 2006

PROSE

Preoccupations: Selected Prose 1968–1978, Faber and Faber, 1980; Farrar, Straus and Giroux, 1980

The Government of the Tongue: The 1986 T. S. Eliot Memorial Lectures and Other Critical Writings, Faber and Faber, 1988; Farrar, Straus and Giroux, 1989
The Place of Writing, Atlanta, Ga: Scholars Press, 1989
The Redress of Poetry: Oxford Lectures, Faber and Faber, 1995; Farrar, Straus and Giroux, 1995
Crediting Poetry: The Nobel Lecture 1995, Loughcrew, Co. Meath: The Gallery Press, 1995; Farrar, Straus and Giroux, 1996
Finders Keepers: Selected Prose 1971–2001, Faber and Faber, 2002; Farrar, Straus and Giroux, 2002

DRAMA

The Cure at Troy: A Version of Sophocles' 'Philoctetes', Field Day Theatre Company and Faber and Faber, 1990; Farrar, Straus and Giroux, 1991
The Burial at Thebes: Sophocles' 'Antigone', Faber and Faber, 2004; Farrar, Straus and Giroux, 2004

TRANSLATIONS

Sweeney Astray, Field Day Theatre Company, 1983; Faber and Faber, 1984; Farrar, Straus and Giroux, 1984
The Midnight Verdict, The Gallery Press, 1993
Laments (by Jan Kochanowski), Faber and Faber, 1995; Farrar, Straus and Giroux, 1995 (co-translated with Stanisław Barańczak)
Beowulf, Faber and Faber, 1999; Farrar, Straus and Giroux, 2000
Diary of One Who Vanished: A Song Cycle by Leoš Janáček, Faber and Faber, 1999; Farrar, Straus and Giroux, 2000
The Testament of Cresseid: A Retelling of Robert Henryson's Poem, London: Enitharmon Editions, 2004

ANTHOLOGIES

Soundings, Belfast: Blackstaff Press, 1972
Soundings 2, Blackstaff Press, 1974
Co-edited with Ted Hughes:
The Rattle Bag, Faber and Faber, 1982
The School Bag, Faber and Faber, 1997

SELECT INTERVIEWS

Adair, Tom, *Linen Hall Review*, 6.2, Autumn 1989, pp. 5–8
Allen, Paul, BBC Radio 3, 12 April 2004
Anonymous, *The Economist*, 22 June 1991, pp. 104–8

Anonymous, *Stage Two*, 1.1, Spring 2004, p. 4

Armitage, Simon, BBC Radio 4, 16 September 1995

Bailey, Anthony, *Quest*, 2.1, January/February 1978, pp. 38–46 and 92–3

Baldinger, Jo Ann, *Pasatiempo/Santa Fe New Mexican*, 26 September–2 October 2003, p. 16

Battersby, Eileen, *Irish Times* 'Weekend', 29 September 1990, p. 5

— *Irish Times*, 2 May 1996, p. 13

— *Irish Times* 'Weekend Review', 3 April 2004, p. 6

Bragg, Melvyn, ITV, 26 October 1991

Brandes, Randy, *Salmagundi*, 80, Fall 1988, pp. 4–21

Breathnach, Páraic, RTE Radio 1, 16 January 2007

Brennock, Mark, *Irish Times*, 9 October 1995, p. 7

Brown, John, *In the Chair: Interviews with Poets from the North of Ireland* (County Clare: Salmon Publishing, 2002), pp. 75–85

Browne, Vincent, *Irish Times*, 31 March 2001, p. 10

Campbell, James, *Guardian* 'Review', 27 May 2006, pp. 4–5

Carty, Ciaran, *Sunday Independent*, 14 October 1979, p. 31

— *Sunday Tribune* Magazine, 7 April 1996, p. 10

Cole, Henri, *Paris Review*, 144, Fall 1997, pp. 89–138

Cook, Christopher, BBC Radio 4, 25 March 2001

Cooke, Harriet, *Irish Times*, 28 December 1973, p. 8

Covington, Richard, *Salon*, online [www.salon.com/weekly/heaney1.html]

Deane, Seamus, *New York Times* 'Book Review', 2 December 1979, pp. 47–8

— *The Crane Bag*, 1.1, Spring 1977, pp. 61–7

de Bréadún, Deaglán, *Irish Times*, 13 September 1984, p. 13

Dorgan, Theo, RTE Radio 1, 19 November 1994

— RTE Radio 1, 8 May 1996

Dungan, Myles, RTE Radio 1, 13 April 2004

— RTE Radio 1, 16 November 2004

— RTE Radio 1, 7 April 2006

Eyres, Harry, *The Times*, 2 April 1991, p. 16

Farndale, Nigel, *Sunday Telegraph* Magazine, 1 April 2001, pp. 20–25

Freeman, John, *Philadelphia Inquirer*, 1 June 2006

Gammage, Nick, *Thumbscrew*, Autumn 2001, pp. 2–11

Garland, Patrick, *The Listener*, 8 November 1973, p. 629

Gish, Nancy K., in *Hugh MacDiarmid: Man and Poet* (Orono: The National Poetry Foundation; Edinburgh: Edinburgh University Press, 1992), pp. 63–70

Greig, Geordie, *Sunday Times* 'Books', 8 October 1995, pp. 7–8

Haffenden, John, *Viewpoints: Poets in Conversation* (Faber and Faber, 1981), pp. 57–75

Hanly, David, RTE 1, 11 April 1989

— RTE Radio 1, 9 October 1995

Hartigan, Patti, *Boston Globe* 'Living', 4 November 1995, p. 21

Hilton, Isabel, BBC Radio 3, 15 January 2007

Hitch, Susan, BBC Radio 3, 28 March 2006

Homen, Rui Carvalho, *European English Messenger*, X.2, Autumn 2001,
 pp. 24–30

Hosey, Seamus, *Speaking Volumes* (Dublin: Blackwater Press, 1995), pp. 35–9

Huey, Michael, *Christian Science Monitor*, 9 January 1989, p. 16

Johnson, Shaun, *Independent* 'Review', 31 October 2002, pp. 4–5

Kavanagh, Terry, *Irish Independent*, 8 May 1991, p. 8

Kellaway, Kate, *Observer* 'Review', 10 September 1995, p. 17

— BBC Radio 4, 4 May 1996

Kelly, John, RTE 1, 18 April 2006

Kinahan, Frank, *Critical Inquiry*, 8.3, Spring 1982, pp. 405–14

Kirsch, Adam, *Harvard Magazine*, November/December 2006, p. 55

Koo, Jason, *Gulf Coast*, Summer/Fall 2004, pp. 203–8

Landesman, Cosmo, *Sunday Times*, 30 January 2000, p. 5

Lawson, Mark, *Guardian* '2', 30 April 1996, pp. 2–3

Lee, Hermione, BBC Radio 3, December 1988

Leith, Sam, *Daily Telegraph* 'Books', 25 March 2006, pp. 1–2

Lysaght, Patricia, BBC Radio 3, 2 March 2004

Marr, Andrew, BBC 1, 16 March 2008

McAuley, Roisin, BBC Northern Ireland, 30 October 1997

McCartney, Jenny, *Sunday Telegraph* 'Seven', 9 September 2007, pp. 8–11

McCrum, Robert, *Books Quarterly*, 20, 2006, pp. 21–5

McKendrick, Jamie, *W*, 15, Autumn 1998, pp. 11–17

Miller, Karl, *Seamus Heaney in Conversation* (London: Between the Lines,
 2000), pp. 17–56

Mooney, Bel, *The Times*, 11 October 1984, p. 8

— BBC Radio 4, 15 November 1988

Moreton, Cole, *Independent on Sunday* 'Culture', 4 April 1999, p. 11

Moriarty, Gerry, *Irish Press*, 19 June 1987, p. 11

Morrison, Blake, *Independent on Sunday* 'Review', 19 May 1991, pp. 26–7

Muir, Marie-Louise, BBC Radio Ulster, 17 April 2006

Murphy, Mike, RTE Radio 1, 13 April 1989

— RTE Radio 1, 10 October 1995

— RTE Radio 1, 16 December 2000

— in Clíodhna Ní Anluain (ed.), *Reading the Future: Irish Writers in
 Conversation* (Dublin: The Lilliput Press, 2000), pp. 81–97

Naparstek, Ben, *The Times* 'Books', 25 March 2006, p. 6

O'Donnell, Mary, RTE Radio 1, 2 September 1997

O'Donoghue, Donal, *RTE Guide*, 12 April 1996, pp. 10–11

O'Driscoll, Dennis, *Hibernia*, 11 October 1979, p. 13

— RTE Radio 1, 25 February 1984

— DVD recording, Georgetown University, Washington, 2007

O'Shea, Helen, *Quadrant*, September 1981, pp. 12–17

O'Toole, Fintan, *Irish Times* 'Weekend Review', 30 October 1999, p. 10

— *Sunday Tribune* 'Inside', 20 November 1983, p. 12

— *Sunday Tribune* 'Inside', 30 September 1984, pp. 2 and 6

Polukhina, Valentina, *London Magazine*, August/September 2007, pp. 58–66

Purcell, Deirdre, *Sunday Tribune* 'People', 4 November 1990, p. 25

Randall, James, *Ploughshares*, 5.3, 1979, pp. 7–22

Ratiner, Steven, *Giving Their Word: Conversations with Contemporary Poets* (Amherst and Boston: University of Massachusetts Press, 2002), pp. 95–107

Remnick, David, *Washington Post*, 3 May 1985, p. C1

Ross, Michael, *Sunday Times* 'Culture', 24 October 1999, pp. 4–5

Shine Thompson, Mary, *The Poets' Chair* (video), Poetry Ireland, 2004

Silverblatt, Michael, *Lannan Literary Video Library*, 27 (Santa Fe: The Lannan Foundation, 1991)

— KCRW Radio, 19 August 2004

Silverlight, John, *Observer* 'Review', 11 November 1979, p. 37

Spinou, Pary, *Friends of Classics*, online [www.friends-classics.demon.co.uk], 13 January 2004

Thomas, Harry, *Talking with Poets* (New York: Handsel Books, 2002), pp. 43–67

Tóibín, Colm, RTE Radio 1, 29 June 1987

Wagner, Erica, *The Times*, 11 September 1998, p. 21

Walsh, Caroline, *Irish Times*, 6 December 1975, p. 5

Walsh, John, *Sunday Times* 'Review', 7 October 1990, pp. 2–4

Williamson, Nigel, *The Times* 'Metro', 27 March–2 April 1999, pp. 16–17

Wilmer, Clive, *Poets Talking: 'Poet of the Month' Interviews from BBC Radio 3* (Manchester: Carcanet Press, 1994), pp. 77–82

Wright, Patrick, BBC Radio 3, 29 March 2001

Wroe, Nicholas, *Guardian* 'Review', 9 October, 1999, pp. 6–7

Biographical Glossary

Allingham, William (1824–89): Poet and diarist. Born Ballyshannon, Co. Donegal. Worked for many years in the Customs service. Friend of Carlyle, Tennyson and Dante Gabriel Rossetti. Author of the narrative poem *Lawrence Bloomfield in Ireland* (1864), his best-known poems include 'The Fairies' – learned by SH at school – and 'Four Ducks on a Pond'. *Diary* (1907).

Alvarez, A. (1929–): Poet, novelist, anthologist, critic, memoirist. Born London. Poetry editor of the *Observer* (1956–66). Edited *The New Poetry* (1962); advisory editor of Penguin Modern European Poets (1965–75). Reviewed *Field Work* in the *New York Review of Books*. *Under Pressure: The Writer in Society* (1965); *The Savage God: A Study of Suicide* (1971); *Where Did It All Go Right? An Autobiography* (1999); *New & Selected Poems* (2002); *The Writer's Voice* (2005); *Risky Business* (2007).

Asmal, Kader (1934–): Politician, lawyer and academic. Born Stanger, Kwa-Zulu Natal. Lecturer in Law at Trinity College Dublin (1963–90). Founder and Chairman of the Irish Anti-Apartheid Movement. Minister for Water Affairs and Forestry (1994–9) and Minister for Education (1999–2004) in South African government.

Barańczak, Stanisław (1946–): Poet, critic, translator, anthologist and academic. Born Poznań, Poland. Founder-member of the dissident KOR (Workers' Defence Committee). Author of many poetry collections in Polish, and principal translator into Polish of SH's poetry. Co-translator into English, with SH, of *Laments* by Jan

Kochanowski. With Clare Cavanagh, he has translated Wisława Szymborska's poetry and translated/edited the anthology *Polish Poetry of the Last Two Decades of Communist Rule* (1991). Alfred Jurzykowski Professor of Polish Language and Literature at Harvard University.

Bishop, Elizabeth (1911–79): Poet, essayist, short-story writer, translator, anthologist. Born Worcester, Massachusetts. Lived in Brazil for many years (from 1951). Dedicatee of SH's uncollected poem 'A Hank of Wool'. *The Complete Poems* (1983); *The Collected Prose* (1984); *One Art: Letters* (1994); *Poems, Prose, and Letters* (2008). Co-editor, with Emanuel Brasil, of *An Anthology of Twentieth-Century Brazilian Poetry* (1972). Taught poetry at Harvard (1970–7).

Brandes, Rand (1956–): Academic, critic and bibliographer. Born Indiana. Dedicatee, with his wife Beth, of SH's poem 'The Rain Stick'. Co-author, with Michael J. Durkan, of *Seamus Heaney: A Reference Guide* (1996) and *Seamus Heaney: A Bibliography 1959–2003* (2008). Professor of English at Lenoir-Rhyne University, North Carolina.

Bredin, Hugh (1939–): Philosopher, academic. Born Co. Derry. Recalled – as a student in St Columb's College, Derry – by SH in 'The Real Names'. Co-author with Liberato Santoro-Brienza of *Philosophies of Art and Beauty* (2000) and translator of works by Umberto Eco. Former Senior Lecturer in Scholastic Philosophy at Queen's University Belfast.

Brodsky, Joseph (1940–96): Poet, essayist, playwright, translator. Born Leningrad. Left Russia, an involuntary exile, in 1972 and lived in the US. SH published a posthumous tribute to Brodsky in the *New York Times* (reprinted in *Finders Keepers*) and elegized him in 'Audenesque'. A conversation between the two poets, on poetry and politics, appeared in *Magill* in 1985. *To Urania: Selected Poems 1965–85* (1988); *So Forth* (1996); *Collected Poems in English* (2000). Essays: *Less than One* (1986); *On Grief and Reason* (1995). Poet Laureate of the USA (1991–2). Nobel Prize for Literature (1987).

Brookeborough, Viscount [Sir Basil Brooke] (1888–1973): Politician. Born Co. Fermanagh. Prime Minister of Northern Ireland (1943–63).

Browne, Hon. Garech (1939–): Founder of Claddagh Records and member of the Guinness brewing family. Born Dublin. Established Claddagh in 1959, recording Irish traditional musicians. Claddagh Records have also issued recordings of poets, mainly from Ireland and Scotland, including SH with John Montague on *The Northern Muse* (1968) and SH with Liam O'Flynn on *The Poet and the Piper* (2003).

Buckley, Vincent (1925–88): Poet, critic, memoirist, editor, academic. Born Victoria, Australia. Founded the Committee for Civil Rights in Ireland in 1969. Published a memoir of his Irish experiences and friendships, *Memory Ireland* (1985). *Last Poems* (1991) contains 'Birthday Suite for Seamus Heaney'. *Selected Poems* (1981). *Poetry and the Sacred* (1968). Edited *The Faber Book of Modern Australian Verse* (1991). Held a personal Chair in Poetry at Melbourne University.

Carey, John (1934–): Critic and academic. Born Barnes, England. Has extensively reviewed SH's work in the *Sunday Times*. *John Donne: Life, Mind and Art* (1981); *Original Copy: Selected Reviews and Journalism 1969–1986* (1987); *What Good Are the Arts?* (2005). Merton Professor of English at Oxford University (1976–2001).

Clarke, Austin (1896–1974): Poet, verse-playwright, novelist, critic, broadcaster. Born Dublin. *Collected Poems* (1974); *Collected Plays* (1963). Autobiographies: *Twice Round the Black Church* (1962); *A Penny in the Clouds* (1968).

Cooke, Barrie (1931–): Painter. Born Cheshire. Has lived in Ireland since 1954. SH, whose portrait he has painted, published a number of catalogue notes on his work. Dedicatee of SH's poem 'Cairn-Maker'; subject of poem 'xi' of the 'Lightenings' sequence; his 'godbeam' paintings are referred to in 'Saw Music'. His work featured on the dustjacket of the Faber edition of *Beowulf* and in a number of limited editions by SH, including *Bog Poems* (1975). Has exhibited in Ireland and internationally.

Corkery, Daniel (1878–1964): Critic, novelist, playwright, short-story writer, academic. Born Cork. Proponent of a nationalist view of Irish literature, expounded in *Synge and Anglo-Irish Literature* (1931). In *The Hidden Ireland* (1924), he recreated the world of the eighteenth-century Gaelic poets of Munster. Professor of English, University College, Cork.

Crotty, Patrick (1952–): Critic, anthologist, academic. Born Co. Cork. Editor of the anthologies *Modern Irish Poetry* (1995) and *The New Penguin Book of Irish Verse* (2009). Editor, with Alan Riach, of the annotated *Complete Poems of Hugh MacDiarmid*. Contributor to *The Cambridge Companion to Seamus Heaney* (2008). Director of the Yeats International Summer School (2006–8). Professor of Irish and Scottish Literature at University of Aberdeen.

Currie, Austin (1939–): Politician and civil rights activist. Born Co. Tyrone. Member of Northern Ireland Civil Rights Association. Founder member of the Social Democratic and Labour Party (1970). Elected to various Northern Ireland parliamentary assemblies, first becoming a Stormont MP in 1964. Elected, for the Fine Gael party in the Republic of Ireland, to the Dáil (1989–2002). Candidate for the Irish Presidency in 1990.

Deane, Seamus (1940–): Poet, novelist, critic and academic. Born Derry. Attended St Columb's College and Queen's University with SH. Dedicatee of SH's poem 'The Ministry of Fear' and co-dedicatee, with Thomas Flanagan, of *Preoccupations*. A director of Field Day Theatre Company, he was general editor of *The Field Day Anthology of Irish Writing* (1991). *Selected Poems* (1988); *Reading in the Dark* (1996); *A Short History of Irish Literature* (1986). *Celtic Revivals* (1985) includes an essay on SH. Professor of Irish Studies at University of Notre Dame (1993–2006).

Delaney, Tom (1947–79): Archaeologist, founder member of the Association of Young Irish Archaeologists. Born Dublin. After appointment to Ulster Museum staff, became friend of SH. Commemorated in Section VIII of 'Station Island' and 'Scrabble' in *Seeing Things*.

Evans, Matthew [Baron Evans of Temple Guiting] (1941–): Publisher, honorary chairman of cultural organizations, peer. Born Suffolk. Chairman (1981–2003) of Faber and Faber, which he joined in 1964. Created life baron, 2000; Labour Party spokesman in the House of Lords. Dedicatee, with his wife – the literary agent, Caroline Michel – of *Electric Light*. Chairman of Royal Court Theatre (1984–90), Governor of British Film Institute (1982–97), Chairman of Arts and Humanities Research Board (1998–2003) and Museums, Libraries and Archives Council (2000–2003).

Fallon, Peter (1951–): Poet, translator, editor, publisher. Born in Germany, but grew up in Ireland. In 1970, he founded The Gallery Press, which published a number of SH's books, including *Hailstones* (1984), *The Midnight Verdict* (1993) – dedicated to Fallon and his wife, Jean Barry – and *The Riverbank Field* (2007). Fallon's poetry includes *News of the World: Selected and New Poems* (1998) and *The Company of Horses* (2007). Translator of *The Georgics of Virgil* (2004), reviewed by SH in the *Irish Times*. Co-editor, with Derek Mahon, of *The Penguin Book of Contemporary Irish Poetry* (1990).

Farren, Robert [Roibeárd Ó Faracháin] (1909–84): Poet, verse-playwright, short-story writer, critic, broadcaster. Born Dublin. *Selected Poems* (1951); *The Course of Irish Verse in English* (1948).

Ferguson, Sir Samuel (1810–86): Poet and translator. Born Belfast. An acknowledged influence on Yeats, he wrote narrative and lyric poetry, often on themes drawn from Irish mythology.

Fiacc, Padraic [pseudonym of Patrick Joseph O'Connor] (1924–): Poet and anthologist. Born Belfast. *Ruined Pages: Selected Poems* (1994). Editor of *The Wearing of the Black: An Anthology of Contemporary Ulster Poetry* (1974).

Flanagan, T. P. [Terry] (1929–): Painter, principally of landscapes. Born Enniskillen. Dedicatee of SH's poem 'Bogland'. Head of Art Department at St Mary's College of Education, Belfast (1965–83), where he first met SH.

Flanagan, Thomas (1923–2002): Critic, novelist and academic. Born Connecticut. Professor of English at University of California, Berkeley, when SH was guest lecturer there (1970–1). Dedicatee of SH's poem 'Traditions' and co-dedicatee, with Seamus Deane, of *Preoccupations. The Irish Novelists 1800–1850* (1959); *The Year of the French* (1979); *There You Are: Writings on Irish and American Literature and History* (2004), preface by SH – who also wrote an obituary notice on Flanagan for the *New York Review of Books*. Professor of English, State University of New York, Stony Brook (1978–96).

Friel, Brian (1929–): Playwright and short-story writer. Born Omagh. Dedicatee of SH's poem 'The Real Names' and *Station Island*. Co-founder, with Stephen Rea, of Field Day Theatre Company (1980). Member of Irish Senate (1987–9). *Selected Stories* (1979); *Translations* (1980); *Selected Plays* (1984); *Dancing at Lughnasa* (1990). *Volunteers* (1975) is dedicated to SH.

Hadzi, Dimitri (1921–2006): Artist. Born New York. His etchings were reproduced in a number of limited editions of SH's poetry and his work featured on the dust jacket of the Farrar, Straus and Giroux edition of *The Burial at Thebes*. He and his wife, Cynthia Hadzi, were on a vacation in Greece with SH and Marie Heaney when the award to SH of the 1995 Nobel Prize for Literature was announced. The Hadzis are the dedicatees of SH's poem 'Mycenae Lookout'. Dimitri Hadzi, who was Professor of Visual and Environmental Studies at Harvard University (1975–89) and a widely exhibited sculptor, is recalled in 'Sonnets from Hellas'.

Hammond, David (1928–2008): Singer, song collector, broadcaster, founder of Flying Fox film company. Born Belfast. Co-dedicatee with Michael Longley of *Wintering Out*, he is the singer in SH's poem 'The Singer's House'. Participated with SH and Michael Longley in 1968 Arts Council of Northern Ireland tour, Room to Rhyme. A director of Field Day Theatre Company. Directed television films – for schools and general audiences – at BBC (Northern Ireland) in which SH featured; 'Something to Write Home About', in *Finders Keepers*, was SH's script for a Flying Fox documentary by Hammond, broadcast in 1998.

Herbert, Zbigniew (1924–98): Poet, essayist, editor. Born Lvov. As an opponent of communism and of socialist realism, resigning from the Polish Writers' Union in 1951, he was unable to publish his poetry in Poland until a 'thaw' in 1956. Later a supporter of the opposition Solidarity movement. The subject of SH's poem 'To the Shade of Zbigniew Herbert', an essay on his work is included in *Finders Keepers*. His poetry in English translation includes *Selected Poems* (1968); *Report From the Besieged City* (1985); and *The Collected Poems 1956–1998* (2007). Essays: *Barbarian in the Garden* (1985); *Still Life with a Bridle* (1991).

Hewitt, John (1907–87): Poet, art critic and art curator. Born Belfast. Art Director of the Herbert Art Gallery and Museum, Coventry (1957–72). SH's poem 'The Schoolbag' is dedicated to his memory and his 'appreciation' of Hewitt appeared in the *Sunday Tribune* in 1987. Hewitt's poem 'The King's Horses' is discussed in *Finders Keepers*. *Collected Poems* (1991); *Selected Poems* (2007). *Ancestral Voices: Selected Prose* (1987).

Hobsbaum, Philip (1932–2005): Poet, editor, critic and academic. Born London. While teaching at Queen's University Belfast, he founded and directed (October 1963 to March 1966) a writing workshop, 'The Group', which SH – who dedicated the poem 'Blackberry-Picking' to Hobsbaum – attended regularly. Taught at Glasgow University (1966–97). Publications included three collections of poetry; *Metre, Rhythm and Verse Form* (1995); and *Reader's Guides* to Charles Dickens (1972), D. H. Lawrence (1981) and Robert Lowell (1988).

Holland, Jack (1947–2004): Novelist, historian and journalist. Born Belfast, where he was taught by SH at St Thomas's Secondary Intermediate School. Lived and worked in New York for many years. *The Fire Queen* (1992); *Hope Against History* (1999); *Misogyny* (2006).

Holub, Miroslav (1923–98): Poet, essayist and scientist. Born Pilsen. Worked (from 1972) at the Institute for Clinical and Experimental Medicine in Prague (becoming Head of Immunology in 1990) and published scientific papers and monographs. SH's essay on Holub's poetry is included in *The Government of the Tongue*. Poems by Holub, in English translation, are collected in *Poems Before & After* (1990 and 2006). Essays: *The Dimension of the Present Moment* (1990); *The Jingle Bell Principle* (1992); *Shedding Life* (1997).

Horgan, John (1940–): Journalist, academic, former Labour Party politician and biographer of Irish politicians. Born Co. Kerry. Member of Irish Senate (1969–77), Dáil (1977–81) and European Parliament (1981–3). Lectured in journalism at Dublin City University (1983–2006). Appointed Press Ombudsman in 2007.

Hughes, Ted (1930–98): Poet, children's writer, translator, critic, anthologist, playwright. Born Yorkshire. SH's translation of *Beowulf* and his poems 'On His Work in the English Tongue' and 'Stern' are dedicated to Hughes's memory. Essays on Hughes are included in *Finders Keepers*. SH and Hughes co-edited *The Rattle Bag* (1982) and *The School Bag* (1997). Appointed Poet Laureate in 1984. *The Hawk in the Rain* (1957); *Birthday Letters* (1998); *Collected Poems* (2003); *Selected Translations* (2006). *Winter Pollen: Occasional Prose* (1994). *Shakespeare and the Goddess of Complete Being* (1992). *Letters* (2007). His version of *The Oresteia* was premiered at the National Theatre, London in 1999.

Hume, John (1937–): Politician. Born Derry and educated at St Columb's College while SH was also a student there. Member of European Parliament (1979–2004), House of Commons (1983–2005), and of a number of Northern Ireland elected assemblies (from 1969). Co-founded Social Democratic and Labour Party (1970), of which he became leader (1979–2001). Shared 1998 Nobel Peace Prize with David Trimble.

James, Clive (1939–): Broadcaster, critic, memoirist, travel writer, novelist, poet. Born Sydney. *The Metropolitan Critic* (1974) reprinted his *TLS* review of *Door into the Dark*. *Unreliable Memoirs* (1979); *Brilliant Creatures* (1983); *Reliable Essays* (2001); *Cultural Amnesia* (2007). *The Book of My Enemy: Collected Verse 1958–2003* (2003) includes the satirical *Peregrine Prykke's Pilgrimage*, in which 'Seamus Feamus' features.

Kavanagh, Patrick (1904–67): Poet, novelist and essayist. Born Inniskeen, Co. Monaghan, he is among the ghosts encountered by SH in 'Station Island' and is quoted in SH's poem 'The Ministry of Fear'. Essays on his work in *Preoccupations* and *The Government of the Tongue*. *Collected Poems* (2004); *Collected Pruse* (1973); *The Green Fool* (1938); *Tarry Flynn* (1948).

Kennelly, Brendan (1936–): Poet, editor, translator, anthologist, novelist, critic, academic. Born Ballylongford, Co. Kerry. *Cromwell* (1983); *The Book of Judas* (1991); *Familiar Strangers: New and Selected Poems 1960–2004* (2004). *Journey Into Joy: Selected Prose* (1994). Editor, *The Penguin Book of Irish Verse* (1970). Professor of Modern Literature, Trinity College Dublin (1973–2005).

Kinsella, Thomas (1928–): Poet, translator, critic and anthologist. Born Dublin, receiving the Honorary Freedom of the City in 2007. *The Government of the Tongue* and *Finders Keepers* include essays on his work by SH. *Collected Poems 1956–2001* (2001); *Marginal Economy* (2006); *Belief and Unbelief* (2007); *Man of War* (2007). *A Dublin Documentary* (2006). *The Dual Tradition* (1995). Translator of *The Táin* (1969) and *An Duanaire* (1981). Editor of *The New Oxford Book of Irish Verse* (1986). Professor at Temple University, Philadelphia, for many years (from 1970).

Landweer, Sonja (1933–): Artist. Born Amsterdam. Living in Ireland since the 1960s. Dedicatee of SH's poem 'To a Dutch Potter in Ireland'. Her ceramics, jewellery and sculptures have been exhibited in Ireland and internationally.

Larkin, Philip (1922–85): Poet, novelist, anthologist, critic and librarian. Born Coventry. Essays on his work by SH – who, in his poem 'The Journey Back', meets 'Larkin's shade' – are included in *Finders Keepers*. *Collected Poems* (1988). *Required Writing: Miscellaneous Pieces* (1983). Novels: *Jill* (1946); *A Girl in Winter* (1947). *Selected Letters* (1992). Edited *The Oxford*

Book of Twentieth-Century English Verse (1973). Sub-Librarian, Queen's University Belfast (1950–55); Librarian, Hull University (1955–85).

Lerner, Laurence (1925–): Poet, critic, academic. Born Cape Town. Lectured in English at Queen's University Belfast (1953–62) and was subsequently a Professor of English at the Universities of Sussex and Vanderbilt. *Domestic Interior* (1959); *The Man I Killed* (1980); *Selected Poems* (1984). *The Truest Poetry* (1960).

Longley, Edna (1940–): Critic, editor, anthologist, academic. Born Dublin. SH's writings are among the topics discussed in her collections of critical essays: *Poetry in the Wars* (1986); *The Living Stream* (1994); *Poetry & Posterity* (2000). Edited *The Bloodaxe Book of 20th-Century Poetry* (2000). *Louis MacNeice* (1988). Married to the poet Michael Longley. Emeritus Professor of English at Queen's University Belfast.

Longley, Michael (1939–): Poet and (from 2007) Ireland Professor of Poetry. Born Belfast. SH is co-dedicatee with Derek Mahon and James Simmons of *An Exploded View* (1973), which includes Longley's verse letters to the three poets. Dedicatee of SH's poem 'Personal Helicon' and co-dedicatee with David Hammond of *Wintering Out*, he took part – with Hammond and SH – in 1968 Room to Rhyme tour. SH reviewed his *Poems 1963–1983* in 1985. *Collected Poems* (2006). *Tuppeny Stung*: essays (1994). Worked in the Arts Council of Northern Ireland (1970–91) where he was Combined Arts Director.

Lowell, Robert ('Cal') (1917–77): Poet, translator, playwright, critic. Born Boston. Imprisoned as a conscientious objector to military service in 1943. In 1965, in protest against American foreign policy, he publicly refused an invitation to a White House Festival of the Arts from President Lyndon B. Johnson. During his final years, Lowell and his third wife, Lady Caroline Blackwood, lived near Kent and in an apartment at Castletown House, a Georgian mansion near Dublin, mentioned in SH's uncollected poem 'Pit Stop near Castletown'. SH's poem 'Elegy' commemorates the poet; his critical writings on Lowell are included in *Preoccupations* and *The Government of the Tongue*.

Collected Poems (2003); *Collected Prose* (1987); *Letters* (2005). Taught poetry at Harvard University (1963–77).

MacDiarmid, Hugh [Christopher Murray Grieve] (1892–1978): Poet, essayist, memoirist, political activist. Born Langholm, Scotland. Champion of Scottish cultural nationalism and of a native literature written in Scots. Co-founded the National Party of Scotland (1928), but became a member of the Communist Party a few years later. Among SH's writings on MacDiarmid are an Oxford lecture, included in *The Redress of Poetry*, and the poem 'An Invocation'. An interview with SH, about the poet, was published in *Hugh MacDiarmid: Man and Poet* (1992). *A Drunk Man Looks at the Thistle* (1926); *Complete Poems* (1978); *Selected Prose* (1992); *New Selected Letters* (2001). Autobiography: *Lucky Poet* (1943).

Maclean, Sorley [Somhairle MacGill-Eain] (1911–96): Poet in Gaelic. Born Raasay, Scotland. SH, who translated Maclean's poem 'Hallaig', elegized the poet in ' "Would They Had Stay'd" ' and delivered a lecture on his work at the 2002 Edinburgh Festival. *Dàin do Eimhir* (1943); *From Wood to Ridge: Collected Poems in Gaelic and English* (1989).

Mahon, Derek (1941–): Poet, critic, playwright, translator, anthologist. Born Belfast. Dedicatee of *Seeing Things*. He and SH participated in a 1977 Arts Council of Northern Ireland tour, In Their Element. His poetry includes *Collected Poems* (1999) and *Harbour Lights* (2005). *Adaptations* (2006). *Journalism* (1996) includes his review of *The Government of the Tongue*. *High Time*, his version of Molière's *The School for Husbands*, was performed by Field Day Theatre Company in 1984. His poem 'Lives' and his version of Sophocles' *Oedipus* (2005) are dedicated to SH. Edited *The Sphere Book of Modern Irish Poetry* (1972) and co-edited, with Peter Fallon, *The Penguin Book of Contemporary Irish Poetry* (1990).

Mangan, James Clarence (1803–49): Poet, prose writer and translator. Born Dublin. Author of a large body of verse, much of it written while earning a precarious living as a freelance writer, his best-known poems include the patriotic 'Dark Rosaleen', translated from the Irish, 'A Vision of Connaught in the Thirteenth Century' and 'Siberia' – all published in the Young Ireland journal, the *Nation*. SH's bicentenary reflections on Mangan's work were published in 2003 in *Poetry Ireland Review*. *Collected Works of James Clarence Mangan* (1996–2002). *Autobiography* (1882).

McCabe, Bernard (1923–2006): Academic and writer. Born Middlesbrough. Dedicatee, with his wife Jane, of *The Haw Lantern*. Professor of English at Tufts University before retiring to England. His publications include *W. B. Yeats: Images of Ireland* (1991), *James Joyce: Reflections of Ireland* (1993) and three books for children. SH's poem 'The Birch Grove' is set in the McCabes' garden in Ludlow.

McFadden, Roy (1921–99): Poet, editor and lawyer. Born Belfast. Worked as a solicitor. Co-editor (1948–53) with Barbara Hunter of the literary journal *Rann*. *Collected Poems 1943–1995* (1996), introduced by Philip Hobsbaum.

McGahern, John (1934–2006): Novelist, short-story writer, playwright, memoirist. Born Dublin. His six novels included *The Barracks* (1963), *The Dark* (1965), *Amongst Women* (1990) and *That They May Face the Rising Sun* (2002) [published in the USA as *By the Lake* (2002)]. *Collected Stories* (1992). *Memoir* (2005) [published in the USA as *All Will Be Well* (2006)]. SH reviewed his short-story collection *High Ground* in 1985.

McLaverty, Michael (1904–92): Novelist and short-story writer. Born Carrickmacross. Headmaster of St Thomas's Secondary Intermediate School in Belfast, where SH taught (1962–3). Dedicatee of 'Fosterage', he is one of the 'masters' encountered by SH in 'Station Island'. SH wrote the introduction to his *Collected Short Stories* (2002) and an obituary tribute, published in the *Irish Times*.

Miller, Karl (1931–): Editor, critic, memoirist. Born near Edinburgh. Co-dedicatee, with his wife Jane Miller, of *Field Work*. From 1964, while literary editor of the *New Statesman*, and as editor of *The Listener* (1967–73), he published early poems by SH. Founded

London Review of Books in 1979. His 'Between the Lines' inter-
view with SH appeared in 2000. *Cockburn's Millennium* (1975);
Doubles (1985); *Rebecca's Vest* (1993); *Dark Horses* (1998);
Electric Shepherd (2003). Professor of Modern English Literature,
University College London (1974–92).

Miłosz, Czesław (1911–2004): Poet, novelist, essayist, critic, mem-
oirist, anthologist, translator, literary historian. Born Lithuania, to a
Polish-speaking family. Participated in the Warsaw underground dur-
ing the Second World War. Worked as diplomat for the Polish Foreign
Service (1946–51), before breaking with the Communist regime and
living in exile: in France, initially, and, from 1960, in the US, where he
became Professor of Slavic Languages and Literatures at the
University of California, Berkeley. Spent his final years in Krakow.
SH – who, in 1999, nominated Miłosz as 'The Giant at My Shoulder'
in an RTE Radio series of that title – dedicated the poem 'Out of This
World' and the translation 'What Passed at Colonus' to his memory.
An essay on Miłosz's work was included in *Finders Keepers* and a
posthumous tribute by SH appeared in the *New Republic* and the
Guardian. Miłosz's review of *Laments* was published in the *New
York Review of Books* in 1996. *New and Collected Poems* (2001).
The Captive Mind (1953). Editor and translator of the anthology
Post-War Polish Poetry (1965). *Native Realm: A Search for Self-
Definition* (1959); *The Witness of Poetry* (1983); *To Begin Where I
Am: Selected Essays* (2001). Nobel Prize for Literature (1980).

Montague, John (1929–): Poet, short-story writer, memoirist, trans-
lator, critic, anthologist. Born in New York, but grew up in Co.
Tyrone. Dedicatee of SH's poem 'The King of the Ditchbacks', his
'Hearth Song' is dedicated to SH. He and SH recorded their work
for Claddagh Records on *The Northern Muse* (1968). *Collected
Poems* (1995); *Smashing the Piano* (1999); *Drunken Sailor* (2004).
The Figure in the Cave: Essays (1989). Memoirs: *Company* (2001);
The Pear is Ripe (2007). Edited *The Faber Book of Irish Verse*
(1974). Lectured in English at University College, Cork (1972–88).
Appointed first Ireland Professor of Poetry in 1998.

Monteith, Charles (1921–95): Director (from 1953) and chairman
(1976–80) of Faber and Faber. Born Lisburn, Co. Antrim.

Accepted *Death of a Naturalist*, for publication by Faber and Faber, in 1965. Dedicatee of *The Government of the Tongue*. Also introduced Philip Larkin, Richard Murphy, Douglas Dunn, Paul Muldoon and Tom Paulin to the Faber poetry list.

Moore, Brian (1921–99): Novelist. Born Belfast. Lived in North America – initially in Canada, later in the United States – from 1948. Dedicatee of SH's poem 'Remembering Malibu'. Reviewed *Station Island* in the *Los Angeles Times*. [*The Lonely Passion of*] *Judith Hearne* (1955); *The Emperor of Ice-Cream* (1965); *The Mangan Inheritance* (1979); *Lies of Silence* (1990).

Muldoon, Paul (1951–): Poet, anthologist, critic, editor, librettist, lyricist, musician. Born Co. Armagh. As a student of English at Queen's University, his lecturers included SH, to whom his poems 'The Briefcase', 'A Telegram for Seamus Heaney' and 'A Grand Tour' are dedicated. Dedicatee of SH's poem 'Widgeon' and the subject of reviews in *Preoccupations* and *Finders Keepers*, he has lived since 1987 in the United States, where he is a Professor at Princeton University and Chair of the University Center for the Creative and Performing Arts. Professor of Poetry at Oxford University (1999–2004); his lectures, collected in *The End of the Poem* (2006), include a study of SH's 'Keeping Going'. Poetry editor of the *New Yorker*. *Poems 1968–1998* (2001); *Moy Sand and Gravel* (2002); *Horse Latitudes* (2006). Edited *The Faber Book of Contemporary Irish Poetry* (1986). Member of rock music group Rackett.

Mulholland, Carolyn (1944–): Sculptor. Born Lurgan. Her work includes commissions for churches and public places in Ireland. Among her portrait sculptures is a bust, in bronze, of SH. Dedicatee of SH's poem ' "Poet's Chair" ', based on her sculpture of that name, she created a work in bronze incorporating his uncollected poem 'A Keen for the Coins'.

Murray, Les (1938–): Poet, verse novelist, critic, editor, anthologist. Born Nabiac, New South Wales. *The Paperbark Tree: Selected Prose* (1992) includes his review of *The Haw Lantern*. Literary Editor of *Quadrant* and editor of *The New Oxford Book of Australian Verse*

(1986) and *Anthology of Australian Religious Poetry* (1986). *Collected Poems* (2002); *The Biplane Houses* (2006). Verse novels: *The Boys Who Stole the Funeral* (1980) and *Fredy Neptune* (1998). He is the subject of a biography, *Les Murray: A Life in Progress* (2000) by Peter F. Alexander.

Newmann, Joan [Joan Watton] (1942–): Poet and teacher. Born Co. Down. Participated in The Group. *Coming of Age* (1995); *Prone* (2007). Co-director, with Kate Newmann, of Summer Palace Press.

O'Brien, Conor Cruise (1917–): Writer, editor, diplomat, politician, academic. Born Dublin. United Nations representative in Katanga (1961). Vice-Chancellor, University of Ghana (1962–5). Minister for Posts and Telegraphs in Irish government (1973–7). Editor-in-chief of the *Observer* (1979–81). *Maria Cross* (1952); *States of Ireland* (1973); *Passion and Cunning* (1988); *Memoir* (1998). Alluded to by SH in 'Whatever You Say Say Nothing'. Reviewed *North* in *The Listener*. Married to Máire Mhac an tSaoi.

O'Brien, Máire Cruise [Máire Mhac an tSaoi] (1922–): Poet, translator, memoirist, diplomat. Born Dublin. Served in Department of External Affairs in Ireland and abroad. Assisted Tomás de Bhaldraithe on *English–Irish Dictionary* (1959). Poetry collections in Irish: *Margadh na Saoire* (1956); *Codladh an Ghaiscígh* (1973); *An Galar Dubhach* (1980); *Shoa* (1999). Memoir: *The Same Age as the State* (2003). Translations: *A Heart Full of Thought* (1959); *Trasládáil* (1997).

O'Donoghue, Bernard (1945–): Poet, translator, critic, academic. Born Cullen, Co. Cork. Dedicatee with his wife, Heather O'Donoghue, of *The Redress of Poetry* and author of *Seamus Heaney and the Language of Poetry* (1994). His translation of *Sir Gawain and the Green Knight* appeared in 2006 and was reviewed by SH in the *Irish Times. Selected Poems* (2008). Edited *Oxford Irish Quotations* (1999) and *The Cambridge Companion to Seamus Heaney* (2008). Fellow of Wadham College Oxford.

O'Donoghue, Heather (1953–): Critic and academic. Born Middlesbrough. *The Genesis of a Saga Narrative* (1991); *Old Norse-Icelandic Literature* (2004); *Skaldic Verse and the Poetics of Saga Narrative* (2005); *From Asgard to Valhalla* (2007). Fellow of Linacre College Oxford.

O'Flynn, Liam (1945–): *Uilleann* piper. Born Kill, Co. Kildare. Former member of the music group Planxty. O'Flynn and SH have collaborated, in Ireland and internationally, on performances of music and poetry; their joint CD *The Poet and the Piper* was issued in 2003.

O'Malley, Mary (1918–2006): Theatre producer and director. Born Co. Cork. With her husband, Pearse O'Malley, she established the Lyric Theatre, Belfast (1951), which initially specialized in verse drama, notably the works of W. B. Yeats and Austin Clarke. Founded (1957) and edited *Threshold* magazine, an issue of which SH guest-edited in 1969.

Ó Rathaille, Aodhagán (c. 1670–1729): Irish-language poet. Born Co. Kerry. His writings include poems lamenting the decline of the old Gaelic order and poems in the *aisling* mode, including 'Gile na Gile', which has been translated by SH as 'The Glamoured'. *Dánta Aodhagáin Uí Rathaille* (1911).

Ó Riada, Seán (1931–71): Composer, arranger, musician, broadcaster. Born Cork. The subject of SH's poem 'In Memoriam Sean O'Riada', he is credited with the modern revival of interest in traditional Irish music, notably through his work with the group Ceoltóirí Chualann. His own compositions include three Masses, *Nomos* (1957–66), musical arrangements for the films *Mise Éire* (1959) and *Saoirse?* (1961) and a setting of SH's 'Lovers on Aran' (1968). Lecturer in music, University College Cork (1963–71).

Ó Suilleabháin, Eoghan Ruadh (1748–84): Irish-language poet. Born Co. Kerry. Composed satires, lyrics and poems in the *aisling* mode. SH alluded to him in 'Midnight Anvil' and translated his 'Poet to Blacksmith' in *District and Circle*. Lived as wandering labourer and schoolteacher and also served in the British navy and army.

Ó Tuama, Seán (1926–2006): Poet and playwright in Irish, critic, academic, editor, anthologist. Born Cork. *Rogha Dánta / Death in the Land of Youth: New and Selected Poems* (1997); *An Grá in Amhráin na nDaoine* (1960); *Repossessions: Selected Essays on the Irish Literary Heritage* (1995). Edited *Nuabhéarsaíocht* (1950) and *An Duanaire* (1981). Member of Irish Arts Council (1973–81) during SH's tenure on the Council. Professor of Modern Irish Literature, University College Cork.

Paisley, Revd Ian (1926–): Politician, clergyman. Born Armagh. Founded Free Presbyterian Church in 1951. Co-founder (1971) and, until 2008, leader of Democratic Unionist Party. Member of the House of Commons (from 1970), the European Parliament (1979–2004) and various Northern Ireland parliamentary assemblies (from 1970). First Minister of the Northern Ireland Executive (2007–8).

Parker, Stewart (1941–88): Playwright for stage and radio. Born Belfast. Participated in The Group. *Spokesong* (1975); *Catchpenny Twist* (1977); *Northern Star* (1984). *Pentecost* was performed by Field Day Theatre Company in 1987.

Paulin, Tom (1949–): Poet, critic, broadcaster, translator, playwright, anthologist, academic. Born in Leeds, he grew up in Belfast. A director of Field Day Theatre Company. Among his poetry collections are *A State of Justice* (1977); *Liberty Tree* (1983); *The Wind Dog* (1999), dedicated to Seamus and Marie Heaney; and *The Invasion Handbook* (2002). His critical books include studies of Thomas Hardy and William Hazlitt; *Writing to the Moment: Selected Critical Essays 1980–1996* (1996), *Crusoe's Secret* (2005) and *The Secret Life of Poems* (2008). His *Faber Book of Vernacular Verse* (1990) was reviewed by SH in the *Sunday Times*. Fellow of Hertford College Oxford (from 1994).

Raine, Craig (1944–): Poet, librettist, critic, editor, academic. Born Co. Durham. Poetry editor at Faber and Faber (1981–91). Editor of *Areté* (since 1999). His profile of SH appeared in *Vanity Fair* (1991). His reviews and essays are collected in *Haydn and the Valve Trumpet* (1990) and *In Defence of T. S. Eliot* (2000), which includes a review of *The Spirit Level. Collected Poems* (2000). *T. S. Eliot* (2007). Fellow of New College Oxford.

Rea, Stephen (1946–): Actor. Born Belfast. Co-founder, with Brian Friel, of Field Day Theatre Company (1980). Appeared in a number of Neil Jordan's films, including *The Crying Game* (1992) and *Michael Collins* (1996). Co-director of SH's *The Cure at Troy* (1990). Played the role of Sweeney in BBC Radio broadcast of *Sweeney Astray* (1990).

Reid, Christopher (1949–): Poet, children's writer, critic, anthologist and editor. Born Hong Kong. Poetry editor at Faber (1991–9). His poetry collections include *Arcadia* (1979); *Katerina Brac* (1985); *Mermaids Explained* (2001); *For and After* (2003); *Mr Mouth* (2006). Edited two anthologies: *Sounds Good* (1998) and *Not to Speak of the Dog* (2000); and *Letters of Ted Hughes* (2007).

Ricks, Christopher (1933–): Critic, editor and academic. Born Beckenham. He was among the earliest reviewers of SH's poetry. *The Force of Poetry* (1984); *T. S. Eliot and Prejudice* (1988); *Beckett's Dying Words* (1993). Edited editions of Tennyson and Housman. Editor, *The New Oxford Book of Victorian Verse* (1987) and *The Oxford Book of English Verse* (1999). Professor of Humanities at Boston University and (since 2004) Professor of Poetry at Oxford University.

Różewicz, Tadeusz (1921–): Poet and playwright. Born Radomsko, Poland, he has lived much of his life in Wroclaw. Translations of his poetry into English include *The Survivor* (1976), *They Came to See a Poet* (1991), *Recycling* (2001) and *New Poems* (2007).

Ryan, Richard (1946–): Diplomat and poet. Born Dublin. A director of Claddagh Records. Has served as Ireland's ambassador to the United Nations and to a number of countries including Korea, Spain and The Netherlands. *Ledges* (1970); *Ravenswood* (1973).

Saddlemyer, Ann (1933–): Biographer, critic, editor, academic. Born Saskatchewan. Dedicatee of *District and Circle* and 'Glanmore

Sonnets', she is represented as Augusta in 'Glanmore Eclogues'. Former owner of Glanmore Cottage in Co. Wicklow, which she rented to SH and his family in the early 1970s and sold to the Heaneys in 1988. Her books include *Becoming George: The Life of Mrs W. B. Yeats* (2002) and editions of the work of Lady Gregory and J. M. Synge. Professor Emeritus of the University of Toronto.

Simmons, James (1933–2001): Poet, editor, critic, academic, musician, songwriter. Born Derry. Founded (1968) and edited the *Honest Ulsterman*. *Poems 1956–1986* (1986); *Mainstream* (1995); *The Company of Children* (1999). His critical study of Sean O'Casey appeared in 1983. Lecturer at New University of Ulster. In 1990 – with his wife, Janice Fitzpatrick Simmons – he established The Poets' House, a creative writing school.

Simpson, Louis (1923–): Poet, translator, critic, novelist, playwright, memoirist, academic. Born Jamaica. He is the 'stranger' in SH's poem 'Making Strange'. *The Owner of the House: New Collected Poems 1940–2001* (2003). *Selected Prose* (1989). Memoirs: *North of Jamaica* (1972); *The King My Father's Wreck* (1995). Taught English at Columbia University, the University of California, Berkeley and (from 1967) the State University of New York, Stony Brook.

Szymborska, Wisława (1923–): Poet, critic and essayist. Born in Kórnik, Poland, she has lived in Krakow since 1931. Her poetry has been translated into English as *Poems* (1981), *People on a Bridge* (1990), *Poems New and Collected 1957–1997* (1998), *Miracle Fair* (2001) and *Monologue of a Dog* (2006). *Nonrequired Reading: Prose Pieces* (2002). Nobel Prize for Literature (1996).

Thomas, R. S. (1913–2000): Poet, clergyman, essayist, memoirist, anthologist, Welsh nationalist. Born Cardiff; grew up in Holyhead. Ordained in 1937 as a priest of the Anglican ministry. Ministered in remote rural and coastal parishes in Wales until his retirement in 1978. Championed Welsh independence and the advancement of the Welsh language. His autobiographical prose, written in Welsh, was published in English translation as *Autobiographies* (1997). His poetry was written in English: *Collected Poems 1945–1990*

(1993), *Collected Later Poems 1988–2000* (2004). *Selected Prose* (1983). Edited *The Penguin Book of Religious Verse* (1963). SH paid tribute to Thomas's work – which influenced his own early writing – at the memorial service for the poet in Westminster Abbey in March 2001.

Tracy, Robert (1928–): Critic, translator and academic. Born Massachusetts. Has taught at the University of California, Berkeley, since 1960 and was a colleague of SH during his temporary teaching appointments there. Regular visitor to Ireland since 1958, with his wife Rebecca Tracy. *Stone* (1981), his translation into English of Osip Mandelstam's first poetry collection, is discussed by SH in *The Government of the Tongue*. *Trollope's Later Novels* (1978). *The Unappeasable Host: Studies in Irish Identities* (1998).

Vendler, Helen (1933–): Critic, anthologist and academic. Born Boston. Dedicatee of two SH books, his interim collection *Hailstones* and *The Spirit Level*. Her critical work, *Seamus Heaney*, appeared in 1998. Essays on SH are included in *The Music of What Happens* (1988), *Soul Says* (1995), *The Breaking of Style* (1995) and the chapbook, *Seamus Heaney and the Grounds of Hope* (2004). Author of studies of W. B. Yeats, Wallace Stevens, George Herbert, John Keats and Shakespeare's sonnets, she edited *The Harvard* [and *Faber*] *Book of Contemporary American Poetry* (1985). Professor of English at Harvard University (from 1981).

Walcott, Derek (1930–): Poet, playwright, essayist and painter. Born St Lucia. SH's review of Walcott's *The Star-Apple Kingdom* (1979) is included in *The Government of the Tongue*. *Collected Poems* (1986); *Omeros* (1990); *The Bounty* (1997); *Tiepolo's Hound* (2000); *The Prodigal* (2004). *Three Plays* (1986). *What the Twilight Says: Essays* (1998). *The Arkansas Testament* (1987) is dedicated to SH. Nobel Prize for Literature (1992). Professor of English at Boston University (from 1985).

Index

Works in the index are by SH unless otherwise stated.

relations with girls, 45, 406; meets
Marie, 45; courtship, 53, 62–3, 68, 169,
222; turns down chance of studentship
at Oxford, 68–9; holiday job in Passport
Office, xxii, 86, 418–19; reading of
1960s writers, 51–2, 112–15; new
acquaintances through the Lyric, 53–4;
publishes first poems, xxi, 37, 78–81;
first journey abroad, xxi; becomes
teacher, xxi–xxii, 52, 68–72, 96, 193;
homes while teacher and before
marriage, 67–8; first publications, xxii,
37, 78–81; involvement with The Group,
xxii, 73–8, 80, 105–6; becomes English
lecturer, xxii, 63, 68, 103; wedding,
xxii, 253–4; honeymoon, 83, 253; early
married life, 61, 62; first book published,
xxii, 61–2; as lecturer at QUB, 41,
102–7; becomes speaker and
broadcaster, xxii, 151, 164, 201; home
in Ashley Avenue, 115–16; children
born, xxii, xxiii, xxiv, 68, 168–9; coping
with newborns, 96–7; summer abroad
(1969), xxiii, 100, 182–4; participates in
protest meetings and marches, xxiii,
119–20; first trip to USA, xxiii; visiting
lecturer at Berkeley, xxiii, 136–43,
145–7; US poets read by, 145–7; gives
up day job and moves to Glanmore,
xxiii, 148–55, 156, 167–8, 197–201,
207–9; Dublin acquaintances, 152–3;
holidays in West Donegal, 117, 177;
starts as presenter of Imprint, xxiii, 151;
visits to Scotland, Copenhagen and
Jutland, xxiv, 163; appointed member of
Irish Arts Council, xxiv; first visit to
Grasmere, xxiv, 162; second cousin
assassinated by Loyalists, xxiv, 220–2;
returns to Berkeley as Beckman
Professor, xxiv, 144, 146; as lecturer at
Carysfort, xxiv, xxv, 193, 226–7,
228–30; moves to Strand Road, Dublin,
193–4, 226–8, 230–1; resigns from
Carysfort, xxv, 265–6; visiting lecturer
at Harvard, xxiv–xxv; teaches one
semester per year at Harvard, 265;
Massachusetts friends, 267–9; mother's
death, xxvi, 312; becomes Boylston
Professor of Rhetoric and Oratory at
Harvard, xxvi, 270; father's death, xxvi,
322; first visit to Japan, xxvi; memorial
lectures for Eliot and Ellmann, xxvi,
429–30; year's sabbatical (1988–9),
xxvi, 322; fiftieth birthday, xxvi, 323–4,
412; elected Professor of Poetry at
Oxford, xxvi, 429–35; year's leave of
absence from Harvard (1994–5), xxvii;
resigns as Boylston Professor and is

appointed Emerson Poet in Residence at
Harvard, xxvii, 269; Nobel celebrations,
xxvii, 355, 368–73; guest of honour at
White House, xxviii, 353–4; features on
Irish stamp, xxix; visited by Emperor
and Empress of Japan, xxix; mild stroke
causes twelve-month cancellation of
engagements, viii, xxix, 461–3; resigns
as Emerson Poet in Residence, xxix
– AS A WRITER: becoming full time,
148–55, 156, 167–8, 197–201, 207–9;
best time of day to write, 464–5;
classical allusions and Latin, 293–6; on
commissions, 291; dialect words, 128–9,
365, 402–3; early pseudonym, 37; east
European influences, 297–8, 300, 386–7;
eclogues, 389; effect of working as
academic, 104, 272–3; experimentation,
408; on failings as poet, 467; first real
experience of writing, 35–6; fitting
writing round teaching, 96–7; on form,
447–8; forty poems in a week, 147;
humour in his poetry, 450; influences
and exemplars, xi, xiii, 36–41, 64, 72,
100, 191–5, 292–3; on inspiration, 320;
inspiration for lighter verses, 110–11;
inspirations, 407–8; on length of
collections, 285; and negative criticism,
161–2; on phases in writer's life, 323–4;
phoneticism, 124–6; poetic development,
97–8, 126–7; on poetic technique, 204;
preferred rhyme forms, 448–9; on prose
poems, 180–1, 408; sectarianism as
impulse to write, 65–7, 86; on self-
consciousness and self-forgetfulness,
218–19; self-consciousness while writing
second book, 88–9; self-doubts, 99; on
sestinas, 361–2; shift from 'I' to 'we',
89–90; and social realism, 251; on
sound of words, 449; sprint poems,
261–2; Strand Road workplace, 230–1;
on subject matter, 449–50; translations
of own work, 428–9; as translator,
217–18, 296, 313–14, 420–8, 435–43;
US influences, 141, 283; verse letters,
123–4; voice, 40, 90; on work–life
balance, 206; on writing, 444–52; on
writing in later life, 345–6, 466; on
writing procedure, 202; writing tools,
468; see also poetry, SH on
Heaney, Sheena (SH's sister), 23, 29, 30, 31
'Heaney in Limboland' (TV programme),
149
Hecht, Anthony, 379
Hellman, Lilian, 137
Hemingway, Ernest, 38, 184
Henri, Adrian, 101
Henry, Mick, 434

Photograph Credits